Approaches to Social Research

Approaches to Social Research

SIXTH EDITION

Royce A. Singleton, Jr.
College of the Holy Cross

Bruce C. Straits
University of California, Santa Barbara

New York   Oxford

OXFORD UNIVERSITY PRESS

Oxford University Press is a department of the University of Oxford. It furthers
the University's objective of excellence in research, scholarship, and education by
publishing worldwide. Oxford is a registered trade mark of Oxford University Press in
the UK and certain other countries.

Published in the United States of America by Oxford University Press
198 Madison Avenue, New York, NY 10016, United States of America.

For titles covered by Section 112 of the US Higher Education
Opportunity Act, please visit www.oup.com/us/he for the latest
information about pricing and alternate formats.

Library of Congress Cataloging-in-Publication Data

Names: Singleton, Royce, author. | Straits, Bruce C., author.
Title: Approaches to social research / Royce A. Singleton, Jr., College of
    the Holy Cross, Bruce C. Straits, University of California, Santa Barbara.
Description: Sixth edition. | New York : Oxford University Press, 2017. |
    Includes bibliographical references and index.
Identifiers: LCCN 2017007201 | ISBN 9780190614249 (hardcover : alk. paper)
Subjects: LCSH: Social sciences—Research. | Social sciences—Methodology.
Classification: LCC H62 .S4776 2017 | DDC 300.72—dc23
LC record available at https://lccn.loc.gov/2017007201

Printing number: 9 8 7 6 5 4 3 2 1

Printed by Edward Brothers Malloy, United States of America

Contents

Preface

To the Student

Of all the courses we have taught, none is more important than research methods. Methodology is the heart of the social sciences; more than anything else, it is what distinguishes social science from journalism and social commentary, from the humanities and natural sciences. Understanding social research methods, therefore, should give you a better sense of sociology and related disciplines and of exactly what it is that social scientists do. To facilitate your understanding, in this book we have described an abundance of actual research studies that cover the full range of social science disciplines.

Besides deepening your understanding of social science, a knowledge of social research is essential for making informed decisions about our daily lives. Social scientific methods and findings influence us in numerous ways. Many government social programs are shaped and evaluated by social research; businesses constantly rely on consumer research for key marketing and management decisions; the popular press daily reports research findings on the most personal aspects of people's lives—from altruism to zero population growth. One of the goals of this book is to help you understand the logic and limitations of social research so that you can evaluate it effectively.

Finally, the study of social research methods should not only sharpen your powers of critical thinking but also enable you to become a more intelligent gatherer of information. Social research consists of activities and ways of thinking in which everyone frequently and profitably can engage. Realizing that most readers will not become social scientists, we have linked many topics to familiar subjects and frames of reference so that you can see how broadly social research may be applied.

The book is organized in four sections. Part I describes the scientific foundations of social research (Chapter 2) and the ethical issues that arise (Chapter 3). Thereafter, the organization generally follows the process of conducting research. Part II introduces the basic terminology of social research (Chapter 4) and then examines two key considerations in planning or designing a study: measurement (Chapter 5) and sampling (Chapter 6). Part III, on data collection, examines the four basic approaches to social research: experiments, surveys, field research, and the use of available data. The four main chapters (Chapters 7, 9, 11, and 12) describe the distinctive process of executing a study with each approach; two other chapters (Chapters 8 and 10) discuss technical features of experiments and surveys; and the last two chapters in this section present strategies for combining methods and approaches (Chapter 13) and for applying research methods to the evaluation of social programs and interventions (Chapter 14). Part IV deals broadly with the interpretation phase of research. Here we discuss data processing and elementary data analysis (Chapter 15) and more advanced, multivariate analysis (Chapter 16), as well as the writing of research reports (Chapter 17).

The book has several special features. Key terms are in boldface type when they first appear in the text and are also listed at the end of each chapter. If you are unsure of the meaning of a term introduced earlier in the text, you can refer to the comprehensive glossary in the back of the book. Main ideas are highlighted in two ways: key points are offset throughout the text, and each chapter ends with a summary. To test your understanding and ability to apply what you have learned, each chapter also contains a set of practical exercises. Finally, boxes are inserted to complement and expand the text; these boxes present interesting research examples, provide additional aids to learning, or discuss the historical, social, and political contexts of research.

As a further aid, we have constructed a companion website for this textbook (www.oup.com/us/singleton-approaches) designed for students at all levels of learning. The site posts the glossary of terms. For each chapter the site also contains the following:

- Answers to selected textbook exercises
- True–false and matching quizzes
- An annotated list of Web resources

To the Instructor

This book has several distinguishing features. First, it is neither a cookbook for conducting social research nor a treatise on epistemology. Rather, we have attempted to strike a balance between the "how to" of research methods (providing information for conducting research) and the "wherefore" (teaching critical analytical skills for reading and evaluating research). Chapter exercises reflect this dual purpose. Some exercises ask students to carry out their own research; others ask them to read and think critically about specific articles reporting empirical studies.

Second, recognizing the broad audience for social research methods, we discuss dozens of actual studies drawn from sociology, social psychology, communications, demography, history, education, and political science. Many of these studies are classics, and others are very recent; all are carefully chosen to heighten students' interest.

Third, in contrast to many methods books these days, we do not endorse the post-modernist critique of sociology as a science. In Chapter 2 we discuss the growth of "qualitative research" in the late twentieth century and its challenges to a natural science model of social scientific inquiry. But otherwise, we do not make a distinction between so-called qualitative and quantitative methods. Instead, we assume that all social research is driven by the same search for understanding, operates from similar epistemological bases, and addresses similar methodological concerns regarding reliability, validity, and generalizability. Major differences among research methods reside in general research strategies. Therefore, this book focuses on the four basic approaches to social research: experimentation, survey research, field research, and the use of available data. We discuss the advantages and disadvantages of each approach, treat the approaches as complementary rather than mutually exclusive, and ultimately advocate a multiple-methods strategy.

Focusing on overall approaches to conducting social research has several pedagogical advantages. First, it enables readers to see each approach not as a method of data collection per se, divorced from research design and analysis, but as a fundamental choice that affects the entire research process. Other methods books tend to separate issues of design and data collection or discuss certain design issues only in relation to specific approaches. For example, sampling techniques are described as survey methods, or measurement is described merely in terms of self-report questionnaire items. However, because measurement and sampling must be addressed in all research, we discuss these issues in relation to each basic approach. Second, a reader's sense of both the logic and the mechanics of doing research is enhanced by understanding the unique process of executing a study with each approach. Unlike the present text, other methods texts disregard the field administration phase of survey research, limiting the discussion to sampling and/or questionnaire design. Similarly, other texts discuss experiments merely in terms of experimental design without describing their basic parts or staging. A focus on the basic approaches, we believe, gives readers a better sense of the integrity of social research and a greater appreciation for both its power and its limitations.

Teaching research methods is challenging. The challenges lie in doing justice to the complexities of research, in going beyond the simplest techniques to provide enough information for readers to become intelligent consumers of research, in developing an understanding not only of each individual stage of research but also of the interrelatedness of all phases, and in presenting information about the "nuts and bolts" of research (e.g., how to draw a sample and how to code data) while not losing sight of the logic of inquiry or the overall research process. Much of what researchers do is informed by their understanding of the entire research process so that elements of research design are dictated by a knowledge of the means of data collection and analysis. Thus, researchers precode questionnaires to facilitate data processing, and in anticipation of multivariate analysis, they include seemingly irrelevant background items in a questionnaire. Getting students to comprehend the overall process is perhaps our greatest challenge, and we believe that this challenge is best met by focusing on basic approaches to social research.

Aside from our emphasis on the four major approaches, we cover essentially the same topics in most other methods texts in approximately the same sequence. We tell students what makes social research scientific, discuss ethical considerations, introduce basic terminology, and then provide chapters on measurement, sampling, the major methods of data collection (i.e., the four approaches), data analysis, and report writing. Unlike some other texts, we also provide extended treatments of experimental designs, survey pretesting and field administration, multiple methods (triangulation), and evaluation research.

Because we subsume methods of data collection under the four approaches, we do not have separate chapters on quasi-experimental research, which we discuss in relation to experimental design (Chapter 8) and evaluation research (Chapter 14); on observational methods, which we cover in our discussion of field research (Chapter 11); and on historical document research and content analysis, which we include in the general strategy of using available data (Chapter 12). Rather than present largely outdated material, we have chosen not to devote a full chapter to index and scale construction. Instead, we discuss technical aspects of scaling relatively briefly in connection with multiple methods (Chapter 13). In general, we have tried to present current methodology in ways that complement modern statistical approaches to measurement, sampling, and data analysis. And, in a similar fashion, our presentation of data analysis emphasizes consumption and understanding rather than the production of statistical analysis.

Advanced topics are included but may be skipped without any loss of continuity. This provides considerable flexibility in using the text, allowing instructors to adopt it for either a one- or a two-term course, for a lower- or an upper-level undergraduate course, or for a graduate course. One can skip Chapter 2 and/or 3 and go directly from Chapter 1 to Chapter 4. Other advanced chapters are 8 and 10, in which we discuss technical design issues related to experimentation and survey research, respectively. For instructors who want to examine the logic of experimental design, Chapter 8 introduces sources of invalidity and basic true, factorial, and quasi-experimental designs. For instructors who emphasize survey research and have students collect data, we have found Chapter 10 on survey instrumentation to be effective in preparing students to design their own questionnaires. Another option for undergraduate courses is to assign Chapters 8 and 10, but omit the more technical end sections on quasi-experimental designs and survey pretesting, respectively. Chapter 13 on multiple methods, Chapter 14 on evaluation research, and especially Chapter 16 on multivariate analysis also are advanced. Instructors teaching one-term courses may easily skip all or portions of the more advanced chapters.

To further serve instructors' needs, the Ancillary Resource Center at arc2.oup-arc.com/ provides a variety of resources, prepared by Royce Singleton. These include (1) lecture, discussion, and exercise ideas, (2) an annotated list of Web resources (with URLs), (3) answers to textbook exercises, and (4) test items for each chapter. The student companion website also contains two sets of quizzes. We welcome comments and suggestions for further improving the book and making it better serve your needs. Just send a message to either of our e-mail addresses: rsinglet@holycross.edu or straits@soc.ucsb.edu.

The Sixth Edition

Although *Approaches to Social Research* contains the same chapters and pedagogical approach as the previous edition, we have revised the book extensively to enhance its value. To give you an idea of how extensive the changes are, let us first consider the revision by the numbers. The sixth edition

- contains 184 new references, with an average publication date of 2007;
- deletes 75 references from the previous edition, which had an average publication date of 1987;
- introduces 22 new research examples, 15 of which replace dated examples from previous editions;
- updates the data presented in 10 tables and 1 figure; and
- adds 11 new key terms.

Many of the changes we made are subtle but important. This includes editing every chapter to improve the clarity and flow of the text, replacing dated everyday examples, presenting the latest data where appropriate, and referencing the latest editions of key sources. Other changes are more substantive. Three chapters (Chapters 3, 11, and 14) were thoroughly revised. In Chapter 3, we added a discussion of the Tuskegee Syphilis Study and revised and expanded discussions of informed consent, deception, confidentiality, and values in social research. As part of our reorganization of Chapter 11, we expanded our discussion of features of field research. And in Chapter 14, we introduced a new core research example that has been integrated throughout our discussion of evaluation research.

Other substantive changes include the following:

New sections and subsections within chapters. In Chapter 2, we expanded the discussion of critiques of science to include qualitative researchers' epistemological challenges to a natural science model of social "science." In Chapter 3, we extended the section on values in social science by adding a subsection, "Managing Personal Values," in which we present an analysis of studies on the effects of homosexual versus heterosexual parenting. We also added new sections: "Big Data" in Chapter 12 and "Publishing a Research Paper" in Chapter 17.

Chapter reorganizations. To achieve consistency in our coverage of the basic approaches to social research, we moved discussions of uses and limitations of surveys (Chapter 9), field research (Chapter 11), and available-data research (Chapter 12) to the end of the respective chapters. Now all three chapters begin with a description of key features, move on to a discussion of the stages in carrying out the approach, and conclude by outlining strengths and limitations.

New interesting and rigorous examples of social research. From the first edition, an important feature of *Approaches* has been the use of diverse empirical studies, carefully chosen as rigorous examples of social research that students would find interesting and relevant to their lives. Therefore, in every edition, we have added new studies and replaced studies on less current topics or on topics unfamiliar to young readers. Among the nearly two dozen new empirical studies introduced in this edition are an audit study of job discrimination against gay men, a content analysis of changes in parental role portrayals in children's picture books, field research on the help-seeking behavior of children in elementary schools, an evaluation study of the Gang Resistance Education and Training program, and a quantitative (path) analysis of the effects of alcohol consumption and sleep on academic performance.

We trust that these changes have improved the book, providing an ever more accessible introduction that presents the latest developments in methodology.

Acknowledgments

Approaches to Social Research has unfolded over a period of nearly 40 years. During that time we have benefited greatly from the comments of numerous persons. Although it is impossible at this point to list everyone to whom we are indebted, several individuals deserve special mention. Ron McAllister, provost emeritus of Elizabethtown College, initiated the project and coauthored the first edition. Margaret Miller Clark, another former coauthor, also made major contributions to the first edition. Many of our students and colleagues at Holy Cross and the University of California, Santa Barbara, have provided inspiration and ideas. For this edition, we benefited greatly from our collaboration with Jeff Dixon of Holy Cross, our coauthor of *The Process of Social Research*, which was a source of several ideas for revising *Approaches*.

Over the years, we have received many helpful suggestions from instructors and scholars of research methods. Beginning with the fourth edition, revisions in our description of the General Social Survey were based on feedback from Tom W. Smith of the National Opinion Research Center. Three instructors reviewed the book for the fourth edition: Ed Hackett of Arizona State University, Megan Sweeney of the University of California, Los Angeles, and Michael Turner of the University of North Carolina at Charlotte. Four reviewers helped us as we prepared to write the fifth edition: Stephanie Bohon, University of Tennessee; Kristen Harknett, University of Pennsylvania; Kathleen Warberg, Wittenberg University; and Ken Watkins, University of South Carolina.

Finally, we thank the reviewers for the sixth and current edition:

Emily Barman, Boston University;
Kebba Darboe, Minnesota State University-Mankato;
Barbara Hart, University of Texas at Tyler;
Lindsey A. Harvell, James Madison University;
Terrence D. Hill, University of Arizona;
Nalin Johri, Seton Hall University;
Hisako Matsuo, Saint Louis University;
Jonathan Matusitz, University of Central Florida;
Zachary Neal, Michigan State University;
Jason Rodriquez, University of Massachusetts-Boston;
Erin Ruel, Georgia State University;
Yvonne Vissing, Salem State University.

Approaches to Social Research

1

Introduction

Social research consists of the process of formulating and seeking answers to questions about the social world. Consider some of the questions investigated in studies reported in this book.

- Recent studies indicate that high school athletes generally receive higher grades and test scores than do nonathletes. Beckett Broh (2002) asked why. Does this finding validate the conventional wisdom that sports participation teaches discipline, perseverance, and a strong work ethic, which promote academic achievement? Or does sports participation benefit athletes' social networks, placing them in a peer group of academically oriented high achievers or helping to establish relations among parents and teachers that facilitate and encourage achievement?
- Bibb Latané and John Darley (1970) speculated about why 38 people in Queens, New York, watching the brutal attack of a woman from their apartment windows, failed to come to her aid in time to save her life. Was it the general apathy of people in modern, urban environments, as many experts claimed? Or was there something about the situation that inhibited people from helping? Why do bystanders sometimes fail to aid people immediately in a crisis situation?
- The outcome of presidential elections, many campaigners now believe, depends on which party has the superior grassroots organization or "ground game" for getting out the vote. Until recently, however, little was known about how best to mobilize turnout. Then, Donald Green and Alan Gerber (2008) asked, Which is most effective and cost-efficient: personal canvassing, telephone calls, or direct-mail appeals?

- As the number of homeless people on the streets of U.S. cities increased visibly in the early 1980s, interest in the problem of homelessness grew. Peter Rossi (1989) asked, What is the extent of the problem—that is, how many homeless individuals are there—and what forces increased the number of homeless in the 1980s? David Snow and Leon Anderson (1993) wondered how the homeless lived. What were their daily lives like? What sort of material, interpersonal, and psychological strategies helped them to survive?
- The famous witchcraft hysteria that swept through Salem, Massachusetts, in 1692 has interested writers, historians, and other social scientists for many years. Kai Erikson (1966) wondered whether the crime wave was consistent with the sociologist Emile Durkheim's theory on the relationship between deviance and social order. Did the community response to deviance demonstrate shared values and enhance community solidarity?
- Since the late twentieth century there has been considerable debate regarding the proper police response to misdemeanor domestic assaults. Should police end the dispute by asking one of the parties to leave the premises? Should they attempt to mediate to de-escalate the conflict? Or should they arrest the assailant? Feminists have pressed for more arrests. But Lawrence Sherman and Richard Berk (1984) wondered whether this was the best policy. More generally, they pondered the effects of punishment on behavior. Will punishment, such as an arrest, deter an individual from repeating the crime? Or will punishment make individuals more likely to commit crimes?

To answer such questions, social scientists have devised basic guidelines, principles, and techniques. The purpose of this book is to introduce you to these "methods" as they are applied in the social sciences. As you will see, however, the research process is much more broadly applicable. The methods of social research can be applied to investigate any curiosity, and our understanding of them can make us smarter consumers, better informed voters, and better students. Let's begin by considering the value of studying research methods.

Why Study Research Methods?

The "why study" question may be asked more often about research methods than about any other area of study in the social sciences. Often, we hear students say, "I don't intend to go to graduate school. And I don't intend to do research. Why do I need to study ('suffer through') methods?" The irony in such a statement is that, beyond providing a foundation of knowledge for those who do become social scientists, the study of research methods may provide more immediate and useful information than any other single course of study. A knowledge of methods can benefit you as both a consumer and a producer of research evidence.

Consuming Research Evidence

You may be a consumer of research in several positions: as a student reading research reports and journal articles to satisfy your curiosity or to meet course requirements and write term papers; as a social worker, educator, librarian, journalist, manager, or other professional keeping up to date in your field and acquiring knowledge to guide you in making decisions; or as an average citizen attempting to deal with the varied claims that are purported to be based on research. To make intelligent decisions about much day-to-day information, you must be able to understand and evaluate it. It is unfortunately true that much research evidence reported in professional journals as well as in newspapers and on television either is itself in error or is misinterpreted. Let us consider some of the kinds of misinformation to which you are likely to be exposed.

In April 2009, Aryn Karpinski (2009a), a graduate student at Ohio State, presented a research paper at a professional meeting in which she reported that students who use Facebook have lower grades than those who do not. Karpinski's study generated a media frenzy, triggering such headlines as "Sad but true: Using Facebook can lower your GPA" and "Facebook dumbs you down." Although they are attention grabbing, these headlines are misleading. To conclude from this type of study that being on Facebook *causes* bad grades violates a cardinal principle of social research: A relationship between two phenomena does not mean that one thing caused the other. In fact, Karpinski (2009b) herself was careful to note this limitation: Her study merely showed an *association* between using Facebook and grades; it did not demonstrate that using Facebook *causes* one's grades to drop. An equally likely interpretation is that receiving bad grades leads you to become a Facebook user. Still another possibility is that there is no causal link between Facebook and grades. Facebook use may be a symptom of procrastination. Or, the association could be due to a common factor, such as a student's major. For example, critics of Karpinski's study pointed out that science majors, who were more likely to use Facebook than humanities and social science majors, also may tend to get lower grades, perhaps because of more stringent grading standards in the sciences (Pasek, more, and Hargittai, 2009). Studying research methods will enable you to apply this reasoning as well as identify other limitations of reported research.

A knowledge of research methods also can make you aware of the mischievous use of research evidence by advertisers. For example, how seriously should we take the television pitch that "75 percent of doctors interviewed prescribed drug X for relief of arthritic pain?" Among the questions that a careful researcher could raise about this "fact" are these:

1. How many doctors were interviewed? (The 75 percent statistic could be based on as few as four interviews.)
2. What were the doctors asked about their prescription of drug X? (If they were asked, "Have you ever prescribed drug X?" they may be just as likely to have prescribed drugs A, B, C, and D as well.)
3. Who interviewed the doctors? (If the manufacturers of drug X did the interviewing, then they may have influenced, wittingly or unwittingly, the doctors to favor their product.)

Advertisers are not the only source of misleading information. Another culprit is self-selected opinion surveys. To make money, attract new customers, and increase reader or viewer involvement, the media frequently conduct mail-in and call-in polls (Crossen, 1994:123). For example, in April 1993 *Parade Magazine* invited its readers to voice their opinions about crime in America by calling a 900 number (*Parade Magazine*, 1993). In all, 15,028 readers took up the invitation, paying a nominal fee to call in. Some 38 percent ("more than a third of Americans," according to *Parade*) said that they did not feel safe in their homes, 35 percent did not think the police were doing a good job, 81 percent did not have faith in the legal system, and 85 percent supported the death penalty. Although *Parade* noted that the results were based on a call-in survey, the magazine also implied that the results were representative of U.S. public opinion. But how representative is this sample? Because it was not randomly selected, the sample is not representative of any population other than the 15,028 callers. As a source of information about public opinion, therefore, it is worthless. Indeed, social scientists have derived the acronym SLOP to describe self-selected listener or reader opinion polls. It seems plausible that *Parade*'s callers would tend to be more concerned about the problem of crime than the average U.S. resident. On at least two issues, data from random samples of the U.S. adult population support this conclusion: In 1992, 11 percent, compared with 38 percent in the *Parade* poll, did not feel safe and secure in their homes (Warr, 1995:305); and in 1993, 72 percent, as opposed to 85 percent in the *Parade* survey, supported the death penalty (T. W. Smith, Marsden, and Hout, 2016).

Because social science findings are reported in the media every day, we can scarcely avoid being consumers of social research evidence. Yet, as the above examples illustrate, we cannot assume automatically that conclusions based on statistical evidence from purported scientific studies are credible. It is therefore important to be able to make judgments about the quality of the data and the limits of the conclusions that might be drawn. As every good social scientist knows, research findings must be interpreted and applied with great care. Whether you are in a position where you need to know the policy implications of research findings or you are simply an ordinary citizen wanting to be better informed about such findings, the study of research methods can help you develop the ability to understand and evaluate the validity and limits of social scientific knowledge.

Producing Research Evidence

In addition to being consumers, we are gatherers and producers of research evidence. We manufacture evidence every time we seek out others' opinions about an issue, attempt to estimate the prevailing opinion within a particular group, or draw conclusions about persons and events on the basis of our own observations. As a producer of information, in this introduction to social research you will find principles and techniques that can be applied at levels of sophistication ranging from casual observation to the conduct of small-scale research projects.

Suppose you are trying to decide whether to take a course from professor X or professor Y. Gathering evidence to help you decide, you solicit opinions about the professors from fellow students. A knowledge of research principles not only could increase your awareness of the limitations in this approach but also could facilitate the collection of more trustworthy information. Research principles suggest, for example, that the trustworthiness of your information will depend on (1) the number of opinions solicited, (2) the consistency of those opinions, (3) whether informants' opinions are formed and solicited independent of one another, and (4) how questions are posed when asking for opinions about professors X and Y.

At a less mundane level, a knowledge of research techniques is essential for nonscientists who must acquire reliable information about a particular group. This occurs more often than you might think. For example, politicians often need to determine what their constituents think about an important legislative issue; corporate executives may need information about their clients' or employees' reactions to proposed policy changes; journalists may want to know something about the makeup of their newspaper's or magazine's readership or may want to determine a community's attitude toward certain services or policies as part of a story they are preparing; students may want to collect data about student body behaviors or opinions as part of a term project or student newspaper article. None of these endeavors entails the kind of massive research effort that would require expert researchers and statisticians. Yet each endeavor calls for the systematic collection of information, which is precisely what research methods are all about.

Methodological Approaches to the Social World

As our opening set of questions reveals, the topics of social research range broadly. In fact, whether a topic or research question is a legitimate object of social research hinges on two obvious criteria. First, the topic must concern *social* phenomena. This means that the research subject involves people—how they act, think, and feel and how they interact with one another. It looks also at the groups that people form (from bowling clubs to leagues of nations), at relations within and among such groups, and at how the groups adapt to changes in society. Second, because social research is *scientific*, it must be possible to address the topic or answer the question by making appropriate observations. In Chapter 2, on the nature of science, we distinguish scientific from nonscientific questions as we discuss the similarities among all fields of scientific inquiry. Then, in the remainder of the book, we concern ourselves with research as it is practiced in such fields as anthropology, communications, economics, education, history, political science, psychology, and sociology.

Among these disciplines there are four principal research strategies for understanding the social world: experiments, surveys, field research, and the use of available data. Each discipline tends to favor one particular strategy. For example, psychologists typically conduct experiments, sociologists most often do survey research, anthropologists characteristically conduct field research, and historians tend to make use of available data. However, all four strategies are important to the world of social research because any of the four can be used to study most social science topics. In fact, one of the early tasks of researchers is to decide which approach or approaches to take.

A discussion of the four basic strategies or approaches to social research comprises the central core of this book (see Chapters 7–12). As each strategy is discussed, you will see that each has certain strengths and weaknesses that make a researcher favor one or another in different situations. Sometimes one strategy may not be feasible for ethical reasons (see Chapter 3). Sometimes an approach will be ruled out because of constraints of time, personnel, space, or some other resource. Furthermore, many researchers argue, as we do in Chapter 13, that it is best, whenever feasible, to study a given problem with a variety of methods so that the weaknesses of one strategy may be canceled out by the strengths of another. But it is often possible to study a social science topic using any one of the four basic research strategies. To demonstrate this, we will consider the topic of altruism.

Some Preliminary Research Questions

Although altruism has been most intensively investigated during the past 50 years, its study is almost as old as social science itself. The man who coined the word "sociology," Auguste Comte, also introduced the term "altruism" more than 150 years ago. Comte thought of altruism as a sympathetic instinct or motive, in contrast to the egoistic motive of self-interest. Today, popular usage of the term still resembles his original concept. Here, for example, is one dictionary definition:

> **al-tru-ism** (al'troo iz em), *n*: 1. Unselfish concern for the welfare of others . . . opposed to *egoism*. (*Webster's New World College Dictionary*, fourth edition, 2008)

Let us suppose that you are interested in the subject of altruism. As a social scientist, your special interest is in understanding altruism as a social phenomenon: What are the patterns of altruism? When, where, and how is it likely to occur? Why are people altruistic? These are the sort of grand questions that motivate all scientific inquiry. To begin your study of altruism, however, you would need to formulate questions that narrow the topic, reducing these original grand questions to manageable proportions. For example, instead of asking, What explains altruism?, suppose you ask, Does urban crowding inhibit people's willingness to help others? Are people more likely to help others who are similar to them? Will first-aid training increase the likelihood that someone will help another in an emergency? How does a person's emotional mood influence his or her willingness to help? What is the family background of committed altruists? These are narrow, specific, and consequently *answerable* research questions.

There are a limitless variety of interesting and worthwhile questions that might be investigated. In Chapters 2 and 4 we will consider the form of scientifically meaningful questions. Researchable questions derive from various sources: a researcher's personal values and goals, intuition, observation of dramatic events, and the current state of scientific knowledge. Eventually, your questions would be refined on the basis of a thorough review of the relevant social science literature. Here is where you would establish the theoretical and practical relevance of the research question. Here also is where you would begin to grapple with several preliminary methodological issues that will shape your study.

One of the most important issues involves the process of definition. As it turns out, dictionary definitions are not satisfactory for research purposes. A dictionary would not be helpful in distinguishing between altruism and similar concepts such as "empathy" or "helping," nor would it tell you how and where to observe instances of altruism. Your literature review would thus be important in revealing how other researchers have defined altruism conceptually and identified it empirically. A thorough review is likely to identify the following citation:

Dovidio, John F., Jane Allyn Piliavin, David A. Schroeder, and Louis A. Penner. *The Social Psychology of Prosocial Behavior*. Mahwah, NJ: Lawrence Erlbaum, 2006.

Reading this book would reveal that it provides a comprehensive review of theory and research on helping, altruism, and cooperation, so this is an important reference. In the preface you would learn that the authors are social psychologists, that each author has studied various forms of prosocial behavior for more than 30 years, and that this book updates a 1995 volume entitled *The Psychology of Helping and Altruism: Problems and Puzzles*.

The topic of greatest interest in the book is helping, which the authors define as "an action that has the consequence of providing some benefit to or improving the well-being of another person" (Dovidio et al., 2006:22). Altruism is a type of helping that takes into account the helper's intentions, benefits, and costs. Definitions of altruism vary, but social scientists generally reserve the term for helping that is motivated purely by a desire to benefit others, without anticipation of personal rewards and often at a cost to the helper. This is more precise than our dictionary definition; however, altruism is a more elusive concept than mere helping. And as Dovidio and colleagues point out, it is not always possible to characterize a particular act of helping as altruistic.

Conceptual clarification is crucial. Still, to study altruism scientifically we must move beyond abstract definitions to specific, concrete observations. To do this is to *operationalize* the concept. One of many possible operational definitions is donating blood; another is giving money to a charitable organization. Both of these acts are intended to help others and incur some cost to the actor. Dovidio and colleagues' book offers many other examples as it reports numerous empirical studies on specific helping acts. In Chapter 5, we discuss the process of conceptually defining and operationalizing concepts as well as criteria for evaluating the quality of "operational definitions."

For now, you can get a better idea of this process as we consider how the topic of altruism might be investigated using each of the four basic approaches highlighted in this book: experiments, surveys, field research, and available data research. All four of our examples focus specifically on volunteering—either informally volunteering to participate in an experiment or formally volunteering by giving freely of one's time and effort to a nonprofit organization. As you will see, each study tailors its basic approach to a specific research question regarding volunteering. Together they provide complementary answers to the general question, What explains altruism?

An Experimental Answer

As we discuss in Chapter 7, **experiments** frequently offer the best approach for investigating the causes of phenomena. One possible cause of altruistic acts may be a sense of belonging to others. Jean Twenge and associates (2007:56) argued that altruistic behavior "depends on believing that one is part of a community in which people mutually seek to aid, to support, and, occasionally, to love each other." When people feel excluded, they are much less likely to help others. To test this idea experimentally, the researchers needed to systematically manipulate exclusion so that some people would be made to feel excluded and others not and then to observe how these people would respond when given the opportunity to behave altruistically.

The manipulation of exclusion required several steps. First, the investigators had research participants, all of whom were psychology students who participated for partial course credit, meet together in groups of four to six to get to know one another. After the discussion, the students filled out forms that requested background information and asked them to name the two people in their group with whom they would most like to work. Finally, after collecting this information, the experimenter told each participant that either everyone or no one in their group had chosen him or her as someone they'd like to work with. In this way, half the participants felt accepted and the other half felt rejected. To observe how this manipulation affected altruism, the experimenter then asked all participants if they would be willing to volunteer to participate in up to three additional experiments, each taking about 15 minutes, for which they would not receive extra credit. The experimenters' operational definition of "altruistic behavior" consisted of the number of extra experiments for which each participant volunteered. Supporting their hypothesis, 90 percent of the "accepted" participants volunteered to help by doing at least one experiment compared with only 20 percent of the "rejected" participants.

The essential feature of this study that illustrates the experimental approach is that a potential influence on altruism—a feeling of social exclusion—was isolated and systematically varied from participant to participant, whereas other factors that might affect altruism were held constant or remained the same for all participants. For example, the same experimenter used the same instructions and same procedures. But what purpose does it serve to hold these features constant? Why was it necessary to include *two* groups, one of which was made to feel accepted and the other to feel excluded? How did the experimenters decide who would be made to feel excluded? And how is this deception ethically justified?

The experiment described here is one of seven experiments reported by the investigators. In other experiments, they found that socially excluded participants donated less money to a "student emergency fund" and were less likely to help pick up pencils accidentally spilled on the floor; they further found that social exclusion reduces helping by lowering empathy toward others (see Chapter 13 for a further description of these experiments). As you will learn, conducting multiple tests of hypotheses is common in experimental research and enhances the generalizability of the findings. But why go to the trouble of contriving and conducting an experiment when there are many naturally occurring acts of altruism that can be studied? In Chapter 7 we examine the logic of the experimental approach, the ways in which experiments are staged, and the advantages and disadvantages of this form of research. In Chapter 8 we look at different types of experimental designs.

An Answer from Survey Research

A second approach to studying altruism that might be taken is the **survey**. Survey research involves the administration of questionnaires or interviews to relatively large groups of people. One purpose of surveys is to describe the frequency of certain characteristics among groups or populations. For example, a survey might tell you how many people at your college or in your organization have voluntarily given blood, have done volunteer work, or have contributed money to charities. Such information can be related to other characteristics of respondents, such as their gender, age, marital status, religion, and occupation, thereby enabling a survey researcher to understand as well as describe the incidence of altruism.

An example of the use of survey research in the study of altruism is a survey on volunteering in the United States that has been conducted annually in September since 2002. Each volunteering study is part of the Current Population Survey (CPS), a monthly survey conducted by the U.S. Census Bureau for the Bureau of Labor Statistics. For more than 75 years, the CPS has been the primary source of labor force statistics for the U.S. population, providing estimates of unemployment, earnings, hours of work, and other important information. In addition to collecting data on the labor force, the CPS includes supplemental questions on topics such as voting and registration, participation in the arts, and cell phone use. The CPS adds these questions on behalf of federal agencies or other sponsors. The sponsor for the Volunteer Supplement to the CPS is the Corporation for National and Community Service, a federal agency established in 1993 whose mission is "to improve lives, strengthen communities, and foster civic engagement through service and volunteering" (Corporation for National and Community Service, 2016).

The purpose of the Volunteer Supplement is to obtain information on the frequency of volunteering and the characteristics of volunteers in the United States. As in each CPS, Census Bureau staff attempt to carry out interviews with members of approximately 60,000 occupied households. The households are selected using rigorous scientific methods to ensure that they are representative of the nation as a whole. Using a laptop computer into which the interview is programmed, interviewers introduce the survey topic by telling respondents that they are "interested in volunteer activities, that is, activities for which people are not paid, except perhaps expenses," and "which they did through or for an organization." Respondents then are asked whether they have done volunteer work in the past year and, if so, how many hours they volunteered, for what kinds of organizations they volunteered, and what types of activities they performed. Other CPS questions identify several demographic characteristics such as age, gender, race, marital status, and labor force status. Among the findings are the following (Inter-university Consortium for Political and Social Research, 2016): In 2015, women were more likely to volunteer than men; 27.8 percent of college students, compared with 24.5 percent of the general population, volunteered; almost one-quarter of college-student volunteering took place in religious organizations; and the most common volunteer activities among college students were tutoring, mentoring, fundraising, preparing or serving food, and engaging in general labor.

In addition to asking people questions, a key feature of survey studies is that information is collected from part of a group (persons residing in 60,000 households) to make generalizations about the whole group (the U.S. population). However, such generalizations are hazardous unless procedures are carefully followed in deciding whom to include in the study. The number of households in the CPS is unusually large for surveys; collecting information from this many people would exceed the budgets for most research. In Chapter 6 we discuss sampling techniques for choosing respondents that are designed to increase accuracy and reduce costs.

Many questions can be raised about survey research in general and the CPS in particular. Why does the Census Bureau conduct personal interviews, which are more costly than mailed questionnaires? What are the advantages of administering the interviews on a laptop computer rather than with pencil and paper? How do survey researchers decide which questions to ask, how best to word the questions, and in what order to ask them? These are the kinds of issues we address in Chapters 9 and 10.

An Answer from Field Research

Field research is essentially a matter of immersing oneself in a naturally occurring (rather than a "staged") set of events to gain firsthand knowledge of the situation. Anthropologists who live in remote communities for long periods to study the culture of the inhabitants are engaged in this form of research, as are other social scientists who voluntarily become members of organizations and groups or take jobs for the sake of conducting social research. In such settings, a field researcher seeks to understand the world as his or her subjects see it and to collect information without unduly influencing its shape and content.

Field research on altruism seldom has been conducted, although there are numerous settings where this approach could be applied. For example, one could work in a blood donor center or join the Red Cross or some other emergency relief organization. One also might do volunteer work, as Rebecca Allahyari (2000) did, at a charitable and nonprofit organization. Allahyari volunteered at the two largest organizations in Sacramento, California, that provide meals for the poor: the Catholic Worker–inspired Loaves & Fishes and the Salvation Army Shelter Services Center. Interested initially in "how homeless people experience social control" (ix) in their daily lives, Allahyari shifted her focus from the homeless to the volunteers who served them when she found herself struggling with moral questions about her volunteer work and relationships. She then went on to explore how the organizational cultures of these two charities shaped the moral self-definition of the volunteers.

To carry out her study, Allahyari relied primarily on her own direct experiences and observations. For 3 years, from 1991 to 1993, she volunteered regularly, preparing and serving food, cleaning up, talking informally to clients and other volunteers, and forming personal relationships. As she found, the two sites had distinct "visions of charity" grounded in different ideological orientations that affected how clients were viewed and how volunteers defined the meaning of their work.

Loaves & Fishes was founded on the Catholic Worker ethic of "personalist hospitality" in which the poor are viewed as guests—"ambassadors of God"—to be treated with dignity and respect. Guests at this site dined at tables set with flowers, were not explicitly indoctrinated, and had few rules to follow. Volunteers—mostly white, middle-class women—were formally introduced to the Catholic Worker philosophy by the staff and constructed moral selves based on gratitude for their own prosperity, commitment to feeding the urban poor, and building an ecumenical community. The Salvation Army viewed the homeless and hungry as souls to be saved by helping them better themselves through hard work and self-discipline. Within the Salvation Army Shelter Services Center, clients were expected to follow strict rules that limited their autonomy and to take measures, such as abstaining from drinking, to redeem themselves. Volunteers, who were mainly working-class males and included many former clients and others performing court-mandated community service, "received disciplining into a work ethic that valued sobriety and productivity" (Allahyari, 2000:153) as they sought physical and spiritual salvation.

Allahyari's study typifies field research. Unlike studies based on other approaches, she reported her research in a book rather than a journal article. The book provides a rich description that is difficult to convey in a brief summary. Her research objective, established once she was in the field, was to understand the meaning that the volunteers attached to caring for others. The "data" that she reports consisted of accounts of events and quotations from those she encountered, both of which were taken from a running log of observations recorded at the end of each day. In addition to her observations as a volunteer, Allahyari formally interviewed staff and examined written documents such as a monthly newsletter produced by Loaves & Fishes staff and the Salvation Army's bimonthly magazine. In Chapter 11 we consider the key issues that Allahyari and other field researchers face: selecting an appropriate setting or group for study and then gaining entry to and getting along with others in the setting; deciding what to observe and record and when and how to record one's observations; and handling, organizing, and analyzing the observational record.

An Answer from Available Data

The final approach to studying the social world discussed in this volume is the use of **available data**—that is, data that have been generated for purposes other than those for which a researcher is using them. Prominent among such data sources are written records, from letters and diaries to newspapers and government documents; but available data also includes nonverbal physical evidence such as paintings, clothing, tools, and other artifacts. Even tombstones could be considered data in this sense since they are created for one purpose (to mark graves) but could be used for others (e.g., to study the diffusion of sculptural styles over several generations). How might altruism be studied with this approach?

A study of volunteering in the wake of the September 11, 2001, attacks on the World Trade Center and the Pentagon shows the difference between anecdotal information and systematic research based on the analysis of available data. Following this unprecedented event, numerous media reports described altruistic acts such as direct physical aid and cash donations to victims of the attacks and their families. Louis Penner and associates (2005) asked whether volunteering was affected by the September 11 attacks and, if so, for how long. They were able to answer this question empirically because they discovered and were given access to the database of an organization that uses an Internet website (VolunteerMatch) to connect volunteers with service organizations.

Several features of the website made it possible to track changes in volunteering over time and to answer the researchers' question. First, the website was launched in August 1997 and was fully functional by the end of that year, so it existed before and after the attacks. Second, the organization maintained a database that recorded key information about users of its website. Visitors to the website who are seeking volunteer opportunities are led through a sequence of steps to detailed information about specific organizations that are located in the person's zip code. After selecting one of these organizations, the person receives a template for his or her e-mail address. If the person wants to volunteer, he or she simply clicks "Send" and his or her name and e-mail address are sent to the organization.

The database maintained by VolunteerMatch contained a daily record of the number of people who had contacted an organization to express an interest in volunteering. Penner and colleagues were provided data from August 7, 1997, through December 31, 2001. Analyzing weekly totals, they found 4 weeks in which volunteering showed unusually high rates. The first of these, December 5, 1999, was a week in which Oprah Winfrey's television show included a segment on VolunteerWatch; the other 3 weeks spanned September 9 through September 29, 2001. During that period, more than 30,000 people signed up to work as volunteers, which was more than double the rate of any other 3-week period during the 4 years analyzed.

The database also grouped service organizations according to their general purpose or targets—for example, children and youth, crisis support, disabled, health and medicine—which enabled the researchers to answer a second question: Was volunteering for certain charities differently affected by the attacks? Although they found that volunteering rates increased substantially for all kinds of charity/service organizations, rates for crisis-related organizations (e.g., the local chapter of the Red Cross) were about two to three times as great as rates for other categories.

Discovering the VolunteerWatch website and gaining the organization's cooperation made it possible for Penner and his colleagues to answer some important questions about the impact of the September 11 attacks on altruism. Indeed, simply finding appropriate available data is a major problem with this approach. It often requires considerable imagination and ingenuity just to think of and uncover the kind of information that can be used to address research questions. And once the data are in hand, still other problems arise involving data handling and analysis. The most fundamental of these problems is how to codify the data in a systematic fashion; another common problem is what to do when the information is insufficient or not comparable from one case to another. On carefully examining the VolunteerWatch database, for example, Penner and colleagues discovered several anomalies in the first few months of the website's existence, including no entries at all for several days, which, they surmised, was caused by working problems with the site in its early stages. This led them to exclude data from all but 4 days of 1997 and to focus on the remaining 4 years. Because of the recency of their data, Penner and colleagues knew precisely how the information had been gathered and tabulated; however, questions about the authenticity and accuracy of available data often arise. This is especially true for historians relying on documentary evidence from the distant past. In Chapter 12, after describing a vast array of available data, we consider these and other issues related to this approach.

Conclusions

Our goals in this introduction have been to demonstrate the value of studying research methods and to describe the general nature of social research. Social research helps us to understand the social world by producing scientifically valid answers to questions. You may seek "answers" from social research in your student and professional lives, and you inevitably will be exposed to various answers through the media. Media reports of social scientific studies, however, sometimes distort the facts and sometimes draw erroneous or misleading conclusions. Moreover, there is inevitably some degree of uncertainty and error in social research. Studying research methods will cultivate your skepticism about research evidence. But this skepticism is healthy because enhancing your ability to understand and evaluate how research findings are arrived at will enable you to identify whether they are based on more or less sound methods of inquiry and whether they warrant strong or weak conclusions.

Exploring how social scientists have investigated the topic of altruism introduced an important theme of this book. That is, although social scientists have developed a variety of approaches to social research, no one approach is inherently superior to another and all approaches may be understood within the framework of scientific inquiry and the quest for understanding. To be sure, the four most basic approaches differ in many ways, and each has its distinctive strengths and weaknesses. Yet, we believe that all approaches must address the same central methodological issues and are subject to the same underlying logic of inference. That the sources of error vary from one approach to another only underscores the value in combining approaches and using them in complementary ways to validate knowledge.

KEY POINT

A variety of approaches may be taken to study social phenomena; the best strategy is to use multiple approaches that do not share the same weaknesses.

An Overview of the Book

Approaches to Social Research is divided into four main sections. The first section describes the scientific and ethical contexts of social research. As we explain the nature of science in Chapter 2, we assume the essential unity of all the sciences, drawing examples from physics, chemistry, and biology as well as sociology and psychology. This does not mean that there is a unified method or "cookbook" for conducting scientific research. It means, rather, that all scientific disciplines abide by the same epistemic requirements for judging the credibility of theories and evidence. Similarly, all scientists are expected to be ethical and to follow widely accepted ethical principles regarding the conduct and reporting of scientific findings and the treatment of human subjects. In Chapter 3 we examine these principles and discuss the process of ethical decision making as well as scientists' responsibility to consider the social consequences of research and to educate others on the appropriate interpretation and application of scientific findings.

The remainder of the book roughly follows the stages in conducting research, from the formulation of a problem or question to data collection to analysis and interpretation. The second section covers the major ingredients of the overall research plan. Focusing on problem formulation, Chapter 4 introduces the basic language of social research and outlines the various purposes of conducting social research and the overall research process. Chapter 5 describes how social scientists operationalize concepts and evaluate the quality of operational definitions. Chapter 6 describes the scientific principles and methods of selecting a representative set of cases. The goal of social research is to answer questions about the social world by producing *valid* empirical evidence. Accordingly, each chapter in this section addresses a key issue in determining the validity of social scientific evidence: the validity of causal inferences (Chapter 4), the validity of operationalizations of concepts (Chapter 5), and the generalizability of findings (Chapter 6). As we discuss these issues, we draw on the first study mentioned at the beginning of the chapter: Broh's (2002) analysis of the impact of sports participation on academic achievement.

Each of the three validity issues is addressed again in the third section of the book with respect to the four basic approaches to social research. Four chapters outline the essential features, variants, steps in conducting, and distinctive advantages and disadvantages of each approach: experiments (Chapter 7), surveys (Chapter 9), field research (Chapter 11), and research using available data (Chapter 12). Two chapters elaborate on special technical features of experiments and surveys. Chapter 8 outlines a framework for analyzing the validity of causal conclusions and various experimental designs that serve as ideal models for establishing causal relationships. Chapter 10 describes the elements of designing a questionnaire. Chapter 13 then examines how two or more of the four basic approaches to social research may be combined effectively to strengthen the validity of research findings. Finally, the concluding chapter of this section examines the special features and problems of conducting evaluation studies, which are aimed at assessing social intervention programs and policies.

Throughout this section we use several studies to illustrate the process and problems of conducting social research. Thus, here is where you will read about the other studies mentioned at the beginning of this chapter: Latané and Darley's (1970) experiments on bystander intervention in emergencies (Chapter 7), Green and Gerber's (2008) field experiments on getting out the vote (Chapters 7 and 13), Snow and Anderson's (1993) field research on homelessness (Chapter 11), Erikson's (1966) analysis of the Salem witch hysteria (Chapter 12), and Sherman and Berk's (1984) analysis of the impact of arrests in cases of domestic assault (Chapters 13 and 14).

The fourth section deals broadly with the processing, analysis, and interpretation of data. Chapter 15 outlines the steps in processing data for quantitative analysis and describes elementary statistical analyses. Chapter 16 considers various statistical techniques for analyzing causal relationships. Because almost all social research ultimately becomes known and is interpreted by others through the reading of reports, books, and articles, in the final chapter (Chapter 17) we examine the writing of research.

Key Terms

All key terms are defined in the glossary at the end of the book.

experiment	field research
survey	available data

Exercises

1. Find a story or article in the media (e.g., newspaper, magazine, television) that reports the findings of a social scientific study or of a contention (e.g., an advertising claim) purportedly based on social scientific evidence. What information, if any, is given about the methods of the study or the limitations of the findings? Does the author report where the data came from, how they were collected, or how many observations the findings were based on?
2. Select a recent issue of a major social science journal, such as the *American Sociological Review*, *American Political Science Review*, or *Social Psychology Quarterly*. Based on your reading of the abstracts of each article, identify the basic approach (experiment, survey, field research, or use of available data) that is used in each study reported in the issue. Which approach is most common?

Web Resources

The website for *Approaches to Social Research*, sixth edition (www.oup.com/us/singleton-approaches), contains several resources for each chapter: (1) answers to selected exercises; (2) true–false and matching quizzes; and (3) annotated lists of Web resources.

PART I

The Scientific and Ethical Contexts of Social Research

The next two chapters describe two important contexts within which social research takes place. Chapter 2 considers the basic elements of science, for social research is fundamentally a scientific enterprise. As such, we believe it is essential to understand what unites the social sciences with the natural sciences. Obviously, it is neither the subject matter nor the specific research techniques. What unites science are its objectives, presuppositions, general methodology, and logic. That is what we focus on in Chapter 2—the epistemological foundations of science that transcend specific subject matters, guiding the efforts of researchers in many different disciplines.

Social research also has a moral foundation. At the same time that social researchers follow the canons of scientific inquiry, they must be sensitive to the ethical choices that they make. Ethics are especially relevant when scientific research involves human beings because researchers are obligated to treat research participants with respect, protect them from harm, preserve their rights, and ensure their well-being. Social scientists also have ethical obligations to their profession to conduct their research with honesty and integrity, as well as to the general public to promote the beneficial application of research findings. In Chapter 3 we consider these ethical concerns, giving special attention to the treatment of human research participants, and describe regulations and codes that guide ethical decision making in social research.

2

The Nature of Science

When you think of a "scientist," what do you think of? For many years, Royce Singleton asked his sociology methods students this question. If you are like most of Singleton's students, you associate science foremost with the natural sciences—chemistry, physics, and biology. Moreover, you probably picture a scientist in a white lab coat in a laboratory, surrounded by test tubes and microscopes (Singleton, 1998).

In short, students rarely conjure images of sociologists or other *social* scientists as scientists. The American public distinguishes between natural and social sciences in a similar way: Whereas 71.6 percent of a national sample of adults thinks that biology is "very scientific," only 8.9 percent say the same of sociology (T. W. Smith, Marsden, and Hout, 2016). Yet disciplines such as sociology and psychology aspire to be scientific (American Sociological Association, 2017; American Psychological Association, 2017). Therefore, to understand how social scientists do what they do, we must understand how science guides their activities. In this chapter, we identify the characteristic product and process of inquiry that defines and unifies all the sciences—natural and social.

Most broadly, this chapter deals with issues of **epistemology**: what constitutes knowledge in the social sciences and how it is created. Standard scientific inquiry reveals what we regard as the essential epistemological foundations of social science. There are alternative epistemologies, however; so in the end we consider some of these challenges to a unified model of science.

The Aim of Science

The word "science" comes from the Latin *scientia*, which means "knowledge." The aim of science is to produce knowledge, to understand and explain some aspect of the world around us. But accumulated knowledge per se does not distinguish science from mythology. What, then, makes an endeavor scientific? Basically, it is a matter of *how* and *why* knowledge is accepted by the scientific community. Two interrelated sets of criteria determine acceptance or rejection. One set of criteria pertains to the form or logical structure of knowledge and the other to the evidence on which it is based. In discussing the nature of science, therefore, we distinguish among the laws, principles, and theories that constitute the *product* of science and the methods and logic of inquiry that comprise the *process* through which scientific knowledge is created, tested, and refined.

Although the analogy is imperfect, it may help in following our discussion to think of a factory or industrial plant in which certain raw materials are processed to create a finished product. One of the differences between industry and science lies in what is processed: Industries manufacture material things; science processes *ideas*. Of course, science has made possible innumerable technological advances, whose material fruits, perhaps because of their visibility, are often seen as the essential end product of science. But these practical results are mere by-products of scientific inquiry. The real goal of science is to achieve understanding; the basic product is ideas.[1] We will see the form that these ideas take as we first consider science as a product. Then we will turn our attention to the science process.

Science as Product

Scientific disciplines differ in terms of their objects of study. Physics is concerned with matter and energy, biology is concerned with the life processes of plants and animals, psychology is concerned with human and animal behavior, and sociology is concerned with properties and processes of social groupings. As a consequence, each of these disciplines has developed its own unique concepts, laws, and theories. Yet, despite such differences, all scientific knowledge, regardless of the field of study, shares certain defining characteristics, the first of which is the type of questions that may be addressed.

Scientific versus Nonscientific Questions

Whether a question can be approached scientifically depends on whether it is possible to make observations—which others also are capable of making—that can answer the question. This means that philosophical questions about essence, existence, or morality are beyond the realm of science. Answers to some philosophical questions do become the fundamental postulates, or assumptions, of science, but these cannot be investigated scientifically. Thus, scientists can only assume that the world exists, that empirically verifiable knowledge is possible, that we can know the world through our senses, and that there is an order to the world. Having made such assumptions, what scientists try to do is describe and explain the order that they assume to exist.

It would be proper for a social scientist to ask such questions as Why do some people watch pornographic films? Why is one type of organization more efficient than another? Are sibling relationships related to adult sexual preference? But it would *not* be within the realm of science to ask, Is pornography morally wrong? Should efficiency be valued over morale? Is homosexuality contrary to God's will? The difference between these two sets of questions is that the former deal with how and why regular patterns of events occur, whereas the latter ask what is desirable. Questions of value and morality are worth asking and speculating about; but they fall within the purview of philosophy and religion. They are not scientific because they cannot be framed in such a way that *observations* can be made to answer them.

Both philosophers and scientists ask about the "why" of things. But to scientists, as the psychologists Michael Doherty and Kenneth Shemberg (1978:6) note, "the 'why' is just shorthand for, What is the relationship between . . . or, Under what conditions . . ." When we can use these phrases, "then the question could be a legitimate scientific question, provided the other terms in the question meet the test of observability." Thus, we can "observe" (i.e., gather data on) whether people view pornographic films, and we can try to determine the "conditions" (e.g., a person's gender and age, relationships with others, occupation) under which this is likely to occur. Likewise, we can determine what the relationship is between the type of organization and efficiency, assuming we can decide how to distinguish different forms of organization and decide on the pattern of observations that represents "efficiency." No such appeals to objective evidence, however, will enable us to decide whether purveyors of pornography should be legally prosecuted or left alone or to decide the relative importance of efficiency and morale.[2]

In short, scientific questions are questions that can be answered by making observations that identify the conditions under which certain events occur. Still, to qualify as scientific knowledge, the *answers* to such questions must take a particular form, a form that meets the requirements of description, explanation, prediction, and understanding.

Knowledge as Description

The first step in producing scientific knowledge is description. We must describe objects and events before we can understand and explain the relationships among them. Each discipline therefore develops its own special language or set of concepts.

Concepts are abstractions communicated by words or other signs that refer to common properties among phenomena. The term "weight," for example, symbolizes a conception of a property of all physical objects. Likewise, the sociological term "status" is an abstraction that points to a property of a social structure or group. The first rule about the scientific use of concepts is one word, one concept. The sociologist George Zito (1975:21) noted that in everyday language one word may stand for many different things; "mass," for example, may mean the quality of size and weight, the main part, a Christian religious ceremony, or something else entirely. To a physicist, however, "it means only the quantity of matter in a body as measured in relation to its inertia." Because everyday language is so vague and full of multiple meanings, scientists find it necessary to restrict or redefine the meaning of common words or to invent new terms (sometimes called "constructs"), thereby creating highly technical vocabularies.

Scientists' second rule about concepts is that there must be agreed-on ways of tying them to tangible objects and events. This rule extends the first rule by stating that concepts must be defined directly or indirectly in terms of precise, reliable observations. It would be scientifically unacceptable to describe something as "heavy," not only because this term has many different connotations (i.e., it refers to more than one concept) but also because as a symbol for any single concept it is imprecise. People may agree or disagree when the weight of an object is described as heavy; however, they can readily agree when the object is placed on a scale and its weight is described as 50 pounds. By the same token, many concepts (e.g., "energy," "electron," "wavelength") that are not simply and directly observable are scientifically acceptable because they imply characteristics that are observable. For example, physicists cannot directly observe the movement of molecules postulated by the kinetic theory of gases; however, using a pressure gauge, they can measure the pressure that this movement implies. Linking concepts to observable events, called "measurement," is something we will have much more to say about in Chapter 5.

To a large extent, the language we use determines what we see in the world. Research has shown, for example, that people have better recognition memory for colors that they can label with familiar words (Lucy and Shweder, 1979). Similarly, the words or concepts that scientists develop indicate their usefulness for describing and explaining phenomena of interest. The existence of the term "social class" thus reflects its utility for explaining sociological concerns such as social order and social change. This implies a third rule about language usage in science: Concepts are judged by their usefulness. Scientists are not dogmatic about concepts. Once a concept has outlived its usefulness or the explanation in which it is embedded has been superseded by a better explanation, it is discarded.

Knowledge as Explanation and Prediction

Explanations, according to the sociologist Gwynn Nettler (1970), are attempts to satisfy curiosity. Depending on the type of question and the needs of the interrogator, curiosity may be satisfied in several ways: by labeling (as when the appropriate term is given in response to a child's question about what something is), by defining or giving examples (as when new terms are clarified with familiar terms and images), by evoking empathy (as when people offer motives or other "good reasons" for their conduct), by appealing to authority (as when something is attributed to "God's will"), or by citing a general empirical rule (as when we say that this book falls when dropped because it is denser than air, and all objects denser than air fall when dropped). Only this last form of explanation is capable of meeting the twin objectives of scientific knowledge—to *explain* the past and present and to *predict* the future.

The "empirical rules" with which scientific explanations are built consist of abstract statements, or propositions, that relate changes in one general class of events to changes in another class of events under certain conditions. Consider, for example, the following two propositions, the first a part of the ideal gas law from chemistry and the second a generalization from social psychology known as the "social facilitation effect":

1. If the volume of a gas is constant, then an increase in temperature will be followed by an increase in pressure (Reynolds, 1971:5).
2. If a task is simple or well learned, then an individual will perform it better in the presence of others than in isolation.

According to each of these propositions, a change in one set of events (temperature of a gas, absence or presence of others) is followed by a change in another set of events (pressure of the gas, performance of an individual) under specified conditions (constant volume, simple or well-learned task). The propositions are abstract in two senses. First, since they may refer to past, present, or future changes, they make no reference to historical time. Second, each proposition pertains to a *general* class of events: gases of a constant volume in one instance and individuals performing simple tasks in the other. The second proposition would be less abstract if it made reference only to males and still less abstract if it applied only to males with high self-esteem. Level of abstractness is important because the ideal in science is to develop the most general understanding: to establish propositions capable of explaining and predicting the widest possible range of events.

Scientists use various terms to denote propositions such as the ideal gas law and social facilitation effect. They may be called **empirical generalizations** when they are derived from observations or **hypotheses** when they have been proposed but not tested. To the extent that the propositions have been repeatedly verified and are widely accepted, they may become known as scientific **laws**. In any case, as scientific explanations, they describe, explain, and predict particular phenomena. The terms contained within the propositions are the concepts that describe—organize and classify—the phenomena to be explained. Thus, the ideal gas law classifies gases according to their volume, temperature, and pressure; the social facilitation effect organizes individual behavior in terms of the concepts of task simplicity, presence or absence of others, and level of performance. Furthermore, each proposition explains and predicts by identifying the conditions (e.g., constant volume, increase in temperature) under which particular events occur (increase in pressure).

Scientific explanation does not end here, however, for although specific events are explained by empirical laws, the regularities expressed by these laws themselves require explanation. The ideal gas law raises the question of *why* increases in temperature invariably increase the pressure of gases under constant volume. Similarly, with respect to the social facilitation effect, why should the presence of others facilitate one's performance on simple tasks?

To answer such questions, and generally to explain empirical generalizations or laws, science introduces theories. **Theory** is one of the most elusive and misunderstood terms in science. It does not mean, as it is popularly understood, "idle speculation or conjecture." A scientific theory consists of a set of interconnected propositions that have the same form as laws but are more general or abstract. Note how the following set of propositions, called the "kinetic theory of gases," explains the ideal gas law by showing how it follows from the "conception of a gas as a collection of molecules in constant motion" (adapted from Reynolds, 1971:8):

As the temperature increases, the kinetic energy of the gas molecules increases.

As the kinetic energy increases, there is an increase in the velocity of the motion of the molecules.

As the molecules travel faster, but are prevented from traveling further by a vessel of constant volume, they strike the inside surface of the vessel more often and with more force.

As the molecules strike the sides of the vessel more frequently, the pressure on the walls of the vessel increases.

Therefore, assuming a constant volume, as the temperature increases, the pressure increases.

Scientific theories may be stated in various ways. The above set of propositions is arranged in a logical network that shows how the law may be deduced from the theory. In chemistry and physics, theories often take the form of mathematical formulas. For example, the formula $PV = nRT$ represents the ideal gas law. Aside from economics, theories in the social sciences usually are stated less formally. What is most critical, from the standpoint of science, is not how the theory is presented but that it is logically consistent and empirically testable.

Still, it is possible to have several logically coherent theories that explain a given empirical regularity and that make the same or similar testable predictions. This is true of the social facilitation effect, for which no established theoretical explanation exists, although several theories have been proposed. One theory holds that an audience enhances performance on simple tasks because the mere physical presence of others increases one's physiological arousal. According to another theory, enhanced performance occurs when persons believe that the other persons present are judging or evaluating their behavior. Scientific research often is directed toward testing such alternative theories, but ultimately one theory is judged superior to other competing theories to the extent that it (1) involves the fewest number of statements and assumptions, (2) explains the broadest range of phenomena, and (3) makes the most accurate predictions.

KEY POINT

Scientific concepts describe *what* is being studied; scientific hypotheses and theories explain *how* and *why* patterned events occur.

Knowledge as Understanding

Finally, many scientists maintain that, in addition to making testable predictions, scientific laws and theories must provide a sense of understanding. Although there is no consensus on the meaning or necessity of the "understanding" criterion, social scientists generally agree that this sense is gained by describing the causal process that connects events (Reynolds, 1971). A theory often meets this criterion in explaining a law or empirical generalization. The connection between temperature and pressure in the ideal gas law, for example, seems more understandable once we know the underlying process, described by the kinetic theory, by which temperature causes an increase in kinetic energy, which causes an increase in the velocity of molecules, and so on. Similarly, a law or hypothesis is thought to be scientifically meaningful when it describes a **causal relationship**—that is, a relationship in which a change in one event forces, produces, or brings about a change in another. In fact, unless a true causal relationship is identified, generalizations cannot meet the dual requirement of explanation and prediction. We can see this by examining some scientifically inadequate generalizations.

Many so-called scientific generalizations purport to explain but have no readily observable consequences and, hence, cannot predict. Standard examples abound in Freudian psychology. For instance, Freud suggested that all dreams represent the fulfillment or attempted fulfillment of a wish and that all persons have a death wish (Hall and Lindzey, 1970). The problem with these generalizations is that they too readily "explain" things after the fact. We can always find some wish with which to interpret or explain a dream, once it has occurred. Similarly, every suicide or accident can be attributed to a death wish. This is like placing your bet after the race is over. Once an event has occurred, any number of plausible, intuitively appealing explanations can be offered. Post hoc generalizations thus give us a false sense of understanding. The trick is also to indicate what to expect under given conditions. Without this kind of objective testability, it is impossible to tell if one event has caused the other.

It is also possible to predict an event on the basis of empirical generalizations without understanding the connection between generalization and prediction. Astronomical predictions of the movement of the stars were accurate long before satisfactory explanations for the movement existed. Today, the healing powers of aspirin are put to use although the reason for aspirin's effectiveness is not well understood; election outcomes can be predicted accurately although their explanation remains unsatisfactory; and, more mundanely, people continue to use a variety of time-tested, reliable, yet seemingly inexplicable predictors of weather changes. It is a folk wisdom, for example, that the leaves of trees show their light green undersides when a storm is imminent. Generalizations such as these, unlike those that explain but do not predict, can be tested and are useful in certain contexts. However, their utility is limited. Once we have an adequate theory that describes the causal process connecting events, we get not only a better sense of understanding but also more accurate and more useful predictions.

Many examples from the history of science show how identifying causal processes enhances the utility of knowledge. One of the more interesting cases is the discovery of the cause and cure of rickets (Loomis, 1970). Rickets is a disease resulting in the softening and bending of growing bones. It is caused by a deficiency of solar ultraviolet radiation, which is necessary for the synthesis of a calcifying hormone released into the bloodstream by the skin. Without this hormone (calciferol), an insufficient amount of calcium is deposited in growing bones, causing the crippling deformities of rickets. Either adequate sunlight or the ingestion of minute amounts of calciferol will prevent and cure rickets. Before the causal process underlying rickets was understood, scientists could, in a sense, predict its occurrence. They noted, for example, seasonal variations in rickets—that is, its rise during the "darker" winter months. They observed its greater prevalence in cities than in rural districts and in northern industrial nations as opposed to northern nonindustrialized nations.

Identifying such patterns eventually led to the conclusion that sunlight had the power to prevent and cure rickets. But it was not until the sun's role in the production of calciferol was understood—until the complete causal process was identified—that rickets could be eradicated completely, even in areas where the sun's ultraviolet radiation is absent.

Thus, explanation in social science generally boils down to a search for causes. Knowing when and how to infer causality is a prerequisite for most social research. One of our goals, therefore, is to enhance this ability, which we will begin to do in Chapter 4 when we discuss criteria used to establish causality.

KEY POINT

Scientific hypotheses and theories provide a sense of understanding by describing the underlying causes of phenomena.

Tentative Knowledge

The psychologist B. F. Skinner (1953:11) argued that "science is unique in showing a cumulative progress," which enables each succeeding generation of scientists to begin a little further along. Thus, according to Skinner, "our contemporary writers, artists, and philosophers are not appreciably more effective than those of the golden age of Greece, yet the average high school student understands much more of nature than the greatest of Greek scientists" (11).

To the extent that this is true, it is largely a result of the *tentative* nature of scientific knowledge. Scientists never achieve complete understanding, nor do they assume access to indubitable truths. One reason is that every answer leads to new questions, and every new fact, law, or theory presents new problems so that no matter what the present state of scientific knowledge, there is always more to know. When or where this progression ends is impossible to tell; however, it is clear that science has barely scratched a very large surface.

Aside from the vast amount that there is to know, scientific knowledge is tentative and uncertain for another, more definitive reason. Unlike mathematics or logic, where the "truth" of statements either is assumed or rests on other statements that are assumed to be true, science bases the truth of its statements on observable evidence. And such evidence is always open to change through reinterpretation or to possible contradiction by new evidence. In other words, at some point a scientific proposition is accepted because it describes or interprets a recurring, observable event. But just because an event has occurred on several occasions, there is no guarantee that it will continue to occur. This can be seen from the following parable from Garvin McCain and Erwin Segal (1977:70):

> Once upon a time there lived a very intelligent turkey. He lived in a pen and was attended by a kind and thoughtful master. All of his desires were taken care of and he had nothing to do but think of the wonders and regularities of the world. He noticed some regularities—for example, that mornings always began with the sky getting light, followed by the clop, clop, clop of his master's friendly footsteps. These in turn were always followed by the appearance of delicious food and water within his pen. Other things varied: sometimes it rained and sometimes it snowed;

sometimes it was warm and sometimes cold; but amid the variability footsteps were always followed by food. This sequence was so consistent it became the basis of his philosophy concerning the goodness of the world. One day, after more than 100 confirmations of the turkey's theories, he listened for the clop, clop, clop, heard it, and had his head chopped off.

Since it is apparent that regularity does not guarantee certainty, scientific propositions, which are based on such regularity, cannot be proven. "Knowledge," therefore, "is understood to be the best understanding that we have been able to produce thus far, not a statement of what is ultimately real" (Polkinghorne, 1983:2). Theories are accepted by the scientific community as more or less reasonable and credible according to the accuracy of their predictions and the frequency with which they have been supported by empirical evidence. Let us now examine how such evidence is processed.

KEY POINT
Scientific knowledge cannot be proven as the search for understanding is uncertain and unending.

Science as Process

The word "process" signifies a series of operations or actions that bring about an end result. In industry, the longer phrase "manufacturing process" describes the sequence of steps through which raw materials are transformed into a finished product. The process differs according to what is manufactured; furthermore, technological advances, shifting consumer demands, and the like lead to periodic changes in the sequence and in its products. But in a given industry, for long periods of time, the process is repeated over and over again along the same line from beginning to end. In science, by contrast, change is built into the process. The product itself—knowledge—is never "finished" but is constantly remodeled to fit the facts. Furthermore, the sequence of steps followed in one scientific investigation is seldom repeated precisely in another, and the end of one investigation often marks the beginning of another. Thus, although the industrial process typically follows a linear progression from raw materials to completed goods, the most characteristic feature of the scientific process is its cyclical nature.

According to John Kemeny (1959:85), the great physicist Albert Einstein, whose own scientific contributions were theoretical, repeatedly emphasized that science "must start with facts and end with facts, no matter what theoretical structures it builds in between." In other words, at some point scientists are observers collecting data and recording facts; next, they try to describe and explain what they see; then, they make predictions on the basis of their theories, which they check against their observations (i.e., the facts or data) again. This chain of events is diagrammed in Figure 2.1. Where we begin in this chain is arbitrary. But at some point, theories generate predictions or hypotheses, hypotheses are checked against data, the data produce generalizations, and the generalizations support, contradict, or suggest modifications in the theory.

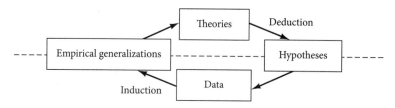

FIGURE 2.1. The scientific process.

KEY POINT

The essence of science is neither a body of knowledge nor a method of inquiry; rather, it is a cyclical process involving a continuous interplay between theory and research.

The horizontal dashed line in the diagram bisecting empirical generalizations and hypotheses separates the world of theory from the world of research. The development of theory, as we have seen, is the goal of science. Research supports this goal through systematic observation that generates the data from which theories are inferred and tested. In the remainder of the text, we are concerned almost exclusively with the research side of science. The important point to remember, however, is that science is a process involving the continuous interaction of theory and research. (To see the interesting turns that scientific inquiry can take, read Box 2.1.)

BOX 2.1 The Serendipity Pattern in Science

Scientific inquiry, for the most part, works within the framework of a theory. Hypotheses are derived, research is planned, and data are gathered and interpreted to test and elaborate theories. Occasionally, however, unanticipated findings occur that cannot be interpreted meaningfully in terms of prevailing theories and that give rise to new theories. Robert Merton (1957) refers to such discoveries as the **serendipity pattern**. In the history of science, there are many cases of scientific discoveries in which chance, or serendipity, played a part. One of these is Pasteur's discovery of immunization.

> Pasteur's researches on fowl cholera were interrupted by the vacation, and when he resumed he encountered an unexpected obstacle. Nearly all the cultures had become sterile. He attempted to revive them by sub-inoculation into broth and injection into fowls. Most of the sub-cultures failed to grow and the birds were not affected, so he was about to discard everything and start afresh when he had the inspiration of reinoculating the same fowls with a fresh culture. His colleague Duclaux relates: "To the surprise of all, and perhaps even of Pasteur, who was not expecting such success, nearly all these fowls withstood the inoculation, although fresh fowls succumbed after the usual incubation period." This resulted in the recognition of the principle of immunization with attenuated pathogens. (Beveridge, 1957:27)

Social science has had its share of serendipitous findings also. The well-known "Hawthorne effect," which refers to the impact that a worker's awareness of being under study has on his or her performance, was an unanticipated finding of a series of studies carried out between 1927 and 1932 at the Western Electric Hawthorne plant in Chicago (Roethlisberger and Dickson, 1939). In one of the studies, six women with the task of assembling telephone relays were placed in a special test room for observation. The idea of the study was to determine the effects of various changes in working conditions (e.g., method of payment, number and length of rest pauses, length of working day) on productivity, as measured by the number of relays completed. Over an extended period of time, numerous changes, each lasting several weeks, were introduced while the women's output was recorded. To the researchers' surprise, however, the changes were not related systematically to output. Instead, the women's output rate rose slowly and steadily throughout the study, even when working conditions introduced early in the study were reintroduced later. After questioning the women, the researchers concluded that their increased productivity was a response to the special attention given to them as participants in what was considered an important experiment. The fun of the test room and the interest of management simply had made it easier to produce at a higher rate. This was an important result in the history of social research for it indicated that subjects' awareness of being under study could affect the very actions that an investigator wishes to observe. Experiments, in particular, must take into account such effects, as we discuss in Chapter 7. (Interestingly, most scholars still trace the discovery of this effect to the Hawthorne study, although the conclusions eventually were shown to be unsupported by the evidence [see Carey, 1967].)

Durkheim's Study of Suicide

The French sociologist Emile Durkheim's classic study *Suicide* (1951), first published in 1897, nicely illustrates the interplay between theory and research. Durkheim lacked many of the tools of contemporary data analysis, and his evaluation of evidence has been criticized on several grounds (Douglas, 1967; Pope, 1976; Stark and Bainbridge, 1996). Yet his study is widely regarded as a model of social research.

Suicide was one of the most widely studied social problems of the nineteenth century (Giddens, 1965:4). Although early philosophical treatments focused on the moral implications of the act, it became the subject of intense empirical study when European nations began to routinely collect statistics on suicide in the late eighteenth century. Before Durkheim's time, several persons had collected and published data relating suicide rates to such factors as occupation, urbanization, religion, rate of social change, race, and climate. Durkheim relied extensively on these works as data sources, especially a study by the Italian physician Henry Morselli, who himself built on the work of the German scholar Adolf Wagner. Although Durkheim examined many of the same relationships as Wagner and Morselli, Durkheim's work gained prominence for its coherent sociological theory of suicide that accounted for a broad range of established findings.

In the introduction to *Suicide*, Durkheim highlights an interesting pattern in the suicide rates among different European countries: Whereas the general mortality rate was similar from one country to another, suicide rates varied considerably. Moreover, the sui-cide rate for each country tended to be stable over time. For example, from 1866 to 1870 the suicide rates in Italy, France, and Denmark were 30, 135, and 277 per million, respectively; and from 1871 to 1875, the rates in these same countries were 35, 150, and 258 per million (Durkheim, 1951:50). Finally, Durkheim notes the steady rise in suicide rates, a point of concern that many writers attributed to the passing of the traditional social order typified by rural and village life and the growth of large industrialized cities. *Suicide* represents an attempt to explain this stability and variation in suicide rates. For Durkheim, these were social facts that required sociological explanation.

To begin, Durkheim considered existing theories of suicide based on nonsocial fac-tors such as insanity, alcoholism, and climate. In each case, he challenged the theory dia-lectically and empirically. First, he argued against the theory on purely logical grounds; then, he presented data to test his reasoning. For example, he reasoned that if suicide were the result of insanity, the same groups with high rates of insanity ought to have high rates of suicide. Contrarily, available statistics showed that although women outnumbered men in insane asylums, men were far more likely to commit suicide; Jews had the highest rates of insanity but the lowest rates of suicide; and there was no correlation between the rates of insanity and suicide among 10 European countries. Thus, here Durkheim moved from theories to hypotheses to data, as depicted on the right side of Figure 2.1.

After rejecting nonsocial explanations of suicide, Durkheim turned to social fac-tors. He first noted that Catholic countries like Spain, Portugal, and Italy had lower rates of suicide than Protestant countries such as Germany, England, and Denmark. Know-ing that other systematic differences among these countries—for example, their level of industrialization—could account for the differences in suicide rates, Durkheim next com-pared Catholic with Protestant areas within the same country, first Germany and then Switzerland. In each case, he found that Catholic areas had lower suicide rates than Prot-estant areas. From such data, he theorized that Protestantism allows "greater freedom to individual thought" and "has fewer beliefs and practices" than Catholicism (Durkheim, 1951:159), so individuals feel less of a bond with others. More generally, the weaker the inte-gration of the religious community, the more likely that an individual will commit suicide. And so, in this part of his analysis, Durkheim moved from data to generalization, as shown on the left side of Figure 2.1.

Having introduced the concept of social integration to explain Catholic–Protestant differences, Durkheim proceeded to show how this concept also could account for other variations in suicide. Statistics from France indicated that unmarried persons were more likely to commit suicide than married persons and that childless persons were more likely to kill themselves than people who have children. Other data revealed that the suicide rate declined during periods of political crises. Each of these findings may be explained, Durkheim argued, by the theory that "suicide varies inversely with the degree of integra-tion of the social groups of which the individual forms a part" (1951:209). Married per-sons experience more intense interpersonal attachments, and hence integration, than do single persons; the same is true of persons with children compared with those without chil-dren. Furthermore, social upheavals such as revolutions and wars tend to "rouse collective sentiments, stimulate partisan spirit and patriotism, political and national faith, alike, and concentrating activity toward a single end, at least temporarily cause a stronger integration of society" (208).

The end result of this scientific study is a theory based in fact or data. The theory is abstract enough to account for several empirical generalizations that relate suicide to religion, marital status, family size, and social change. Durkheim called this the theory of "egoistic suicide" because the cause of suicide springs from "excessive individualism" or lack of social integration. Although he went on in *Suicide* to develop a more comprehensive theory that included a fourfold typology of causes, the theory of egoistic suicide, synthesized as follows by Whitney Pope (1976:23), has received the greatest attention:

> The higher the rate of social interaction, the stronger the collective sentiments.
> The stronger the collective sentiments, the stronger social integration.
> The stronger social integration, the more individuals act in the service of social interests.
> The more individuals act in the service of social interests, the more meaning they find in life and the lower the suicide rate.

Although our description of *Suicide* shows how it encapsulates the scientific process, a single study such as this is part of a continuous, unending cycle of inquiry. Just as Durkheim built on the work of Wagner, Morselli, and others, numerous studies since Durkheim have questioned, refined, and tested his insights. Scholars have offered several methodological criticisms (one of which, called the "ecological fallacy," we take up in Chapter 4); have reinterpreted and refined his theory, especially the pivotal concept of social integration; and have repeatedly tested all of his hypotheses. Subsequent research shows that some of the patterns Durkheim found continue to hold: For instance, men have higher rates of suicide than women (see Wray, Colen, and Pescosolido, 2011), and divorce rates and nonmarried status are positively related to suicide rates (see Breault, 1994). However, some of Durkheim's interpretations and other findings have been challenged. In the late twentieth-century United States, suicide rates in areas heavily populated with certain Protestant groups, such as evangelical Protestants, were similar to those in areas with large concentrations of Catholics (Pescosolido and Georgianna, 1989; Pescosolido, 1990).

The thread running through all of this work, beyond the interplay between theory and data, is a mode of inquiry that distinguishes scientific research from other forms of research. Some people refer to this as "the scientific method." But this unfortunate phrase implies a definitive, orderly procedure that simply does not exist in science. What characterizes scientific inquiry is a commonly understood logic of justification and a set of standards that all scientists follow in generating and assessing the evidence on which their theories are based.

Logical Reasoning

Scientists are expected to follow the principles of logical reasoning. This does not mean that logic can tell scientists how to think or reason; rather, once an act of reasoning has taken place and is communicated, logic provides the criteria for evaluating the correctness of the reasoning. Durkheim began his study with a collection of facts or data on suicide and with the idea that social facts warranted a sociological explanation. He identified several empirical generalizations and then, using his imagination, came up with the theory of egoistic suicide. There are no logical rules that Durkheim could have followed to devise his theory; however, once he had formulated the theory, it became possible for others to assess its logical consistency and to logically deduce its testable predictions.

When people reason, they make inferences; that is, they draw conclusions based on information or evidence. The two main types of logical reasoning, inductive and deductive, differ in terms of the strength or certainty with which the evidence supports the conclusion. In **deductive reasoning**, the conclusion is absolutely certain if the evidence is true. In **inductive reasoning**, the conclusion is uncertain even if the evidence is true because its content goes beyond the evidence.

Consider the following examples of each type of reasoning:

Inductive: Hubert, Walter, and Joan, who are union members, are Democrats. Therefore, all union members are Democrats.
Deductive: All union members are Democrats. Joan belongs to the union. Therefore, Joan is a Democrat.

Note that the first conclusion goes beyond the information at hand. Therefore, we cannot know for certain that the conclusion is true; we can only judge how probable it is, based on the evidence. Even if the evidence is true, it is always possible that new information will show that some union members are *not* Democrats. (Remember the parable of the turkey.) By contrast, according to the rules of deductive logic, the second conclusion— "Joan is a Democrat"—must be true *if* the statement about union members being Democrats is true and *if* we have accurately identified Joan as a union member.

It is sometimes said that induction moves from specific instances to general principles, whereas deduction moves from the general to the specific.[3] Thus, in our example of induction, we observe that specific union members are Democrats and infer from this the general conclusion that they *all* are. In the example of deduction, we began with the general proposition that *all* union members are Democrats and deduced that a particular union member is a Democrat.

Scientists reason inductively when they infer empirical generalizations from data. This type of reasoning describes Durkheim's thinking when he inferred that Protestants were more likely to commit suicide than Catholics based on the fact that predominantly Protestant countries had higher suicide rates than predominantly Catholic countries. It also describes the formulation of his theory to account for generalizations relating suicide rates to religion, marital and family status, and political crises. In the scientific process depicted in Figure 2.1, inductive reasoning is a "bottom-up" process, moving from data to empirical generalizations to theories.

Scientists reason deductively when they show how a hypothesis explains or predicts specific facts. Thus, deductive reasoning represents a "top-down" process in Figure 2.1, proceeding from general principles to specific observations or facts. The following set of propositions shows how, by deduction, Durkheim's hypothesis explains the fact that the suicide rate is lower among Catholics than among Protestants:

> If one group is more socially integrated than another, then its suicide rate will be lower. (HYPOTHESIS)
> Catholics are more socially integrated than Protestants.
> Therefore, the suicide rate is lower among Catholics than among Protestants. (FACT)

Each type of reasoning is evaluated according to different rules and criteria. Inductive inferences are analyzed in terms of the *degree* to which the evidence supports the conclusion. The degree of support, moreover, can be increased or decreased by adding information or evidence. For example, the above inductive inference that "all union members are Democrats" becomes more probable when we increase the number of observed cases or individuals who are both union members and Democrats. The inference also is strengthened to the extent that the observed cases are dissimilar but weakened when they are similar to one another. For example, if the observed individuals are of different ages, live in different cities, and are employed in different industries, we would be more confident in the conclusion than if the individuals were all more than 40 years old, lived in Detroit, and worked in the automotive industry. The more diverse sample eliminates the possibility that the inference applies only to union members of a certain age or residence or occupation. Similarly, Durkheim increased the strength of his generalization regarding religion and suicide by showing that suicide rates were higher not only in Protestant than in Catholic countries but also in Protestant than in Catholic areas of Germany and Switzerland.

Scientists have devised logical rules for evaluating the soundness of many forms of inductive reasoning. Indeed, social science methodology is basically a system of logical rules and procedures for conducting research and evaluating knowledge claims. We introduce logical principles throughout the book as we discuss, for example, the criteria for inferring cause-and-effect relationships (Chapter 4), the means of determining the reliability and validity of social measurements (Chapter 5), and the bases for estimating population characteristics from sample statistics (Chapter 6).

Unlike inductive inferences, which may vary in strength or probability, deductions are either valid or invalid. A conclusion logically follows from a general proposition or it does not; a hypothesis is logically consistent with the facts, as is Durkheim's hypothesis, or it is not. Checking for deductive validity or sound logical reasoning is an essential first step in evaluating hypotheses and theories; however, when a hypothesis or theory is logically consistent with the facts, this does not mean that it is necessarily true. Logically, some other hypothesis might explain the facts just as well. The sociologist Arthur Stinchcombe (1968) points out, for example, that explanations other than Durkheim's social integration theory can account for the higher suicide rate of Protestants. This observation "might be explained by their occupations, by the lesser emphasis on the sin of suicide in Protestant theology, by the fact that confessors are available to every Catholic in times of trouble and crisis, and so forth" (18).

Ultimately, Durkheim strengthened the support for his hypothesis in several ways: by replicating the findings with different data sets, as when he reproduced the Protestant–Catholic difference within different countries; by testing a wide variety of predictions, as when he showed a higher incidence of suicide among single than among married persons and a reduction in suicides during periods of parliamentary crisis; and by eliminating major alternative explanations, as when he presented results that discounted the mental illness explanation. In science, however, the verification of a hypothesis is really never complete. No matter how strong the evidence, it is always possible for the evidence to be true and the hypothesis false. It is also possible for the evidence itself to be in error. To avoid these possibilities, scientists must (1) repeatedly conduct research to build up a large and diversified "body of confirming evidence, or to find disconfirming evidence if there is any," and (2) take all steps necessary to ensure accurate, unbiased evidence (Salmon, 1973:116). In the ensuing chapters, we point out these steps. For now, we describe three key principles to which scientists adhere in gathering and evaluating evidence: empiricism, objectivity, and control.

KEY POINT

Deductive reasoning, as when deriving a hypothesis from a theory, is either valid or invalid; *inductive reasoning*, as when generalizing from specific observations, is more or less sound depending on the scope of the observations.

Empiricism

As we noted earlier, scientists limit themselves to problems and issues that can be resolved by making observations. This means that scientific inquiry is based on empiricism. **Empiricism** is a way of knowing or understanding the world that relies directly or indirectly on what we experience through our senses: sight, hearing, taste, smell, and touch. In other words, pieces of information or data are acceptable in science only insofar as they can be observed or "sensed" in some way under specifiable conditions by people possessing the normal sensory apparatus, intelligence, and skills. Claire Selltiz, Lawrence Wrightsman, and Stuart Cook (1976), for example, point out that whereas people can see a baseball, they cannot see a neutron. However, "people can see neutrons indirectly, by observing photographic representations of paths neutrons leave. Under no normal conditions can people regularly observe ghosts. Nor do ghosts leave any other observable or tangible manifestations. Thus, we can have scientific theories about baseballs and neutrons but not about ghosts" (22). To say that science is based on empiricism, therefore, is to say that the only admissible evidence for or against a scientific hypothesis or theory must be observable, directly or indirectly, through some tangible manifestation.

This statement implies that appeals to authority, tradition, revelation, intuition, or other nonempirical ways of knowing, which may be acceptable in other endeavors (such as theology and philosophy), cannot be used as scientific evidence. Scientists do not accept a statement or generalization about the world simply because an authority or expert says it is true or because tradition and common sense say it is so or because it seems intuitively plausible. As Jeffrey Katzer, Kenneth Cook, and Wayne Crouch (1998:17) say,

> Evidence is paramount. If the results of well-conducted studies disagree with the authorities, then the authorities may very well be wrong. The proper method for an expert to appeal this verdict is to conduct another study. Or, if two research reports disagree, then additional studies need to be conducted to resolve the issue. The point is that knowledge about the world is best obtained by carefully looking at the world, not by looking at someone's idea of the world.

It should be noted that the terms "observable" and "empirical" have broader meaning in science than in philosophy. To a philosopher, observable applies to properties like "red," "round," or "hot," which can be perceived directly by the senses. To a scientist, observables are anything that can be related to the results of perceived measurements. For example, a temperature of 98.6 degrees Fahrenheit is considered observable to a scientist because it can be related to the height of a column of mercury in a thermometer. It is not observable to a philosopher, however, because there is no direct sensory perception of such a magnitude. One cannot feel or "see" temperature directly; one can only see a pointer reading on a thermometer (Carnap, 1966). Thus, empiricism in science often takes the form of *indirect* observation, whereby instruments are employed that aid and extend the scientist's ability to observe. What passes for empirical data also extends to records of observations made by others, such as the official statistics on suicide used by Durkheim.

Objectivity

Empirical evidence is assumed to exist outside of scientists themselves. Therefore, it is sometimes held that scientists are, or should be, objective. However, in the usual sense of the term (to mean observation that is free from emotion, conjecture, or personal bias), **objectivity** is rarely, if ever, possible. Social psychologists have demonstrated that we do not see the world simply "as is." Rather, we learn to see. The light waves impinging on our eyes must be interpreted by our minds, and our interpretations depend on the sum total of our past learning and present experiences—including everything from our culture and language to our beliefs and expectations. Thus, our observation—or, more properly, our interpretation—of the world is inevitably distorted to some extent by factors not under our conscious control. For this reason, scientists agree that objectivity, in the sense of observation free from bias, is a practical impossibility.

Fortunately, scientists assign a limited and far more useful meaning to the term "objective." To a scientist, it merely means agreement on the results of a given observation. In other words, it must be possible for two or more independent observers working under the same conditions to agree that they are observing the same thing or event. The technical term for this is **intersubjective testability**. Doherty and Shemberg (1978:5) provide the following example of its application in social research:

> If you were to send two observers into a classroom and instruct them to rate a child on "hostility," you may well expect to get two very different ratings. The term

hostility is open to many different interpretations. So the observations would not be very objective. On the other hand, suppose you instructed the observers to count the number of times that a particular child punched or hit other children, defined what you meant by punched or hit, maybe showed the observers a training film to sharpen the definition, and *then* turned them loose to make the observation. You would very likely get very high agreement among the observers. That's objectivity.

Because of the requirement of objectivity, scientists are supposed to describe their research in detail, outlining their logic and methods of observation in such a way that other scientists may evaluate and repeat the investigation. In this way, others can decide for themselves whether a researcher's subjectivity has distorted the conclusions. In fact, ultimately "objectivity is the product of a community of thinkers, each offering unsparing criticisms of . . . claims that the others make. For no one scientist engaged in this process of criticism is infallible, and each has his [or her] own peculiar intellectual or emotional bias" (Nagel, 1967:9–10).

Although it does not diminish his contribution, some analysts now contend that Durkheim's presentation and interpretation of evidence was biased. For example, Rodney Stark and William Sims Bainbridge (1996) strongly imply that Durkheim knowingly disregarded discordant data, including higher Catholic than Protestant suicide rates in some German states, and that he was grossly misinformed about England, a Protestant nation that, in fact, had one of the lowest suicide rates in Europe. Because Durkheim's didactic intent was to legitimize sociology as a scientific discipline, he also proposed a less-than-complete and hardly dispassionate explanation of the fluctuations in the suicide rate. By restricting his attention to social causes, he ignored the full range of factors that contribute to this complex phenomenon (D. P. Phillips, Ruth, and MacNamara, 1994). Durkheim might well deny such biases and argue that nonsocial causes of suicide simply were not empirically supported. The important point is that the determination of objectivity and the acceptance of scientific knowledge ultimately depend on the judgment of the scientific community. (For an example of how the public nature of science contributes to its objectivity, see Box 2.2.)

Control

As we have noted, the influence of certain biases is unavoidable, for language itself can structure our perceptions of the world. During the course of research, however, there are many ways in which scientists attempt to control for and minimize bias to maximize the trustworthiness of their observations. The use of control procedures that rule out biases is the principal way in which scientific inquiry differs from casual observation. In fact, the principle of **control** lies behind virtually every procedure and technique introduced in the remainder of this book. To get a glimpse of how scientists apply this principle, let us examine some applications from medical research.

Until the twentieth century, nearly all medications had little, if any, beneficial pharmacological effect on those who were treated (Shapiro, 1960). Whatever positive effect they seemed to have was probably due to the power of suggestion or because people improve naturally from many ailments, irrespective of the medical treatment they receive. If most

BOX 2.2 A Case of Scientific Fraud

The importance of the public nature of science, and the way in which it contributes to its objectivity, can be seen in the evaluation and reanalysis of some studies by the late British psychologist Cyril Burt (Kamin, 1974; Dorfman, 1978; Lewontin, Rose, and Kamin, 1984). For several decades—from the 1930s to the 1960s—Burt was an influential figure in the scientific research on intelligence and its genetic basis. His research on identical twins reared apart was a principal source of support for the theory that intelligence is determined primarily by heredity. Burt's data were compelling to hereditarians for several reasons (Lewontin, Rose, and Kamin, 1984:101). Because identical twins have identical genes, one way to demonstrate the hereditary basis of a trait such as intelligence is to study twins who do not share the same environment. If they resemble one another closely on a trait, the resemblance is logically attributable to that which they have in common: their identical genes. Not only did Burt report a very high correlation between the IQs of twins reared apart, supporting the heredity argument, but also his data were supposedly based on the largest sample of separated twins ever studied. Furthermore, in contrast to the environmental similarity of separated identical twins that is almost always found, the environments of the separated twins in Burt's study were reported to be very dissimilar. This last point is crucial to the heredity argument because it eliminates the possibility that similar environments rather than genetic identity account for the high correlation in IQ scores.

Beginning in the early 1970s, Burt's published studies underwent a close scrutiny that revealed several highly implausible and inconsistent results. For example, it was noted that each time Burt reported his data on separated twins, the number of twin pairs went up, from 21 in the first full report in 1955 to "over 30" in 1958 to a final report of 53 in 1966, whereas the reported correlation between IQs—.771—remained the same. Moreover, this remarkable tendency for IQ correlations to remain the same to the third decimal as sample size increased was also true of Burt's published statistics on nonseparated identical twins and on other types of relatives. When a long-awaited and carefully researched biography of Burt appeared in 1979, the question of his fraudulence was beyond doubt. The evidence uncovered in the book indicated that Burt had collected no data during the period when the twin studies were reported and that he had, in fact, fabricated the figures.

In science, fortunately, fraud is extremely rare. This is ensured because of science's public nature. Because of Burt's preeminence, scientists accepted his findings uncritically for many years, especially hereditarians who were eager to see their theories supported. This demonstrates the subjective element involved in judging the work of others. But these intersubjective judgments also provide a basis for correction and revision. And so, eventually the public scrutiny of Burt's work led to the rejection of his data as scientific evidence.

prescriptions were pharmacologically ineffective, however, why did so many people believe they were beneficial? The answer probably rests with the faulty evidence on which such beliefs were based. For example, it was widely held at one time that cold saltwater baths were beneficial to people suffering from high fevers. This belief appears to have been based on repeated observations of improvement in the condition of people subjected to this treatment. But this evidence is insufficient to establish the validity of the cure because it is possible that people who did *not* take cold saltwater baths showed similar improvement. Without comparing the course of the disease in patients receiving the treatment with its course in a control group who did not receive it, there was no rational basis for deciding whether the observed improvement could be attributed to the treatment (Nagel, 1967).

Yet even this kind of comparison may be inadequate for testing the efficacy of a new treatment or drug. When a treatment group is compared with a group that has received no treatment at all, there is still no control for the psychological effect of merely receiving some form of medication. A substantial part of medical practice appears to be based on the physician's and the patient's faith in the power of drugs to cure. It has been observed, for example, that persons given an inert substance such as a saline solution or sugar pill, called a "placebo," often react as favorably as persons given real medication. It is important, therefore, to control for such placebo effects. One way that this is often done in medical research is through the use of "double-blind" investigations.

In a double-blind study, several doctors are asked to prescribe and administer the drug being tested to their patients. The doctors receive the drug from the researcher in individual vials that are identified by number and contain only enough of the drug for one patient. Half of the vials contain the actual drug and half contain a placebo. Since neither doctors nor patients know which they are receiving, their beliefs about the drug cannot influence its effectiveness. That is, any difference observed between those receiving the drug and those receiving the placebo cannot be attributed to either the doctors' or the patients' expectations about the drug.

Still, even if a double-blind procedure were used, there may be other problems of interpretation. One of the most important of these problems stems from the simple fact that people are different; they react differently to various treatments and drugs, so most medications are not 100 percent effective. Therefore, if the patients used for testing tend to be people for whom a drug just happens not to work, the researcher may underestimate its effectiveness; and if the patients tend to be people for whom the drug does work, the researcher may overestimate its effectiveness. Fortunately, social researchers have devised methods—random selection procedures, discussed in Chapters 6 and 7—that control for this problem by determining whether chance can account for study results.

Research findings are often open to a variety of interpretations. The idea of control is to employ procedures that effectively rule out all explanations except the one in which the researcher is interested. In medical research, this takes the form of placebo groups and double-blind techniques designed to rule out the possibility of doctors' and patients' expectations contributing to the effectiveness of a treatment. In social research, as you will see, the application of the concept of control takes many forms. Durkheim was one of the first sociologists to control for alternative interpretations through data analysis. As we mentioned, he repeated his analysis of the relation between religion and suicide rates, first examining suicide rates among countries with varying proportions of Protestants and Catholics and then considering areas with varying Protestant and Catholic populations within particular countries. By analyzing the relation between religion and suicide *within* countries, he controlled for some of the factors that varied *among* countries. In the case of Switzerland, he took advantage of the fact that some French- and German-speaking areas were largely

Catholic and others were largely Protestant. This allowed "him to hold constant the effect of language as well as of nationality ('race') while examining the effect of religion on suicide" (Selvin, 1965:114).

Other control procedures in social research include (1) using several independent observers, not only to check for interobserver agreement (i.e., objectivity) but also to cancel out the personal biases of any particular observer; (2) withholding information from subjects, who may respond differently if they knew specifically what the researcher was investigating; and (3) employing instruments like tape recorders and counters or systematic observational methods that eliminate errors of omission and commission on the part of human observers. As we turn our attention exclusively to *social* research, we not only will introduce you to such techniques but also will help you to identify the sources of error and bias for which the techniques are intended to control.

KEY POINT

Scientific inquiry is guided by *empiricism* (reliance on observational evidence), *objectivity* (the ability of two or more people to agree on an observation), and *control* (use of procedures that eliminate sources of error and bias).

Critiques of Scientific Inquiry

In this chapter, we have presented an epistemology drawn from many philosophers who have analyzed the scientific process. Some social scientists believe, however, that this epistemology does not or should not apply to social research. At the least, others argue, it conveys an unrealistic impression of what social scientists actually do. Such views, we believe, fail to acknowledge a crucial fact: This model of inquiry unifies and guides the activities of all scientists even if their work falls short of the ideal. Still, we would be remiss if we did not point out challenges to, as well as some of the more important realities of, science, especially as practiced in the social sciences.

The Ideal and the Reality of Scientific Inquiry

Admittedly, we have presented a somewhat idealized view of science. The first reality is that theoretical knowledge is not well developed in the social sciences. There are those who claim that, at best, the social sciences have established only a few low-level principles and certainly nothing comparable to the ideal gas law examined earlier. As a consequence, social scientific theories tend to be stated less formally than the logical deductions used in this chapter or the mathematical equations often found in the natural sciences. Also, although we have defined "scientific theory" as a set of interrelated propositions from which testable hypotheses can be deduced, the term has a much looser meaning in the social sciences. In these fields, theory may refer to all sorts of speculative ideas offered as explanations for phenomena, and it is common to see the terms "theory" and "hypothesis" used interchangeably.

It is also important to dispose of a popular misconception of scientific theory that the ideal view of science may serve to perpetuate. That is, theories do not have to make precisely accurate predictions to be judged as scientifically useful. Scientific predictions are seldom, if ever, exactly confirmed. There is always some degree of error. How much error depends on the level of development of both theory and research technology, which explains why theoretical predictions in the physical sciences, more advanced in both areas, are generally so much more accurate than in the social sciences. But this lesser degree of accuracy does not make social science theory any less scientific. In all sciences, decisions between rival theories are seldom based on observational evidence alone. Rather, theories are evaluated and compared not only in terms of the accuracy of their predictions but also with respect to their explanatory scope and logical coherence.

Our idealized depiction of science also may foster some distorted impressions about the practice of scientific inquiry. Scientific investigations seldom proceed along a smooth path from theory to hypothesis to observation to generalization, and so on. Reports of scientific research tend to follow this format, but that is mostly the product of hindsight and the condensation of a great many activities. Rather, the course of inquiry tends to be irregular and circuitous, with no typical scenario. For example, a scientist may begin with a theoretical deduction, test the deduction, find that it is not confirmed, mull over the inconsistent results, revise the theory, test a new theoretical deduction, and so forth. Or a scientist may begin with a problem from everyday life, make an educated guess about a suspected relationship, investigate the relationship, find that it does not hold, revise the idea, and formulate a new hypothesis for further study.

The sociologist Walter Wallace (1971:18–19) also points out that the process of scientific inquiry may occur

> (1) sometimes quickly, sometimes slowly; (2) sometimes with a very high degree of formalization and rigor, sometimes quite informally, unselfconsciously, and intuitively; (3) sometimes through the interaction of several scientists in distinct roles (of say, "theorist," "research director," "interviewer," "methodologist," "sampling expert," "statistician," etc.), sometimes through the efforts of a single scientist; and (4) sometimes only in the scientist's imagination, sometimes in actual fact.

As you can see, there is nothing mechanical or programmed about scientific work. The development of theory, the formulation of empirical tests of hypotheses, and the application of methods to carry out the tests all involve a great deal of imagination and insight and can generate tremendous excitement and frustration.

This last observation brings us to an important aspect of the reality of scientific practice. Whereas the image of scientists projected by the ideal view is that of detached and dispassionate observers of the world, there is a pervasive subjective element in science. Scientists are not merely passive recorders of the social world or the world of nature. Rather, they actively interpret what they see on the basis of socially shared ideas and assumptions. And far from being detached, scientists naturally develop an intense commitment to their work, which may lead them to overlook or reject evidence that is contrary to their own ideas. In fact, such commitment may affect entire scientific disciplines. It has been shown that disciplines may adhere to theories for long periods in the face of much contradictory evidence and that major theories are displaced only after prolonged "scientific revolutions" (Kuhn, 1962).

This reinforces our earlier point about objectivity. That is, as much as scientific norms and the scrutiny and skepticism of the scientific community foster objectivity, it is impossible to eliminate completely the influence of personal values and biases. Value judgments intrude on scientific inquiry in several ways, affecting problem selection, decisions about research procedures, and the interpretation of results. In the mid-1970s, for example, many scholars began to point out the impact of sexism on social research. They noted that gender differences often were ignored, studies of one sex were presented as if they were applicable to both sexes, and problems were selected and findings interpreted from a male-dominant perspective that treated women as passive objects rather than as fully human subjects (Eichler, 1988). We believe that these problems are, to a large extent, correctable because the very nature of scientific inquiry enables its own critique (Sprague and Zimmerman, 1989). As long as scientists are committed to accurate reporting and to making their assumptions and biases as explicit as possible, others can critically review research findings. And by considering alternative explanations and alternative research strategies, scientists can exercise the power of self-correction.

KEY POINT

Scientists' personal values may influence what they choose to study, how they conduct their research, and how they interpret evidence.

Alternative Models of Social "Science"

As we noted, some scholars are critical of likening social "scientific" inquiry to natural science. Some of these critiques of the natural science model are as old as the social science disciplines themselves. In the late twentieth century, however, two developments resulted in renewed attacks on the viability of this model. One development, European in origin, occurred among social theorists who debated philosophical questions about the nature of scientific knowledge (e.g., Agger, 1991; Seidman and Wagner, 1992). Several different schools of thought offered a range of criticisms, including the following:

- Critical theory, which claims that science reflects an investment in the status quo and fails to promote economic and social change that could transform social relations and empower the powerless (see Agger, 1991);
- Historicism, which denies the possibility of general laws insofar as observed regularities are always tied to time and place (see D'Amico, 1989; Gergen, 1973);
- The "discourse" school, which emphasizes the ways that language structures and limits knowledge (see Foucault, 1970; Rabinow and Sullivan, 1987); and
- Postmodernism, which rejects the possibility of abstract explanation, challenges systematic empiricism, and sees one description of reality as no more valid than another (Rosenau, 1992).

Despite their important methodological implications, for the most part these critiques have been ensconced within philosophy and social theory; consequently, their impact on the practice of social research has been limited.

The second development was the emergence of **qualitative research**. Although there were forerunners of this approach in the first half of the twentieth century, use of the term "qualitative research" began to appear in the 1950s and 1960s and became widespread in the last quarter of the century (Allwood, 2012). Today, discussions of social research methods often are framed by the quantitative/qualitative distinction. In this book, we have chosen to disregard this distinction. We believe, like the sociologist Barbara Hanson (2008:97), that differences between so-called qualitative and quantitative methods "are more apparent than real" and that recognizing the distinction may be counterproductive. Nonetheless, there is no denying the influence of qualitative research on social scientific inquiry.

The conventional wisdom is that quantitative research transforms observations into numerical values and qualitative research reports observations in ordinary language in the form of text and visual images. These data are generated by different methods and require different analytic techniques: quantitative research typically involves surveys, experiments, and statistical analysis, and qualitative research involves field research, in-depth interviews, analysis of historical documents, and textual analysis. Finally, discussions of the quantitative/qualitative divide often attempt to establish a link between epistemology and the methods and techniques applied by each approach (Lincoln and Guba, 1985; Morgan, 2007). And when this comparison is made, quantitative research is equated with natural science as outlined in this chapter.

The several versions of the qualitative approach vary in their philosophical underpinnings (Allwood, 2012). Here we consider three epistemic assumptions that underlie most versions. First, a basic tenet of qualitative research is that human action has distinctive qualities that make the social and natural sciences fundamentally different. The inanimate or nonhuman objects in the natural sciences "are not expected to interpret themselves or the environment or field in which they are located and move" (Gurwitsch, 1974:129). Therefore, a natural scientist can invoke interpretations without regard to how the objects of study may interpret their own worlds. Human beings, in contrast, act with intentionality; their actions have purpose and meaning. Because of this—because the objects of study themselves act on their own interpretations of the world—social scientists should aim to understand human behavior from the subject's frame of reference. Otherwise, their interpretations of the social world are bound to be erroneous or inadequate.

Second, whereas natural science develops knowledge about an objective reality that is assumed to exist independent of the investigator, qualitative research assumes that what we observe or know about the world is a social construction. In other words, knowledge does not constitute an objective reality that is waiting to be discovered; rather, it is created or "constructed" by social actors. The strict version of social constructionism holds that the only reality is our conception or perception of it; a more common view is that concepts do correspond to something real in the world (Brown, 1995). In either case, qualitative researchers focus on how social actors define and shape conceptions of reality.

An example of social constructionism is the perspective of medical sociologists that what gets labeled an illness or disease "is often socially negotiated" (Conrad and Barker, 2010:S68). This is most evident when the concept of disease is examined historically. Some diseases, such as neurasthenia, no longer exist, and other illnesses, such as chronic fatigue syndrome and fibromyalgia, are contested in that "sufferers claim to have a specific disease that many physicians do not recognize or acknowledge as distinctly medical" (S70).

Third, whereas the aim of natural science is to develop universal laws that generalize across events, qualitative research often aims to describe each event or entity as a singular culture- and time-bound reality. These aims are commensurate with the distinction between *nomothetic* and *idiographic* explanations. **Nomothetic explanations** identify common causes among classes of events. **Idiographic explanations** describe the unique set of conditions that account for the actions of a single person or set of actors at a particular time and place. An example of a nomothetic explanation is the hypothesis that in cases of misdemeanor domestic assault, offenders are less likely to repeat the offense if they are arrested. As we discuss in Chapter 13, this hypothesis was partially supported in a series of studies with data from a large number of cases. An example of an idiographic explanation is a narrative account of all the factors and conditions—age, gender, prior arrest record, employment status, and so forth—that led to the commission of a single act of domestic assault.

Following Randall Collins (1989), we take the position that although these criticisms have contributed to the development of social scientific theory and method, they have not undermined the basic scientific approach. For example, we agree that it is important to understand the subject's point of view in addressing many social scientific questions. In fact, the distinction between nonhuman and human actors has many methodological consequences. We can ask people questions, probing the reasons for their behavior. We can participate in their worlds to gain their perspective, as field researchers do. We also must consider how people's awareness of being questioned or observed may affect what they say and do. Consistent with a qualitative approach, we see certain methodological approaches as more amenable to understanding human motivation and cognition than other approaches. However, many social scientific issues and types of analysis need not take into account the subject's view of social reality (e.g., social class differences in morbidity and mortality). And regardless of whether one does incorporate the subject's interpretation into one's analysis, it is always best to use a variety of methodological approaches.

Furthermore, accepting the idea that knowledge is socially constructed does not deny the existence of an external reality that scientists aspire to understand. The social construction of knowledge applies no less to the natural than to the social sciences. As Michael Lynch and David Bogen (1997:489) point out, natural scientists do not "directly observe a pre-given nature while social scientists must contend with symbolic orders created by other human beings." Rather, "the data examined in the laboratory . . . require complex instruments, visual records, and interpretive practices." Yet, social constructions such as laboratory data are about real things; scientists can study phenomena as both real and socially constructed. Andrew Abbott (2004:189) suggests that once researchers have identified how concepts and ideas are socially constructed, the next step is to examine "the real consequences of that construction." And as Peter Conrad and Kristin Barker (2010:S77) further note, regarding illness, "the social forces constructing the definition and treatment of illness are themselves real phenomena that can be studied empirically."

Similarly, one type of explanation does not preclude the possibility of another. Science always begins with description, and that description may involve a narrative account (i.e., an idiographic explanation) of why a particular event occurs. But for natural science, descriptions and narrative accounts are not enough; the ultimate goal is to develop abstract causal explanations that go beyond particular events. Nonetheless, descriptions, including idiographic explanations, are the building blocks on which abstract analysis rests. A clear example is comparative historical analysis, which involves the development of causal explanations of social change. To arrive at a nomothetic explanation, analysts systematically compare a relatively small number of carefully selected case studies, usually in the form of historical narratives or idiographic explanations.

Summary

- To know and understand the world around us, science addresses questions that can be answered by identifying the conditions under which observable events take place.
- Answering scientific questions requires concepts that describe the phenomena of interest and general laws and theories that identify patterned relationships.
- Ideally, events to be explained can be logically deduced from laws and theories so that it is possible both to explain the past and present and to predict the future.
- Scientific theories satisfy our curiosity and render a sense of understanding by positing causal processes that connect events.
- Because observed patterns are always subject to change or reinterpretation, there are no ultimate explanations in science, and it follows that scientific theories should not be judged as true or false, only *useful*.
- The process of producing scientific knowledge involves a constant interplay between theory and data (or research).
- Throughout this process, scientists follow the principles of logic, reasoning inductively when they infer generalizations from specific observations and reasoning deductively when they show how theories and hypotheses imply specific facts or predictions.
- The conduct of scientific research is guided by three canons of inquiry: empiricism, objectivity, and control.
- Empiricism means that the only admissible evidence is that which we can know directly or indirectly through our senses.
- Objectivity amounts to intersubjective testability—the capability of independent observers to agree on the results of observations.
- Ultimately, objectivity is a product of science's public nature, for knowledge rests with the consensus of scientists who carefully scrutinize individual claims.
- So far as possible, scientists control for bias and error in the course of their research.
- Theory in social science seldom takes the form of a deductive system of propositions and rarely, if ever, matches the accuracy of the natural sciences.

- Research can be haphazard, sometimes exhilarating, and sometimes frustrating, so doing scientific work requires a deep emotional commitment that can influence the process of inquiry.
- Some social scientists, most of whom are engaged in qualitative research, reject the natural sciences as a model for social research.
- Qualitative researchers assume that the social and natural sciences differ because humans have the capacity to act intentionally based on their interpretations of the world, knowledge is a social construction that differs from "objective reality," and it is not possible to develop universal laws of social life.

Key Terms

epistemology	inductive reasoning
concept	empiricism
explanation	objectivity
empirical generalization	intersubjective testability
hypothesis	control
law	qualitative research
theory	nomothetic explanation
cause/causal relationship	idiographic explanation
deductive reasoning	serendipity pattern

Exercises

1. Give examples of scientific and nonscientific questions that could be asked about the following topics: (a) capital punishment, (b) abortion, (c) intelligence.
2. Indicate whether each of the following inferences represents *deductive* or *inductive* reasoning.
   a. A survey researcher interviews 2500 people from a random sample of U.S. adults and finds that 69 percent say that they are in favor of capital punishment. He concludes that 69 percent of the U.S. adult population favors capital punishment.
   b. The presence of others strengthens people's dominant (prevalent or most likely) responses. If the dominant response is correct, people will perform better in the presence of an audience than when they perform alone. (This is called the social facilitation effect.) Assuming the latter statements are true, it follows that good pool players will make a higher percentage of their shots when an audience is watching them play than when they are shooting pool by themselves.
   c. Research with University of Hawaii students found that women, Asians, and students living at home were less likely to smoke marijuana than men, non-Asians, and students not living at home, respectively. Noting that each of the former groups has more to lose (e.g., is likely to experience more disapproval) from smoking marijuana, the researcher concluded that the more social constraints a student has, the less likely it is that he or she will smoke marijuana.
3. You have been listless for the past 2 weeks. You do not have much of an appetite. Your friends bore you, and you can't seem to get interested in anything. Your grades are beginning to go down. Formulate a hypothesis to account for this situation and then show how the facts of the situation can be deduced from your hypothesis (adapted from Runkle, 1978:281).
4. In this chapter we have assumed a unitary view of science, claiming that the basic aims and process of scientific inquiry apply equally well to the social and natural sciences. But as we noted in the end, this view, sometimes called the "logical-empiricist philosophy of science," has been challenged on several fronts. Familiarize yourself with the following critiques by finding information in your

library (see Chapter 17 for guidance on conducting a literature search). In each case, how does the alternative paradigm challenge logical empiricism?

discourse theory

feminist standpoint methodology

historicism

postmodernism

social constructivism

sociology of scientific knowledge

Notes

1. A distinction sometimes is made between basic or pure science, concerned exclusively with the production of knowledge, and applied science, involving the application of principles to specific, limited problems (see Chapter 14). The heart of science, however, is the search for understanding, not the solution of existing problems.
2. On the other hand, it would be possible to investigate scientifically the effects of prosecution on the incidence of pornography or the relationship between efficiency and morale.
3. Although generally true, there are exceptions to this distinction. As John Kemeny (1959:112) notes, an inductive conclusion need not be a generalized statement. From careful observations of electoral politics, a political scientist may reason that a Democrat will be elected president in the year 2020. This is a particular event, and yet it is also an inductive conclusion. Furthermore, Kemeny notes, "Deduction need not start with a generalization either. For example, from 'there are at least five students in the course' and from 'there are at most seven students in the course' we can deduce that 'there are either 5, 6, or 7 students in the course'"(112).

3

Research Ethics

As scientists, social researchers are expected to follow general standards of scientific inquiry, emphasizing logical reasoning, objectivity, and control for bias and error. In the ensuing chapters we introduce methods and principles that apply these standards to social research. But as we consider these technical aspects, we must also be aware of another dimension of social science—the moral dimension. When we think about how to conduct research, we must think not only of using the *right* techniques but also of *rightly* using the techniques that we learn. We must think about research ethics.

Ethics is both a subject matter and a discipline (Solomon, 1984). The subject matter consists of standards of right and wrong; ethics tells us how to act in moral and responsible ways. Being ethical means acting in accord with ethical principles, but it also means understanding and continuously examining the reasons we act as we do. Ethicists—those who study ethics—take this understanding to another level by analyzing the origins, meaning, and underlying principles of moral conduct.

Research ethics involves the application of ethical principles to scientific research. Research ethics comes from two sources: society at large and research professions. An important part of what we learn as human beings is the system of dos and don'ts that distinguish right from wrong. We learn as children, for example, that it is right to be honest and wrong to lie. Each profession also has standards of moral conduct that apply to people in their professional roles. Scientists are supposed to conduct their research with care, be truthful in reporting findings, and be open to criticism and new ideas (Resnik, 1998). Survey researchers have a special obligation to maintain the confidentiality of their clients (Groves et al., 2009). For the most part, professional standards are "determined and limited by generally accepted concepts of morality" (Shuler, 1982:165); however, ethical issues arise when the pursuit of a research question or the application of research procedures conflicts with general ethical principles. One of the most controversial practices in the social sciences, for example, is the use of deception, which is thought to be necessary to study certain forms of human behavior, even though it violates the moral principle that one should not lie.

Historically, social researchers attended to the development of scientific methods long before they seriously considered research ethics. It was widely assumed that social science could be pursued without regard for its impact on others, and it was left to individual investigators, using their personal standards of morality, to deal with ethical issues that arose from their research (Sieber, 1982:4). These views were forcefully challenged, however, beginning with the Nuremberg trials, which revealed gross violations of subjects' rights by German physicians during World War II. Accused of crimes against humanity, the physicians had conducted experiments on prisoners that caused great pain and suffering and resulted in numerous deaths. In one experiment subjects were kept naked outdoors in below-freezing temperatures until parts of their bodies froze; in others, they were infected with malaria, typhus, poisons, and bacteria in deliberately inflicted wounds (J. Katz, 1972).

Influenced by the atrocities committed by Nazi scientists, professional organizations developed codes of ethical standards to guide scientific work; the American Psychological Association (APA) was one of the first, formally adopting its initial ethical code in 1953 (Reese and Fremouw, 1984). But it was not until the 1960s and early 1970s that the federal government and other professional associations put into place the current system for the protection of human research subjects. Much of the discussion and debate about ethics during this period was stimulated by several controversial studies in the United States that aroused public concern about human rights violations. For example, a study that tracked the course of untreated syphilis in African American sharecroppers was condemned for its failure to provide informed consent; a study of obedience to authority led social scientists to question the standard use of deception in laboratory experiments; a study that secretly taped jury deliberations and an observational study of homosexual acts in public restrooms raised concerns about invasions of privacy; a study funded by the U.S. Army to determine the conditions for insurgency in Latin American nations provoked suspicions about the intended use and possible negative consequences of the findings. As we consider research ethics in this chapter, we describe these and other studies that were instrumental in establishing the federal regulations and professional ethical codes that guide ethical decision making in social research.

There are three broad areas of ethical concern in scientific research: the ethics of data collection and analysis, the ethics of treatment of participants, and the ethics of responsibility to society (Reese and Fremouw, 1984). First, researchers are expected to be careful and forthright in observing, analyzing, and reporting findings. Being ethical in this sense is synonymous with being a good research scientist. Second, scientists have ethical obligations regarding the treatment of human subjects. Basic ethical principles accepted in our cultural and legal tradition demand that research participants be treated with respect and protected from harm. Third, ethical concerns arise from the relationship between science and society, especially regarding the uses of scientific knowledge. Many social scientists believe that researchers have a responsibility to assess the possible uses of scientific findings, to promote their beneficial application, and to speak out against their destructive application.

In this chapter, we consider each of these areas of ethical concern; however, we give the greatest attention to the treatment of research participants. It was clashes between scientific practice and the rights and welfare of research participants that led to the codification and adoption of federal regulations regarding research practices.

Data Collection and Analysis

Conducting ethical social research involves, first, researchers' obligations to one another and to their discipline to make sure that their data are sound and trustworthy. Because scientific progress rests on the trustworthiness of findings from the work of many investigators, dishonesty and inaccuracy in conducting and reporting research undermine science itself. Scientific norms therefore demand intellectual integrity. Scientists are expected to be "unremittingly honest" in their observations and analyses; to be tolerant, questioning, and willing to admit error; and to place the pursuit of knowledge and understanding above personal gain or the promotion of a particular philosophy or ideology (Cournand, 1977).

Some social scientists consider careless errors and poorly conducted research violations of this ethical standard. For example, Robert Groves and colleagues (2009) contend that survey researchers have an ethical obligation to follow best practices to ensure valid results. Otherwise, it would be "unethical to burden respondents with a request for participation" (372). Likewise, the psychologist Robert Rosenthal (1994:127) sees a close relationship between ethics and scientific quality: "The lower the quality of the research, the less justified we are ethically to waste research participants' time, funding agencies' money, and journals' space." Other social scientists maintain, however, that judgments about ethics should be separated from judgments about the scientific quality and utility of research (Sears, 1994). Although sloppy research and unintentional errors are unfortunate, they generally are not considered unethical.

Clearly unethical actions in the conduct of research, referred to as **research misconduct**, are fabrication, falsification, and plagiarism (Steneck, 2007). *Fabrication* consists of making up data and reporting them. The most common form of *falsification* is manipulating data so that recorded results do not accurately represent actual findings. *Plagiarism* is appropriating another person's ideas, results, or words without giving proper credit. We discuss plagiarism in Chapter 17. Here we examine data falsification and fabrication.

Unethical data manipulation can occur in many ways. A researcher may exclude certain cases from the analysis to achieve a desired outcome, fail to report results that contradict a favored hypothesis, and apply inappropriate statistical tests that improve the appearance of the data by yielding significant results (for an example, see Berry [1991]). The extent to which data are obscured in these ways is unknown; however, more extreme ethical violations involving the complete fabrication of data are thought to be exceedingly rare in science (Marshall, 2000). When, in 2001, the social psychologist Karen Ruggiero retracted articles in two journals because she had fabricated the data, the editor of one journal remarked that he had never seen a retraction of this sort in the social psychology literature (Biernat and Crandall, 2001).

The Ruggiero case reveals the gravity of scientific fraud. Ruggiero's work, published in some leading psychology journals between 1995 and 2000, drew a great deal of attention. One 1995 paper was cited in more than 50 studies. Her provocative central thesis—that racial and sexual discrimination are more widespread than most people think—also had important policy implications. Before the revelation of fraud, Ruggiero was a rising star in the discipline. After completing her PhD at McGill University in 1996, she became an assistant professor at Harvard and then moved to the University of Texas in 2000, where she quickly gained a reputation as an excellent teacher and colleague (Biernat and Crandall, 2001). Apparently, suspicions about the validity of her research arose when others could not replicate her findings. When a former research assistant asked Harvard to investigate, she admitted to using "invalid data" in her research studies at Harvard (Holden, 2001).

The impact of scientific fraud is far-reaching. For a scientist who is discovered to have published false data, the consequences are severe. Ruggiero was subjected to professional disgrace and to public humiliation from media coverage of the incident. She resigned her faculty position and almost certainly ended her career as a research scientist. "The ripple effect on the field," as Chris Crandall (2001:20) points out, "can be even worse." Because scientists build their research on the work of others, false leads can result in the loss of considerable time, money, and energy for those who pursue them. Similarly, the publication of fraudulent data harms everyone associated with it: Graduate students working in the researcher's lab lose time and the trust of colleagues; the institution where the fraud took place must investigate the case and, if the research was supported by external funding, possibly return the funds; the image of the discipline may be tarnished; and the validity of the work of everyone who cites the invalid articles may be questioned.

Science is a public activity, carried out by a community of scholars who constantly evaluate each other's work. In the end, it was this scrutiny, specifically the inability of others to replicate her findings, which called into question Ruggiero's research. So, in one sense, the case shows that science's system of checks is working. Still, incidents of data manipulation and fabrication may be difficult to uncover. Although fraud would seem most likely to surface when the research gains prominence, as did Ruggiero's, fraudulent data may remain undetected for years. It was well more than a decade before it was discovered that Cyril Burt's data on twins (see Box 2.2), which were highly influential in research on the heritability of intelligence, were fabricated. Furthermore, replication may not be the most effective means of preventing or detecting fraud. Exact replications are not highly valued as scholarly work, they are expensive, and varying conditions may confound the interpretation of failures to replicate. Therefore, social researchers must resort to other methods to prevent scientific fraud.

KEY POINT

By promoting cooperation and trust among researchers, honesty in research makes it possible to achieve scientific goals.

To enhance transparency and reduce the likelihood of scientific fraud, beginning in the 1990s many professional associations introduced the standard of **data sharing** into their ethical codes. The Code of Ethics of the American Sociological Association (ASA), for example, states, "sociologists share data and pertinent documentation as a regular practice." If not placed in a public archive, the data for completed projects or published research should be available "for a reasonable period of time" to others (ASA, 1999:13.05), who may seek to verify the findings through reanalysis. A policy of data sharing is also included in the submission guidelines for many social science journals. It is impossible to know the extent to which this policy has prevented data fabrication and falsification; however, there are cases of reported studies in which a reanalysis of the data has uncovered irregularities that could only lead to the conclusion that the data were faked (e.g., see Broockman, Kalla, and Aronow, 2015).

Part of the fallout from the Ruggiero case was a discussion of measures that should be taken by social scientists to prevent scientific misconduct. Among the recommendations were the following (B. Murray, 2002; also see Sterba, 2006):

- Research institutions should educate students about scientific misconduct. Ethics training is mandatory for professional psychology programs accredited by the APA and is required for students working on National Institutes of Health (NIH) research grants. The topic of research ethics also should be an integral part of all courses in social research methods.
- Institutions, funding agencies, and individual researchers should periodically check data. The NIH conducts regular research audits. But because universities do not have the resources for intensive audits that the NIH has, we recommend at least random quality checks by principal investigators. Survey researchers, for example, should validate a sample of interviews for every interviewer.
- Investigators should prescribe specific criteria for the inclusion or exclusion of certain data, such as outliers (see Chapter 15), before data are collected and analyzed.
- In papers submitted for publication, researchers should provide detailed information on how they collected, processed, and analyzed their data, and journal editors should insist on such detailed accounting.

We cannot overemphasize the importance of carefully conducting research and honestly reporting findings. For scientists, this is the most fundamental ethical dictum.

Treatment of Human Subjects

Four problem areas have been identified most often regarding the ethical treatment of human subjects: potential harm, lack of informed consent, deception, and privacy invasion (Diener and Crandall, 1978). Each of these problems arises when research practices violate basic human rights. It is considered a violation of basic rights to harm others, to force people to perform actions against their will, to lie to or mislead them, and to invade their privacy. In this section, we review these four issues to sensitize readers to research situations that are potentially unethical as well as to strategies and guidelines that help to ensure subjects' rights. Then, we discuss the process of making ethical decisions.

Harm

All new physicians take an oath of ethical, professional behavior attributed to the Greek physician Hippocrates (460–377 BC). One of the first provisions of the Hippocratic oath is that the doctor "abstain from whatever is deleterious"—that he or she do no harm. Likewise, the first right of any participant in a research project is the right to personal safety. Ethical researchers recognize this right and are careful to respect it. Research that would endanger the life or physical health of a human subject is simply not acceptable in the social science community. Even research that harms animals, although it might directly benefit humans, is opposed by some scientists on ethical grounds (see, e.g., Rowan [1995] and Beauchamp [1997]).

The issue of harm is not as simple and straightforward as it may appear, however. Harm is sometimes difficult to define. Given the nature of social science research projects, physical harm to subjects is highly unlikely. But people can be harmed personally (by being humiliated or embarrassed), psychologically (by losing their self-esteem), and socially (by losing their trust in others) through their participation in research that might never threaten their physical well-being (Diener and Crandall, 1978:17f). Moreover, it is often difficult to predict whether, or the extent to which, one's investigative procedures will be harmful to research participants. The prison simulation study of Philip Zimbardo and colleagues (1973) is a good example. These investigators created a mock prison in the basement of a Stanford University building in which male student volunteers role-played prisoners and guards. The study was scheduled to run 2 weeks but had to be terminated after only 6 days because of its unanticipated adverse effects on the participants. Guards physically and psychologically abused prisoners, and prisoners broke down, rebelled, or became servile and apathetic. The participants got so caught up in the situation and became so absorbed in their roles that they began to confuse role-playing and self-identity. Although Zimbardo and colleagues intended to study how the roles of "guard" and "prisoner" influenced subjects' reactions, they never anticipated such extreme effects.

In addition to the difficulty of predicting harm, few scientists adhere to the dictum that no harm whatsoever should ever come to research participants. Rather, researchers are expected to weigh potential harm against the benefits that might be derived from the research. The guiding principle, supported by professional codes and government regulations, is that "risks to subjects are reasonable in relation to anticipated benefits" (Code of Federal Regulations, 2009:46.111). If there is little or no scientific value from a study that knowingly exposes subjects to harm, the study should not be done, no matter how small the harm. But if a study has considerable scientific merit, some degree of potential harm may be justified. In biomedical experiments, for example, a new treatment that threatens the lives of volunteers may be justified if it promises a cure for a dreaded disease such as cancer.

A major difficulty with a **cost–benefit analysis** of this sort is the ability to assess the full extent of costs and benefits. Costs and benefits may be impossible to predict, as seen in the prison simulation study, or to measure. How costly is personal stress or embarrassment?

How do you quantify the benefits of testing a theory? It also may be difficult to balance costs and benefits because of the many recipients who stand to benefit. In addition to subjects, investigators gain knowledge that may contribute to professional success and recognition; the profession advances scientific understanding, which may lead to the betterment of humanity. Research seems most justifiable when the person exposed to the risks will also receive the benefits of potentially harmful procedures. However, this situation is much more likely to apply to biomedical than to social research (Diener and Crandall, 1978).

Despite these problems, a cost–benefit analysis is an important first step in evaluating the ethics of a proposed study. One should also be sensitive to areas of study and to research procedures that pose the greatest risk of harm. The potential for doing harm to subjects may be highest in social research that investigates negative aspects of human behavior (e.g., aggression, obedience to malevolent authority, cheating). Much of the research on these topics takes place in laboratory experiments, where research participants may suffer a temporary loss of self-esteem or experience a high degree of stress and, as a result, may become upset or angry about their involvement in research.

KEY POINT
Researchers should evaluate the risk of harm to research participants and decide whether the benefits justify the risks or the risks are too great to justify the research.

Consider, for example, the work of Stanley Milgram (1974) on obedience to authority. Under the guise of a teacher–learner experiment, Milgram asked subjects playing the role of teacher to deliver to learners what the subjects thought were dangerously high levels of electric shock. It goes without saying that the learner, a confederate of the experimenter, was not actually being shocked. But to the subjects, this was a highly stressful conflict situation: Should they obey the experimenter in administering the shocks, or should they refuse to continue in the experiment? The subjects showed many obvious signs of stress; indeed, one subject had a convulsive seizure that made it necessary to terminate his participation. Milgram, in turn, was severely criticized for not protecting his subjects from potential harm. For example, he made no effort to determine before their participation whether subjects should be excluded from the experiment for physical or psychological reasons. Some researchers also questioned the long-term effects that the experiment might have had on subjects' self-concepts. What would subjects think of themselves knowing that they were capable of inflicting pain on another person?

The laboratory setting at least guarantees a certain amount of control over subjects' behavior, allowing for intervention if participants are about to experience harm. That control may be altogether absent in studies conducted in natural settings. Bibb Latané and John Darley (1970), for example, staged a crime (looting of a liquor store) to explore the conditions under which bystanders intervene to help. When other investigators replicated this study in the Midwest, one bystander telephoned the police, who showed up with guns drawn to arrest the researchers (Diener and Crandall, 1978:73). This was a situation in which considerable harm could have come to both subjects and researchers.

The ethical issue of harm is much less a problem in nonexperimental research such as surveys and the use of available data. Still, researchers must be alert to the potential for doing harm. Survey researchers can harm people by asking questions about illegal behaviors such as drug abuse, which could prove embarrassing or put participants at risk for criminal prosecution if the information is disclosed. Similarly, researchers should consider whether research findings might reflect negatively on the particular group or population they are studying.

Aside from assessing the risk of harm to research participants and designing one's research to minimize such risks, researchers must be aware of several widely adopted ethical practices that are designed to protect participants from harm (see Diener and Crandall, 1978).

1. Researchers should inform subjects of any reasonable or foreseeable risks or discomforts before the study begins and should give subjects sufficient opportunity to consider whether to participate. Federal regulations mandate such "informed consent," discussed in the next section, for all federally funded research. A major criticism of Milgram's experiment, which predates the latter regulation, is that he did not obtain prior permission from participants to allow him to place them in a highly stressful conflict situation.

2. Where appropriate, researchers should screen out research participants who might be harmed by the research procedures. In their prison simulation study, Zimbardo and associates (Zimbardo, 1973) gave several personality tests to volunteers to select subjects with "normal" personality profiles and thereby minimize the possibility of destructive effects. Another criticism of Milgram's experiment is that he failed to administer examinations before the experiment to determine whether subjects suffered from psychological or physical problems that might have excluded their participation.

3. If stress or potential harm is possible, measures should be taken to assess harm after the study, and research participants should be informed of procedures for contacting the investigator. As discussed in the section on deception, virtually all laboratory experiments include a debriefing session immediately following the study, which is designed to assess as well as ameliorate negative reactions. But if long-lasting effects are possible, the researcher has a special obligation to conduct follow-up interviews and possibly to provide counseling. Zimbardo (1973) held an encounter session after his study to allow subjects to express their feelings. He also conducted follow-up interviews to assess the impact of the experience and found no evidence of long-term negative effects. Indeed, most subjects regarded the experiment as a valuable learning experience. Milgram (1974) also carefully questioned his subjects, interviewing all of them immediately after the experiment and sending them reports of the study and follow-up questionnaires asking for their reactions to their participation in his research. His ultimate ethical justification for this research was that it was judged acceptable by those who took part in it.

Informed Consent

The second ethical issue arises from the value placed on freedom of choice in Western societies. For moral and legal reasons, subjects should not be coerced into participating in social research. To the military tribunal at Nuremberg, "the voluntary consent of the human subject" was the most fundamental ethical principle of biomedical research violated by Nazi scientists (J. Katz, 1972:305). Not only must subjects understand that their participation is *voluntary*; they also must be given enough information about the research to make an *informed* decision about whether to participate. In other words, researchers should obtain the explicit or implicit **informed consent** of their subjects to take part in an investigation.

Both aspects of this principle were violated in the Tuskegee Syphilis Study, which was conducted over 4 decades by the U.S. Public Health Service. The purpose of the study was to follow the course of untreated syphilis, a sexually transmitted and life-threatening disease. The research participants were 600 African American men, many of whom were "uneducated sharecroppers." Of these men, about two-thirds had the disease when the study began in 1932; the other third did not. The men were told that they had "bad blood," a local term that described a range of ailments not limited to syphilis; they agreed to participate on the promise of medical care for "minor ailments," burial insurance, and other benefits (Jones, 1981:chapter 1; Centers for Disease Control and Prevention, 2013). But for those who had syphilis, according to the historian James Jones (1981:7), "there was nothing to indicate that . . . [they] knew they were participating in a deadly serious experiment." When penicillin became an accepted treatment in the late 1940s, the men were not given it. It was not until 1972 that the study was exposed and terminated (Jones, 1981; Centers for Disease Control and Prevention, 2013).

"Informed" means that research participants must be given enough information about the research to make a rational decision about whether to participate. In the case of Tuskegee, participants were given incomplete and misleading information (i.e., bad blood) and they did not know that treatment for their true underlying condition would be withheld. "Consent" refers to voluntary participation. To volunteer is to have the freedom to choose to participate and to discontinue participation; however, firsthand accounts indicate that the men at Tuskegee were discouraged from seeking treatment, and they would lose benefits if they withdrew from the study (Jones, 1981:5–7).

What information about the research must be conveyed for subjects to exercise their *informed* consent? Table 3.1 lists the basic requirements for informed consent outlined in the Code of Federal Regulations. These include descriptions of the research purpose, potential risks and benefits from participation, how confidentiality of records will be maintained, and a statement that participation is voluntary. Some requirements are open to interpretation; for example, full disclosure of the research purpose and procedures is usually not necessary. Minimally, subjects must be told that their participation is voluntary and that they are free to withdraw from the study at any time; moreover, they must be given a clear description of the risk of harm involved and of personal rights that might be jeopardized by their participation. Milgram's subjects, for example, should have been told that the experiment might be stressful and that this stress conceivably could have harmful effects.

Ethical regulations for federally funded research dictate that a *written* consent form, signed by the subject or the subject's legal guardian, must be used when more than "minimal risk" of harm is anticipated. Minimal risk refers to risks that are no greater than those ordinarily encountered in daily life (CFR, 2009). In such cases, informed consent protects both subjects and researchers. Subjects are protected from harm by being able to make

TABLE 3.1. Informed Consent Checklist

1. A statement that the study involves research, an explanation of the purposes of the research and the expected duration of the subject's participation, a description of the procedures, and identification of any procedures that are experimental;
2. A description of any reasonably foreseeable risks or discomforts;
3. A description of any benefits to the subject or to others that may reasonably be expected;
4. A disclosure of appropriate alternative procedures or courses of treatment;
5. A statement describing the extent, if any, to which confidentiality of records identifying the subject will be maintained;
6. For research involving more than minimal risk, an explanation as to whether and what type of compensation and medical treatments are available if injury occurs;
7. An explanation of whom to contact for answers to pertinent questions about the research, subjects' rights, and research-related injury; and
8. A statement that participation is voluntary and the subject may discontinue participation at any time without penalty or loss of benefits.

Source: Code of Federal Regulations (2009:46.116).

up their own minds about the risks of participation; researchers are legally protected by subjects' explicit voluntary agreement. However, although written informed consent is accepted practice in biomedical research, it has several limitations as an ethical safeguard and is not always desirable in social research.

It is often difficult, even in biomedical research, truly to inform subjects about all the risks of research since the risks are not always known. Moreover, a subject's consent to participate does not remove a researcher's responsibility to minimize danger to the subject, and it should never be used to justify other unethical practices. Finally, the use of informed-consent procedures presents methodological problems for several kinds of studies. Research has shown that surveys requiring a signature on a consent form reduce the chances that people will participate (Singer, 1978, 2003) and make them more likely to give socially acceptable (as opposed to truthful) responses (Singer, 1978). And in laboratory experiments, the provision of full information about a study can completely undermine its validity because subjects who are told the true purpose of the study may not behave naturally (Trice, 1987). It is not surprising, then, that studies that convey hypothesis-related information in their informed-consent procedures have failed to replicate findings of studies not containing such information (Adair, Dushenko, and Lindsay, 1985).

Although it is clear that documentation of consent and full disclosure of research purposes and procedures can present methodological problems, there are ways of circumventing these problems while following the doctrine of informed consent. According to the Code of Federal Regulations (2009:46.117), a written consent form may be waived if (1) the only record linking the subject to the research is the consent form and the principal risk would result from a breach of confidentiality or (2) the research presents no more than minimal risk of harm and involves no procedures for which written consent is normally required outside the research context. The second exception applies to most surveys, except when respondents are asked about sensitive topics such as sexual behavior, drug abuse, and illegal conduct for which disclosure could put them at risk for criminal or civil liability or damage their reputation. In fact, Robert Groves and colleagues (2009:389) assert that when risk is minimal or nonexistent in surveys, written or signed consent should not be obtained. Minimal-risk surveys almost always satisfy informed-consent requirements with introductory statements read orally by interviewers or written into self-administered questionnaires (Groves et al., 2009:390). For example, in a series of campus surveys, Royce Singleton had interviewers read the following statement to respondents: "Before we start, I would like to assure you that this interview is confidential and completely voluntary . . . If we should come to any question that you don't want to answer, just let me know and we'll go on to the next question."

Federal regulations also provide for a waiver of documentation or an alteration of some of the elements of informed consent when they would adversely affect the study. However, the waiver of documentation can be made only when the research involves minimal risk to subjects. Finally, it is common in medical and experimental research today to forewarn subjects that a full disclosure of the purposes of the research is not possible until after their participation. They might be told, in addition, that they may be in one of two groups (e.g., an experimental treatment and a placebo or control) but that the study results would be invalid if participants knew their assigned group prior to the conclusion of the research.

KEY POINT
Researchers should give research participants the opportunity to make a voluntary and informed decision about whether to take part in research.

Experiments conducted in natural settings and disguised or covert observation of private domains present the greatest ethical risk from the standpoint of informed consent. In both types of studies, a researcher's desire to observe subjects' spontaneous and natural behavior is incompatible with the acquisition of consent: To obtain informed consent destroys subjects' naivete and defeats the purpose of the study. Whether such research is regarded as unethical depends, for some people, on other ethical considerations, such as invasion of privacy, risk of harm, and the costs incurred in terms of time and money. If the research does not invade the subjects' privacy, is harmless, and is not costly to the subjects, informed consent may be ethically unnecessary. In this sense, testing the effects of different appeals when soliciting donations for a charitable organization, such as Robert Cialdini and David Schroeder (1976) did, would not be considered ethically questionable because subjects—those asked to donate money—were not at risk and their rights were not violated. However, Latané and Darley's 1970 experiment involving the staging of a crime would be ethically questionable because subjects were exposed to considerable stress and risk of harm.

One of the most controversial studies involving covert observation was Laud Humphreys's study (1975) of sexual encounters in public restrooms. Humphreys posed as a voyeur and "watchqueen," whose job was to warn homosexuals of intruders as they engaged in fellatio. He also recorded the license numbers of these men, traced their identities through the Department of Motor Vehicles by misrepresenting himself as a market researcher, and later interviewed them in their homes after changing his appearance so that he would not be recognized. Although Humphreys carefully guarded the confidentiality of his subjects, this study now is considered ethically indefensible by many social scientists. Among several other problems, Humphreys failed to obtain his subjects' informed consent and risked doing serious damage to their psyches and reputations.

Disguised observation studies such as the one by Humphreys are relatively rare and do not always pose such dangers. No matter what the apparent risk of harm, however, this kind of research is invariably controversial. Indeed, some social scientists take the absolutist position that research simply should not be done where investigators deliberately misrepresent their identity to enter an otherwise inaccessible social situation. The sociologist Kai Erikson (1967:368), for example, argues that this kind of research "can injure people in ways we can neither anticipate in advance nor compensate for afterward"; that it "may be painful to the people who are . . . misled; and even if that were not the case, there are countless ways in which a stranger who pretends to be something else can disturb others by failing to understand the conditions of intimacy that prevail in the groups he has tried to invade." Regarding this kind of research, Erikson (1967:368) also reiterates one of the most basic assumptions of informed consent:

> If we happen to harm people who have agreed to act as subjects, we can at least argue that they knew something of the risks involved and were willing to contribute to that vague program called the "advance of knowledge." But when we do so with people who have expressed no readiness to participate in our researches (indeed, people who presumably would have refused if asked directly), we are in very much the same ethical position as a physician who carries out medical experiments on human subjects without their consent.

Deception

Deception, the third area of ethical concern, in some ways is the most controversial. To deceive is, to put it bluntly, to lie. Deception violates the moral obligation that people have toward one another to tell the truth, which is necessary to develop meaningful, trusting relationships. Yet, deception is a widely used and accepted practice in social research, especially in experiments. In social psychology, where it is most common, the percentage of studies reported in major journals that used some form of deception peaked in the 1970s at around 70 percent and then declined. Although less frequent today, studies employing deception are still prevalent, accounting for about one-third to one-fifth of all research in social psychology (Hertwig and Ortmann, 2008a).

As we noted, the principle of informed consent does not require researchers to reveal everything about a study to the research participants, provided that there is minimal risk of harm. Consequently, withholding information about the hypothesis or not revealing all the design features of a study generally would not be considered deceptive. Deception occurs when researchers deliberately mislead or misinform subjects about some aspect of a study. In this sense, participants in Milgram's experiment were deceived in several ways. They agreed to participate in what they thought was a learning experiment, but was instead a study on obedience. As the study began, participants chose a card designating whether they would be the "teacher" or "learner." The drawing was rigged, with teacher written on both cards. Thus, research participants ended up playing the teacher role, whereas an actor, who was a confederate of the experimenter, played the role of learner. Participants were then told they would be reading word pairs to the learner, and when the learner responded incorrectly, the teacher was to shock him or her by pressing a lever on a "shock generator." The shocks, the experimenter told the research participants, could be extremely painful but would not cause permanent damage; however, in reality, the learner did not receive any shocks.

Aside from misinforming subjects and using confederates to mislead subjects about research purposes and tasks, as in Milgram's study, another frequent form of deception in experiments is providing false feedback about subjects' own behavior as a way of manipulating their feelings and thoughts. For example, to temporarily raise or lower subjects' self-esteem, they might be told that they performed well or poorly on a bogus test of academic aptitude. Deception also occurs in field research when a researcher deliberately misrepresents his or her identity, as in the Humphreys study.

The rationale for deception is that it is necessary to place research participants in a mental state where they will behave naturally. If subjects know the true purpose of a study, they may act in a way to present the most favorable impression of themselves or to help the researcher by confirming the hypothesis. Deceiving subjects about the true purpose of a study diverts their attention from the hypothesis by giving subjects a believable and engrossing explanation for what they are doing. Defenders of deception also maintain that, without it, one simply could not effectively study many forms of behavior, especially behavior that people normally find objectionable, such as aggression, conformity, cheating, or obedience to a malevolent authority. Had Milgram informed his research participants that he was studying obedience, they almost certainly would have disobeyed. Only by deceiving them about the true purpose of his research could he observe their naturally obedient behavior.

However, there is strong and vocal opposition to deception. The most thoroughgoing critique is offered by the psychologist Diana Baumrind (1985:165), who argues that "intentional deception in the research setting is unethical, imprudent, and unwarranted scientifically." According to Baumrind, deception is unethical because it violates a subject's right to informed consent (i.e., consent obtained by deceit, by definition, cannot be informed) and violates the trust implicit in the investigator–subject relationship. It is imprudent because it ultimately damages the credibility of behavioral scientists as well as trust in other expert authorities. And it is unwarranted scientifically because deceptive practices do not accomplish the scientific objectives that justify their use. Baumrind claims that the almost routine use of deception in experiments is common knowledge among some groups of subjects (presumably college students), which makes them suspicious. Because of this, deception may not produce the naive and spontaneous behavior that it is designed to elicit, thereby making experimental results inherently ambiguous.

Despite these objections, the prevailing sentiment among social scientists is not to rule out deception entirely. Most agree that Milgram's use of deception went too far because he misled participants about the *potential risk of harm*, thereby clearly violating the principle of informed consent. However, both ASA and APA ethical codes allow for deception. The ethical defense of deception is that it is permissible so long as it is used as a last resort after careful consideration of alternative procedures, the information to be gained outweighs the negative impact of deceiving subjects, and care is taken to inform subjects of the deception and ensure that they leave the study in a positive frame of mind. The ASA ethics code (1999:12.05) states that

(a) Sociologists do not use deceptive techniques (1) unless they have determined that their use will not be harmful to research participants; it is justified by the study's prospective scientific, educational, or applied value; and that equally effective alternative procedures that do not use deception are not feasible . . .
(b) Sociologists should never deceive research participants about significant aspects of the research that would affect their willingness to participate, such as physical risks, discomfort, or unpleasant emotional experiences.
(c) When deception is an integral feature of the design and conduct of research, sociologists attempt to correct any misconception that research participants may have no later than at the conclusion of the research.

John Adair and colleagues (Adair, Dushenko, and Lindsay, 1985) point out that the negative consequences in deception research are usually minimal and that there is a lack of viable alternative methodologies. Therefore, the deception dilemma may be rectified best by the ASA's point (c)—adequate debriefing.

Debriefing

Debriefing serves methodological and educational as well as ethical purposes; ideally, it should occur in all studies with human participants, not just those studies involving deception. By interviewing subjects after their participation, researchers may gain valuable information about subjects' interpretations of research procedures; furthermore, by understanding the nature of the study, subjects can gain a greater appreciation for their research experience. If subjects are deceived, however, then the debriefing session becomes critically important. Not only must researchers explain the true purpose of the study and the reasons for the deception, but they must do so with great care and sensitivity.

Researchers must be alert to the fact that, when exposed to the truth, subjects may feel embarrassed or angered about having been "fooled" and may harbor resentment toward the investigator and toward social research in general. To obviate such feelings, investigators have developed elaborate debriefing techniques (see Carlsmith, Ellsworth, and Aronson, 1976; Mills, 1976). We will not describe these techniques in detail, but certain common aspects deserve mention. First, it is best to debrief subjects as soon after their participation as possible, especially if the deception or its revelation is likely to cause discomfort. Second, the debriefing should be carried out slowly and deliberately, first eliciting subjects' reactions and then gradually explaining the nature of the experiment until subjects fully understand every point. Third, since negative feelings about being deceived are worsened when the deceiver is smug about it, researchers can relieve some of their subjects' discomfort by expressing their own discomfort about the necessity of using deception to arrive at the "truth." Fourth, researchers should point out to subjects that if the experiment works well, virtually *everyone* is fooled. Finally, above all, researchers should follow Herbert Kelman's

(1968:222) guideline: "A subject ought not to leave the laboratory with greater anxiety or lower self-esteem than he [or she] came in with."

KEY POINT
Researchers should use deception as a last resort, carefully considering alternative methods and sensitive ways to debrief research participants.

Research on the effects of deception and debriefing indicates that, in general, carefully administered debriefing is effective. Stevens Smith and Deborah Richardson (1983) found that subjects who were deceived and subsequently debriefed reported more positive experiences—for example, greater enjoyment and greater educational benefit—from their research participation than did subjects who were not deceived and, as a consequence, received less adequate debriefing. An earlier study drew similar conclusions:

> it appears that subjects are willing to accept or tolerate certain discomfitures or unpleasantries if they are viewed as necessary elements of a scientific enterprise. Thus, learning that they had been deceived . . . *enhanced* the subject's assessment of the experiment's scientific value; elaborate deceptions are apparently viewed as good social science methodology! (Straits, Wuebben, and Majka, 1972:515)

At the turn of the century this seemed to be the final word on deception: that it was deemed acceptable by research participants. The deception debate is far from over, however, as indicated by several articles that present renewed challenges (see Hertwig and Ortmann, 2008a, 2008b; Sell, 2008). The current principal argument against deception is that its known use makes subjects suspicious; and if they are suspicious of deception, they will not believe the experimental scenario, and their actions will not be as naive and spontaneous as is assumed. For this reason, experimental economists have effectively banned the use of deception. Others maintain that this position is, in a sense, easy for economists to take because deception is unnecessary when one assumes, as economists do, that human decision making and behavior are driven primarily by rational choice and when one is merely measuring reactions to induced monetary rewards. By contrast, a "ban on deception would make it impossible or extremely difficult to investigate nonrational aspects of behavior" (K. S. Cook and Yamagishi, 2008). As the debate continues, Ralph Hertwig and Andreas Ortmann (2008b:225) propose that the evaluation of deception should be evidence based and that more studies are needed to determine the extent to which participants in contemporary studies "harbor suspicion or feel distressed about being deceived" and how this affects research findings. To this end, a recent study showed that exposure to deception did not affect the validity of experimental results (Barrera and Simpson, 2012).

Privacy

The idea of the right to privacy goes back to antiquity. For example, Hippocrates' oath promises, "Whatever . . . I see or hear, in the life of men, which ought not to be spoken of abroad, I will not divulge as reckoning that all such should be kept secret." Despite its ancient origins, however, the moral claim to privacy was not widely respected as a fundamental right until the past few centuries. The Industrial Revolution made physical privacy possible, and political democracies granted and increasingly protected the privacy of individual belief and opinion (Ruebhausen and Brim, 1966). Today, invasion of privacy remains a public concern because of the controversial use of various forms of electronic surveillance.

The right to privacy is the individual's right to decide when, where, to whom, and to what extent his or her attitudes, beliefs, and behavior will be revealed. Social research presents many possibilities for invading the privacy of research participants, and it is essential that researchers be sensitive to the ways in which their actions can violate this basic right.

The dramatic case of the Wichita Jury Study in 1954 shows how social research can come into direct conflict with the value of privacy (Vaughan, 1967). In an effort to understand and perhaps even improve the operations of juries, researchers secured the permission of judges to record six actual jury deliberations in Wichita, Kansas, without the knowledge of the jurors. When news of the study became known, it was roundly criticized by columnists and commentators across the country and investigated by a Senate subcommittee, which led ultimately to the passage of a law prohibiting the recording of jury deliberations. The argument against this study was that jury deliberations must be sacrosanct to protect the inalienable right to trial by impartial jury. Surveillance "threatens impartiality to the extent that it introduces any question of possible embarrassment, coercion, or other such considerations into the minds of actual jurors" (Vaughan, 1967:72).

As this study shows, one way in which subjects' privacy can be invaded is through the use of concealed devices such as one-way mirrors, microphones, and cameras. If such devices are used with subjects' knowledge and consent, they pose no problem. If they are used without subjects' knowledge to record behavior in public places (e.g., restaurants and waiting rooms), they also are acceptable to many researchers so long as subjects remain anonymous and are not at risk. But when hidden recording devices are used to observe behavior in private settings to which a research participant would not ordinarily allow a researcher access, an invasion of privacy occurs. In addition to juries, other settings that are considered private are homes, personal offices, closed meetings, and physicians' examining rooms (Diener and Crandall, 1978).

Closely related to the use of concealed recording devices is the use of a false cover to gain information that subjects would not reveal if their informed consent were obtained. This became a major problem in the second phase of Laud Humphreys's study, mentioned previously, when he got the names of men he had observed performing homosexual acts and interviewed them in their homes. When Humphreys observed these men in public restrooms, he did not know their names or other details of their private lives. But the identifying information he subsequently obtained intruded on his subjects' privacy and, in the worst of circumstances, could have led to legal difficulties or even blackmail.

Whether access to information is defined as an invasion of privacy depends on how private that information is. Humphreys's research drew attention not only because he used questionable means to procure information but also because he was investigating a sensitive area—sexual behavior. Some types of information are considered more private or sensitive than others. Among the most sensitive and threatening areas are sexual behavior and illegal activities. Researchers investigating these areas have a special obligation to protect the privacy of their informants.

Anonymity and Confidentiality

No matter how sensitive the information, ethical investigators protect the right to privacy by guaranteeing **anonymity** or **confidentiality**. Information given anonymously secures the privacy of individuals, but this safeguard is usually possible only in surveys using self-administered questionnaires without names attached or in some available data studies. Most often an investigator can identify each individual's responses; therefore, the principal means of protecting research participants' privacy is to ensure confidentiality. A researcher can do this in a variety of ways: by removing names and other identifying information from the data as soon as possible, by not disclosing individuals' identities in any reports of the study, and by not divulging the information to persons or organizations requesting it without the research participant's permission.

Laud Humphreys defended his research partly in terms of the steps he took to ensure confidentiality, such as destroying all data containing personally identifying information after the completion of his study. Likewise, the researchers in the Wichita Jury Study acted to protect privacy by destroying the original recording of each jury deliberation after transcribing the recording and editing the transcript to avoid the identification of any of the persons involved. The Census Bureau protects confidentiality in a variety of ways, for example, by not releasing individual responses to the census of population and housing for 72 years—a person's average lifetime—and by suppressing identifying information when releasing data.

KEY POINT

Researchers should respect individuals' right to privacy by gathering information anonymously or by taking measures to ensure that the information is confidential.

Field research usually requires more ingenuity to safeguard anonymity and confidentiality. The traditional approach is to use fictitious names for individuals, groups, and locations, although this alone may not be sufficient to prevent people from recognizing themselves and others. For example, in a study of conflict over an anti-gay ballot measure in "Timbertown," a small town in Oregon, Arlene Stein (2010) promised her informants confidentiality, telling them that she would assign them a pseudonym, so that no individuals would be identified in printed reports. However, when Stein published her research in a book, *The Stranger Next Door*, a columnist for the local paper wrote that it was easy to "recognize who she's writing about" (563). According to Stein (558), after someone in the town circulated a copy of the book in which the pseudonyms had been crossed out and real names assigned, "lots of people were upset." One resident was so offended by Stein's portrayal of her that she asked the city council to pass a resolution condemning the book. When that failed, she took her concerns to the local media, where the newspaper ran an editorial claiming, "people are so easy to identify [in the book] that we had to question Stein's sincerity in wanting to protect her sources' identity" (560).

Stein reports that she faced an ethical dilemma, which she later realized was heightened by doing research in a small town where informants knew one another. On the one hand, confidentiality would be compromised unless she made major changes in the descriptions of individuals and the town; on the other hand, the more she "changed identifying characteristics, the less compelling" her story would be (Stein, 2010:557). To remove the possibility of identification, researchers may alter some of the information about people, such as their family background, occupation, or other intimate details of their lives, or they might develop composite characters based on more than one informant. None of these methods is foolproof, however, which led Stein to wonder whether researchers should abandon the promise of making individuals anonymous. Perhaps the best solution is to ask the subjects themselves if the material considered for presentation or publication is acceptable to them. This was the strategy adopted by Bettylou Valentine (1978) in her study of a community called "Blackston."

Valentine (1978:166) believed that some intimate details of people's lives involving family size, family structure, and interrelationships were relevant to important points she wanted to make. She "did not see how it would be possible to disguise the people enough to make them unrecognizable even to themselves and at the same time accurately illustrative of the Blackston community." Therefore, after she had completed a draft of her manuscript, she sent copies to all the major characters. She explained that her story might be published in the future, and she asked each person (1) whether her account was accurate and fair; (2) whether any material would be embarrassing to anyone; and (3) whether they had any comments, corrections, or other reactions. Finally, she subsequently returned to Blackston to talk to several of the persons involved. As a result of these contacts, Valentine not only worked out additional disguises that protected the privacy of her informants but also gained valuable insights and suggestions for her book.

Ensuring the confidentiality of information traceable to individual research participants becomes especially important when disclosure can cause harm; therefore, researchers must be aware of challenges to this safeguard. The most serious challenge comes from law enforcement authorities. Unlike physicians, lawyers, and the clergy, social scientists are subject to subpoena and cannot guarantee research participants legal immunity. When threatened with criminal penalties for not divulging confidential information, a few researchers have staunchly resisted. The sociologist Rik Scarce spent 159 days in jail when he refused to testify about conversations he may have had with an animal-rights activist. He had met the activist in the course of research for his book *Eco-Warriors: Understanding the Radical Environmental Movement*. Scarce (1999:981) believed that sociologists should "treat confidential information as confidential *no matter what*," citing the 1984 code of the ASA, which stated that the confidentiality of information should be maintained even when it "enjoys no legal privilege and legal force is applied."

To protect researchers from prosecution when they refuse to betray confidential sources, Scarce (2005) favors a federal "shield law," which many states have enacted to protect journalists. A few states have shield laws for certain kinds of research (Palys and Lowman, 2002), but these laws would not apply to most social scientists. Another source of protection are certificates of confidentiality (U.S. Department of Health and Human

Services, 2016), which the federal government issues to research institutions. The certificates protect researchers from being compelled by legal authorities to disclose identifying information. Researchers who study sensitive topics such as mental health, sexual practices, substance abuse, and other illegal activities may apply for the certificates through their research institution.

Making Ethical Decisions

Ethical issues arise in social research when conflicts occur between societal values, such as freedom and privacy, and scientific methods aimed at obtaining the highest quality data. In the preceding sections we have identified some areas of potential conflict—harm to participants, involuntary participation, intentional deception, and invasion of privacy. We also have examined some current resolutions of these ethical issues. It should be clear from our discussion that there are no easy answers; indeed, frequently there is considerable disagreement among scientists about the ethicality of research (Ceci, Peters, and Plotkin, 1985). With this in mind, how does a researcher decide what to do?

Some social scientists, such as Diana Baumrind (1971:890), take the position that "scientific ends, however laudable they may be," should never justify the use of means, such as lying to subjects, that violate fundamental moral principles or sacrifice the welfare of research participants. In philosophy, this ethical position is known as *deontology*: Basic moral principles should allow no exceptions, no matter what the consequences. By contrast, the operating ethical philosophy of most social scientists today—the philosophy behind professional ethical codes and federal ethical guidelines for research—is basically *teleological*: The morality of acts should be judged in relation to the ends they produce. Thus, a study that sacrifices subjects' welfare, such as through deception or risk of harm, may be justified ethically, provided that its benefits outweigh its costs. The underlying principle, from the teleological theory of utilitarianism, is the "greatest good for the greatest number."

Investigators planning research should anticipate a study's benefits and costs; if potential costs exceed anticipated benefits, the ethical decision would be to not conduct the study. As we pointed out in our discussion of risk of harm, however, cost–benefit analyses are not at all simple and straightforward. Consequently, this approach alone cannot justify potentially harmful studies. Although it provides a workable framework, for further direction and guidance in making ethically responsible decisions researchers rely on professional codes, government regulations, and personal judgment.

In the previous section, we frequently referenced ethical codes developed by professional societies such as the ASA. There are as many professional societies—and therefore ethical codes—as there are varieties of social science disciplines; however, the codes are similar enough that they give "a clear idea of the essential ethical concerns" when doing social research (Kimmel, 1996:27). Box 3.1 provides excerpts from the ethical codes of three such societies: the American Anthropological Association (AAA), the APA, and the ASA. These codes cover ethical responsibilities not only to those studied but also to the profession, the public, and students.

BOX 3.1 Codes of Professional Ethics

The following statements are excerpts from the professional codes of ethics of three national organizations: the American Anthropological Association (AAA), the American Psychological Association (APA), and the American Sociological Association (ASA). You can read the complete codes of ethics on their websites.

Professional Practice in the Conduct of Research

> In their capacity as researchers, anthropologists are subject to the ethical principles guiding all scientific and scholarly conduct. They must not plagiarize, nor fabricate or falsify evidence, or knowingly misrepresent information or its source. (AAA)

> Psychologists seek to promote accuracy, honesty, and truthfulness in the science . . . of psychology. In these activities psychologists do not steal, cheat, or engage in fraud, subterfuge, or intentional misrepresentation of fact.

> Psychologists do not fabricate data.

> If psychologists discover significant errors in their published data, they take reasonable steps to correct such errors in a correction, retraction, erratum, or other appropriate publication means.

> Psychologists do not present portions of another's work or data as their own. . . . (APA)

> Sociologists adhere to the highest scientific and professional standards and accept responsibility for their work. . . .

> In planning and implementing research, sociologists minimize the possibility that results will be misleading.

> Sociologists do not fabricate data or falsify results in their publications or presentations.

> In presenting their work, sociologists report their findings fully and do not omit relevant data. They report results whether they support or contradict the expected outcomes.

> Sociologists take particular care to state all relevant qualifications on the findings and interpretation of their research. Sociologists disclose underlying assumptions, theories, methods, measures, and research designs that might bear upon findings and interpretations of their work. (ASA)

Treatment of Research Participants

> A primary ethical obligation shared by anthropologists is to do no harm. It is imperative that, before any anthropological work be undertaken . . . each researcher think through the possible ways that the research might cause harm. Among the most serious harms that anthropologists should seek to avoid are harm to dignity, and to bodily and material well-being, especially when research is conducted among vulnerable populations. Anthropologists should not only avoid causing direct and immediate harm but also should weigh carefully the potential consequences and inadvertent impacts of their work. When it conflicts with other responsibilities, this primary obligation can supersede the goal

of seeking new knowledge and can lead to decisions to not undertake or to discontinue a project.

Anthropological researchers working with living human communities must obtain the voluntary and informed consent of research participants. Ordinarily such consent is given prior to the research, but it may also be obtained retroactively if so warranted by the research context, process, and relations. The consent process should be a part of project design and continue through implementation as an ongoing dialogue and negotiation with research participants. (AAA)

When psychologists conduct research . . . they obtain the informed consent of the individual or individuals using language that is reasonably understandable to that person or persons except when conducting such activities without consent is mandated by law or governmental regulation or as otherwise provided in this Ethical Code.

Psychologists discuss with persons . . . and organizations with whom they establish a scientific . . . relationship (1) the relevant limits of confidentiality and (2) the foreseeable uses of the information generated through their psychological activities.

Psychologists do not conduct a study involving deception unless they have determined that the use of deceptive techniques is justified by the study's significant prospective scientific, educational, or applied value and that effective nondeceptive alternative procedures are not feasible.

Psychologists do not deceive prospective participants about research that is reasonably expected to cause physical pain or severe emotional distress.

Psychologists explain any deception that is an integral feature of the design and conduct of an experiment to participants as early as is feasible, preferably at the conclusion of their participation, but no later than at the conclusion of the data collection, and permit participants to withdraw their data. (APA)

Sociologists have an obligation to ensure that confidential information is protected.

Informed consent is a basic ethical tenet of scientific research on human populations.

Sociologists take steps to implement protections for the rights and welfare of research participants and other persons affected by the research.

In their research, sociologists do not encourage activities or themselves behave in ways that are health- or life-threatening to research participants or others. (ASA)

Responsibility to the Public

Anthropologists should be clear and open regarding the purpose, methods, outcomes, and sponsors of their work.

Anthropologists have an ethical obligation to consider the potential impact of both their research and the communication or dissemination of the results of their research. Anthropologists must consider this issue prior to beginning

(continued)

(continued)

research as well as throughout the research process. Explicit negotiation with research partners and participants about data ownership and access and about dissemination of results, may be necessary before deciding whether to begin research.

Results of anthropological research should be disseminated in a timely fashion. It is important to bear in mind that these results may not be clear cut, and may be subject to multiple interpretations, as well as susceptible to differing and unintended uses. (AAA)

Psychologists are committed to increasing scientific and professional knowledge of behavior and people's understanding of themselves and others and to the use of such knowledge to improve the condition of individuals, organizations and society. . . . They strive to help the public in developing informed judgments and choices concerning human behavior.

If psychologists learn of misuse or misrepresentation of their work, they take reasonable steps to correct or minimize the misuse or misrepresentation. (APA)

Sociologists are aware of their professional and scientific responsibility to the communities and societies in which they live and work. They apply and make public their knowledge in order to contribute to the public good. When undertaking research, they strive to advance the science of sociology and to serve the public good. (ASA)

Professional ethical codes articulate general principles and rules that apply to research situations often encountered in a particular discipline. They are designed at once to protect the welfare of the individuals with whom scientists work and to guide researchers in making ethically responsible choices. Aside from barring membership, professional associations lack the means of enforcing ethical codes. By contrast, the second source of direction for ethical decision making, federal regulations, is legally binding. In the United States, regulations covering scientific misconduct and the use of humans in research stem from several congressional acts. The most significant of these was the National Research Act (1974). This act led to the *Belmont Report*, which set forth basic ethical principles for protecting human research participants and to a set of formal regulations.

The *Belmont Report* (National Commission, 1979) identifies three broad, unifying ethical principles that formed the basis for specific regulations: respect for persons, beneficence, and justice. *Respect for persons* means that researchers must treat individuals as "autonomous agents" who have the freedom and capacity to decide what happens to them. It also requires that those with diminished autonomy, such as children and mentally retarded individuals, are entitled to protection. An application of this principle is the doctrine of informed consent. *Beneficence* requires researchers to consider the welfare of participants so that they "maximize possible benefits and minimize possible harms." Included in this consideration are longer-term benefits that may result from the advancement of knowledge and betterment of humankind. *Justice* means that the benefits and burdens of research should be fairly distributed. In particular, the burdens of research should not fall on one group while the benefits accrue to another. The exploitation of unwilling prisoners as research subjects by Nazi scientists is an extreme example of injustice.

Based on the *Belmont Report* and other work, the Department of Health and Human Services (then known as the Department of Health, Education, and Welfare) codified its regulations for protecting research participants under Title 45 of the Code of Federal Regulations, Part 46 (45 CFR 46). Over time, these regulations have been revised, and in 1991 most federal agencies that support or conduct human subjects research adopted a common set of regulations as Subpart A of 45 CFR 46, informally called the "Common Rule" (Steneck, 2007). (Other subparts outline additional protections for special research areas and populations such as pregnant women, prisoners, and children.)

The **Common Rule** provides information about the application of regulations, defines terms such as "human subject" and "minimal risk," and presents criteria for approval of research, including the requirements for informed consent that we outlined earlier. To ensure compliance with regulations, this policy also requires that all applicable institutions establish a committee (called an **institutional review board**, or **IRB**) to review and approve research involving human (and animal) subjects. Virtually every college and university in the United States and most tax-exempt private research foundations have IRBs. Although at first IRB approval was required only of federally funded research, it now pertains to *all* human subjects research, whether funded or not, conducted at institutions that receive federal funding (Singer and Levine, 2003).

According to the Common Rule, each IRB has at least five members, with varying backgrounds to ensure the adequate review of research proposals. To provide a diversity of expertise, the members must include at least one nonscientist (such as a lawyer, ethicist, or member of the clergy) and at least one member not affiliated with the research institution, as well as persons competent to review specific research activities (such as a social scientist in the case of social research). Investigators submit written documents to the IRB that describe the proposed research and specifically outline how research participants' rights are to be protected, such as provisions for informed consent and measures to ensure confidentiality. The IRBs then approve, disapprove, or require modifications to secure approval of research according to their interpretation of federal regulations.

Below in abbreviated form are the main criteria for IRB approval that are specified in Section 46.111 of the Common Rule:

- Risks to subjects are minimized;
- Risks to subjects are reasonable in relation to anticipated benefits, if any, to subjects, and the importance of the knowledge that may reasonably be expected to result;
- Selection of subjects is equitable;
- Informed consent will be sought from each prospective subject or the subject's legally authorized representative;
- Informed consent will be appropriately documented;

- When appropriate, the research plan makes adequate provision for monitoring the data collected to ensure the safety of subjects;
- When appropriate, there are adequate provisions to protect the privacy of subjects and to maintain the confidentiality of data.

When research proposals are submitted to the IRB, the board or IRB chair must decide initially whether the research is exempt from federal regulations or qualifies for an expedited review. Exempt research includes some anonymous surveys, studies involving normal educational practices or educational testing, and the use of existing data and observations of public behavior (when recorded data cannot be linked to individuals). If nonexempt research involves no more than minimal risk to subjects (or if minor changes are being made to previously approved research), the IRB may perform an **expedited review**. Under this procedure, the review is carried out not by the entire IRB, but by the IRB chairperson or by one or more IRB members designated by the chairperson. Otherwise, the full committee reviews a proposal to decide whether to approve, disapprove, or require modifications to secure approval.

By design, the Common Rule is flexible enough to apply to many different research situations and was intended for social and behavioral as well as biomedical research. However, it was written with clinical medicine in mind, and IRBs have tended increasingly to apply regulations from this perspective (Singer and Levine, 2003). As a result, some social scientists have been critical of the operation of IRBs, seeing them as imposing unnecessary hurdles that impede research without enhancing subjects' protection. This is particularly true of the requirement of informed consent. In medical research, subjects routinely sign a written consent form. But in social research, obtaining written or explicit consent may be inconvenient and embarrassing and disturb the flow of interaction. For example, Michael Rowe (2007) describes a field study of British policing in which he accompanied police officers as they went about their normal activities. Although he was candid with the officers about the nature of his study and was sure to obtain their consent, it often was not feasible to seek the consent of victims, witnesses, and others whom he encountered. To clarify officers' brief description of his role to others or to get others' full consent would have damaged his relation with officers and gotten in the way of their main business. Rowe contends that the ethical dilemmas he encountered were mitigated by recording minimal personal details and no full names or precise locations and by keeping his research notes in a secure place.

If you are undertaking social research, you should familiarize yourself with relevant professional ethical codes as well as federal regulations in the Common Rule. These sources will sensitize you to ethical issues and to established safeguards for protecting research participants. Still, research decisions cannot rest on the rigid application of ethical codes. Ethical principles tend to identify what is most desirable or clearly unacceptable; they do not cover every situation that arises in research, and their application often requires considerable interpretation. Ethical decision making therefore ultimately depends on the critical judgment of researchers themselves. Throughout the research process, ethical researchers should recognize that alternative approaches may be taken, and they should select the methods that best meet research objectives while respecting the rights and preserving the well-being of research participants.

KEY POINT

Ethical decision making requires a considered judgment regarding appropriate research procedures based on human rights, ethical codes, and government regulations.

Importantly, when making difficult ethical decisions, it is always a good idea to solicit others' opinions. In addition to asking the opinions of others in the field, Celia Fisher and Denise Fryberg (1994) argue that researchers should seek the opinions of participants, especially in deception research. To assess the potential impact of deception as well as enhance the protection of subjects, they propose that researchers survey prospective participants on ethical issues at the initial stages of planning a study. Subjects could be asked, for example, about the scientific value of the study, the relative advantage of deception and alternative procedures, their psychological reactions to experimental manipulations, and the efficacy of debriefing procedures in alleviating psychological discomfort. In this way, research participants become partners in the process of ethical decision making.

Values in Social Research: Science and Society

A third area of research ethics arises from the relationship between science and society. Ethical codes of social scientific disciplines such as psychology and sociology state that their disciples are committed to increasing scientific knowledge for the ultimate purpose of improving human welfare. Principle E of the ASA code (1999) states, for example, that "when undertaking research, [sociologists] strive to advance the science of sociology to serve the public good." How social scientists should fulfill this obligation has been the subject of debate for some time. Deciding what will better humankind is necessarily a value judgment; therefore, the debate centers on how values enter into social research, which is where we begin.

The Issue of Value Neutrality

In the interest of promoting the scientific side of social research, some scholars once held that social science should be "value-free." According to this position (Lundberg, 1961), we can and should make a sharp distinction between the roles of scientist and citizen. Science is nonmoral. The methods of science are designed to eliminate personal preferences and values; and "there is nothing in scientific work, as such, which dictates to what ends the products of science shall be used" (Lundberg, 1961:32). Scientists' only imperative is "to say what they know"—to present relevant findings and theoretical interpretations. In their capacity as citizens, scientists may take moral positions, campaigning, for example, against nuclear weapons, environmental pollution, or racial oppression. But if social scientists are to be taken seriously as scientists, they should not confuse this role with that of a citizen and should not let their personal values affect their research.

This value-free ideology is no longer tenable for two main reasons. First, it is now clear that values have a substantial influence on the research process. Personal values and political beliefs inevitably affect how scientists select and conceptualize problems and how they interpret their findings. As we discuss in Chapter 4, many nonscientific factors affect problem selection: personal interests and ideologies, the availability of funding, the climate of opinion in society, research fads and fashions. Similar factors affect the perspective that researchers take and the kinds of questions they ask, which in turn determine the kinds of answers they will find. When IQ tests were first administered on a large scale during World War I, the prevailing belief in both scientific and nonscientific circles was that ethnic groups migrating from southern and Eastern Europe were inferior to earlier immigrant groups. Consequently, when the former groups scored consistently lower than Americans of northern and western European ancestry, this was seen not only as proof of existing beliefs about ethnic differences but also as a validation of the tests as measures of innate intelligence. Of course, neither of these interpretations is acceptable today because social scientists have demonstrated conclusively the effects of language, culture, and socioeconomic factors on test scores.

The value-free ideology alleges that as scientists, social researchers can remain neutral in accumulating facts about social life that are of equal utility to Democrats and Republicans, liberals and conservatives. The second problem with this position is that although claiming to be value-neutral seemingly protects the scientist's self interest and autonomy, in effect it places researchers in the service of others' values, such as those of research sponsors or anyone else who chooses to use their findings. Those who advocated complete value neutrality took physical scientists as their model, claiming that these "real" scientists could serve equally well under fascistic or democratic political regimes (Lundberg, 1961). But the moral bankruptcy of this position comes into sharpest focus when we consider such real scientists under the Nazi regime. German physicians apparently operated out of a value-free model of science when they "systematically froze human beings in tubs of ice and, in the conduct of sterilization experiments, sent electrical charges through female ovaries" (Gray, 1968:179). This example is extreme; no one today would argue that value neutrality justifies harming others. More to the point, scientists have come to realize that they bear some responsibility for applications of their research. Physicists who worked on the atomic bomb did not do so out of a value-free ideology but out of patriotism and a belief that Japan and Germany had to be stopped. However, many of them had second thoughts about helping to build the bomb, especially after they saw its destructive effects.

Both of these problems of maintaining value neutrality are exacerbated for social scientists, who typically study problems that have immediate relevance to people's lives. More often than a chemist or physicist, a social researcher is drawn to the study of particular phenomena for their social as well as their scientific significance. The nature of the problems selected and the motivation to study them are inherently value-laden in social research. Social scientists, therefore, must be aware not only of the influence of personal values and political ideology on their own work but also of the implications of their findings for constructive or destructive use by others.

Managing Personal Values

Among social scientists, anthropologists probably have been most keenly aware of the impact of values on the research process. They developed the sensitizing concept of "cultural relativity" to guard against the tendency to judge other cultures in relation to one's own cultural worldview. **Cultural relativity** is the idea that cultural values—standards of truth, morality, beauty, correct behavior, and so forth—vary widely and must be judged in relation to a given society. In addition, anthropologists have pointed out the importance of language—that Western scientific language may not be appropriate for "translating" the behavior of another culture and that it is therefore necessary to understand how people perceive the world in their own terms.

In sociology, one the founding fathers of the discipline, Max Weber (1949), believed that personal values should not influence the collection and analysis of data. Otherwise, social scientists' findings will not be seen as credible and valid, but rather as a projection of their personal beliefs. Avoiding biases in the use and interpretation of evidence may be easier said than done, however. A case in point is research on differences in children raised by homosexual versus heterosexual parents.

Research on same-sex parenting has generated considerable ideological debate. Some states explicitly or implicitly prohibit the adoption of a child by a same-sex couple. In court cases and in drafting legislation, advocates and opponents have used research evidence to support their causes. In this context, Judith Stacey and Timothy Biblarz (2001) reviewed studies of the effects of homosexual versus heterosexual parenting, asking, "(How) does the sexual orientation of parents matter?" At first, they point out how researchers' political beliefs affect their selection of evidence and interpretation of findings. For example, researchers with political views hostile to homosexual adoption report that gay parents subject their children to disproportionate risks for a variety of negative outcomes. Among other issues, Stacey and Biblarz note that this research has extrapolated inappropriately "from studies of single-parent families to portray children of lesbians as more vulnerable to everything from delinquency [and] substance abuse . . . to teen pregnancy [and] . . . suicide" (162). By contrast, research seemingly motivated by political views sympathetic to homosexual parenting has emphasized the consistent absence of differences in children raised by homosexual and heterosexual parents, even though such a finding is theoretically puzzling and unlikely. In effect, Stacey and Biblarz argue, the broader political and social climate has put sexuality researchers on the defensive. Because differences between children of homosexual versus heterosexual parents are assumed to be *deficits*, scholars who support gay rights may ignore differences.

When Stacey and Biblarz analyzed 21 of the better studies as of 1998, they found that researchers frequently downplayed differences, especially regarding children's gender and sexual preferences and behavior. Some studies showed, for example, that children of homosexual parents were less likely to engage in traditional sex-typed behavior in dress and play than children of heterosexual parents. Such findings raise important theoretical questions. Most of the differences, Stacey and Biblarz contend, are likely the effects of parental gender rather than sexual orientation. For example, children of co-mother parents "should develop in less gender-stereotypic ways than would children with two heterosexual parents" (177). Furthermore, some differences may not be the result of parenting practices but of other factors associated with the stigma of homosexuality, which makes gay parents more likely to be older, urban, highly educated, and in less stable relationships.

Some critics of the value-free ideology suggest that researchers "hide behind" the veil of "value-free" research when their research is anything but value-free. One way to address this criticism is to admit one's values and biases up front and allow the audience to evaluate the research with that information in hand. Stacey and Biblarz agree, noting that especially for ideological and emotional subjects such as gay parenting it is "incumbent on scholars to acknowledge the personal convictions they bring to the discussion" (161). Thus, they stated in their article that they "personally oppose discrimination on the basis of sexual orientation or gender" (161).

Acknowledging personal and political sympathies is especially important in sociological studies of marginalized groups that are outside the societal mainstream, such as deviants, the poor, and racial/ethnic and sexual minorities. Charles Ragin and Lisa Amoroso (2011:114) point out that field research often is undertaken and is best suited to give voice to these groups, whose views are rarely heard by mainstream audiences and whose lives are often misrepresented. In trying to understand reality from the perspective of marginalized individuals, field researchers may become sympathetic with their point of view. The way to deal with this, as the sociologist Howard Becker (1967) contends, is to adhere to the standards of good scientific work but also carefully consider "whose side we are on." This does not mean that one should always present all sides or should avoid taking sides. These options are seldom, if ever, possible. What we should do, according to Becker, is admit whose side we are on, use our theories and techniques impartially—taking precautionary measures designed to guard against bias—and make "clear the limits of what we have studied, marking the boundaries beyond which our findings cannot be safely applied" (247). Part of this "sociological disclaimer," Becker believes, should be a statement

> in which we say, for instance, that we have studied the prison through the eyes of the inmates and not through the eyes of the guards or other involved parties. We warn people, thus, that our study tells us only how things look from that vantage point— what kinds of objects guards are in the prisoners' world—and does not attempt to explain why guards do what they do or to absolve the guards of what may seem, from the prisoners' side, morally unacceptable behavior. (247)

Becker does not argue that social scientists should stand pat with their "one-sided" views of reality. In fact, he sees the long-term solution to an enlarged understanding of institutions as the accumulation of many one-sided but different views of reality. This position is analogous to the methodological principle of triangulation, discussed in Chapter 13, in which multiple methods are applied to the same research problem. However, whereas triangulation techniques are used to eliminate methodological biases and errors, here we suggest that these techniques also might be used to shed light on personal values that may be embedded in a particular methodological approach or view of reality.

The Application of Research Findings

Guarding against the intrusion of values in research and carefully noting the limitations of conclusions do not comprise the extent of social scientists' ethical responsibility to society. They also must be aware of and, some believe, provide direction regarding how others use their research findings. There is little question that the public will use social science research. Such research already has had and will continue to have a major impact on social policy. To cite one prominent example, the U.S. Supreme Court decision of 1954 (*Brown v. Board of Education of Topeka*), which declared that separate educational facilities for blacks and whites were inherently unequal, was based in large part on social science findings. The unanimous opinion cited several studies showing that segregation had a detrimental psychological effect on black children.

In the 1960s, 1970s, and 1980s, social scientists continued to be among the staunchest and most vocal supporters of racial integration and civil rights, with many testifying in cases involving school desegregation, busing, and affirmative action. Similarly today, social scientists often present evidence in cases involving sexual discrimination, sexual harassment, and gay rights. These scholars have taken the initiative in offering their expert advice in areas of social policy. For the most part, they have attempted to show how social science findings supported positions that most of their colleagues favored, and their political involvement is noncontroversial. The hard ethical debate concerns how much responsibility researchers bear for applications that are destructive or contrary to prevailing scientific and public sentiment. That is the question that physicists debated after the bomb. Should one try to foresee possible misuses and abuses of scientific findings? If one can foresee misuse or abuse, should the research be conducted at all? And if such research is conducted, how active a role should the researcher play in the dissemination of the findings? Is the researcher responsible for the way information is presented and for assessing the public's reaction?

The most controversial studies in the annals of social science raise just these issues. For example, Project Camelot, a multimillion-dollar research study funded by the U.S. Army, was designed to measure and forecast the causes of revolution and insurgency in underdeveloped areas of the world (I. L. Horowitz, 1967). Because of its huge scope, the project drew a large team of respected social scientists. Some, seeing the project as an unprecedented opportunity to do fundamental research on a grand scale, may not have inquired deeply into the ultimate purpose of the project. Others believed for various reasons that they were, in no sense, "selling out" to the military. They believed that they would have great freedom in handling the project, that there was a possibility of improving conditions in underdeveloped nations, and that they could have an enlightening influence on the military (I. L. Horowitz, 1967). What they failed to envision was the "uses to which the United States Army or Central Intelligence Agency could have put the information, such as fostering revolutions against regimes hostile to the United States. They failed to recognize the grave concern those in other countries would have over such potential uses" (Diener and Crandall, 1978:108). Indeed, in July 1965, 7 months after the project began, after its revelation made it a cause célèbre in Chile, Project Camelot was canceled by the Defense Department.

It is precisely this potential (and actual) abuse of findings that led many social scientists to condemn the research of the educational psychologist Arthur Jensen. In 1969, Jensen published an article in the *Harvard Educational Review* entitled "How much can we boost IQ and scholastic achievement?" In arguing that IQ was determined largely by heredity, Jensen concluded that genetic differences accounted for the higher scores of whites than blacks on IQ tests and that no amount of compensatory education could undo this difference. Such a view had not been propounded in respectable academic circles for many years prior to Jensen's article; as a result, the article created a furor. Many scholars severely criticized Jensen's conclusions on methodological grounds. But the point here is that Jensen apparently failed to consider the uses to which his article might be put. Although he himself was opposed to segregation and argued that his research suggested the need for educational programs tailored to individual differences (Edson, 1970), others seized upon Jensen's research to oppose integration. Less than a week after a report of his article made headlines in Virginia newspapers, defense attorneys quoted heavily from Jensen's article in a suit in federal district court to integrate schools in two Virginia counties (Brazziel, 1969). Their main argument was that differences in intelligence between whites and blacks were innate; that white teachers could not understand blacks; and that black children should be admitted to white schools strictly on the basis of standardized tests.

Still another study demonstrates the ethical tightrope that researchers traverse when their research concerns an important policy issue. Lawrence Sherman and Richard Berk (1984) were duly circumspect about the policy implications of their domestic violence experiment, reported in Chapters 13 and 14, which showed that arrest reduced the likelihood of a repeat offense. The clearest implication was that police should no longer be reluctant to make arrests in domestic assault cases. But Sherman and Berk also cautioned against routinely requiring arrests in such cases. They noted the unique features of the jurisdiction of the study and concluded that, even if their findings were replicated in other jurisdictions, arrest may work better for certain types of offenders and in certain types of situations. Still, many activists, law professors, and others who favored mandatory arrest laws attacked Sherman and Berk's position on the policy implications of their study (Sherman, 1993). At the same time, others were critical of Sherman in particular because they perceived his dissemination of the study's results to the media as an effort to influence policy toward mandatory arrest (Binder and Meeker, 1993). The latter critics became especially vocal when replication experiments failed to show consistent beneficial effects of arrest. (See Sherman [1993] and Berk [1993] for rejoinders to this criticism.)

What are the ethical implications of such controversies? At least three principles are spelled out in the ethical codes of professional associations. First, social scientists have an obligation to consider how their findings will be used. For example, as the 2009 AAA Code of Ethics stipulates, "Anthropological researchers . . . must consider carefully the social and political implications of the information they disseminate. They must do everything in their power to insure that such information is well understood, properly contextualized, and responsibly utilized" (AAA, 2009:III.C.1). Second, consistent with the principle of data sharing, mentioned earlier, and given that eventual applications often are unknown, scientists should disseminate knowledge to the widest possible audience to increase public knowledge and encourage debate, so that no one group can exploit the knowledge for its own welfare (Diener and Crandall, 1978). Third, when research has obvious and immediate applications, scientists have a special obligation to actively promote appropriate uses and to prevent misuses of their findings. Thus, an APA ethical principle states, "If psychologists learn of misuse or misrepresentation of their work, they take reasonable steps to correct or minimize the misuse or misrepresentation." (From this standpoint, we believe that Sherman and Berk were ethically responsible.) Finally, scientists can assume responsibility collectively for the application of research through organizations that communicate on their behalf and provide a forum for the discussion of policy-related issues (Diener and Crandall, 1978). One such organization is the Society for the Psychological Study of Social Issues; another is the Society for the Scientific Study of Social Problems.

KEY POINT
Scientists cannot isolate themselves from the political context of research; they bear responsibility for the interpretation and application of research findings.

Summary

- Research ethics consists of moral principles against which the actions of scientists are judged.
- Three major areas of research ethics are the ethics of data collection and analysis, the ethics of the treatment of human subjects, and the ethics of responsibility to society.
- The ethics of data collection and analysis prescribes that scientists carry out their research and report their findings honestly and accurately; violations of these ethical principles undermine the advancement of science.
- To protect the rights and welfare of research participants, researchers should consider how best to carry out a study while considering issues of harm, informed consent, deception, and invasion of privacy.
- Researchers should not expose participants to substantial risk of physical or psychological harm unless the benefits of participation exceed the risks and subjects knowingly choose to participate.
- Participants should be informed that their participation is voluntary and should be told about any aspects of the research that might influence their willingness to participate.
- If deception is deemed necessary, researchers must gently and fully inform subjects of the deception as soon after their participation as possible.
- Researchers should avoid invasions of privacy and use all possible means to protect the confidentiality of information provided by research participants.
- Most researchers must submit protocols to IRBs to pass judgment on the ethics of proposed research. Before and after institutional approval, researchers are guided in their decisions by federal regulations and professional ethical codes.
- The third area of research ethics, which involves the relationship between values and scientific research, advises scientists to promote the general welfare.
- Although it was once believed that social science could be value-free, this view is now widely rejected because of the apparent influence of values on the research process and because so-called value neutrality makes scientists subject to others' values.
- Researchers should guard against the intrusion of personal values in the conduct of research and carefully point out the limitations of their research.
- Where appropriate, researchers should promote beneficial applications and fight against harmful applications of research findings.

Key Terms

ethics
research ethics
research misconduct
data sharing
cost–benefit analysis
informed consent
debriefing

anonymity
confidentiality
Common Rule
institutional review board (IRB)
expedited review
cultural relativity

Exercises

1. Discuss the ethical problems raised by the following research examples.
    a. (Hypothetical) A criminologist meets a professional fence through an ex-convict he knows. (A *fence* is someone who buys and sells stolen goods.) As part of a study, the researcher convinces the fence to talk about his work—why he sticks with this kind of work, what kind of people he deals with, how he meets them, and so forth. To gain the fence's cooperation, the researcher promises not to disclose any personal details that would get the fence in trouble. However, when subpoenaed, he agrees to reveal his informant rather than go to jail. Has the researcher violated an ethical principle in agreeing to talk?
    b. (Hypothetical) A researcher gains access to a clinic serving AIDS patients by responding to a call for volunteers. While working at the clinic, she makes a record of patients' names and later approaches them, identifies herself as a social scientist, fully explains the nature of her research, and asks for their cooperation in her in-depth survey of AIDS victims. Most patients agree, although some react negatively to the request. What aspects of the researcher's strategy are ethically problematic?
    c. Stephen West, Steven Gunn, and Paul Chernicky (1975) tested a proposition from attribution theory in social psychology regarding the way people perceive reprehensible acts. To do this, they tempted subjects to participate in a burglary and then tested whether those who agreed to participate differed from those who refused and from subjects who were not approached with regard to their perceptions (attributions) about this illegal act. One of the experimenters, posing as a local private detective, contacted students and presented an elaborate plan for burglarizing a local advertising firm. Two groups of subjects were told that the burglary was to be committed for a government agency; another group was promised $2000 for their participation. The subject's agreement or refusal to take part in the burglary and his or her reasons for the decision were the major dependent variables. The researchers did not actually carry out the crime. What ethical problems does this study pose? Describe how you would debrief subjects in this study.
2. If you are preparing a research proposal or if you simply want to become more familiar with ethical codes and guidelines for conducting social research, visit Chapter 3 of the textbook website (www.oup.com/us/singleton-approaches) and examine the annotated list of Web resources. Among the resources are links to the Federal Code of Regulations, codes of various professional associations, and an informed-consent checklist. You also will find a free online tutorial on the rights and welfare of research participants, offered by the NIH Office of Extramural Research, which satisfies the NIH human subjects training requirement for obtaining federal funds.

PART II

Research Design

Thus far we have placed social scientific inquiry in the contexts of science and ethics. We have outlined the goals and norms that guide scientific inquiry as well as the ethical considerations that must be taken into account. Having filled in the background, we are now ready to learn about the details of social research.

Science is the process of producing generalized understanding (theory) through systematic observation (research). Research involves the planning, execution, and interpretation of scientific observation. The three chapters in this section deal with the planning phase. Focusing on the selection and formulation of the research question, Chapter 4 introduces the basic terminology of social research. Chapters 5 and 6 then address two major problems in planning a study: devising operations to measure the phenomena of research interest and selecting cases for observation. Together, these chapters specify the key elements and considerations in the overall plan, called the *research design*. The overview they provide will set the stage for the treatment of the execution and interpretation phases of research in the remainder of the book.

The language of social research introduced in Chapter 4 represents a shift in terminology from our discussion of the nature and logical structure of scientific theory in Chapter 2. As you will see, the tools of thinking on the abstract, theoretical level (concepts, propositions) differ somewhat from the tools of research on the empirical level (variables, hypotheses). The process of moving from the abstract to the concrete is itself an essential part of social research that we consider still further in Chapter 5.

4

Elements of Research Design

All social research focuses on a particular topic and addresses specific research questions. We begin this chapter by considering the social forces and personal motives that affect topic selection. We then consider three main concerns as a researcher narrows in on researchable questions: (1) what entities (e.g., individual people, groups, formal organizations, nations) are to be studied, (2) what aspects or characteristics of these entities are of interest, and (3) what kinds of relationships among the characteristics are anticipated. By considering these key elements of research design, we can grasp the language of social research and what it means to state the problem in researchable terms.

Origins of Research Topics

The starting point for research is the selection of a topic. Once a topic is chosen and the research question is set, we can consider guidelines for conducting research that will generate the most valid data and the most definitive answers. Given that anything that is "social" and "empirical" could be the subject of social research, the variety of potential topics is nearly endless. So, *how* are specific topics likely to emerge in the social sciences? We have identified five factors that explain the origin of most topics.

1. *The structure and state of the scientific discipline.* With the scientific goal of advancing knowledge, most researchers select topics suggested by the ongoing development of theory and research in their particular fields of study. The organization of disciplines casts the framework for topic selection. Social psychologists, for example, divide their discipline with respect to various forms of social behavior, such as aggression, altruism, interpersonal

attraction, and conformity, which act as organizing themes or areas of research interest. Similarly, sociologists frequently study aspects of various institutions, like religion, politics, education, and the family, around which the discipline is organized. As knowledge in an area develops, inconsistencies and gaps in information are revealed that researchers attempt to resolve.

2. *Social problems.* The focus and development of the social sciences are intimately related to interest in basic problems of the "human condition." Historically, this has been a major source of research topics, especially in sociology. The most eminent sociologists of the nineteenth and early twentieth centuries—people like Emile Durkheim, Karl Marx, Max Weber, and Robert Park—concerned themselves with problems emanating from great social upheavals of their day, such as the French and Industrial revolutions and massive foreign immigration to the United States. The problems wrought by these events—alienation, deviance, urban crowding, racism, and many others—have remained a major focus of the discipline. Indeed, many people are attracted to the social sciences because of their perceived relevance to social problems.

3. *Personal interests of the researcher.* Carrying out a research project, with its inevitable complications, obstacles, and demands for time and money, requires considerable interest and commitment on the part of the investigator. What sustains this interest more than anything else are highly personal motivations for doing research on a particular topic. Thus, an investigator may choose a topic not only because it is considered theoretically important, novel, or researchable but also because it stimulates his or her interest. According to the social psychologist Zick Rubin (1976:508–9), one reason for his embarking on the study of romantic love was that he was "by temperament and avocation, a songwriter. Songwriters traditionally put love into measures." And so he set out to find a way of measuring love scientifically. In a similar fashion, it is not surprising that members of particular groups often have pioneered research on those groups; for example, women have led the way in research on women and African Americans in research on blacks (King, Keohane, and Verba, 1994:14).

4. *Social premiums.* There are also powerful social determinants of topic selection. Through the availability of supporting funds, the prestige and popularity of the research area, and pressures within the discipline and within society, social premiums are placed on different topics at different times. Typically, these premiums will reinforce one another, with the social climate affecting funding, which in turn affects prestige. This was certainly true of the space program in the 1960s. Today, in the social sciences, the aging of the population as a whole has raised interest and support for research on the elderly, just as it has caused a dramatic increase in federal expenditures on and services available to older people. Similarly, in the 1970s the women's movement spurred a dramatic increase in research on gender issues that has continued into the twenty-first century.

5. *Practical considerations.* An overriding concern in any research project is cost. Research requires time, money, and personnel. Limitations on these resources, as well as other practical considerations such as the skill of the researcher and the availability of relevant data (see Chapter 12), will shape both the nature and the scope of the problem that the researcher can pursue.

The choice of any given research topic may be affected by any or all of the factors mentioned. Consider a study by Beckett Broh (2002), which examined the effects of participation in extracurricular activities on high school academic achievement. Using data from a national survey of high school students, Broh's study was designed to determine who benefits from participating in sports and other school activities and why. The study continued a line of inquiry on the impact of the extracurriculum of theoretical interest to sociologists of education and sport. Social scientists, school officials, and the general public have long debated whether sport, in particular, builds character and has positive educational benefits. Given the costs of extracurricular programming, especially school sports, and the public concern about boosting academic achievement, Broh's study also had important practical implications. Finally, the topic was of special personal interest to Broh. She had been a high school athlete, and after her collegiate athletic career was cut short by an injury, she turned to coaching middle and high school basketball in Michigan and Ohio. These experiences naturally sparked her interest in sport and education as a PhD student in sociology. And when her mentor suggested that she look at the questions in the National Educational Longitudinal Study, she found the means of testing some of her ideas about the impact of athletes' network of relationships on their academic achievement.

Once a general topic has been chosen, it must be stated in researchable terms. This involves translating the topic into one or more specific questions or hypotheses. We'll discuss the process of moving from general topics to specific questions later. First, it is important to understand that the formulation of a researchable problem or question boils down to deciding what *relationships* among what *variables* of what *units* are to be studied. We will now turn our attention to these important terms.

Units of Analysis

The entities (objects or events) under study are referred to in social research as **units of analysis**. Social scientists study a variety of units (sometimes called "elements" or "cases"). These include individual people; social roles, positions, and relationships; a wide range of social groupings such as families, organizations, and cities; and various social artifacts such as books, periodicals, documents, and even buildings. Ordinarily, the unit of analysis is easily identified. The unit is simply what or who is to be described or analyzed. For example, a researcher wanting to determine whether larger organizations (in terms of the number of employees) have more bureaucratic rules and regulations than smaller ones would treat the *organization* as the relevant unit and would gather information on the size and bureaucratic complexity of different organizations. In Broh's study of the impact of extracurricular activities on academic achievement, the unit of analysis was *individuals* or, more precisely, individual high school students.

In much social research the individual person is the unit of analysis. Social scientists are less interested in individual differences, however, than in the impact of the social context on people in general, the social relationships that individuals form, and large-scale social processes. To analyze "the social" often requires units beyond individual human beings. Consider Fred Markowitz's (2006) study of psychiatric deinstitutionalization. Before the

1960s substantial numbers of mentally ill persons were treated in large, publicly funded hospitals. But as a result of developments in psychiatric drugs, stricter standards for involuntary commitment, and federal funding cuts, the number of resident patients in state and county psychiatric hospitals sharply declined over the next few decades. Studies of *individuals* seem to indicate that this deinstitutionalization movement increased the number of mentally ill who are arrested or imprisoned. For Markowitz, this raised a question about social control: If the behavior of mentally ill persons, who are more likely than others to be both perpetrators and victims of crime, cannot be managed by the mental health–care system, will the mentally ill tend to end up in the criminal justice system? Mental health–care and criminal justice *systems* refer to *social* units; social systems are aspects of communities or nations, not individuals. Markowitz thus chose to analyze cities. Examining the number of psychiatric beds in hospitals and the crime and arrest rates in 81 U.S. cities, he found that the lower a city's capacity to place the mentally ill in public psychiatric hospitals, the higher the city's crime and arrest rates.

Data on individuals also may be inadequate for investigating social and cultural change, especially in the distant past. At mid-twentieth century, the sociologist David Riesman (1950) published an influential book, *The Lonely Crowd*, in which he theorized a general trend toward "other-directedness." Because of changes wrought by the Industrial Revolution, such as the expansion of white-collar and service jobs, increasing material abundance, and the development of mass media of communication, people's actions were becoming less motivated by intrinsic values and more influenced by the actions of others. But how can one study long-range trends in individual motivation when it is impossible to analyze individuals from the past? One social scientific solution is to rely on various social artifacts such as the media and to assume that their visual or verbal imagery reflects the individual values and behavior of direct interest. To test Riesman's theory, for example, researchers have chosen advertisements in mass-circulation magazines as their units of analysis. One study analyzed more than 4000 ads in three women's magazines (*McCall's*, *Ladies' Home Journal*, and *Good Housekeeping*) for the period 1890–1984 (Zinkhan and Hayes, 1989). Results showed that the advertising appealed increasingly over time to the standards of others (other-directedness).

Aggregate Data

One way of identifying the unit of analysis in reported research is to determine the properties or traits that are being described. Individual people have traits such as age, race, and gender; have attitudes and opinions; and act in certain ways, such as saying that they voted in the last civic election, committed a felony, or did volunteer work last week. Only social aggregates such as groups, organizations, cities, and nations have a size, average age, percentage who voted, or crime rate. It can be confusing, however, when individual-level data are combined to describe a social unit to which the individuals belong.

Information about one set of units that is statistically combined to describe a larger social unit is called **aggregate data**. Each year, *U.S. News and World Report* uses aggregate data to rank America's best colleges: They gather information about individual students at each college to characterize the college as a whole. Among their indicators of academic quality, for example, is each school's graduation rate, which is calculated by dividing the number of enrollees in a given class into the number who graduate within 6 years of their enrollment. Other aggregate measures include average SAT or ACT test scores; the proportion of enrolled freshmen who graduated in the top 10 percent of their high school classes; and the acceptance rate, the ratio of the number of students admitted to the number who apply.

In *U.S. News* rankings, the unit of analysis is colleges; that is what is being described and compared. But the use of aggregate data does not always imply a collective unit of analysis. In another study of adolescents' extracurricular participation, Andrew Guest and Barbara Schneider (2003) wondered whether the effect of such activities depended on the social context of the school and community. For example, sports may have a greater effect on academic achievement in lower-class communities, which value sports as paths to financial gain, than in upper-class communities, which value sports for their health and aesthetic benefits. Guest and Schneider's unit of analysis, as in Broh's study, was individual high school students; however, they created aggregate measures to study the impact of the community and school context. Their measure of the community's socioeconomic class was based largely on the average income and education of the neighborhoods where the students lived, and a school context measure consisted of the percentage of students from each student's high school who went on to 4-year colleges after graduation.

Thus, when information about individuals is aggregated to describe groups or collectivities, the unit of analysis may be either the individual or the group. How can you tell? In their analyses, researchers ordinarily compare a number of instances of a particular unit—for example, a number of individuals, a number of cities, or a number of colleges. To identify the unit of analysis, therefore, ask yourself what is being described in each instance and what sorts of units are being compared—individuals or groups. If the aggregate data are used to compare different groups, the unit of analysis is the group. If the data are used to compare individuals who belong to different groups, the unit is the individual.

One reason it is important to identify accurately the unit of analysis is that confusion over units may result in false conclusions about research findings. Generally speaking, assertions should be made only about the particular unit under study. (Actually, assertions should be even more circumscribed than this, as we will see in Chapter 6.) To draw conclusions about one unit on the basis of information about another is to risk committing a logical fallacy.

Ecological Fallacy

The most common fallacy involving the mismatching of units is the **ecological fallacy** (Robinson, 1950). This occurs when relationships between properties of groups or geographic areas are used to make inferences about the individual behaviors of the people within those groups or areas. This is similar to what logicians call the "fallacy of division": assuming that what holds true of a group also is true of individuals within the group. Knowing that Sally attended a college whose students had relatively low average SAT scores, you would commit this fallacy if you assumed that Sally herself had low SAT scores.

Political analysts who use aggregate data from elections to study individual voting behavior are particularly susceptible to the ecological fallacy. Suppose, for example, that a researcher wanted to know whether registered Democrats or Republicans were more likely to support an Independent Party candidate in a city election but that the only information available was the percentage of votes the candidate received and the percentages of Republican and Democratic voters *in each precinct*. In short, the researcher wants to draw conclusions about *individual voters* but has collective information only about *precincts*. Knowing that the candidate received a relatively larger number of votes in precincts with greater percentages of Republicans does not permit the conclusion that Republican voters were more likely to support the candidate than were Democratic voters. In fact, it is plausible that Democrats in predominantly Republican precincts were more likely to support the Independent Party candidate than were Democrats in other precincts. Because the unit of analysis here is the precinct and not the individual voter, we simply do not know how individual voters within each precinct voted.

At one time, social scientists frequently performed ecological analyses such as the one above. For example, criminologists analyzed crime and delinquency rates in relation to other characteristics of census tracts to draw conclusions about characteristics of individual criminals and delinquents. A typical erroneous conclusion might be that foreign-born persons commit more crimes than native-born persons because the crime rate is higher in areas with greater proportions of foreigners. But such a conclusion is clearly unwarranted because we do not know who actually committed the crimes—foreign or native-born persons. Similarly, Durkheim's classic study of suicide was subject to the ecological fallacy by inferring that Protestants commit more suicides than Catholics from the observation that suicide rates were higher in predominantly Protestant nations than in predominantly Catholic ones.[1]

It is not always wrong to draw conclusions about individual-level processes from aggregate or group-level data. Social scientists have identified conditions under which it is reasonable to make such inferences (e.g., Firebaugh, 1978), but it is often difficult to determine whether these conditions are met. The implications of the ecological fallacy are clear: Carefully determine the units about which you wish to draw conclusions and then make sure that your data pertain to those units. If you are interested in individuals but only aggregate data are available, then draw conclusions tentatively, recognizing the possibility of an ecological fallacy.

KEY POINT

If data describe social units (e.g., schools), one must be cautious in drawing conclusions about individuals (students within the schools).

Variables

Although researchers observe units of analysis, it is relationships among characteristics of units that are of primary interest. Characteristics of units that vary, taking on different values, categories, or attributes for different observations, are called **variables**. Variables may vary over cases, over time, or over both cases and time. For example, among individuals, any set of characteristics that may differ for different people, such as age (range of years), gender (male and female), and marital status (single, married, divorced, widowed, etc.), is a variable. And for an individual, any characteristic that may vary from one time period to the next, such as age, level of education (first grade, second grade, etc.), and income (dollars earned per year), is a variable.

It is not unusual to see some confusion between variables and the attributes or categories of which they consist. "Gender" is a variable consisting of the categories male and female; "male" and "female" by themselves are not variables but simply categories that distinguish persons of different gender. Likewise, "divorced" and "Republican" are not variables but categories of the variables "marital status" and "political party affiliation," respectively. To keep this distinction clear, note that any term you would use to describe yourself or someone else (e.g., sophomore, sociology major) is an attribute or category of a variable (academic class, major).

KEY POINT

Social scientists study *relationships* among *variables*; variables depict and differentiate *units of analysis*.

You are now in a position to test your understanding of the concepts of unit of analysis and variable. Table 4.1 is designed to help you do this. The first column presents eight research questions or hypotheses; the second and third columns identify the relevant units of analysis and variables. Read the first column while covering up the second and third columns and record the unit of analysis and variables on a separate sheet of paper. Then check your answers by examining the full table.

Types of Variables

Social scientists find it necessary to classify variables in several ways. One type of classification is necessitated by the complexity of social phenomena. For any given research problem, a researcher can observe and measure only a few of the many potentially relevant properties. Those variables that are the object of study—part of some specified relationship—are called **explanatory variables**, and all other variables are **extraneous** (Kish, 1959).

There are two types of explanatory variables: dependent and independent. The **dependent variable** is the one the researcher is interested in explaining and predicting. Variation in the dependent variable is thought to depend on or to be influenced by certain other variables. The explanatory variables that do the influencing and explaining are called **independent**. If we think in terms of cause and effect, the independent variable is the presumed cause and the dependent variable the presumed effect. Independent variables are also called "predictor variables" because their values or categories may be used to predict the values or categories of dependent variables. For example, when Broh (2002) studied the impact of extracurricular involvement on academic achievement, her independent variable consisted of whether students participated in specific school activities such as interscholastic sports and her dependent variable was level of academic achievement. One research question was whether sports participation explained (or predicted) differences in academic achievement.

TABLE 4.1. **Sample Research Questions, Units of Analysis, and Variables**

Research question/hypothesis	Unit of analysis	Variables
[WHAT ONE WANTS TO KNOW]	[WHAT ENTITIES ARE DESCRIBED AND COMPARED]	[WITH RESPECT TO WHAT CHARACTERISTICS]
Are older people more afraid of crime than younger people?	Individuals	Age, fear of crime
The greater the growth of air passenger traffic at a city's airport, the greater the economic growth.	Cities	Growth of air traffic, economic growth
The higher the proportion of female employees, the lower the wages in nineteenth-century factories.	Factories	Proportion of employees who are female, average wage
Does economic development lower the birth rate?	Nations	Level of economic development, birth rate
The longer the engagement period, the longer the marriage.	Couples (dyads)	Length of engagement, marriage duration
Fan support in the NBA, as measured by attendance, is not related to the proportion of black players on the team.	NBA teams	Racial composition of the team, average attendance
Comic strips introduced in the 1930s were more likely to emphasize powerful heroes than strips introduced in the 1920s.	Comic strips	Whether main characters in strip were powerful, when comic strips were introduced (1920s or 1930s)
When television sports commentators make reference to individual competitors, they are more likely to use first names for female athletes than for male athletes.	References to competitors	Gender of athlete, whether athlete is identified by first name

Research studies in the social sciences often involve several independent variables and sometimes more than one dependent variable. Also, a variable is not intrinsically independent or dependent. An independent variable in one study may well be a dependent variable in another, depending on what the researcher is trying to explain. Finally, it is conventional in mathematics and science for the letter X to symbolize the independent variable and for the letter Y to represent the dependent variable. This is a practice we shall follow in the remainder of the book.

Extraneous variables, which are not part of the explanatory set, may be classified in two important ways. First, in relation to specific independent and dependent variables, they may be **antecedent** or **intervening**. An antecedent variable occurs prior in time to both the independent and the dependent variable; a variable is intervening if it is an effect of the independent variable and a cause of the dependent variable. Antecedent variables in Broh's study were parents' income and a student's race and gender; each of these variables may affect both extracurricular involvement and academic achievement. An intervening variable was students' self-esteem. Extracurricular involvement could affect self-esteem, which in turn could affect a student's academic performance. Figure 4.1 depicts these examples of antecedent and intervening variables. Each arrow in the figure represents causal direction. Thus, "Parents' income → Extracurricular involvement" means that parents' income influences or causes extracurricular involvement, and the absence of an arrow means that one variable does not cause another.

A. Antecedent Variable

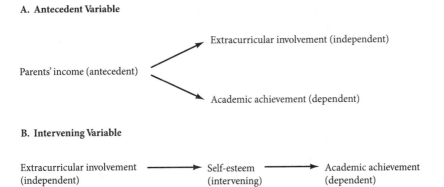

B. Intervening Variable

FIGURE 4.1. Antecedent and intervening variables.

Extraneous variables also may be categorized as controlled or uncontrolled. Controlled or, more commonly, **control variables** are held constant, or prevented from varying, during the course of observation or analysis. This may be done to limit the focus of the research or to test hypotheses pertaining to specific subgroups—for example, all males or all males younger than 18 years of age. Basically, the value or category of a control variable remains the same for a given set of observations. Several techniques for holding variables constant are discussed at length in the following chapters. Examples include selecting only individuals of the same age and gender, observing groups of the same size, creating uniform laboratory conditions or social settings in which to observe people or groups, and statistically controlling for specific attributes.

Whenever a variable is held constant in research, that variable cannot account for (or explain) any of the variation in the explanatory variables. Suppose, for example, that you wanted to explain differences (i.e., variation) between people in their level of aggression. If you controlled for gender by studying only males, then the variable "gender" could not account for any of the observed variation in aggression. Holding variables constant thus simplifies complex social situations. It is a means of ruling out variables that are not of immediate interest but that might otherwise explain part of the phenomenon that the investigator wishes to understand. One aim of efficient research design is to identify potentially relevant extraneous variables to measure and control as many as is feasible. Broh measured numerous extraneous variables, including parents' income and students' race, gender, and self-esteem. This enabled her to statistically control and test the effects of these variables on the relationship between extracurricular activities and academic achievement.

Another important distinction is made between quantitative and qualitative variables. This is a crude way of pointing to some significant differences in the numerical representation of variable categories. We make more precise distinctions along these lines in the next chapter, but for now we appeal to the common understanding of quantitative and qualitative. A variable is **quantitative** if its values or categories consist of numbers and if differences between categories have numerical value. For example, the variable "income," measured in dollars, signifies a quantitative difference—a certain number of dollars—between people with different incomes. **Qualitative variables** have discrete categories, usually designated by words or labels, and nonnumerical differences between categories. For example, the variable gender, consisting of the discrete categories male and female, makes a categorical, but not a numerical, distinction between people.[2]

Relationships

Social scientists' ultimate objective is to make sense of the social world by discovering enduring relationships among phenomena. Much research is therefore aimed directly at developing and testing relationships. There are other, more immediate purposes for which research is conducted, such as exploration and description, which we discuss later in the chapter. Yet, even when a researcher's goal is discovery or description, research findings will depend to a large extent on what particular *relationships* are anticipated. Research is not like the kind of fishing trip in which you drop your line anywhere, hoping you will catch something. Investigators do not make random observations. Whatever their goals, they must decide what to observe or ignore, how to go about making their observations, and how to interpret them. Such decisions inevitably are based on a researcher's expectations about how variables are related to one another.

Consider an investigator who wants to study "everything" about families but "let the facts speak for themselves" (Batten, 1971:9–11). Without *any* expectations, how is the researcher to decide what constitutes a "family"? Should first cousins be included even if they live far away or seldom keep in touch? Should a family include all persons living in the same household, no matter how remote the blood tie (Batten, 1971)? When collecting data, should the researcher include the hat size and shoe size of each family member? Such considerations ultimately depend on the social researcher's *expectations* about salient properties and *relationships* regarding families.

Facts never speak for themselves. Not only which facts are sought but also how they are interpreted depends again on anticipated relationships—on what particular answers the researcher expects the data or "facts" to provide. A classic everyday example (although likely apocryphal) of how one can draw very different conclusions from the same facts is "contrasting newspaper coverage of a two-car race between Soviets and Americans during the Cold War. An American newspaper described the race this way: 'American car beats out Soviet competitor.'" By contrast, a Russian newspaper described the exact same facts "differently: 'Soviet car finishes second; American car is next-to-last'" (D. Murray, Schwartz, and Lichter, 2001:86). Similarly, pundits and politicians often refer to the number of jobs "created" in the United States during a president's term of office. The most frequently cited numbers are estimates of employment drawn from a Bureau of Labor Statistics survey of businesses and government agencies. Conclusions drawn about these data, however, must take into account factors such as population growth and women's level of participation in the labor market, and they depend on assumptions about who is responsible for job growth (e.g., Congress, the president, global economy). Without considering the complex set of relationships among factors affecting employment, different conclusions may be drawn.

Given that all research carries expectations about the nature of what is being investigated, anticipated relationships and guiding theoretical explanations should always be identified as far as possible. Beckett Broh's (2002) selection of variables for her study was guided largely by three theoretical explanations of the link between sports participation and educational achievement: (1) developmental theory—sports teaches skills, such as a strong work ethic and perseverance that help students achieve in the classroom; (2) the leading crowd hypothesis—athletes gain social status and membership in a peer group of disproportionately college-oriented high achievers, which facilitates higher academic performance; and (3) social capital theory—sports create strong social ties among students, parents, and teachers that provide educational benefits. Broh derived the social capital model in part from her experience as a basketball coach; she noted that her players tended to spend more time with their parents and had better relationships with them than other students.

Thus far we have relied on the reader's intuitive grasp of the term "relationship." Everyone has experienced relationships at some point. One might think of relationships among kin; "serious" relationships, as between lovers; and relationships among the members of teams and work groups. We also have a sense of a relationship when one event regularly precedes or follows the occurrence of another, for example, when the appearance of dark clouds is regularly followed by rain. All such relationships have two features. First, they always involve two or more entities: persons, objects, or events—such as parent and child, leader and follower, or clouds and rain. Second, the pairs or combinations of things usually occur together and change together; thus, the appearance of one thing signals the appearance of the other and the absence of one implies the absence of the other. For example, by definition, every parent has a child and every child has (or had) a parent; we cannot have one without the other. Also, by observation we know that certain kinds of clouds produce rain and that without clouds it cannot rain.

KEY POINT

Facts or data do not speak for themselves; they must be interpreted based on anticipated and predicted relationships.

The kind of relationships with which social scientists are concerned, **relationships among variables**, have these same two features. Two or more variables are related, or form a relationship, to the extent that changes in one are accompanied by systematic changes in the other(s). Since the manner in which the variables change or vary together will depend on whether the variables are qualitative or quantitative, we will consider the nature of relationships separately for each of these types of variables.

Relationships among Qualitative Variables

Consider the two qualitative variables race and political party affiliation. If two individuals have the same party affiliation, say Democrat, then the category of this variable does not change as we look from one individual to the other. If they have different affiliations, say one is a Democrat and the other is a Republican, then the category of the variable does change. Assuming similar statements about race, we would say that a relationship exists between race and political party affiliation if a comparison of a pair of individuals reveals that a change in race is accompanied by a change in party affiliation. More generally, the basic

Table 4.2. Varying Degrees of Association between Two Qualitative Variables: Race and Political Affiliation

A. Perfect association	White	Black	Total
Democrat	0	10	10
Republican	10	0	10
Total	10	10	20
B. Moderate association	White	Black	Total
Democrat	3	7	10
Republican	7	3	10
Total	10	10	20
C. No association	White	Black	Total
Democrat	5	5	10
Republican	5	5	10
Total	10	10	20

idea of a relationship, or association, between qualitative variables can be incorporated into two assertions (Leik, 1972:26): (1) if one variable changes, the other variable changes, and (2) if one variable does not change, the other does not change. If these two assertions were true for all pairs of cases, the result would be a perfect one-to-one correspondence between the categories of one variable and the categories of the other. Table 4.2A depicts a perfect relationship between race and political party affiliation among 20 individuals.

In actual research, of course, we never see such perfect associations. To a researcher, therefore, the important question is not whether a given pair of variables is perfectly associated but how strongly they are related. That is, how closely do the data approximate a perfect association between variables? Statistical techniques to assess this are called "measures of association." These techniques, as well as the concept of "strength of relationship," are best understood if assertions about concomitant changes in variables are treated as predictions. Table 4.2A suggests two predictions: (1) if a person is black, then he or she will be a Democrat, and (2) if a person is white, then he or she will be a Republican. The proportion of times such predictions are correct for all cases is an index of the strength of the relationship. A high proportion indicates that the variables are strongly related; a low proportion indicates a weak relationship. Furthermore, if the proportion is so low that knowledge of one variable is of no use in predicting the other, the variables are said to be unrelated. The rest of Table 4.2 gives a possible combination showing a moderate relationship between race and political party affiliation (Table 4.2B) and a distribution indicating no relationship (Table 4.2C). Statistical indices of association may be computed for each of these distributions. Ordinarily, these indices will range from 0, indicating no relationship, to 1.00, indicating a perfect relationship.

Relationships among Quantitative Variables

As we move from qualitative to quantitative variables, it becomes possible to say whether a change in a variable represents an increase or a decrease in value. With this additional property, we can measure not only the strength of the relationship but also two other aspects: direction and linearity.

A relationship may be either positive or negative in direction. A **positive** or **direct relationship** between variables exists if an increase in the value of one variable is accompanied by an increase in the value of the other or if a decrease in the value of one variable is accompanied by a decrease in the value of the other. In other words, the two variables consistently change in the same direction. We would expect a positive relationship between sons' heights and fathers' heights (the taller a father, the taller his son will tend to be) and between students' scores on the SAT and their college grade-point averages (as scores increase, grades tend to increase). A **negative** or **inverse relationship** between variables exists if a decrease in the value of one variable is accompanied by an increase in the value of the other. Thus, changes in one variable are opposite in direction to changes in the other. We would find a negative relationship between a person's age and how long he or she is expected to live (as age increases, life expectancy decreases) and between the speed and accuracy with which people perform many tasks (the faster one does something, the less accurately one is likely to do it).

Relationships among quantitative variables are usually depicted with graphs, such as those in Figure 4.2. The lines in these two graphs illustrate the characteristic of "linearity." The straight line in Figure 4.2A depicts a *linear* relationship. (Specifically, this line depicts a *positive linear* relationship. A straight line running from the upper left corner to the lower right corner would depict a *negative linear* relationship.) Note that one variable changes at the same rate and in the same direction (positive) over the entire range of the other variable. The curved line in Figure 4.2B depicts a *curvilinear* relationship. In this case, the rate of change in one variable is *not* consistent over all values of the other: Variable Y increases more rapidly for low values than for high values of variable X and then reverses direction. We would expect this pattern of relationship to occur between the age and annual earnings of adult workers. Earnings will generally increase with age up to retirement and then will decline.

Tabular and graphic representations of relationships between variables and other statistical analyses are discussed further in Chapter 15. There, as well as elsewhere in the book, we focus on linear relationships since this pattern is most often assumed and analyzed in the social sciences. A common statistical measure of the strength and direction of linear relationships between two quantitative variables is the Pearson product-moment coefficient of correlation, or **correlation coefficient** for short. Symbolized by the letter r, the correlation coefficient may vary between -1.00 and $+1.00$. The signs $-$ and $+$ indicate the direction of the relationship, positive or negative; the magnitude of the coefficient, ignoring the sign, indicates the strength of association. Again, strength of association can be construed as accuracy of prediction. Relationships between two quantitative variables are represented in graphs such as Figure 4.2; however, when each case is plotted according to its values on the independent and dependent variables, the plots seldom form a perfectly straight line, as in Figure 4.2A. Rather, the plots cluster to varying degrees about the best-fitting line. If we use this line to predict Y values from X values, then the more closely the plots cluster about the line, the more accurate the prediction and the stronger the association. Figure 4.3 shows two possible outcomes. In Figure 4.3A, where the plots cluster fairly tightly around the line, there is a relatively strong correlation of .74 between variable X and variable Y. This is the

A. Linear relationship

B. Curvilinear relationship

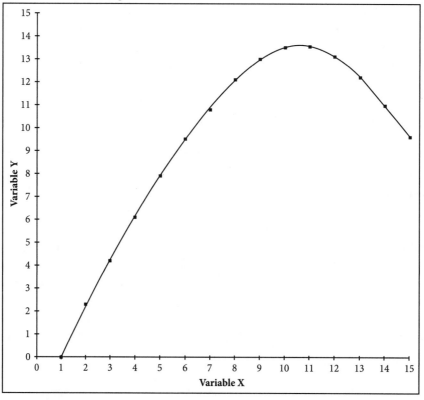

FIGURE 4.2. Linear and curvilinear relationships between two quantitative variables.

A. Strong correlation, $r = .74$

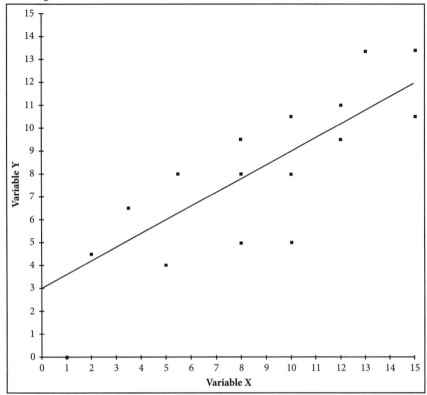

B. Weak correlation, $r = .08$

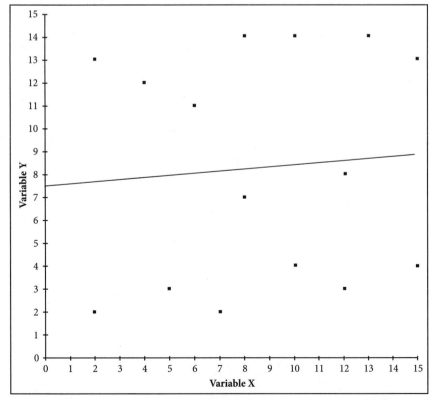

FIGURE 4.3. Strong and weak correlations between two quantitative variables.

same correlation that Broh (2002) found between students' grades in English and grades in math. In Figure 4.3B, where the plots are loosely clustered about the line, the correlation is .08. This is the correlation Broh found between number of hours spent on homework and grades in English.

Relationships between a Qualitative and a Quantitative Variable

Another method of assessing relationships is used when both qualitative and quantitative variables are involved. Most often in such cases, especially in experiments, the independent variable is qualitative and the dependent variable is quantitative. This is the type of relationship considered here.

It will be helpful, once again, to think in terms of predictions. A relationship is said to exist if the different categories of the independent variable predict different values for the dependent variable. Thus, if each category of the independent variable is treated as a distinct group, then a relationship can be described in terms of the *differences among groups* on the dependent variable. We might compute an average value of the dependent variable for each group. No differences in these averages across groups would then indicate no relationship. And, in general, the larger the differences, the stronger the relationship.

For example, suppose a researcher was interested in examining the relationship between race and annual income. Since annual income, as measured in dollars earned, is a quantitative variable, average incomes could be computed for each racial group (i.e., for each category of the qualitative variable race), as shown in Table 4.3.[3] Note that there is a difference in the averages across groups: In 2014, whites earned $56,866 on average and blacks earned $35,398. Thus, we may conclude that a relationship exists between race and income.[4]

Statistically Significant Relationships

Social scientists do not ordinarily consider an association between two variables meaningful unless the association is **statistically significant**. Consider the moderate association between race and party affiliation in Table 4.2B. Note that there are only 20 cases in this table. Now suppose that these 20 cases represent a random sample of the U.S. population. It would not be appropriate to conclude from these data that there is an association between race and party affiliation in the general population. Why? Because in a sample this small the difference in party affiliation between blacks and whites easily could have occurred by chance (i.e., as a result of random selection) even if there is no relationship in the larger population.

TABLE 4.3. **Relationship between a Quantitative Variable (Median Income in 2014 Dollars) and a Qualitative Variable (Race)**

	White	*Black*
Median income	$56,866	$35,398

Source: C. DeNavas-Walt and B. D. Proctor. *Income and Poverty in the United States: 2014*. U.S. Census Bureau, Current Population Reports, P60-252. Washington, D.C.: U.S. Government Printing Office, 2015, Table 1.

TABLE 4.4. Race by Political Party Preference,*
2014 General Social Survey

	White	Black
Democrat	49.9%	93.6%
Republican	50.1	6.4
	100.0%	100.0%
(N)	(994)	(266)

*Party preference indicates respondents who described themselves as
either "strong" or "not very strong" Democrats (Republicans); data
exclude those who identified as "independent." Based on 2196 white
and black respondents.

Statistically significant associations are those that are *not* likely to have occurred by chance or random processes. Table 4.4 shows the relationship between race and party affiliation in a recent national sample of the adult population. The respondents in this survey were asked whether they usually thought of themselves as a Democrat, Republican, or Independent. Table 4.4 shows only those respondents who described themselves as either Democrats or Republicans. Blacks were far more likely than whites to identify themselves as Democrats (93.6 percent compared to 49.9 percent); given the size of the sample (2196), this difference is highly unlikely to have occurred by chance and therefore is statistically significant. When this property of relationships is reported in the research literature, it is indicated with an italic lowercase *p* followed by $<$ and a decimal; for example, $p < .01$. This means that the probability is less than 1 in 100 that the relationship could occur by chance, assuming that there is no relationship in the larger population from which the sample is drawn. With odds this low, we would conclude that the association did not occur by chance and therefore that a relationship between race and party affiliation exists in the United States. (See Chapter 15 for a brief discussion of tests of statistical significance.)

It is important to note that statistical significance is not the same as strength of association. Although strong associations are more likely to be statistically significant than weak ones, a very weak association may be significant provided that the sample is large enough. For example, both of the correlations reported above for the Broh (2002) study (see Figure 4.3) were statistically significant, although one (.74) was strong and the other (.08) was very weak. The reason that such a low correlation was significant was that it was based on a sample size of more than 10,000 students. With samples this large, even relatively weak associations are unlikely to occur by chance and, therefore, are likely to differ from a zero association in the population (all high school students) from which the sample was drawn.

So far we have examined some common ways of depicting relationships. Also, we have noted four properties of relationships: strength, directionality, linearity, and statistical significance. The *strength* of a relationship refers to the extent to which variables are associated or correlated. *Directionality* and *linearity* tell us how changes in one variable are related to changes in another. Do the variables change in the same or the opposite direction? Is the rate of change in one variable consistent over all values of the other? Together these two properties describe the *form* of the relationship. Knowing the strength and form of relationships as well as whether it is statistically significant will often satisfy a researcher's curiosity.

However, if our interest is in explaining social phenomena, we also will need to know about the causal link between variables. And these statistical properties are never sufficient to establish a cause-and-effect relationship.

KEY POINT

Relationships may be described by their *form* (how changes in one variable vary with changes in the other), *strength* (how accurately values of one variable predict values of the other), and *statistical significance* (likelihood that the relationship occurred by chance or random processes).

The Nature of Causal Relationships

In Chapter 2 we noted that, for purposes of explanation and prediction, scientists find it helpful to think in terms of cause-and-effect relationships. But how does one identify such a relationship? What is meant by the term "causality"? At first glance, the task of defining causality seems simple. Since we are so accustomed to thinking causally and causal terms are so frequently used in everyday life, the concept would appear to be widely understood. In lay terms, a *cause* is something that makes something happen or change. It seems obvious that a rock thrown against a window will cause the glass to shatter. And the fact that drinking too much soda causes someone to get a stomachache is a **causal relationship** that you can comprehend even if you fortunately have not had the same experience.

In contrast to the implicit understanding of causality that seems to exist in everyday life, the meaning of the concept of "cause" has been hotly debated by philosophers and scientists for centuries. Much of this debate stems from the philosopher David Hume's analysis (1748). Hume argued that all that one can observe is a constant or stable association between events. From such association we infer a causal connection; however, there is no way of logically or empirically showing that a causal connection actually exists. A causal relationship exists only in the observer's mind; it is something inferred from an observed association between events. Following Hume's line of reasoning, some philosophers and scientists have argued against the use of the concept of cause in science. Yet many scholars regard causal relationships as the heart of scientific understanding, at least in the social, behavioral, and biological sciences (Woodward, 2016). Furthermore, even if such relationships cannot be "proven" empirically (just as no generalization can be proven by scientific evidence), researchers have found working with causal hypotheses to be a productive way of doing science (Blalock, 1964:6).

The important point of Hume's analysis, therefore, is that we should understand the bases for making causal inferences. In other words, what kind of evidence supports the belief that a causal relationship exists? Social scientists generally require at least three kinds of evidence to establish causality. These requisites are association, direction of influence, and nonspuriousness.

Association

For one variable to be a cause of another, the variables must have a statistical **association**. If the pattern of changes in one variable is not related to changes in another, then the one cannot be producing, or causing, changes in the other. Thus, for instance, if intelligence is unrelated to delinquency—that is, if adolescents of high and low intelligence are equally likely to be delinquent—then intelligence cannot be a cause of delinquency.

Associations are almost never perfect, so a perfect association between variables is not a criterion of causality. According to logicians, in fact, the very idea of causation implies imperfect associations between events. Causes can have invariable effects only in "closed systems" that exclude all other factors that might influence the relationship under investigation. Many of the laws of physics, for instance, are said to apply exactly only in a vacuum. However, vacuums are not found in nature; neither is it possible in real social situations to eliminate completely the influence of extraneous factors. Perfect associations may be expected, therefore, only under the theoretical condition that "all other things are equal" but not in the "real world" of observations.

Barring "perfect" associations, then, the application of this first criterion necessarily involves a judgment about whether an association implies a meaningful causal relationship. In the social sciences, causal relationships often are implied from comparatively "weak" associations. One reason for this is that many measurements in the social sciences are relatively imprecise. The primary reason, though, is that in explaining human action, multiple causes may independently or jointly produce the same or similar effects. A weak association may mean that only one of several causes has been identified, or it may mean that a causal relationship exists but not under the conditions or for the particular segment of the population in which the weak association was observed. Rather than strength of association, therefore, social scientists rely on tests of statistical significance to determine whether a meaningful, interpretable association exists between variables. Although Broh (2002) found a weak correlation between time spent on homework and grades, because this association was statistically significant, it was interpreted as a cause (among others) of academic performance.

Direction of Influence

A second criterion needed to establish causality is that a cause must precede its effect, or at least the **direction of influence** should be from cause to effect. In other words, changes in the causal factor, or independent variable, must influence changes in the effect, or dependent variable, but not vice versa. For many relationships in social research the direction of influence between variables can be conceived in only one way. For example, characteristics fixed at birth, such as a person's race and gender, come before characteristics developed later in life, such as a person's education or political party affiliation; and it is hard to imagine how changes in the latter could influence changes in the former.

Direction of influence is not always so easy to determine. Suppose you found a correlation between racial prejudice and interracial contact showing that the more contact a person has with members of other races, the less prejudiced he or she is apt to be. One possible interpretation is that racial contact increases familiarity and contradicts stereotypes, thereby reducing prejudice. An equally plausible interpretation is that prejudiced people will avoid contact, whereas tolerant people will readily interact with other races, so that racial prejudice influences racial contact. Without any information about the direction of influence between these variables, there is no basis for deciding which variable is the cause and which is the effect. To take another example, a correlation between grades and class attendance may mean that greater attendance "increases the amount learned and thus causes higher grades" or it may mean that "good grades lead students who obtain them to attend class more frequently" (Neale and Liebert, 1986:89–90).

Direction of influence was an issue in the Broh (2002) study. An association between sports participation and academic performance could mean that playing sports has educational benefits, but it also could mean that higher-achieving, "good" students are more likely to choose or be selected to play sports than other students. Because Broh hypothesized that sports participation had a positive influence on grades, it was important for her to rule out the possibility that superior academic performance leads to sports participation.

The requirement that causes influence effects has two major implications for research: (1) hypothesized relationships should always specify the direction of influence among variables and (2) whenever the direction cannot be established theoretically, it should be tested empirically. As you will see, this task is relatively easy in experiments but often difficult in other kinds of research.

Nonspuriousness (Elimination of Rival Hypotheses)

If two variables happen to be related to a common extraneous variable, then a statistical association can exist even if there is no inherent link between the variables. Therefore, to infer a causal relationship from an observed correlation, there should be good reason to believe that there are no "hidden" factors that could have created an accidental or spurious relationship between the variables. When an association or correlation between variables cannot be explained by an extraneous variable, the relationship is said to be *nonspurious*. When a correlation has been produced by an extraneous third factor and neither of the variables involved in the correlation has influenced the other, it is called a **spurious relationship**.

The idea of spuriousness is obvious when we consider two popular examples in the social sciences. The first is a reported positive correlation in Europe between the number of storks in an area and the number of births in that area (Wallis and Roberts, 1956:79). This correlation might explain how the legend that storks bring babies got started, but it hardly warrants a causal inference. Rather, the correlation is produced by the size of the population. Storks like to nest in the crannies and chimneys of buildings; so as the population and thus the number of buildings increases, the number of places for storks to nest increases. And as the population increases, so does the number of babies. We also would expect to find a positive correlation between the number of firefighters at a fire and the amount of damage done. But this does not imply that firefighters did the damage. The reason for the correlation is the size of the fire: Bigger fires cause more firefighters to be summoned and cause more damage.

In these examples the original relationship is an incidental consequence of a common cause: an antecedent extraneous variable. In the first example, the size of the population accounts for *both* the number of storks and the number of births; in the second, the severity of the fire determines *both* the number of firefighters and the amount of damage. These relationships are depicted in Figure 4.4. The examples are intuitively obvious, and the third factor is fairly easy to identify.

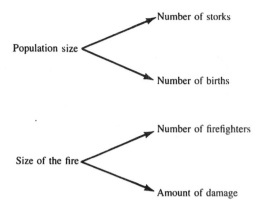

FIGURE 4.4. **Examples of spurious relationships.**

In actual research, spurious relationships are much less apparent, and the possibility often exists that an unknown variable may have produced an observed association. For many years, numerous studies have shown that children who are breastfed tend to have higher IQ scores than those who are not. Proponents of breastfeeding (which does have many other benefits for mother and child) have inferred a causal connection, contending that the effect may be due to a component of breast milk or perhaps to the physical interaction between mother and baby. Recent research suggests, however, that this association is spurious. Both breastfeeding and child intelligence are influenced by the mother's intelligence: Mothers with high IQs are more likely to breastfeed *and* more likely to have children with high IQs (Der, Batty, and Deary, 2006).

To infer that a relationship is nonspurious, researchers must identify and control for extraneous variables that might account for an association. We can see how this works by considering the relationship between cigarette smoking and lung cancer. Based on studies of U.S. men and women over age 55, the Centers for Disease Control and Prevention (2015) reported that those who smoked cigarettes were 25 times more likely to get lung cancer than people who did not smoke. But the reason scientists now believe that there is a causal link between smoking and cancer is not based simply on this association; rather, it is based on the fact that smokers' greater risk of getting cancer remains about the same when the effects of other variables are removed.

Suppose we control for the variable urban–rural residence. This could create a spurious association between smoking and cancer if urban areas have more smokers as well as sources of lung cancer (e.g., greater air pollution) than rural areas. To control for extraneous variables we must remove their effects, such as by computing the incidence of lung cancer among smokers and nonsmokers separately for urban and rural residents. A finding of no difference in the cancer rate between smoking and nonsmoking urban dwellers and between smoking and nonsmoking rural residents would suggest that urban–rural residence produced a spurious association between smoking and cancer. If we found, however, that both urban and rural smokers were more likely to develop lung cancer than nonsmokers in these areas, we would be more confident that the relationship is nonspurious.

To infer nonspuriousness, researchers must show that the relationship is maintained when all extraneous variables are held constant. Circumstances seldom allow for the control of all variables; therefore, researchers attempt to control the effects of as many as possible. The greater the number of variables that are controlled without altering a relationship, the greater the likelihood that the relationship is not spurious. Thus, we would become even more confident in a causal link between smoking and lung cancer if the incidence of lung cancer among smokers and nonsmokers remains the same when examined separately for men and women, people of low and high socioeconomic status, people of different races, and so forth. (Box 4.1 provides another example of the importance of the nonspuriousness criterion. In this case, the causal interpretation that exercise reduces the risk of heart attacks was challenged by several rival explanations.)

KEY POINT
An association between variables does not necessarily imply that the variables are causally related. In addition to association, causal inferences require evidence of direction of influence and nonspuriousness.

In one way or another, tests for spuriousness entail controlling for extraneous variables. The type of statistical control employed in our smoking–cancer example is common in nonexperimental research. Its major drawback is that one can control statistically only for those variables that have been observed or measured as part of the research. Hence, the effects of any unknown or unmeasured variables cannot be assessed. A stronger test of nonspuriousness is provided in experiments through a process called "randomization" that makes it theoretically possible to control for all extraneous variables. Experimental controls are discussed in Chapter 7, and causal analysis techniques involving statistical manipulation of nonexperimental data are discussed in Chapter 16.

BOX 4.1 Problems in Causal Interpretation: The Case of Exercise and Heart Attacks

Of the three criteria needed to establish a causal relationship, the most difficult to assess is nonspuriousness. One can never be sure that a causal connection exists between correlated variables. Indeed, mistaken impressions of causality may remain undetected for years. An interesting example of this problem in social science research is related by the psychologists Schuyler Huck and Howard Sandler (1979:151, 152, 227).

In recent years there has been much interest in the relative benefits of regular exercise. One controversial claim is that exercise can reduce the risk of heart attacks. An early study by J. N. Morris of London shows, however, just how difficult this is to establish. Examining drivers and conductors of London's double-decker buses, Morris found that the drivers were far more likely to suffer from heart disease and to die from coronaries than were the conductors. Since the drivers sat in their seats all day while the conductors ran up and down stairs to collect fares, he concluded that it was the differential amount of exercise inherent in the two jobs that brought about the observed differences in health. Before reading further, you might try to think of variables other than exercise that could have produced the difference in heart problems between the drivers and conductors. Morris uncovered one variable in a follow-up study, and Huck and Sandler mention two others.

Some time after the publication of the above results, Morris examined the records maintained on the uniforms issued to drivers and conductors and discovered that drivers tended to be given larger uniforms than conductors. Therefore, he concluded, differences in weight rather than exercise might be the causal factor. That is, heavier men, who were more coronary-prone to begin with, may have chosen the sedentary job of driver, whereas thinner men chose the more physically active job of conductor.

Another explanation is related to the amount of tension associated with the two jobs. As Huck and Sandler (1979:227) point out,

> The conductors probably experienced very little tension as they went up and down the bus collecting fares from the passengers; the worst thing that they probably had to deal with in their jobs was a passenger who attempted to ride free by sneaking around from one seat to another. Normally, however, we suspect that the conductors actually enjoyed their interaction with other people while on the job.
>
> But on the other hand, each driver had the safety of everyone on the bus as his responsibility. And as anyone who lives in or visits a city knows, driving in rush-hour traffic is anything but restful. Having to dodge pedestrians, being cut off by other vehicles, watching for signal changes—these activities can bring about temporary outbursts of anger and chronic nervousness. Imagine how it would affect your heart to be in the driver's seat of a bus for eight hours each working day!

Finally, a third variable that could account for the different rate of heart problems is age. If mobility or seniority or some other function of age were related to job assignment, then employees assigned to the driver jobs may have been older and those assigned to the conductor jobs younger. And since we would expect more heart attacks among older persons, age rather than the nature of the job could be the causal variable.

In this example it is impossible to tell which cause—exercise, weight, job stress, or age—may have produced the observed differences in health between drivers and conductors. Since both weight and age are antecedent to job type and heart disease, either of these uncontrolled extraneous variables could have created a spurious relationship. However, if exercise or job stress were the correct interpretation, then the original relationship would not be spurious, since exercise and job stress specify intervening variables through which the job itself can make a person more or less susceptible to heart problems. The following diagram shows the difference in these two outcomes.

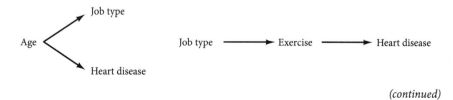

(continued)

(continued)

It is possible that two or more of these variables are operating jointly to produce the health differential between the two groups. The only safe conclusion is that we really do not know which interpretation is correct.

In general, correlation does not imply causation. All correlations must be interpreted; like any fact, they do not speak for themselves. To infer a causal relationship from a correlation, an investigator must detect and control for extraneous variables that are possible and plausible causes of the variable to be explained. The fatal flaw in Morris's study is that relevant extraneous variables were not controlled; without directly assessing the effects of such "hidden" causes, we cannot tell which interpretation is valid.

Causation, Intervening Variables, and Theory

Recall that extraneous variables may be either antecedent or intervening in relation to the independent and dependent variables. An antecedent variable, which is causally prior to both the independent and the dependent variable, can produce a spurious relationship. By contrast, the identification of an intervening variable or mechanism linking the independent and dependent variables strengthens the causal inference. Indeed, this is sometimes advocated as a fourth criterion—in addition to association, direction of influence, and nonspuriousness—for establishing that one variable causes another (see Hyman, 1955). For example, one may argue that the belief that smoking causes lung cancer will be enhanced considerably if and when it is established that certain chemical agents from cigarettes produce cancerous cells. Knowing the causal process through which smoking produces cancer would provide one last shred of evidence against a spurious correlation. However, once the criterion of nonspuriousness is firmly established, a causal relationship is generally inferred even if the intervening mechanisms are not known. Few scientists today doubt that smoking causes cancer. Thus, although specifying the intervening variables in a relationship may lead to a better theoretical understanding and more accurate prediction, it is "not part of the minimum requirements for demonstrating causality. Holding a match to a pile of leaves is a cause of their bursting into flame, even if one cannot describe the intervening chemical reactions" (Hirschi and Selvin, 1967:38).

KEY POINT
Antecedent variables may create spurious associations; *intervening variables* clarify the causal connection between variables.

Although not a necessary causal criterion, the identification of intervening variables is nonetheless an essential part of scientific inquiry. Often, in fact, this is what the development and testing of theory is all about. For example, Durkheim's theory of suicide stipulated the intervening causal mechanism—social integration—for a number of relationships. The reason that fewer suicides are found among Catholics than among Protestants and that there are fewer suicides among married than among single people, according to the theory, is that being a Catholic and being married each engenders a greater sense of social integration, which in turn reduces the likelihood that anyone within the group will commit suicide. Broh (2002) tested the effects of several intervening variables. Having found that participation in interscholastic sports benefits students' academic performance, she also showed that this relationship was best explained by developmental and social capital theories. High school athletes develop a greater work ethic and sense of control over their lives than do nonathletes, and their athletic participation generates stronger ties among students, parents, and teachers, all of which have positive effects on academic performance.

Yet, theory plays a much larger role in causal analysis than specifying intervening variables. Theories not only render a more complete understanding of the causal processes that connect events but also provide the general framework for investigating the nature of all relationships. Theories tell a researcher which relationships to observe, what extraneous variables are likely to affect the relationships, and the conditions under which a causal relationship is likely to exist. It is only in terms of some theory, in short, that a researcher can determine how to assess the meaningfulness of a weak association and how to test for direction of influence and nonspuriousness. Thus, we see again the importance of the interplay between theory and research in science. Theory guides research, and research provides the findings that validate and suggest modifications in theory.

Formulating Questions and Hypotheses

Having introduced the language of units of analysis, variables, and relationships, we are now ready to return to formulations of research questions. According to Glenn Firebaugh (2008), research questions should meet two fundamental criteria: They should be researchable and interesting. A researchable question is one that is answerable through empirical research. As we saw in the preceding chapters, some questions cannot be answered because they are beyond the realm of science (e.g., Does God exist? Is capital punishment morally wrong?) or because ethical considerations rule them out. Other questions may be too grand. Novice as well as experienced researchers often begin with questions that are so broad in scope that they provide little or no immediate direction for research. For example, Stanley Schachter, well known in part for his work on affiliation, was interested in what motivates people to be around others (Evans, 1976:159), a question nearly as encompassing as the entire field of social psychology. Before Schachter could begin to do research, he had to reformulate this question so that it pointed to identifiable variables and relationships. After reading and speculating about "affiliative tendencies," Schachter eventually focused on the question of how fear affects the desire to be with others.

Firebaugh's second criterion for good research questions is that they should be interesting to you and, especially, to others. What makes a question interesting? Primarily it should contribute to ongoing conversations in a scientific field of study. The only way to know whether your question speaks to such conversations is to learn about the latest research through a thorough review of the literature. Here is where you will find the major theories, key findings, and unresolved issues in the field. Beckett Broh's (2002) literature review revealed several studies that found a positive association between high school students' participation in sports and grades. Relatively few studies, however, had examined the effect of other extracurricular activities, and even fewer had attempted to test theoretical explanations of how sports participation enhances educational achievement. After considering various theories, Broh formulated three unanswered research questions:

- Why does sports participation boost students' achievement? Does sports participation benefit students' development and social networks, and are these the mechanisms that link participation to educational outcomes?
- Are the educational benefits of sports participation unique to sports, or do nonsports extracurricular activities also promote achievement?
- Do nonsports extracurricular activities benefit students' development and social networks? (Broh, 2002:73)

Broh's research questions were "interesting" because they extended prior research in new directions. (Also of interest, albeit much less common, are research questions that challenge well-established findings.) Her questions extended research in two ways: by broadening the question to include participating in nonsports activities as well as interscholastic sports and by identifying an intervening variable (social capital) that accounts for the effect of sports participation on grades. Two other ways of extending prior research suggested by Firebaugh (2008) are investigating whether a finding applies to a new population (imagine Broh replicating her study outside the United States) and whether a finding applies to a new time period (e.g., would a similar association be found in the first half of the twentieth century?).

The tentative answers to research questions are called "hypotheses." Formally defined, a **hypothesis** is an expected but unconfirmed relationship between two or more variables. Hypotheses come from a variety of sources, including everything from theory to direct observation to guesses and intuition. Sometimes the formulation of hypotheses is the principal outcome of research. At other times, hypotheses are never made explicit, even though they implicitly guide research activities. However, whenever the research objective is clearly one of testing relationships among variables, hypotheses should be stated formally and precisely so that they carry clear implications for testing the stated relations.

Although they may be stated in a variety of ways, all hypotheses should speculate about the nature and form of a relationship. An adequate hypothesis statement about two variables should indicate which variable predicts or causes the other and how changes in one variable are related to changes in the other. For example, if we thought that education generally increases tolerance, we might hypothesize that "an increase in education will result in a decrease in prejudice." This statement implies two features about the relationship: first, which variable causes, explains, or predicts the other (education predicts prejudice); and second, how changes in one variable are related to changes in the other (as education increases, prejudice decreases). Hypotheses that specify the form of the relationship are said to be testable because it is possible, assuming each variable has been measured adequately, to determine whether they are true or false or at least whether they are probably true or probably false.

There are several ways of expressing testable hypotheses, such as the one relating education and prejudice:

1. *"If–then" (conditional) statements.* These statements say that if one phenomenon or condition holds, then another will also hold. An example is "If a person has a high level of education, then he or she will have a low level of prejudice." Alternately, one could say, "If a person has a low level of education, then he or she will have a high level of prejudice." In logic, such statements are called **conditionals**. A conditional consists of a connection between two simple statements, each pointing to a condition or category of a variable. As used in science, the connection asserted by a conditional is that the condition (or variable category) following the "if" *causes* the condition (or variable category) following the "then." Social research hypotheses seldom are specified in this form. Still, it is always possible to restate testable hypotheses as conditionals; and using this standard logical form, some scientists contend that it is easier to ascertain the kinds of inferences that legitimately can be made from research findings to the hypothesis (McGuigan, 1993:37).

2. *Mathematical statements.* Some hypotheses may be stated in the form of the standard mathematical formula $Y = f(X)$, which reads "Y is a function of X." An example is Einstein's famous formula $E = mc^2$ (i.e., energy equals mass times the speed of light squared). Although it was once a hypothesis, $E = mc^2$ is now called a scientific "law" because it has been confirmed repeatedly. Mathematical formulas represent precise formal statements of hypotheses. Because variables in social research generally are measured with less precision than in the physical sciences, social scientists seldom state hypotheses in this form. Nonetheless, mathematical formulas are the ideal in science because they yield precise predictions and express complex relationships parsimoniously. The mathematical form is also equivalent to the conditional. $Y = f(X)$ merely says "If (and only if) X is this value, then Y is that value" (McGuigan, 1993:38).

3. *Continuous statements.* Hypotheses of the form "The greater the X, the greater (or lesser) the Y" indicate that increases in one variable (X) are associated with increases (or decreases) in another variable (Y). For example, as education increases, prejudice decreases; or, expressed in slightly different form, the higher the level of education, the lower the prejudice.

4. *Difference statements.* Statements in this form assert that one variable differs in terms of the categories of another variable. For example, people with high education are less prejudiced than people with low education. Whether "continuous" or "difference" statements are used to express a hypothesis will depend on whether the variables in the hypothesis are quantitative or qualitative. If both variables could be "quantified," then the relationship could be stated in the continuous form. But if either variable consisted of discrete categories, such as "high" and "low" prejudice, then the relationship would need to be stated in the difference form. In either case, it is easy to transform the hypothesis statement into a conditional. For example, the statement "The higher the level of education, the lower the level of prejudice" becomes "If education is high, then prejudice will be low."

Both continuous and difference statements clearly specify the *form* of the relationship. However, both types of statements are ambiguous about the causal connection between variables. Ordinarily, a statement of the form "The greater the X, the greater the Y" is meant to imply that X causes Y. But it also can mean that Y causes X or that X and Y cause one another. As noted in our discussion of causation, it is important to know which variable is presumed to cause the other; in addition, since most hypotheses take the form of continuous or difference statements, the causal linkage can be problematic. Fortunately, in most research articles and reports, researchers make this connection clear in their discussions of the hypothesis.

At this point we should reiterate an important tenet of scientific research. Although all of the above forms of expression appear to assert that the relationship is absolutely true or false, hypotheses in science can only have probabilistic, not exact, confirmation. Thus, although the statement "If X, then Y" logically can only be true or false, it is assumed that observations will show it to be "probably true" or "probably false."[5] One often sees this kind of assumption built into statements of hypotheses in the form of qualifiers such as "tends to" or "in general." For example, one might say that "increased education will *tend* to reduce prejudice." Such statements acknowledge that tests of hypotheses are always restricted by the limited accuracy of measures and the inability to specify and control all the variables affecting events.

The idea that hypotheses can only be judged to be *probably* true or *probably* false gives rise to another type of hypothesis associated with tests of statistical significance. Significance tests indicate the probability that an observed relationship between two variables is due to chance variation; if a test is significant, this means that there is a low probability, say less than 5 in 100, that the relationship occurred by chance, and we therefore conclude that the relationship exists or is real. In statistics, the hypothesis that a relationship is a chance occurrence, which is the opposite of the hypothesized relationship, is called the **null hypothesis**. In other words, evidence supports the research hypothesis only insofar as the null hypothesis is rejected with a known probability of error. Researchers do not always make reference to the null hypothesis when testing relationships; however, it is central to the logic of significance testing and is always implicit.

How a hypothesis is expressed in a given study will depend on several factors: the researcher's discretion, the current state of knowledge about the research problem, and whether qualitative or quantitative variables are involved. Regardless of how hypotheses are expressed, however, they should indicate at least the form of the relationship between variables and, ideally, should specify the causal linkage between variables; ultimately, it is causal relationships in which scientists are interested.

Research Purposes and Research Design

In the previous pages we have emphasized the role of relationships in social research. The sense that social scientists make of the social world is expressed in terms of relationships among variables. Furthermore, although they may be only vaguely defined or implicit and unknown to the researcher, anticipated relationships structure a researcher's every activity, from deciding which variables to measure to deciding how observations should be made and interpreted. Not all research is conducted for the immediate purpose of testing relationships, however. Research is undertaken for three broad purposes: (1) to *explore* a phenomenon such as a group or setting to become familiar with it and to gain insight and understanding about it, frequently to formulate more precise research questions for further study; (2) to *describe* a particular community, group, or situation as completely, precisely, and accurately as possible; and (3) to examine and formally *test relationships* among variables. Whether a study is conducted primarily for the purpose of exploration, description, or testing relationships is important to know because these three functions have different implications for research design.

Exploratory research is undertaken when relatively little is known about something, perhaps because of its "deviant" character or its newness. Falling into this category of research are observational studies of street gangs and radical political and religious movements; clinical case histories of persons, groups, and events; and anthropological accounts of entire cultures. When exploring a topic or phenomenon about which one knows very little, one necessarily begins with a general description of the phenomenon. This sounds easy but in fact is probably the most difficult kind of study for a novice researcher to undertake. There are no clearly delineated independent and dependent variables and, therefore, no preset categories of observation and analysis. A researcher may have few, if any, guidelines to help determine what is important, who to interview, or what leads to follow. For these reasons, the research plan in an exploratory study is more open than in other kinds of research. Decisions are made about the kinds of instruments needed (e.g., photographic equipment, tape recorders) and the key persons with whom one will need to speak at first, but the paths down which these initial steps may lead are almost impossible to foresee. In Chapter 11, on field research, we discuss some data-gathering approaches that entail exploration.

The objective of a **descriptive research**, as the name implies, is to describe some phenomenon. All scientific research involves description at some level. Exploratory field research, for example, usually attempts to describe in detail the setting or cultural group under study. A purely descriptive study, however, is much more structured. It is basically a fact-finding enterprise, in which information is gathered from a set of cases that are carefully selected to enable a researcher to make estimates of the precision and generalizability of the findings. Examples of descriptive studies are the various censuses conducted periodically at the local and national levels. A census may provide information about everything from the age and racial composition of a community to its employment and housing costs. Also having a descriptive purpose are the ubiquitous opinion polls that attempt to estimate the proportion of people in a specified population who hold certain opinions or views or who behave in certain ways. For example, how many favor capital punishment? How many say they will vote for candidate A in the next election?

The third purpose for which research is conducted is to test relationships. Research with this purpose is sometimes called **explanatory research** because it formally seeks to explain why phenomena occur by identifying causes and effects. Since all research involves description, the primary difference between descriptive and explanatory studies lies in the scope of the description. Purely descriptive research operates at a lower level of description by merely seeking information about isolated variables, whereas explanatory research goes beyond this step to a description of relationships among variables. A survey that simply reports attitudes toward gun control is descriptive, but one that examines why people favor or oppose gun control is explanatory.

Both descriptive and hypothesis-testing research are highly structured and must be carefully planned. With these kinds of research it is important, therefore, to have a complete, detailed strategy worked out before the data are collected. This preliminary strategy or outline is what we have called the **research design**. The research design consists of a clear statement of the research question as well as plans for gathering, processing, and interpreting the observations intended to answer the question. To formulate a research design is to anticipate the entire research process, from beginning to end. To do this, one must have an adequate knowledge of every stage of social research. Examining these stages now will serve not only to clarify the key components of research design but also to introduce the reader to the remainder of the book.

Stages of Social Research

Recall from Chapter 2 that the scientific process consists of the cyclical interplay between theory and data. At some point, scientists work deductively from theory to data in testing hypothesis; at another point, they interpret data and infer theories. Thus, scientific inquiry is alternately deductive and inductive. Figure 4.5 outlines the major steps that apply to deductive explanatory research, which is the primary focus of this book. Although most deductive inquiry follows this pattern, steps may be omitted, depending on the research

FIGURE **4.5. The stages of social research.**

approach, and there may be numerous feedback loops. In short, this is an idealized model; some research is much less orderly than it implies.

Stage 1: Formulation of the Research Question

Research begins with a question. Questions initially chosen almost always require more precise formulation to be amenable to research. From a general idea, one must decide more specifically what one wants to know and for what purpose one wants to know it. The best ideas for formulating questions are likely to be found in the scientific literature. In addition to helping to narrow and refine the research question, a review of the literature may reveal its broader theoretical significance. Literature reviews also may help to identify relevant control variables and should suggest pertinent methods and procedures by indicating how other researchers have addressed the question.

Stage 2: Preparation of the Research Design

Once the question has been clearly formulated, a researcher must develop an overall plan or framework for the investigation. To do this, he or she must, in effect, anticipate all of the subsequent stages of the research project. Preliminary decisions must be made about what sort of observations are needed to answer the research question or to provide an adequate test of the hypothesis. The researcher must then select an appropriate strategy for making the observations—experiment, survey, field research, or use of available data. Each of these approaches has its unique strengths and weaknesses that determine its suitability for given questions. Often, the best strategy, as we argue in Chapter 13, is a combination of approaches. Within the context of selecting an overall strategy, decisions also must be made on the unit of analysis, on which variables to observe and control and how they should be measured, and on how best to analyze the data. Thinking through all of these issues in advance should prevent serious mistakes and omissions in a study. Not all problems can be foreseen, however, especially in exploratory research, and many of the decisions at the design stage will be arbitrary and subject to change.

Two issues—measuring variables and selecting units of analysis—warrant special attention and are ordinarily worked out in detail after the basic research design is complete. These are therefore considered separate, concurrent stages.

Stage 3: Measurement

Part of the research plan involves devising operations that will link specific concepts to empirically observable events. This process of operationalization and measurement as well as techniques for assessing the quality or goodness of measures will be taken up in Chapter 5.

Stage 4: Sampling

In addition to deciding on the unit of analysis, researchers must also determine how many units should be selected and how to go about choosing them. The problems and methods related to sampling are addressed in Chapter 6.

Stage 5: Data Collection

In designing a study, researchers first decide on a general approach to data collection, which affects decisions about measurement and sampling. As we have pointed out, there are four basic choices: experiment, survey, field research, and use of available data. The underlying logic of each of these approaches, as well as their distinctive issues, advantages, and disadvantages, is covered in Chapters 7 through 12.

Stage 6: Data Processing

Having made the observations, a researcher is ready to analyze and interpret them. Prior to analysis, the data must be transformed or processed. Chapter 15 begins with a discussion of data processing, giving special attention to the preparation of data for statistical analysis.

Stage 7: Data Analysis and Interpretation

Once the data are ready for analysis, they must be manipulated further so that their meaning and bearing on the questions and hypotheses that initiated the inquiry can be extracted. There are several types of analysis, many of which involve statistical tests that are beyond the scope of this textbook. Without any training in statistics, however, one can learn how to read and to present data properly in tables and graphs and when it is appropriate to apply certain statistical procedures. Also, it is possible to develop a solid understanding of the logic of analyzing causal relationships. These topics are also covered in Chapters 15 and 16. Having analyzed the data, one draws conclusions about the hypotheses and theory that guided the research and, if appropriate, assesses the practical implications of the findings. Finally, one reports the results.

Summary

- There are many sources of ideas and factors affecting topic selection, including theoretical and practical relevance, social premiums, and the personal values and resources of the researcher.
- General topics are refined and research questions emerge in the course of working out the overall study plan, or research design, the key elements of which are units of analysis, variables, and relationships.
- Units of analysis are the entities about whom or about which a researcher gathers information. These include individual people, groups and organizations of all kinds, communities, nations, and social artifacts.
- Researchers often aggregate information about individuals to describe the social unit that the individuals comprise. In general, conclusions should be restricted to the unit of analysis to which the data pertain. In drawing conclusions about individuals from group-level data, one risks committing an ecological fallacy.
- Variables are the characteristics of units that may vary in successive observations. Research focuses on explanatory variables while attempting to eliminate the influence of extraneous variables.
- The dependent variable is the explanatory variable that a researcher tries to explain or predict; an independent variable is a presumed cause of the dependent variable.

- Other variables may be either antecedent or intervening in relation to specific independent and dependent variables and either controlled or uncontrolled during the course of the study.
- Quantitative variables have categories that express numerical distinctions, whereas qualitative variables involve differences in kind rather than in number.
- Anticipated and predicted relationships guide all social research.
- Relationships occur when the changes in two or more variables form a predictable pattern. This pattern has two properties, strength and form, which are depicted differently according to whether the variables are qualitative or quantitative.
- In addition to statistical measures of strength of association, such as the correlation coefficient, tests of statistical significance indicate whether a relationship is likely to exist or whether it is likely to be the product of random processes.
- To establish that variable *X causes* variable *Y*, one must show that *X* and *Y* are statistically associated, that the direction of influence is from *X* to *Y*, and that the association between *X* and *Y* is nonspurious. Theories that identify intervening variables also may strengthen the inference that *X* causes *Y*.
- Research questions should be scientifically answerable and also interesting by contributing to ongoing research. Questions ask about a relation between variables, whereas a hypothesis is a conjecture about the nature and form of a relationship.
- In social research, a hypothesis may take the form of a conditional, a mathematical equation, a continuous statement, or a difference statement.
- Although much social research is undertaken to test hypotheses, it also may be done for the purposes of exploration and description.

Key Terms

unit of analysis
aggregate data
ecological fallacy
variable
    explanatory variable
    extraneous variable
    dependent variable
    independent variable
    antecedent variable
    intervening variable
    control variable
    quantitative variable
    qualitative variable
relationships among variables
    positive (direct) relationship

negative (inverse) relationship
correlation coefficient
statistical significance
causal relationship
    association
    direction of influence
    spurious relationship
    nonspuriousness
hypothesis
conditional
null hypothesis
exploratory research
descriptive research
explanatory research
research design

Exercises

1. Suppose an anthropologist studies several villages in southern India. For each village she has data on the number of people and the average age of men and women, and she has computed an index of

the monetary value of various consumer goods in the village (e.g., the value of the total number of refrigerators, televisions, and air conditioners divided by the size of the population). An analysis of these data reveals that the villages with populations having the lowest average age also have the highest average dollar value of modern consumer goods (Bernard, 1994). What is the unit of analysis in this study? Can the anthropologist conclude from this association that young people purchase more modern consumer goods than older people? Why or why not?

2. For each of the following research questions or hypotheses, identify the *unit of analysis, independent variable*, and *dependent variable*.

   a. Boys whose parents are divorced or separated have more behavior problems than boys living with both biological parents.

   b. The number of sexually explicit magazines (such as *Hustler* and *Playboy*) sold in each of the 50 states is positively correlated with the number of reported rapes.

   c. Residents of rural communities are less tolerant of people holding controversial views than are urban residents.

   d. How does the level of economic development of a country affect the level of human services provided to its people?

3. The contact hypothesis, described recently as "one of the most durable ideas in the sociology of race and ethnic relations," has been investigated extensively over the past 50 years. In its simplest form, the hypothesis is that contact between members of different races fosters positive racial attitudes. Imagine you want to test this hypothesis. Specifically, you hypothesize that prior interracial contact in schools and neighborhoods will lead to greater racial diversity in one's current circle of friends. Assume you are going to do a survey at your college (or a local college).

   a. Suppose you find a correlation of .23 between prior interracial contact and racial diversity of friends. What does this indicate about the relationship?

   b. Now suppose the correlation was significant at $p < .01$. What does this information reveal about the relationship?

   c. An important control variable in your study would be race. Restate the hypothesis with race as a control variable.

4. In a campus survey, a researcher finds a statistically significant correlation of $-.22$ between frequency of exercise and depression; that is, the more students exercise, the less depressed they are. Can he conclude from these data that lack of exercise is one cause of depression? Why or why not? Now carefully explain how gender could create a spurious association between frequency of exercise and depression.

5. Based on a national survey, Christopher Ellison and Kristin Anderson (2001) examined the relationship between religious involvement and domestic violence among U.S. couples. Several previous studies had shown that regular religious attendance is inversely related to abuse among both men and women. The researchers analyzed several extraneous variables including respondents' age, education, employment status, and psychological depression.

   a. Select one of these variables and explain how it could create a *spurious association* between religious involvement and partner violence.

   b. The researchers hypothesized that "religious communities may reduce the risk of abuse by enhancing the levels of social integration and support enjoyed by their members." Are they hypothesizing that the relationship between religion and abuse is spurious? Explain.

6. Formulate three hypotheses, each relating two variables from the following list. For each hypothesis, specify the independent and dependent variables.

Gender (male/female)	Party identification (Republican/
Level of education (highest grade	Democrat/Independent/none)
completed)	Belief in life after death (yes/no)
Marital status (married/widowed/	Attitude toward capital punishment
divorced/separated/never married)	(favor/oppose)

7. Express one of the hypotheses formulated in Question 6 in the form of a (a) conditional, (b) continuous statement (if possible), and (c) difference statement.

Notes

1. When Frans van Poppel and Lincoln Day (1996) tested Durkheim's theory with individual-level data from the Netherlands at roughly the same period as Durkheim, they found that the Catholic–Protestant difference in suicide rates could be accounted for by how the causes of deaths were recorded. Catholic deaths were far more likely than Protestant deaths to be recorded as "sudden death" or "death from ill-defined or unspecified cause"; these deaths would have been categorized as suicides had they occurred among Protestants. Although Durkheim's theory may be supported by other data, this analysis shows the pitfalls of using group-level data to make inferences about individuals.

2. We caution readers not to confuse this distinction with the distinction between quantitative and qualitative research or quantitative and qualitative measurement. Both quantitative researchers (typically survey researchers and experimenters who rely on numbers and statistical methods) and qualitative researchers (who do intensive interviews, participant observation, and depth analyses of historical materials and rely on discursive methods) use both kinds of variables in their analyses (see King, Keohane, and Verba, 1994).

3. Table 4.3 reports a type of "average" called the "median," which is equal to the 50th percentile: Half of the group earn less and half earn more.

4. Determining the level of confidence that a relationship exists, as well as estimating the strength of the relationship, is the job of statistics and is therefore beyond the scope of this textbook. In general, confidence and strength will be greater to the extent that (a) the observed differences between groups are large, (b) the computed averages are based on a large number of people, and (c) people in the same group are similar to one another and different from those in other groups.

5. Determining whether a statement is probably true or probably false, like assessing the existence and strength of a relationship, is a matter of applying the laws of probability, which is the subject of statistics.

5

Measurement

Measurement is the process of assigning numbers or labels to units of analysis to represent conceptual properties. This process should be familiar to readers even if the definition is not. For example, we measure every time we "rate" something, such as a movie, restaurant, or blind date: "The movie was 'pretty good'"; "the new restaurant definitely merits a four-star rating—the decor, service, and food are excellent, and the price is right"; "on a scale of 1 to 10, I would give him a 2—not the worst date I have ever had but close to it." In a somewhat more refined manner, you may have "measured" someone's "intelligence" by his or her grade-point average, and you probably have measured your weight on a bathroom scale. Each of these examples contains the essentials of measurement: Labels or numbers ("pretty good," "four-star," a "2," a particular grade-point average, a pointer reading on a scale) are assigned to objects (movies, restaurants, people) to represent properties (the overall quality of a movie, restaurant, or date; intelligence; weight).

There is a difference, however, between these everyday examples of measurement and the process of measurement in social research. In the examples, the rules for assigning labels or numbers to objects are more or less intuitive, whereas in social research these rules must be spelled out in detail. Scientific norms require that we fully describe our methods and procedures so that others can repeat our observations and judge the quality of our measurements. In this chapter we outline the measurement process, provide several examples of measurement in social research, and then discuss three criteria for evaluating the nature and quality of measurements.

The Measurement Process

The measurement process begins as a researcher formulates his or her research question or hypothesis. Every question or hypothesis contains terms—concepts or variables—that refer to aspects of reality in which a researcher is interested. Measurement involves thinking about what these terms mean in both an abstract and an empirical sense. The ultimate goal of measurement is to specify clearly observable referents of the terms contained in one's hypothesis, but to get to this point one must first consider the abstract meaning of the terms. Thus, the entire measurement process moves from the abstract (concepts) to the concrete (measures of concepts).

Conceptualization

Recall Beckett Broh's (2002) study of extracurricular involvement and academic achievement, which we introduced in Chapter 4. Broh theorized that extracurricular activities increase social capital, which in turn enhances academic achievement. This theory relates three terms: "extracurricular activities," "social capital," and "academic achievement." The terms are merely labels for concepts. To understand fully what the theory means and to arrive at an appropriate set of observations for testing it, one must know the meaning of these concepts. Thus, the initial step in measurement is to clarify the concepts embedded in one's theories and hypothesis with words and examples, ultimately arriving at conceptual (also called "theoretical") definitions.

Broh considered the meaning of each of her key concepts. She relied on common understandings of extracurriculum and academic achievement. *Academic achievement* generally refers to "cognitive learning outcomes which are products of [school] instruction or aimed at by [such] instruction" (Helmke and Schrader, 2001:13552); the *extracurriculum* pertains to school activities outside the set of courses offered at a school. *Social capital*, according to Broh (2002:72), "is generally recognized as the ability to accrue benefits through membership in social networks."

Theoretical definitions of this sort direct the search for appropriate measures of concepts, establish a basis for judging the quality of one's measures, and enable others to evaluate the meaning of one's research findings. Such definitions, however, are not worked out anew with each research project, nor are they the arbitrary invention of each individual investigator making sure that others understand what he or she means. If this were so, there would be no basis for developing a shared body of knowledge. Rather, the process of formulating and clarifying concepts, called **conceptualization**, is linked to theory testing and construction. This ongoing process may occur prior to any particular empirical investigation, and it usually continues through research as theories and their constituent concepts are refined and elaborated.

Broh derived her theoretical definition of social capital from analyses of this concept by, among others, the sociologists James Coleman and Alejandro Portes. Coleman (1990:304) distinguished social capital, "embodied in the relations among persons," from human capital, "embodied in the skills and knowledge acquired by an individual." He also argued (Coleman, 1988) that the family is a primary site of social capital, whereas Portes

(1998) analyzed important extrafamilial networks. Taking into account these theoretical analyses, Broh (2002:72) concluded that "participation in sports and other extracurricular activities may serve to create social capital within the family by providing opportunities for increased social interaction between the parents and the child"; these activities further create social capital outside the family "by offering opportunities for the formation and intensification of social ties among students, parents, and the school." Operating through these networks, social capital facilitates academic achievement in two ways: It exerts social control over students by encouraging them to comply with school norms and values, and it provides channels for students to acquire important educational information and resources.

The conceptualization of complex concepts such as social capital often involves making careful distinctions among similar ideas and breaking down the concept into various components or dimensions. Thus, in her conceptualization, Broh distinguished between social capital and "human capital," and she identified different social ties—parent–child, parent–teacher, student–teacher, and student–student—in which social capital is grounded. With regard to the extracurriculum, she carefully noted the numerous activities in which students participate, such as sports, drama, music, and vocational clubs; and she further distinguished between types of sports activities, such as interscholastic sports, intramural sports, and cheerleading. This sort of analysis further clarifies the meaning of concepts and generates more precise statements of problems and hypotheses. Beginning with the general theoretical relationship between the extracurriculum and social capital, Broh concentrated on the less abstract relationship between participation in interscholastic athletics and social ties among parents, students, and teachers.

Two aspects of concepts are especially relevant to the measurement process. First, a concept may signify a single category, such as "male" or "B student," or a concept may imply several categories or values, such as "gender" or "grade in English." Measurement assumes the possibility of assigning *different* values or categories to units of analysis; hence, we measure concepts that vary, which we refer to as "variables." Second, many social science concepts are not directly observable. For example, we cannot "see" social capital or academic performance in the same sense that we can see a table or a horse or the color red. On the other hand, although we cannot see school performance, we can observe how many questions students answer correctly on standardized tests and the grades they receive in core academic subjects such as English and math. After conceptualization, the next step is to identify such manifestations of one's concepts, and it is at this point that we move from a language of concepts to a language of variables.

Just where this shift in language occurs is difficult to pinpoint, and researchers often use the terms "concept" and "variable" interchangeably. Still, it is important to realize that these terms connote different levels of abstraction. Once a researcher begins to speak in terms of a variable, he or she generally has some observable events in mind that represent the underlying concept.

Operationalization

Once the meaning of a concept has been clarified and the concept is construed as a variable, a researcher begins the process of **operationalization**. The counterpart of a conceptual definition is an operational definition. An *operational definition* describes the research operations that specify the values or categories of a variable. Broh operationalized the variables in her study using responses to survey questions from the National Educational Longitudinal Study (NELS), which administered questionnaires to students in the 8th, 10th, and 12th grades. In both the 10th and the 12th grades, for example, students were asked whether they had participated on an interscholastic sport team—that is, "your school team competes with other schools' teams." Based on these questions, Broh (2002:74) operationally defined *participation in interscholastic sports* as "whether a student participated in interscholastic sports during both the 10th and 12th grades (1 = participated in both years, 0 = did not participate in both years)."

To understand better the notion of operational definitions, let us consider a simple illustration from everyday life. Suppose your friend bakes you a delicious carrot cake. You ask your friend how he made it because you would like to make one. Your friend says, "Oh, you take some carrots, flour, sugar, eggs, and so forth, add some nuts, bake it, and voilà!—you have a carrot cake." Would you be able to make an identical cake with these directions? Not likely. What you need is an operational definition of your friend's concept of "carrot cake." You would need to have the complete directions—that is, details such as all of the ingredients, the amount of each ingredient to use, the steps necessary to combine the ingredients, the oven temperature, and baking time. In short, your friend's operational definition should look like an ordinary recipe. Using the recipe (operational definition), you should be able to produce a similar cake.

Many operational definitions are possible; social scientists must choose or develop one that they believe corresponds reasonably well to the concept in question. To return to the carrot cake example, how could you be certain that your friend's recipe represented an "authentic" carrot cake? Are nuts really an essential ingredient? Suppose you substituted whole-wheat flour for white; would you still have a carrot cake? If you compared his recipe with others, you would no doubt find some differences. How are you to conclude which is the correct recipe? In the end, you would find that there is no correct recipe, but you would still have to decide for yourself whether your friend's operational definition (recipe) "really" corresponded to your idea of what a carrot cake is. As you can see, operational definitions, so essential to social research, are somewhat arbitrary and restricted expressions of what a concept really means.

KEY POINT

Measurement begins with *conceptualization*, the clarification of the meaning of a concept, and ends with *operationalization*, a procedure detailing the observational categories or values representing the concept.

When creating operational definitions, a researcher may consider many different empirical representations or indicators. An **indicator** consists of a single observable measure, such as a single questionnaire item in a survey. If each indicator classified units in exactly the same way, the choice would be wholly arbitrary. However, no two indicators measure a given concept or variable in the same way, and no one indicator is likely to correspond perfectly to its underlying concept. Indicators provide imperfect representations of concepts for two reasons: (1) they often contain errors of classification and (2) they rarely capture all the meaning of a concept. Consider one indicator of social capital in Broh's study: whether students talk to their teachers outside class about their school work. Whether this promotes social capital will depend on why students speak with their teacher. Are they doing so for disciplinary reasons at the insistence of the teacher or because they seek guidance on an assignment? And there are many sources of social capital other than student–teacher relations, including students' relations with other students and with parents and parent–teacher relations.

Because of the imperfect correspondence between indicators and concepts, researchers often choose to rely on more than one indicator when operationalizing a concept. Sometimes several indicators of a given concept are analyzed separately, yielding multiple tests or cross-checks of a hypothesis. At other times, indicators are combined to form a new variable, as when answers to several questions, each a distinct indicator, are combined to create the variable "IQ score." Researchers generally use several indicators to operationalize a complex concept like social capital. To measure social capital between students and parents, Broh summed the responses to three questions, which asked students how often they talked to their parents about school courses, programs and activities, and studies. With simpler concepts like "participation in interscholastic sports," a single indicator will suffice. James Davis (1971:18) suggests this rule for deciding whether to use single or multiple indicators to represent a concept: "If you have to ponder about the best way to measure a key [concept], it is worth measuring in two or more different ways." (See Box 5.1 for examples of different ways to operationally define the concept of "religiosity.")

BOX 5.1 Operationalizing the Concept of "Religiosity"

The sociologist Ronald Johnstone (1983:289–304) provides an excellent illustration of the processes of concept clarification and measurement with respect to the concept of "religiosity." Johnstone notes, first, that the conceptualization of religiosity should begin with a definition of *religion*: "Religion is a set of beliefs and practices, centered around a belief in the supernatural and an orientation toward the sacred, that are shared by members of a group" (290). Having defined religion, one could say that religiosity is the concept of "being religious." This conceptual definition suggests several ways of operationalizing religiosity:

1. The group affiliation approach focuses on the religious group to which a person belongs. In this case, a person is religious if he or she professes to be a member of some religious group, such as a Protestant or Catholic, whereas nonmembers are nonreligious. The General Social Survey (GSS) (T. W. Smith, Marsden, and Hout, 2016) asks respondents, What is your religious preference? Is it Protestant, Catholic, Jewish, some other religion, or no religion? Those who answer "no religion" would be devoid of religiosity, but this fails to capture the intensity of belief or degree of religious interest, which is closer to the concept of individual religiosity.

2. Single indicators of individual religiosity typically have emphasized "ritual participation"—in particular, the frequency of attendance at formal religious services. The GSS includes such a measure:

How often do you attend religious services?
[ ] Never
[ ] Less than once a year
[ ] About once or twice a year
[ ] Several times a year
[ ] About once a month
[ ] 2–3 times a month
[ ] Nearly every week
[ ] Every week
[ ] Several times a week

Related questions tap frequency of prayer or extent of involvement in the total organizational life of the congregation. The problems with such measures are that they (1) are subject to bias and (2) assume that religiosity is a one-dimensional phenomenon. Attendance may reflect, for example, family or other group pressures, habit, or the desire to socialize with friends after services, rather than religious commitment. Moreover, people who rank high on one dimension of religiosity may rank low on another, so different conclusions about the impact of religion could be reached, depending on which measure of religiosity is used. For example, Stephen Ainlay and James Hunter (1984) found that although church attendance declined with age among persons older than 50, nonchurch participation measures such as Bible reading and listening to religious radio programs increased with age.

3. An example of the multidimensional approach is Charles Glock's (1962) identification of five dimensions of religiosity: experiential, ritualistic, ideological, intellectual, and consequential. Joseph Faulkner and Gordon DeJong (1966) have developed sets of questions for measuring each of Glock's dimensions. For example, the experiential dimension concerns the degree of emotional attachment to the supernatural. Items developed by Faulkner and DeJong to measure this dimension include the following:

Would you say that one's religious commitment gives life a certain purpose which it would not otherwise have? (1) Strongly agree; (2) Agree; (3) Disagree; (4) Strongly disagree.

All religions stress that belief normally includes some experience of "union" with the Divine. Are there particular moments when you feel "close" to the Divine? (1) Frequently; (2) Occasionally; (3) Rarely; (4) Never.

4. The final two approaches identified by Johnstone conceive of religiosity in terms of (1) open-ended "ultimate concerns" and (2) intrinsic–extrinsic religious orientation. The ultimate-concern approach attempts to define religiosity in terms of basic religious

(continued)

(continued)

feelings, without reference to traditional religious forms or institutionalized religious groups. The intrinsic–extrinsic concept distinguishes between extrinsically motivated persons for whom religion represents a self-serving instrumental conformity to social conventions and intrinsically motivated persons for whom religion provides a framework for living and understanding life. Here are two sample items from Joe Feagin's (1964) intrinsic–extrinsic religious orientation scale:

The church is most important as a place to formulate good social relationships. (1) I definitely disagree; (2) I tend to disagree; (3) I tend to agree; (4) I definitely agree.

My religious beliefs are what really lie behind my whole approach to life. (1) This is definitely not so; (2) Probably not so; (3) Probably so; (4) Definitely so.

Operational Definitions in Social Research

There are two general kinds of operational definitions in social research: manipulated and measured. *Manipulation* operations are designed to change the value of a variable, whereas *measurement* operations estimate existing values of variables. Both types are illustrated in a study of job discrimination against openly gay men in the United States. To investigate the level of discrimination, Andras Tilcsik (2011) sent fictitious resumes to 1769 postings of white-collar, entry-level job openings. All the resumes described a male, graduating college senior having similar traits, qualifications, and experiences with one exception: an experience signaling a gay sexual orientation. The independent variable, sexual orientation, was *manipulated* by indicating in one-half of the resumes that the applicant was the treasurer of a campus gay and lesbian organization ("Gay and Lesbian Alliance") and in the other half that the applicant was the treasurer of a left-wing campus organization ("Progressive and Socialist Alliance"). To operationalize the dependent variable, employment discrimination, Tilcsik used a *measured* definition: whether the applicant was invited for an interview. Among other findings, the study showed that heterosexual applicants had a greater chance of being invited for an interview than gay applicants (11.5% versus 7.2%).

With respect to the manipulation of sexual orientation, Tilcsik points out that being a member of a left-wing campus organization is an effective control because participation in a gay organization tends to be associated with progressive or liberal political views. In addition, the position of treasurer entailed financial and managerial skills that were relevant to the job. To emphasize this point, the resume item listed four responsibilities associated with the position of treasurer; for example, "managed budget and all corresponding accounts" and "wrote grant proposals, increasing grant revenue by 25% from previous years." Unless investigators explicitly spell out the details of their manipulations and measurements, other researchers will not be able to replicate or judge the quality of the research.

Manipulation of an independent variable is by definition experimental, and we will have a good deal more to say about this in Chapter 7. For now, let us examine some of the various approaches to operationalization of measured variables.

Verbal Reports

By far the most common form of social measurement is the **verbal** or **self-report**: replies to direct questions, usually posed in interviews or on questionnaires. Self-reports provide simple and generally accurate measures of background variables such as age, gender, marital status, and education. They also are used extensively to measure subjective experiences, such as knowledge, beliefs, attitudes, feelings, and opinions.

All the variables in Beckett Broh's study were operationalized by means of self-reports. She used a single item from the first year of the NELS survey to measure parents' income: What was your total family income from all sources in 1987? (possible responses ranged from 1 = none to 15 = $200,000 or more).

Composite Measures

In self-report attitude measurement, responses to several questions frequently are combined to create an **index** or **scale**. As we noted earlier, it is best to use several indicators to measure complex concepts. Scales and indexes condense or reduce the data generated by multiple indicators into a single number or scale score. This not only simplifies the analysis but also increases precision and provides a means of assessing the quality of the measurement.

Broh created several composite measures in her study, combining from two to seven questions. For example, she added together the amount of time students reported spending on homework each week in school and out of school. To operationalize self-esteem, Broh drew on seven items from Morris Rosenberg's (1965) widely used self-esteem scale. Respondents were asked to indicate whether they strongly agree, agree, disagree, or strongly disagree with each of the following seven statements. Values between 1 and 4 were assigned to the response categories, with 4 representing strong agreement with a positive statement about the self (or, conversely, strong disagreement with a negative statement).

1. I feel good about myself. (Strongly agree = 4)
2. I feel I am a person of worth, the equal of other people. (Strongly agree = 4)
3. I am able to do things as well as most other people. (Strongly agree = 4)
4. On the whole, I am satisfied with myself. (Strongly agree = 4)
5. I feel useless at times. (Strongly disagree = 4)
6. At times I think I am no good at all. (Strongly disagree = 4)
7. I feel I do not have much to be proud of. (Strongly disagree = 4)

An individual's responses to these seven questions were added together to produce a single scale score that could range from 7 (low self-esteem) to 28 (high self-esteem).

As with most scale construction, the development of the Rosenberg self-esteem scale involved some sophisticated statistical techniques that are beyond the scope of this book.

Because of the difficulty of creating scales and because there are literally thousands of scales and indexes, we recommend that a beginning researcher use well-validated scales to measure attitudes, opinions, and other subjective experiences whenever possible. Chapter 13 contains a more advanced discussion of the underlying logic of scaling.

KEY POINT

Many operational definitions (or indicators) are possible, but rarely does any one indicator perfectly represent a concept; therefore, it is usually preferable to use multiple indicators.

Verbal reports vary widely with respect to question wording and response formats. The number of response categories ranges from two to seven for most attitude measures, but a researcher may provide many more categories or none at all. Instead of labeling all response categories, as in the self-esteem scale, investigators may ask respondents to place a check mark along a line whose end points represent opposite ends of a continuum.

Verbal reports also are elicited with pictures and diagrams, which can simplify complex issues and are particularly useful with children. To measure attitudes toward residential integration, for example, Maria Krysan and Reynolds Farley (2002) presented respondents five cards with diagrams depicting neighborhoods containing 14 homes. Each card showed a different interracial mixture ranging from all black to all white, with three racially mixed neighborhoods. Respondents "were asked to imagine that they had been looking for a house and found a nice one they could afford." (945). Then they were asked to rank the cards from the most to least attractive and to indicate whether they would not want to move into any of the neighborhoods.

Because slight changes in phrasing can drastically alter the meaning of a question, wording is very important. We will discuss question formats and wording at length in Chapter 10, which deals with interview and questionnaire construction.

Observation

Tilcsik measured employment discrimination by direct observation of behavior: He recorded whether employers contacted applicants to set up an interview. Lesley Joy and her colleagues (Joy, Kimball, and Zabrack, 1986) developed an observational measure of children's aggression to compare a Canadian town before and after it first received television reception in 1974 with two similar "control" towns that had one or several television channels prior to this time. Trained observers recorded grade school children's physically aggressive behavior (hitting, pushing, chasing, etc.) and aggressive words (threatening, arguing, insulting, etc.) on school playgrounds during recess. Summary measures of physical and verbal aggression (average number of acts per minute of playground observation) increased for both sexes following the introduction of television.

Observation provides direct and generally unequivocal evidence of overt behavior, but it also is used to measure subjective experiences such as feelings and attitudes. For example, one could measure interpersonal attraction by observing and recording the physical distance that two people maintain between themselves, with closer distances indicative of greater liking. Similarly, Zick Rubin (1970) operationally defined "romantic love" by observing the length of time couples spent gazing into one another's eyes.

In addition to firsthand observation, hardware such as videotapes, audiotapes, and counters are commonly used for recording purposes. To measure which television programs people watch, the Nielsen Organization attaches an electronic monitoring device to the television set of each person in their sample, which automatically records, minute by minute, the channel to which the set is tuned.

Archival Records

Archival records, which refer to existing recorded information, provide another invaluable source of measurement. The various types of archival data, discussed in Chapter 12, include statistical records, public and private documents, and mass communications.

Using public data from the U.S. censuses, John Logan and Brian Stults (2011) found that black–white residential segregation in metropolitan areas peaked around 1960 or 1970 and has declined slowly but steadily since then, with segregation historically lowest and declines greatest in areas where blacks constitute less than 5 percent of the population. "Residential segregation" was operationally defined by the index of dissimilarity, which indicates the percentage of whites (or blacks) who would have to change their census block of residence to produce zero segregation. Among the 50 metropolises with the largest black populations in 2010, the index of dissimilarity ranged from 80 for Detroit (the most segregated) to 36 for Las Vegas (the least segregated). This means that in Detroit either 80 percent of whites or 80 percent of blacks would have to move to eliminate residential segregation and thereby reduce the index to zero.

Another example of an operational definition derived from archival records comes from a study of parental role portrayals in twentieth-century children's picture books. Amy DeWitt, Cynthia Cready, and Rudy Seward (2013) analyzed parental roles that appeared in 300 "easy" storybooks selected to represent six time periods, from pre-1960 to the year 2000. Based on illustrations and narrative text, they determined whether mother and father characters were depicted in five parental roles: companion, disciplinarian, caregiver, nurturer, and provider. Each role was operationally defined in terms of specific behaviors; for example, nurturing behaviors included "physically or verbally express affection for the child," "verbally encourage the child," and "comfort the child"; caregiving behaviors included "prepare meals for and/or feed the child," "clean the child," and "pick out clothes and/or dress the child." Unexpectedly, they found little change in parental roles over time as traditional roles continued to dominate, with mothers acting as nurturers and caregivers and fathers as providers.

Selection of Operational Definitions

Given that you have a concept in mind, how do you decide on an appropriate operational definition? First, your decision will be made in the context of an overall research strategy, the choice of which depends to a degree on the specific research question or hypothesis. As we shall see, each of the four basic approaches has its distinctive strengths and limitations, which must be taken into account. Some hypotheses, for example, contain variables that may be impractical or unethical to manipulate and, hence, to study experimentally. No one would propose inducing varying amounts of emotional suffering in people to study effects on physical health.

Each of the different approaches favors certain types of operational definitions. For the most part, survey research involves verbal reports; field research entails observational measurement; and the use of available data, by definition, includes archival records. Experiments, in contrast, use a combination of measures—verbal reports and/or observation in addition to manipulation procedures. Field researchers often supplement their observations with verbal reports. And survey researchers sometimes use observational measures; for example, an interviewer may observe the type of household and neighborhood in which an interviewee resides as a measure of social class.

With an overall research strategy in mind, the most basic requirement is to select an operational definition that fits the concept well. Although we have said that no operational definition can capture a concept's meaning perfectly or completely, this does not license a researcher to select just any measure. It is still desirable to get the best possible fit between concept and measure, and the best way to do this is by carefully considering the meaning of the concept, especially as it relates to the theory in which it is embedded.

An example of a study in which theory guided the selection of an appropriate operational definition is Albert Pierce's test (1967) of Durkheim's (1951) hypothesis that suicide rates increase in periods of rapid economic change independent of the direction of change (boom or bust). Durkheim theorized that marked economic changes can disturb the existing goals and norms toward which people orient their lives, can thrust individuals into new social settings in which they are ill-suited to manage, and hence can increase the probability of suicide. Data for white males during the peacetime years 1919 to 1940 were examined. At first, Pierce correlated the suicide rate with various *objective* measures of economic change, based on income, percentage of labor force unemployed, and housing construction, with indecisive results. Finally he struck upon the notion of using a measure—the "index of common stock prices"—that would reflect the *public definition* of the economic situation, which is more in tune with Durkheim's theory. That is, rapid fluctuations of stock-market prices may be viewed as indicators of public economic uncertainty, resulting in disruption or discontinuities in perceived goals and norms. Pierce's analysis revealed that suicide rates correlated highly with the rate of change in the public definition of economic conditions as operationally defined by the index of stock-market prices.

Beyond attending to the basic research strategy and the concept's meaning, the choice of operational definitions is largely a matter of creativity, judgment, and practicality. One's selection also should be aided by considering three characteristics that describe the nature and quality of information provided by operational definitions: levels of measurement, reliability, and validity.

Levels of Measurement

Speaking in terms of variables, we can define *measurement* as "the assignment of numbers or labels to units of analysis to represent variable categories." For example, in measuring participation in interscholastic sports, Broh assigned the number 1 to "participated in both the 10th and 12th grades" and 0 to "did not participate in both grades"; and she assigned a number between 7 and 28 to represent a student's level of self-esteem. However, unlike the numbers derived from the measurement of length, time, mass, and so forth in the physical sciences, the numbers applied to social measurement do not always have a simple and straightforward interpretation. **Levels of measurement** indicate the various meanings of these numbers, which reflect basic empirical rules for category assignment. The four general levels usually identified are nominal, ordinal, interval, and ratio.

Nominal Measurement

The lowest level, **nominal measurement**, is a system in which cases are classified into two or more categories on some variable, such as gender, race, religious preference, or political party preference. Numbers (or more accurately, numerals)[1] are assigned to the categories simply as labels or codes for a researcher's convenience in collecting and analyzing data. For example, political party preference might be classified as follows:

1. Democrat
2. Republican
3. Independent
4. Other
5. No preference

With nominal measurement, the empirical rule for assigning units to categories is that cases placed in the same category must be *equivalent*. Thus, we can say that all 1s share the same political preference and that 1s differ from 2s in their political preference. However, because we are merely using numbers as labels, no mathematical relationships are possible at the nominal level: We cannot say that $1 + 2 = 3$ (Democrat plus Republican equals Independent) or that $1 < 2$ (Democrats are "lower" on political preference than Republicans).

Nominal measurement has two characteristics that apply to all levels of measurement: Variable categories must be both exhaustive and mutually exclusive. To be **exhaustive** means that there must be sufficient categories so that virtually all persons, events, or objects being classified will fit into one of the categories. The following set of categories for the variable "religious preference" does not meet this criterion:

1. Protestant
2. Catholic

You can probably think of other categories needed to make this measure exhaustive, especially if you happen to have no religious preference or if you are Jewish or Muslim or a member of some other religion. Even if one expected few non-Catholic or non-Protestant respondents, one should at least add the categories "None" and "Other" to cover all the possibilities.

The criterion of **mutual exclusivity** means that the persons or things being classified must not fit into more than one category. Suppose that a researcher hastily came up with the following categories for the variable "place of residence":

1. Urban
2. Suburban
3. Rural
4. Farm

You can see that some persons would fit into both categories 3 and 4. The following set of categories would be an improvement:

1. Urban
2. Suburban
3. Rural, farm
4. Rural, nonfarm

Ordinal Measurement

In **ordinal measurement**, numbers indicate the rank order of cases on some variable. The psychologist S. S. Stevens (1951), who developed the idea of measurement level, used hardness of minerals as one example of ordinal measurement. We can determine the hardness of any two minerals by scratching one against the other: Harder stones scratch softer ones. By this means, we could number a set of stones, say five, from 1 to 5 according to their hardness. The numbers thus assigned, however, would represent nothing more than the order of the stones along a continuum of hardness: "1" is harder than "2," "2" is harder than "3," and so on. We could not infer from the numbering any absolute quantity, nor could we infer that the intervals between numbers are equal; in other words, we could not say how much harder one stone is than another.

Another example of ordinal measurement would be an individual's ranking of certain leisure activities in terms of the pleasure derived from them. Suppose you ranked three activities as follows:

1. Playing tennis
2. Watching television
3. Reading sociology

From this ordering we could not make any statements about the intervals between the numbers; it may be that you enjoy watching television almost as much as playing tennis but that reading sociology is not nearly as pleasurable as watching television. In this sense, ordinal measurement is like an elastic tape measure that can be stretched unevenly; the "numbers" on the tape measure are in proper order, but the distances between them are distorted.

One virtue of ordinal measurement, as Julian Simon (1978:231) notes, is "that people can often make an accurate judgment about one thing *compared to another*, even when they cannot make an accurate *absolute* judgment." Simon (231) illustrates the accuracy of comparative judgments with a familiar example:

> You can often tell whether or not a child has a fever—that is, when the child's temperature is two or three degrees above normal—by touching the child's face to yours and comparing whether her skin is warmer than yours. But you would be hard-put to say whether the temperature outside is 40° or 55°F, or whether a piece of metal is 130° or 150°F.

Similarly, in the realm of social measurement one can probably say with some certitude whether security or chance for advancement is the more important job characteristic, without being able to say just how important either characteristic is.

On the one hand, the ability of human observers to make such comparative judgments permits a wide range of reasonably accurate social measurements at the ordinal level—for example, measures of socioeconomic status, intelligence, political liberalism, various preference ratings, and attitude and opinion scales. On the other hand, ordinal measurement is still rather crude. At this level we cannot perform most mathematical (statistical) operations in analyzing the data. We cannot add, subtract, multiply, or divide; we can only rank things: $1 < 2, 2 < 3, 1 < 3$.

Interval Measurement

Interval measurement has the qualities of the nominal and ordinal levels plus the requirement that equal distances or intervals between numbers represent equal distances in the variable being measured. An example is the Fahrenheit temperature scale: The difference between 20°F and 30°F is the same as the difference between 90°F and 100°F—10 degrees. We can infer not only that 100°F is hotter than 90°F but also how much hotter it is. What enables us to make this inference is the establishment of a standard measurement unit, or *metric*. For Fahrenheit temperature, the metric is degrees; similarly, time is measured in seconds, length in feet or meters, and income in dollars.

When numbers represent a metric, the measurement is "quantitative" in the ordinary sense of the word. Thus, we can perform basic mathematical operations such as addition and subtraction. However, we cannot multiply or divide at the interval level. We cannot say, for example, that 100°F is twice as hot as 50°F or that 20°F is one-half as hot as 40°F. The reason is that interval measures do not have a true or absolute zero but an arbitrary one. That is, the zero point on the scale does not signify the absence of the property being measured. Zero degrees Fahrenheit does not mean that there is no temperature; it is simply an arbitrary point on the scale. Its arbitrariness is illustrated by comparison with another interval scale designed to measure the property of temperature: 0°F equals about −18°C (Celsius or centigrade), and 0°C equals 32°F.

Although social researchers often aim to create interval measures, most of what passes for this level of measurement is only a rough approximation. IQ score, for example, is sometimes treated as an interval-level measure, even though it makes no sense to add IQ scores or to infer that equal numerical intervals have the same meaning. (Is the difference between

IQ scores of 180 and 190 equal to the difference between 90 and 100?) The empirical rule defining interval measurement is to create equal intervals between numbers. Some attitude scaling techniques attempt to do this, although most scales (e.g., Rosenberg's self-esteem scale) have ordinal-level measurement.

Ratio Measurement

The fourth level, called **ratio measurement**, includes the features of the other levels plus an absolute (nonarbitrary) zero point. The presence of an absolute zero makes it possible to multiply and divide scale numbers meaningfully and thereby form ratios. The variable income, measured in dollars, has this property. Given incomes of $20,000 and $40,000, we can divide one into the other (i.e., form a ratio) to signify that one is twice (or one-half) as much as the other.

Many measures in social research have a well-defined metric and a zero point that meaningfully signifies none of the property being measured. Besides income, other examples are age in years, number of siblings, and years of employment. Ratio-level measures often are obtained by simply counting—for example, number of courses taken in sociology, number of siblings, number of people in a social network. Also, aggregate variables, which characterize collectivities of people, frequently are measured at this level by counting and then dividing by a population base—for example, crude birth rate (number of births per 1000 people in the total population), divorce rate (number of divorces per 1000 existing marriages), percentage of labor force unemployed, percentage Democrat.

KEY POINT

Level of measurement indicates the kinds of inferences that can be made when comparing different categories or values of a variable: *nominal* allows one to infer differences, *ordinal* to infer rank order, *interval* to infer distances, and *ratio* to infer ratios.

Discussion

The level of measurement achieved depends on the empirical procedures used to operationalize a concept. A field researcher, for example, may obtain an ordinal measure of age using people's appearance, manner, and other observed characteristics to classify them as "children," "young adults," "middle-aged," and "seniors." Or date-of-birth information might be used to measure age as a ratio scale.

It is interesting to note that the four levels of measurement themselves form an ordinal scale with regard to the amount of information they provide. Each level has the features of the level(s) below it plus something else. Table 5.1 illustrates this.

In most social science research, the distinction between interval and ratio levels of measurement is not very important compared with the differences among interval, ordinal, and nominal measures. Many older statistical techniques (including Pearson's correlation coefficient) assume interval measurement and are therefore inappropriate for lower levels of measurement. Some newer techniques are well suited for drawing meaningful inferences about nominal and ordinal measures.[2]

TABLE 5.1. **Information Provided by the Four Levels of Measurement**

Information provided	Nominal	Ordinal	Interval	Ratio
Classification	X	X	X	X
Rank order		X	X	X
Equal intervals			X	X
Nonarbitrary zero				X

Finally, researchers may use words rather than numbers to represent gradations in conceptual properties (Sorokin, 1937:21–22). If a historian describes the extent of political unrest in various epochs as "low," "high," and "extremely high," an ordinal scale is being used to measure political unrest. If a field researcher classifies the homeless as "mentally ill," "drug-dependent," and "other," the categories represent a nominal scale. The use of words rather than numbers to represent variable categories does not imply poorer or better measurement (King, Keohane, and Verba, 1994:151–52). Whether words or numbers are used, the quality of a measure is judged in terms of reliability and validity, as explained below.

Reliability and Validity

We have seen that for any concept several operational definitions are possible and that creative insight, good judgment, and relevant theory aid in the development of operational definitions. Admittedly, these aids are subjective in nature; however, once an operational definition is selected, there are more objective ways to evaluate its quality. Social scientists use the terms "reliability" and "validity" to describe issues involved in evaluating the quality of operational definitions.

Reliability is concerned with questions of stability and consistency. Is the operational definition measuring "something" consistently and dependably, whatever that something may be? Do repeated applications of the operational definition under similar conditions yield consistent results? If the operational definition is formed from a set of responses or items (e.g., scores on the self-esteem scale), are the component responses or items consistent with each other? An example of a highly reliable measuring instrument is a steel tape measure. With this instrument, a piece of wood 20 inches long will be found to measure, with negligible variation, 20 inches every time a measurement is taken. A cloth tape measure would be somewhat less reliable in that it may vary with humidity and temperature and in that we can expect some variation in measurements depending on how loosely or tightly the tape is stretched.

Measurement **validity** refers to the congruence or "goodness of fit" between an operational definition and the concept it is purported to measure. Does this operational definition truly reflect what the concept means? Are you measuring what you intend to measure with this operational definition? If so, you have a valid measure. An example of a valid measure is amniocentesis, a technique for determining various genetic characteristics of an unborn child, including sex. It is a valid measure of biological sex because it can determine with virtually perfect accuracy whether the unborn child has a Y chromosome and hence will be a boy or a girl. At one time, many invalid "measures" of the unborn's sex existed in the form of folk wisdoms. One belief, for example, involves tying a string to the pregnant woman's wedding band and holding the band suspended over her abdomen. If the band swings in a circle, the baby will be a girl; if the band swings back and forth, the child will be a boy.

A highly unreliable measure cannot be valid—how can you measure something accurately if the results fluctuate wildly? But a very reliable measure still may not be valid; that is, you could be measuring very reliably (consistently) something other than what you intended to measure. To take a facetious example, let us suppose we decide to measure the intelligence of students by standing them on a bathroom scale and reading the number off the dial (Davis, 1971:14). Such an operational definition would be highly reliable as repeated scale readings would yield consistent results. However, this obviously would not be a valid measure of an individual's intelligence.

KEY POINT

Reliability is synonymous with "consistency"; *validity* is synonymous with "accuracy." A valid measure is necessarily reliable, but a reliable measure may or may not be valid.

Sources of Error

When we apply an operational definition to a set of cases, we use different labels, ranks, ratings, scores, and so forth to represent differences or variation among the cases. There are three potential sources of variation. By examining these sources, we can better understand the ideas behind reliability and validity assessment. The three sources of variation in any measurement are expressed in the following equation:

Observed value = true value + systematic error + random error

The first source of variation is *true differences* in the concept the operation is intended to measure. One would hope that this would account for most of the variation in the measurements; after all, this is what validity is all about! In the ideal situation, with a perfectly valid operational definition, *all* of the measured variation would reflect differences in the concept under study. Observed differences in IQ scores obtained with an IQ test, for example, ought to reflect only true differences in intelligence and nothing else. However, since perfect measurement is unobtainable, a realistic approach is to be aware of other possible sources of variation and to try to eliminate or reduce their effects as much as possible.

Social scientists refer to sources of variation other than true differences in the variable being studied as "error." The main problem in interpreting the observed variation is to determine what part of it can be explained by true differences and what part is due to one or more sources of error. There are two basic types of measurement errors: systematic and random.

Systematic measurement error results from factors that systematically influence either the process of measurement or the concept being measured. Assuming interval-level measurement, systematic error would be reflected in ratings or scores that are consistently biased in one direction—either too high or too low. A cloth tape measure that has stretched with wear would create error in the form of constant underestimates of length. An example of systematic error in social measurement is the cultural bias of IQ tests. Most IQ tests contain problems and language that tend to favor particular groups in society. Given the same "true" intelligence level, a person familiar with the test problems and language will always score higher than a person who is unfamiliar with the test problems or who speaks a different language from the one in which the test is communicated. Thus, differences in IQ scores may reflect a systematic error introduced by the cultural bias of the test, as well as differences in intelligence.

Many of the systematic errors that contaminate social measurement arise from respondents' reactions to participating in research. When a respondent's sensitivity or responsiveness to a measure is affected by the process of observation or measurement, we refer to this as a **reactive measurement effect** (Webb et al., 2000:12). Just as people behave differently alone than in front of an audience, or with friends than with strangers, they tend to react differently when in a research setting. Awareness of the presence of a social scientist "observer," for example, can increase or decrease the incidence of some observed behaviors.

It has been shown that people are less willing to admit to holding undesirable positions and attitudes when they are aware of being "tested." This is why verbal report measures generally underestimate (a systematic error) the prevalence of socially unacceptable traits, behaviors, and attitudes such as psychiatric symptoms, deviant behaviors, and racial prejudice. A good example is John McConahay's (1986) Old-Fashioned Racism Scale. This measure asks respondents whether they agree or disagree with palpable racist statements: For example, "Blacks are generally not as smart as whites"; "If a black family with about the same income and education as I have moved next door, I would mind it a great deal." In this post–civil-rights era, however, it is no longer socially acceptable to support acts of open discrimination or to endorse blatant racist beliefs about black intelligence, ambition, and other stereotyped characteristics. Consequently, many white Americans, knowing the socially desirable answers, may not express their true feelings when responding to the Old-Fashioned Racism Scale or similar measures. Indeed, it is precisely for this reason that researchers have questioned evidence of a decline in racial prejudice in the late twentieth century. That is, the apparent decline may be a function of social desirability effects rather than of real changes in attitudes (Crosby, Bromley, and Saxe, 1980).

In addition to this **social desirability effect**, other response tendencies can introduce systematic measurement error. Respondents are more likely to agree than to disagree with statements, irrespective of their content (called the "acquiescence response set"); also, when sequences of questions are asked in a similar format, respondents tend to give stereotyped responses, such as endorsing the right-hand or left-hand response (Webb et al., 2000). Such tendencies produce systematic error when they correspond to variation in the measured property. For example, if a question measuring political liberalism is worded such that agreement indicates a liberal view, then the researcher could not be sure whether a person's agreement indicated a liberal view or simply a tendency to agree with statements regardless of their content.

Systematic errors differ from the true value of a variable by a constant amount. Therefore, they bias measurements in a particular direction, underestimating or overestimating the true value, which affects their accuracy or validity. Because of their constancy, however, systematic errors do not adversely affect reliability. Reliability is undermined by inconsistencies in measurement that arise from random errors.

Random measurement error is unrelated to true differences in the concept being measured. It is the result of temporary, chance factors, such as transitory upswings and downswings in the health and mood of research subjects, temporary variations in the administration or coding of a measure, or momentary investigator fatigue. A tired or bored respondent, for example, may give erroneous responses by not attending carefully to the questions asked. Similarly, an ambiguously worded question will produce random errors by eliciting responses that vary according to respondents' interpretations of the question's meaning.

Such error is random because its presence, extent, and direction are unpredictable from one question to the next or from one respondent to the next. Thus, random errors in a measure of the variable "age" would not be consistently high or low but rather would fall on either side of respondents' real ages so that the average error would be zero. Random error could be demonstrated by asking someone whose visual acuity is impaired (perhaps by drunkenness) to measure the length of an object several times. It is likely that this person's measurements will vary about the object's true length. Sometimes the errors will vary in one direction (overestimating length) and sometimes in the other (underestimating length); sometimes they will be large and sometimes small. Random errors produce imprecise and inaccurate measurements, affecting reliability; however, because they are unsystematic, random errors tend to cancel each other out with repeated measurements. Thus, they do not bias the measure in a particular direction.

In Figure 5.1, a target is used to illustrate the relationship among reliability, validity, and the two sources of measurement error. Measurement is an attempt to hit the bull's eye, which represents the theoretical definition of the concept. A tight pattern, irrespective of its location on the target, reflects a reliable measure because it is consistent. Validity is a reflection, however, of how closely the shots cluster about the bull's eye. Random error affects the tightness of the pattern as well as distance from the center, hence both reliability and validity; systematic error affects only the distance of shots from the bull's eye, hence only validity.

KEY POINT

A completely valid measure is free of both systematic and random error; a completely reliable measure is free of random error but may contain systematic error.

Low reliability	High reliability	High reliability
Low validity	Low validity	High validity
High random error	Low random error	Low random error
Low systematic error	High systematic error	Low systematic error

FIGURE 5.1. Analogy of target to reliability, validity, and measurement error.
Adapted from Babbie (1995).

Reliability Assessment

So far we have said that reliability indicates consistency, or the extent to which a measure does not contain random error. Because we can never know for certain the precise true value of that which we measure, measurement errors can be examined only indirectly. In fact, we infer random error from the degree of consistency observed across measurements. If a measure yields the same result time after time, then it is free of random error; furthermore, the greater the variation in repeated measurements, the greater the random error. Reliability assessment is essentially a matter of checking for such consistency—either over time (as when the same measurements are repeated) or over slightly different but equivalent measures (as when more than one indicator or more than one observer/interviewer/recorder is used).

Test–Retest Reliability

The simplest method for assessing reliability, the **test–retest** procedure, involves testing (i.e., measuring) the same persons or units on two separate occasions.[3] For example, a researcher might administer the self-esteem scale to the same group of students on consecutive days. One then calculates the statistical correlation between the sets of "scores" obtained from the two measurements, and the resulting value serves as an estimate of reliability. Such correlations range from 0 (indicating a completely unreliable measure with total random error) to 1.00 (indicating a perfectly reliable measure subject to no random error). For the test–retest procedure, the correlation tends to be high, with anything less than .80 considered dangerously low for most measurement purposes. Test–retest reliability checks of the self-esteem scale have produced correlation coefficients of .82 to .88 for 1- and 2-week intervals (M. Rosenberg, 1979; Gray-Little, Williams, and Hancock, 1997); however, test–retest reliability coefficients for this scale are much lower for longer periods of 6 months (.63) and 1 year (.50) (Gray-Little, Williams, and Hancock, 1997).

Although simple in principle, the test–retest method has several problems that limit its usefulness as an estimate of reliability. First, either the persons responding to questions or the persons recording observations may remember and simply repeat the responses they gave the first time, thereby inflating the reliability estimate. Second, real change in the concept being measured may occur in the interim between the two "tests." In attitude measurement, new experiences or new information may result in a shift in attitude. For example, positive or negative experiences between administrations may raise or lower a respondent's self-esteem; the loss of a job may change one's attitude toward unemployment insurance or social welfare programs. Because such true changes are inseparable from random errors in test–retest correlations, they falsely lower the reliability estimate. Third, the first application of a measure may itself bring about conceptual changes in the persons under study. Suppose, for example, that a scale designed to measure traditional sex-role attitudes is administered on two occasions to the same group of persons. If, after the first administration, the persons began to think through some of their assumptions about women and consequently changed some of their beliefs, a subsequent administration of the scale would yield different scores and a lowered estimate of reliability.

To a certain extent, these problems are manageable. For example, one can try to time the second measurement optimally so that responses to the first testing will have been forgotten but little real change in the concept will have had time to occur. Also, the above difficulties may be more or less problematic depending on the type of measure under study. Using a test–retest reliability estimate for an attitude measure would be fraught with problems because such measures tend to be highly reactive and genuine changes in attitudes are likely to take place over time. However, the test–retest procedure provides a good evaluation of the reliability of many relatively stable concepts such as characteristics of organizations or political units and individual background variables.

Split-Half and Internal Consistency Reliability

Rather than obtain a *stability* estimate based on consistency over time, as in test–retest reliability, a second set of procedures for assessing reliability estimates the agreement or *equivalence* among the constituent parts or items of a multi-item measure. If we assume that each component of a measure represents the same underlying concept, a lack of agreement among the components would indicate a high degree of random error, hence low reliability. Like the test–retest estimate, all of the statistical estimates of equivalence yield coefficients that run from 0 to 1.00.

A commonly used equivalence estimate is the **split-half method**. In this procedure, a scale or index (i.e., a measure containing several items) is applied once to a sample of cases, after which the items of the scale are divided into halves, usually by random selection; each half is then treated as a subtest with the results of the two subtests correlated to obtain an estimate of reliability. The higher the correlation, the more equivalent the halves and the greater the reliability of the measure.

The split-half technique assumes the existence of equivalent subsets of items. From there, it is a short step to the assumption that every item in a scale is equivalent to every other item. This gives rise to another technique for assessing reliability, called **internal consistency**. With this approach, a researcher examines the relationships among all the items simultaneously rather than arbitrarily splitting the items. The basic question is, To what extent are the items homogeneous—that is, to what extent do they measure the same concept? The most common estimate of internal-consistency reliability is Cronbach's alpha, which is based on the average of the correlations among the responses to all possible pairs of items. Numerous studies have reported Cronbach's alpha for the self-esteem scale, ranging from a low of .72 for a sample of men 60 years or older to a high of .88 for a group of college students (Gray-Little, Williams, and Hancock, 1997).

Intercoder Reliability

A second type of equivalence measure examines the extent to which different observers or coders using the same instrument or measure obtain equivalent results. Assuming that the different users have been properly trained, a reliable operational definition must yield comparable results from user to user. Estimates of equivalence are calculated by comparing the records of two or more researchers who independently apply the same operational definition. For example, in the aforementioned study of parental roles (DeWitt,

Cready, and Seward, 2013), several coders were trained to code role behaviors in a subset of 84 books. When their codes were compared with those of the researcher, the level of agreement, or **intercoder reliability**, was very high, with coefficients well above .90 on all behaviors.[4]

It is the norm in social research to check for intercoder reliability whenever measures are derived from systematic observation or from archival records. With regard to the other types of reliability, the split-half and internal consistency techniques are the most frequently used, although they are limited to multi-item measures. The test–retest approach is less common, not only because of the problems mentioned above but also because of the impracticality of applying the same measure twice to the same sample of cases.

KEY POINT
Reliability assessment examines consistency (1) across repeated applications of a measure over time, (2) among the constituent parts or items comprising the measure, or (3) among different observers or coders applying the measure.

Improving Reliability

At some point in this discussion of reliability assessment you might have wondered, What can be done if your measure turns out to have low reliability? Should you discard it and start over with another measure? In some cases you may decide to do just that. However, there are ways to raise the reliability of an operational definition to an acceptable level.

1. Exploratory studies, preliminary interviews, or pretests of a measure with a small sample of persons similar in characteristics to the target group are ways to gain crucial information about whether the measure is clearly understood and interpreted similarly by respondents. The need for preliminary work with actual respondents before the final form of an instrument is completed cannot be overstated. Indeed, it is a topic we will consider again in relation to experiments and survey research.

2. Simply adding items of the same type to a scale will usually increase reliability. Other things being equal, a composite measure containing more items will normally be more reliable than a composite measure having fewer items. There are two reasons for this. First, as we noted earlier, random errors deviate on either side of the true value. Thus, with repeated measurements or additional items, such errors will tend to cancel each other out, yielding a more stable and accurate measure of the true value. Second, since any given set of items represents a sample of the possible measures of a concept, adding items increases sample size. As you will see in the next chapter, a basic principle of sampling is that the larger the sample, the more reliable the estimate.

3. An item-by-item analysis will reveal which items discriminate well between units with different values on a particular variable. Those items that do not discriminate appropriately should be omitted. For instance, on a test measuring knowledge of research methods, students with the highest scores should be more likely to answer a given question correctly than students with the lowest scores. If both those scoring high and those scoring low on the test are equally likely to answer the question incorrectly, the question may be

ambiguous or misleading. By retaining only those items or questions that correlate highly with the total score, reliability may be greatly improved.

4. Clues for improving reliability may be found in the instructions to respondents. Are they clear, or is there some room for misinterpretation? One should also examine the conditions under which the instrument is used or administered. Are they consistent? Finally, one might question whether the users of the instrument have been adequately and uniformly trained.

It is important to bear in mind that although a highly unreliable measure cannot be valid, it is possible to have highly reliable but invalid measures. Therefore, unless validity has been demonstrated, caution should be used in drawing conclusions about the goodness of even the most reliable measure.

Validity Assessment

Reliability assessment is relatively simple; the major forms that we have outlined use straightforward procedures that yield precise estimates of consistency and random error. These procedures are independent of the theories under investigation; that is, they can be applied and interpreted without regard to what is actually being measured. Validity assessment, by contrast, is more problematic. Systematic errors, which affect validity but not reliability, are more difficult to detect than random errors. And the issue of measurement validity generally cannot be divorced from larger theoretical concerns; sooner or later you must ask what the nature of your concept is, what it means, and whether your operational definition faithfully represents this meaning or something else.

Validity cannot be assessed directly. If it could—if we knew a case's true value on a variable independent of a given measure—then there would be no need for the measure. Or if we had perfectly valid, established measures of concepts, assessing validity would simply be a matter of checking to see if the application of a new operational definition corresponded with the application of an existing one. If we invented a new measure of length, for example, we could easily check its validity by determining whether we get the same results with standard instruments—tape measure, yardstick, transit, and so on—for measuring length. But there are few established operational definitions of concepts in the social sciences. Therefore, to assess validity, one must either (1) subjectively evaluate whether an operational definition measures what it is intended to or (2) compare the results of the operational definition with the results of other measures with which it should or should not be related. As you will see, the relevant kinds of subjective judgments and objective evidence depend on the purpose of measurement.

Subjective Validation

There are two methods of validity assessment based on subjective evaluation of an operational definition: face validity and content validity. **Face validity** refers simply to a personal judgment that an operational definition appears, on the face of it, to measure the concept it is intended to measure. In some cases this claim alone would seem reasonable to establish a measure's validity. Few would dispute the face validity of common indicators of variables such as age, gender, and education. Many observational measures of behavior have similar palpable validity—for example, "hitting another person" as an indicator of aggression and "offering assistance to a stranger" as an indicator of helping. As a method of validity assessment, however, face validity is generally not acceptable. Most operational definitions have it. After all, why would an instrument be offered as a measure of some concept if it did not appear to be valid? Face validity is based solely on personal judgment rather than objective evidence. Furthermore, it suggests that validity is an all-or-none matter when, in fact, measures have degrees of validity. For example, several operational definitions of age are possible. One could ask respondents directly what their age is, ask for their age at their last birthday, or ask them when they were born. Although these all have face validity, they are not equally accurate.[5] One would not know which operationalization is most accurate without resorting to a validation method other than face validity.

A more acceptable form of subjective evaluation, **content validity**, concerns the extent to which a measure adequately represents all facets of a concept. This type of validation is used most often in psychology and education, where it is applied to measures of skill, knowledge, and achievement. An instructor testing the reader's knowledge of this chapter, for example, ought to be concerned with the test's content validity—that is, with whether it includes questions on all sections of the chapter. Such a test would not have content validity if it omitted questions on reliability and validity and contained only questions on the measurement process and levels of measurement.

Psychologists and educators speak of the performance or content "domain" in relation to content validity. To demonstrate content validity, one must be able to identify clearly the components of the total domain and then show that the test items adequately represent these components. This is not difficult for most tests of knowledge. With respect to knowledge of the current chapter, one could list all the major topics and subtopics and then develop test items for each one, making sure that the number of items per topic is proportionate to the breadth of coverage. However, such a process is considerably more complex when measuring the abstract concepts typical of the social sciences. The domain of concepts like social capital, alienation, and social status is not easily specified; therefore, it is difficult to determine how adequately the domain has been tapped by specific indicators.

To some extent, the problems associated with face and content validity are not unique. All forms of validation are subjective in the sense that judgments on the validity of an operational definition ultimately rest with the verdict of the scientific community. However, social scientists generally do not find content validity evidence as persuasive as the kinds of "external" evidence provided by the validation procedures examined in the next two sections. Evidence that is external to the investigator is less subject to unintentional distortion and is easier to verify.

Criterion-Related Validation

Criterion-related validity applies to measuring instruments that have been developed for some practical purpose other than testing hypotheses or advancing scientific knowledge. One may wish to devise measures that will identify children with learning disabilities, determine a person's ability to fly an airplane or drive a car, or predict success in college. Under these circumstances, an investigator is not interested in the content or apparent meaning of the measure but in its usefulness as an indicator of a specific trait or behavior. The trait or behavior is called a *criterion,* and validation is a matter of how well scores on the measure correlate with the criterion of interest. The higher the correlation, the more valid the measure with respect to that criterion. As Jum Nunnally (1970:34) notes, with this form of validation the criterion variable is the only necessary standard of comparison: "If it were found that accuracy in horseshoe pitching correlated with success in college, horseshoe pitching would be a valid measure for predicting success in college."

The selected measure may indicate an individual's *current* or *future* standing on the criterion variable. For example, a mental health inventory designed to identify those in need of psychiatric care could be given to a sample of "well" persons and a sample of persons currently under psychiatric care. Its validity would be indicated by the degree to which the inventory distinguishes between the current two groups. Or the measure may predict a person's future standing on the criterion variable. A college entrance examination, for example, might be validated by comparing the exam scores of high school students with a criterion measure of their later success in college, such as grade-point averages or whether they graduate.

Since criterion-related validity rests on the correspondence between a measure and its criterion, it is only as good as the appropriateness and quality of the criterion measure. Unfortunately, this may present major difficulties. By what standards do you choose the criterion? What if no reasonable criterion exists? What if the criterion exists but practical problems prevent using it? For example, how would you demonstrate the validity of a county civil service test developed to assist in the hiring of probation officers? Logically, you could suggest that the county hire high-, average-, and low-scoring persons; then, at a later time, you could compare some measure of their job performance, such as supervisors' ratings, with their scores on the civil service test. Most likely, however, the county will hire only the top scorers and, regardless of their performance on the job, you would not know how it might have compared with the job performance of those who scored average or low. Thus, you could not assess the criterion-related validity of the measure.

Despite such problems, evidence of criterion-related validity is crucially important when a test or measure serves a specific, practical end. Thus, if a test is designed to screen and select candidates for certain jobs or to place students in ability tracks or special programs, then it is important to know how well it works for the given purpose. Except for applied areas of psychology and education, however, social science measures are not developed to help solve practical problems of this sort. Operational definitions are created to reflect the meaning of certain concepts, and there is seldom a clear and adequate criterion variable for evaluating validity.

Construct Validation

When neither a pertinent criterion of prediction nor a well-defined domain of content exists for determining validity, investigators turn to construct validation. (The term "construct" is interchangeable with the term "concept"; a concept developed for scientific purposes is sometimes called a construct.) **Construct validation** emphasizes the meaning of the responses to one's measuring instrument. How are they to be interpreted? Is the instrument measuring the intended concept (or construct), or can it be interpreted as measuring something else? Although this sounds like face validity, the orientation is different; construct validity is based on an accumulation of research evidence and not on mere appearances.

According to the logic of construct validation, the meaning of any scientific concept is implied by statements of its theoretical relations to other concepts. Thus, the validation process begins by examining the theory underlying the concept being measured. In light of this theory, one formulates hypotheses about variables that should be related to measures of the concept. At the same time, one considers other variables that should *not* be related to measures of the concept but might produce systematic error. Then one gathers evidence to test these hypotheses. The more evidence that supports the hypothesized relationships, the greater one's confidence that a particular operational definition is a valid measure of the concept.[6]

An example of construct validation is Morris Rosenberg's validation (1965) of his self-esteem scale. *Self-esteem* refers to an individual's sense of self-respect or self-worth: Those with high self-esteem have self-respect; those with low self-esteem lack self-respect. Rosenberg reasoned that, if his "scale actually did measure self-esteem," then scores on it should "be associated with other data in a theoretically meaningful way" (18). Thus, because clinical observations indicated that depression often accompanies low self-esteem, people who score low on the scale should report more depressive feelings such as unhappiness and gloom and appear more depressed to outside observers. Also, given the sociological proposition that an individual's self-esteem is determined largely by what others think of him or her, students with high self-esteem scores should be chosen more often as leaders by classmates and described more often as commanding the respect of others. Evidence confirmed these and other theoretical expectations, thereby supporting the construct validity of the self-esteem scale.

Table 5.2 depicts the differences between construct validation and criterion-related validation. The test of criterion-related validity is the ability of the measure to classify, group, or distinguish persons (or other units of analysis) in terms of a single criterion. What the measure means aside from its ability to make such distinctions is of little concern. What is important is the strength of the correlation between the predictive measure and a measure of the criterion; the stronger the correlation, the higher the validity.

TABLE 5.2. **Comparison of Criterion-Related and Construct Validity**

	Criterion-related validity	*Construct validity*
Validity a matter of:	Ability to classify units with precision	Ability to capture the meaning of the concept
The measure is used for:	Practical application	Theoretical application
Assessment a matter of comparison with:	A single, agreed-on independent criterion	No clear, single criterion
Degree of validity a matter of:	Predictive accuracy	A consistent pattern of relationships

In construct validation, however, one is less interested in the accuracy of a prediction per se than in what a relationship reveals about the meaning of the concepts being measured. One does not necessarily expect the correlation between measures of two theoretically related concepts to be extremely high because the two concepts do not mean exactly the same thing. That is why it is important to examine the relation of the measure in question to several other variables rather than base the assessment of validity on a single prediction. All the tested relations contribute to the evaluation of construct validity; it is their cumulative effect that supports or disputes the validity of the measure.

Evidence of construct validity consists of any empirical data that support the claim that a given operational definition measures a certain concept. Because such evidence may be derived from a wide variety of sources, construct validation is not associated with a particular approach or type of evidence. We will now consider four of the more common types of evidence used to establish construct validity. Remember, though, that no single study or piece of evidence is sufficient; the construct validity of a concept is only as compelling as the amount and diversity of evidence supporting it.

1. *Correlations with related variables.* If a measure is valid, it should correlate with measures of other theoretically related variables. M. Rosenberg (1965) validated his self-esteem scale in this way by showing that scores on it were correlated with symptoms of depression and with peer ratings.

2. *Consistency across indicators and different methods of measurement.* Different measures of the same concept should be correlated, and because each methodological approach (e.g., self-reports, observation, archival records) is subject to different sources of systematic error, measures of concepts should not be tied to a particular method. Thus, one of the most convincing signs of construct validity is the correspondence of results when a concept is measured in different ways. This is called **convergent validity** because the results converge on the same meaning, namely, that conveyed by the underlying concept.

Abundant evidence supports the convergent validity of the Rosenberg Self-Esteem Scale. For example, based on a sample of 9th and 10th graders, David Demo (1985) showed that scores on Rosenberg's scale were positively associated with scores on another popular scale, the Coopersmith Self-Esteem Inventory, and with peer ratings of each individual's self-esteem. Other studies similarly have found positive associations between the Rosenberg Self-Esteem Scale and the Lerner Self-Esteem Scale (Savin-Williams and Jaquish, 1981) and with an indicator of general self-regard (Fleming and Courtney, 1984).

3. *Correlations with unrelated variables.* A valid operational definition should separate the concept being measured from other concepts from which it is intended to differ. In other words, there are some variables (representing systematic errors) with which a measure should not be highly correlated. This is called **discriminant validity**.

A good example is Zick Rubin's validation (1970) of his 13-item Love Scale. A valid measure of love should differentiate love from liking because the two concepts are empirically related but conceptually distinct. Rubin therefore developed a parallel scale of liking. When both the love and the liking scales were administered, he found that their scores were only moderately correlated. Also, whereas respondents liked their dating partners only slightly more than they liked their friends, they loved their dating partners much more than their friends. Additional evidence showed that the Love Scale tapped an attitude toward a specific other person rather than a general response tendency. For example, Love Scale scores were uncorrelated with scores on the Marlowe–Crowne Social Desirability Scale, designed to measure the tendency to give socially desirable responses.

4. *Differences among known groups.* When certain groups are expected to differ on the measure of a concept, one source of validating evidence would be a comparison of the groups' responses. Richard Contrada and colleagues (2001) used this approach to test the validity of a measure of perceived ethnic discrimination. Respondents were instructed to indicate on a 7-point scale ranging from 1 (never) to 7 (very often) how often over the past 3 months particular forms of ethnic discrimination had been directed at them. One item asked, "How often have others implied that you must be dishonest because of your ethnicity?" Another asked, "How often have others had low expectations for you because of your ethnicity?" When this measure was administered to students at Rutgers University, nonwhites, as expected, were significantly more likely to report ethnic discrimination. (See Box 5.2 for an example of construct validation that uses a variety of evidence.)

Although construct validation is now considered the model validation procedure for most social measurement, it is not without its problems. It is cumbersome and requires abundant evidence; more important, however, it can lead to inconsistent and equivocal outcomes. On the one hand, if a prediction is not supported, this may mean that the measure lacks construct validity. On the other hand, such negative evidence may mean that the underlying theory is in error or that measures of other variables in the analysis lack validity. Only if one's theoretical predictions are sound and the measures of other variables are well validated can one confidently conclude that negative evidence is due to a lack of construct validity (Zeller and Carmines, 1980).

BOX 5.2 Validation of the Attitudes toward Feminism Scale

At the height of the Women's Liberation Movement in the mid-1970s, Eliot Smith, Myra Marx Ferree, and Frederick Miller (1975) developed a 20-item scale to measure attitudes toward feminism. Each scale item consists of a profeminist or antifeminist statement; for example, "Women have the right to compete with men in every sphere of activity," and "A woman who refuses to bear children has failed in her duty to her husband." Respondents indicate their level of agreement with each statement, numbers are assigned to the answer categories, and then scale scores are calculated by adding up responses to the 20 items. The numerical range of the answer categories is 1 to 5, with the highest number representing a profeminist response; so the scale has a possible range of 20 (extreme antifeminism) to 100 (extreme profeminism). (See Box 13.1 for a description of how the authors created this scale.)

There is unusually good evidence validating this measure, called the FEM Scale (an acronym based on the authors' first names). The creators of the FEM Scale tested its reliability as well as its construct validity with data from 100 Harvard summer school students. Royce

(continued)

(continued)

Singleton and John Christiansen (1977) also assessed the scale's validity with data from a larger, more heterogeneous sample of respondents. Following is a summary of the evidence regarding the scale's reliability and validity.

Reliability

Both of these studies obtained a reliability estimate, based on internal consistency, of .91, which is quite acceptable for attitude measurement.

Intercorrelations and Convergent Validity

Smith, Ferree, and Miller tested the validity of the FEM Scale by correlating it with three other variables: measures of identification with the Women's Movement, activism in the movement, and the Rubin–Peplau Just World Scale. High scores on the latter scale reflect a belief that the world is a just place and that people generally get what they deserve. Smith, Ferree, and Miller reasoned that feminists are unlikely to view the world in general as a just place since they tend to perceive that women have been treated unjustly. Consistent with expectations, the results showed that FEM Scale scores were positively correlated with the identification and activism measures (evidence of convergent validity) and negatively correlated with scores on the Just World Scale.

Singleton and Christiansen correlated scores on the FEM Scale with measures of dogmatism, antiblack prejudice, and identification with the Women's Movement. They reasoned that dogmatism, a tendency to adopt traditional views, would include an antifeminist orientation. Also, prejudice toward blacks would reflect a general tendency toward prejudice with which antifeminist attitudes would be consistent. The correlations of individuals' scores on the FEM Scale with their scores on these other measures were moderately high, as expected.

Discriminant Validity

In addition to the above measures, Smith, Ferree, and Miller administered the Rotter I–E Scale to their respondents. "I–E" stands for internal–external locus of control. High "internals" are persons who believe that they have a great deal of personal control over their lives; high "externals" are persons who tend to believe that their lives are controlled by forces outside themselves. Because there was reason to expect that feminism would be mildly correlated with both of these tendencies, Smith, Ferree, and Miller expected no correlation with the FEM Scale when internality and externality were treated as a single scale. Once again, the results supported their prediction.

Known-Groups Validity

Singleton and Christiansen also administered the FEM Scale to members of two groups with opposing views on women's issues: the National Organization for Women and Fascinating Womanhood. The National Organization for Women (NOW) was the largest and most prominent organization in the Women's Movement; Fascinating Womanhood was an antifeminist organization of the early to mid-1970s that strongly advocated a traditional, dependent role for women. FEM Scale scores of the members of these two organizations were widely divergent, as expected. Recall that the scale has a range of 20 to 100. Members of NOW had an average score of 91, whereas members of Fascinating Womanhood had an average score of 51.

KEY POINT
Objective validity assessment examines the degree to which the operational definition is correlated with a current or future criterion (*criterion-related validity*) or forms expected relationships with other measures and variables (*construct validity*).

A Final Note on Reliability and Validity

The procedures for assessing validity and reliability may seem so complex and cumbersome that one may wonder if investigators ever pass beyond this stage of research.[7] Fortunately, many investigators avoid the issue by borrowing, from previous studies, measures that have established records of validity and reliability. Also, few researchers apply more than one of the simpler procedures to ascertain the reliability or validity of their new measures. Sometimes a measure is tested or validated by others. At other times, new measures are introduced (perhaps with minimal evidence of reliability or validity) and widely used until invalidating features are found (such as the middle-class bias of IQ tests) and the instrument is revised or replaced. Thus, validity and reliability assessment is not confined to intrastudy or intrainvestigator efforts but is an ongoing process that extends across studies and investigators and over a considerable length of time.

It is also true that the most elaborate procedures were developed in response to the difficulties of operationalizing some concepts, such as attitudes, that are relatively unstable and pose reactivity and other measurement problems. More stable and less reactive measures are not as problematic.

In speaking about the issues validity raises, James Davis (1971:14–15) aptly observes that at "the extreme [validation] constitutes a philosophical thicket which makes a dandy hiding place from which antiempirical social scientists can ambush the simple-minded folk who want to find out what the world is like rather than speculate about it." Although it is true that such difficulties can immobilize die-hard perfectionists, for most social scientists the validation problem presents challenging opportunities to exercise their creativity. No measure is perfect, but an imperfect measure is better than none at all. Or, as Davis further notes, "Weak measures are to be preferred to brilliant speculations as a source of empirical information" (15).

Summary

- *Measurement* is the process of assigning numerals or labels to units of analysis to represent conceptual properties.
- The measurement process involves *conceptualization* (the development and clarification of concepts) followed by *operationalization* (the description of the research procedures necessary to assign units to variable categories to represent concepts).
- Because single indicators do not correspond perfectly to concepts, researchers often use multiple indicators, which may be combined to create an index or scale.
- Operational definitions may be formed either by experimentally manipulating a variable or through nonmanipulative procedures such as verbal reports, observations of behavior, and archival records.
- One selects operational definitions in the context of an overall research strategy with an eye toward obtaining the best possible fit with the concept being measured.

- Operational definitions are described in terms of their level of measurement and are evaluated with respect to their reliability and validity.
- Measurement level alerts us to the various ways that we can interpret the numerals assigned to different variable categories.
- In nominal measurement, the numbers are simply labels that signify differences of kind.
- In ordinal measurement, different numbers indicate the rank order of cases on some variable.
- In interval measurement the numbers form a metric so that different numbers imply not only rank order but also countable distances.
- In addition to all the features of lower measurement levels, ratio measurement contains an absolute zero point, making it possible to form ratios of the numbers assigned to categories.
- *Reliability* refers to the stability or consistency of an operational definition, whereas *validity* refers to the goodness of fit between an operational definition and the concept it is purported to measure. A valid measure is necessarily reliable, but a reliable measure may or may not be valid.
- A completely valid measure reflects only true differences, which means that it is free of both systematic and random error. A completely reliable measure is free of random error but may reflect true differences and/or systematic error.
- We assess reliability by calculating the correlation between (1) repeated applications of the measure (test–retest reliability) and (2) responses to subsets of items from the same measure (split-half reliability); by (3) examining the consistency of responses across all items (internal consistency); or by (4) observing the correspondence among different observers or coders who apply the same measure (intercoder reliability).
- We assess validity by subjectively evaluating an operational definition, by checking the correspondence between the operational definition and a specific criterion, or by determining whether the operational definition of a given construct correlates in expected ways with measures of several other constructs.
- Subjective validation involves judgments of either whether an operational definition appears to be valid (face validity) or whether it adequately represents the domain of a concept (content validity).
- Criterion-related validation applies to measures (or tests) that are intended to indicate a person's current or future standing on a specific behavioral criterion. It is especially important to assess when a measure is a practical, decision-making tool.
- Construct validation is based on an accumulation of research evidence, including differences among groups known to differ on the characteristic being measured and correlations with related variables, with different measures of the same concept (convergent validity), and with measures from which the concept should be differentiated (discriminant validity).

Key Terms

conceptualization
operationalization
indicator
verbal (self-) report
index/scale
level of measurement
    nominal
    ordinal
    interval
    ratio
exhaustive
mutually exclusive
reliability
validity
systematic measurement error

reactive measurement effect
social desirability effect
random measurement error
test–retest reliability
split-half reliability
internal-consistency reliability
intercoder reliability
subjective validation
    face validity
    content validity
criterion-related validation
construct validation
    convergent validity
    discriminant validity

Exercises

1. Look up an article in a social science journal that reports an empirical study that investigates one of the concepts listed below, as either an independent variable or a dependent variable. Do the researchers provide a *theoretical definition* of the concept? What is the researchers' *operational definition*? What is the source of their operational definition (self-report, observation, or records)?

alienation	liberalism/conservatism
fear of crime	political participation
group cohesion (or cohesiveness)	racial prejudice

2. In Chapter 1 we introduced the topic of altruism. "Altruism" refers to helping behavior that is motivated purely by a desire to benefit others without anticipation of personal rewards. Helping behavior provides some benefit to or improves the well-being of another person. Assuming you were going to conduct a campus survey, how would you operationalize altruistic behavior? Give examples of at least two indicators.

3. Indicate the level of measurement of each of the following variables.
    a. *Seriousness of criminal offense*: measured by having judges rank offenses from the most to the least severe
    b. *Political activism*: measured by the total number of politically related activities in which an individual participates
    c. *Ethnic group membership*: measured by having respondents check one of these categories: black, Hispanic, Oriental, Caucasian, other
    d. *Educational attainment*: measured by asking respondents to check one of the following categories: 8th grade or less; 9–11 years; high school graduate; some college; college graduate
    e. An item measuring an attitude or opinion that uses the following response format: strongly agree, agree, undecided, disagree, strongly disagree

4. Suppose that members of a class in research methods were given an examination on this chapter. Assuming that the examination is designed to measure students' knowledge of the material in the chapter, describe three possible sources of measurement error (either systematic error or random error) in the set of examination scores. For each source of error, explain whether it is likely to affect measurement validity, reliability, or both.

5. One problem with many studies of domestic violence, including child abuse, is that they have relied on self-reports. Because domestic abuse is socially stigmatized and can result in criminal charges, individuals may be tempted to underreport abusive conduct. What kind of measurement error (random or systematic) does this introduce? What effect would this have on the reliability and/or validity of such self-report measures?

6. Below are three of the items you are considering for your campus survey of altruism (see Question 2). First, using your personal judgment and keeping in mind that all measures are subject to some degree of error, evaluate the validity of each item; that is, indicate why you believe the item is likely to be a valid or invalid measure of altruism. Second, let's assume you create a composite measure of altruism in which you ask respondents whether they engaged in several different altruistic actions during the past year (besides the possible items below, other items might include giving money to charity, helping carry a stranger's belongings, and giving food or money to a homeless person). How would you assess the reliability and validity of your composite measure?
    a. Have you ever donated blood?
    b. Have you ever helped someone pack and move?
    c. Have you ever been a "big brother" or "big sister" to a child who was not a sibling?

Notes

1. At times we will use the word "number" where technically the term "numeral" is more accurate. The difference, simply put, is that numbers are abstract concepts (such as the number 2), whereas

numerals are the squiggly lines used to represent the concepts. In the nominal level of measurement, numerals do *not* represent the number concept but rather are arbitrarily assigned to categories for coding purposes.

2. Choosing an appropriate statistical technique, however, is not always easy because an actual measure may fall between two levels of measurement. One might think of educational attainment (years of schooling), for example, as providing more information than an ordinal scale but not attaining the interval-scale level.

3. As the terminology suggests, most of the procedures for determining reliability were developed in connection with psychological testing.

4. DeWitt, Cready, and Seward (2013) used Cohen's kappa coefficient to calculate interrater reliability. Kappa is thought to be a better measure than simple percent agreement because it takes into account agreement that could occur by chance.

5. Studies have shown that if a single question is used, it is best to ask respondents in what year they were born. However, the way to get the most accurate measure is to ask both date of birth and age at last birthday, check one against the other, and then inquire about any discrepancies (Sudman and Bradburn, 1982).

6. As you can see, this process is similar to general hypothesis testing. In fact, construct validation "is not simply a matter of validating a [measure]. One must try to validate the theory behind the [measure]" (Kerlinger, 1973:461).

7. The foregoing discussion of reliability and validity does not exhaust the use of these concepts in the social sciences, for in addition to judging the adequacy of operational definitions, the terms are applied in the evaluation of other aspects of a research study. For example, the term "validity" is used in reference to the adequacy of a research design (Chapters 7 and 8). The concept of "reliability" is used frequently in judging the quality of a sample (Chapter 6).

6

Sampling

Sampling, whether we are aware of it or not, is part of everyday life. For instance, after eating at one of a chain of restaurants, a person may decide that all the restaurants in the chain serve poorly prepared food and provide poor service. A student's decision to take a given course may be based on the opinions of friends who have already taken it. Having met a few people from New York, someone may conclude that New Yorkers are pushy and aggressive. In each of these examples, inferences about a whole class of objects are made from observations of a subset of such objects. The examples implicitly contain the basic idea behind sampling:

1. We seek knowledge or information about a whole class of similar objects or events (usually called a **population**).
2. We observe some of these (called a **sample**).
3. We extend our findings to the entire class (Stephan and McCarthy, 1958:22).

Though simple in principle, sampling can be fraught with difficulties in practice. Consider some possibilities. The restaurant patron may have picked a day when the head cook had quit and had been replaced by the busboy, or she may have patronized the worst franchise in the chain. The student talked to friends, who are likely to have highly similar opinions that may differ markedly from the opinions of other students who have taken the course. Finally, characterizations of groups of people, like the one of New Yorkers, seldom apply to even a majority of the group. Generalizations such as these, drawn from casual observation, are likely to be in error because they are based on inadequate samples of information. In this chapter we discuss some rigorous yet surprisingly simple techniques that are designed to reduce the hazards of generalizing from incomplete information.

Chapter 5 discussed the measurement of variables. Before actual measurements are taken, researchers must select an appropriate set of units (or cases). Selecting a set of cases raises several crucial questions. The first of these questions was addressed in Chapter 4: What is the unit of analysis—individual people, married couples, newspaper editorials, cities? The answer to this question, recall, hinges largely on the research question, which determines what the researcher seeks to describe and compare. Thus, research on the relationship between a nation's literacy rate and its economic development would use nations as units; a study of the influence of years of schooling on prejudice would concern individuals. The decision about *what type of unit* to examine will not be considered further in the current chapter; we will assume that the appropriate type of unit has been determined. The interests here will be with *how many* such units of *what particular description* should be *chosen by what method*. But before examining each of these issues, let us take a brief look at some of the reasons that sampling in social research, as in everyday life, is a practical necessity for informed decisions.

Why Sample?

Scientists seek to establish the broadest possible generalizations, applicable to infinitely large classes of events. Yet, it is impossible to observe all relevant events. In the physical sciences, the nature of the elements studied simplifies this problem. Particular physical and chemical elements are assumed to be identical or nearly identical with respect to pertinent properties. Thus, any sample of one or more cases suffices; one test tube of hydrogen, distilled water, or nitroglycerine will be like any other. As we move from the physical to the biological and social sciences, however, this assumption of homogeneity becomes increasingly risky. Because people and other social objects vary widely on nearly every imaginable property, studying any one case simply will not suffice as a basis for generalizing. The heterogeneity of cases requires careful procedures designed to ensure that the range of variation in the population will be represented adequately in one's sample of observations.

Beyond the need to represent population variability adequately, practical considerations usually necessitate sampling. Researchers often want to know something about a specific social group or population that, for reasons of size, time, cost, or inaccessibility, cannot be studied in its entirety. Indeed, unless a researcher is willing to restrict his or her inferences to a very small set of narrowly defined cases or unless one has unlimited time and funds, there is no getting around sampling.

To interview the entire 20,000-student population at a university, a population that is relatively small by survey research standards, would require a long period of time or a large number of interviewers. However, time is often of the essence. A lengthy period of data collection would render some data, such as attitudes about current issues or voter preferences, obsolete by the time the information was completely in hand. Moreover, the responses of persons interviewed late in the investigation could not be considered comparable to those of persons interviewed early. Responses could be affected by current events, or rumors and scuttlebutt about the ongoing survey may influence the responses of persons interviewed late. A large staff of interviewers also would present problems. It would add to the total costs of the study; it would be more difficult to train and supervise interviewers adequately; and one may be forced to hire some interviewers who are not well qualified, thereby reducing the accuracy of the data.

This last point brings us to a third reason for sampling. Paradoxically, the attempt to observe all cases may describe a population less accurately than a carefully selected sample of observations, especially in survey studies of large populations. The reason is that the planning and logistics of observation are more manageable with a sample. Greater attention can be given to the design of interviews or questionnaires, to procedures for locating difficult-to-find respondents, and, once again, to the hiring, training, and supervision of a competent staff of interviewers, all of which will increase the quality of the data collected.

A case in point is the decennial census, a complete enumeration of the U.S. population made every 10 years. The census is an enormous undertaking; the 2010 Census, which counted 308.7 million people, cost an estimated $14.7 billion to collect, edit, and present (databases and publications); and the Bureau of the Census hired about 565,000 interviewers just to track down those people who did not return their census forms in the mail (Williams, 2012). With considerable effort, the 2010 Census was the most accurate ever. Yet, the Census Bureau estimated 16 million omissions, that is, people who were either missed or could not be identified because of incomplete responses. According to estimates, significant undercounts occurred in several categories, including renters, young children, and minorities, which included about 1.5 million black Americans and Hispanics (U.S. Census Bureau, 2012). As James Gleick (1990:22) said about the 1990 Census, there were simply "too many doors to knock on, and too many people living without doors . . . [and too high] a rate of noncooperation." These obstacles are much easier to overcome in a sample. That is why data from some sample surveys, such as the 60,000-household Current Population Survey (CPS), are considered more accurate for many purposes than the census. A postenumeration sample survey is used to estimate the accuracy of the census and to make statistical adjustments to the count. To increase accuracy and reduce costs, many statisticians recommend that the census be replaced with a survey of a large sample.[1]

We hasten to add that only in the case of extremely large populations would we expect a sample to yield more accurate information about a population than a survey of the whole population. But the justification for sampling need not rest on a claim of greater accuracy. More to the point, carefully selected samples are an efficient way of producing accurate information. You can see this for yourself on the next election day. Note the accuracy with which the major news networks predict certain election outcomes, long before all the votes have been tabulated. This accuracy is made possible by the careful sampling procedures of expert pollsters. (The polls have not always been so accurate, however, as revealed in Box 6.1.)

Population Definition

After determining the unit of analysis, the first task in sampling is to define the population of interest—to describe the particular collection of units that make up the population. The sociologist Kenneth Bailey (1982:86) notes that an experienced researcher always gets a clear picture of the population before selecting the sample, thus starting from the top

BOX 6.1 Sources of Error in Survey Sampling: Two Notorious Failures in Political Forecasting

Every 4 years in the United States, the accuracy of public opinion polls is put to the test. Why? Because unlike most surveys, in which there are no external criteria for assessing the validity of sample estimates, pre-election poll forecasts can be judged against the actual outcome of the election (Martin, Traugott, and Kennedy, 2005). Based on samples, polls cannot be expected to predict an outcome perfectly; but given random sampling, they should be within an expected margin of sampling error. Taking this into account, social scientists have devised various methods for assessing poll accuracy (see Martin, Traugott, and Kennedy, 2005). These analyses indicate that most polls do well, with estimates off by no more than the expected margin of error—a few percentage points. In 2008, 19 final polls, all conducted within a few days of the election, had Barack Obama winning the presidential election by 5 to 11 percentage points; Obama's actual margin of victory was 7 points. Election polls, however, have not always been so accurate, as two infamous examples from the annals of sample surveys reveal.

Perhaps the biggest polling debacle occurred in the presidential election of 1936, when *Literary Digest* magazine predicted that Alfred Landon would be a landslide winner, by 57 to 43 percent, over Franklin Roosevelt. At this time, the *Literary Digest* was well known for its polls on public issues and enjoyed considerable prestige, having predicted the winner in every presidential election since 1920. Its 1932 poll erred by less than 2 percentage points. However, in 1936 it missed calling the election by a wide margin. What went wrong? With more than 2 million individuals polled, the *Digest's* sample was certainly large enough. Indeed, it was enormous by current standards. In 2008, a sample of only 2000 to 3000 people was required to predict accurately the voting behavior of more than 130 million voters.

There were two major reasons for the failure of the *Literary Digest* poll. The first was the manner in which the sample was selected, which produced *coverage error* (see p. 183). The *Digest* conducted its polls by mailing ballots to millions of people. The names and addresses of these people came from a variety of sources, including phone books, automobile registration lists, and the *Digest's* own subscription list. Because such sources tended to exclude poor individuals, who could not afford telephones or automobiles, the sample did not provide a representative cross-section of American voters. With rich and poor voting similarly before 1936, this bias against the poor population apparently had little effect on the predictions. But in 1936, rich individuals tended to vote for Landon, poor persons voted overwhelmingly for Roosevelt, and the bias inherent in the *Digest's* initial sample contributed to the error.

A second problem with the *Digest* poll has to do with what is called *nonresponse bias* (see p. 183). With any survey, there will be a certain percentage of the selected sample who do not respond or who cannot be contacted. Studies have shown that these nonrespondents tend to differ in important ways from respondents. For example, both lower-class and upper-class people are less likely to respond to questionnaires or personal interviews than are middle-class people. Respondents are also likely to have a stronger interest in the survey topic than do nonrespondents. Although the *Digest* mailed 10 million sample ballots to prospective voters, it based its predictions on 2.4 million responses. Peverill Squire (1988) has shown that this low response rate combined with a nonresponse bias produced a substantial error in the 1936 poll. Feeling more strongly about the election than did the pro-Roosevelt majority, the anti-Roosevelt minority was more likely to respond to the *Digest* poll.

Another notorious polling failure occurred in 1948, known as "the year the polls elected Thomas E. Dewey President." All three major polls—Gallup, Crossley, and Roper—that covered the 1948 campaign projected that Dewey would be the winner with 50 percent or more of the popular vote, but he ended up with just over 45 percent. Several factors combined to produce this failure. For one thing, those who were undecided about their election choice when the polls were taken went predominantly for Truman. Critics of the 1948 polls, however, agree that the way the samples were selected also contributed to the prediction error.

By this time the pollsters were using a procedure called "quota sampling" (see p. 173). With quota sampling the population is divided into subgroups (e.g., men and women, blacks and whites), and interviewers are assigned a fixed quota of persons to interview in each of the subgroups. For example, an interviewer might be required to interview three men under 40 years of age and four over 40, as well as four women under 40 and four over 40. Quotas are determined to guarantee that the sample will be representative of the voting population with respect to important characteristics thought to affect voting behavior. One shortcoming of this method is that the quotas are theoretical; they are an indirect means of creating a representative sample of the voting population *before the election*. However, demographic characteristics of the voting population cannot be known with certainty until after the election is held. Another problem is that the interviewers, who are free to choose anyone they like within the assigned quota, may be subject to selection bias. In fact, Gallup and Crossley poll results from 1936 to 1948, based on quota sampling, revealed that interviewers consistently preferred Republicans (D. Katz, 1949). With the Democratic candidate, Roosevelt, possessing a large lead in 1936, 1940, and 1944, Gallup and Crossley were able to predict the winner despite the Republican bias of their polls. But this was too much to overcome in an election as close as that of 1948.

(population) and working down (to the sample). "In contrast, novice researchers often work from the bottom up." Rather than making explicit the population they wish to study, they select a predetermined number of conveniently available cases and assume that the sample corresponds to the population of interest. Consider a sample consisting of "randomly" chosen passersby at a shopping center on a Saturday afternoon. What could this sample possibly represent? There is simply no way of knowing. It almost certainly would not be representative of people in the surrounding community. For one thing, weekend shoppers would probably overrepresent people who work during the week and underrepresent the retired and unemployed. And if the shopping area happens to be a luxurious shopping mall, the sample is likely to be heavily weighted in favor of the financially well-off. At best, this sample would represent Saturday afternoon shoppers at the shopping center in question on the day the data were collected, which is a strange definition of the population and surely not one in which a researcher would be interested.

Defining the population is a two-step process. First, one must clearly identify the **target population**, that is, the population to which a researcher would like to generalize his or her results. To define the target population, the researcher must specify the criteria for determining which cases are included in the population and which cases are excluded. The relevant criteria depend on the type of unit and the research question. With individual people, some combination of locale, age, and selected demographic variables such as gender, race, employment status, and age is ordinarily used (Sudman, 1976:12). For example, in a study of aging and religion, Stephen Ainlay, Royce Singleton, and Victoria Swigert (1992:179-80) defined the target population as "noninstitutionalized residents of Worcester, Massachusetts, who were 65 years of age or older."

For the National Education Longitudinal Study (NELS), which Beckett Broh (2002) used to analyze the relationship between extracurricular activities and academic achievement, the target population for the base year, 1988, consisted of students enrolled in "all public and private schools containing eighth grades in the fifty states and District of Columbia" (Spencer et al., 1990:6). This definition was clarified further by taking into account several pragmatic considerations, as the researchers note:

> Excluded . . . are Bureau of Indian Affairs (BIA) schools, special education schools for the handicapped, area vocational schools that do not enroll students directly, and schools for dependents of U.S. personnel overseas. The student population excludes students with severe mental handicaps, students whose command of the English language was not sufficient for understanding the survey materials (especially the cognitive tests), and students with physical or emotional problems that would make it unduly difficult for them to participate in the survey. (6)

If the unit is groups or organizations, then organizational type and size as measured by number of members or employees are often specified. For instance, to study factors influencing the adoption of maternity-leave policies, Erin Kelly and Frank Dobbin (1999) limited the population to public, nonprofit, and private-sector establishments with 50 or more workers in three states: California, New Jersey, and Virginia. Studies of families also invoke unique definitional criteria: for example, the presence or absence of children, number of generations, and intact or single parents. Which set of criteria is used depends on the researcher's purposes.

Two defining characteristics that always implicitly or explicitly define the target population are its geographic and time referents. Each of the above examples of target populations has a clear political or geographic boundary (city of Worcester, United States, three states), and each has a distinctive time frame (1989, 1987–88 academic year, 1986).

Researchers next must find a way of making the target population operational. This involves the second phase of population definition: constructing the sampling frame. The **sampling frame** denotes the set of all cases from which the sample is selected. Since the term can be misleading, please note that the sampling frame is *not a sample*; rather, it is the *operational definition of the population* that provides the basis for sampling.

There are two ways of constructing a sampling frame, which correspond to the two ways to define a set (or subset) in logic: (1) listing all cases and (2) providing a rule defining membership. For example, in a city telephone survey, the sampling frame could consist of the city phone book (a listing) or the set of all telephone numbers with certain telephone exchanges (a rule). In survey research, establishing a sampling frame often amounts to obtaining an adequate listing—either of the population as a whole or of subgroups of the population. But listing is not always possible or preferable. As long as cases can be identified, a rule procedure can usually be devised for finding and selecting cases. Suppose you wanted to observe the behavior of inmates in a mental institution. Listing all acts before they occur is impossible. However, if we consider that all acts within the institution occur at specified places, days, and times, then this would provide the basis for a three-dimensional rule (site, time, and day) for identifying and selecting cases. Similarly, if you wanted to interview people attending a rock concert, the fact that everyone must arrive at the concert at a particular time allows you to establish a rule based on time of arrival.

It is a researcher's hope that the sampling frame and the target population will be identical. Unfortunately, this usually occurs only for very small, geographically concentrated populations. Because it is often impossible or impractical to create an accurate list of the target population, one must rely on existing lists; and such lists are inevitably incomplete. For the aging and religion study, the sampling frame consisted of the 1989 Worcester city census, which provided names, addresses, and birth dates. However, not only was it likely that many people were not counted in the census, but also, through deaths and migration in and out of Worcester, the target population was bound to have changed somewhat by the time the interviews were conducted. Thus, the sampling frame could not have matched precisely the target population.

KEY POINT
To draw a sample, first specify the target population and then find a sampling frame, usually a list, identifying all cases within the population.

Strictly speaking, inferences should be made only about the population represented by the sampling frame. Yet, it is the target population to which we wish to generalize. Therefore, one should always evaluate the extent to which cases in the target population have been omitted from the sampling frame. How many omissions are there? How are they likely to differ from cases included in the sampling frame? Because they frequently differ in a systematic way from those included in the frame, excluded cases can seriously bias findings. The infamous *Literary Digest* poll (see Box 6.1), which erred by a large margin in predicting the 1936 presidential election, used several frames, including phone books and automobile registration lists, all of which tended to exclude the poor. Whenever such biases are known to exist, researchers should decide whether to use the list or to find an alternative sampling frame. Regardless of the frame that is used, however, the nature of possible excluded cases should be acknowledged and carefully taken into account when making inferences about the target population.

The problem of omitted cases is solved best by finding a good list to begin with. Despite its flaws, the annual Worcester city census provided a reasonably accurate frame. For sampling individuals, many small and mid-size U.S. cities have population and household directories. If the target population consists of a local professional association, union, school, church, or some other institution, membership directories are usually available and provide excellent frames. But at the national level, few lists exist. An explicit list of all 8th-grade students in the United States, for example, is simply not available. To sample national populations, researchers generally break the target population down into natural groupings for which lists are available or can be constructed at low cost. For the NELS, the researchers obtained a list of public and private schools in the United States, a sampling frame that comprised an implicit list of all 8th-grade students. We discuss this sampling strategy further under "Sampling Designs."

Often, there is no single list that adequately enumerates the population. This is particularly true for organizations as a unit of analysis. Although national lists exist for special populations such as hospitals, newspapers, and businesses, no one has tallied American voluntary associations (Knoke, 1990) or all public organizations, let alone all types of organizations. The sampling frame in the Kelly and Dobbin study of maternity-leave policy was compiled from several sources (see Dobbin et al., 1993). First, 13 sectors were chosen to represent different parts of the economy, including publishing, banking, retail trade, and transportation. Then, the most complete published list of organizations for each sector was selected. Among the frames were Dun's *Million Dollar Directory* (for various private-sector organizations), the directory of the American Hospital Association (for hospitals), and the *Encyclopedia of Associations* (for nonprofits). To enumerate organizations in the public sector, the investigators used commercial telephone directories as well as official state and federal government directories.

Equally problematic is finding or constructing sampling frames for studies of rare or special target populations, such as Vietnam War veterans, people with a particular illness or disability, or people with incomes above or below a given amount. If a list of the general population is available, it may be possible to screen the rare population from the larger sampling frame. In the Worcester study of the elderly, the sampling frame for the general population was culled to include only people older than 64 years of age. Alternatively, members of the special target population, such as people older than age 64, could be identified at the data-collection stage.

Finally, some populations defy identification and listing. Imagine trying to identify for sampling purposes members of a terrorist group or other radical political groups, such as white power skinheads, or deviant populations such as drug abusers, criminals, or delinquents. For obvious reasons, political radicals and deviants tend to resist identification by anyone outside their own group. In studying such populations, therefore, the process of population definition breaks down because an adequate sampling frame is unobtainable.

Sampling Designs

Ideally, in sampling we would like to obtain a sample that will be representative of the target population. To be "representative" means to provide a close approximation of certain characteristics of the target group. If the population consists of the students at Alpha College, then a perfectly representative sample would be like Alpha College students in all respects. The sample would contain the same proportion of first-, second-, third-, and fourth-year students, the same proportion of commuter students, the same proportion of sociology majors, and so forth, as is contained in the student body as a whole.

Although it is intuitively appealing, the concept of "representativeness" has nearly disappeared from the technical vocabulary of sampling. Not only is it extremely unlikely that one will be able to draw a *perfectly* representative sample; it also is rarely possible to evaluate a specific sample in terms of its overall representativeness. Because the populations we study are not known in all respects (which is, of course, the reason we study them), there is no way of knowing just how representative a given sample is. Therefore, we use the term representative in reference to specific, known population characteristics but not in reference to the overall quality of the sample.

The quality of a sample must be judged in terms of the procedure that produced it, that is, in terms of its sampling design. **Sampling design** refers to that part of the research plan that indicates how cases are to be selected for observation. Sampling designs are generally divided into two broad classes: probability and nonprobability. **Probability sampling** is scientifically more acceptable, although it is not always feasible or economical. Its essential characteristics are that all cases in the population are randomly selected and have a known probability of being included in the sample. In **nonprobability sampling**, the chances of selecting any case are not known because cases are nonrandomly selected.

Probability sampling designs offer two major advantages over nonprobability sampling designs. The first advantage is that they remove the possibility that investigator biases will affect the selection of cases. The second advantage is that, by virtue of random selection, the laws of mathematical probability may be applied to estimate the accuracy of the sample. With probability sampling, one knows to which population the sample may be generalized as well as the limits of generalizability; but with nonprobability sampling, the population itself is undefined and the laws of probability do not apply.

Probability Sampling

Random Selection

Probability sampling always involves the process of **random selection**. In popular usage, "random" describes something that occurs or is done without plan or choice; random events or choices are haphazard or nondeliberate. As used in sampling, however, random has a more specific, technical meaning. It refers to a process that gives each element in a set, such as each case in a population, an equal chance of being selected. If for any reason the selection process favors certain cases or if the selection of one case increases or decreases the likelihood that another case will be selected, then the selection is *biased*. By this definition, your circle of friends would clearly be biased as a sample of the student population at your college. So also would a variety of other, more or less haphazardly chosen samples, such as the students enrolled in introductory sociology classes, students who happen to be in the library on a weekday night, or those students who pass in front of the campus center at a given time. In each of these samples, it is a good bet that certain types of students are more likely to appear than others; therefore, they are not random samples of the student body.

To satisfy the condition of randomness, an investigator cannot simply pick cases haphazardly or in any hit-or-miss fashion; subtle and often unconscious biases will invariably enter into the selection process. Rather, mechanical or electronic aids should be used to ensure that chance alone dictates selection. One popular "mechanical" procedure is the lottery method. All cases are numbered; the numbers are written on equal-size objects, such as balls or disks; the objects are thoroughly mixed in a container; and then the requisite number of "cases" is selected one by one. This method is cumbersome and impractical, however, when applied to populations of social scientific interest.[2] In actual practice, social researchers usually draw random samples using a computer program that generates random numbers or selects cases randomly from a computerized list of the population.

KEY POINT

The quality of a sample rests on the procedure for selecting cases; good "representative" samples always involve *random selection*.

Simple Random Sampling

The basic probability sampling design that is incorporated in all of the more elaborate probability sampling designs discussed below is called a **simple random sample**. The defining property of a simple random sample is that every possible *combination* of cases has an equal chance of being included in the sample. For example, in a population of four cases, numbered 1, 2, 3, and 4, there are six possible samples of size 2: (1, 2), (1, 3), (1, 4), (2, 3), (2, 4), and (3, 4). In a simple random sample, each of these pairs of cases would have the same chance of selection. To guarantee this property, two requirements are necessary: (1) a complete list of the population and (2) the random selection of cases.

With the concepts of "random selection" and "simple random sampling" now in mind, we are in a position to examine the principles of probability sampling theory. Although a complete understanding of the theory would require advanced training in statistics, readers can gain a good intuitive grasp of the essential concepts through the following small-scale hypothetical example.[3]

Suppose that you are interested in conducting a study of alcohol consumption on your campus. Your interest perhaps stems from recent reports that problem drinking is increasing among college-age youth. Limited time and resources prevent you from studying the student population as a whole, so you focus instead on all the students who live in your off-campus condominium. There are eight residents in all, which makes it easy to create a list of the target population. You realize that you would not need to draw a sample of such an incredibly small population. But to understand how samples vary, let us look at some characteristics of samples drawn from this imaginary population. Your dependent variable is alcohol consumption, which you measure by administering a questionnaire in which you ask each resident how many drinks he or she consumes on a typical weekend night. (You also tell your respondents to consider one drink a bottle or glass of beer, a glass of wine, a wine cooler, a shot glass of liquor, or a mixed drink.)

The following tabulation contains hypothetical data for the population of eight students:

| Variables | *Ana* | *Bea* | *Cam* | *Dora* | *Ezra* | *Fred* | *Greg* | *Huan* |
	A	B	C	D	E	F	G	H
Gender	F	F	F	F	M	M	M	M
Class standing	U	G	U	G	U	G	U	G
Number of drinks	3	1	0	2	3	4	6	5

Note that, in addition to alcohol consumption, information is given on gender and undergraduate versus graduate student status. There are four females (F) and four males (M) and four undergraduates (U) and four graduate (G) students. These two variables will be considered later.

Characteristics of a population are called **parameters**. For our population of eight students, we are interested in the average (or mean) number of drinks consumed. We determine this parameter by adding up all of the reported drinks (24) and dividing by the number of cases (8), which equals 3.0. In the real research situation, the parameter would not be known, and our task would be to obtain an estimate from a sample of observations. Sample estimates of population parameters are called **statistics**. Just as we calculated the mean number of drinks consumed in the population, we can estimate the population mean by calculating the mean number of drinks consumed in a sample. To get an idea of how such sample estimates will vary, let us examine all possible simple random samples of two students and of four students that could be drawn from the population. By seeing how the sample statistics vary in relation to the population parameter, we also can see the kinds of generalizations about a population that are possible from a single sample.

There are 28 possible combinations of two cases each that can be drawn randomly from eight cases; thus, there are 28 simple random samples of size 2. You can check this for yourself by systematically arranging the possibilities in the following manner: AB, AC . . . AH, BC, BD . . . GH. We have done this for you in Table 6.1, which also gives the mean number of drinks for each combination.

Similarly, there are 70 simple random samples of size 4. To see how the estimates of alcohol consumption will vary from sample to sample, let us calculate the mean number of drinks consumed for each possible sample of size 2 and size 4. Calculating a statistic, such as the mean, for all possible samples of a given size results in a **sampling distribution**. The sampling distributions of the means for samples of size 2 and size 4 are presented in Figure 6.1 and in columns 2 and 4 of Table 6.2. Note first the sample of two cases: Only one combination (BC) yields a sample mean of 0.5 (Bea has 1 drink and Cam has 0, for an average of 0.5); only one combination (CD) has a sample mean of 1.0; three combinations (AC, BD, CE) have sample means of 1.5; and so on. Now, examining samples of four cases, two combinations (ABCD and BCDE) yield sample means of 1.5, two combinations (ABCE and BCDF) yield sample means of 1.75, and so on.

From the sampling distributions one can calculate the probability that any given sample will be selected. (Probabilities, which range from 0 to 1, correspond to percentages. Thus, an event with a probability of .40 is likely to occur 40 percent of the time.) Recall that with simple random sampling, each possible combination of cases is equally likely to be selected. This means that the likelihood, or probability, of selecting any particular combination of two cases (e.g., BC) from the above population will be equal to 1 divided by the total number of combinations (or 1/28 = .036).[4] This is also the probability of drawing a sample with a mean of .5 or of drawing a sample with a mean of 1.0 since each of these means is the result of one and only one combination of two cases. To get the probability of selecting a sample with a mean of 1.5, we simply add the probabilities of each combination that yields a mean of 1.5 (1/28 + 1/28 + 1/28 = .107), which, as you can see, equals the

TABLE 6.1. List of All Possible Samples of Size 2

Combination of cases	Mean number of drinks	Combination of cases	Mean number of drinks
AB (Ana, Bea)	2.0	CE (Cam, Ezra)	1.5
AC (Ana, Cam)	1.5	CF (Cam, Fred)	2.0
AD (Ana, Dora)	2.5	CG (Cam, Greg)	3.0
AE (Ana, Ezra)	3.0	CH (Cam, Huan)	2.5
AF (Ana, Fred)	3.5	DE (Dora, Ezra)	2.5
AG (Ana, Greg)	4.5	DF (Dora, Fred)	3.0
AH (Ana, Huan)	4.0	DG (Dora, Greg)	4.0
BC (Bea, Cam)	0.5	DH (Dora, Huan)	3.5
BD (Bea, Dora)	1.5	EF (Ezra, Fred)	3.5
BE (Bea, Ezra)	2.0	EG (Ezra, Greg)	4.5
BF (Bea, Fred)	2.5	EH (Ezra, Huan)	4.0
BG (Bea, Greg)	3.5	FG (Fred, Greg)	5.0
BH (Bea, Huan)	3.0	FH (Fred, Huan)	4.5
CD (Cam, Dora)	1.0	GH (Greg, Huan)	5.5

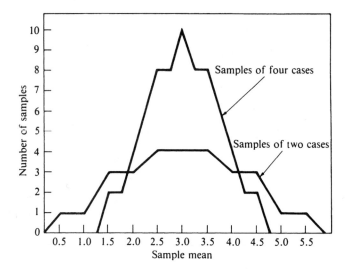

FIGURE 6.1. Frequency distributions of sample means for simple random samples of two cases and four cases drawn from a hypothetical population of eight cases with a mean of 3.0.

number of such combinations (3) over the total (28). The remaining probabilities are given in columns 3 and 5 of Table 6.2. Note that the probability of obtaining a particular sample mean increases as the estimate approaches the actual population mean of 3.0 drinks. By the same token, the more a sample mean deviates from the population mean, the lower its probability of selection.

It is also possible to calculate the probability of obtaining sample estimates within a given range of the population mean. For example, there are 18 samples (count them) of two

TABLE 6.2. **Means and Probabilities of Simple Random Samples of Two Cases and Four Cases Drawn from a Hypothetical Population of Eight Cases with a Mean of 3.0**

SAMPLE MEANS	Sample of two cases		Sample of four cases	
	NUMBER OF SAMPLES	PROBABILITY	NUMBER OF SAMPLES	PROBABILITY
0.50	1	.04		
0.75				
1.00	1	.04		
1.25				
1.50	3	.11	2	.03
1.75			2	.03
2.00	3	.11 ⎫	4	.06 ⎫
2.25			6	.09
2.50	4	.14	8	.11
2.75			8	.11
3.00	4	.14 ⎬ .64	10	.14 ⎬ .89
3.25			8	.11
3.50	4	.14	8	.11
3.75			6	.09
4.00	3	.11 ⎭	4	.06 ⎭
4.25			2	.03
4.50	3	.11	2	.03
4.75				
5.00	1	.04		
5.25				
5.50	1	.04		
Total number of samples	28		70	
Mean of sample means	3.0		3.0	

cases with means between 2.0 and 4.0; thus, the probability of obtaining a sample mean within this range is 18/28 = .64. Similarly, with samples of four cases, the probability of getting a sample mean within the range of 2.0 to 4.0 is 62/70 = .89; and with samples of six cases (not shown), the probability is 1.0 (i.e., all samples have means between 2.0 and 4.0). This illustrates an important principle in sampling theory: The larger the sample, the closer its mean is likely to be to the population mean.

The amount that a given sample statistic deviates from the population parameter it estimates is known as **sampling error**. For example, in our hypothetical population, a sample mean of .5 has a sampling error of 2.5 because this is how much it differs from the known population mean of 3.0. Similarly, a sample mean of 1.5 has a sampling error of 1.5 (3.0 − 1.5 = 1.5). The statistical measure of the "average" of such errors for an entire sampling distribution is called the **standard error**. Using this concept, then, another way of stating the principle about sample size is the larger the sample, the smaller the standard error.

KEY POINT

As sample size increases, the *standard error* (a measure of the "average" sampling error) decreases.

So far, we have demonstrated that knowledge of the sampling distribution of the mean enables one to make the following kinds of statements regarding the accuracy of a sample mean: The probability is .89 that the mean of a randomly selected sample of four cases will deviate from the population mean by 1 or less (i.e., will fall within the range 2.0–4.0). In the above example, the sampling distributions were constructed by calculating means for all possible random samples from a *known* population. In actual research, we select only one sample to estimate an *unknown* population characteristic. The key to being able to make the same kind of statement about sample accuracy in the actual research situation is provided by the mathematical theory behind probability sampling. According to this theory, the sampling distributions of various statistics (such as the mean) form stable, predictable patterns. Consequently, even though the population parameter is not known, the theory indicates *how* sample estimates will be distributed (by specifying the sampling distribution) and provides a statistical formula for calculating the standard error, a measure of *how much* the sample estimates will tend to vary.

More rigorous accounts of sampling theory and sample estimation procedures can be found in the inferential statistics section of most statistics textbooks. In actual research, sample inferences about a population parameter are arrived at in the following manner. From a single sample, drawn randomly:

1. The sample statistic (e.g., the sample mean) is considered the best single estimate of the population parameter (e.g., the population mean).
2. The extent to which the sample statistic tends to deviate from the population parameter, indicated by the standard error, is calculated on the basis of variation within the sample.
3. Theoretical knowledge about the sampling distribution is utilized to attach a probability, or level of confidence, to a calculated range within which the population characteristic is likely to fall.

This range, called a **confidence interval**, is established around the sample statistic. What the confidence interval tells us is that interval estimates obtained with this procedure are likely to contain the population parameter 95 percent of the time. In presenting the results of opinion polls, newspapers and magazines usually give the margin of error for an unstated 95 percent level of confidence; for example, when reporting the percentage of respondents who gave a particular opinion, they may note that the "margin of error is plus or minus 4 percentage points, based on a sample of 750 adults."

KEY POINT
The *confidence interval* indicates the range of values within which the estimated population value is likely to lie. The *level of confidence* is the probability (e.g., 95 percent) that the interval contains the population value.

A major advantage of probability sampling is that the size of the confidence interval (i.e., sample precision), or the amount by which the sample statistic is likely to differ from the population parameter, can be estimated *before* a study is carried out. Recall that the possible error in sample statistics is a function of sample size: The larger the sample, the smaller the standard error. Therefore, one can get a more precise sample estimate by selecting a larger sample. Sample precision also may be increased using a more complex sampling design known as "stratified random sampling."

Stratified Random Sampling

In **stratified random sampling**, the population is first subdivided into two or more mutually exclusive segments, called **strata**, based on categories of one or a combination of relevant variables. Simple random samples then are drawn from each stratum, and these subsamples are joined to form the complete, stratified sample.

To illustrate, let us return to our hypothetical data. Note that the population of eight cases can be broken down into two strata—male and female—according to categories of the variable "gender" or into two strata—undergraduate and graduate—according to categories of the variable "student status." A stratified random sample of four cases could be drawn by randomly selecting an equal proportion of males and females. In other words, one could draw independent random samples of two cases from each stratum, male and female, and then combine them into a single sample. This process would not produce a simple random sample since there are several combinations of cases that are not possible—for example, the combinations of all females (ABCD) or all males (EFGH). There are 36 possible stratified random samples of four cases with equal proportions of males and females. By computing the mean number of drinks consumed for each of these possible samples, we again obtain a sampling distribution of the mean. This distribution can be compared with the sampling distribution based on simple random sampling to demonstrate the effect of stratifying on sample precision.

Table 6.3 presents the sampling distributions for samples of four cases based on simple random sampling, stratified random sampling with gender as the stratification variable, and stratified random sampling with student status as the stratification variable. Note by examining the last two rows of Table 6.3 that, compared with simple random sampling, sampling with gender stratification yields a distribution of sample means that cluster more tightly about the population mean. Thus, it is possible for a stratified sample to yield a better estimate than a simple random sample. In contrast, stratifying by student status offers no such improvement; indeed, the percentage of sample means between 2.5 and 3.5 (i.e., that deviate from the population mean by as little as .5) is lower—44 percent—than in simple random sampling—60 percent.

As these comparisons reveal, stratifying can contribute to sampling efficiency. Whether it does depends on whether the stratifying variable is related to the study variable.

TABLE 6.3. Means of Samples of Four Cases Drawn by Simple Random
Sampling and Stratified Random Sampling with Gender
and Student Status as Stratifying Variables

Sample means	Simple random samples	Samples stratified by gender	Samples stratified by student status
1.50	2		2
1.75	2		
2.00	4	1	2
2.25	6	2	6
2.50	8	5	2
2.75	8	6	2
3.00	10	8	8
3.25	8	6	2
3.50	8	5	2
3.75	6	2	6
4.00	4	1	2
4.25	2		
4.50	2		2
Total number of samples	70	36	36
Mean of sample means	3.0	3.0	3.0
Percentage of sample means between 2.5 and 3.5	60	83	44
Percentage of sample means between 2.0 and 4.0	89	100	89

In our hypothetical population, gender is related to alcohol consumption but student status is not; that is, men tend to drink more than women, whereas undergraduate and graduate students drink about the same amount. Consequently, stratifying by gender increases sample precision but stratifying by student status does not.

Technically speaking, stratifying by variables correlated with the study variable increases the precision of estimates because it systematically controls relevant sources of variability (or heterogeneity) in the population. The effect of this is to eliminate a source of sampling error—for example, the error that could occur if our sample of students contained all men or all women. Thus, when there are differences across strata, stratified sampling ensures that these differences are accounted for and are not free to vary within the sample. In fact, in the extreme instance, when all the variation in the dependent variable is across strata and each stratum is completely homogeneous, a researcher needs to sample only one case per stratum for a perfectly accurate estimate. In our hypothetical population, this would occur if, say, each woman had one drink and each man drank five drinks. The population mean would be 3.0, and a sample of one woman and one man would yield a mean estimate of 3.0 $[(5 + 1)/2 = 3.0]$.

If the stratifying variable is related to the variable under study, a stratified random sample will be more precise and, hence, more efficient than a simple random sample of the same size. But since we also can increase sample precision by increasing sample size, the greater efficiency of stratifying depends on whether the cost of stratifying is low relative to the cost of sampling more cases. Obtaining a stratified sample necessitates classifying cases according to categories of the stratifying variable *prior to drawing the sample.* Therefore, the sampling frame must contain information on the stratifying variable. Otherwise, you cannot draw separate samples from each stratum. Often, however, the information needed to stratify is not available and is either impossible or too costly to obtain, which limits the use of stratified random sampling.

In addition to increasing efficiency, stratified random sampling may be used to guarantee that variable categories with small proportions of cases in the population are adequately represented in the sample. Suppose, for example, that we wanted to examine ethnic differences in alcohol consumption on a campus where 90 percent of the students are white, 5 percent are black, and 5 percent are Asian. A simple random sample of 100 would yield, on the average, 90 whites, 5 blacks, and 5 Asians. However, the number of cases in the latter two sampled groups is so small that statistical estimates derived from them would be unreliable. To get around this problem, we could obtain a stratified random sample in which we select a greater proportion of blacks and Asians for our sample than are found in the population. We might select 40 whites, 30 blacks, and 30 Asians. This is called **disproportionate stratified sampling** because the proportion of cases in each stratum of the sample does not reflect the proportion in the population.

When strata are sampled proportionate to the population composition, each case has an equal probability of being selected and one can generalize directly from sample to population. But with disproportionate sampling, the probability of selection varies from stratum to stratum and one must make a statistical adjustment before estimating population parameters.[5] Disproportionate stratified random sampling still constitutes a probability sample because the probability of case selection is *known.* Furthermore, probability sampling theory applies since the subsamples drawn from each stratum are simple random samples.

Cluster Sampling

Both simple random sampling and stratified random sampling assume that a complete list of the population is available. What do you do, however, when your target population is so large that it is either impossible or impractical to list all its members? The only lists of the U.S. population—income tax forms and census forms filed every 10 years—are confidential and not available to the public. Lists of most city and all state populations simply do not exist, and it would be prohibitively expensive to compile lists of these and other very large populations. In such instances, researchers often are able to obtain a sample in stages, using a method called **cluster sampling**.

In cluster sampling, the population is broken down into groups of cases, called "clusters." The clusters generally consist of natural groupings, such as colleges and churches, or geographic areas, such as states, counties, cities, and blocks. Unlike stratified sampling, which draws cases from each stratum, cluster sampling draws cases only from sampled clusters. To draw a cluster sample, one first selects at random a sample of clusters. Then one obtains a list of all cases within each selected cluster. If all the cases in each sampled cluster are included in the sample, the design is called a *single-stage cluster sample* in that sampling occurs once—at the cluster level. More frequently, cluster sampling involves sampling at two or more steps or stages, hence the term **multistage cluster sampling**. An example of a two-stage cluster sample would be a random selection of 4-year colleges (first stage), followed by a random selection of students within each sampled college (second stage). The sampling units in the first stage of a multistage sample are termed **primary sampling units**; units in the second stage are termed *secondary sampling units*, and so on.

Whereas stratified random sampling is used either to increase sample precision or to provide a sufficient number of cases in small strata, the principal reason for cluster sampling is to reduce the costs of data collection. In face-to-face interview studies of large, widely scattered populations, two major costs are interviewer travel and the listing of population elements. Simple random and stratified random methods produce isolated interviews at dispersed localities, which can create substantial travel costs to reach respondents. However, clustering concentrates interviews within fewer and smaller geographic areas, thereby spreading the travel costs over several cases and reducing the costs of any one interview.

Since the listing of population elements is a prerequisite for simple random or stratified random methods, clustering also can reduce costs by limiting the compilation of lists of cases to selected clusters rather than compiling a list of the entire population. Moreover, multistage cluster sampling may be the only viable method of drawing a probability sample when an exhaustive list of population elements is unavailable or impractical to create. Often, when this occurs, it is possible to obtain lists of subpopulations (clusters) into which the population is naturally grouped or can be subdivided. For example, although a single list of all 8th-grade students does not exist and would be difficult and extremely costly to compile, a complete and accurate list of public and private schools in the United States is maintained by Quality Education Data, Inc. The NELS used this database to draw a two-stage cluster sample for the 1988 base-year survey. From the nearly 40,000 schools nationwide, the NELS obtained a sample of 1057 schools; then, from each participating school, 26 students were randomly selected (Spencer et al., 1990). (Box 6.2 provides an example of a multistage sampling design for a national survey of the adult population.)

Multistage sample designs may involve either simple random sampling or stratified random sampling at each stage of the design. In other words, one can stratify clusters just as one stratifies individual cases. The NELS stratified clusters because schools were divided into several strata according to four variables: school type (public, Catholic private, other private), region of the country, urbanicity (whether the school's location was urban, suburban, or rural), and percentage minority. A number of schools were then selected within each stratum.

KEY POINT
Stratified sampling increases efficiency by reducing sampling error (provided that the strata are related to the study variable). *Multistage cluster sampling* increases efficiency by reducing costs.

One problem with cluster sampling is that natural clusters often vary considerably in the numbers of cases they contain. This, in fact, was true of the schools in the NELS. There are two ways of handling this problem to reduce potential error. First, you can stratify

BOX 6.2 Sampling Design for a Nationwide Survey

Survey organizations such as the Survey Research Center at the University of Michigan use multistage cluster sampling to conduct nationwide surveys. The steps involved in selecting the Survey Research Center's national sample in the 1970s are roughly diagrammed in the accompanying figure. The steps are numbered and labeled according to the type of unit selected.

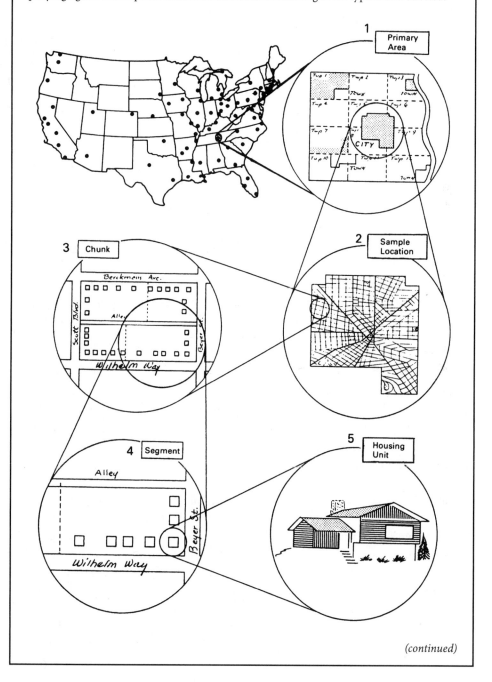

(continued)

(continued)

Step 1. The United States is divided into *primary areas* consisting of counties, groups of counties, or metropolitan areas. These areas are stratified by region, and a proportionate stratified sample of 74 areas is selected.

Step 2. The 74 areas are divided into *locations* such as towns, cities, and residual areas. After these have been identified and stratified by population size, a proportionate stratified sample of locations is drawn within each area.

Step 3. All sample locations are divided into *chunks*. A chunk is a geographic area with identifiable boundaries such as city streets, roads, streams, and county lines. After division into chunks, a random sample of chunks is drawn.

Step 4. Interviewers scout each sample chunk and record addresses and estimates of the number of housing units at each address. They then divide the chunks into smaller units called *segments*, and a random sample of segments is selected.

Step 5. Within each sample segment, either all or a sample of the housing units, usually about four, are chosen for a given study. Finally, for every housing unit in the sample, interviewers randomly choose one respondent from among those eligible, which ordinarily consists of all U.S. citizens 18 years of age or older.

Source: Survey Research Center, 1976. *Interviewer's Manual*, rev. ed., p. 36. Ann Arbor: Institute for Social Research. Used by permission.

clusters by population size. In this way, relatively few clusters with extremely large populations can be sampled from a separate stratum to guarantee that they are represented in the sample. Otherwise, with simple random sampling one runs the risk of not selecting clusters that account for a major proportion of the population. Imagine, for example, drawing a cluster sample, with counties as the primary sampling units, of the population of Nevada, in which more than 80 percent of the people reside in 2 of the state's 16 counties. Any sample that excludes these 2 counties would be a biased sample of Nevada residents. Yet the chances are high that neither of the state's 2 largest counties would be included in a simple random sample of counties (e.g., the probability that neither would be selected is 55 percent in a sample of 4 counties and 23 percent in a sample of 8 counties). The best procedure, therefore, would be to stratify by county size, placing the 2 most populous counties in the topmost stratum, and then sample 100 percent from this stratum (i.e., select both counties).

When clusters vary in size, another common solution is to make the selection of clusters or cases within clusters proportionate to the size of the cluster. This method, called **probability proportionate to size sampling**, was applied to the selection of schools in the NELS. One way this method works is to assign each cluster a probability of selection proportionate to the number of cases in the cluster. Thus, a school with 1000 students would be twice as likely to be selected as a school with 500 students. If an equal number of students is selected from each school, then each student in the population has an equal probability of being selected.[6]

Table 6.4 compares multistage cluster sampling with stratified random sampling. Although cluster samples are more cost efficient, they are less precise, size for size, than

TABLE **6.4. Comparison of Stratified and Multistage Cluster Sampling**

	Stratified random sampling	*Multistage cluster sampling*
Purpose	Reduce margin of error; sample small subsets of population	Reduce costs
Population breakdown	By variable categories (strata)	By geographical units or natural groupings (clusters)
Sampling	Within every stratum	Within randomly selected clusters
Optimally efficient	When there are large differences between homogeneous strata	When there are small differences between heterogeneous clusters

either simple random or stratified random samples. The latter designs have a single source of sampling error; however, there are sampling errors associated with each stage of a multistage cluster sample. For example, in a two-stage cluster sample of college students at 4-year colleges, the sample of 4-year colleges would represent the population of colleges within a range of error, and the sample of students within a selected college represents all students in the college within a range of error. The sampling error in the total sample is thus compounded and can be large relative to the error produced by one simple random selection.

In stratified sampling, efficiency increases to the extent that strata are internally homogeneous; for example, the drinking behavior of women is similar and the drinking behavior of men is similar. By contrast, the ideal in cluster sampling is for clusters to be internally *heterogeneous* compared with the differences between clusters. Because you are selecting a *sample* of clusters, you essentially want each cluster to be a replica of the population. But this is rarely the case. In fact, there generally is much less variability (hence sampling error) within than across natural clusters. For example, residents in a single block are likely to be fairly homogeneous with respect to income, but quite different in terms of average income from the residents in another block. For this reason, one way of increasing efficiency is to select more clusters and fewer elements within the clusters. By increasing the number of clusters, sampling error is reduced at the stage that is subject to the greatest error.[7]

Although increasing the number of clusters generally decreases sampling error, it also increases the cost of cluster sampling. A greater number of clusters means more widely scattered interviews, hence more time and expense invested in travel and more time and expense required for listing elements within the selected clusters. Reducing costs is the reason for cluster sampling. Consequently, researchers are likely to resolve this dilemma by simply selecting as many clusters as they can afford (Babbie, 1995:215).

Systematic Sampling

Before the computer age—before random number programs and computerized lists became available—social scientists often used a technique called "systematic sampling" to closely approximate simple random sampling. Simple random sampling requires not only a complete sampling frame, such as a list, but also the numbering of population elements. (In effect, one selects random numbers that correspond to case numbers.) A list in a computer file meets both of these requirements. But if you only have an unnumbered hard-copy list of the population and the list is long, such as a university student directory, it is much easier to draw a systematic sample than a simple random sample.

Systematic sampling consists of selecting every Kth (e.g., 15th or 20th) case from a complete list or file of the population, starting with a randomly chosen case from the first K cases on the list. Such a procedure has two requirements: a sampling interval (K) and a random start (Sudman, 1976). The **sampling interval** is merely the ratio of the number of cases in the population to the desired sample size. A *random start* refers to the process of randomly selecting the initial case between 1 and K. For example, suppose you wanted to draw a sample of 100 students from the 2500 students listed in the campus directory. Dividing 2500 by 100, you obtain a sampling interval of 25. You would then select at random a number between 1 and 25 and, starting with that number, select every 25th student thereafter. Suppose the random number turns out to be 19. Your sample then would consist of cases numbered 19, 44, 69, 94, 119 . . . 2494.

Although each case in a systematic sample has an equal chance of being selected, each *combination* of cases does not. (There are only 25 possible combinations in this example.) Technically speaking, therefore, a systematic sample is not the equivalent of a simple random sample. It is a random sample, however, and in practice researchers regard it as a close approximation of a simple random sample.

A potential problem as well as a potential advantage with systematic sampling arises from the fact that most available lists are not random but, rather, are ordered in some fashion, such as alphabetical or by rank, age, or size of unit. The danger is that the available population listing may have a periodic or cyclical pattern that corresponds to the sampling interval. A classic example is a World War II study in which a 1-of-10 systematic sample of soldiers was drawn. The list from which the sample was drawn, however, was ordered by squads of 10 soldiers, with each squad ordered by rank (sergeants, corporals, privates). When the sample was drawn, the interval of 10 corresponded to all the sergeants on the list.

Fortunately, the danger of periodicity in a systematic sample is actually quite small. More often, an ordered list is advantageous because it provides an implicitly stratified sample; if the list is ordered in terms of a variable correlated with the study variable, this will increase precision. For example, organizational size—in terms of either assets or number of employees—is a key variable in studies of organizations. Therefore, if a list of business establishments is ordered by number of employees, a systematic sample will implicitly stratify the businesses by size.

Nonprobability Sampling

Nonprobability sampling refers to processes of case selection other than random selection. Without random selection, nonprobability samples have two basic weaknesses: (1) they do not control for investigator bias in the selection of units and (2) their pattern of variability cannot be predicted from probability sampling theory, thereby making it impossible to calculate sampling error or to estimate sample precision. However, although one should be mindful of these weaknesses, it would be a mistake to rule out nonprobability sampling. In many instances, this form of sampling either is more appropriate and practical than probability sampling or is the only viable means of case selection.

1. Consider the situation in which very few cases can be included in the sample. For an investigator doing an intensive study in which the unit of analysis is a city, corporation, or university, the expense of studying more than one or a few cases would be prohibitive. Similarly, the length of interviews in an intensive interview study may limit an investigator to a relatively small number of cases. As we have seen, probability sampling is less reliable the smaller the sample. With extremely small samples of one or few cases, generalization from sample to population essentially becomes a matter of judgment. The selection of cases is therefore better left to expert judgment (in other words, nonrandom selection) than to the whims of chance (Wallis and Roberts, 1956:117–18).

2. When studying past events, an archaeologist or historian often finds only a fraction of relevant materials available or accessible. Similarly, in contemporary societies, certain individuals or institutions may refuse to cooperate in an inquiry. Under these circumstances, a researcher must either accept a nonprobability method of case selection or abandon the study altogether.

3. In the early stages of investigating a problem, when the objective is to become more informed about the problem itself, probability sampling simply may be unnecessary. It will suffice to select a range of cases nonrandomly without concern for precise statistical generalization.

4. If the population itself contains few cases or if an adequate sampling frame cannot be obtained or constructed, there is no point in considering probability sampling. With small populations (say, fewer than 100), each case should be studied in its own right in comparison with all others. If the population is unknown or not readily identifiable, as in many sociological studies of deviance, sampling generally will consist of studying any and all identifiable and cooperative units.

Because nonprobability sampling is a residual category pertaining to any method of *non*random case selection, the various types of nonprobability samples are far ranging and less precisely defined than the probability sampling designs examined in the previous section. With this in mind, let us now examine three primary types of nonprobability samples: convenience, purposive, and quota.

KEY POINT
Probability sampling is preferred over *nonprobability sampling* because it controls for selection bias and allows for the calculation of sampling error; however, it is not always necessary or feasible.

Convenience Sampling

In this form of sampling (also called "haphazard," "fortuitous," and "accidental" sampling), researchers simply select a requisite number from cases that are conveniently available. In terms of the study of campus alcohol consumption, you might decide to (1) ask a professor for permission to administer a questionnaire to all the students in his or her classes, (2) interview whoever comes down the dormitory hall when you happen to be there, or (3) find a convenient spot in the campus pub from which to observe behavior. Television stations and newspapers wanting to tap public opinion on specific issues may interview conveniently available commuters, shoppers, store clerks, and others (Chein, 1981). Such methods of case selection are easy, quick, and inexpensive. If the research is at an early stage and generalizability is not an issue, then they may be perfectly appropriate. However, convenience sampling is a matter of catch-as-catch-can. There is no way of determining to whom, other than the sample itself, the results apply. Consequently, such samples should be avoided whenever the goal is to make inferences about a population.

Purposive Sampling

In this form of sampling, an investigator relies on his or her expert judgment to select units that are representative or "typical" of the population. The general strategy is to identify important sources of variation in the population and then to select a sample that reflects this variation. One might select a single unit or subpopulation that is thought to be typical of the population in important respects or select a few units that correspond to key population differences. For example, in his study of "community ideology"—the values and beliefs associated with different kinds of communities—David Hummon (1990) selected residents of four distinct communities in northern California: a central city, an upper-class suburb, a working-class suburb, and a rural small town. Because the type of community in which people lived was likely to affect their community ideology, this was a crucial variable in Hummon's study. He therefore wanted to be sure that it was represented adequately in his sample. Furthermore, in selecting the specific communities, Hummon carefully examined census data to identify typical areas or towns and to avoid populations that contained relatively large proportions of aged, minority, or institutionalized persons. Such purposive sampling fit the aims of the study extremely well because Hummon's interest was not in estimating the distribution of various beliefs about communities within a particular population but in identifying the key elements in various community ideologies.

Another purposive sampling technique, applied to election forecasting, is the selection of "barometer" states or precincts that have served as reliable predictors of overall election returns in previous years. Still another is the selection of deviant or extreme cases to discover why they deviate from the norm. Finally, one may select both typical and extreme instances within the same study. For example, if one were testing an innovation in schools, it would be wise to investigate at least one instance of the "typical school" in a particular city (or state or nation) and at least one instance of the best and worst problem schools (T. D. Cook and Campbell, 1979:76). If comparable results were found in all three instances, one would have a reasonably firm basis for inferring that the effect applies to the full range of schools.

As with any nonprobability method of case selection, purposive sampling for heterogeneity and/or typicality is an unacceptable substitute for probability sampling when precise and accurate generalizations are required. However, with studies of more limited scope or in situations that preclude random selection, purposive sampling is an acceptable alternative. It generally offers much stronger, less tenuous inferences than convenience sampling, although such inferences are very much dependent on a researcher's expert judgment. The major weakness of purposive sampling is that making an informed selection of cases requires considerable knowledge of the population before the sample is drawn.

Quota Sampling

Quota sampling is a form of purposive sampling that bears a superficial resemblance to stratified random sampling. Like the latter, quota sampling divides the population into relevant strata such as age, gender, and race. Once the strata are established, each interviewer is given quotas for each category of people that he or she is supposed to interview within a specified geographic area. For example, an interviewer covering an area of Boston might be assigned quotas of one man under the age of 30, three men 30 and older, three unemployed women, and two employed women. To fill the quotas, the interviewer is free to choose anyone who meets the quota requirements.

The difference between quota sampling and stratified random sampling lies precisely in how cases are selected once quotas have been set. In stratified random sampling, the requisite number of cases within each stratum must be drawn by simple random sampling. But in quota sampling, the quota of cases within a stratum may be filled in whatever way the investigator chooses. Each stratum in a quota sample thus constitutes a convenience sample of the corresponding stratum of the population (Chein, 1981:426); moreover, the total sample is also a convenience sample, albeit one that resembles the population with respect to some key characteristics.

Quota categories ordinarily are chosen so that the sample will be representative of the population on important characteristics. By agreeing with the population on these characteristics, the method assumes that the sample will be like the population in other ways as well. Experience has shown, however, that this is an unsafe assumption. Interviewers allowed to self-select respondents are subject to several kinds of bias. If left to their own devices, they will interview their friends in excessive proportions; they also have been known to fill quotas by concentrating on areas where there are large numbers of potential respondents, such as transportation or entertainment centers, college campuses, and business districts (Chein, 1981:426). When quotas are filled by home visits, interviewers tend to select houses that are perceived as more attractive or as housing persons with relatively high incomes (Carter, Troldahl, and Schuneman, 1963). The potential biases in such procedures are obvious: Friends are likely to resemble closely the interviewers themselves; people who gravitate to population centers may differ sharply from those who do not; and a preference for nicer neighborhoods and homes will almost certainly create a strong socioeconomic bias. Thus, representative quotas on some characteristics do not ensure representation on others.

For some years before the election forecast failure in 1948 (see Box 6.1), quota sampling was the predominant sampling design in opinion surveys. Eventually, however, probability sampling became the standard for sample surveys, and quota samples are no longer acceptable "when important actions may be taken as a result of the survey estimates" (Brick, 2011:883). Yet, despite its weaknesses, quota sampling is still popular in many countries

(Brick, 2011) and continues to be used by some market research and opinion survey organizations because of two main advantages (Kalton, 1983). First, unlike probability sampling, there is no need to construct a sampling frame for selecting respondents. Second, whereas probability sampling requires that interviewers make several call-backs, if necessary, to contact predesignated respondents who are not at home, call-backs are unnecessary in a quota sample. The interviewer must simply find any eligible person according to the relevant quota criteria. For these two reasons, interviewing can be completed more quickly, more easily, and at much lower cost in quota sampling studies. To reduce the hazards of the quota technique, investigators have introduced tight geographic controls, specifying the section of the city, block, and even household where respondents may be selected. This will not eliminate sample biases entirely, but it does refine quota sampling to the point that it "is clearly superior to loose judgment or convenience samples" (Sudman, 1976:200).

Other Sampling Designs

In addition to the foregoing "pure" forms, investigators have developed a variety of other sampling techniques and designs. Each of these methods addresses a recurring problem in social research: what to do when research purposes require the rigorous, systematic selection of cases but available resources or other practical problems preclude the use of conventional probability sampling designs.

Consider, for example, the Chicago Homeless Study (Rossi et al., 1987; Rossi, 1989), which attempted to estimate the composition and size of Chicago's homeless population. Because of the difficulties in conducting empirical research on the homeless population, estimates of the extent of homelessness vary widely and knowledge of the conditions that produce it is minimal. Conventional probability sampling in surveys assumes "that persons can be enumerated and sampled within their customary dwelling unit"; however, this assumption fails by any definition of the homeless. For the Chicago study, therefore, the investigators devised a strategy that sampled persons from nondwelling units at times of maximum separation between homeless individuals and those with homes. The sampling design consisted of two complementary probability samples: (1) a systematic sample of persons spending the night in more than 20 shelters provided for homeless persons and (2) a one-stage, stratified cluster sample of the 19,409 census blocks within the Chicago city limits. Blocks were stratified by the expected number of homeless to be found on each block, according to police estimates. Within each selected block, between the hours of 1:00 AM and 6:00 AM, interviewers conducted thorough searches of every conceivable place, including alleys, hallways, roofs, basements, and parked cars. All persons encountered were first given a short screening interview to determine if they were homeless. If so, the person was given a 15- to 20-minute interview.[8]

John Watters and Patrick Biernacki (1989) devised a different strategy for sampling another "hidden" population—injecting drug users. This group is at high risk for the transmission of the HIV that causes AIDS. Because of the clandestine nature of illicit drug use, members of this target population are difficult to locate. One option rejected by Watters and Biernacki was the use of a convenience sample of injecting drug users enrolled in methadone maintenance treatment programs. Although this option would have provided easy access to some of the target population, there was reason to believe that persons in methadone clinics were a biased sample of drug users who differed in many ways from those users outside the clinics.[9] The sampling strategy they decided on, which they called "targeted sampling," contained several steps: (1) through observation and the use of several sources of information, they determined which neighborhoods had the highest concentrations of drug users and drug-related activity; (2) on the basis of intensive observation and interaction with people in these areas, they identified potential respondents; and (3) they established field sites in each area and developed specific plans for recruitment. During the course of the study, Watters and Biernacki were careful to select adequate numbers of particular groups of respondents and were sensitive to the effects of time and field site location on recruitment.

Combined Probability and Nonprobability Sampling

To reduce the costs associated with probability sampling, probability and nonprobability sampling may be combined in one design. This is possible whenever sampling is carried out in stages (Chein, 1981:438–39). Cases can be selected according to nonprobability procedures at one stage and by probability procedures at another. Two combinations are common in social research. The first involves multistage probability sampling of clusters, with a quota sampling of individual respondents at the final stage. Thus, one might "select a probability sample of counties in a state; within each of these counties, a probability sample of neighborhoods; and within each of the selected neighborhoods, a quota sample controlled for, say, age and sex" (Chein, 1981:438). Although it is sometimes called "probability sampling with quotas," such a design produces, strictly speaking, a *non*probability (quota) sample—with geographic restrictions that sharply reduce interviewer selection bias.

The second combination reverses the first strategy by drawing a probability sample of cases within a nonprobability (purposive) sample of areas. For example, in their study of maternal leave policies, Kelly and Dobbin (1999) collected information on the history of personnel policies from 279 organizations. All the establishments were located in three states: California, New Jersey, and Virginia. Within each state, they randomly selected organizations from 13 sectors or types of establishments with 50 or more workers; however, the states themselves formed a purposive national sample, carefully "selected for their varying legal environments" (Kelly and Dobbin, 1999:475). With this design, mathematical sampling theory applies to inferences from each probability sample to its respective sector and state population, although more risky investigator judgment must be used in making generalizations to all organizations nationwide.

Referral Sampling

Another set of techniques has been developed for sampling target populations that comprise small subgroups of the larger population (see Sudman and Kalton, 1986; Sudman, Sirken, and Cowan, 1988): for example, users of a particular service or product, members of a minority ethnic group that is widely dispersed in a larger population, laid-off workers, or persons with AIDS. If resources are plentiful and members of the target population are readily identifiable, probability sampling can be carried out simply by choosing a large enough fraction of the larger population and screening for members of the target population. However, extensive screening is costly and time-consuming, and it is possible to miss persons because they are incorrectly identified.

Often, the sampling technique devised to handle these problems utilizes some form of referral, wherein respondents who are initially contacted are asked to supply the names and addresses of members of the target population. In **network sampling**, respondents initially contacted in screening a probability sample of the larger population are asked to identify members of the target population who are socially linked to the respondent (e.g., relative, neighbor, co-worker, friend). In a study of male Vietnam veterans, for instance, George Rothbart, Michelle Fine, and Seymour Sudman (1982) first selected respondents by screening the larger population for eligible persons. Each respondent to a screening call was then asked if he or she had a son, brother, or nephew who was a veteran. The sample of 1011 consisted of 535 veterans who were directly contacted and 476 veteran kin who were nominated in the initial screening process. Since veterans living within initially contacted households comprised only 6.2 percent of the larger population, a sample of 1011 would have required 16,439 interviews without network sampling. With network sampling, however, the number of screening interviews was slightly more than half this total—8698. Thus, the major advantage of this technique is a reduction in screening costs. On the other hand, the final probability sample creates unequal selection probabilities that increase sampling error and that must be taken into account in the analysis, and failures by informants to identify members of the target population may result in bias.

Another referral technique, called **snowball sampling**, uses a process of chain referral: When members of the target population are located, they are asked to provide names and addresses of other members of the target population, who are then contacted and asked to name others, and so on. A basic assumption of snowball sampling is that members of the target population often know each other. This technique has been used to create sampling frames (Sudman and Kalton, 1986) and is sometimes associated with probability sampling (Goodman, 1961), but most applications involve nonprobability methods of selection. For example, D. Michael Lindsay (2008) used snowball sampling to examine the role of public leaders and elite actors in the American evangelicalism movement. Initially, he interviewed 157 religious and nonprofit leaders from a diverse group of organizations within the movement; then, at the end of each interview, he asked these informants to identify other leaders who shared their religious commitments. Thus, with the help of the early informants, he contacted and interviewed a total sample of 360 elites.

Patrick Biernacki and Dan Waldorf (1981:144) note that snowball sampling is particularly applicable to studies of deviant behavior, where "moral, legal, or social sensitivities surrounding the behavior in question . . . pose some serious problems for locating and contacting potential respondents." In these studies, members of the target population are often socially invisible by virtue of their illicit, clandestine activities. Their characteristics, therefore, are unknown, and drawing a probability sample is virtually impossible. Often the best that one can do is to use all available means to find eligible respondents and start referral chains. The quality of the sample ultimately depends on a researcher's ability to develop initial contacts and referral chains that represent a range of characteristics in the target population.

Factors Affecting Choice of Sampling Design

Now that we have examined the basic sampling designs, let us look more closely at some of the factors that enter into a researcher's selection of an appropriate design. Which sampling design is adopted depends on several preliminary considerations:

1. What is the stage of research?
2. How will the data be used?
3. What are the available resources for drawing the sample?
4. How will the data be collected?

As you will see, these considerations are interrelated and vary in their relative importance in affecting the choice of a sampling design.

Stage of Research and Data Use

The first two considerations—stage of research and data use—dictate how accurate the sample must be as a description of the population (Sudman, 1976). Accuracy is least important in the exploratory phases of research, when the goal is to discover interesting patterns and generate hypotheses for later study. In fact, in these circumstances, generalizing to a specified population and estimating sample precision are usually unimportant or irrelevant. A researcher often must rely on his or her judgment in drawing a sample and may end up selecting cases because of availability or willingness to participate in the research; therefore, convenience or purposive sampling is appropriate.

Accuracy would appear to be most important in large-scale fact-finding studies that provide input for major policy decisions. Perhaps the best example of this is the aforementioned CPS. The CPS is the only up-to-date source of information on a number of important characteristics of the total population—providing, for example, monthly estimates of unemployment and employment. As Seymour Sudman (1976:3) notes, "major government economic and welfare programs are influenced by changes of a few tenths of a percent in CPS data from month to month." Consequently, a very large (approximately 60,000) and carefully controlled probability sample is necessary to guarantee a high degree of precision.

The desired level of precision in most studies lies somewhere between exploratory data gathering and the CPS. The important point here is that a researcher must have some sense of how good the sample must be to meet the objectives of the research. For example, if you need to assess opinions about student government among students at your school for the purpose of documenting support for government reforms, a haphazard, poor-quality sample would be inappropriate. You would need to make sure that the sample is adequate for the task of making reasonably accurate generalizations about the student population. However, if you merely wanted to get some sense of the variability in opinions about student government for a class project, a small-scale convenience sample would suffice.

Available Resources

If sample accuracy were the sole criterion, selecting an appropriate sampling design would be a simple matter of using the procedure that yields the smallest margin of error. However, accuracy ultimately must be balanced against cost. Available resources such as time, money, materials, and personnel place limitations on how cases can be selected. The primary reason for multistage cluster sampling, as we have seen, is that it reduces time and expense resulting from interviewer travel and the compilation of necessary case listings. Therefore, some form of this design is recommended for all large-scale surveys. Because it requires less time, systematic sampling sometimes is used in lieu of simple random sampling. And the only viable rationale for quota sampling similarly rests on critical savings in time and expense in comparison with probability sampling.

For a student doing unfunded research, such comparisons probably seem irrelevant. The underlying message, however, is that one should make efficient use of available resources in designing one's sample. The sampling design should be appropriate for available resources, but lack of funds should not be used as an excuse for drawing a haphazard, low-quality sample. As a general rule, one should define the target population to fit the scope of the study; if the study is small enough, a well-designed and executed sample is possible with limited resources.

Method of Data Collection

A common impression of sampling is that it is only a tool of survey researchers. Social scientists who employ the other major forms of data collection (experimentation, field research, and documentary research) have been seen as having a peripheral interest in sampling. In truth, however, all researchers must deal with case selection. The four data-collection strategies simply handle the issue of sampling in different ways. As you will see in subsequent chapters, convenience sampling is the rule in experiments, which tend to use small samples drawn from readily available populations. Some form of probability sampling is found in most surveys, purposive or judgmental sampling typifies field research, and—to the extent that the population is definable—probability sampling often is used in the analysis of available data.

Factors Determining Sample Size

Having carefully defined the target population, obtained a good sampling frame, and come up with an appropriate sampling design, a researcher finally must decide on an adequate sample size. As with the choice of a sampling design, several interrelated factors affect the decision about sample size: (1) heterogeneity of the population, (2) desired precision, (3) type of sampling design, (4) available resources, and (5) number of breakdowns planned in data analysis. The most sophisticated research applications enter these factors into mathematical equations for determining sample size. Although such technical matters are largely beyond the scope of this book, understanding some of the statistical sampling theory underlying sample size considerations is important. The few mathematical principles that we introduce in the following discussion apply directly to simple random sampling. However, they also apply, in a more complex fashion than we discuss, to other forms of probability sampling and, in both a logical and an intuitive sense, to nonprobability sampling designs.

Population Heterogeneity

Heterogeneity refers to the degree of dissimilarity (and, conversely, homogeneity to the degree of similarity) among cases with respect to a particular characteristic. In general, the more heterogeneous the population with respect to the characteristic being studied, the more cases required to yield a reliable sample estimate. The logic of this principle can be seen by considering the extremes: If all cases were exactly alike, a sample of one case would suffice; and if no two cases were alike on a given characteristic, only a complete census could satisfactorily represent the population.

The best statistical measure of population heterogeneity for a quantitative variable is the **standard deviation**, conventionally symbolized by the Greek letter sigma (σ). There is a direct link between this measure and the concept of standard error, introduced earlier in our discussion of probability sampling theory. The standard error, recall, indicates the degree of error in a sample estimate (the "average" amount by which a sample estimate deviates from the population value it estimates). The formula used to calculate the standard error is $\sigma/\sqrt{N}$, that is, the standard deviation divided by the square root of the sample size N. From this formula one can see that the standard error is directly related to the heterogeneity of the population as measured by σ and is inversely related to sample size. Thus, the greater the heterogeneity of the population, the larger the sample necessary to achieve a given level of precision.

KEY POINT
As heterogeneity, or variation, of a variable increases, the standard error increases.

Desired Precision

Technically speaking, *precision* refers to the degree of variability or error in a sample estimate, hence to the standard error. The concept of "precision" is perhaps best conveyed in terms of the size of the confidence interval used to estimate a population value. Thus, it is more precise to say that the average number of drinks consumed is likely to fall between 2.0 and 4.0 than to say that the average is likely to fall between 1.0 and 5.0. For a given confidence level (say, 95 percent), the size of the confidence interval is directly related to the standard error; that is, the smaller the standard error, the smaller the confidence interval and the *more* precise the sample estimate. Of course, the larger the sample, the smaller the standard error. Therefore, it follows that the larger the sample, the greater the precision of the sample estimate.

Two facts about this relationship are especially noteworthy because they defy intuition to a certain extent. First, ordinarily it is the absolute size of the sample rather than the proportion of the population sampled that determines precision. As long as the population is relatively large, the proportion of the population sampled has a negligible effect on precision. For example, in 2010 the population of Vermont was a little more than 625,000 and the population of Massachusetts was more than 6.5 million. Now, if one were to take a simple random sample of 2000 in each of these states, the sample proportion of the total population would be about 1 of every 300 persons in Vermont and about 1 of every 3000 persons in Massachusetts. Yet, based on these samples, an estimate (say, of average income) would be just as precise for Massachusetts as for Vermont.

We can get a mathematical understanding of this relationship by reexamining the formula for the standard error. Although the formula given above shows that the standard error is determined only by the standard deviation and sample size, this formula actually applies to populations of theoretically infinite size. For finite populations, the formula should be multiplied by a correction factor equal to $\sqrt{1-f}$, where f is the **sampling fraction**, or the proportion of the population included in the sample (Kish, 1965:43–44). Note, however, that if the sampling fraction is very near zero, then the correction factor becomes $\sqrt{1}$, or 1, which has no effect on the standard error. In most practical examples, the population is so much larger than the sample that f is extremely small—near zero—and the correction factor can be ignored. For example, with a sample of 2000, $f = .0032$ for Vermont and .0003 for Massachusetts. Only with small populations would we expect f to be much larger than zero; however, for a small population, a small f implies a small sample size, and it is the latter that has the greater impact on the standard error.

Although precision is governed primarily by the absolute numerical size of the sample rather than by the proportion of the population sampled, the sample need not be enormous in size to yield very precise results. This is the second crucial fact about precision and sample size. The sampling error tends to be quite small for a sample of size 2000 to 3000, and increasing the sample size beyond this number decreases the error by so little that it usually is not worth the additional cost.

The mathematical explanation for this once again can be found in the standard error formula. Note that the standard error goes down as the *square root* of the sample size goes up. Because of the square root function, each time we wish to decrease the standard error by one-half we must increase the sample size fourfold. At this rate, the precision gained with increased sample size reaches a point of minute, diminishing returns after a few thousand cases. Consider, for example, how sample size affects the standard error of a percentage, such as the estimated percentage of the vote a candidate will receive in an election. With two candidates and an evenly split vote, the standard error will be 5.0 percent for a sample size of 100. This error decreases to 2.5 percent when the sample reaches 400 and to 1.0 percent when the sample reaches 2500, as Table 6.5 shows. To get the error down to 0.5 percent we would need a sample size of 10,000.

TABLE 6.5. **Standard Error of a Percentage of 50 Percent, Broken down by Sample Size***

Sample size	Standard error (%)
100	5.0
400	2.5
2500	1.0
10,000	0.5

*Standard errors are smaller for percentages greater than or less than 50 percent.

Readers should now begin to understand how election forecasters can make accurate predictions using samples of a few thousand of millions of voters. The huge size of the population has no effect on the precision of sample estimates. And a sample size of 2000 to 3000 is large enough to predict accurately all but the closest elections.

KEY POINT
The margin of sampling error in a sample estimate nearly always depends on the absolute size of the sample and *not* on the size of the sample relative to the population.

We hasten to add that 2000 to 3000 should not be regarded as *the* standard size for reliable sample results. Not only does sample size depend on factors other than precision, but also necessary levels of precision vary widely from one study to the next. At one extreme, the CPS requires a sample of some 60,000 housing units, so that "a change of 0.2 percentage point in the unemployment rate [is] significant at a 90-percent confidence level" (U.S. Bureau of Labor Statistics, 2016a). At the other extreme, 30 cases generally is regarded as minimally adequate for statistical data analysis, although most social researchers would probably recommend at least 100.

Sampling Design

The type of sampling design also affects decisions about sample size. Recall that one way of increasing precision other than selecting a larger sample is to use stratified rather than simple random sampling. In other words, for the same level of precision, a stratified random sample requires fewer cases than a simple random sample. A cluster sample, however, requires a somewhat larger number of cases for precision equal to that of a simple random sample. A nonmathematical explanation for these comparisons rests on the concept of "heterogeneity."

Remember that stratified random sampling provides greater sampling efficiency (or precision) when the stratifying variable is related to the variable one is estimating. If it is related, much of the variation or heterogeneity in the estimated variable resides in differences between the strata, and each stratum tends to be relatively homogeneous. With respect to alcohol consumption, for example, there is much less variability among men or among women than between men and women. By sampling every stratum, the effect of stratified random sampling is to eliminate this *between* source of heterogeneity, leaving only the variation within the strata. And because the strata are relatively homogeneous, the standard error of each stratum is small in comparison with the population as a whole, and stratified sampling produces a smaller margin of error than a simple random sample of the same size.

Although cluster sampling has the advantage of low cost, it lacks efficiency in precision. In two-stage cluster sampling, for example, there is variability both between and within the clusters. By taking a sample of clusters, the "between source" of heterogeneity that was eliminated in stratified sampling is still present. If the variability between clusters tends to be large compared with the variability within the clusters, then the sampling error could be considerable, depending on how many clusters are selected. (For this reason, we want clusters to be heterogeneous compared with differences between the clusters—the opposite of the strategy in stratified sampling.) Furthermore, each stage in a multistage cluster design contributes a source of variability or error to the total sample; consequently, the more stages, the larger the total sampling error tends to be and the larger the sample required for a given level of precision.

Available Resources

Each individual case requires an expenditure of available resources. Consequently, at some point, cost must enter into the equation for determining sample size. When a fixed amount of money and/or time has been allocated for a project, Sudman (1976:88–89) offers the following rule of thumb for survey research: Allocate one-half of both money and time to data collection (and the other half to data analysis). Once the data-collection procedure is specified, the sample size can be determined on a time- and cost-per-case basis. That is, the number of cases will be equal to the total time for data collection divided by the time per case or the total funds for data collection divided by the cost per case.

KEY POINT

The two overriding factors in choosing a sampling design and an appropriate sample size are how precise sample estimates need to be and the cost of sampling.

Number of Breakdowns Planned

The number of variables and variable categories into which the data are to be grouped and analyzed also must be taken into account in determining sample size. In general, the more breakdowns planned in the analysis—the more complex the relationships under investigation or the more distinct subcategories of separate interest—the larger the sample must be. Consider, for example, what happens when a sample of 1000 is divided into males/females, then into blacks/whites, then into people older/younger than 18 years of age, then into urban/rural residence. If we were interested in describing rural black young men, we might find that a breakdown of the 1000 cases looks something like this:

Sample	1000
Males	489
Black males	60
Young black males	20
Rural young black males	4

With just 4 cases available, the sample would be too small for a reliable analysis of this particular subgroup. To avoid this kind of problem, it is important to estimate the number of breakdowns to be made during data analysis and to make sure that the total sample size will provide enough cases in each subcategory. If the requisite sample size turns out to be large, it might be more efficient to sample the relevant subcategories separately, as in stratified and quota sampling.

Final Notes on Sampling Errors and Generalizability

In the sections on probability sampling and sample size considerations, we spoke repeatedly of sampling error—the deviation of a sample estimate from the true population value. The sampling error referred to in our discussions is random error, produced by the random selection of elements. Although unavoidable in sampling, this error can be estimated and reduced by increasing the size or efficiency of one's sample. There is, however, another type of sampling error, called **sample bias**,[10] which is nonrandom, difficult to detect, and often much more damaging to sample accuracy.

In probability sampling designs, the two most common sources of sample bias are **coverage error** due to incomplete sampling frames and **nonresponse bias** due to incomplete data collection. As an example of coverage error, we mentioned earlier that telephone directories provide inadequate sampling frames to the extent that they exclude the poor, who cannot afford telephones, and the more wealthy, who tend to have unlisted numbers. There are two forms of nonresponse. *Unit nonresponse* occurs when, through refusals to cooperate, unreturned questionnaires, missing records, or some other means, the sample turns out to be a fraction of the number of cases originally selected for observation. *Item nonresponse* occurs when a respondent fails to answer a specific survey question. Either form creates bias when nonobservations differ in systematic ways from observations. Thus, in surveys, mail surveys in particular, highly educated respondents are more likely to cooperate than poorly educated ones. Also, those people who feel most strongly about the topics or issues of a study are more likely to respond than those in the middle (see Box 6.1).

Researchers should try to reduce the likelihood of these biases. For coverage error, researchers should assess how the sampling frame may differ from the target population and consider how such differences may affect survey estimates. To reduce unit nonresponse bias, the conventional wisdom has been to increase **response rates**, the proportion of people in the sample who actually complete the survey. It is assumed that nonresponse bias increases as the response rate declines. Robert Groves (2006) has shown, however, that the correlation between response rates and nonresponse bias is relatively weak and that this bias depends primarily on "how strongly correlated the survey variable of interest is with . . . the likelihood of responding" (670). This makes it incumbent on survey researchers to consider variables that might be related to responding and to seek data that can be used to estimate and reduce nonresponse effects. In a study of voluntarism, for example, knowing that women are more likely to volunteer than men, you should examine the response rates of men and women and adjust survey estimates based on these rates. Otherwise, if men are overrepresented among nonrespondents, estimated rates of voluntarism will be too high.

Groves cautions against "the blind pursuit of high response rates in probability samples" (2006:668), and recent evidence shows that "efforts to reduce nonresponse can lead to poorer-quality data" (Fricker and Tourangeau, 2010:934). Still, high response rates continue to be valued (Peytchev, Baxter, and Carley-Baxter, 2009). Some researchers and sponsors have more confidence in the representativeness of a survey with a high response rate than in one with a very low rate. Two trends indicate, however, that survey researchers may have to shift the emphasis from obtaining a very high response rate to assessing non-response bias and adjusting survey estimates based on variables that are likely to be related to the tendency to respond. First, as we note in Chapter 9, response rates in most surveys are declining. Second, some procedures used to increase response rates, such as multiple contacts and recontacting people who initially refuse to participate, have raised ethical concerns among institutional review boards (Dillman, 2007:28).

The underlying issue addressed in this chapter is generalizability. Advances in knowledge depend on our ability to generalize. With this in mind, readers should be aware of two limitations to sampling in social research. First, although social scientists would like to make the broadest possible generalizations, for reasons of convenience and economy they often study local or special populations. Investigators in the Worcester aging and religion study, for example, were not interested specifically in religion among older Worcester residents, which turned out to be their target population, but rather in religion and aging in the United States and beyond. They chose Worcester because that was the city in which the investigators were teaching. Drawing a probability sample made their results generalizable (within an estimable margin of error) to all Worcester residents 65 years and older. But inferences beyond this population are based on little more than intuition.

The second limitation concerns generalizing from samples to populations. As we have seen, the manner of selecting cases determines to whom and with what level of precision research results may be applied. Sample generalizability is the primary generalization issue addressed in social science research, especially survey studies, which are often called "sample surveys" because the sampling of units is such an integral part of the research design. Survey researchers are also largely responsible for the development of many of the sampling techniques discussed in this chapter. So it is no wonder that most of our examples came from survey studies and involved people as units.

However, the issue of generalizability is not limited to units of analysis, nor is the sampling of units solely the province of survey research. Generalizability pertains to all features of research, including the time of the study, the research setting, and the operational definitions. We might ask, for example, whether the same results would be obtained if a different set of questions were asked or if the study were conducted in a different place or at a different time of day or year. The social scientific ideal is to establish theoretical propositions that hold under all conditions—that do not pertain to any particular population, time, or setting. With this goal in mind, social researchers have no particular target population as the focus of their research. To establish the broadest possible generalizations, researchers use a variety of techniques in addition to random sampling, which we discuss in later chapters. These include replication (Chapter 7), theoretical sampling (Chapter 11), and triangulation (Chapter 13).

Summary

- *Sampling* is the process of selecting a subset of cases to draw conclusions about the entire set.
- It is usually impossible for practical reasons to examine all cases, and observing a sample of cases is simply more efficient anyway: It saves time and money and can be as accurate as research purposes demand.

- Sampling begins with a description of the target population, the collection of units about which one wishes to generalize.
- There is often an imperfect fit between the target population and the sampling frame, which consists of either (1) a list of cases from which the sample is actually selected or (2) a rule defining membership that provides a basis for case selection.
- The procedure for selecting a sample, called the "sampling design," may involve either probability or nonprobability sampling.
- Probability sampling, which is based on a process of random selection, eliminates investigator bias in selecting cases and permits the application of mathematical probability theory for estimating sample accuracy.
- Probability sampling designs include simple random sampling, stratified random sampling, cluster sampling, and systematic sampling.
- In simple random sampling, random selection from the entire population makes it equally possible to draw any combination of cases.
- The distribution of a statistical property for all possible combinations of random samples of a fixed size is called the "sampling distribution."
- A given sample statistic differs from the estimated population value by an amount known as the "sampling error"; an index of the size of such errors in a given sampling distribution is called the "standard error." In general, the larger the sample, the smaller the standard error.
- To take into account random sampling error, researchers use interval estimates, called "confidence intervals," in making inferences from a sample statistic to its population parameter.
- In stratified random sampling, the population is divided into strata and independent random samples are drawn from each stratum. The number of cases in each stratum of the sample may be either proportionate or disproportionate to the number of cases in the population.
- Stratifying improves sampling efficiency, provided that the stratifying variable is related to the variable under study and that the cost of stratifying is low compared with the cost of increasing the sample size. It also may be used to increase the number of cases in subpopulations that would prove too small if a simple random sample were drawn.
- In cluster sampling, the population is divided into natural groupings or areas, called clusters, and a random sample of clusters is drawn. When this is done in stages, as it usually is, moving from larger to smaller clusters, it is referred to as "multistage sampling."
- Clustering reduces the costs of interviewer travel and sampling frame construction, but it does so at a loss of sample precision.
- Systematic sampling, which often provides a reasonable approximation to simple random sampling, consists of selecting cases from an available list at a fixed interval after a random start.
- Nonprobability sampling designs include convenience, purposive, and quota samples.
- Convenience sampling is a rubric for various nonrandom and unsystematic processes of case selection that offer no basis for generalizing.
- Purposive sampling involves the careful selection of typical cases or of cases that represent relevant dimensions of the population.
- Quota sampling allocates quotas of cases for various strata and then allows for the nonrandom selection of cases to fill the quotas.
- If selection can be done in stages, using probability sampling at one stage and nonprobability sampling at another can reduce costs.
- For rare target populations, sampling may entail a process of referral. Network sampling asks respondents to identify members of the target population who are socially linked to the respondent in a specified way. Snowball sampling uses a chain of referrals, with initial contacts asked to name other members of the target population with particular characteristics, who are asked in turn to name others, and so on.
- Factors affecting the choice of a sampling design include (1) the stage of research and data use, with research in later stages intended to provide accurate population descriptions requiring the most sophisticated probability sampling designs; (2) available resources such as time, money, and personnel; and (3) the method of data collection.

- In general, the more heterogeneous the population, the greater the desired precision and available resources, and the larger the number of breakdowns planned during the data analysis, the larger the sample should be.
- Holding sample size constant, one will generally get the greatest precision with a stratified sample, followed by a simple random sample, and then a cluster sample.
- The quality of a sample ultimately depends not only on sample variability resulting from random selection but also on sample bias in the form of coverage error and nonresponse error.

Key Terms

population	multistage cluster sampling
sample	primary sampling unit
target population	probability proportionate to size sampling
sampling frame	systematic sampling
sampling design	sampling interval
probability sampling	nonprobability sampling
random selection	convenience sampling
simple random sampling	purposive sampling
parameter	quota sampling
statistic	network sampling
sampling distribution	snowball sampling
sampling error	heterogeneity
standard error	standard deviation
confidence interval	sampling fraction
stratified random sampling	sample bias
stratum	coverage error
disproportionate stratified sampling	nonresponse bias
cluster sampling	response rate

Exercises

1. This exercise will help familiarize you with some types of probability sampling. First, using the A section of the latest issue of your campus telephone directory as a starting point, draw up a sampling frame composed of the first 50 names listed.

   a. *Simple random sample.* Select a random sample of 10 names using the Research Randomizer (http://www.randomizer.org/). List all the random numbers you select, and then list the 10 names in your sample. Repeat this procedure in drawing a random sample of 5 names.

   b. *Stratified systematic sample.* Divide the names in your sampling frame into strata on the basis of gender. Now select a one-of-five systematic sample within each stratum. Begin with a random start and indicate the random number in each stratum with which you began. List the names that you obtain.

2. Each election year, the press relies on exit polls to forecast and analyze election outcomes. Exit polls are surveys of voters immediately after they have cast their votes at their polling places. The polling places (or precincts) are randomly selected to represent each state and, for national polls, the nation as a whole. Interviewers give selected voters a questionnaire that takes only a couple minutes to complete. It asks for whom they voted, about important issues, and about demographics such as gender, age, and race. Participation is voluntary and anonymous. Interviewing starts when the polls open and continues throughout the day until about an hour before they close at night.

   In one national election exit poll, voters were selected in the following way. Within each state, a complete list of precincts was obtained. The precincts were divided up into counties, and within each county precincts were selected randomly so that the odds of being selected were proportionate to the number of people who typically voted in that precinct. At each selected precinct, one or sometimes two interviewers stood outside and attempted to randomly select roughly 100 voters during the day as they exited from voting. The interviewers accomplished this task by counting voters as they left the polling place and selecting every voter at a specific interval (say, every third or fifth voter). The interval was chosen so that the approximately 100 interviews were spread evenly over the course of the day.

   a. What is the overall sampling design? (Be specific. This is a complex design, involving more than one sampling method.)
   b. What sampling frame was used in the design?
   c. Is stratification incorporated into the design? If so, what was the stratifying variable?
   d. What sampling method was used to select voters within each selected precinct?
   e. Some journalists and commentators would like to have had mid-day numbers or estimates from the exit polls. Why would the mid-day numbers have a much larger margin of error than when the polls were completed at the end of the day? Give *two* possible reasons, one involving random sampling error and the other involving sampling bias.
   f. Evaluate the sampling strategy with respect to coverage error; assume that the target population is all voters in the national election.

3. The GSS, which we describe throughout Chapter 9, consists of a personal interview survey of adults (18 years and older) living in households in the United States. Read about the sampling design of the GSS in Appendix A of the GSS Codebook, which can be found online (http://www.gss.norc.org/documents/codebook/GSS_Codebook_AppendixA.pdf). Briefly describe the overall design of the 2010 GSS. How has the design changed from 1972 to the present? When did the GSS switch from a "block quota" sample to a full probability sample?

4. Suppose the governor hires you to conduct a survey of state firefighters. The state plans to launch an advertising campaign to hire more firefighters. The goals of the survey are to describe the state population of firefighters in terms of basic demographic characteristics such as age, race, religion, and social class and to determine what leads people to become firefighters. You want to be able to estimate margins of error, and you also would like to have reliable information on female firefighters, who are estimated to make up only 5 percent of firefighters statewide.

   a. What is your target population for this survey?
   b. Assume you decide to do a personal interview survey. No complete list of all firefighters in the state is available; however, you have found a website with a complete directory of state fire departments. How would you go about selecting a probability sample of *firefighters*? In other words, what sampling design would you use? Keep in mind the goals of the survey. Be specific and be sure to fully describe how you would draw the sample.
   c. Now assume that you are going to do a mail questionnaire survey and that you were able to obtain a complete list of firefighters working in the state. However, the list contains no information other than each firefighter's name, address, and length of service. What sampling design would you use? Be specific and be sure to fully describe how you would draw the sample.

5. Because of your developing methodological expertise, someone who is about to conduct a random sample survey asks you, "What proportion of the population should I sample to give me adequate precision?" How would you respond to this question?

Notes

1. The U.S. Constitution mandates a complete enumeration of the population every 10 years. The primary purpose of the census is to reapportion seats in the U.S. House of Representatives. In 1999, the Supreme Court ruled that a plan to use statistical sampling in the census to determine congressional apportionment violates the Census Act (U.S. Census Bureau, 2009). Apparently, it will require a constitutional amendment to replace the census with a sample survey of the U.S. population.

2. The lottery method also has proven inadequate on occasion because of insufficient mixing. Two dramatic examples of this problem are the military draft lotteries of 1940 and 1970. Statistical analyses

convincingly have shown that both lotteries were biased, apparently a result of the failure of physical mixing to achieve randomness (Fienberg, 1971). The 1970 lottery, based on birthdays, was set up in the following way: 366 cylindrical capsules with rounded ends were used; slips of paper with the January dates were inserted in 31 capsules and placed in a large, square wooden box; the February dates were inserted and then placed in the box and mixed with the January dates, and this procedure was repeated for each of the remaining months, in turn; the box then was shut and shaken several times; finally, the 366 capsules were poured from the box into a large bowl, from which they were drawn. When the lottery drawing sequence was analyzed, it was shown that the sequence was not random but, rather, a reflection of "the order in which capsules were placed in the wooden box during the initial mixing procedure" (Fienberg, 1971:260). As a result, those with birthdays in the later months of the year had lower lottery numbers, hence were more likely to be drafted, than those with birthdays in the early months of the year.

3. This example is modeled after presentations by Morris James Slonim (1957, 1960) and Isidor Chein (1981).
4. If each one of a set of events is equally likely to occur, then the probability of any one event occurring is defined as 1 divided by the number of events. Assuming a perfect coin, for example, we have two events—a head and a tail—with the probability of one event (say, a head) in a single flip equal to 1/2.
5. This is accomplished by a weighting procedure that compensates for oversampling in some strata. The necessary mathematical formulas can be found in Kish (1965).
6. The following example illustrates how the probabilities are equal. Suppose that the total number of students in the population is 500,000 and that 100 schools are selected. The probability of selecting a school A, with 1000 students, is $100 \times 1000/500,000$, or .20. The probability of selecting a school B, with 500 students, is $100 \times 500/500,000$, or .10. If 50 students are selected from each school, the probability of selecting a student from school A is $.20 \times 50/1000$, or .01, which is the same as the probability of selecting a student from school B ($.10 \times 50/500 = .01$).
7. Another problem with cluster sampling is that, except for rare cases in which clusters are equal in size, the probabilities of case selection may vary widely from cluster to cluster. Consequently, estimates of population characteristics require some complex statistical solutions, which are beyond the scope of this book.
8. Richard Appelbaum (1990:13), who contends that counting the homeless population is an intractable problem and that "every effort is likely to produce an undercount," criticized the Rossi street survey on two counts. First, since homeless individuals were self-identified, there is the strong possibility of response bias—through avoidance of interviewers, refusals to be interviewed, or unwillingness to admit to being homeless. Second, the survey reached only the visible homeless population, which excludes the sizeable number of people in rooming houses, jails, and halfway houses, as well as people riding trains and buses.
9. Despite the potential bias, studies of noninstitutional hidden populations are rare. Indeed, "classic studies of deviance have depended largely or wholly on populations captured in the nets of institutions of social control" (Watters and Biernacki, 1989:417).
10. These two types of error—random sampling error and sample bias—are analogous to random and systematic measurement error.

PART III

Methods of Data Collection

The chapters in this section cover the four most distinctive and widely used approaches to social research: experiments, surveys, field research, and research using available data. Several factors influence an investigator's selection of an approach: the research question, available resources, and disciplinary and personal preferences. All too often a researcher is ideologically committed to one means of making observations. Indeed, each approach has developed largely independent of the others and, as a consequence, tends to have its own distinctive terminology for describing various features of the method. This is reflected, for example, in the terms applied to units of analysis, which are labeled variously as "subjects" or "participants" (experiments), "respondents" (surveys), "informants" (field research), and "items" (available data research).

Once a given approach is selected, it has an overriding effect on nearly every other facet of the research, from measurement and sampling to data analysis. Thus, although we already have dealt broadly with elements of research design, in the following chapters we will return again and again to design issues. In fact, we devote whole chapters to technical design features of experiments (Chapter 8) and surveys (Chapter 10). Otherwise, our principal aim in the four main chapters (Chapters 7, 9, 11, and 12) is to describe each approach's unique process of executing a study. Then, in Chapter 13, we present strategies for using a combination of methods and approaches. Throughout most of this section we assume the goal of basic social research—to understand the social world. In the final chapter (Chapter 14), we examine a form of applied social research called "evaluation research," whose aim is to assess social programs and policies.

7

Experimentation

People readily associate the term "experiment" with scientific research. Typically they have read about or conducted experiments in elementary and high school science courses. Many have learned that experimentation is the hallmark of "the scientific method." In fact, we have found that some students refer to any scientific study as an experiment. This usage of the term, however, is technically incorrect and can be misleading. Much of social research is nonexperimental; the word experiment denotes studies with several distinctive features.

The key features of the experimental approach are manipulation and control. To test hypotheses, experimenters deliberately introduce changes into the environment of subjects and observe or measure the effects of the changes. Because greater control is exercised over the conditions of observation than in any other research strategy, experiments more effectively eliminate the possibility of extraneous variables offering alternative interpretations of research findings. For this reason, experimental studies long have been regarded as the optimal way to test causal hypotheses. Even when a "true" experiment is impractical or impossible and some other approach must be used, the logic of experimentation serves as a standard by which other research strategies are judged.

In this chapter we introduce the essential features and causal logic of experiments as found in social research. We outline the process of "staging" an experiment and then discuss the social nature of experiments, including ways to prevent the social aspect from adversely affecting their scientific value. Finally, we discuss some variants of the experimental approach: experiments conducted in natural settings, the application of experimental design to social surveys, and the use of units of analysis other than individuals.

The Logic of Experimentation

The main reason for doing an experiment is to test a hypothesis that one variable affects another variable. Thus, all experiments possess certain basic requirements that permit strong inferences about cause and effect. Research designs that fill these requirements are called **true experimental designs**; those that do not, which are discussed in Chapter 8, are called "pre-experimental" or "quasi-experimental" designs. In this section we focus on the logic of experimentation by first identifying those essential features that make true experiments a model for testing causal relationships, and then we relate these features to the criteria for inferring causality.

Testing Causal Relations

The basic features of an experimental design are nicely illustrated by a simplified version of Ellis Page's study (1958) of teacher comments and subsequent student performance. Page wanted to determine whether teacher comments written on test papers would motivate students to improve their scores on the next test. (This seems like a relevant question to study in view of the hours teachers spend writing comments on students' papers!) To conduct the experiment, Teacher "Smith" gave one of her classes a scheduled objective test and scored the tests in her usual way, assigning grades A through F. Then she assigned the test papers, by tossing a coin, to one of two piles. One pile of papers received the experimental treatment, a specified comment that depended on the letter grade, as follows (Page, 1958:174):

A: Excellent! Keep it up.
B: Good work. Keep at it.
C: Perhaps try to do still better?
D: Let's bring this up.
F: Let's raise this grade!

Papers assigned to the second pile received no comment, providing a control group. The effect of the comments on student performance was judged by comparing the scores of students in the two groups on a subsequent test given and scored in the usual way. Results showed that the group that had received the written comments scored higher on the second test than the group that had received no comments.

What basic features of an experimental design are illustrated in the foregoing experiment? A *manipulated* independent variable (whether or not the teacher wrote comments on the first test) is *followed by* a measured dependent variable (student performance on the second test). There are two groups: One receives the experimental **treatment**, and another, the control, does not receive the treatment. Except for this experimental manipulation, the treatment and control groups are treated *exactly alike* to avoid introducing extraneous variables and their effects. Finally, subjects (or in this case their first test papers) are assigned to one or the other group *randomly*.

How do these features meet the requirements of causal inference? Although we can never prove beyond all doubt that two variables (say, X and Y) are causally related, recall that certain types of empirical evidence are regarded as essential for causal statements: (1) association (i.e., evidence that X and Y vary together in a way predicted by the hypothesis); (2) direction of influence (evidence that X affected Y rather than Y affected X); and (3) the elimination of plausible rival explanations (evidence that variables other than X did not cause the observed change in Y). The first two kinds of evidence show that X could have affected Y; the third kind shows that the relation between X and Y is nonspurious—that other variables are not responsible for the observed effects. Let us refer back to our simplification of Page's experiment to see how these types of evidence were provided.

1. *Association.* It was found that the independent variable, teacher comments, was associated with the dependent variable, scores on the subsequent test, in the manner hypothesized. That is, the treatment group, which received comments, scored higher on the test than the control group, which received no comments.

2. *Direction of influence.* Evidence that the independent variable (X) influenced the dependent variable (Y) and not the other way around is based on time order in experiments: Y cannot be the cause of X if it occurred after X. In the Page experiment, we know that the subsequent test scores (Y) could not have caused or affected the teacher comments (X) because the experimenter made sure that the comments occurred first.

3. *Elimination of rival explanations.* What might be plausible reasons that one group of students would score higher than another group on a test? Personal qualities such as intelligence and motivation might have an effect; experiences such as having a cold on the test day, missing breakfast, or being distracted by another student also might affect individual scores. These extraneous variables are controlled by random assignment of persons to the treatment and control groups. **Random assignment** means that the procedure by which subjects are assigned (in this case, tossing a coin) ensures that each subject has an equal chance of being in either group. By virtue of random assignment, individual characteristics or experiences that might confound the results will be about evenly distributed between the two groups. Thus, the number of students who are bright or dull, motivated or unmotivated, fully nourished or hungry, attentive or distracted, and so forth, should be about the same in each group.

In addition to controlling pre-experimental differences through random assignment, researchers make every attempt to ensure that both groups are treated exactly alike during the experiment except for the experimental treatment that one group receives. In the Page experiment, the tests given, time of testing, and intervening classroom experiences were the same for both groups. Examples of violations of this principle would have been if the treatment and control groups had not had the same teacher or if students had been told that they were in an experimental or control group.

In an airtight experimental design, there is only one rival explanation: The results could have occurred by chance. This would mean that the process of randomly assigning persons to the experimental and control groups resulted, by chance, in an unequal distribution between the groups of variables related to test performance, such as intelligence, interest in school, and health. The lower test scores of the control group in the Page experiment, for example, could have resulted from the chance assignment of fewer of the brighter students to this group than to the treatment group.

KEY POINT

Experiments provide strong inferences about cause and effect because they control the conditions of observation: The independent variable is manipulated *before* the dependent variable is measured, and groups are made equivalent through random assignment.

To assess the likelihood that the results of an experiment could have occurred by chance, experimenters use a **test of statistical significance**. Recall from Chapter 4 that significance tests indicate the likelihood or probability that an association is the result of random processes. Such tests express this probability in decimal form. So, when we read that the results of an experiment were found to be significant at the .05 level, this means that only about 5 percent of the time, or 5 times in 100, would differences this large between the experimental and control groups occur by chance when the experimental variable actually has no effect. With such a low probability it would be reasonable to rule out prior differences uncontrolled by the randomization process as a plausible rival explanation of the experimental results. However, if the results were not found to be statistically significant, it would not be reasonable to rule out differences due to chance assignment and we could not be confident that the experimental treatment caused the effects. In short, a statistical test of significance assesses the likelihood that the observed difference between the groups is real (significant) and not of a magnitude that would occur frequently by chance.[1]

Matching and Random Assignment

Some researchers attempt to eliminate prior differences between groups by **matching** subjects on characteristics that logically seem to be related to the experimental outcome. If, for example, an experimenter wanted to learn which of two methods of teaching Russian is more effective, potential students for the two language methods groups might be matched on variables such as grade-point average and verbal aptitude test scores. For each student with, say, above-average verbal aptitude and average grades, a second student who scored nearly the same on the two variables would have to be found. Then, each matched pair would be split so that one of the pair would be in each group, thus ensuring that the composition of the groups would be highly similar on the matching variables.

Readers should note carefully that matching should be used in conjunction with, and *not* as a substitute for, randomization. Matching is a powerful technique whose objective is similar to that of stratification in random sampling: to increase the efficiency of the experimental design by creating treatment groups that are similar with respect to characteristics related to the dependent variable. However, matching on some characteristics does not guarantee an equal distribution on other possibly relevant extraneous variables. For example, in the study of language-teaching methods, another variable that might affect the learning of a foreign language is auditory discrimination, the ability to discriminate similar sounds. Only with randomization can one be sure of the approximate equivalence on *all* extraneous variables, including those unknown to the researcher.

One problem with matching is that researchers do not always know what variables to match or control for. Another problem is that, unless the pool from which the subjects are drawn is extremely large, it may be difficult to find enough pairs of subjects who are alike on the relevant variables to make up similar matched groups. In other words, it may be difficult to form treatment groups large enough to produce reliable results. This is especially the case when more than one or two matching variables are involved.

There are several ways to assign subjects randomly to experimental and control groups. The method previously mentioned was tossing a coin for each subject; "heads" meant one group and "tails" meant the other. For experiments with more than two groups we recommend using a computer program that generates random numbers. The important point is that "random" does not mean haphazard; it is a technical term meaning that every case has an equal and independent chance of being assigned to any experimental condition. If matching procedures are used, one should first match subjects on relevant variables and then randomly assign the members of each matched pair to different groups.

A final word of caution relates to the difference between the random *assignment* of subjects in experiments and the random *selection* of cases in probability sampling. Although both processes invoke randomness, they occur at different points in the research process and serve different purposes. Sampling occurs first, for example, when a pool of subjects is selected for an experiment; although random sampling facilitates inferences from sample to population, it is seldom used in experiments. Random assignment occurs after the sample has been selected, when subjects are assigned to different experimental groups; its function is to make groups approximately equal on all uncontrolled extraneous variables, and it is an essential aspect of true experiments.

KEY POINT
Random assignment, the process of placing subjects in experimental conditions, should not be confused with *random sampling*, which is one means of selecting research subjects from an eligible population.

Internal and External Validity

Ellis Page concluded from his experiment that writing "encouraging" comments on student papers, at least among secondary students, causes learning to improve. For readers of Page's published study (and for all students of research methods), the question is, Does the evidence support this conclusion? Is this a valid test of the hypothesis? The answer boils down to evaluating three aspects of a study: measurement validity, internal validity, and external validity.

As we saw in Chapter 5, measures are valid when they correspond well to the theoretical concepts under study. Did Page's operational definitions of the independent and dependent variables measure what they were intended to measure? To manipulate the independent variable, he had teachers write precisely defined comments on some test papers but not on others; to measure the dependent variable, the teachers recorded scores and grades on objective tests administered in the usual course of instruction. Because students were unaware that they were in an experiment, Page eliminated the possibility of a reactive measurement effect, a major concern in laboratory experiments, which we consider later in the chapter. We might question how students interpreted the written comments; for example, were they seen as encouraging? And had Page found that the comments had no effect, we might wonder how many students actually read them. But on the face of it, Page's study passes the test of measurement validity.

The second validity concern is whether a study provides sound evidence of a causal relationship. When it does and we are confident that a change in the independent variable caused a change in the dependent variable, a study is said to be high in **internal validity**. We evaluate internal validity in terms of the overall study design. True experiments such as the Page study possess the following design requirements:

- Random assignment
- Manipulation of the independent variable
- Measurement of the dependent variable
- At least one comparison or control group (i.e., at least two groups, experimental and comparison)
- (Excluding experimental manipulations) The constancy of conditions across groups

Experiments with these minimum characteristics are internally valid because they rule out the possibility that extraneous variables, rather than the manipulated independent variable, are responsible for the observed outcome of the study. As we saw in the Page study, experiments eliminate rival explanations associated with extraneous variables in two ways. First, effects of prior differences between subjects, such as personal qualities and experiences, are "neutralized" by randomly assigning subjects to treatment and control groups, thus initially ensuring approximate equivalence of the groups. Second, aside from the introduction of the experimental variable, treatment and control groups are treated exactly alike, thus ensuring equivalence of the groups during the experiment.

A related concern is that experiments have **external validity**. This is a question of generalizability, or what the experimental results mean outside of the particular context of the experiment. For example, regarding Page's study, we might question whether the same results would be obtained with different classes, teacher comments, subject matter, or age groups. At this point we will describe the Page study more completely as it also provides an excellent example of an experiment high in external validity.

For his experiment, Page selected 74 teachers at random from 12 secondary schools (grades 7–12) in three school districts. These teachers were given detailed instructions in how to carry out the experiment, including the random selection of one of her or his classes for the experiment. This procedure ensured that the experiment would include a great variety of subject matter as well as students at every grade level. More than 1200 students participated, unaware that they were experimental subjects.

In addition to the "no comments" group (the control group) and the "specified comments" group that received the comments listed in our earlier discussion, a third group, called the "free comments" group, received whatever comments the teachers felt were appropriate in the circumstances. Random assignment of the initial set of test papers to one of the three groups was carried out by means of a specially marked die. The specified comments group scored significantly higher than the no comments group on the subsequent set of tests, with the free comments group scoring highest of all. Analysis of the data showed consistent results regardless of the particular class, school, or grade level (grades 7–12). Because of the consistency of the experimental results in different settings, with different teachers and students, we can say the experiment was high in external validity.

Of the latter two types of validity, internal validity takes precedence. If an experiment lacks internal validity—and we cannot confidently infer that manipulating the independent variable caused changes in the dependent variable—it makes no sense to consider whether the results can be generalized. Therefore, the primary concern in designing experiments is to make sure that they provide a sound test of a causal hypothesis. Still, because social scientists' interests go beyond the specific subjects and situations that they study, external validity does matter. The extent to which it matters and how it matters depend on the nature of the theory or hypothesis being tested.

KEY POINT
Laboratory experiments are high on *internal validity* but tend to be low on *external validity*.

In Page's study, external validity was especially relevant because the hypothesis applied to a particular population and setting. The hypothesis that written comments enhance test performance clearly pertained to students in the school classroom. So, it was important to show that it was supported with numerous teachers teaching a variety of subjects at several grade levels. Had Page tested the hypothesis with a single teacher in a single classroom, we would be much less confident about its generalizability. Whenever a specific target population and setting is the object of study, researchers should incorporate design features that enhance external validity, such as the use of multiple testing sites, as in Page's study, or the use of probability sampling.

Aside from applied research, most experiments are not designed to generalize *to* a specific population or setting. Rather, they have the broader scientific goal of testing hypotheses that are assumed to be universally true and therefore apply *across* people, places, and times. The extent to which a hypothesis, tested in a single study, may be generalized in this sense depends initially on the underlying theory that is tested. Consider, for example, the intergroup contact hypothesis—that contact between members of different groups, such as racial groups, reduces prejudice (see Pettigrew, 1998). In one experimental test of this hypothesis (S. W. Cook, 1984), white female college students operated an imaginary railroad system with a black co-worker who was a confederate of the experimenter. After prolonged interaction—more than 40 sessions—in which the co-workers shared responsibility for decisions and eventually won bonus money, interacting subjects expressed more favorable views toward African Americans than control subjects. The aim of this study was not to generalize to U.S. white, female college students who play management games with African Americans; rather, it was to test a theory of intergroup relations. According to the theory, when members of different groups engage in socially sanctioned, equal-status contact in the cooperative pursuit of common goals, they are likely to develop more positive attitudes toward members of the other group. An experiment provides a sound test of the theory when all these conditions are met. And, with these conditions present, we would expect the theory to generalize across subjects, groups, and settings. Whether it does is usually established over time in repeated studies.

All experiments involve a particular group of subjects and take place at a specific time and setting with a certain set of procedures, observers, and experimenters. Because all these aspects limit the external validity of any one experimental test, the best strategy for increasing the generalizability of theories and hypotheses is **replication**. That is, the experiment is repeated—by the same or another investigator who conducts the research at a different time, in a different setting, with slightly different procedures, or with a different sample of subjects. Indeed, the strongest argument for generality is that widely varying experimental tests have produced similar results. (A technique called "meta-analysis," discussed in Chapter 13, enables researchers to synthesize and summarize the results of numerous studies addressing the same research question, thereby providing systematic evidence of external validity.)

Sampling in Experiments

Although external validity is gained primarily though replication, it also may be enhanced within a given study through certain features of the research design. Foremost is the selection of a sample. One of the most persistent criticisms of experiments is that they are short on external validity because they tend to rely on convenience samples of college students (Sears, 1986; Henry, 2008a). Because experimental manipulation often involves a laboratory setting and/or elaborate staging, it is usually impractical either to sample subjects over wide areas or to utilize a large number of subjects. As a consequence, experimenters tend to use small samples drawn from readily available populations. And because most experimentation is done in universities, most often the subjects are college students. How often? In social psychology, a discipline based heavily on experimental research, analyses of three major journals showed that between 1990 and 2005 more than 90 percent of the articles reported studies with college student samples (Henry, 2008a).

The heavy reliance on college student samples is a long-standing controversy in the social sciences (Mook, 1983; Sears, 1986). Some scholars argue that the sample of subjects does not matter because the phenomena studied are so basic that they are universally true. In fact, much reported research implicitly makes this assumption. Others maintain that no matter what sample is used, the key to generalizing is identifying the theoretical conditions that constrain the ability to generalize (Lucas, 2003; Blanton and Jaccard, 2008). Knowing these conditions and how they operate in different populations enables researchers to generalize from one sample to another. Still others, however, see problems in experimenters' narrow participation base.

College students differ from people in general on several dimensions, including socioeconomic level, age, occupational goals, education, and interests. Research across the life span suggests that "compared with older adults, college students are likely to have less-crystallized attitudes, less-formulated senses of self, stronger cognitive skills, stronger tendencies to comply with authority, and more unstable peer group relationships" (Sears, 1986:515). Moreover, apart from the personal characteristics that set them apart, college students are immersed in a distinctive culture, the university setting, that differs from other social environments (Henry, 2008b). Given these differences, David Sears (1986:520) went so far as to say that the narrow database of college students may be producing "mistaken conclusions about human nature." He pointed out, for example, that some relationships may be limited to or stronger among college students; others may be true of adults in ordinary life but not of students.

Sears's argument remains mostly speculative because little research has systematically compared results obtained with college and noncollege samples. In one survey of such comparisons across a variety of relationships, it was found that about half differed substantially, with relationships generally stronger among college students than among nonstudents (R. A. Peterson, 2001). An interesting example, which shows how the use of college student samples may affect theory development, comes from research on the intergroup contact hypothesis. An analysis of more than 500 studies showed that the relationship between intergroup contact and prejudice reduction was significantly stronger for college students than for adults (Pettigrew and Tropp, 2006). Such a finding raises important theoretical questions (Dasgupta and Hunsinger, 2008). Is it because college students are more open to change than older adults, as Sears surmised? Or are students more likely to benefit from contact than nonstudents because campus norms favor egalitarianism more strongly than the norms of other communities (Dasgupta and Hunsinger, 2008)?

The implication is that broadening the subject population benefits research not only by increasing external validity but also by helping to develop theories (Glick, 2008). Several scholars therefore recommend conducting more experiments with adult samples. One increasingly popular way of doing this, described later in this chapter, is to carry out an experiment within a population-based sample survey. Another possibility is to conduct a laboratory experiment but draw a more heterogeneous sample via probability or purposive sampling. According to inductive logic, the broader the range of cases included in the sample, the more generalizable the findings. Thus, the inferences that could be drawn from a study with a homogeneous sample of college sophomores enrolled in introductory psychology are far more restricted than the inferences possible from a probability sample of people from the town where the college is located. One might therefore draw the latter sample, not because it is meaningful to generalize to all residents of the town, but because the greater heterogeneity among town residents permits stronger inferences about generalizability.

KEY POINT

External validity refers to the generalizability of research findings both *to* specific populations and *across* populations, settings, and time. Probability sampling can increase the first type of external validity; replication increases the second type.

Finally, convenience samples of American college students also constitute a narrow cultural base from which to generalize about human social behavior (Fish, 2000).

Recent research in social psychology has shown that robust findings from research in American and Western cultures may not apply to non-Western cultures (Choi, Nisbett, and Norenzayan, 1999; Henrich, Heine, and Norenzayan, 2010). Therefore, to further increase external validity, more experimental research must be carried out in non-Western cultures.

Staging Experiments

Experiments are most frequently conducted in laboratory settings to which an experimenter brings subjects to have them participate in individual or social activities. Planning and carrying out a laboratory experiment is much like producing a play. There are "scripts" to write and rewrite; a sequence of "scenes," each contributing something vital to the production; a "cast" of experimental assistants to recruit and train; "props" and "special effects"; and "rehearsals." And once the stage is set, the experimenter must publicize the experiment and sell potential subjects on participation, for without an audience there can be no play.

FIGURE 7.1. Key points in planning and conducting an experiment.

In writing a play the playwright must consider how each scene will contribute to the success of the play; likewise, a researcher designing an experiment must consider how each part of the experiment will contribute to the entire production. Figure 7.1 shows the key points in planning and conducting an experiment. The main parts are (1) introduction to the experiment, (2) manipulation of the independent variable, (3) measurement of the dependent variable, and (4) concluding activities, which usually include a debriefing and sometimes a postexperimental interview. To illustrate these parts, we first summarize an experiment and then refer back to it as we describe each part.

An Example: Who Will Intervene?

Why do bystanders sometimes fail to aid people immediately in crisis situations? This was the question that the social psychologists John Darley and Bibb Latané asked after a widely publicized incident in New York City in 1964. A young woman named Kitty Genovese was brutally murdered while, according to news reports, 38 of her neighbors watched from their windows without so much as calling the police until her attacker had departed.[2] Trying to understand how people failed to act in time to save the woman, Darley and Latané (1968) hypothesized that the more bystanders who witness an emergency, the less likely it is that any one bystander will come to the victim's assistance and the greater the amount of time that will elapse before intervention.[3] To test this hypothesis, they launched a highly influential program of research. One of their earliest experiments involved a simulated group discussion where an experimental subject witnessed (over an intercom system) and believed others to be witnessing an apparent epileptic seizure of one of the discussants.

Subjects were men and women enrolled in introductory psychology courses at New York University. The subjects participated to fulfill part of a class requirement but were not told the nature of the experiment before reporting to the laboratory. On arrival they were met by an assistant to the experimenter, who led them down a corridor to a small room, seated them, and had them fill out a background information form. Each subject was then given headphones with a microphone attached and was instructed to listen for further directions. Over the intercom system the experimenter stated that the research involved the personal problems of college students and that, because of the personal nature of the discussion in which he or she would be participating, measures had been taken to minimize embarrassment for the students and to protect their privacy. First, anonymity would be preserved by their physical separation. (In reality, the separation permitted tape-recorded simulation of other subjects' participation and of the emergency.) Second, the experimenter would not be listening to the discussion but would obtain the participants' reactions afterward. (This explanation permitted the experimenter's absence from the scene of the emergency.)

The experimenter went on to say that some organization of the discussion was necessary and that each person in turn would present his or her problems to the group. Next, each person in turn would respond to the others' remarks, with further discussion at the end. Each person's microphone would be on for 2 minutes and then would automatically shut off, allowing only one person to be heard at a time. (These instructions ensured that the subjects would realize two things at the time of the "emergency": only the "victim's" microphone was on, and they had no way to determine what the other discussants were doing.)

The simulated discussion then began. The victim spoke first and, among other problems, mentioned a proneness to seizures. Then the other "participants" and the subject spoke. In the second round of the discussion, the victim made several comments and then, after about 70 seconds, began in a distressed and somewhat incoherent voice to ask for help because he was having a seizure. After 125 seconds the victim's speech was cut off. The length of time it took the subject to report the emergency was measured from the start of the apparent epileptic fit.

The number of other people the subject believed to be in the group discussion was the major independent variable. The discussion groups (three treatment conditions) consisted of two persons (the subject and the victim), three persons, or six persons. The major dependent variable was the length of time from the onset of the seizure until the subject left the room. If the subject did not leave the room in 6 minutes, the experiment was ended.

Subjects who left the room before 6 minutes had elapsed found the experimental assistant seated in the hall. As soon as the emergency was reported, or at the end of 6 minutes, debriefing began. The real purpose of the experiment was then explained and the subject's emotional reactions were discussed. Then, the subject was asked to complete a questionnaire and several personality trait scales.

Briefly, results showed that the number of discussants believed to be participating strongly affected subjects' reporting of the incident. All subjects in the two-person groups reported the emergency, with approximately 80 percent of those in the three-person groups and 62 percent of those in the six-person groups reporting. In regard to speed of response, subjects in the three-person groups reported about as quickly as those in the two-person groups; the small difference obtained was not statistically significant. However, subjects in the six-person groups took significantly longer to report.

The Darley and Latané experiment provides an excellent example of the work and planning involved in staging an experiment. The subject is brought into the setting where the production will take place. Appropriate props have been prepared and are in place: desk, chair, headphones, microphone, background information form, prerecorded tapes, chair in hallway, and additional scales and a questionnaire. There is a cast of characters. In addition to the experimenter and persons clearly perceived by subjects to be assistants to the experimenter, frequently there are "confederates," or persons who appear to be subjects participating in the experiment but who are actually persons trained by the experimenter to play the subject role to affect the real subject in some way. The Darley and Latané experiment had a cast consisting of the experimenter's assistant, the experimenter, and confederates posing as subjects. (In this experiment the subject's only contact with the experimenter and confederates was through the tapes.) The cast carefully follows a script memorized in advance; only the subject is free to vary his or her behavior, some measure of which is the dependent variable. Every effort is made to ensure that the same "play" is presented to each subject to preserve internal validity. (For a further description of Darley and Latané's program of research on bystander intervention, see Box 7.1.)

BOX 7.1 EXTERNAL VALIDITY AND THE SOCIAL INHIBITION OF HELPING

The epileptic seizure experiment was part of a program of research carried out by the social psychologists Bibb Latané and John Darley (1970) on bystander intervention in emergencies. The program consisted of a series of experiments, each designed to examine the kinds of factors that influence a person's decision to help or not to help another. Additional experiments by Latané and Darley show how successive experimentation can increase external validity as it extends our knowledge of a social phenomenon.

Latané and Darley believed that a key factor in determining whether a bystander will intervene in an emergency is the presence of other bystanders. They hypothesized that as the number of bystanders increases, any one bystander will be less likely to *notice* an emergency incident, less likely to *interpret* it as an emergency, and less likely to *intervene* or take action. In ambiguous situations, which most emergencies are, people tend to look to others to gauge their reactions. Thus, others' apparent lack of concern and inaction will inhibit helping. When others are present, one also runs the risk of embarrassment by misinterpreting the situation. Moreover, the costs for not helping are reduced because one feels less personally responsible for taking action.

In their initial test of this explanation, Latané and Darley had subjects fill out questionnaires in a waiting room, either alone or in the presence of two strangers. As the subjects worked, smoke was piped into the room through a wall vent. The experimenters, observing subjects' reactions through a one-way mirror, found that the majority of subjects who were alone noticed the smoke in less than 5 seconds and reported it to the experimenter in less than 2 minutes; subjects in the presence of others took an average of 20 seconds to notice, and most failed to report before the 6-minute experimental period had ended. In a postexperimental interview, the researchers also found that many of the latter subjects had interpreted the smoke as a nondangerous event—that is, as something other than fire. The "smoke" was explained variously as "steam or air-conditioning vapors," "smog, purposely introduced to simulate an urban environment," and "truth gas."

A second experiment, involving a woman in distress, was similar in design to the smoke-filled-room study. After setting subjects to work on a questionnaire, a female researcher exited the waiting room through a curtained doorway to work next door in her office. Four minutes later she could be heard climbing up on a chair (to reach a book) and then crashing to the floor and screaming as the chair fell over. She then cried, "Oh, my God, my foot . . . I . . . I . . . can't move . . . it. Oh, my ankle, I . . . can't . . . can't . . . get . . . this thing off . . . me." This was followed by moaning and struggling for about 2 minutes until she limped out of her office door. The main dependent variable was whether subjects intervened to help the victim: 70 percent of the alone subjects did, but in only 40 percent of the pairs of strangers did either person offer help to the injured woman.

Besides these two studies and the epileptic seizure study, Latané and Darley conducted several other experiments on the social inhibition of helping, each producing similar findings. These experiments utilized a wide range of emergency situations. The situations varied in their seriousness. Some, such as the smoke-filled room, involved danger to the subject, whereas others, such as the fall and the seizure, involved danger to the victim. The experiments also

(continued)

(continued)

utilized a range of subject populations. In addition to the above experiments in which male and female college students participated, other studies included men and women from the general public. Finally, Latané and Darley performed field experiments as well as the laboratory experiments reported here. Thus, the external validity of the basic finding, which would be low in any one experiment, was made impressively high by a succession of studies that varied in their settings, procedures, measures, and samples.

In the decade following the publication of Latané and Darley's research, more than 50 studies were performed on bystander intervention in emergencies. About 90 percent of these showed that the presence of others inhibits helping (Latané and Nida, 1981). More recently, a meta-analysis of 53 articles reporting 105 independent tests provided clear support for the bystander effect (Fischer et al., 2011). This research not only further documents an important social phenomenon, but also extends our knowledge by refining theoretical understanding and by identifying conditions under which the effect is reduced or eliminated. It is now clear, for example, that the presence of others is much less inhibiting in dangerous than in non-dangerous situations (in part because dangerous situations are more likely to be defined as clear-cut emergencies in which help is needed) and when the bystanders know one another.

Subject Recruitment and Acquisition of Informed Consent

Before the start of the "production," subjects must be recruited and the investigator must obtain the subjects' informed consent to participate. As is typical of experiments, Darley and Latané's subjects were a convenience sample of college students who participated to fulfill a course requirement. Frequently, subjects volunteer or are paid for their participation. This experiment predates federal regulations regarding informed consent, and Darley and Latané give no indication that they told subjects about foreseeable risks and discomforts before they agreed to participate. Nowadays, subjects must be given an informed-consent form that (1) explains the experimental procedures and potential risks and benefits to the participants or to others and (2) informs them that their participation is voluntary and that they have the right to leave the experiment at any time without penalty.

Introduction to the Experiment

The first scene of an experiment consists of some sort of introduction to the study. This involves an explanation of the purpose or nature of the research, together with instructions to the subject. In the bystander intervention study, subjects were told that the research involved the personal problems of college students and that to avoid embarrassment they would carry on a discussion with other students who were physically separated from them. Then they were told how the discussion would proceed.

All subjects are likely to want to understand what the study is about, and they will expect to be given some sort of explanation. If they are told the actual hypothesis, subjects may behave as they think they should rather than as they would ordinarily. However, subjects must be given some explanation; otherwise, they may try to guess the hypothesis and "help" the experimenter by behaving in a way that confirms the guessed hypothesis.

Therefore, a false explanation, or **cover story**, such as Darley and Latané offered, is thought to be necessary to prevent preoccupation with the true purpose of the study. A good cover story must make sense to subjects; that is, it must be understandable and believable. The first scene, including the cover story, also should have enough impact on the subject to arouse interest. If the subject is not paying attention to the directions or to the events being staged, experimental "findings" will be worthless.

The Experimental Manipulation

The manipulation of the independent variable may be thought of as the second scene of the experiment. This is the point at which some set of stimuli is introduced that serves as an operational definition of the researcher's independent variable and to which the subject is expected to respond. The major independent variable in the foregoing study was the size of the simulated discussion group. There were three levels of the independent variable or three conditions to which subjects were assigned randomly: the two-person condition, the three-person condition, and the six-person condition. (Random assignment may occur at any time before the experimental manipulation.) The group size was manipulated by means of an assistant's comments pertaining to the size of the group and by the number of voices heard over the earphones.

A major concern in experiments is the possible meaning that subjects may attribute to the experimental manipulation. Essentially a matter of measurement validity, this has been referred to as the problem of "multiple meanings" (Aronson and Carlsmith, 1968). For example, a manipulation meant to arouse embarrassment in the subject is invalid if it produces disgust or anger instead. In general, the more complex the set of stimuli presented to a subject, the less sure a researcher may be that a manipulation appropriately measures the independent variable. When interpreting the results of any experiment, therefore, one must be sensitive to possible alternative explanations for any effects found. Evidence that the manipulation had the intended effect is gained by conducting a series of experiments in which the same theoretical concept is operationally defined differently and by performing manipulation checks.

Manipulation Checks

An immediate way to obtain evidence that the manipulation of the independent variable was experienced or interpreted by subjects in the way the experimenter intended is to incorporate some sort of **manipulation check** into the experiment. This might involve asking subjects, either directly or by means of a written instrument, what they felt or thought during or immediately after the experimental manipulation. A manipulation check may also be used to determine whether subjects understood or recalled essential directions or facts related to the manipulation.

In the Darley and Latané study, subjects were given a 15-item checklist of thoughts that might have occurred to them during the seizure. In addition, subjects were asked whether at the time of the seizure they had been aware of other persons who might be witnessing it— an awareness crucial to the meaning of the independent variable. (Data from two subjects who found the seizure unconvincing were not included in the statistical analysis.)

Different viewpoints exist regarding the best place in an experiment to administer a manipulation check. Frequently, a manipulation check is taken after the independent variable is manipulated but before the dependent variable is measured. The advantage here is that the manipulation is still fresh and the subject's memory of it has not been distorted by later events. However, it may not be feasible at this point, as in the Darley and Latané study, where the check was made part of the postexperimental interview. (Certainly, it was more appropriate for the subjects to respond at once to the "emergency" than to a checklist!) An additional problem with having a check administered between the experimental manipulation and the dependent variable is that of reactivity; that is, the manipulation check may alter subjects' subsequent behavior (the dependent variable) by calling attention to or emphasizing the manipulation.

One solution to this dilemma may be found through pretesting. Some studies of racial discrimination have manipulated the race of target persons in written vignettes using racially connected names, such as "Tyrone" for blacks and "Todd" for whites. In one experiment (Ford, 1997), the validity of this manipulation was checked, before the experiment was performed, by asking 45 subjects who did not take part in the experiment to indicate the race that was likely to be associated with a list of 25 names, including Tyrone and Todd. All of the subjects reported that the name Tyrone implied African American and Todd implied white European. Alternatively, an experiment might be tried out on a number of subjects. Pretest subjects might be run in the usual manner through the manipulation of the independent variable and then interviewed as to how it affected them (Aronson and Carlsmith, 1968). In this way, a manipulation check is carried out without affecting the data of the actual experiment. This procedure makes good sense also in view of the fact that there would still be time to make changes in the experiment before it is conducted with actual subjects whose data would be collected and analyzed.

Measurement of the Dependent Variable

The dependent variable, which always follows the introduction of the independent variable, is measured in experiments with either self-reports or observations of behavior. Darley and Latané used behavioral observation, with the dependent variable consisting of the length of time from the onset of the seizure until the subject left the room to report the emergency. A behavioral measure of the dependent variable—grades on a second test—also was used in the Page study of the effect of teacher comments on student performance.

The use of verbal versus observational measures of the dependent variable is a controversial point among experimenters. Our examples notwithstanding, verbal reports are more common, although they often contain serious weaknesses. Verbal measures have the advantage of being easy to devise, allowing for more numerous and varied assessments of the dependent variable. They also tend to be high in face validity. Using a verbal measure, for example, an experimenter interested in willingness to help could simply ask, "To what extent are you willing to help?" There are two major problems with such self-reports, however: first, subjects may censor their responses, especially when they construe the "truth" to reflect negatively on themselves; second, research consistently has shown differences between what people do and what they think and say they will do (Deutscher, Pestello, and Pestello, 1993).

With observations of behavior, however, subjects tend to be less aware or even unaware of the measure. Behavioral measures also can be more precise; recall that Darley and Latané recorded the length of time to respond to the emergency in seconds. Finally, when a specific behavior (e.g., helping) is of interest, it is better to get a direct measure of that behavior than an indirect measure of how subjects *say* they will behave.

KEY POINT

In experiments, measurement validity is assessed through manipulation checks and through replications that apply different operational definitions of the same theoretical concept.

Debriefing

The closing scene of the experiment is a **debriefing** session in which an experimenter discusses with a subject what has taken place. When subjects have been deceived, it is ethically imperative that they be told at this point about the nature of and reasons for the deception and that their feelings about being deceived be explored fully (see Chapter 3). Experimenters also may try to learn what subjects experienced throughout the experiment: Did the subject understand the directions? If a cover story was used, did the subject believe it? Why did the subject respond as he or she did to the experimental manipulation? Did the subject experience psychological stress or discomfort? How does the subject feel about the experiment as a whole?

Experimenters should be aware that the manner in which the debriefing session is conducted may make a great deal of difference in subjects' feelings about being deceived (if the subjects have been deceived), about this research and researcher, and about social science research in general. Thus, experimenters should explain the real purpose of the research and why it is of importance. If deception has been used, subjects must be gently informed of this and the reasons it was necessary. If the manipulation aroused a subject's emotions, this too should be justified and every effort made to relieve any remaining discomfort. Any negative feelings of subjects toward the study should be brought into the open and discussed. Subjects should be encouraged to ask questions about the study.

Because many subjects in their experiment experienced stress and conflict, Darley and Latané took great care in explaining the necessity of the deception and seeing that subjects left the experiment feeling positive about their participation. Although they did not gather systematic information about subjects' reactions to the experimental experience, Shalom Schwartz and Avi Gottlieb (1981) administered an "ethics questionnaire" to measure subjects' feelings about their participation in three different experiments on bystander intervention, including a close replication of the Darley and Latané study. Very few subjects felt any negative effect such as being upset, embarrassed, or nervous or feeling angry at the experimenter; and subjects generally evaluated their experience favorably. The vast majority found their participation enjoyable, believed that the research was ethically justified, and were not resentful about having been deceived. The relative absence of negative reactions, Schwartz and Gottlieb contend, was most probably due to the thorough debriefing provided in all three experiments.

Finally, subjects must be convinced not to talk to others about the experiment. This is a serious problem in that frequently potential subjects are acquainted with one another. Experiments requiring deception will not yield valid results if subjects coming to the experiment have been informed of its true purpose. Even experiments not requiring deception will usually suffer if subjects previously have been told the hypothesis or what the experimental manipulation is. If the debriefing process has been an open, satisfying experience for a subject up to this point, he or she is likely to respect the researcher's wishes in regard to secrecy.

Pretesting

Pretesting an experiment may be compared to rehearsals of a play in that the pretests provide an opportunity for the director of the research to (1) train the cast; (2) test the props, instructions, and cover story; (3) check whether the manipulation has the intended effect; and (4) revise and practice the script. Pretests are carried out on a few preliminary subjects to see how the experimental procedures affect them. Feedback provided by pretest subjects may be used to modify the manipulation of the independent variable (e.g., by increasing the level of a stimulus such as praise or by changing the behavior of confederates in some way), to change the dependent measure, or to improve some other part of the experiment such as the instructions, setting, or cover story. The time it takes for the actual performance of a play is usually a fraction of the time required to write the play and prepare for its performance. Similarly, the amount of time spent by a researcher in planning and pretesting an experiment will typically be many times greater than the time spent running subjects through the experiment.

Experimental and Mundane Realism

One thing an experimenter may learn from pretesting is the extent to which pretest subjects become involved in the experiment—that is, whether they are compelled to attend to it and take it seriously or, on the other hand, to remain detached. When an experiment is found to have impact on subjects and to seem real to them, it is said to have **experimental realism** (Aronson and Carlsmith, 1968). The bystander intervention study achieved a high degree of experimental realism for subjects. As Darley and Latané (1968:381) report,

> Subjects, whether or not they intervened, believed the fit to be genuine and serious. "My God, he's having a fit," many subjects said to themselves (and were overheard via their microphones) at the onset of the fit. Others gasped or simply said "Oh." Several of the male subjects swore. One subject said to herself, "It's just my kind of luck, something has to happen to me!" Several subjects spoke aloud of the confusion about what course of action to take, "Oh God, what should I do?"

This type of experiment is sometimes called an *impact experiment* (Aronson, Brewer, and Carlsmith, 1985) because the event in question—witnessing an emergency by hearing an apparent epileptic seizure—happened to the subjects themselves. Impact experiments tend to be high in experimental realism, although the stimuli presented are often complex, increasing the likelihood of multiple meanings from subject to subject. By contrast, *judgment experiments*, in which subjects make judgments about stimulus materials presented by an experimenter, have little direct impact on subjects. For example, subjects might be asked to indicate how much they like a stimulus person about whom they read a description or whom they see on film. This type of experiment allows substantial control over the events or stimuli presented, but the gain in control may undermine subject involvement and thereby lower experimental realism. In general, there often is a tension between the goal of experimental realism and the goal of control over the experimental situation. Ways to increase experimental realism include using a "live" experimenter rather than tape-recorded or written instructions, making the cover story more interesting, selecting a confederate with substantial acting ability, and developing elaborate apparatus or other props.

A second type of realism that experiments may have to different degrees is called **mundane realism** (Aronson and Carlsmith, 1968). This type of realism refers to the similarity of experimental events to everyday experiences. The Page experiment on teacher comments, which took place in a natural setting, was clearly high in mundane realism. Receiving general comments on exams has happened to every student. The Darley and Latané experiment, however, was low in mundane realism. Carrying on a highly regulated discussion with unseen peers over an intercom is not likely to be a common experience.

Experiments may be high in both experimental and mundane realism, high in one type of realism but low in the other, or low in both. Of the two types, mundane realism is considered less important in that an experiment is by nature a contrived situation (Aronson and Carlsmith, 1968). Therefore, mundane realism is of less concern in planning and pretesting. To control many variables and isolate others for study, some degree of mundane realism must be sacrificed. However, as long as an experiment is properly designed, so that the relationship between variables is interpretable, its findings will be important even if it is artificial in a mundane sense.

The Experiment as a Social Occasion

Unlike an audience for a stage play, who assume a passive role, subjects in a laboratory experiment are both audience and active participants. As participants, they bring to the experimental setting their own personal qualities, needs, and expectations. And as they interact with the experimenter (or the experimental assistants), the event takes on social as well as scientific aspects.

Scientifically, an experiment is an occasion to measure subjects' responses to certain intentionally and systematically varied stimuli. However, other stimuli related to the social aspects of the occasion may have unintended effects, which account for subjects' responses as much as or more than the intended experimental manipulation. A good example of this was the famous Hawthorne experiments, mentioned in Chapter 2 (see Box 2.1). Measuring the production rate of workers in response to a series of changes in working conditions (e.g., working hours, temperature, method of payment), the investigators (Roethlisberger and Dickson, 1939) found to their surprise that every change introduced resulted in an increase in productivity. This heightened productivity was a response not to the specific changes, however, but to the special attention given the group of workers as participants in an important experiment.

In Chapter 5, we referred to the responses that result from subjects' awareness of being studied as **reactive measurement effects**. An example was the self-censoring that occurs with verbal report measures. Although such effects are present in varying degrees in survey and field research, they are most problematic in laboratory experiments. Subjects in a laboratory experiment are acutely aware that they are participants in an experiment. Usually, their participation has brought them to a place they have never been to interact with people whom they have never met. They realize that they may be asked to do some strange things in the name of scientific inquiry, and they are likely to suspect that the true nature of the experiment is being concealed from them. They are aware that they are being observed and that certain behaviors are expected of them. Let us take a look now at how such thoughts and expectations might affect subjects' behavior.

Demand Characteristics

In any situation, from classroom to athletic field to experimental laboratory, norms and role expectations govern behavior. Subjects entering an experiment, for example, implicitly agree to place themselves under the control of an experimenter and to perform a wide range of tasks without questioning their purpose or duration (Orne, 1962). These expectations were strikingly demonstrated by the psychologist Martin Orne (1962) in the course of his research on hypnosis. To study the difference between the degree of control inherent in the hypnotic relationship and that in a waking relationship, Orne tried to develop boring, meaningless, or unpleasant tasks that waking subjects would refuse to do or would stop doing after a short period of time. However, Orne found instead that subjects would persist hour after hour in apparently meaningless tasks. In one of these, subjects were instructed to perform additions of adjacent numbers on a sheet filled with hundreds of random numbers, to tear up the sheet in a prescribed manner, and then to go on to the next sheet and do the same thing, continuing in this manner until told to stop. Despite many efforts, Orne could find no task that would be refused or quickly discontinued by subjects once they agreed to participate in an experiment.

To Orne, these results revealed that a previously unimagined degree of control exists in the experimental setting. As a consequence of "being in an experiment," subjects feel justified in carrying out all sorts of tedious, noxious, or even dangerous tasks. In one experiment, Orne and Frederick Evans (1965) found that subjects fearlessly complied with a request to reach into a cage containing a poisonous snake, only to be prevented from doing so by an invisible pane of glass. The reason subjects will perform such tasks is that the "demands" placed on them in an experiment go beyond an experimenter's verbal instructions. Because of the knowledge that one is in an experiment, endlessly boring tasks are viewed as endurance tests and seemingly dangerous acts are seen as really safe.

The particular cues in an experimental situation that communicate to subjects what is expected and what an experimenter hopes to find are called **demand characteristics** (Orne, 1962, 1969). These cues, which may be subtle, range broadly. They can be communicated through campus scuttlebutt about the experiment, information provided during the recruiting of subjects, experimenter qualities such as appearance, the laboratory setting, experimental procedures, and communications during the experiment. According to Orne (1962), what makes subjects especially susceptible to such cues is their determination to play the role of "good subject." A good subject believes in the value of social science research and hopes by his or her participation to make a contribution toward the advancement of science. Whatever the purpose of the experiment, he or she assumes it to be worthwhile. Such subjects will gladly comply with virtually any request of the experimenter. And to help the experimenter, they are sensitive, consciously or unconsciously, to cues that indicate how to behave so as to validate the experimental hypothesis. Consistent with the good-subject role, we have found during debriefing that subjects sometimes express concern about whether they have "performed" as expected, saying something like, "I hope I didn't ruin the experiment."

The crux of the problem is that, in some experiments, unintended demand characteristics may influence subjects' responses more than the intended experimental manipulation. Consider, for example, laboratory studies of the effect of persuasive messages on attitude change. When presented with a message or argument, followed by attitude or opinion measures, most subjects realize that their acquiescence to the message is being studied. If they are motivated to conform to an experimenter's expectations, then compliance to demand characteristics rather than the persuasiveness of the message accounts for their responses. One study in which this was demonstrated (Silverman, 1968) presented subjects with a 250-word report advocating the use of closed-circuit television tapes to present lectures in large classes. It was found that subjects showed more agreement with the message when they were told that they were in an experiment than when this fact was not explicitly conveyed to them.

Evaluation Apprehension

In addition to their concern about being helpful and cooperative, subjects in experiments often experience anxiety about being evaluated. Viewing the experimenter, typically a psychologist, as having special skills to determine their true character or personality, subjects come to experiments expecting the possibility that they will be evaluated. When this suspicion is confirmed, they are likely to experience **evaluation apprehension**. According to Milton J. Rosenberg (1965:29), who coined the term, subjects whose evaluation apprehension is aroused are concerned that they "win the positive evaluation of the experimenter, or at least that [they] provide no grounds for a negative one." This may cause the subject to be overly sensitive to cues regarding what constitutes a good, healthy, able, or "normal" performance of the task and, thus, to not respond spontaneously to the independent variable.

Evidence that subjects may behave in a way that is thought to project a favorable image comes from an experiment by M. J. Rosenberg (1969). Subjects who believed they were participating in a social perception study were asked "to judge how much they liked or disliked various pictured persons." Before carrying out this task, however, one group of subjects was told that past research indicated that psychologically mature and healthy people show greater liking for strangers than do immature people, whereas a second group was told the opposite. For both groups, subjects' "liking" judgments reflected their beliefs about how psychologically mature individuals would respond.

For many subjects in the Rosenberg experiment, "looking good" may have seemed consistent with "being a good subject" and complying with demand characteristics. What happens, however, when there is a conflict between projecting a favorable image and confirming the experimenter's hypothesis? The evidence suggests that subjects will choose to look good. In one experiment (Sigall, Aronson, and Van Hoose, 1970), for example, subjects who knew the experimenter's hypothesis responded so as to disconfirm it when they thought that cooperating would reveal an unfavorable personality type.

KEY POINT

Being aware that they are in an experiment, subjects may try to guess the true purpose of the study so that they might behave in ways that project a favorable image or that help the experimenter confirm the hypothesis.

Other Motives of Experimental Subjects

Motives of experimental subjects are not limited to those of the good subject who carefully attends to demand characteristics to help the experimenter or to the anxious subject intent on putting his or her best foot forward. When 110 experienced subjects were questioned regarding what they liked about the last experiment in which they participated (Straits and Wuebben, 1973), responses referred to the nature of the experimental task or the experimenter, the challenge of a new experience or of being successful in the experiment, the opportunity to learn something, and figuring out the experiment's purpose. Other common motivators are course credit or pay.

Another possible subject role is that of the negative or "bad" subject who tries to sabotage the research by deliberately providing useless or invalid responses. Chris Argyris (1968:188) wrote, for example, that

> in one major university, a formal evaluation was made of the basic psychology course by nearly 600 undergraduates [and] the students were very critical, mistrustful, and hostile to the requirement [that they had to participate in experiments]. In many cases they identified how they expressed their pent-up feelings by "beating the researcher" in such a way that he never found out.

Why would subjects feel this way? Argyris, borrowing from organizational theory, has argued that experiments "tend to place subjects in situations that are similar to those organizations create for the lower level employees" (193). Unaccustomed to being subordinates in a highly authoritarian system, research subjects may react by adopting employee ploys such as covert withdrawal or opposition.

Despite Argyris's claim, negativistic subjects seem to be less prevalent than apprehensive or good subjects (S. J. Weber and Cook, 1972). On the other hand, studies on the motivation of experimental subjects, taken together, seem to suggest that human subjects are too complex and diverse to describe by simple models presuming good, bad, or anxious subjects. For example, subjects may hold both hostile and favorable feelings toward experimentation and the social sciences. Certain features of experiments, such as required participation or unpleasant tasks, may evoke bad subject motives and behavior; other features, such as an impressive or attractive experimenter, may stimulate good subject motives. One cannot assume that a subject will be a passive responder to the experimental manipulation. Furthermore, there is always the strong possibility of subject bias whenever experimental procedures make the hypothesis transparent.

Experimenter Effects

Another source of bias due to the social nature of experiments is the experimenter. Experimenters can affect the results of their research in many ways that are not unique to experimentation, for example, by making recording errors, computational errors, and errors of interpretation or by intentionally falsifying their data (recall from Chapter 2, Box 2.2, the case of Cyril Burt). However, the most problematic experimenter effects are influences on subjects' behavior. Robert Rosenthal (1966, 1967, 1969), who investigated such effects extensively, showed that numerous experimenter traits, including gender, race, status, anxiety, and warmth, affect the behavior of subjects. Just what effects these traits have depend on the particular experiment and on characteristics of the subject. Also, to a certain extent, such effects can be limited through training and appropriate controls.

More unsettling and operating at a more subtle level are effects resulting from an experimenter's expectations about how the experiment will turn out. Several studies by Rosenthal and others have shown an **experimenter expectancy effect**—that experimenters may unintentionally communicate to subjects their expectations about how the subjects "should" respond so as to confirm their hypotheses. One study involved a "person-perception" task (Rosenthal and Fode, 1963). Graduate student experimenters, who believed they were replicating a previous study, were told to present a set of photographs of individuals and ask subjects to rate each photograph as to how successful the individual appeared to be. The pictures had been selected on the basis of pretests to include only individuals who appeared neither especially successful nor unsuccessful. However, half the experimenters were informed that subjects would generally perceive the persons photographed as experiencing success (high ratings); the other half were led to expect that subjects would perceive the individuals as unsuccessful (low ratings). Although the experimenters read identical instructions to their subjects, those experimenters expecting high success ratings tended to get higher ratings from their subjects than those expecting low ratings.

The means by which experimenters communicate their expectancies to subjects is not well understood, although there have been a number of studies on this question. Some studies have demonstrated the importance of auditory cues—voice quality or tone of voice. For example, Edward Zoble and Richard Lehman (1969) showed that if subjects performing Rosenthal and Fode's (1963) person-perception task were denied visual contact with the experimenter, about one-half of the expectancy effect remained. This study, as well as others (Rosenthal, 1969:253–54), also provides indirect evidence that visual cues such as facial expressions and gestures may mediate expectancy effects.

Fortunately, although there is little question of the existence of experimenter expectancy effects, it is doubtful that such effects are either strong or widespread. Those studies designed to demonstrate an expectancy effect, such as the study involving person perception, differ from most other experiments in two regards: (1) the stimulus was highly ambiguous, which may have caused the subject to pay unusual attention to any possible cues from the experimenter, and (2) the experimenters for the most part ran subjects in one experimental condition only. Elliot Aronson and J. Merrill Carlsmith (1968:67) have pointed out that an experimenter would be less likely to bias subject behavior when running subjects in more than one condition because he or she would probably notice any systematic differences in his or her behavior toward subjects. Still, the general problem of experimenter bias is one that researchers can ill afford to ignore.

Minimizing Bias Resulting from the Social Nature of Experimentation

Although experiments provide an ideal model for testing causal relations, the success of that model depends on an experimenter's ability to eliminate or minimize potential biases emanating from an experiment's social nature. Several strategies have been developed for handling the problems raised by demand characteristics and experimenter bias.

The most straightforward way of detecting demand characteristics is simply to ask subjects about their perception of the experimental situation (Orne, 1969). Did the subjects entertain any hypotheses? Did it appear to them that the experimenter expected them to behave in a certain way? How do they think others might have reacted in the situation? This sort of probing could take place in a pretesting phase, in which subjects are asked for their impressions at different points in the experiment, or during the debriefing.

The most widely used means of controlling for demand characteristics is a cover story that provides subjects with a false hypothesis about the purpose of the study. If a cover story satisfies subjects' suspicions about the purpose of the experiment, the subjects will not be busily trying to figure out the true hypothesis; therefore, they will be less likely to act deliberately in ways consistent or inconsistent with it. Similarly, experiments high in experimental realism (partly achieved with a good cover story) have such an impact on subjects that there is little chance for them to be distracted by evaluation apprehension or other suspicions.

A second approach to circumventing the problem of demand characteristics is to measure the dependent variable in a setting different from the one in which the independent variable is manipulated. By separating these processes physically, experimenters hope the subjects will dissociate the events psychologically. For example, M. J. Rosenberg (1965) arranged for subjects to participate in two apparently unrelated studies conducted by different experimenters. In the first study, conducted in the education department, subjects were paid to write essays counter to their own views on a particular issue, with the size of the payment being the independent variable. Then, in a subsequent opinion survey, conducted in the psychology department, subjects' attitudes on the same issue were measured. A less elaborate separation of these parts of the experiment occurred in three studies testing the hypothesis that guilt increases compliance (Freedman, Wallington, and Bless, 1967). The investigators first manipulated subjects' feelings of guilt. Then, when the experiment appeared to be over and the subject was about to leave the laboratory, they measured compliance by asking subjects if they would be willing to take part in another study, without pay, being conducted by another person in the department.

A third technique for controlling demand characteristics is to keep subjects unaware that they are participating in an experiment. In this way, subjects should behave naturally without wondering about the true nature of the situation. The best place to conduct such "disguised experiments" is in a natural rather than a laboratory setting (Campbell, 1969). A good example is the Page experiment on teacher comments.

Finally, there is some evidence that the effects of demand characteristics can be minimized by asking subjects to adopt the role of the "faithful subject." Faithful subjects believe that they should follow instructions scrupulously, regardless of their suspicions about the true purpose of the experiment (S. J. Weber and Cook, 1972). Getting subjects to adopt this role, however, might be difficult if the experiment is likely to evoke a high level of evaluation apprehension.

Several approaches also have been developed to eliminate or reduce bias introduced by experimenters. One possibility, the **double-blind technique**, prevents experimenters from knowing which condition a subject is in. This would be akin to studies of new drugs in which neither the subject nor the research assistant interviewing the subject knows whether the subject received the drug or a placebo (inert substance). With this method, a coding system enables research supervisors to keep track of which subjects received which treatment.

In most studies it is not possible to keep the experimenter blind to the subjects' condition because differences in the treatment conditions are obvious to the experimenter. In these cases, a partial solution may be to utilize two or more experimenters, with each "blind" to some part of the experiment. For example, when the manipulation of the independent variable is separated from the measurement of the dependent variable, as in the guilt-compliance study mentioned earlier, these two processes could be carried out easily by different experimenters.

Another effective means of controlling the effects of experimenter bias is to have a single experimental session that includes all subjects. The experimenter might read general instructions to all subjects but manipulate the independent variable by varying additional written instructions. If the latter instructions were randomly assigned, the experimenter could not systematically influence the subjects in any one group.

Finally, one could reduce the amount of contact between the experimenter and subjects by using taped recordings or written instructions. This averts the possibility of an experimenter unknowingly introducing differences in the intended manipulation through slight variations in voice quality, inflections, and volume; by smiling more at some subjects than at others; and so forth. This approach also would reduce experimental realism, however, because subjects are likely to be more attentive to a live experimenter.

Experimentation outside the Laboratory

In the last two sections we have focused on experiments carried out in a laboratory. By far the most common setting for the experimental approach, the laboratory permits substantial control—control over subject assignment and of the events to which subjects are exposed. Control is obtained, however, at some cost: The sample of subjects is usually small and from a highly restricted population; the setting is often unrealistic in the mundane sense; and the subjects are aware that the experimenter has created the situation to test some hypothesis about their behavior.

Some experimental designs avoid these problems by moving outside the laboratory into a more natural social setting. When experiments take place "in the field," mundane realism tends to be high and demand characteristics are minimized because subjects often are unaware that they are participating in a study. Experimental designs also may be incorporated into nonexperimental research approaches, such as social surveys. Finally, as further evidence of the versatility of the experimental approach, the subjects randomly assigned to experimental conditions may consist of social units such as families, classrooms, clinics, and organizations, as well as individuals.

Field Experiments

Field experiments refer to studies that meet all the requirements of a true experiment but are conducted in a natural setting. As in a laboratory experiment, there is a staging of events in a field experiment. But this staging occurs in an environment that is familiar to the subject and is rendered in such a way that it appears to be a "natural" (albeit slightly out of the ordinary) part of that environment. For an example we turn to one of numerous field experiments on bystander intervention.

One way to overcome the ambiguity and diffusion of responsibility that are inherent in many emergencies and that inhibit people from helping is to focus responsibility for helping onto one person. A situation where this commonly occurs is public places in which one stranger asks another to watch his or her possessions while he or she leaves the area for a short time. Thomas Moriarty (1975) tested the effectiveness of such a request by staging a series of thefts at Jones Beach, New York, in the summer of 1972. To set up the manipulation of "commitment to help," a confederate placed a blanket on the beach near the subject, turned on a portable radio, and proceeded to sunbathe. After reclining for a few minutes, the confederate spoke briefly to the subject, asking him or her either to watch his belongings while he was away for a few minutes (commitment condition) or for a match as he left for a walk (control condition). A few minutes later, a second confederate walked by, picked up the radio from the victim's blanket, and walked quickly away. Two dependent measures were used: noticing the theft and intervening to stop it. Noticing the theft was measured in a postexperimental interview; of the 56 subjects, 16, all of whom were in the control condition, reported that they had not noticed the radio being taken. Among the 40 subjects who noticed the theft, 95 percent of those who had accepted responsibility to help intervened compared with only 20 percent of those who were not committed to help.

Social researchers have gone outside the research laboratory to conduct experiments in a wide variety of settings. In the study of helping behavior alone, field experiments have been performed in department stores and municipal parking lots (Forgas, Dunn, and Granland, 2008; Shotland and Stebbins, 1983), in a suburban shopping mall (C. J. Taylor, 1998), in a college library (Isen and Levin, 1972), in elevators (Latané and Dabbs, 1975), on a highway (Bryan and Test, 1967), and in the New York City subway (Piliavin and Piliavin, 1972). Conducting experiments in such settings offers several advantages. Without being aware that a study is in progress, subjects should not respond self-consciously to demand characteristics. External validity generally increases, not only because the setting is more realistic but also because it is possible to observe the behavior of a more heterogeneous sample of subjects. Field experimentation also lends itself well to applied research—that is, research intended to provide input into problem solving. Some of the field experiments on helping behavior, for example, have been directed at factors affecting blood donating (Goette and Stutzer, 2008) and charitable contributions (Simpson, Irwin, and Lawrence, 2006). (To learn about the fruitful application of field experimentation to the study of voter mobilization, read Box 7.2.)

KEY POINT

Field experiments tend to be higher in external validity and mundane realism than laboratory experiments.

With these advantages, one may wonder why the field has not supplanted the laboratory as the primary setting for experimental research. Alas, there are disadvantages, the major drawback being the lower degree of control in field experiments. Often, researchers can only approximate a true experimental design in the field. It may not be possible to assign subjects (or other units of analysis) randomly to the various treatment conditions. Sometimes it is not possible to have a true control group because of ethical considerations or subject preferences. Furthermore, field experimenters often relinquish some control over the experiment by their dependence on other persons such as administrators or teachers to carry out parts of the study. Consequently, it is much more difficult outside the laboratory to ensure that there are no systematic differences in the experiences of subjects other than those resulting from the manipulation of the independent variable.

A related problem with field experimentation is that the manipulation of the independent variable may be less controllable and more open to interpretation. This is apparent in studies that attempted to evaluate the educational impact on American preschoolers of the television series *Sesame Street* (Ball and Bogatz, 1970; T. D. Cook and Conner, 1976; Liebert, 1976). Ideally, to investigate the effects of viewing, it would be desirable to have a treatment group that viewed the series and a control group that did not. However, because there was no practical way to prevent the control group children from viewing the series in their homes, it was decided that the experimental treatment would be "encouragement to view." This treatment included weekly visits by trained staff who encouraged parents and children to watch the programs and who brought along literature, toys, and games designed to stimulate viewing. The control group children received no encouragement and could view or not. Both groups of children were given a battery of tests before the first viewing season and at its end, and the results showed that the group that was encouraged to view made greater gains on the posttests. Unfortunately, this did not establish that viewing the programs caused the gains because there were systematic differences in the experiences of the two groups aside from the viewing experience; that is, the effects of viewing were confounded with the effects of encouragement. It is possible that the social and intellectual stimulation provided by the encouragement alone was sufficient to cause the gains.[4]

BOX 7.2 FIELD EXPERIMENTATION ON VOTER MOBILIZATION

How to increase voter turnout draws broad interest—from nonpartisan groups wishing to promote civic involvement and strengthen democracy, from political consultants and campaign organizers seeking to win elections, and from social scientists theorizing about patterns of political participation. Until recently, however, there was little hard evidence about how best to get out the vote. The advice from professional campaigners ran from election-day phoning to mail reminders, leafleting, personal canvassing, and other methods. But nobody really knew what worked. Then, the political scientists Donald Green and Alan Gerber launched a program of field experiments, the results of which have transformed the way that people think about getting out the vote.

Gerber and Green (2000) performed their first field experiment in New Haven, Connecticut, at the time of the 1998 general election. They designed the experiment to test the effects of three methods of mobilizing turnout: personal canvassing, telephone calls, and direct mail appeals. From a complete list of registered voters, they randomly assigned nearly 30,000 voters to one or more of these get-out-the-vote (GOTV) strategies.

All three strategies were carefully developed based on input from professional campaign consultants. Paid canvassers contacted voters during each weekend for 4 weeks before the election; between one and three mailings, each consisting of a three-color postcard, were sent 15, 13, and 8 days before the election; and telephone calls were made by a telemarketing firm 1–2 days before or on the day of the election. In all cases, one of three nonpartisan appeals was made: civic duty, close election, and neighborhood solidarity. In the civic duty version, for example, the script read, "We want to encourage everyone to do their civic duty and exercise their right to vote. Democracy depends on the participation of our country's citizens" (Gerber and Green, 2000:656).

To assess effects, Gerber and Green determined through public records who voted in the election and who did not. The results showed that the content of the messages made no difference in voter turnout, but how the messages were delivered did. Personal canvassing was estimated to increase voter turnout by 9.8 percentage points, direct mail raised turnout by .6 percentage points per mailing, and telephoning had no effect.

Prior to this study, experimental research was rare in political science. But after demonstrating the value of field experiments for studying voting behavior, Gerber and Green's research generated a rapidly growing literature based on this methodology. In contrast to other research approaches, experiments offer the most effective means of testing causal claims. If done properly, with randomized comparisons, they leave little doubt about what works and what doesn't. Conducting the experiments in the field—in a real-world setting—also enhances external validity, and using public records to measure voter turnout improves on studies that rely on self-reports. Furthermore, the sample in voter turnout experiments is huge compared with that in most other field experiments. With nearly 30,000 voters, Gerber and Green were able to detect small differences in the effectiveness of GOTV techniques and to make precise estimates of their costs.

Since the New Haven field experiment, scores of field experiments on GOTV drives have been carried out. They have been done in local, state, and general elections; in numerous areas throughout the United States; among voters of different ethnicity; with both nonpartisan and partisan efforts; and with a range of mobilization strategies (see Green and Gerber,

2008). Although we now know much more about what works, the central finding of the first experiment still applies. The best way to mobilize voters is through personal contact: "the more personal the interaction between campaign and potential voter, the more it raises a person's chances of voting" (Green and Gerber, 2008:10). As Gerber and Green (2000:653) hypothesized in their initial study, the lack of personal canvassing may account for the decline in voter turnout in U.S. elections in the last quarter of the twentieth century, when mobilization efforts became "increasingly impersonal, and messages that once might have been delivered in person [were] communicated using mass marketing techniques." By the same token, Bergan et al. (2005:760) attribute part of the increased turnout in the 2004 general election to a marked change in campaign strategy, "with both parties placing an unusual emphasis on voter mobilization."

By 2004, the effort to get supporters to the polls on election day, known as the "ground game" by campaign professionals, was considered an essential strategy for winning elections. Republican campaigners believed that their ground game was decisive in re-electing President Bush in 2004, just as President Obama's supporters claimed that their superior grassroots mobilization was the key to victory in 2008. Neither party can know for sure. But anyone who wants to know which GOTV approaches work best and at what cost should read Green and Gerber's (2008) *Get Out the Vote: How to Increase Voter Turnout.*

Finally, field experiments often raise ethical and legal issues. Is it ethical or legal, for example, to expose passersby to a crime or to someone who collapses or feigns a heart attack, as has been done in bystander intervention research? Imagine the risk of harm in the theft experiment. What if the subject, perhaps an off-duty police officer, used physical force to apprehend the "thief"? Or what if someone called the police? To Moriarty's (1975) credit, he took precautions to limit the risk of harm, stationing an observer nearby to record subjects' reactions and to stop the interaction between subject and thief once the subject had intervened. He also told subjects as soon as possible that the theft was not real. Still, we wonder how many institutional review boards these days would approve this study.

In laboratory experiments, subjects' rights are protected by obtaining their prior consent to participate and by debriefing. But these safeguards may be impossible to incorporate in a field experiment. Obtaining informed consent, for instance, in many cases would destroy the cover for the experiment. Thus, there is a greater demand on field experimenters to demonstrate that their research presents no more than minimal risk of harm to subjects.

Experimental Designs in Survey Research

The versatility of the experimental approach is evidenced not only by extensions into the field but also by the use of experimental design in survey research. For example, numerous surveys have investigated the effects of slight changes in the wording of a question during an interview. Generally, as part of a larger survey, a mini-experiment is conducted by directing a question with one wording to a randomly selected subsample of respondents and directing a differently worded question to the remaining respondents. (See Box 10.1 for a specific example.)

As long as surveys involved questionnaires that had to be printed in advance, the experiments incorporated into surveys tended to be simple; most often they were limited to two conditions (or questionnaire forms) in what was called a "split-ballot design." But two innovations, the advent of computer-assisted interviewing (see Chapter 9) and the development of the vignette method, have greatly expanded the application and complexity of experimental designs in large-scale surveys (Sniderman and Grob, 1996). The following two studies illustrate these developments.

An example of an experiment embedded in a larger survey is Jon Hurwitz and Mark Peffley's (2005) study of the impact of racialized code words on support for punitive crime policy. For much of U.S. history, candidates for political office have explicitly "played the race card" to gain voter support. That is, they have used racial words to express antiblack sentiments and racial stereotypes and to arouse fears of African Americans. But according to Tali Mendelberg (2001), as the norm of racial equality strengthened in the last half of the twentieth century, explicit appeals became unacceptable and were unlikely to garner support because they made people aware of the racist content of the message. Mendelberg argues, however, that "when a society has repudiated racism, yet racial conflict persists, candidates can win by playing the race card" through implicit appeals that "prime racial stereotypes, fears, and resentments while not appearing to do so" (4).

To test whether the subtle phrase "inner-city," which has strong racial connotations, would implicitly prime whites' racial concerns, Hurwitz and Peffley (2005) experimentally manipulated the phrase in a 2001 national telephone survey of non-Hispanic whites. In a set of questions about crime, they asked respondents how they would prevent crime committed by "violent criminals": by spending money on new prisons or antipoverty programs. A randomly selected one-half of respondents were asked about violent criminals, whereas the other half were asked about "violent *inner-city* criminals." The survey also included sets of questions about racial attitudes, punitiveness, fear of crime, and background measures. As hypothesized, whites' racial attitudes were significantly related to punitive policies (new prisons instead of antipoverty programs) only in the inner-city cue condition. In the absence of the inner-city phrase, whites' racial attitudes were unrelated to their crime-policy preferences.

An experimental design also may be incorporated into surveys through the use of different sets of questionnaires (see Navazio, 1977) and vignettes. *Vignettes* are short, detailed, and concrete descriptions of situations that contain references to factors that are thought to be important in decision making. Some survey researchers believe that vignettes produce more valid responses than the briefer but more general or abstract questions normally used in opinion surveys (see Alexander and Becker, 1978; Mutz, 2011). To test experimentally which factors in a given situation significantly affect respondents' decision making, a number of versions of the vignettes are developed by systematically varying the details of the situation. The different versions are then randomly assigned to respondents. For example, to study college women's fertility plans, Bruce Straits (1985) used six vignettes, each of which described a married woman facing a decision directly or indirectly bearing on her childbearing plans. The information that was varied in each vignette concerned the direct costs of children due to changes in earning power and living standards, the indirect costs of children due to the loss of other opportunities for self-fulfillment (e.g., forgoing further schooling or occupational advancement), and the perceived cultural support for parenthood. Contrary to some journalistic accounts, Straits found that the college women in his sample had a strong commitment to motherhood that took precedence over a career and other direct and indirect costs of childbearing.

Surveys typically draw large numbers of respondents through probability sampling from a designated target population (see Chapter 9). As the political scientist Diana Mutz (2011) points out, experiments embedded in such surveys afford many advantages. In general, such studies benefit by combining the high internal validity of experiments with the high external validity of probability samples. Larger samples make it easier to investigate the effects of multiple independent variables as well as differences among population subgroups. Moreover, survey experiments may be designed to inform public policy and, because they can be carried out quickly, to investigate reactions to real-world events (see Mutz, 2011:12–20).

Units of Analysis Other Than Individuals

Experimental designs do not always use individuals as the unit of analysis. Numerous laboratory experiments performed over the years have treated pairs of subjects or small groups as units. Although less common, experimental units of analysis also have consisted of larger groupings such as organizations or neighborhoods.

One illustrative field experiment on patrol staffing in San Diego, California, used police "beats" as the units, assigning them to either a one-officer or a two-officer condition. The object of this study was to evaluate whether staffing police patrol cars with two officers as opposed to one officer resulted in increased quality of service, efficiency, and safety, making the practice cost-effective (Boydstun, Sherry, and Moelter, 1978). It had been determined that the difference in cost between fielding a two-officer patrol unit and a one-officer patrol unit was more than $100 per unit for an 8-hour period. Pairs of beats were matched on various characteristics and then randomly assigned to the one-officer or two-officer staffing condition, with 44 patrol units involved. The findings revealed that quality of performance and efficiency were as high with the one-officer units as with the two-officer units and that the two-officer units were more often associated with suspects resisting arrest or assaulting officers. The study concluded, therefore, that the staffing ought to be primarily one-officer units.

Sometimes the use of social units can be more economical than the use of individuals. Kevin Arceneaux (2005) demonstrated this in a study of voter mobilization in Kansas City, Missouri. An advocacy group used voting precincts as units of analysis when it conducted a door-to-door canvassing campaign to persuade voters to vote for a ballot proposal that would increase the sales tax to support the bus service. As we describe in Box 7.2, in field experiments on getting out the vote, typically registered voters are randomly assigned to experimental conditions. In testing the effects of door-to-door canvassing, for example, trained canvassers would visit only those individuals assigned to the treatment condition. However, as Arceneaux (2005:169) notes, this increases the geographic area to be covered, and it "requires a great deal of care in constructing walk lists" and training canvassers to avoid contact with individuals who are not targeted. Alternatively, he suggests randomly assigning clusters, such as voting precincts, to treatments rather than individuals. This would not only reduce costs but also make it possible to study the effects of voter mobilization on voter *preferences* as well as turnout. In both types of experiments, publicly available voter files are used to measure turnout, but the files reveal only whether individuals voted, not *how* they voted. Because precinct-level data are available on voter choices, it is possible to compare preferences across precincts. In Kansas City in 2003, it was found that door-to-door canvassing had a small but nonsignificant effect on mobilizing supporters for the proposal.

Summary

- Because of its greater degree of control, experimentation is the preferred approach for testing causal hypotheses.
- Experiments control for extraneous variables by (a) randomly assigning subjects to treatment and control groups (which ensures that pre-experimental differences are distributed approximately evenly among the groups) and (b) making sure that treatment and control group subjects experience the same events during the experiment except for the manipulation of the independent variable.
- By providing relatively strong inferences about cause and effect, experiments are high in internal validity; however, the laboratory context and narrow subject pools limit their generalizability and lower their external validity.
- External validity is sometimes increased by using more heterogeneous samples; more often it is achieved through replications that test the same hypothesis but in a different setting, with different variable manipulations and measures and with subjects drawn from different populations.
- The staging of an experiment has four main parts: (1) an introduction, which provides instructions and a rationale for the experimental procedures; (2) manipulation of the independent variable, ideally followed by a manipulation check; (3) measurement of the dependent variable; and (4) a debriefing session, which is intended to explain the purpose of the experiment, explore subjects' reactions, and assuage subjects' anxieties about their participation.
- Before experiments are carried out, they should be pretested on preliminary subjects to check the efficacy of the procedures.
- A study's experimental realism refers to the extent to which the experiment engages and has an impact on subjects; its mundane realism refers to the similarity of experimental procedures to "real-world" events.
- Subjects' actions in an experiment may be determined by their sensitivity to cues, called "demand characteristics," which may communicate the hypothesis being tested; by their apprehensiveness about being evaluated; or by their resentment about being "coerced" into taking part in an experiment.
- Subject biases might be detected by pre- and postexperimental interviews; they may be controlled most effectively using a good cover story that inhibits subjects' suspicions.
- Experimenters may nonverbally communicate their own expectations to subjects. Such biases are controlled most effectively by keeping experimenters blind to the subjects' conditions or using two experimenters, each blind to a part of the experiment, or carrying out the experiment in a single session.
- One other means of controlling for biases and also increasing external validity is to perform an experiment in a natural setting, where subjects are unaware that a scientific investigation is taking place. However, field experiments may sacrifice control and usually make it more difficult to protect subjects' rights and safety.
- Experiments may be incorporated into sample surveys and may use of units of analysis other than individuals.

Key Terms

true experimental designs
treatment
random assignment
test of statistical significance
matching
internal validity
external validity
replication
cover story
manipulation check

debriefing
pretesting
experimental realism
mundane realism
reactive measurement effects
demand characteristics
evaluation apprehension
experimenter expectancy effect
double-blind technique
field experiment

Exercises

1. In the March 2006 issue of *Social Psychology Quarterly* (vol. 69, pp. 97–107), Jeffery Lucas, Corina Graif, and Michael Lovaglia report an experiment that examined the question of why misconduct occurs more frequently in the prosecution of severe than mild crimes. Read the article and then answer the following questions.
   a. What was the independent variable in all three hypotheses? How was it manipulated? Did the investigators perform a manipulation check?
   b. How did the experimenters measure the dependent variable "personal importance of attaining a conviction"?
   c. Aside from the manipulation of the independent variable and measurement of the dependent variable, how does this study meet the requirements of a true experiment?
   d. Evaluate this experiment from the standpoint of measurement validity, internal validity, and external validity.
   e. Evaluate the experiment in terms of experimental and mundane realism.
2. To investigate racial discrimination in the labor market, two researchers conducted a study in which they answered help-wanted ads in Boston and Chicago newspapers by sending resumes. They sent two sets of resumes to each ad, with each set of resumes randomly assigned either a very African American–sounding name or a very white-sounding name (e.g., Tyrone versus Todd). Finally, they tested the effect of race by counting the number of call-backs for interviews. (For a more complete description of this study, see Box 8.1.)
   a. Is this a true experiment? Carefully explain.
   b. What is the independent variable in this study? How was it manipulated?
   c. Explain how this study effectively controls for demand characteristics and experimenter effects.
   d. In discussing the weaknesses of the study, the investigators note that (1) newspaper ads represent only one channel for job searches and (2) there are other measures of racial discrimination that they could not use, such as whether applicants got a job and the wage they were offered. Explain whether these criticisms pertain to the internal validity or external validity of the study.
3. In addition to several laboratory experiments, Latané and Darley (1970) did a field study on bystander intervention. They performed the study by staging a theft at a discount beverage store in Suffern, New York, which sold beer and soda by the case. "Robbers" acted out the theft when either one or two other customers were in the store and near the checkout counter. When the cashier, who was in cahoots with the robbers, left the checkout counter to get something in the back of the store, the robbers picked up a case of beer, remarked "They'll never miss this," and walked out the door. Soon thereafter the cashier returned to the checkout counter and resumed waiting on the customers; the dependent measure was whether customers reported the theft to him. As in laboratory experiments, customers were more likely to report the emergency (the theft) when they were the only witness than when someone else also saw it.

    a.   What feature of a true experiment is missing from this study? What problems does this present in interpreting the results of the study?

    b.   Evaluate this study from the standpoint of research ethics. What ethical issues does it raise?

4.   Suppose you want to test the hypothesis that flattery increases helping—that is, people who are flattered and thereby made to feel good about themselves are more likely to help someone than are people who are not flattered. Design an experiment to test this hypothesis. How will you manipulate the independent variable? How will you measure helping behavior? Why would it be better to conduct your experiment in the field than in the laboratory?

Notes

1.   Note that in this sense the word "significance" does not refer to the importance or triviality of the research findings.

2.   Although this account of the Genovese case appears in numerous social psychology textbooks, analyses of court transcripts and other legal documents fail to support the existence of 38 unresponsive eyewitnesses (R. Manning, Levine, and Collins, 2007). Nonetheless, the incident stimulated research on one of the most robust findings in social psychology: the bystander effect.

3.   This hypothesis is explained partly by the theory that the presence of others at an emergency is likely to create a "diffusion of responsibility" for helping. That is, with others present, we feel less personally responsible for taking action and are more likely to rationalize that "someone else is doing something."

4.   This study is a good example of how a group of subjects who receive "no treatment" is not always an appropriate comparison group. Ideally, the experiences of the treatment and control groups should be similar in every way except for the variable the researcher intends to manipulate. A better comparison group for the *Sesame Street* study would be one in which families also received weekly visits with toys and games but in which the content of the materials was not designed to encourage viewing *Sesame Street*.

8

Experimental Designs

By now you should have some clear ideas about the experimental approach—its key features, strengths and weaknesses, and the steps in carrying out an experiment. This chapter
will provide additional knowledge necessary to become an informed consumer of research.
Understanding the language and logic of experimental designs should be especially valuable to you as a citizen, as experimental designs increasingly are applied to the study of
social policy issues. Reading this chapter is, in fact, a prerequisite to reading Chapter 14, on
policy assessment research.

Although the topic of experimental design may sound formidable and some experiments with their statistical baggage do appear complex, the basic principle of good design
is simply the idea of "doing only one thing at a time." For the results of an experiment to
be as unequivocal as possible, the only plausible explanation of changes in the dependent
variable must be the manipulated independent variable. Therefore, a good design is one
that rules out explanations of the results other than the effect of the independent variable.
We learned in Chapter 7 that this is best accomplished by randomly assigning subjects to
experimental conditions (thereby controlling for pre-existing subject differences) and by
making sure that the events occurring within each experimental condition are exactly the
same except for the manipulated independent variable (thus controlling for extraneous factors and experiences during the experiment). The principle, then, is to allow only one factor,
the independent variable, to vary while controlling the rest.

In this chapter, the first three designs we consider are inadequate; they do not follow
the principle of good design. Before we examine the flaws in these "pre-experimental"
designs, we identify the kinds of uncontrolled variables, or threats to internal validity, that
provide plausible rival explanations of study results. Next, we consider three basic, true

experimental designs, which stand up better against threats to validity and thereby yield less ambiguous results. Then, we examine designs for testing the joint effects of two or more independent variables. The need for these more complex "factorial" designs exists because in the "real world," unlike in the typical laboratory experiment, many variables may be at work simultaneously. Finally, we examine some "quasi-experimental" designs, used when it is not practical or possible to meet all the requirements of true experiments.

Threats to Internal Validity[1]

In Chapter 7 we introduced the notion of internal validity. Recall that an experiment has internal validity when one can make strong inferences about cause and effect, inferring with confidence that the independent variable, rather than an extraneous variable, has produced the observed differences in the dependent variable. When we cannot separate the effects of the independent variable from possible effects of extraneous variables, we say that the effects are *confounded*. A subtle example of confounding is a taste-preference study sponsored by Pepsi-Cola (Huck and Sandler, 1979). In an early version of what became known as the "Pepsi Challenge," people were asked to taste two beverages, Pepsi and Coca-Cola, and indicate which they preferred. Ostensibly to prevent bias, the study sponsors concealed which beverage was Pepsi and which was Coke by marking the glasses with a letter, and perhaps to simplify the analysis, they used the same letters throughout the test: "M" for Pepsi and "Q" for Coke. Although Pepsi was reported to have won the Pepsi Challenge, the test lacked internal validity because the letter on the glass was confounded with the beverage in it. Indeed, when the study was replicated with Coke in *both* glasses, participants preferred the letter "M" over the letter "Q." Thus, letter preference rather than taste preference could have accounted for the original results.

The ideal research design effectively controls extraneous variables that threaten the internal validity of a study. We say "threaten" because uncontrolled extraneous variables pose explanations of study results that rival the hypothesized effects of the independent variable. To facilitate the evaluation of research designs, investigators have classified several common **threats to internal validity**, which we will now consider. Each of these threats signifies a distinctive class of extraneous variables.

KEY POINT
The internal validity of a study is threatened when the possible effects of the independent variable are confounded with the effects of extraneous variables.

One threat to internal validity is **history**. This consists of events in the subjects' environment, other than the manipulated independent variable, that occur during the course of the experiment and that may affect the outcome. In this sense a "historical event" may be a major event of social or political importance, such as an assassination of a public figure or a prolonged strike, or it may be a minor event that occurs within the experimental setting and has no significance outside it, such as a hostile remark by a subject. For example, suppose that you are studying the impact of a series of written persuasive communications on attitudes toward U.S. immigration policies. During the course of your experiment, many of your subjects happen to view a feature television program on the plight of illegal immigrant workers. Should the results of your study show that subjects' attitudes toward U.S. immigration policies have changed, it would be impossible for you to tell whether this change was caused by your independent variable (written communications) or by the television program. The confounded effects of the experimental manipulation and *history* preclude a clear causal interpretation of the results.

Another frequent rival explanation for research findings is **maturation**. By this we mean any psychological or physical changes taking place within subjects that occur with the passing of time regardless of the experimental manipulation. Even during a 1- or 2-hour experiment, subjects may become hungry or tired. Over a long-term experiment, subjects may grow physically or intellectually, become more rigid or more tolerant, or develop health problems or improved health. The effects of such maturational factors may be confounded with treatment effects. For example, in a study of the effectiveness of a new physical therapy program for stroke victims, any progress that the stroke victims would make naturally over time without therapeutic intervention (a phenomenon known as "spontaneous remission") might incorrectly be attributed to the therapy.

Testing represents a third possible source of internal invalidity. Similar to reactive measurement effects discussed in Chapters 5 and 7, testing refers to changes in what is being measured brought about by reactions to the process of measurement. Typically, people will score better or give more socially desirable or psychologically healthier responses the second time a test or scale is administered to them. This is true even when a different but similar measure is used. There are several reasons this occurs. On some measures, such as intelligence tests, the tasks simply become easier after practice. Attitude scales, on the other hand, may alert subjects to the purpose of the scale, causing them to give socially desirable responses or perhaps to re-examine their own attitudes. Such effects are potentially confounded with the effects of the independent variable whenever subjects are measured twice in the same study and the initial measurement arouses their awareness of being studied.

A fourth threat to internal validity, **instrumentation**, refers to unwanted changes in the measuring instrument or procedure. This threat is most likely to occur in experiments when the "instrument" is a human observer, who may become more skilled, more bored, or more or less observant during the course of the study. Instrumentation effects also may occur when different observers are used to obtain measurements in different conditions or parts of an experiment. Such an effect would be analogous to a shift in an instructor's grading standards while grading a set of essays or to inconsistent standards on the part of two instructors grading subsets of the same essays.

The fifth threat to internal validity is **statistical regression**, the tendency for extreme scorers on a test to move (regress) closer to the mean or average score on a second administration of the test. Also known as *regression toward the mean*, this phenomenon is likely to affect experimental results when subjects are selected for an experimental condition because of their extreme scores. Consider, for example, an experiment to assess the effectiveness of an assertiveness-training program in helping shy, introverted persons become more socially outgoing. Subjects are given a previously validated scale of extroversion, and the most introverted subjects—those who score in the bottom quartile—are assigned to the experimental condition, where they undergo an 8-week assertiveness-training program. The remaining subjects serve as a control group, receiving no such training. At the end of 8 weeks, both groups are retested. Assuming that subjects in the experimental group showed more significant gains in extroversion, on average, than the control group, we cannot confidently attribute this difference to the assertiveness-training program. The students chosen for assertiveness training were those scoring in the bottom 25 percent on a measure of extroversion. Because of this, the observed increase in extroversion scores may have been due to statistical regression rather than the training program.

Statistical regression can explain many events in everyday life. An example should clarify how its effects occur. Suppose that Instructor Young gives his class two exams. In each case the average grade is B. Table 8.1 compares the performance of individuals on the two tests. Young is disappointed to see, from the first row of Table 8.1, that of the 15 persons who received As on Exam I, only 10 received As on Exam II, with 4 receiving Bs and 1 receiving a C. He concludes that 5 of the students became overconfident after the first exam and slacked off. Then he looks at the C scorers and is delighted to see that of the 15 who scored C initially, 2 raised their scores to A and 4 to B. He feels some satisfaction that at least these students hit the books to bring their grades up. Such conclusions could be correct, but it is more likely that the results are due to regression toward the mean.

Because measurement error is always present, there is never a perfect correlation between scores from separate administrations of the same test or measure. A relatively large amount of measurement error will be reflected in a low correlation of scores and will result in more regression toward the mean. Another way to think of it is that the extreme scorers, as a subgroup, are affected more by chance factors we might call luck. On the first exam, some of the high scorers are particularly lucky, whereas some of the low scorers are particularly unlucky. But it would be rare for extremely lucky students on the first exam to repeat their good fortune on the second exam (or for unlucky students to repeat their misfortune), which results in subgroup scores closer to the mean. Initially average scorers, on the other hand, are likely to include about as many lucky as unlucky individuals so that changes in luck will tend to cancel out and not influence results on the second test.

A sixth threat to internal validity, **selection**, is present whenever there are systematic differences in the composition of the control and experimental groups. Selection bias is especially likely when naturally existing groups are studied. Suppose, for example, a study

TABLE 8.1. **Grade on Exam II by Grade on Exam I (Hypothetical Data)**

	Exam II grade			
Exam I grade	A	B	C	Total
A	10	4	1	15
B	3	22	5	30
C	2	4	9	15
Total	15	30	15	60

compared 1-year recidivism rates of apparently recovered alcoholics who received help through Alcoholics Anonymous with the recidivism rates of those who received in-hospital treatment. One possible systematic difference in the two groups that might affect absti- nence is economic standing. If economic well-being aids recovery and if those choosing in- hospital treatment were in fact more affluent, then the hospital treatment group might have a better record of recovery because of their economic status, apart from any benefits of the treatment. Another possibility, also a matter of selection, is that the people entering the two treatment programs differed in the severity of their alcohol abuse, with more severe cases, who were also less likely to be "cured," receiving in-hospital treatment.

An additional example where selection would be a confounding factor is a study com- paring the academic progress of pupils in an alternative school with that of pupils in a conventional school. Even if attempts were made to match the alternative school with a con- ventional school on such relevant characteristics as class size and socioeconomic status of pupils, there still might be confounding differences between the two groups. For example, the parents of the alternative-school children might be more permissive or differ in other unknown ways from the parents of the conventional-school pupils. Whenever the groups are not equivalent at the beginning of the experiment, it is difficult to interpret differences on the dependent variable.

Another rival explanation for experimental results involves the loss of subjects from the experimental groups. The reasons for subjects dropping out range from illness or moving out of the area to disenchantment with the experience of being a subject. The loss of subjects in an experiment is called **attrition**.[2] Attrition poses the greatest threat to internal validity when there is **differential attrition**—that is, when the conditions of an experiment have different dropout rates. Invariably, those subjects who drop out differ in important ways from the ones who remain so that the experimental conditions are no longer equiva- lent in composition; thus, differential attrition undermines the effects of random assign- ment. In an experiment to test the effectiveness of behavior-modification techniques on smoking cessation, for example, smokers might be randomly assigned either to the experi- mental treatment or to the control group. But what if the heaviest smokers drop out of the experimental group? The measure of smoking (say, number of cigarettes smoked per day) at the end of the treatment will tend to reflect greater success than if all subjects had remained in the experimental group. Thus, the effect of differential attrition will be confounded with the treatment.

Finally, experimental findings may be confounded by an *interaction* between two or more of the threats to internal validity we have discussed. This simply means that two of these threats, say selection and maturation, act together to affect the outcome on the depen- dent measure. You will recall the example we used to illustrate the possible confounding effects of maturational processes, a hypothetical study of the effectiveness of a new physi- cal therapy program for stroke victims. We pointed out that some degree of spontaneous remission might be confounded with the therapy effects. Now suppose that patients were allowed to select either the new therapy program, where treatment took place at a hospital, or the usual program, which involved visits by a physical therapist to the patient's home. We can conjecture how this process of selection might interact with effects of the normal recovery process (maturation). Those patients who volunteered for the new treatment program would differ from those who did not in one obvious way: They would have to have transportation to the hospital. For most patients, this would mean a family member or some other person available and willing to take them and wait for them while they had the therapy. Perhaps stroke victims who have someone around who is willing to make such an effort are also receiving more social and emotional support (and perhaps other benefits) than are those patients who do not have such a person available. Such benefits could possibly facilitate spontaneous remission for patients in this therapy group. Thus, the interaction effects of selection (differences between patients choosing and not choosing the new program) and maturation (spontaneous remission) would be confounded in this study with the effects of the therapy program.

We now examine three research designs in which threats to internal validity pose rival explanations for the results, thus preventing meaningful interpretation. Because these designs lack one or more features of true experimental designs, they are termed pre-experimental.

Pre-experimental Designs

Design 1: The One-Shot Case Study

$$X \qquad O$$

In the simplest possible design, the **one-shot case study**, some treatment is administered to a group, after which the group is observed or tested to determine the treatment effects. The above diagram illustrates this design; X stands for the treatment condition of the independent variable and O stands for the observation or measurement of the dependent variable. Time moves from left to right.

To illustrate this design, imagine a teacher who is having a problem with her 4th-grade pupils frequently talking out of turn. She decides to conduct the following "experiment" one day. Every time a child speaks out of turn, the teacher says, "You are talking out of turn," and then immediately turns her attention to the pupil who was interrupted or to another who is modeling desirable behavior. (This is the treatment, symbolized by the letter X in the diagram.) Toward the end of the day a teacher's aide carefully records the number of incidents for each child and finds that few children are talking out of turn and that the number of incidents is low. (This is the measurement of the dependent variable, symbolized by the letter O.) The teacher concludes that her treatment is effective and recommends it to other teachers.

Unfortunately for the teacher's efforts, such a conclusion is unwarranted; several other explanations may account for the apparent change in behavior. Maybe one of the more recalcitrant talkers left after lunch for a date with the dentist; this would result in an attrition effect. Maturational variables also might threaten the study's internal validity if, for example, some of the children were particularly tired that day. Finally, history could offer an alternative explanation for the results; perhaps early in the day the class had a music lesson in which they let off steam by doing a lot of energetic singing and so felt less inclined to interrupt during class discussions. Attrition, maturation, and history represent threats to the internal validity of any study based on the one-shot case study design.

The critical flaw in this design is that it provides no adequate basis for comparison, and some process of comparison is essential to scientific inference. We cannot tell in our example what the incidence of talking out of turn would have been with a different intervention, with no intervention, with a different group of students, or on a different day. All we know is that the teacher intuitively sensed that talking out of turn decreased.

Many of our day-to-day assumptions about causality are based on experiments similar to one-shot case studies. Suppose a jogger buys a new brand of running shoes and afterward finds that she is running faster than before. Concluding that the shoes have "helped" her, she recommends them to you. Can you think of other explanations for her increase in speed?

Design 2: The One-Group Pretest–Posttest Design

$$O_1 \quad X \quad O_2$$

A second pre-experimental design, the **one-group pretest–posttest design**, involves observing or measuring a group of subjects (the pretest), introducing a treatment (the independent variable), and observing the subjects again (the posttest). The pretreatment observations are represented by O_1, the independent variable by X, and the posttreatment observations by O_2. For example, the performance of a group of joggers might be timed before (O_1) and after (O_2) they received a new brand of running shoes (X). Design 2 is commonly found in educational, organizational, and clinical research. It is an improvement over design 1 because it provides a basis of comparison, but it is still subject to major sources of invalidity.

We may illustrate this design by changing our design 1 example slightly. Suppose the teacher's aide counted talking-out-of-turn incidents on the day before as well as the day of the experiment. How would this change in design affect the study's internal validity? First, the attrition threat is controlled effectively in design 2 studies because only the data from those subjects observed both before and after the treatment would be used in analyzing the effects of the independent variable. In addition, the pretreatment observation makes it possible to determine whether those who dropped out before the second observation differed initially from those who remained.

Two other threats found in the one-shot design, maturation and history, also are found in the one-group pretest–posttest design. In fact, the longer the period between pretest and posttest, the greater the likelihood that either of these threats will confound the results. If in our example a weekend or holiday intervened between pretest and posttest, the children might be "talked out" or worn out on the posttest day.

Additional threats to internal validity—testing, instrumentation, and sometimes statistical regression—may present rival explanations to the hypothesis in design 2 studies. To continue with our example, it is possible that recording talking-out-of-turn incidents could inhibit children who notice their behavior is being observed and recorded; this would be a testing effect. Instrumentation would threaten internal validity if the teacher's aide was not consistent in measuring the problem behavior. For instance, he might record every incident zealously during the pretest but become bored during the posttest and fail to count some incidents. Or, he might be more accurate on the second day of observation as a result of practice. Finally, statistical regression can be a problem in design 2 studies if a group representing an extreme position on the dependent variable is used. This was not the case in our classroom example since the whole class served as subjects.[3]

Design 3: The Static Group Comparison

$$X \quad O_1$$

$$O_2$$

A third pre-experimental design, the **static group comparison**, like design 2, is an improvement over the one-shot case study in that it provides a set of data with which to compare the posttreatment scores. Whereas design 2 provided pretreatment scores on the same group, design 3 provides the scores of a control group. As symbolized above, the rows represent separate groups: X stands for the experimental treatment, the blank space under X stands for the no-treatment control, and O represents the dependent-variable measure. Note that each group is measured just once.

Our classroom example again may be altered slightly to fit this design. Let us suppose that, because of rapid growth in the area, the school is on double sessions so that the teacher has one class in the morning and a different one in the afternoon. On the treatment day she tries out her new approach on the morning class only but records talking-out-of-turn incidents for the pupils in both groups.

Although the static group comparison does a better job of controlling threats to internal validity than do the other two pre-experimental designs, some threats remain. The threat of history confounding the findings is controlled, for the most part, because the two groups should experience the same major environmental events. Since there is no pretest, the threats of testing and statistical regression are absent. And as long as measurements are equally reliable and valid for the two groups, instrumentation is not a problem. On the other hand, selection is a serious threat to internal validity, for without the random assignment of subjects to the experimental and control groups, there is no control of possible pretreatment differences. Attrition also is uncontrolled and there are no pretest data by which one may learn whether subjects who drop out of a group are similar or dissimilar to those who remain. Groups that were similar in all important aspects at the beginning of a study may become dissimilar through differential attrition. Finally, maturation also may be a threat if maturational factors are operating differently in the two groups. Indeed, it seems plausible that the afternoon class will be less lively and less likely to talk out of turn than the morning class, simply because it is later in the day.

We turn now to a discussion of true experimental designs, in which threats to internal validity are better controlled.

KEY POINT

Specific threats to valid causal inference depend on the research design: Testing, history, and maturation are the main threats in a one-group pretest–posttest design; selection is the main threat with static group comparison.

True Experimental Designs

The designs described in this section differ from the pre-experimental designs in that there are always two or more groups and subjects are assigned to them randomly to ensure approximate equivalence of the groups.

Design 4: The Pretest–Posttest Control Group Design

$$R \quad \begin{matrix} O_1 & X & O_2 \\ O_3 & & O_4 \end{matrix}$$

The **pretest–posttest control group design** involves measuring the experimental group before and after the experimental treatment. A control group is measured at the same time but does not receive the experimental treatment. As symbolized before, the rows represent separate groups, and time moves from left to right: the R to the left indicates that subjects are randomly assigned to the groups, each O stands for an observation, the X symbolizes the treatment condition of the independent variable, and the blank space under the X indicates the no-treatment control condition.

Our earlier example of the study of assertiveness-training effectiveness may be altered to illustrate this design. In the original example, which was not a true experiment, subjects who scored in the bottom 25 percent on an extroversion scale were assigned to the experimental treatment, with the remaining 75 percent serving as controls. To fit design 4, the entire pool of available subjects would be randomly assigned to the treatment and control groups. Both groups then would be given the extroversion scale (O_1 and O_3 pretest measurements). Only the experimental treatment group would receive the assertiveness training; at the conclusion of the training, both groups would again be given the extroversion scale (O_2 and O_4 posttests).

How does this design deal effectively with the common threats to internal validity? To consider history first, any event in the general environment that would produce a difference between the pretest and posttest in the experimental group (O_1–O_2) would produce about the same difference in the control group (O_3–O_4).[4] Similarly, changes resulting from maturation, testing, or instrumentation would be felt equally in both groups. Therefore, these factors cannot account for differences between the posttests, O_2 and O_4. Random assignment also eliminates the factors of selection and regression, within the limits of chance error. Comparison of O_1 and O_3 provides a check on the randomization procedure with regard to initial differences on the dependent variable. And even if the subject pool consisted only of extreme scorers—for example, all introverts—random assignment of these subjects to experimental and control groups should ensure initially equivalent groups that regress about the same amount on the posttest. Finally, this design permits the assessment of possible attrition effects; one can compare both the number of subjects and the pretest scores of those who drop out of each group.

Since true experimental designs adequately control threats to internal validity (without which we cannot tell whether the independent variable was responsible for the results), it is appropriate to examine these designs for possible threats to *external validity*. You will recall that external validity refers to the extent to which a study's findings have meaning outside the particular circumstances of the experiment—that is, the extent to which the results may be generalized.

The pretest–posttest control group design suffers from the external-validity threat of testing interacting with the independent variable, called *testing-X interaction* or *testing-treatment interaction*. This simply means that the effect of the independent variable may be different when a pretest is present compared to when it is not. Sometimes an independent-variable effect can be produced only with subjects who have been sensitized to the experimental treatment by pretesting. To continue with our example, it may be that the assertiveness training is effective in helping people become more socially outgoing only when they have been made particularly conscious of their introversion (or extroversion) by responding to the pretest extroversion scale. If that were true, results of the study could be generalized only to other similarly pretested groups.

KEY POINT

In a pretest–posttest control group design, the effect of the treatment may depend on the presence of a pretest. Known as *testing–treatment interaction*, this limits external validity.

The extent to which one need be concerned about an interaction between testing and treatment depends on the experimental situation. In educational settings, where test taking is the norm, the effects of a testing–treatment interaction would probably be negligible; and the learning situations to which one would be generalizing are likely to involve testing. The classroom experiment described in Chapter 7 on the effects of teacher comments on student achievement (Page, 1958) is an example of the usefulness of the pretest–posttest control group design. Since regular classroom tests and procedures were used in this study, there is no reason to believe the pretests interacted with the treatment to any significant extent. However, in studies of attitude change or persuasion, a pretest may very well alert subjects to the treatment to follow in such a way as to make them more receptive (or resistant) to it. In such cases, the findings would have little external validity, and it would be better to use the following design.

Design 5: The Posttest-Only Control Group Design

$$X \quad O_1$$
$$R$$
$$O_2$$

The simplest of the true experimental designs, the **posttest-only control group design** incorporates just the basic elements of experimental design: random assignment of subjects to treatment and control groups, introduction of the independent variable to the treatment group, and a posttreatment measure of the dependent variable for both groups. Note that, except for one crucial difference—subject randomization—design 5 resembles the pre-experimental static group comparison design. Unlike this design, however, design 5 controls for the common threats to internal validity adequately.

Some researchers seem to feel more confident that groups are equivalent before the experimental manipulation when they can check pretest scores. Yet, in reality, the random assignment of subjects is sufficient to ensure approximate equivalence. Therefore, under most circumstances, design 5 is preferable to design 4, the pretest–posttest control group design. By eliminating the pretesting step, design 5 has two major advantages. First, it is more economical. Second, and more important, it eliminates the possibility of an interaction between the pretest and the experimental manipulation. Still, there are special situations requiring a pretest and other situations in which a pretest would be useful. Imagine, for example, a long-term experiment in which you expect a higher than usual number of subjects to drop out. In such a situation, pretest scores on each group would help in determining whether there was an interaction between attrition and the experimental manipulation.

Design 6: The Solomon Four-Group Design

$$O_1 \quad X \quad O_2$$

$$O_3 \qquad O_4$$

$$R$$

$$X \quad O_5$$

$$O_6$$

A third true experimental design, the **Solomon four-group design** is really a combination of designs 4 and 5, as may be seen in the above symbolic representation. Here we have an experimental group and a control group that are pretested, along with an experimental and a control group that are not pretested.

The Solomon four-group design has the advantages of both of the two previously discussed experimental designs; information is available regarding the effect of the independent variable (O_2 and O_5 compared with O_4 and O_6), the effect of pretesting alone (O_4 versus O_6), the possible interaction of pretesting and treatment (O_2 versus O_5), and the effectiveness of the randomization procedure (O_1 versus O_3). Although this design provides more information than either of the other two experimental designs, the requirement of two extra groups makes it much more expensive to use.

Within-Subjects Designs

Each of the three true experimental designs requires the random assignment of subjects to conditions. Randomization is intended to create groups that are equivalent on uncontrolled extraneous variables. Another solution to the problem of equivalence is to have the same subjects participate in both the treatment and the control conditions of the experiment. In other words, an experimenter might expose subjects to a treatment (X_1), apply the measure of the dependent variable (O_1), expose the same subjects to a control (or comparison treatment) condition (X_2), and then measure the effect a second time (O_2), as diagrammed below:

$$X_1 \quad O_1 \quad X_2 \quad O_2$$

This type of study is called a **within-subjects design** because each subject acts as his or her own control—that is, O_1 is compared with O_2 for each subject. By contrast, designs 4–6 are called **between-subjects designs** because different groups of subjects are compared with one another.

Within-subjects designs have a long history in the natural sciences and are used in some areas of psychological research such as sensation and perception. They have two principal advantages. First, they require fewer subjects; a within-subjects design with a treatment and a control condition, for example, would require half as many subjects as design 5. Second, by having each individual experience and react to every condition of the experiment, they reduce the error associated with how different people react to these conditions. But, within-subjects designs also create threats to internal validity that often make them inappropriate for social research. A study by R. Brent Gallupe and associates (1992) illustrates these threats and the general strategy for estimating their effects.

Gallupe and colleagues sought to compare the effectiveness of traditional brainstorming with electronic brainstorming. From the time it was introduced in the 1950s, brainstorming has been a popular method for enhancing group creativity. To stimulate ideas through group discussion, members of brainstorming groups are asked to express as many ideas as they possibly can while withholding comments and criticisms. Despite its widespread use, however, research has shown that brainstorming groups do not outperform noninteracting individuals. Group researchers attribute this to various inhibitors, such as evaluation apprehension, present in interacting groups. To reduce these inhibitors, they recently have introduced a new technique called "electronic brainstorming" in which group members simultaneously type ideas into a computer, which then distributes the ideas to all members of the group.

To compare the productivity of traditional verbal brainstorming with electronic brainstorming in a within-subjects design, one simply could have the same groups generate ideas first verbally and then electronically. This is, in part, what Gallupe and colleagues did, and they used the number of nonredundant ideas each group produced as their primary measure of the dependent variable. Suppose more ideas were produced following electronic brainstorming than following verbal brainstorming. Other than the different form of communication, what might account for this effect? One possibility is a testing effect; with practice, groups became better at generating ideas. (Alternatively, if they produced fewer ideas over time, this might be due to fatigue.) Another possibility is that subjects may become aware of the experimenter's hypothesis; if subjects realized after the first, traditional brainstorming session that their idea generation was being compared under two conditions, they might behave differently in the second session, perhaps viewing electronic communication as a novel and more interesting challenge.

More generally, in any within-subjects design, there is always the possibility that observed changes are a result of the sequencing or order of the treatment and control conditions rather than the treatment itself. The principal method of controlling for order effects is **counterbalancing**. This consists of reversing the sequence of the treatment and control conditions so that different groups of subjects experience either sequence. Gallupe and colleagues' experiment was counterbalanced; half the subjects brainstormed verbally first and the other half brainstormed electronically first, with the order determined randomly. With random assignment, the within-subjects design becomes a true experiment, effectively controlling for threats to internal validity. Testing effects should be manifested equally in both sequences, and the effects of the order of the treatment and control condition can be estimated by comparing differences in the measures of the dependent variable in one sequence with differences in the other. But even though testing is manifested equally and order effects can be tested, the randomized within-subjects design does not eliminate these effects. Consequently, if it is likely that participating in one condition of an experiment will influence how subjects respond to another, as often occurs in social psychological experiments, this design should not be used.

Gallupe and colleagues carried out two experiments comparing verbal with electronic brainstorming. In addition to counterbalancing the different forms of communication, both experiments manipulated group size or the number of group members and both used two different idea-generation problems to reduce the testing effect. The researchers found that neither the type of problem nor the order of the brainstorming techniques had an effect, which simplified the interpretation of the findings. Except in two-member groups, electronic brainstorming produced more ideas than verbal brainstorming.

Overview of True Experimental Designs

Many simple variations of experimental designs are possible. Although designs 4 and 5 were presented as having just two groups (an experimental group and a control group), the logic of either design may be extended easily to three or more groups: One might, for example, want to compare several clinical approaches for treating depression or a number of methods of teaching reading. Similarly, groups may be added to vary the intensity of the independent variable; for example, we might induce a high level of frustration in one group, a moderate level in another, and a low level in a third group.

Sometimes ethical considerations preclude withholding treatment from a control group. This is frequently the case in the fields of correction, clinical psychology, medicine, and education. Also, a true no-treatment control group, one that is identical to the treatment group except for the treatment manipulation, is impossible to implement in many situations. The hypothetical study discussed earlier, in which a new approach to physical therapy for stroke victims was compared with a standard approach, illustrates the common variation of experimental design in which there is no true control group; rather, two or more treatments are compared for their relative effectiveness.

We have pointed out the importance of random assignment of subjects as a means of controlling for pre-existing differences (known and unknown) in subjects. However, randomization introduces one other threat to internal validity: The observed results might have occurred by chance rather than being caused by the experimental variable. Recall that tests of statistical significance are used to determine the likelihood of this occurring, thereby screening out trivial results that could have occurred easily by chance. Having noted this, we stress again that the random assignment of subjects is an integral part of any true experimental design.

The matter of external validity warrants further comment. As noted earlier, external invalidity results from an interaction of the treatment, or independent-variable manipulation, with some other variable. The presence of such interaction means that treatment effects apply only under certain conditions inherent in the experiment. Earlier, for example, we discussed the threat of a testing–treatment interaction as a particular concern in the pretest–posttest control group design. This interaction limits the generalizability of results to situations in which subjects have been pretested. External validity similarly may be threatened by interactions of the treatment with characteristics of the subject population, time, or some other feature of the experimental setting. We now elaborate on a few of these sources of external invalidity.

Sample selection often restricts external validity. Because the sample of subjects participating in an experiment typically consists of homogeneous groups such as college students, the possibility of sample selection interacting with the independent variable may be present in any of the experimental designs. Thus, extreme caution must be used in generalizing any effect of the independent variable to dissimilar groups. A cigarette smoking cessation treatment, for example, might succeed with volunteer subjects (who are highly motivated) but be ineffective with the general population of smokers who wish to quit.

Maturation also may interact with the independent variable; that is, the effect of the treatment may occur only with subjects in a certain physical or mental state. For example, the findings of an experiment conducted at four o'clock on a hot summer day may be generalizable only to hot, tired subjects. Solutions to this problem include (1) deliberately varying the conditions that would seem to affect maturational states as part of the experimental design and (2) replicating the basic experiment under varying conditions.

Finally, the effect of the treatment might be peculiar to the historical circumstances surrounding the experiment. For example, a study of the effects of personal experiences on Americans' attitudes toward Muslims might produce significant results only because the experiment took place immediately following a highly publicized attack on U.S. soil by Islamic extremists. Because of the attack, subjects may react differently to the treatment. Replicating experiments under different historical circumstances is an effective way of ruling out the threat of such treatment–history interactions.

KEY POINT
When the effect of a treatment depends on the sample, setting, or time of a true experiment, this limits external validity.

Factorial Experimental Designs

Social events often are caused or influenced by a number of variables. Therefore, it frequently makes sense to study several possible causes, or independent variables, at the same time. When two or more independent variables are studied in a single experiment, they are referred to as *factors*, and the designs that enable us to explore their effects jointly are called **factorial experimental designs**. Although more than one variable is manipulated, it is possible to assess the effect of any manipulated variable while controlling for the impact of other variables. Hence, the basic principle of good design, "doing only one thing at a time," still applies.

An interesting example of a factorial design is Jody Gottlieb and Charles Carver's (1980) experiment on "the anticipation of future interaction and the bystander effect." As you may recall, Darley and Latané (1968) demonstrated the bystander effect—the larger the number of bystanders who witness an emergency, the less likely that any one person will help—in an experiment described in Chapter 7. Gottlieb and Carver's study was similar to that of Darley and Latané. Subjects (college students) were asked to engage in a discussion of the problems of college living with other subjects over an intercom system; the other discussants were tape recorded; the number of discussants varied, either one or five others; and the dependent measure consisted of the length of time that subjects took to respond to a staged emergency (one of the supposed fellow discussants, who apparently had been eating, began choking and struggling for breath and cried out for help). So, one independent variable or factor was the number of discussants, or "bystanders." Gottlieb and Carver reasoned, however, that the bystander effect may occur because of the anonymity of the subjects; that is, they never saw nor did they expect ever to meet their co-subjects face to face. If subjects expected to interact with other bystanders face to face in the future, they might be more willing to help to avoid being blamed by others for their inaction. Thus, Gottlieb and Carver manipulated a second factor, anticipated interaction, by telling some subjects that they would be meeting afterward face to face and telling the others that they would not meet the co-subjects at all.

The Gottlieb and Carver experiment represents the simplest case of a factorial design. Two variables (number of bystanders and anticipated interaction) are manipulated, with each variable having two levels or categories. This design requires 4 experimental conditions, one for each combination of variable categories: one discussant (the emergency victim)/anticipated interaction; one discussant/no anticipated interaction; five discussants/anticipated interaction; and five discussants/no anticipated interaction. When a design has two independent variables, each having two levels, we call it a 2 × 2 (two-by-two) factorial design. A design that had three levels of one factor and four levels of another would be a 3 × 4 factorial design having 12 conditions. In every case the number of conditions of a factorial design may be determined by multiplying the number of levels of the first factor by the number of levels of the second factor and, if there are additional factors, by the number of levels of each in turn. Theoretically, a factorial design may utilize any number of factors, although there are practical limits.

As you can see, factorial designs are simple extensions of the basic experimental designs. In fact, we already have introduced one design, the Solomon four-group design, which may be viewed as a factorial design. We depicted this design as follows, with each row representing a separate group.

$$O_1 \quad X \quad O_2 \quad \text{first group}$$
$$O_3 \qquad\quad O_4 \quad \text{second group}$$
$$R$$
$$X \quad O_5 \quad \text{third group}$$
$$O_6 \quad \text{fourth group}$$

Table 8.2 presents the Solomon four-group design in factorial form. Note that this design has two factors: the treatment and the pretest. Also, like the Gottlieb and Carver

TABLE 8.2. **Solomon Four-Group Design Represented as a 2 × 2 Factorial Design**

Treatment condition (factor A)	Pretest condition (factor B)	
	PRETEST	NO PRETEST
Treatment	First group, O_2	Third group, O_5
No treatment	Second group, O_4	Fourth group, O_6

experiment, both levels (categories) of one factor are combined with both levels of the second, forming the four experimental groups in the cells of Table 8.2. So, this is another example of a 2 × 2 factorial design.

Ideally, each cell will have the same number of subjects. When this is not possible (because of subject attrition or other reasons), the dependent-variable data in the various cells can be analyzed after statistical adjustment has been made to compensate for the uneven number of subjects. As always with true experimental designs, subjects are assigned to the various conditions (cells) by a random device to control for pre-experimental differences.

You may be wondering how the effects of the various factors are determined in a factorial design. To answer this question, let us consider a hypothetical study of the effect of a sympathetic movie portrayal of the gay community (the treatment) on attitudes toward gay rights (the dependent variable). The results from the Solomon four-group experiment are shown in Table 8.3. Each cell contains the average (mean) posttest attitude score for that experimental group. A higher score indicates a more positive attitude toward gay rights.

First, factorial designs provide information about the **main effect** of each factor—that is, the overall effect of the factor by itself. We have labeled the treatment variable "factor A" and the pretest variable "factor B." The main effect of factor A is determined by comparing the overall mean score of subjects who received the experimental treatment (which in this case is 25) with the overall mean score of subjects who did not receive the experimental treatment (in this case 15).[5] Subjects who saw the movie were more supportive of gay rights than those not exposed to the movie. Whether this treatment effect is "significant" would have to be determined by an appropriate statistical test. Let us assume that all effects are statistically significant.

Likewise, the main effect of factor B is determined by comparing the overall mean score of pretested subjects (30) with the overall mean of subjects not pretested (10). Thus, exposure to the pretest also enhanced posttest attitudes toward gay rights. Although this

TABLE 8.3. **Hypothetical Results of a Study Using a 2 × 2 Factorial Design**

Treatment condition (factor A)	Pretest condition (factor B)		Overall means of A
	PRETEST	NO PRETEST	
Treatment	40	10	25
No treatment	20	10	15
Overall means of B	30	10	

result is not unexpected, it is nonetheless discouraging since ideally treatment effects (the movie) should be much more powerful than measurement artifacts (pretesting effects).

Interaction Effects

Note that we determined the main effects of each factor by averaging overall levels of the other. Assessing main effects in this way can be misleading because it may conceal how the two factors, acting together, produce the outcome. A major advantage of factorial designs is that they also provide information about the *joint effects* of the factors. If there is an interaction between two factors, the effect of one factor on the dependent variable varies according to the value or level of the other. In other words, the effects of the factors together differ from the effects of either alone. Because of this possibility, it is always best to check first for an interaction; otherwise, conclusions based on main effects may be incorrect.

The presence of the pretesting effect in our example should lead us to question the generalizability of the movie effect. Specifically, there may be an interaction between the pretest and the movie, with the pretest sensitizing subjects to the topic and thereby enhancing the movie's impact. Inspection of the cell means in Table 8.3, graphed in Figure 8.1, does indeed reveal a testing–treatment interaction: The movie has an impact only on pretested subjects. Consequently, its value outside the laboratory as an attitudinal change agent appears to be limited.

KEY POINT

Interaction effects should be tested before *main effects*; otherwise, one may conclude that *X* consistently affects *Y* when in reality the effect of *X* on *Y* depends on *Z*.

Interaction effects do not always look like the idealized results in Figure 8.1. Some other possible outcomes are graphed in Figure 8.2. The movie treatment may affect all subjects but more so those pretested (Figure 8.2A), may have no effect on pretested subjects (Figure 8.2B), or may even have a reverse effect on pretested subjects (Figure 8.2C). Finally,

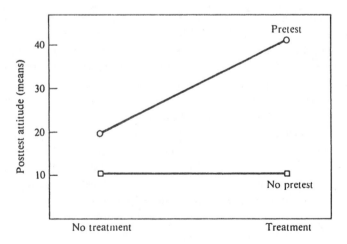

FIGURE 8.1. Graph of cell means from Table 8.3.

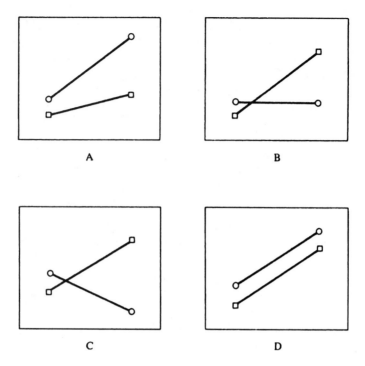

FIGURE 8.2. Illustrative outcomes for 2 × 2 factorial designs.
Symbols are the same as in Figure 8.1.

when there is no interaction, the lines connecting the mean scores for pretested and not-pretested subjects will be parallel, as shown in Figure 8.2D. (Box 8.1 describes a factorial experiment that produced an interaction effect.)

BOX 8.1 Example of a Factorial Design: A Field Experiment on Labor Market Discrimination

Audit studies use experimental methods to investigate discrimination in real-life settings. In a typical study, pairs of auditors or "testers," who differ in race, gender, or age, attempt to rent the same apartments, purchase the same cars, or apply for the same job openings. Although these studies carefully match the pairs on key characteristics such as physical appearance, presentation style, and qualifications, it often is not possible to rule out the possibility that unmeasured observed differences between the testers biased the results. Marianne Bertrand and Sendhil Mullainathan (2004) conducted a field experiment of racial discrimination in the labor market that effectively controlled for such systematic differences between testers.

Rather than use "live" auditors, Bertrand and Mullainathan (2004) sent resumes in response to help-wanted ads in Chicago and Boston newspapers. To create realistic templates for the resumes, they altered actual resumes posted on job-search websites. Then they employed a 2 × 2 factorial design to investigate the effects of two factors: race (African American or white) and the quality of the resume (high or low). Race was manipulated by varying the name on the resume, with half of the resumes assigned a white-sounding name (e.g., "Todd Baker" or "Anne Kelly") and the other half an African American–sounding name (e.g., "Tyrone Jackson" or "Ebony Jones"). The quality of the resume was manipulated by systematically varying several criteria such as labor market experience, skills listed, and existence of gaps in employment. In addition, higher-quality resumes were more likely to have certification degrees, foreign language and extra computer skills, and awards or honors.

The experiment took place between July 2001 and May 2002. During that period, resumes were sent in response to more than 1300 "employment ads in the Sunday editions of *The Boston Globe* and *The Chicago Tribune* in the sales, administrative support, and clerical and customer services sections" (Bertrand and Mullainathan, 2004:996). For each ad, two high-quality and two low-quality resumes were sent, with one resume in each pair randomly assigned to a white name and the other to an African American name. The dependent measure was whether an applicant received a phone or e-mail call-back for an interview.

Figure B8.1 shows both a main effect for race and an interaction effect. First, irrespective of resume quality, African American names were less likely to be called back for an interview than white names. Second, quality of resume made a difference for whites but not for African Americans. Among white applicants, the call-back rate was 11.31 percent with a higher-quality resume and 8.8 percent with a lower-quality resume. Thus, having a higher-quality resume made a statistically significant difference of 2.51 percentage points in whether an applicant received a call-back. Among African Americans, the call-back rate was 6.99 percent with a higher-quality resume and 6.41 percent with a lower-quality resume, which shows a nonsignificant .58 percentage difference. This pattern of discrimination was obtained across occupations and industries in both Boston and Chicago and held as much for employers who listed "Equal Opportunity Employer" in their ad as other employers. The results suggest that racial discrimination still exists and may account for why African Americans continue to do poorly in the labor market.

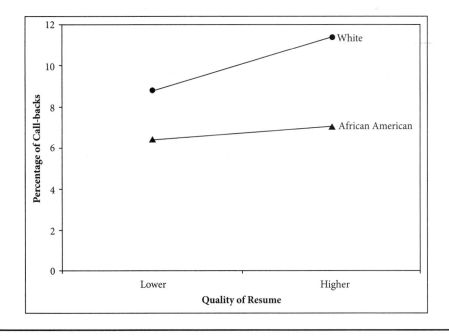

In addition to providing information on interaction effects, factorial designs are cost-efficient. A factorial design can increase the amount of information provided by a study with little increase in cost over a nonfactorial experimental design. Consider the Gottlieb and Carver experiment, for example. By adapting the procedures of the Darley and Latané experiment and manipulating the number of discussants, this study replicated the bystander effect. In effect, it addressed the following question: Does the number of bystanders affect helping in emergencies with a different sample of subjects? But by including another relevant independent variable, anticipated interaction, the factorial design addressed two additional questions: (1) Does anticipated face-to-face interaction affect helping? (2) Will anticipated interaction diminish the impact of the bystander effect—that is, will expected future encounters with bystanders reduce the difference between helping in the absence and presence of bystanders? As it turned out, Gottlieb and Carver did not find an interaction effect, as expected. Rather, there were main effects for both factors: Anticipated interaction reduced the time to respond to the emergency, irrespective of the presence of bystanders, and response time was longer in the bystander than in the nonbystander condition.

A factorial design also may enhance external validity by determining the effects of a key variable under several conditions. When the effects are consistent under diverse conditions, we are more confident that the findings generalize to additional situations. For example, we may want to study the effects of counseling on troubled marriages, with our dependent measure being the percentage of participant couples still together 1 year after completion of counseling. A $2 \times 3 \times 2$ factorial design might utilize two counseling approaches, let us say "behavior modification" and "eclectic"; three counselor conditions, such as "male–female counselor team," "male counselor only," and "female counselor only"; and two cost-of-counseling conditions, perhaps "fixed fee" and "free." Since this design explores the effects of marriage counseling under 12 conditions, the study should be high in external validity.

Finally, in our discussion of external validity in Chapter 7, we noted that experiments embedded in large-scale surveys make it easier to include a large number of experimental conditions, which are necessary in complex factorial designs. For example, to explore subtle racial discrimination, Paul Sniderman, Richard Brody, and Philip Tetlock (1991) randomly varied five attributes of telephone interviewers' descriptions of a "laid-off worker" (race, gender, age, marital status, parental status, and work history), after which respondents were asked how much help in finding a new job the government should give laid-off workers ("none at all," "some," or "a lot"). The $2 \times 2 \times 3 \times 4 \times 2$ factorial design had 96 different versions. In addition to the embedded factorial design, in their analysis Sniderman, Brody, and Tetlock used information about the respondents collected during the telephone survey. One surprising finding was that self-described conservatives were more likely to favor government help if the laid-off worker was black than if she or he was white; the government-assistance position of self-described liberals was unrelated to the racial manipulation.

Quasi-experimental Designs

Legal, ethical, or practical considerations make it impossible to employ a true experimental design in some research situations. Frequently, random assignment of persons (or other units) is not possible. At other times, control or comparison groups cannot be incorporated into the design. Sometimes, random assignment to treatment and control groups can be carried out but researchers cannot exercise the tight control over subjects' experiences required for a true experiment. To deal with these problems, researchers have developed a number of **quasi-experimental designs**, so named because they take an experimental approach without having full experimental control.

In terms of complexity and effectiveness in controlling extraneous threats to validity, these designs generally lie between pre-experimental and true experimental designs. Some of them resemble pre-experimental designs but with added features. Others are similar to true experimental designs but with something lacking, such as a control group or the process of randomization.

An example of the first type is the **separate-sample pretest–posttest design** (Campbell and Stanley, 1963), diagrammed as follows:

$$R \quad \begin{matrix} O_1 & X & \\ & X & O_2 \end{matrix}$$

R in this design signifies random assignment to the time of measurement. The top line represents the group randomly selected for pretreatment measurement. This group receives the treatment but is not measured afterward. The second group is randomly selected for posttreatment measurement. Since the treatment effect is estimated by comparing pretest (first-group) scores with posttest (second-group) scores, this design resembles the pre-experimental one-group pretest–posttest design (O_1 X O_2). However, some of the threats to validity found in the latter (e.g., testing and testing–X interaction) are eliminated using separate samples. The most serious challenge to the internal validity of the design is history.

The separate-sample pretest–posttest design may be useful in those circumstances in which the entire population of interest, such as residents of a city, employees of a large firm, students in a university, or soldiers in a military unit, receives the same treatment. Although one cannot randomly assign subjects to different treatments, the design may be applied if one can determine the timing of the measurement of the dependent variable and randomly select those who are measured before and after the treatment. For example, measurement might take the form of an attitude survey conducted prior to and following alcohol education week (the treatment) at a certain college.

Nonequivalent control group designs exemplify those quasi-experimental designs that are similar to but lack a crucial feature of true experiments. These designs often are used when the experimental treatment is administered to intact groups, such as school classes, making random assignment of individual subjects impossible. In one such design, symbolized below, pretests and posttests are administered both to the experimental group and to a nonequivalent but similar control group.

$$\begin{matrix} O_1 & X & O_2 \\ O_3 & & O_4 \end{matrix}$$

Except for the missing R representing randomization, this design looks exactly like the pretest–posttest control group design. Randomization, of course, should be used if at all possible. But if it is not possible, then this quasi-experimental design is often worth using. The inclusion of a control group, especially one that is highly similar to the experimental group in known respects, makes it superior to the one-group pretest–posttest design. For if the groups are similar in recruitment and history, then the design controls for history, maturation, testing, and regression.

Another important type of quasi-experimental design involves time-series data, which consist of multiple observations of the same or similar units over time. The **interrupted time-series design** resembles the one-group pretest–posttest design except that instead of a single observation before and after the treatment, there are multiple observations before and afterward, as shown below. (*Note*: There are no limitations, other than practical ones, on the number of observations in the series.)

$$O_1 \quad O_2 \quad O_3 \quad O_4 \quad X \quad O_5 \quad O_6 \quad O_7 \quad O_8$$

The treatment may be systematically introduced into the series by a researcher, or it may consist of some naturally occurring intervention. Social researchers often use this design when periodic measurements of an effect of interest are available, such as regularly administered school achievement tests, business records of absenteeism and productivity, or myriad institutional records on events such as automobile accidents, divorces, and crimes. For example, to assess the deterrent effect of a gun-control law mandating 1-year minimum sentences for anyone convicted of carrying a firearm without an appropriate license, one could examine homicide rates several years before and several years after the law went into effect (see S. J. Deutsch and Alt, 1977). If the law had an impact, one would expect an "interruption" or discontinuity in the time series—the homicide rates—at the point where the law was introduced.

The use of several observations makes the interrupted time-series design superior to the one-group pretest–posttest design. Any change from pretest to posttest in the latter design may reflect a long-term trend or a temporary upswing or downswing in a fluctuating pattern. But these effects can be distinguished from treatment effects in a time-series design by comparing the overall pattern with any change at the point of intervention. The biggest threat to internal validity with the interrupted time-series design is history since it is possible that some more or less simultaneous event other than X may have produced the change. Also, if the time series is taken from official records, an instrumentation effect should be ruled out by checking carefully to see whether there has been a change in record-keeping procedures.

The best way to control for history in a time-series analysis is to examine two or more time series, one of which was exposed to the treatment and the others of which were not. This extension of the interrupted time-series design is known as the **multiple time-series design**.

$$O_1 \quad O_2 \quad O_3 \quad O_4 \quad X \quad O_5 \quad O_6 \quad O_7 \quad O_8$$

$$O_1 \quad O_2 \quad O_3 \quad O_4 \qquad O_5 \quad O_6 \quad O_7 \quad O_8$$

The subscripts here represent points in time. Now, if a change from O_4 to O_5 occurs in the first group but does not occur in the second group, the change is not likely to be due to a treatment-correlated historical event. This quasi-experimental design is particularly effective in controlling for sources of invalidity. But like the nonequivalent control group design, which is contained within it, the strength of inferences in a multiple time-series design depends on how comparable the control group is to the interrupted group.

Since the design possibilities are so numerous, we limit further discussion of quasi-experimental designs to some general ideas and a detailed description of two quasi-experimental studies that used one or more of the designs outlined above.[6] The objective of such studies, as with true experiments, is to determine treatment effects by eliminating plausible rival explanations of experimental results. Lacking subject randomization or other features of true experiments, however, quasi-experimental studies use a variety of approaches to establish internal validity. Threats to internal validity are ruled out individually in several ways (T. D. Cook, Cook, and Mark, 1977): (1) including special design features, (2) examining additional data that bear on each threat, and/or (3) reasoning, on the basis of theory or common sense, that a particular threat is an unlikely alternative explanation.

An example of a design feature that strengthens causal inferences in a quasi-experiment is the use of a pretest. This is a nonessential feature in most true experiments because randomization creates initially equivalent groups. But in a quasi-experimental study, a pretest permits a vital check on the initial difference between nonequivalent groups (T. D. Cook, Cook, and Mark, 1977). An example of the second approach—examining additional data—comes from a study of a smoking-cessation treatment (Berglund et al., 1974). The researchers obtained a measure of motivation from pretreatment interviews with participants. By showing that motivation scores were unrelated to subjects' success in quitting smoking, they eliminated one selection threat as a possible rival explanation. Finally, an example of the third approach is ruling out testing as a serious threat in an educational setting where the measures are similar to typical classroom testing procedures.

KEY POINT
Researchers should identify specific threats to the internal validity of *quasi-experiments* and then consider how these threats may be ruled out.

Let us further examine how these approaches are applied in two carefully conducted quasi-experimental studies.

Example 1: Interracial Attitudes and Behavior at a Summer Camp

Can contact between "opposite-race" children under favorable circumstances improve interracial attitudes and behavior? To test this idea, the social psychologist Gerald Clore and his colleagues (1978) set up a summer camp for underprivileged black and white children that was designed to provide a positive interracial experience. Previous research suggested that prolonged, intimate contact between racial groups of equal size and similar socioeconomic background could significantly reduce prejudice. Therefore, the camp was structured so that blacks and whites of similar status were equally represented among the campers, counselors, and staff. For example, children were assigned to tents that accommodated three black and three white campers of the same sex and age group (8–10 or 11–12), as well as one black and one white counselor. In all, 196 children were randomly assigned to attend one of five 1-week camp sessions.

The experimenters used three dependent measures to assess whether the camping experience affected racial attitudes and behavior. First, they administered an attitude measure, based on four questions regarding feelings toward children of the opposite race. The procedure approximated the separate-sample pretest–posttest design, with half the children administered the measure on the first day of camp and the other half near the end (the fifth or sixth day). Results showed the camp to be effective for girls but not for boys. Whereas the girls had somewhat more negative cross-race attitudes at the beginning and shifted toward neutrality, the boys were relatively neutral at the beginning and showed no change.

A second measure, obtained for three of the five weeklong sessions, involved making inexpensive loaded cameras available to the children and allowing them to photograph whatever and whomever they wished. Within age, sex, and race categories, children were randomly assigned to either a pretest group that took pictures on the second day or a posttest group that took pictures on the fifth or sixth day. The dependent variable was the proportion of persons in the resultant photographs who were not of the photographer's race. Thus, this measure, like the first, was based on the separate-sample pretest–posttest design. But unlike the first measure, the photo taking was unobtrusive and behavioral. Analysis of the photos revealed a slight but nonsignificant overall treatment effect: For only one of the three weeks measured did photos taken at the end of the week reveal a significantly higher proportion of cross-race persons than photos taken at the beginning.

A third set of measures, also behavioral, consisted of interpersonal choices the children made in three games played on the first day of camp and again on the fifth or sixth day. Counselors recorded the choices, with the dependent variable being the proportion of choices that were interracial. The design for this measure, referred to by the researchers as a "multiple-group pretest–posttest design," resembled the pre-experimental one-group pretest–posttest design but was an improvement over it in that it was replicated over five camp sessions ("multiple groups"). Results showed a slight shift toward more cross-race choices from the beginning to the end of the sessions. As with the attitude measure, the change was evident for girls only. Although they showed no significant change from pretest to posttest, the boys made a higher proportion of cross-race choices overall than did the girls.

Thus, the dependent measures, taken together, indicated that the camp experience was effective in changing the interracial attitudes and behavior of the girls but not of the boys, who evidenced more positive attitudes and behavior from the beginning. The authors of the study described how they were able to rule out rival explanations to the hypothesis that the camp experience itself caused the observed changes. To do so, they invoked special design features, additional data, and reasoning based on common sense.

Some crucial design features incorporated in the study enabled Clore and co-workers to eliminate several validity threats. These features included the use of two different quasi-experimental designs, three different dependent measures (attitude questions, photographs, and interpersonal choices), and replications. Using more than one quasi-experimental design strengthens a study because different designs ordinarily will not share the same weaknesses. For example, testing effects cannot be ruled out in the multiple-group pretest–posttest design (which produced the shift in cross-race choices) since pretests and posttests are administered to the same persons. However, testing is not a threat in the separate-sample pretest–posttest design (which produced the change in attitudes) since individuals receive either the pretest or the posttest but not both.

The use of dissimilar measures also strengthens inferences by controlling for systematic error in any one measure. Moreover, the measurement processes were replicated three to five times (weekly camp sessions), controlling for the most part the threats of instrumentation and history. Instrumentation could be ruled out because with pretests and posttests repeated over several weeks, it was unlikely that scorers' expertness, effort, or enthusiasm would differ systematically from pretest to posttest across all sessions. And since the measurements were replicated at different times and produced consistent results for both the attitude and the choices measures, the rival explanation of history was ruled out for these two measures. On the other hand, one could not rule out entirely the possibility that historical conditions were responsible for the change in the photo measure, implausible as this explanation seems, since this measure showed significant effects for only 1 week.

Two possible rival explanations for certain of the findings were ruled out through the examination of additional data. First, it was conjectured that the changes in the interpersonal-choices data might be attributable to children making their choices from among their acquaintances. That is, if children were acquainted with more same-race children than cross-race children at the beginning of camp, they might choose more same-race children on the pretests and move toward a higher proportion of cross-race posttest choices as they became acquainted with the cross-race children. Since the names of initial acquaintances of each child were available (the children had been asked in one game to circle the names of all the other children whom they knew), it was possible to test this argument. Data for two camp sessions were reanalyzed, discarding choices of children known to the subject before camp. The results of the reanalysis were consistent with the original findings, ruling out this rival explanation.

A second possible explanation for the choices data, that choices in the posttest games might reflect allegiance to the child's living unit, was also evaluated. The choices data were reanalyzed using the proportion of cross-unit choices as the dependent variable. No significant effects were found, thereby ruling out this second possibility.

Finally, Clore and colleagues were able to rule out other threats through reasoning based on common sense. For example, maturation was an unlikely explanation for the changes because the camp sessions lasted only 1 week each. The threat of regression was implausible because subjects were not selected on the basis of extreme attitudes or behavior.

Example 2: The Connecticut Crackdown on Speeding

In late December 1955, Governor Abraham Ribicoff of Connecticut instituted a crackdown on speeding in the hope of reducing the number of deaths from automobile accidents, which had risen to a high point of 324 in 1955. New, stiffer penalties for speeding involved automatic suspension of the offender's driver's license: 30 days for the first offense, 60 days for the second offense, and indefinitely for the third offense, with a hearing after 90 days. Although opposed by many, the crackdown was carried out and suspensions for speeding increased dramatically. When the number of traffic fatalities declined to 284 in 1956, Governor Ribicoff was quoted as saying, "With the saving of 40 lives . . . we can say the program is definitely worthwhile" (Campbell and Ross, 1968).

But did the program actually cause the reduction in traffic deaths? Donald Campbell and H. Lawrence Ross (1968) addressed this question while demonstrating the utility of quasi-experimental time-series designs. First, they noted that the data Ribicoff cited, although impressive, covered only 2 years—the year before and the year after the crackdown. If these data alone were used in determining whether the crackdown (the treatment) caused the decrease in deaths (the dependent variable), the design would be the one-group pretest–posttest design, which fails to control for most of the common threats to validity.

Because of the weakness of the one-group pretest–posttest design, Campbell and Ross did an analysis based on an interrupted time-series design. Data for this design are graphed in Figure 8.3, which shows the number of traffic fatalities from 1951 through 1959. The decrease in traffic fatalities in 1956 now appears much less impressive in view of the comparable decreases shown in 1952 and 1954 and the unusually high number of fatalities in 1955.

FIGURE 8.3. Connecticut traffic fatalities, 1951–1959.

Source: Campbell and Ross (1968:42). Reprinted by permission of the Law and Society Association and Blackwell Publishing, Ltd.

FIGURE 8.4. Traffic fatalities (per 100,000 persons) for Connecticut, New York, New Jersey, Rhode Island, and Massachusetts.

Source: Campbell and Ross (1968:45). Reprinted by permission of the Law and Society Association and Blackwell Publishing, Ltd.

Campbell and Ross then extended their evaluation by using a multiple time-series design. The researchers obtained traffic fatality statistics for the years 1951 through 1959 for four states adjacent to Connecticut, which were assumed to be similar in weather and driving patterns. Figure 8.4 shows the time-series data for the five states. Note that for the year 1955, four of the five states showed an increase in fatalities over the previous year, with Connecticut showing the greatest increase. All five states showed a decrease for 1956. These facts, as well as the fact that the 1956 decrease in Rhode Island closely resembled that in Connecticut, might argue against the hypothesis that the decrease in Connecticut was caused by the crackdown. However, Connecticut was the only one of the five states to show consistent year-to-year decreases following the crackdown; Rhode Island, by contrast, showed consistent increases after 1956.

Let us now examine how the major threats to validity were dealt with in this study.

History is a possible threat in that some event of 1956 other than the crackdown may have caused the reduction in fatalities. Possible rival explanations included better weather conditions in 1956 than in 1955 and improved safety features on 1956-model automobiles (Campbell and Ross, 1968). Although the researchers reasoned on the basis of available data that neither of these explanations appeared plausible, the threat of history cannot be ruled out altogether, especially in view of the fatality rate decreases for 1956 in all of the four control states. Some event common to all five states still may have caused the decrease in fatalities. However, history is not a plausible rival explanation for the post-1956 decreases in Connecticut since the adjacent states failed to show the same pattern.

Maturation is normally associated with human physical and psychological processes. In the Connecticut study, maturation would be a threat if, for example, the driving population as a whole were becoming more skilled drivers. Although this is implausible, Campbell and Ross extend the idea of maturation to processes external to subjects. Thus, they defined as a maturation threat the possibility of a long-term trend toward a reduction in death rates resulting from such factors as improved medical services and improved highways. But since no such trend appears in the time-series or multiple time-series data, this threat may be ruled out.

The threat of *testing* must also be evaluated: Could the pretest by itself have caused the change? In this case, the pretest consists of the 1955 traffic fatalities statistic. It seems unlikely that mere keeping of records would have much impact on the next year's statistic, but the widespread publicizing of the high 1955 figure conceivably could have increased driver caution, thus lowering the subsequent year's statistic. This threat cannot be ruled out with certainty for 1956; however, it seems implausible that publication of the 1955 figure would result in the continued year-to-year decreases that were observed in Connecticut.

Instrumentation would be a threat if there had been a postcrackdown change in record keeping. Campbell and Ross reported that they found no evidence of this.

Regression is a threat whenever a treatment is administered on the basis of a high pretest score. It may be argued that this was the case with the Connecticut crackdown on speeding, which was instituted following an extreme year. On the basis of data from 1951 through 1956, regression or simple instability of the data would indeed offer a plausible rival explanation. However, since the rate of traffic deaths continued to decrease in the years following the crackdown, these factors do not explain the findings adequately. The Campbell and Ross study is an example of rigorous quasi-experimental research. Although the absence of a true experimental design made it impossible to exert optimal control over the threats to validity, the researchers gained valuable knowledge by making use of better quasi-experimental designs, relevant available data, and common sense. By these means they were able to conclude with a large degree of confidence that the Connecticut crackdown on speeding had some effect.

Summary

- The basic principle of good experimental design is "doing only one thing at a time"—that is, allowing only one independent variable to vary while controlling all other variables.
- Pre-experimental designs violate this principle by permitting a number of variables to go uncontrolled, presenting serious threats to the internal validity of the study. True experimental designs effectively control for these threats, and quasi-experimental designs control extraneous variables imperfectly.
- Experimental designs are evaluated in terms of how well they control for extraneous variables that threaten a study's internal and external validity. Common threats to internal validity, which rival hypothesized study results, include the following classes of extraneous variables:
  - History (specific events other than intended experimental manipulations that occur during the course of an experiment),
  - Maturation (psychological and physiological changes in subjects),
  - Testing (the effects of being measured once on being measured a second time),
  - Instrumentation (unwanted changes in the measuring instrument or procedure),

- Statistical regression (the tendency for extreme scorers on one measurement to move closer to the mean score on a later measurement),
  - Selection (differences in the composition of experimental and control groups), and
  - Attrition (the loss of subjects during the course of an experiment).
- Interactions, such as differences between treatment groups resulting from the combined effect of initial differences and history, maturation, or testing, also may threaten external validity.
- Pre-experimental designs (one-shot case study, the one-group pretest–posttest design, and the static group comparison) lack one or more features of true experiments, such as a comparison group or random assignment; therefore, they are subject to several validity threats.
- Although all the basic true experimental designs (pretest–posttest control group, posttest-only control group, Solomon four-group) are strong in internal invalidity, they may be weak in external validity.
- The external validity of the pretest–posttest control group design suffers from the possibility of a testing–treatment interaction, in which experimental effects occur only for pretested subjects.
- Randomized within-subjects designs offer the advantage of comparing the same individuals in both experimental and control conditions but are seldom used in social research because responses in one condition are likely to affect responses in a subsequent condition.
- Factorial designs, in which two or more independent variables are manipulated, tend to enhance external validity and can test for both main effects and joint effects. Main effects refer to the effects of a single factor by itself; joint or interaction effects refer to outcomes in which the effect of one independent variable depends on the level or value of another.
- Quasi-experimental designs (e.g., separate-sample pretest–posttest, nonequivalent control group, interrupted time-series) lack some feature (usually randomization) of true experiments, but often permit relatively strong inferences about cause and effect by virtue of special design features and supplementary data that test specific validity threats and by rendering threats implausible through reasoning.

Key Terms

threats to internal validity
   history
   instrumentation
   statistical regression
   selection
   attrition
   differential attrition
   maturation
   testing
pre-experimental designs
   one-shot case study
   one-group pretest–posttest design
   static group comparison
true experimental designs

pretest–posttest control group design
posttest-only control group design
Solomon four-group design
within-subjects designs
between-subjects designs
counterbalancing
factorial experimental designs
   main effect
   interaction effect
quasi-experimental designs
   separate-sample pretest–posttest design
   nonequivalent control group design
   interrupted time-series design
   multiple time-series design

Exercises

1. Despite the care taken in devising experiments, some manipulations of the independent variable may inadvertently be confounded with other variables. And sometimes this goes unnoticed until after a study is published. See if you can identify the confounded variable in the following study mentioned by Charles Stangor (2004:245). To test the hypothesis that aerobic exercise reduces depression, Lisa McCann and David Holmes (1984) randomly assigned women with mild depression to one of three conditions: an exercise class that met twice a week, a relaxation treatment (placebo) in which subjects practiced muscle relaxation at home, or a no-treatment control group. When all subjects

were tested after 5- and 10-week periods, only the exercise group showed a significant reduction in depression. What else, besides exercise, may account for this reduction?

2. For each of the following studies, identify the major threat(s) to internal validity and explain how each threat is an alternative explanation of the study's hypothesized effects.

   a. A campus lecturer touting the benefits of transcendental meditation (TM) presents data showing that persons who have practiced TM for 24 months or longer perform better on recall tests and learn more quickly than a group of randomly selected nonmeditators. According to the lecturer, these data show that TM directly improves the ability to learn.

   b. Stephen Schoenthaler (1983) studied the impact of dietary changes on the antisocial behavior of individuals in juvenile detention facilities. In one study, the diet of inmates was changed by replacing sugar with honey; soft drinks and Kool-Aid with fruit juice; and high-sugar cereals, desserts, and snacks with foods lower in simple sugars. Using reliable institutional incident reports, Schoenthaler measured antisocial behavior for each inmate 3 months prior to, as well as 3 months after, the dietary change. The records showed a significant reduction in behavioral problems.

   c. To test the effects of the children's television series *Sesame Street*, viewers were tested for various preschool skills (e.g., recognizing letters of the alphabet) both before and after a season of viewing. It was found that children with the lowest initial test scores showed the greatest gains, which suggests that disadvantaged children benefited more than others from watching the program.

3. The authors give an example of an experiment in which the *interaction* effect of selection and maturation is a threat to internal validity. Imagine the following hypothetical experiment. To study the effects of new writing-intensive courses at a college, a researcher examines two groups of students during a single semester. One group consists of first-year students enrolled in writing-intensive courses, and the other group consists of mostly upper-class students who are not enrolled in such courses. Tests given at the beginning and end of the semester reveal a much greater improvement in writing skills for the group enrolled in writing-intensive courses than for the group not enrolled. How could a selection-maturation effect account for this outcome?

4. One of the nation's most popular programs to control and prevent drug abuse is Drug Abuse Resistance Education (DARE). DARE is a school-based program with a core curriculum that focuses on children in their last year of elementary school (5th or 6th grade), although it has been used with children in kindergarten through 12th grade. Taught by a police officer, the program is designed to increase students' knowledge of drugs, to develop negative attitudes toward drugs, and to enhance students' ability to resist peer pressure to use drugs. Suppose someone tests whether exposure to DARE has these hypothesized effects. Knowing that DARE is being administered in all 6th-grade classes in the local school district, he decides to randomly select 10 classes in which to conduct a study. At the beginning of the school year, he measures attitudes toward drug use among all students in the 10 randomly chosen classes. Then, at the end of the year, after the children have been exposed to the DARE program, he measures their attitudes toward drug use again.

   a. Use the notation introduced in this chapter to diagram the design of this study. What are the main threats to the internal validity of this study, and how could each threat account for the results?

   b. Suppose the investigator decides to do a second study using an alternative design. He learns about another school district where DARE is not administered and decides to compare the attitudes of 6th-graders in this school district with the attitudes of 6th-graders who are exposed to DARE. In this case, he contacts all the 6th-grade classes from each of the two school districts and measures attitudes toward drug use among all students in these classes at the end of the school year. Diagram the design of this study. What new threat to internal validity, not present in the original study, could account for the results?

   c. To carry out an internally valid experimental test of DARE, what features of the study would you need to have control over? Explain.

5. Suppose in the audit study reported in Box 8.1 that the researchers found no interaction effect but that both race and resume quality had statistically significant effects on call-backs for interviews. Graph this outcome in a figure like the one in Box 8.1.

Notes

1. This section and the next three sections draw heavily on Donald Campbell and Julian Stanley's classic treatment of these subjects (1963).
2. Campbell and Stanley (1963) originally used the term "mortality" to describe this source of invalidity. However, "attrition," which is now commonly used, seems better to capture the intended meaning.
3. However, if the teacher initiated the experiment one day because of a sharp increase in talking out of turn, the incidence of this behavior may regress toward a more typical classroom level on the posttest.
4. However, this design does not by itself control for effects of unintended events that might occur *within* a treatment group. For a discussion of this problem and suggestions for dealing with it, see Campbell and Stanley (1963:13–14).
5. Note how the principle of "doing only one thing at a time" applies in interpreting factorial results. The only difference between the first-row and the second-row groups is the factor-A manipulation. The two groups are equivalent on factor B (each row has an equal number of pretested and nonpretested subjects) and should be approximately equivalent on extraneous variables as a result of subject randomization.
6. For a more complete discussion, see Shadish, Cook, and Campbell (2002).

9

Survey Research

Survey research in its many forms has become a common activity in today's world, and most of us have had some experience with it in one form or another. Perhaps you have been stopped on the street by a news reporter and asked your opinion on some issue of local or national importance. You may have responded to a reader survey found in a popular magazine. Or perhaps you have replied to an Internet questionnaire when registering a newly purchased product. You or someone else in your household likely responded to the last U.S. Census, which attempted to enumerate and gather confidential information about every person living in the United States. You have been a consumer of survey research if you have read the results of public-opinion surveys. You have done a little "survey research" of your own if you moved to a new community and asked a number of residents about local restaurants or where to obtain various services.

In addition to their extensive use outside the scientific community, "surveys are the most widely used method of collecting data in the social sciences, especially in sociology and political science" (Bradburn and Sudman, 1988:61). An analysis of the three most prestigious journals in sociology found that 79 percent of the 105 most-cited articles from 2001 to 2010 used data collected from surveys (Porter and Ecklund, 2012). In this chapter we cite numerous survey studies, several of which were conducted or commissioned by the federal government, the single largest user of surveys.

General Features of Survey Research

Surveys differ in the extent to which they conform to these typical features of professional survey research:

1. A large number of respondents are chosen through probability sampling procedures to represent the population of interest.
2. Systematic questionnaire or interview procedures are used to ask prescribed questions of respondents and record their answers.
3. Answers are numerically coded and analyzed.

As we now elaborate on these three features through reference to actual studies, we will also describe exceptions to the general rule for each feature.

Large-Scale Probability Sampling

Professional surveys make use of large samples chosen through scientific sampling procedures to ensure precise estimates of population characteristics. National opinion polls typically number around 1000 respondents, but surveys of national samples can be much larger. In the National Educational Longitudinal Study (NELS), for example, the probability sample interviewed in 1988 consisted of 24,599 8th-graders from 1052 public and private schools. Participating students were asked about a wide range of school, family, and home experiences; and these data were supplemented by information obtained from parents and teachers as well as achievement test scores and school characteristics such as teacher and student composition. Beckett Broh (2002) analyzed the NELS data in her study of the impact of extracurricular involvement on academic achievement. Using data from follow-up surveys of NELS respondents, Thomas Deleire and Ariel Kalil (2002) examined the effect of family structure on four developmental outcomes among teenagers: whether they graduate from high school, attend college, smoke or drink, and initiate sexual activity. As previous researchers had found, youths from nonmarried families did not fare as well as youths from married families on all four outcomes. A major exception to this pattern, however, was youths from single-parent multigenerational families, who did just as well as youths from married families.

The NELS was conducted by the National Opinion Research Center (NORC) on behalf of the National Center for Educational Statistics of the U.S. Department of Education. Such national studies require considerable resources—time, money, and personnel—that are beyond the capacity of independent researchers or small research teams. Many surveys, therefore, involve somewhat smaller samples drawn from state or local populations. Kim Fridkin, Patrick Kenney, and Jack Crittenden (2006), for example, surveyed the political attitudes of 166 Anglo, 37 African American, 125 Latino, and 58 Native American 8th-grade students in six integrated public schools randomly drawn from metropolitan Phoenix. Anglo adolescents were more likely to discuss politics and watch news programs at home, practice democratic skills at school, and hold positive views of government. Among minority adolescents, Native Americans had the fewest opportunities to develop democratic skills at home and school and expressed the greatest distrust of the political system.

Useful surveys also are conducted with nonprobability samples. Patrick Carr, Laura Napolitano, and Jessica Keating (2007), for example, interviewed a purposive sample of 147 delinquent and nondelinquent young men and women living in three high-crime neighborhoods in Philadelphia. Although most of the youth were negatively disposed toward the police because of their personal experiences with law enforcement, they nevertheless favored a tougher and fairer police force as a means of reducing crime in their neighborhoods.

Thus, although large-scale probability samples are the ideal, surveys vary considerably in sample size and sampling design. There are legitimate reasons for doing a small-scale survey, particularly if you have a low budget or some specialized or applied research purpose. Indeed, students can often conduct their own low-budget research if they have a research problem that can be studied appropriately with a brief questionnaire survey of the home campus or a telephone survey of the local dialing area.

At the other end of the spectrum from surveys of local populations are surveys that draw samples from more than one nation. In comparative or **cross-national surveys**, equivalent surveys are conducted in different countries. For example, based on interviews with 9529 married women from 22 different nations, Carrie Yodanis (2005) analyzed whether tolerance of divorce at the national level is associated with enhanced or diminished gender equality within marriage. Her results suggest that wives experience a more equal division of household labor when living in a country in which divorce is accepted and practiced. The ease of divorce in a society was associated with a more equal division of household labor.

Units of Analysis

Although in most surveys the units of analysis are individuals, this is not always the case. An example of a survey treating employers as units is the Current Employment Statistics program, a monthly sample of about 150,000 businesses and government agencies, conducted by the U.S Bureau of Labor Statistics to measure changes in employment, wages, and hours. Another example utilized cities as units to study community decisions about whether to fluoridate water supplies to reduce tooth decay. A controversial issue in many communities in the 1950s, the proposal to fluoridate provided social scientists with an excellent opportunity to study the political decision-making process in cities. To learn how cities had dealt with the issue of fluoridation, Robert Crain, Elihu Katz, and Donald Rosenthal (1969) sent questionnaires to three informants in each of 1181 cities: the public-health officer, the publisher of the largest city newspaper, and the city clerk. One finding was that when the city decided the issue by referendum, the odds against fluoridation were 5 to 1.

Systematic Procedures: Interviews and Questionnaires

Surveys obtain information through interviews and/or self-administered questionnaires. The survey of political attitudes among 8th-graders was based on interviews; the study of youth in high-crime neighborhoods used a combination of interviews and self-administered questionnaires; the study of political decision making in cities made use of questionnaires only.

An additional example of the use of questionnaires is the College Alcohol Study (see Wechsler and Nelson, 2008), a widely cited national survey of American college students' drinking habits. The mail questionnaire, completed by more than 50,000 students at 120 colleges, asked numerous questions about drinking behavior and other health issues. The most controversial findings concerned binge drinking, operationally defined as the consumption of five or more drinks in a row for men and four or more drinks in a row for women during the 2 weeks prior to the survey. In each of the 1993, 1997, 1999, and 2001 surveys, the researchers found that two in five students who responded were binge drinkers. Binge drinkers, especially those who frequently binged, were far more likely than non-binge drinkers to experience a variety of alcohol-related and other health problems, such as engaging in unprotected and unplanned sex, getting in trouble with campus police, damaging property, and getting hurt or injured.

Unstructured versus Structured Interviewing

Regardless of whether a survey researcher makes use of interviews only, questionnaires only, or some combination of the two, the procedures tend to be standardized for all respondents to enhance the reliability of the data. This epitomizes a **structured interview**: The objectives are specific, all questions are written beforehand and asked in the same order for all respondents, and the interviewer is highly restricted in such matters as the use of introductory and closing remarks, transitions or "bridges" from topic to topic, and supplementary questions to gain a more complete response (called "probes"). There are exceptions to this rule, however, as informative and scientifically useful surveys are sometimes carried out in a less formal or structured manner.

In an **unstructured interview**, the objectives may be general, the discussion may be wide ranging, and individual questions will be developed spontaneously over the course of the interview. The interviewer is free to adapt the interview to capitalize on the special knowledge, experience, or insights of respondents. An everyday example of an unstructured interview might be a journalist interviewing a celebrity to learn more about his or her personal background, interests, and lifestyle. Between the two extremes, a **semistructured interview** would have specific objectives, but the interviewer would be permitted some freedom in meeting them. The scope of the interview would be limited to certain subtopics, and key questions probably would be developed in advance.

The choice of a highly structured, semistructured, or unstructured approach depends on the researcher's objectives. For example, in their ongoing study of Mexican migration to the United States, Douglas Massey and associates (1987) wanted to gather quantitatively rigorous data but ruled out a highly structured approach because of the sensitive nature of the study and the respondents' limited background (many are poorly educated or illiterate). Their semistructured interview form lists subtopics or data to collect for each household member. The interviewers are given considerable discretion as to question wording and timing to ensure that the interview is informal and not threatening to the respondents. To make sure that the flexible, semistructured interviews produce comparable or standardized information from each respondent, the interviewers receive extensive training and field supervision. This approach, when combined with annual probability sampling of households in three to five carefully chosen communities, yields precise quantitative information on Mexican migration to the United States.

When the research purpose is not to derive facts or precise quantitative descriptions but to understand the meaning of respondents' experiences, unstructured interviews often are adopted. This approach allows maximum flexibility in the development of hypotheses and theory; however, it seldom is associated with survey research because it invariably involves small nonprobability samples and qualitative analysis. The Carr, Napolitano, and Keating (2007) study of attitudes toward the police relied primarily on unstructured interviews to explore adolescents' complex views of police and law enforcement. To identify emerging themes, the researchers tape recorded, transcribed, and then coded the interviews using qualitative data-analysis software. Two emerging themes were "the police" and "how to reduce crime." Some responses with these themes were the product of direct questioning; however, many of the youth talked about the police in response to other questions, such as when asked to describe their neighborhood and the dangers they encountered in their daily lives. As these answers were probed, it became clear that the attitudes of youth in the high-crime neighborhoods were shaped by their direct experiences with law enforcement.

For some research purposes, a social scientist might utilize two or three sets of interviews, beginning with loosely structured interviews and progressing to a final set of highly structured interviews. A freer interviewing style in the preliminary stages would yield rich and varied information. This approach would assist a researcher in formulating or refining hypotheses, clarifying objectives, and specifying subtopics for subsequent semistructured interviews. Findings from a second set of interviews might be applied to the development of a highly structured questionnaire.

Quantitative Data Analysis

Data-analysis techniques depend on whether the survey's purpose is descriptive, explanatory, or a combination of the two. Surveys that are primarily **descriptive** seek to describe the distribution within a population of certain characteristics, attitudes, or experiences and make use of simpler forms of analysis. **Explanatory** surveys move beyond description to investigate relationships between two or more variables and attempt to explain these relationships in cause-and-effect terms. Sorting out the relationships between the variables in an explanatory survey requires the use of more sophisticated data-analysis techniques. (Data analysis will be dealt with further in Chapters 15 and 16.)

An illustration of a primarily descriptive study is the National Health and Social Life Survey (NHSLS), in which a national probability sample of adults between the ages of 18 and 59 were interviewed about their sexual attitudes and practices (Laumann et al., 1994). Originally prompted by the lack of national statistics on the prevalence of various sexual behaviors relevant to the AIDS epidemic, the NHSLS was transformed by actions of federal agencies and hostile politicians into a study with a broader focus, a much smaller than planned sample (3432 people were interviewed rather than 20,000), and a sponsorship by private rather than by public funding.

Among the interesting NHSLS findings are estimates of same-gender sexual activity and forced sexual behavior. Only 1.4 percent of the women and 2.8 percent of the men during the interview identified themselves as "homosexual" or "bisexual." Yet in a short, self-administered questionnaire that the respondent placed in a sealed envelope, 4.3 percent of the women and 9.1 percent of the men reported having engaged in a sexual act with someone of the same gender since puberty. These and other NHSLS estimates of homosexuality are substantially lower than reported in the Kinsey report and other studies that did not use probability sampling (Laumann et al., 1994:286–90). Perceptions of unwanted sexual activity varied by gender. Although only 2.8 percent of the men reported ever having forced a woman to do something sexual that she did not want to do, 21.6 percent of the women reported forced sex by a man.

The aforementioned NELS represents explanatory survey research. The study began with a baseline survey of students' school and school-related experiences in the 8th grade and continued with follow-up surveys 2, 4, 6, and 12 years later. The general purpose of the NELS was to relate the 8th-grade experiences to high school performance and, in turn, to later achievements in life. The wealth of data enables investigators to examine the impact of numerous factors—for example, students' school experiences and activities; their relationships with peers, parents, and teachers; and characteristics of their schools—on students' academic achievement, persistence in school, participation in postsecondary education, and career choices.

Secondary Analysis of Surveys

In most of the examples presented thus far, each survey had a central topic and the investigators were responsible for all phases of the research project, from the formulation of ideas and research design to the collection, analysis, and presentation of the data. Although this was once the dominant approach, researchers today are more apt to analyze survey data collected by some other person or agency than to conduct an original survey themselves. The analysis of survey data by analysts other than the primary investigator who collected the data is called **secondary analysis**. Analyses of the NELS data by Beckett Broh and others represent this form of research.

One of the many advantages of this research strategy is that sample size can be increased greatly by combining data from several surveys. For example, in their study of the long-term effects of education, Herbert Hyman, Charles Wright, and John Shelton Reed (1975) drew together 54 surveys conducted between 1949 and 1971, involving 76,671 respondents, from three sources: the Gallup poll, the NORC at the University of Chicago, and the Survey Research Center at the University of Michigan. Not surprising, a very strong positive relationship was found between amount of education and correct answers to knowledge questions. However, this was true not only for "academic"-type questions taken from the arts and sciences but also for questions relating to current affairs and popular culture. Furthermore, the relationship persisted over time, suggesting that one of the lasting effects of education is a lifelong openness to learning or tendency to seek information.

The earliest application of secondary analysis was to census data and then, beginning in the 1950s, to opinion-poll data. These data, however, were collected primarily for administrative and journalistic purposes. The major impetus for secondary analysis came in the 1970s with the advent of surveys designed expressly for the purpose of making high-quality data available to the social science research community (Glenn, 1978). The first large-scale survey of this type, the General Social Survey (GSS), began in 1972 and was conducted annually (except for 1979, 1981, and 1992) until 1994. Each GSS involved personal interviews with about 1500 respondents, drawn from a probability sample of the adult population of the United States. Starting in 1994, the GSS shifted to biennial surveys with two 1500-person samples in even-numbered years. Then, in 2006, a third sample was added to create a rotating three-wave panel, for a total sample size of 4510 respondents. The 2006 panel was re-interviewed in 2008 and 2010; henceforth, each GSS contains one new panel and re-interviews with two previous panels.

In contrast to most surveys, which have a central topic, the GSS is eclectic, with questions pertaining to a broad range of attitudes and behavior. A portion of each GSS includes questions that are replicated across years to facilitate research on social trends; time trends are available for 363 variables for 20 or more years between 1972 and 2014. The remainder of each survey is devoted largely to topical and cross-national modules, which comprise blocks of questions relating to special topics. The cross-national modules, which are sponsored by the International Social Survey Program (ISSP), are included in national surveys in more than 50 collaborating countries. The Yodanis comparative study of divorce culture and marital gender equality used the 1994 ISSP module on Family and Changing Gender Roles.

The 2014 GSS contains topical modules on knowledge about and attitudes toward science, quality of working life, shared capitalism, wealth, work and family balance, social identity, social isolation, and civic participation, as well as two ISSP modules, one on national identity and the other on citizenship. The quality of working life module, which replicates questions asked in 2002, 2006, and 2010, includes questions on method of work compensation, work schedule, work–family interference, job characteristics, chances for advancement, job security, relations with co-workers and management, and discrimination. The ISSP module includes questions measuring opinions about what it takes to be a good citizen, attitudes toward civil liberties for dissidents, involvement in various forms of political and social action, group memberships, opinions about people's rights in a democracy, and attitudes toward government and politics.

Data from the GSS are often used in the teaching of sociology and other social science courses, especially statistics (see Babbie, Halley, and Zaino, 2007; Frankfort-Nachmias and Leon-Guerrero, 2015). Moreover, analyses of GSS data can be found in more than 26,000 books, articles, chapters, and PhD dissertations (National Opinion Research Center, 2016). We make extensive use of GSS data in Chapters 15 and 16. In this chapter and the next, we will report some of the survey methods and materials used in producing these data so that readers may become more familiar with this important database.

Survey Research Designs

Research design generally refers to the overall structure or plan of a study. The crucial design features of experiments, with their focus on hypothesis testing, reveal how a given study will test a specific hypothesis. Surveys, however, place much less emphasis on this aspect of research design. The idea of a survey is to measure variables by asking people questions and then to examine the relationships among the measures. The major design option is to ask the questions once or to repeat the questions over time.

Cross-Sectional Designs

The most commonly used survey design by far is the **cross-sectional design**, in which data on a sample or "cross-section" of respondents chosen to represent a particular target population are gathered at essentially one point in time. By "one point in time" we do not mean that respondents are interviewed or that self-administered questionnaires are collected simultaneously (although questionnaires might be in some studies). Rather, the data are collected in as short a time as is feasible. For the 2014 GSS, it took more than 6 months, between April and October, for 151 interviewers to complete interviews with 3842 respondents (T. W. Smith, personal communication, 2016). Most of the studies cited earlier are cross-sectional designs.

Two variations on the cross-sectional survey design have been developed out of sociological interest in studying the influence of social contexts and interpersonal relations on individual behavior. Cross-sectional surveys are limited by the amount and accuracy of the information that individual respondents can capably report about the groups and milieus to which they belong. Contextual designs and social network designs address this problem by studying individuals and relationships found within the same social context.

Contextual designs sample enough cases within particular groups or contexts to describe accurately certain characteristics of those contexts. Doris Entwisle, Karl Alexander, and Linda Olson (1994) employed this design to study whether the gender gap in math achievement favoring boys over girls might be explained by the contextual resources of their schools and their neighborhoods. The investigators first sampled 20 Baltimore elementary schools and then sampled children from each 1st-grade classroom in the selected schools. Student improvement in math skills during the first 2 years of school was predicted from individual-level variables (including initial math reasoning score, race, sex, parents' education, family economic standing) and contextual-level variables (average number of years of schooling for parents of sampled children in each of the 20 schools, racial composition of each school, and median neighborhood household income). The analysis revealed that the boys' gains in math skills were more affected by resources outside the home (school and neighborhood contexts) than were the girls' gains.

Social network designs focus on the relationships or connections among social actors (people, organizations, countries, etc.) and the transaction flows (processes) occurring along the connecting links.[1] Network adherents reject analytical approaches that isolate actors from their social environment (network linkages) and that interpret behavior solely in terms of actor attributes (characteristics). For example, social psychologists may hypothesize that the likelihood of two people becoming friends increases (1) if they share common interests and values (the traditional attribute approach) or (2) if they share a friend in common (the network approach).

Social network designs typically require the interviewing of every person in the group under study. This makes it possible to delineate networks of personal relationships by asking respondents to provide such information as who their best friends are, whom they most like to work with on a certain project, or to whom they would go for advice. In a social network study of a male-dominated advertising firm, Herminia Ibarra (1992) found that women had to form costly, differentiated interactional networks by choosing (1) other women as friends and sources of support and (2) men mostly as instrumental (work-related) resources. The men, in contrast, chose other men for both expressive and instrumental purposes.

Longitudinal Designs

Because cross-sectional designs call for collection of data at one point in time, they do not always show clearly the directi[...] are not well suited to the study of process and change. [...] out the logical relations among variables, and respon[...] and present events. But both of these sources of evide[...] tronger inferences about causal direction and more ac[...] survey researchers have developed **longitudinal desi**[...] re asked at two or more points in time. The question[...] f independently selected samples of the same general p[...]. This results in two main types of longitudinal designs: trend studies and panel studies.

A **trend study** consists of a repeated cross-sectional design in which each survey collects data on the same items or variables with a new, independent sample of the same target population. This allows for the study of trends or changes in the population as a whole. Trend studies may be illustrated by the monthly government surveys used to estimate unemployment in the United States (target population) as well as by repeated public-opinion polls of candidate preferences among registered voters (target population) as an election approaches. An analysis of GSS trends in support for same-sex marriage, for example, shows tremendous changes between 1988, when the question was first asked, and 2014. In 1988, about 12 percent of respondents agreed and 73 percent disagreed that "homosexual couples should have the right to marry one another." By 2010, more people agreed than disagreed, and in 2014, for the first time, a majority (57 percent) agreed (Associated Press–NORC Center for Public Affairs Research, 2015).

Ideally, all trend information would be obtained through measures repeated frequently at regular intervals, as in the GSS. However, much of our trend-survey data come from infrequent replications of studies. For example, in 1993, Danching Ruan and associates (1997) replicated a 1986 social-network survey in urban China to see whether structural changes in Chinese society would be reflected in changes in personal relationships. Both surveys asked respondents to name others with whom they had discussed important matters over the past 6 months. The discussion partners named in 1986 were primarily co-workers (44 percent) and relatives (39 percent). The 1993 replication revealed a dramatic shift in personal connections: More friends and associates and fewer co-workers and relatives were named as discussants. The 1986–1993 changes in people's discussion networks were consistent with concurrent large-scale social changes, including a diminished role of the traditional workplace in people's lives and the new opportunities provided by an emerging market economy.

Most trend studies measure changes in the general population over time. To study the developmental effects of aging as well as chronological changes, it is also possible to focus on a specific cohort of persons. A **cohort** consists of persons (or other units such as organizations and neighborhoods) who experience the same significant life event within a specified period of time (Glenn, 1977). Most often the life event that defines a cohort is birth, but it also might be marriage, completion of high school, entry into medical school, and so forth. Demographers long have analyzed birth cohorts from census data to predict population trends. In the past half-century, social researchers also have begun to do **cohort studies** of various attitudes and behaviors by tracing changes across cohorts in repeated cross-sectional surveys. Cohorts are identified (or tracked) by their birth date; for example, the 1972 cohort would be 18 years old in a 1990 survey, 28 years old in a 2000 survey, and 38 years old in a 2010 survey.

Cohort trend studies enable one to study three different influences associated with the passage of time. To get a sense of these influences and of the difficulty of studying them at a single point in time, consider a cross-sectional survey containing measures of age and attitudes toward premarital sex. The GSS, for example, includes the following question: "There's been a lot of discussion about the way morals and attitudes about sex are changing in this country. If a man and woman have sex relations before marriage, do you think it is always wrong, almost always wrong, wrong only sometimes, or not wrong at all?" If we found that responses to this question became more conservative (premarital sex is always or almost always wrong) with age or time, this could be a result of one of three kinds of influences: *life course* (as people grow older, they become more conservative), *cohort* (older generations are more conservative than younger generations), or *historical period* (the prevailing culture has become more conservative over time, making it less socially acceptable to hold liberal views toward premarital sex).

The problem with cross-sectional data is that one cannot begin to disentangle these various effects. Longitudinal data in general and cohort analyses in particular are generally superior for this purpose, although readers should be aware that these techniques seldom provide clear causal inferences (Glenn, 1977). An example of a cohort study is David Harding and Christopher Jencks' (2003) analysis of age, cohort, and period effects on changing attitudes toward premarital sex. Using GSS data from 1972 to 1998, data from a 1965 NORC survey, and Gallup surveys in 1962, 1969, and 1973, Harding and Jencks broke the samples down into 10-year age cohorts according to the decade when respondents turned 18 years of age, from the 1920s to the 1990s. In general, they found a sharp increase in liberal attitudes toward premarital sex since 1962, with much of the change occurring in the early 1970s, which they attributed to a period effect. Within each cohort, they also found an increase in conservatism after people turned age 30, which they attributed to an aging effect.

Whereas trend studies identify which *variables* are changing over time, **panel studies** can reveal which *individuals* are changing over time because the same respondents are surveyed again and again. Paul Lazarsfeld, Bernard Berelson, and Hazel Gaudet's 1948 classic study of voter behavior, *The People's Choice*, exemplifies the panel method. Before the 1940 presidential election, 600 persons were interviewed repeatedly between May and November. The analysis revealed that persons who expressed a clear preference for the Democratic or the Republican candidates at the first interview were unlikely at the second interview 1 month later to remember having seen or heard any campaign propaganda from the party of the opposing candidate. Because of this phenomenon of selective attention, few voters changed their preferences over the course of the study.

By repeatedly surveying persons over an extended period of time, a panel study can record life histories—schooling experiences, labor force participation, income changes, health conditions, and so forth—much better than retrospective questions from a cross-sectional survey. Some of the early panel studies analyzed data from small, highly selective samples over very long periods of time. Glen Elder's (1999) 30-year follow-up study of the impact of the Great Depression on the life course analyzed data from a panel study that began in 1932 with the selection of 167 5th-grade children from five elementary schools in Oakland, California. These individuals were observed, tested, and questioned more than a hundred times before they graduated from high school in 1939. They then completed a short questionnaire in 1941, were interviewed extensively in 1953–54 and 1957–58, and completed a final follow-up mailed questionnaire in 1964. In a study of attitude change among Bennington College students, women who were surveyed initially in the late 1930s either were interviewed or completed a mailed questionnaire in 1960 and then again in 1984 (Alwin, Cohen, and Newcomb, 1991). A major finding of this study was the persistence of political attitudes over the adult years, as the Bennington women, who were liberalized in the college years, remained politically liberal in later life.

KEY POINT

Panel surveys measure changes in individuals over time, *trend surveys* track general social changes, and *cohort surveys* gauge changes in age groups.

Panel studies of any duration were a rarity in the social sciences until the late 1960s, when the federal government began conducting large-scale longitudinal studies for secondary data analysis. In addition to the NELS, which surveyed a sample of 8th-graders in 1988 and then did follow-up surveys of these same respondents in 1990, 1992, 1994, and 2000, other examples include the Panel Study of Income Dynamics and the National Longitudinal Survey of Youth (NLSY). The Panel Study of Income Dynamics has collected data on a sample of U.S. households annually from 1968 to 1997 and biennially beginning in 1999; following descendants of the initial sample of 5,000 for nearly 50 years of data collection, the study has grown to more than 10,000 families. Starting in 1979 with interviews of more than 12,000 individuals 14–22 years of age, the NLSY re-interviewed this sample annually through 1994 and biennially since then.

Two drawbacks to studies of this magnitude are that they are expensive and that they take considerable time. In addition, panel surveys have two problems not found in cross-sectional designs: respondent attrition and reactivity stemming from repeated measurement (Duncan, 2001). Panel attrition occurs when respondents interviewed in the initial wave do not respond in later waves. The more respondents who drop out, the less likely that follow-up samples will be representative of the original population from which the initial sample was drawn. Therefore, researchers typically make great efforts and devote sizeable resources, including incentive payments, to retain a high percentage of the initial sample in follow-up surveys. The NLSY, for example, offered respondents $10 for their time. In the early years, more than 95 percent of the initial respondents were re-interviewed; by 1992, 13 years after the initial 1979 interview, the NLSY was still able to interview 90 percent of the original sample (Brandon, Gritz, and Pergamit, 1995). No matter what the rate of follow-up response, however, a panel survey is like the experimental pretest–posttest design in its ability to assess and control for the effects of attrition. That is, initial information on respondents who fail to participate in later waves can be used to assess nonresponse bias and to make necessary statistical adjustments.

Interviewing respondents repeatedly also may affect how individuals respond to the survey; two problems are "time-in-sample bias" and "panel conditioning" (Sikkel and Hoogendoorn, 2008). The first bias may occur when panel participation becomes routinized to the point that respondents merely repeat what they have said before, rather than carefully consider their current feelings and actions. Or realizing from previous interviews that a "yes" response leads to follow-up questions, respondents may avoid answering the extra questions by answering "no" (Kalton and Citro, 1993). Panel conditioning may stimulate real attitude or behavioral changes so that respondents' attitudes and behavior are no longer representative of the larger population. In national election studies, for example, voter registration and turnout has been shown to increase with the number of times participants were interviewed (Traugott and Katosh, 1979).

Although some argue that "pervasive behavioral effects" are unlikely in panel surveys, "especially when changes in the behavior under investigation require more effort than making a trip to the polls" (Duncan, 2001:11011), there is nonetheless evidence of panel conditioning on a wide range of behaviors. John Warren and Andrew Halpern-Manners (2012) have theorized about the circumstances under which panel conditioning is likely to occur. Their research suggests, for example, that panel conditioning effects are most likely when repeated surveys are close together in time (Halpern-Manners, Warren, and Torche, 2014).

Steps in Survey Research: Planning

The activities in doing surveys fall into three broad categories: (1) planning, (2) field administration, and (3) data processing and analysis. The remainder of this chapter is devoted to planning and field administration. Chapters 15 and 16 deal with data processing and analysis.

In planning a survey, a few activities may be thought of as key decision points. These activities are represented in the flowchart shown in Figure 9.1. Under each major activity we have indicated the chapters that address it.[2]

The initial stages in planning a survey are essentially the same as in other forms of research. The first step is to select a topic and formulate a problem in researchable terms. One then reviews relevant journal articles, books, and other materials to determine what is known about the topic and what work remains to be done. During the course of this review, a researcher inevitably will refine and further specify his or her objectives; also, he

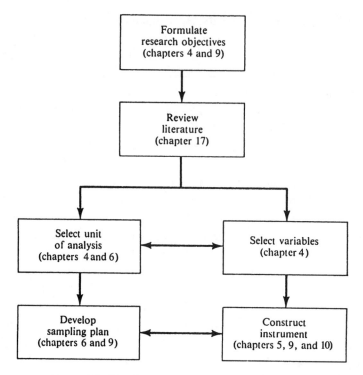

FIGURE 9.1. Key decision points in planning a survey.

or she may become aware of existing measures or scales that may be incorporated into the prospective study. The selection of units of analysis and variables occurs in light of research objectives. In survey research, the units of analysis are either individuals or groups of individuals (including families, organizations, cities); the particular variables selected depend on which characteristics should be studied to meet research objectives.

An effective planning device when thinking about variables is to work backward mentally from the final steps in the study to the earlier steps in the planning phase. Serious mistakes can be avoided by anticipating the data analysis. To do this, one works out the actual data analysis along with the steps likely to be taken in the event of various outcomes. One might ask questions such as these: If the data support my hypothesis, what will I do next? If the data are the opposite of my hypothesis, what will I do next? (I might decide that I need to control additional variables to test the hypothesis properly.) Have I included all the variables I might want to use? By anticipating the data analysis in this way, the survey content can be planned better. (But, then again, this is not as easy as it sounds, as James Davis reveals in his report of a social survey that we recount in Box 9.1.)

Having selected the unit of analysis and identified key variables, a survey researcher turns his or her attention to the development of the sampling plan and survey instrument. As the flowchart in Figure 9.1 shows, these plans are made concurrently as each affects the other and both depend on the objectives and resources of the researcher. Constructing the survey instrument or questionnaire requires a great deal of time and thought and the making of many decisions. We devote the entire next chapter to this aspect of survey design.

BOX 9.1 An Informal Account of a Large-Scale Survey

Researchers do not, as a rule, report the false starts, unsolvable roadblocks, embarrassing problems, and mistakes that are a normal part of the process of doing surveys. James Davis (1964), however, has provided a humor-filled account of a national survey, the Great Books study, from its inception to the publication of a book. Davis describes the events as an illustration of how survey research is carried out in a large research organization.

The parties involved in the Great Books study included the NORC, with James Davis as study director; the Fund for Adult Education, as client; and the object of the study, the Great Books Foundation. Through grants, the Fund for Adult Education, a subsidiary of the Ford Foundation, had been supporting various educational activities and programs, including Great Books. By commissioning an evaluation study, the fund hoped to gain concrete evidence of the value of the Great Books program and to determine whether the continuation or expansion of support was merited. The Great Books Foundation, a non-profit corporation, believed in its program, according to Davis, but seriously doubted the usefulness of a survey in evaluating it. The parties in the study agreed at the outset that the study would be concerned with the effects on participants of participation in Great Books.

The Great Books program in 1957–58 involved approximately 1960 discussion groups throughout the United States, with additional groups in Canada and elsewhere, which met every 2 weeks from September to June. At each meeting, the members discussed a book that they had been assigned to read. Book selections were organized into blocks of 1 year. The size of the groups varied, with a sample average of 11. The groups were sponsored chiefly by public libraries but also by churches, businesses, and individuals. One or two persons served as leaders of each group. No tuition was charged, and no certificates of completion were given. Readings could be bought from the foundation inexpensively if desired.

The design of the study fell naturally into two parts: sampling and questionnaire construction. In regard to sampling, the "ideal" design would have been a field experiment in which a large probability sample of persons were randomly assigned to a control group or to a Great Books discussion group. After a specified period, both groups would be measured on the dependent variables. However, such a design was not feasible. Among other problems, the effects were expected to take a long time to appear, and a report had to be delivered in about a year. The compromise design would use beginning participants as a control group and compare them with advanced-year members on several variables. The sample was stratified to overrepresent the advanced-year groups, where the effects might be expected to show. Groups were asked to distribute and complete self-administered questionnaires at a regular meeting. Thus, although it would have been ideal to have had a sample of randomly assigned *individuals* in and out of the Great Books program, practical considerations resulted in a stratified sample of Great Books discussion *groups*.

Constructing the questionnaire presented more difficulties than devising the sampling plan. The Fund for Adult Education, the Great Books Foundation, and the study director, Davis, had different ideas about the program's effects. The fund, interested in community participation, argued that participants would become more involved in community affairs as a result of their exposure to great literature. Davis and the Great Books Foundation doubted that this was the case. The Great Books Foundation insisted that its program did not have any

(continued)

(continued)

specific purposes that could be evaluated by a survey. Under pressure from Davis, the foundation was able to make some general statements regarding the program's objectives: Participants should become more open-minded, develop more critical-thinking skills, become more intellectually sophisticated, and so forth, effects that would be difficult to measure. Davis was interested in members' philosophies, ideologies, and tastes. He also wanted to include some social network questions to see how a person's acceptance or nonacceptance by the group affected his or her reactions to the program. However, the Great Books Foundation ruled out the social network questions as possibly offensive to participants. Instead, questions were asked about roles played by the respondent and others in the group. The final questionnaire contained items reflecting the Fund's interest in community participation; a few items related to aesthetics, open-mindedness, and critical thinking; measures of tastes, ideologies, and philosophies; and the role questions.

More than 90 percent of the sampled groups returned the questionnaires. Analysis of the survey results showed marked differences in knowledge between beginners and advanced-year members, slight differences in tolerance and open-mindedness, and few behavioral differences.

A report for the sponsor was completed on time in August 1958. The project, however, was not finished. Davis immediately conceived the idea of doing a follow-up study to find out which respondents had dropped out of the groups during the year so that data from these individuals could be subtracted. The remaining data would be reanalyzed to see whether omission of the dropouts affected the findings. The fund agreed to sponsor the follow-up study. Controlling for dropouts had little effect.

A new study then was conceived to analyze the factors associated with dropping out, using the remaining budget money. The idea was not only to learn why Great Books members drop out but also to view the data more broadly as "why some small-scale social systems lose the commitment of their members" (Davis, 1964:228). Davis admitted that through this study, he hoped to impress on his colleagues that he was capable of theory-building research, as opposed to purely empirical work. The study was to lead to the publication of *Great Books and Small Groups*.

The study showed that retention of participants was greatest where a large percentage of members played active roles. Theories that the content of the roles is important were not supported, nor was Davis's hunch that retention was related to a balance of power in the group.

At the end of Davis's account (1964:233–34) of the Great Books study, he gives a beautiful description of the satisfactions of doing research:

> There is a lot of misery in surveys, most of the time and money going into
> monotonous clerical and statistical routines, with interruptions only for squab-
> bles with the client, budget crises, petty machinations for a place in the academic
> sun, and social case work with neurotic graduate students. And nobody ever
> reads the final report. Those few moments, however, when a new set of tables
> comes up from the machine room and questions begin to be answered; when
> relationships actually hold under controls; when the pile of tables on the desk
> suddenly meshes to yield a coherent chapter; when in a flash you see a neat test
> for an interpretation; when you realize you have found out something important
> that nobody ever knew before—these are the moments that justify research.

A critical aspect of survey instrumentation is deciding on the mode of asking questions—interviewer administered (face-to-face [FTF] or telephone surveys) or self-administered (paper-and-pencil or computer-assisted questionnaires) or some combination of these modes. This choice depends partly on other planning decisions such as the research objectives, units of analysis, and sampling plan. For example, in the College Alcohol Study, the sampling plan required contact with a large number of respondents at more than 100 geographically dispersed colleges and universities. These requirements ruled out both FTF and telephone interviews as too expensive, time-consuming, and impractical, and questionnaires were used. In the study of young people's attitudes toward law enforcement, personal interviews were necessitated by the sensitivity and complexity of the topic and by the researcher's need for an approach flexible enough to explore how attitudes were formed.

The choice of survey mode, in addition to the overriding factor of cost, will determine the optimum sampling design. The most expensive and time-consuming mode of survey research is FTF interviewing, the major costs of which are incurred from direct interviewing time and travel to reach respondents. If respondents are widely dispersed geographically, this method also will require an efficient sampling procedure for locating respondents. Under these circumstances, the most cost-efficient procedure usually is multistage cluster sampling. Almost all large-scale surveys are multistage, with stratification at one or more stages. If respondents are reached easily by mail or phone, there is no reason to use clustering. Simple random or systematic sampling may be implemented, with or without stratification, provided that an adequate sampling frame can be obtained.

As you can see, survey planning is not a linear series of decisions. Rather, it requires the simultaneous consideration of the likely costs and benefits of many choices. Also, as planning progresses, revisions in previous decisions and plans frequently are needed. Survey costs and benefits are best viewed from Robert Groves's (1989) "total error perspective," which identifies four types of errors that threaten the accuracy of survey results. We discussed each of these error sources in the chapters on sampling and measurement:

1. *Coverage error*: Differences between the target population and the sampling frame; this is produced when the sampling frame does not include all members of the population, as when a telephone survey omits people without telephones.
2. *Sampling error*: The difference between a population value and a sample estimate of the value that occurs because a sample rather than a complete census of the population is surveyed.
3. *Nonresponse error*: Differences in the characteristics of those who choose to respond to a survey and those who refuse or cannot be contacted because of an insufficient address or a wrong telephone number, they are never at home, or they are on vacation.
4. *Measurement error*: Inaccurate responses associated with the respondent, the interviewer, the survey instrument, and the postsurvey data processing.

Ideally, survey planners effectively allocate available funds and resources to minimize the impact of these potential errors. This is difficult because the errors may be interrelated (reducing one may increase another), certain types of error may be too costly to reduce appreciably, and information on the extent of the errors may be limited or lacking. The choice of a stratified random sampling plan, for example, might reduce sampling error but increase coverage error compared with a simple random sampling design. Reducing nonresponse error by efforts to convert reluctant respondents may inadvertently increase measurement error. Conversely, efforts to decrease measurement error may increase nonresponse error. Survey error can never be completely eliminated. When it is too expensive to reduce a source of error, it may be possible to estimate the magnitude and direction of the error and make suitable adjustments in the data analysis.

KEY POINT

Survey researchers seek to minimize error resulting from construction of the sampling frame (*coverage error*), sample selection (*sampling error*), securing sampled respondents (*nonresponse error*), and data collection (*measurement error*).

We now consider various survey modes. Figure 9.2 lists the four basic data-collection modes along with typical computer-based variations. The modes may be conceptualized as falling along a continuum from the most to the least interactive. At one end of the continuum, involving all channels of communication, is FTF interviewing; this is followed, in turn, by telephone interviews, various computer-assisted self-interviews, and autonomous self-administered questionnaires. Although we focus primarily on the four basic modes, recent technological developments have rapidly expanded the options and encouraged the use of multiple modes of data collection. Therefore, we discuss mixed-mode data collection strategies after comparing the modes shown in Figure 9.2. Each mode, as you will see, has its distinctive advantages and disadvantages, especially with respect to error reduction.

Most
Interactive

Face-to-Face (FTF) Interviews

Computer-assisted Personal Interviewing (CAPI)

Telephone Interviews

Computer-assisted Telephone Interviewing (CATI)

Computer-Assisted Self-Interviews

Internet (Web) Surveys

Computer Self-Administered Questionnaires (CASI)

Interactive Voice Response (IVR) Surveys

E-mail Transmission of Questionnaires

Paper-and-Pencil Questionnaires

Least
Interactive

FIGURE 9.2. Major data-collection modes.

Because sampling error is primarily a function of sampling design, sample size, and population heterogeneity and not a function of the data-collection mode, our concern here is with the other three sources of error, especially coverage error and nonresponse error.

Face-to-Face and Telephone Interviewing

Both FTF interviews and telephone interviews require trained interviewers proficient in the use of the survey's **interview schedule**. The interview schedule consists of instructions to the interviewer together with the questions to be asked and, if they are used, response options. Interviewers and an interview schedule permit much more flexibility than is possible with a self-administered questionnaire. For example, when research objectives necessitate the use of questions that require respondents to answer in their own words, an interviewer usually will be able to elicit a fuller, more complete response than will a questionnaire requiring respondents to write out answers. This is particularly true with respondents whose writing skills are weak or who are less motivated to make the effort to respond fully. In addition, interviewers can easily utilize question formats in which certain questions are skipped when they do not apply to a particular respondent, whereas such a format may be confusing for respondents completing a questionnaire. Furthermore, in cases where it is important that questions be considered in a certain order, a self-administered questionnaire presents problems because respondents may look over the entire form before beginning to answer.

Other advantages of interviewing include the ability of an interviewer to clarify or restate questions that the respondent does not at first understand. An interviewer may also help respondents clarify their answers by using *probes*, such as "I'm not sure exactly what you mean" or "Can you tell me more about that?" Interviewers help to ensure that every relevant item is answered; tedious or sensitive items cannot be passed over easily as in self-administered questionnaires. Even when a respondent initially balks at answering an item, a tactful explanation by the interviewer of the item's meaning or purpose frequently results in an adequate response.

In addition to these characteristics that both modes of interviewing share, each has its own set of advantages and disadvantages.

Face-to-Face Interviewing

The oldest and most highly regarded method of survey research, **face-to-face** or **in-person interviewing**, has a number of advantages in addition to the ones already mentioned. The response rate, the proportion of people in the sample from whom completed interviews (or questionnaires) are obtained, is typically higher than in comparable telephone or mail surveys (de Leeuw, 2008:128–29). Nonresponses, however, have been increasing in Western government and academic FTF surveys (de Leeuw and de Heer, 2002; Brick and Williams, 2013). Since 2000, the overall response rate for the GSS has been around 70 percent; it was 69.2 percent in 2014 (NORC, 2016). Reasons for the high response rate likely include the intrinsic attractiveness of being interviewed (having someone's attention, being asked to talk about oneself, the novelty of the experience); the difficulty of saying "no" to someone asking for something in person; and possibly the fact that the importance and credibility of the research are conveyed best by an FTF interviewer who can show identification and credentials.

This survey mode is appropriate when long interviews are necessary. FTF interviews of 1 hour's length are common, but they sometimes go much longer. In 2014, GSS respondents took about 100 minutes to answer 475 questions (T. W. Smith, personal communication, 2016). With FTF interviewing, one can use visual aids such as photographs and drawings in presenting the questions, as well as cards that show response options. The cards may be useful when response options are difficult to remember or when it is face-saving for respondents to select the option or category on the card rather than to say the answer aloud. Finally, FTF interviewing permits unobtrusive observations that may be of interest to researchers. For example, the interviewer may note the ethnic composition of the neighborhood and the quality of housing.

There are some disadvantages to this method, the greatest of which is cost. The budget for an FTF survey must provide for recruiting, training, and supervising personnel and for interviewer wages and travel expenses, plus lodging and meals in some cases. Groves et al. (2009:173) estimate that national FTF surveys cost 5 to 10 times as much as telephone surveys. The full cost of the 2014 GSS, from sampling through release of the data to the public, was about $1350 per respondent (T. W. Smith, personal communication, 2016).

Another disadvantage is the difficulty of locating respondents who are not at home when an interviewer first calls. In more and more households, no adult is at home during the day. This necessitates call-backs in the evening or, as in the GSS, generally restricting contacts to weekdays after 4:00 PM and on weekends. Even then, many persons in large cities will not open their doors to strangers in the evening, and many interviewers refuse to go into certain areas of cities at night. Fear of strangers and the desire for privacy may be the causes of another disadvantage: The response rate for heterogeneous samples in metropolitan areas has been declining for several years. However, this is not true for rural areas or among specialized target groups.

Staff supervision presents special difficulties. Frequently, interviewers, data coders, and researchers are geographically dispersed. If an interviewer has not recorded responses adequately, effective coding is impossible. Furthermore, many interviews may be completed by an interviewer before feedback gets back to the individual. This is less of a problem when interviewer supervisors go over each interview schedule soon after it is completed. Some of the problems associated with interviewer mistakes may be minimized with **computer-assisted personal interviewing** (CAPI). A computer program, usually on a portable laptop computer, prompts the interviewer with instructions and question wording in the proper order, skips questions not relevant to particular respondents, ensures that the interviewer enters appropriate response codes for each question, may indicate when respondents are giving inconsistent responses to related questions, and may even digitally record random interview segments with a laptop microphone for quality control. CAPI has become the standard for large-scale survey research in the United States; the GSS switched to CAPI in 2002.

Finally, with the personal interview method, interviewers may introduce bias into the data in several ways. For example, they may fail to follow the interview schedule in the prescribed manner or may suggest answers to respondents. Bias also may be introduced through a respondent's reaction to the interviewer's gender, race, manner of dress, or personality. In Chapter 7 we spoke of an experiment as a social occasion and the related possibilities of bias. An FTF interview is no less a "social occasion" than an experiment; consequently, interviewers must be carefully trained to be sensitive to the ways in which they may wittingly or unwittingly affect their interviewees' responses.

Telephone Interviewing

Like FTF interviewing, **telephone interviewing** has its advantages and disadvantages. Substantial savings in time and money are two of the reasons survey researchers choose to use this method. Large survey research organizations that have a permanent staff can complete a telephone survey rapidly, and even those researchers who must hire and train interviewers can complete a telephone survey faster than one requiring FTF interviews or mailed questionnaires. As noted above, the costs for telephone surveys are far less than the costs for FTF interview surveys. However, telephone survey costs will exceed those for mailed questionnaires, even with several follow-up mailings included.

Another major advantage of telephone interviewing is the opportunity for centralized quality control over all aspects of data collection (Lavrakas, 1993, 2010), including question development and pretesting, interviewer training and supervision, sampling and call-backs, and data coding and entry. Administration and staff supervision for a telephone survey are much simpler than for a personal interview survey. No field staff is necessary; in fact, it is possible to have the researcher, interviewers, and coders working in the same office. This arrangement permits supervisors to monitor ongoing interviews, allowing immediate feedback on performance and helping to minimize interviewer error or bias. Coders may be eliminated and the interviewers can enter numbers corresponding to respondent answers directly into a computer terminal. If they are used, coders may provide immediate feedback to interviewers and their supervisors.

In terms of sampling quality, the telephone survey mode falls between FTF interviews and mailed questionnaires. In the past, lists of telephone subscribers were used in the sampling process, creating a problem of coverage error by excluding those who had unlisted telephone numbers or moved too recently to be directory listed (Steeh, 2008:226). The problem of missing those individuals with unlisted numbers was resolved through **random-digit dialing** (RDD) procedures in which telephone numbers are chosen randomly. In the simplest RDD design, telephone prefixes (exchanges) within the target geographic area are sampled and then the last four digits of the telephone number are randomly selected. In actual practice, more complex "list-assisted" RDD procedures are used to screen out nonresidential and other ineligible numbers, and "dual-frame" procedures are used to sample both mobile and landline phones (Groves et al., 2009:132–34; Steeh, 2008:227–28).

In addition to RDD, the introduction of **computer-assisted telephone interviewing** (CATI) in the 1970s greatly enhanced the efficacy of this survey mode (Nathan, 2001). CATI refers to a set of computerized tools that aid interviewers and supervisors by automating various data-collection tasks. The uses of CATI include sampling and dialing phone numbers, scheduling call-backs, screening and selecting the person to be interviewed at each sampled phone number, prompting the interviewer with appropriate introductions and questions in the proper sequence, skipping irrelevant questions, identifying when responses are inconsistent with replies to earlier questions, ensuring that the interviewer enters legitimate response codes for each question, recording the responses into a computer data file, and producing immediate sampling and interviewing updates for supervisors (Lavrakas, 1993). Finally, an added benefit of CATI systems is that complex factorial designs may be seamlessly incorporated into surveys (see Chapter 8).

Still, telephone surveys have their limitations. Response rates for many federal telephone surveys declined from around 70 percent in the 1990s to 50 percent by 2005 (Dixon and Tucker, 2010), and rates for private U.S. survey organizations are even lower, with most telephone surveys between 20 and 50 percent (Holbrook, Krosnick, and Pfent, 2008). Factors contributing to the plunging telephone response rates include the growth of caller ID call-screening and call-blocking technologies, heightened privacy concerns in the face of increased telemarketing calls, and the increase in cell phone–only households (Curtin, Presser, and Singer, 2005; Dixon and Tucker, 2010). In short, many people do not answer their phone, be it landline or cell, unless they recognize and wish to speak to the caller.

Other limitations of telephone surveys are interview duration and the complexity of the questions asked. Conducting a telephone interview longer than 20 to 30 minutes increases the risk of nonresponse and mid-interview termination (de Leeuw, 2008). Although interviewers may repeat a question, it is desirable to develop questions simple enough to be understood and retained by respondents while they formulate an answer. Research also has shown that open-ended questions yield shorter, less complete answers in telephone interviews than in FTF interviews (Groves and Kahn, 1979). Furthermore, questions with multiple response options may present difficulties in that interviewers cannot present the options on cards but must read and, if necessary, repeat options to respondents at the risk of boring them. For these reasons, the telephone survey mode lacks the advantages of the FTF mode in regard to the types of questions that are used.

Another disadvantage of telephone interviews is that it is more difficult for interviewers to establish trust and rapport with respondents than it is in FTF interviews; this may lead to higher rates of nonresponse for some questions and underreporting of sensitive or socially undesirable behavior. Robert Groves (1979) compared the results of two identical telephone surveys based on separate samples with the results of an FTF survey asking the same questions. At the end of the questionnaire were items about respondents' reactions to the interview. Among other questions, respondents were asked whether they felt uncomfortable talking about certain topics, such as income, their income tax refund, political opinions, or racial attitudes. For each of the sensitive topics, more telephone respondents felt uncomfortable, with the largest differences for the income and income tax questions. Not surprisingly, the telephone surveys showed lower response rates to the income questions. Other studies confirm that respondents are less likely to divulge illegal or socially undesirable behavior to an interviewer by telephone than in FTF interviewing (Aquilino, 1994:211, 214; Holbrook, Green, and Krosnick, 2003).

Despite these disadvantages, telephone surveys became the most popular survey method in the United States and Western Europe in the last quarter of the twentieth century. Reduced time and cost are major advantages. Furthermore, closer supervision, developments in RDD and CATI, and the high percentage of households with telephones made the quality of telephone surveys only slightly inferior to that of FTF interviewing. Now, however, unless a solution can be found for rapidly declining telephone response rates, some survey researchers offer a grim prognosis for the long-term future of this survey mode (Kalton, 2000; Curtin, Presser, and Singer, 2005:97). Perhaps the biggest challenge is the rapid proliferation of mobile telephones and the growth of the cell phone–only population. As of 2015, results from the National Health Interview Survey indicated that 47 percent of homes only use cell phones and do not have a landline phone (Blumberg and Luke, 2015). Complex methodological, statistical, legal, and ethical issues must be resolved to develop effective dual-frame sampling of mobile and landline telephones (Lavrakas et al., 2007). In light of these mounting obstacles to telephone surveys, some foresee an increasing reliance on self-administered questionnaires (Dillman, Smyth, and Christian, 2009).

KEY POINT
Compared to telephone interviewing, face-to-face interviewing has higher response rates, allows visual aids, and permits long and complex questionnaires, but is more expensive.

Paper-and-Pencil Questionnaires

Occasionally, the site of a **paper-and-pencil-questionnaire** is a school or organization, where a questionnaire may be hand-delivered and filled out in a group or individually. Most often, however, the setting is a home or a workplace. To get to this setting, almost all self-administered questionnaires are mailed to respondents. Therefore, we will discuss the pros and cons of this method as a *mail survey*.

A mail survey is less expensive than FTF or telephone interviews, although the budget for printing and postage must be sufficiently high to permit follow-up mailings. No interviewers or interviewer supervisors are needed, there are no travel or telephone expenses, and little office space is required. In some surveys, the staff may consist of just one or two persons in addition to the researcher. Groves et al. (2009:173) estimate that mail surveys generally cost 20 to 70 percent less than telephone surveys.

The time required to complete the data-collection phase of the survey is greater than that for telephone surveys but usually less than that for FTF surveys. The sample size may be very large, and geographic dispersion is not a problem. Furthermore, there is greater accessibility to respondents with this method since those who cannot be reached by telephone or who are infrequently at home usually receive mail.

Compared with interviews, self-administered questionnaires offer several advantages to motivated respondents (Mangione, 1995). Respondents are free to select a convenient time to respond and to spend sufficient time to think about each answer. The absence of an interviewer also assures privacy, which may explain why respondents are less willing to reveal illegal or socially undesirable behaviors or other sensitive information to an interviewer than in a self-administered questionnaire (Tourangeau and Smith, 1996:277–79).

On the other hand, coverage and nonresponse error may be magnified with this survey mode. Researchers must sample from a mailing list, which may have some incorrect or out-of-date addresses and which may omit some eligible respondents. Because of the lack of a complete sampling frame, mail surveys rarely have been used in national surveys; however, beginning in the 1990s, the U.S. Postal Service has made electronic files of mailing addresses available to the public though qualified companies, thus making mail surveys more viable either as an alternative or as a multimode complement to RDD telephone surveys (Link et al., 2008; Iannacchione, 2011).

Response rate also tends to be lower with mailed questionnaires than with other survey modes. A meta-analysis of 45 research studies in which two or three data-collection modes were compared found that, on the average, FTF surveys have the highest response rate (70.3 percent), telephone surveys the next highest (67.2 percent), and mail surveys the lowest (61.3 percent) (Hox and de Leeuw, 1994). Still, although rates of 50 percent or lower are common in mail surveys, it is possible to obtain higher response rates by following the highly detailed "tailored design" procedures developed by Don Dillman (2007; Dillman, Smyth, and Christian, 2009).

The most important factors in generating high return rates are reducing the costs for the respondent and increasing the perceived importance and rewards of survey participation (Dillman, Smyth, and Christian, 2009). Costs are reduced by including postpaid return envelopes, enclosing small cash prepayments (rather than monetary incentives conditional on survey completion), and making the questionnaire shorter, visually appealing, and easier to complete. The importance of the survey is impressed on respondents by using stamped rather than metered mail, by making special appeals within the cover letter, by personalizing correspondence (e.g., with real signatures and salutations with respondents' first names), and by making repeated contacts in the form of preliminary notification and follow-ups emphasizing different appeals (Dillman, Smyth, and Christian, 2009; Mangione, 1995).

In addition to a generally lower overall response rate, self-administered questionnaires may introduce nonresponse bias due to response selectivity. Certain groups of persons, such as those with little writing ability and those not interested in the topic, would be less likely to respond to a mailed questionnaire than to a personal interview request. Also, more questions are left unanswered with self-administered questionnaires than with interview methods. The problem of item nonresponse may be alleviated to some extent by instructions explaining the need for every item to be answered, by assurances of confidentiality, and by making items easy to understand.

Although interviewer bias is eliminated, so are the advantages of an interviewer. There is no opportunity to clarify questions, probe for more adequate answers, or control the conditions under which the questionnaire is completed or even who completes it. A mailed questionnaire usually yields the most reliable information when closed questions are used, when the order in which questions are answered is unimportant, and when the questions and format are simple and straightforward.

Mail surveys may serve the research purposes well under the following conditions: with specialized target groups who are likely to have high response rates,[3] when very large samples are desired, when costs must be kept low, when ease of administration is necessary, and when moderate response rates are considered satisfactory.

Computer-Assisted Self-Interviews

The advent of computers and the Internet has spawned several new data-collection technologies. We have already mentioned CAPI and CATI. By automating many tasks and simplifying others, these methods reduce interviewer errors and facilitate the interview process. However, they do not displace the interviewer; they simply make his or her job easier. More recently, researchers have developed a variety of computer-mediated surveys that are self-administered. These include e-mailed questionnaires, interactive voice response (IVR) surveys, computerized self-administered questionnaires, and Internet (Web) surveys (Figure 9.2).

E-mail and Web surveys are conducted over the Internet. Both involve computer-to-computer transmission of a questionnaire; in e-mail surveys the questions are sent as the text of an e-mail message or in an attached file, whereas in Web surveys the questionnaire is on specially designed webpages. IVR surveys are conducted by telephone as respondents listen to prerecorded, voice-read questions and then use Touch-Tone data entry or give verbal answers, which are recorded (see Steiger and Conroy, 2008). In **computer-assisted self-interviewing** (CASI), the questionnaire is transmitted on a program that may be sent to respondents or on a laptop provided by the researcher. Of these innovations, Web surveys have had the broadest application. IVR surveys, which may not be suitable for long or complex questionnaires, have been used extensively in consumer marketing research but have had limited application in general social surveys. CASI often has been used in conjunction with interview-administered surveys. We focus here on the advantages and disadvantages of Web surveys.

One of the greatest advantages of Web surveys is reduced cost. Compared to self-administered questionnaires, the cheapest of the traditional modes, Internet surveys eliminate the costs of paper, postage, assembly of the mailout package, and data entry (Dillman, 2007). The principal costs are computer equipment and programming support, questionnaire development and testing, and Internet service provider fees. For faculty and students, some of these costs are eliminated. And for all researchers, the development of online survey software and questionnaire tools such as SurveyMonkey, Survs, and QuestionPro has facilitated questionnaire construction and delivery. A related advantage is time savings. Web surveys require much less time to implement than other survey modes; compared to mail surveys, which may take weeks or months for questionnaires to be delivered and returned, Web surveys may be completed in only a few days. Finally, Web surveys can substantially reduce the cost of increasing sample size because once the electronic questionnaire has been developed, the cost of surveying each additional person is far less than in an interview or mail survey.

Another advantage of Web surveys, one they share with other computer-mediated methods, is flexibility in the questionnaire design. As Don Dillman (2007:354) points out, a questionnaire can be designed "to provide a more dynamic interaction between respondent and questionnaire" than is possible in a paper-and-pencil survey. Web questionnaires can incorporate extensive and difficult skip patterns, pop-up instructions for individual questions, drop-down boxes with lists of answer choices, feedback on possibly incorrect answers (e.g., birth date "1839"), pop-up word definition screens, and automatic fill-ins for later answers. They can use a great variety of shapes and colors and can add pictures, animation, video clips, and sound (Dillman, 2007:458). When designed carefully, Web survey options and features may be used to motivate and assist respondents and otherwise substitute for the role that an interviewer plays (Couper, Traugott, and Lamias, 2001; Lozar Manfreda and Vehovar, 2008:276–81).

At this point, the great practical advantages and enormous design potential of Web surveys for social research are offset by some major weaknesses. Perhaps the greatest of these weaknesses is coverage error. This error derives from two related problems: the proportion of the general population who are Internet users and the lack of a sampling frame to sample users. By 2015, 75 percent of U.S. households were using the Internet at home or elsewhere. However, a "digital divide" remains, with nonusers being more likely to be black or Hispanic, poorly educated, and older than those with Internet access (Morris, 2016). The second problem, the absence of a good frame for sampling Internet users, is currently handled by limiting professional Web surveys to special populations having membership lists and Web access, such as college students or employees of an organization (Couper and Bosnjak, 2010). Another approach is to use telephone RDD or some other mode to generate a probability sample and then persuade sampled individuals to complete an online questionnaire (Fricker et al., 2005). In the absence of a well-defined probability sampling plan, consumers should be wary of most Web polls and surveys because they are likely to entail self-selected samples that merely reflect the views of those who choose to respond.

Nonresponse error poses another problem, as studies have found response rates for Web surveys to be about 10 percent less than that for mail surveys (Lozar Manfreda et al., 2008; Shih and Fan, 2008). Furthermore, not only is the response rate low (one meta-analysis of 56 Internet surveys found an average response rate of 35 percent [C. Cook, Heath, and Thompson, 2000]), but Internet surveys face problems similar to those underlying declining telephone response rates, including privacy issues, spam and "phishing" scams, and the proliferation of nonprofessional Web surveys. However, studies have shown that Web response rates comparable to mail rates can be achieved with special populations (college students with free e-mail access) and motivational efforts (an advance cover letter explaining the study's purpose) (Kaplowitz, Hadlock, and Levine, 2004).

KEY POINT

Compared to mail questionnaires, Web surveys reduce costs, require less time, and may employ complex interactive questionnaires, but reach more limited populations and have lower response rates.

Despite these coverage and nonresponse problems, Web surveys have developed so rapidly in recent years that some have argued that they eventually will replace mail and interview survey modes. Solutions to some of the problems are being explored. One approach is to employ probability-based, Web-enabled panels designed to be representative of the United States or another target population. In the Web-based Knowledge Networks' panel, members are initially recruited by list-assisted RDD telephone sampling, and then households that agree to participate are given the equipment necessary to access the Internet. In a series of mode experiments, Tom W. Smith and J. Michael Dennis (2004) compared responses to questions asked in the 2000 and 2002 GSS FTF surveys with responses to identically worded questions from the Knowledge Networks panel. Although some of the differences between the FTF and Web surveys were small, Smith and Dennis concluded that "much more information is needed on differences in measurement across modes before results from Web-based surveys and surveys using other modes can be considered generally comparable" (10).

Mixed-Mode Surveys

Choosing a data-collection mode is difficult when none of the primary modes seems optimum for the intended research. An alternative solution is to design a **mixed-mode survey**, which uses more than one mode, either sequentially or concurrently, to sample and/or collect the data. In this way, the weaknesses of one mode may be offset by the strengths of another mode. For example, since 1970 the U.S. decennial census has combined less expensive mail surveys followed by more expensive in-person interviews with people who do not return the mail questionnaires.

The proliferation of modes, among other developments, has fueled a marked increase in mixed-mode designs in the twenty-first century (Couper, 2011). Modes may be combined in many different ways for a variety of reasons. Here we briefly mention three of the most common ways of mixing survey modes (de Leeuw, 2005; Dillman and Messer, 2010).

1. Use one mode to recruit, screen, or contact respondents and another mode to administer the survey. In Web surveys, telephone RDD sampling may be used to screen for Internet access for the purpose of recruiting respondents (Fricker et al., 2005), and sending an advance recruitment letter with a small cash incentive by U.S. mail has been shown to dramatically increased response rates (by 17 percent). In IVR surveys, a telephone interviewer may initially contact and recruit the respondent and then switch the respondent to the self-administered IVR mode (Steeh, 2008). For the Current Population Survey, in which respondents remain in the sample for several months, initially expensive FTF interviewing is used to recruit and motivate respondents to obtain a high response rate; less expensive telephone interviewing is employed in subsequent months. Follow-ups on reluctant respondents, in the form of simple reminders or a longer persuasive message, may involve a different mode (e-mail, telephone, in person) than the main data-collection mode (de Leeuw, Hox, and Dillman, 2008; Millar and Dillman, 2011).

2. Use a second mode to collect data on a subset of questions from the same respondents. A mode shift to self-administered questionnaires—paper-and-pencil or CASI—often is used in FTF surveys to increase privacy in the collection of sensitive information. Typically, an interviewer administers the largest part of the interview but then provides the respondent with either a paper questionnaire to be sealed in an envelope or a CASI laptop to complete the self-administered portion that requests the most sensitive information. In this way, respondents are less susceptible to social desirability biases, which are more likely when questions

are administered by an interviewer. An early application of this strategy occurred in the 1992 National Health Interview Survey–Youth Risk Behavior Supplement, which used an audio questionnaire to collect sensitive information about drug use, sexual intercourse, cigarette smoking, and other unhealthy behaviors from adolescents (Willard and Schoenborn, 1995). Teens listened to the questions on a portable audio headset and recorded their answers on an answer sheet that did not contain any information by which parents or other household members would know the questions being answered. Besides providing privacy to the young respondents, this data-collection mode was more effective than a written questionnaire with younger teens and those with poor reading skills. In addition, the prerecorded questions provided greater standardization (wording, tone of voice, etc.) than when questions are asked by interviewers.

3. Use different modes to survey different respondents. One solution to the coverage problem in Web surveys, for example, is a respondent-specific approach whereby those individuals without Web access are surveyed in person or by mail. Other examples include increasing the response rate of the sampled population by conducting telephone or FTF interviews with those who did not respond to an initial mail questionnaire (Biemer and Lyberg, 2003) and offering a mail follow-up option to those who did not respond initially to a Web survey (Millar and Dillman, 2011). Alternatively, respondent-specific designs may start with a relatively inexpensive mail survey, then follow up on the nonresponses with telephone interviews, and finally attempt to reach the remaining nonrespondents with expensive FTF interviews (de Leeuw, Hox, and Dillman, 2008).

The first two mixed-mode designs have been common practice for some time; their advantages in reducing cost, increasing response rates, and improving data quality are well established. The recent surge of interest in mixed-mode surveys is mainly due to the third design, in which different modes are used with different respondents during the data-collection process (Couper, 2011). The major weakness is the uncertain comparability of respondents surveyed by different modes. Because the various modes may differ in coverage, sampling, nonresponse, and measurement errors, merging the mode subsamples to statistically estimate the target population is a difficult and uncertain undertaking.

Field Administration

Once the planning is completed, fieldwork can begin. This phase of the research begins with the recruitment and training of interviewers, continues with the field interviews, and concludes when follow-up efforts have been completed on initially unresponsive persons in the sample. Figure 9.3 presents a flowchart that summarizes the various aspects of a survey's fieldwork phase.[4] Although we focus on FTF interviewing, the discussion includes some aspects of telephone surveys and other modes.

Interviewer Recruitment and Selection

Although there are no universally agreed-on criteria for the selection of interviewers, experience and common sense suggest that certain qualities are desirable. These qualities include articulateness; a pleasant personality that inspires cooperation and trust; a neat,

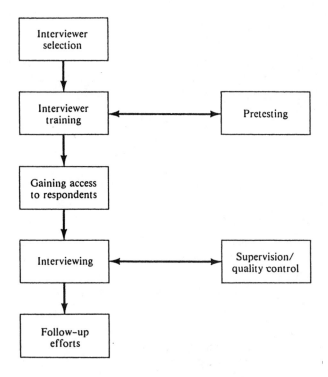

FIGURE **9.3. Flowchart illustrating a survey's fieldwork phase.**

businesslike appearance; freedom from prejudices or stereotypes toward the population being interviewed; interest in the survey topic; familiarity with computers; and the ability to listen, use neutral probes when needed, and record responses accurately. We suspect that the presence of these qualities is evaluated to some degree during the selection and training processes. This should create reasonably well-qualified interview staffs and would explain why research has found no consistent correlates between interviewer characteristics and the quality of interviewing (Fowler, 1991; Groves et al., 2009).

Unless the survey is being done by a large research organization that has a permanent staff, researchers must recruit all the interviewers for a given survey. The process of recruiting interviewers is basically the same as hiring for any job (E. Weinberg, 1983). That is, positions are advertised and applicants are screened and selected. Beyond minimum reading and writing skills, availability and readiness to meet job requirements are the principal selection criteria. Other interviewer attributes are largely dependent on market forces. The majority of interviewers, according to data from a sample of interviewers at U.S. government statistical agencies, do not regard their job as a primary source of income or as a career, perhaps because of the intermittent nature of the work (Groves and Couper, 1998:198). This work feature as well as job requisites also may account for the composition of the interviewer workforce, which is predominantly female and young to middle age, with above-average education. Since such attributes are largely beyond the control of researchers, it is fortunate that they appear to be much less important in determining the quality of a survey than the interviewer's ability achieved through careful training and experience.

Interviewer Training

Interviewers receive training in general interviewing skills and techniques as well as in specific procedures required for a particular survey project. In practice, these two aspects of training often are combined, with survey-specific materials (e.g., questionnaire or sampling procedures) used for practical application (E. Weinberg, 1983; Lessler, Eyerman, and Wang, 2008). More specifically, the training process must accomplish several goals:

1. Provide interviewers with information regarding the study's general purpose, sponsor, sampling plan, and uses or publication plans.
2. Train interviewers in locating households and eligible respondents as prescribed by the sampling design.
3. Teach basic interviewing techniques and rules, such as how to gain respondents' cooperation, establish rapport without becoming overly friendly, ask questions and probe in a manner that will not bias the response, and deal with interruptions and digressions.
4. Acquaint interviewers with the survey instrument and instructions for CAPI or CATI.
5. Provide demonstrations and supervised practice with the interview schedule.
6. Weed out those trainees who do not possess the motivation and ability to do an acceptable job.

Studies of the effects of training on interviewer errors have shown that too little training (less than a day) is inadequate and that better-quality data are associated with more extensive training (Groves et al., 2009:316). A training program for FTF interviewing may combine home study with a series of classroom sessions. The first session might begin with a general introduction to the study, followed by a presentation and instruction in basic interviewing skills and responsibilities. In the second session, the researcher would thoroughly familiarize interviewers with the survey questionnaire, going over the entire instrument item by item, explaining the importance of each item, and giving instructions for recording responses and examples of problematic responses and ways to deal with them. Next, the researcher would conduct a demonstration interview and then divide interviewers into pairs for supervised practice interviewing. Third and subsequent sessions would involve further practice, possibly including field experience, and further evaluation. Experienced interviewers generally receive survey-specific training through home study of the project's special interviewing procedures and survey instrument followed by discussions or mock interviews with a field manager. For an excellent discussion of what trainees should expect in telephone survey training, see Patricia Gwartney's *The Telephone Interviewer's Handbook* (2007).

Pretesting

A pretest consists of trying out the survey instrument on a small sample of persons having characteristics similar to those of the target group of respondents. The main reason for conducting a pretest is to determine whether the instrument serves the purposes for which it was designed or whether further revision is needed. **Pretesting** may be carried out before, at the same time as, or after the interviewers are trained. An advantage to completing the pretest before interviewer training is that the final instrument may be used during training. An advantage to delaying pretesting is that the interviewers can assist with this step, either during the field practice part of interviewer training or after the formal training is completed. A disadvantage to delaying pretesting is that there may be a time gap between the completion of training and the start of the "real" interviews while the instrument is being revised. The subject of pretesting is discussed in more depth in Chapter 10.

Gaining Access

Gaining access to respondents involves three steps: getting "official" permission or endorsement when needed or useful, mailing a cover letter introducing the study to persons or households in the sample, and securing the cooperation of the respondents.

When doing a community interview survey, it is usually a good idea to write a letter to or visit a local official to describe the general purpose of the study, its importance, the organization sponsoring it, the uses to which the data will be put, the time frame, and so forth. In addition, endorsement letters from relevant local organizations may be sought, such as the county medical society if doctors will be interviewed or the chamber of commerce if businesses are being sampled.

Respondent cooperation also will be enhanced by a good **cover letter**. In interview surveys, a cover letter is usually mailed a few days before an interviewer is to call on a respondent. In surveys using mailed questionnaires, a cover letter is sent with the questionnaire either as a separate sheet or attached to the questionnaire. Dillman, Smyth, and Christian (2009) also recommend mailing a brief prenotice letter just prior to a questionnaire mailing. Occasionally, cover letters are mailed out in advance of phone surveys when mailing addresses are known. In an analysis of 29 research studies, sending a letter in advance improved telephone response rates by an average of about 8 percent (de Leeuw et al., 2007). The objective of the cover letter, to persuade respondents to cooperate with the survey, may be met by (1) identifying the researcher and survey sponsor and the phone number of a contact person, (2) communicating the general purpose and importance of the study, (3) showing how the findings may benefit the individual or others (e.g., the results will be used to improve health care or to increase understanding of marriage relationships), (4) explaining how the sample was drawn and the importance of each respondent's cooperation to the study, (5) assuring individuals that they will not be identified and that their responses will be kept confidential and will be combined with those of others for data-analysis purposes, (6) explaining that the questionnaire will take only a few minutes to fill out or that the interview will be enjoyable and will be held at the respondent's convenience, and (7) promising to send respondents a summary of the study's findings. (See Box 9.2 for an example of a cover letter.) Also, response rates may be increased by including a token incentive, such as $1 or $2, with the cover letter (Singer and Ye, 2013).

A third step in interview surveys is gaining the cooperation of respondents. Interviewers must contact or reach the sample person and then persuade him or her to cooperate

BOX 9.2 Sample Cover Letter for Household Survey, with Key Features Identified in the Left-Hand Margin

 Washington State University

Social and Economic Sciences Research Center

Wilson Hall 133
PO Box 644014
Pullman, WA 99164-4014
509-335-1511
FAX 509-335-0116

Date	→	July 8, 1999
Inside address	→	L. T. Hansen 2121 Lincoln Way East Uniontown, WA 99962-2056
The request	→	I am writing to ask your help in a study of new residents being conducted for the state of Washington. This study is part of an effort to learn what draws people to the state, and whether they are happy or unhappy with what they find here.
Why you were selected	→	It's my understanding that you may have moved to Washington state sometime in the last few years. We are contacting a random sample of new residents from every county in the state to ask why they moved, what their employment experience has been, and whether services are meeting their needs.
Usefulness of survey	→	Results from the survey will be used to help state and local government make Washington a better place for new residents like you. By understanding what people want when they move here, public officials can do a better job providing services and improving the state's quality of life. And by knowing more about the job skills of new residents, public agencies and private businesses can help make the most of what new residents contribute to the state's economy.
Confidentiality	→	Your answers are completely confidential and will be released only as summaries in which no individual's answers can be identified. When you return your completed questionnaire, your name will be deleted from the mailing list and never connected to your answers in any way. This survey is voluntary. However, you can help us very much by taking a few minutes to share your experiences and opinions about Washington state. If for some reason you prefer not to respond, please let us know by returning the blank questionnaire in the enclosed stamped envelope.
Token of appreciation	→	We have enclosed a small token of appreciation as a way of saying thanks for your help.
Willingness to answer questions	→	If you have any questions or comments about this study, we would be happy to talk with you. Our toll-free number is 1-800-833-0867, or you can write to us at the address on the letterhead.
Thank-you	→	Thank you very much for helping with this important study.
		Sincerely,
Real signature	→	*Don A. Dillman* Don A. Dillman Professor and Deputy Director

P.S.   If by some chance we made a mistake and you have not moved to
Washington (or back to Washington after living somewhere else) since
January 1990, please answer only the first question in the questionnaire and
return the rest of it blank. Many thanks.

Source: Dillman (2007:162). Copyright 2007 by John Wiley and Sons, Inc. Used by permission.

by completing the survey. Making contact with designated households is primarily a matter of persistence and overcoming barriers. Interviewers vary the time of attempted contacts and may make repeated call-backs, typically at least 6 for FTF surveys and 10 or more for telephone surveys (Fowler, 1993). We will discuss follow-up efforts further as a final phase of fieldwork.

Avoiding refusals is a more difficult problem that requires special interviewer skills. According to Robert Groves and Mick Couper's (1996, 1998) theory of survey participation, which applies mainly to in-person interviews, in the initial moments of a survey encounter, the sample person is actively trying to comprehend the purpose of the interviewer's visit. He or she uses cues from the words, behavior, and physical appearance of the interviewer to arrive at an explanation (or identify a script) and then evaluates the costs of continuing the conversation. Whether the person eventually agrees or refuses to participate depends on the interviewer's ability to quickly and accurately judge the particular script reflected in the householder's initial response and to react accordingly.

The theory is consistent with analyses of interviewer–householder interactions. For example, Robert Groves, Robert Cialdini, and Mick Couper (1992) found that experienced interviewers use two related strategies to convince respondents to participate. First, they tailor their approach to the sample unit, adjusting their dress, mannerisms, language, and arguments according to their observations of the neighborhood, housing unit, and immediate reactions of the householder. Second, they maintain interaction, which maximizes the possibility of identifying relevant cues for tailoring the conversation to present the most effective arguments. In a subsequent analysis, Groves and Couper (1996) concluded that the most effective interviewer adaptations were those that addressed the real concerns of the householder. Moreover, experimental tests of a training program to help interviewers anticipate and address such concerns were shown to increase cooperation (Groves and McGonagle, 2001).

In contrast, tailoring is difficult in telephone interviews due to the absence of visual cues and inadequate time—often a few seconds—to maintain interaction and build up rapport (for an exploratory study, see Couper and Groves, 2002). Nevertheless, phone interviewers are trained to instantly make and maintain a positive impression on respondents through their voice (tone, pitch, speed, and enunciation) and prememorized scripts for introducing the survey and addressing respondents' reluctance to participate (e.g., "I'm not good [at] answering surveys," "I'm too busy," "You are invading my privacy") or other concerns (Gwartney, 2007).

Interviewing

Although we noted earlier that interviews may be more or less structured, nearly all surveys, especially large-scale surveys, use structured or "standardized" interviewing. The goal of standardization is to expose each respondent to the same interview experience so that any differences in recorded answers are the result of differences among respondents "rather than differences in the process that produced the answer" (Fowler and Mangione, 1990:14). To standardize the measurement process, survey instruments consist almost entirely of questions with fixed response alternatives that are presented in the same order for all respondents, and interviewers are instructed to carefully follow prescribed procedures. Ideally, interviewers should be perfectly consistent, neutral intermediaries of the survey researcher. In short, "the goal [of standardized interviewing] is nothing less than the elimination of the interviewer as a source of measurement error" (Groves, 1989:358).

Specific practices vary somewhat from one survey organization to another, but the following four rules of standardized interviewing, according to Floyd Fowler (1991:264; also see Fowler and Mangione, 1990), are given almost universally to interviewers:

1. Read the questions exactly as written.
2. If a respondent does not answer a question fully, use nondirective follow-up probes to elicit a better answer. Standard probes include repeating the question, asking "Anything else?" "Tell me more," and "How do you mean that?"
3. Record answers to questions without interpretation or editing. When a question is open-ended, this means recording the answer verbatim.
4. Maintain a professional, neutral relationship with the respondent. Do not give personal information, express opinions about the subject matter of the interview, or give feedback that implies a judgment about the content of an answer.

(Further, more detailed interviewer guidelines from an FTF community survey are provided in Box 9.3.) For a description of standardized interviewing in CATI surveys, see Gwartney (2007:172–233).

Considerable empirical evidence and sound theoretical arguments justify standardization principles (Fowler, 1991; Fowler and Mangione, 1990). For example, if questions are not asked as worded, one cannot know what question was posed; and numerous experiments have shown that small changes in the wording of questions can alter the distribution of answers (Schuman and Presser, 1981). Also, experiments have demonstrated that suggestive questioning (presenting only a subset of answer alternatives that are presumed to be relevant) and suggestive probing can affect response distributions and relationships with other variables (Smit, Dijkstra, and van der Zouwen, 1997).

Although there is little doubt that standardization reduces an interviewer's contribution to measurement error, a more serious, long-standing concern is that presenting a standard stimulus in and of itself can produce measurement error. According to this view, standardized interviewing stifles interviewer–respondent communication in two ways: (1) it inhibits the ability to establish rapport, which motivates respondents to cooperate and give complete and accurate answers, and (2) it ignores the detection and correction of communication problems (Beatty, 1995; also see Maynard and Schaeffer, 2002).

BOX 9.3 Guidelines for Survey Interviewers

Organizations sponsoring surveys, such as the NORC, which oversees the GSS, usually produce an interviewers' manual that explains rules and procedures to follow to minimize the effects of error. The rules and guidelines outlined below have been adapted from an interviewers' manual used in a community survey conducted in a medium-size city; however, they apply to any well-conducted personal interview survey.

Rules
Three basic rules are suggested.

1. *Courtesy, tact, and acceptance.* It is of utmost importance that your manner be at all times courteous, tactful, and nonjudgmental. Under no circumstances are you to argue or debate anything that is said. The primary function of the interviewer is to learn what the respondent believes about the items on the schedule without judging or influencing that response in any way. No matter what the respondent says, the interviewer should accept it without showing surprise, approval, or disapproval. Respondents will be less likely to share confidential data about their personal lives, for example, with an interviewer who appears to disapprove of them.

2. *Dress.* Three things should be kept in mind in selecting clothing for interviewing: the expectations that surround the role of the interviewer, the persons being interviewed and their probable response to one's dress, and comfort. Within the limits of good taste, the individual interviewer should make adjustments for the neighborhood in which he or she is working.

3. *Confidentiality.* Under no circumstances is the interviewer to give out to anyone except the supervisor any information gathered in the course of interviews. Incidents that occur or any information gained while interviewing are strictly confidential and should not be discussed with anyone who is not part of the project. Project workers should never discuss interview data, even among themselves, in a public place where the conversation could be overheard.

Procedures in Conducting an Interview
The following procedures have been found to be helpful in conducting interviews and obtaining accurate, honest responses. In many cases, deviating from these procedures will influence the respondent and introduce bias.

1. *Initiate the interview.* When the respondent comes to the door, introduce yourself by name. Show identification. Explain briefly what the study is about and whom it is you wish to interview. Be prepared to answer briefly questions regarding who is sponsoring the study and how or why the respondent was chosen. Letters of endorsement and newspaper clippings may be presented.

Proper groundwork by the researcher and a positive approach on the part of the interviewer will help to minimize the problem of refusals. In addition, the interviewer can frequently overcome an initial refusal by listening to the respondent's concerns and then

(continued)

(continued)

addressing those concerns. For example, is the respondent "too busy"? Stress the brief and enjoyable nature of the interview or, when necessary, make an appointment to call back. Does the respondent appear suspicious about the uses to which the data will be put? If so, explain again the study's purpose, provide an assurance of confidentiality, and explain that the data will be combined so that no individual's responses can be identified or linked to that person. Of course, firm refusals must be respected.

2. *Put the respondent at ease.* This is a major part of successful interviewing. A conversational, convivial attitude may help put the respondent at ease. Try to be relaxed and "natural."

3. *Be businesslike.* While it should be relaxed, an interview should not be long-winded. Remember that you and the respondent are busy people. If the respondent strays far afield from the point of a question, politely pull him or her back on the track.

4. *Keep the interview situation as private as possible.* If you are in a room with other people, do not let your attention wander to other parts of the room. Direct your questions to the respondent, and maintain eye contact. This will help both you and the respondent focus on the task.

5. *Avoid stereotyping.* Do not try to "categorize" the respondent as your preconceptions may interfere with your objectivity and may influence the respondent. You can also help to prevent the respondent from stereotyping you by not identifying yourself with any particular group or ideology.

6. *Be thoroughly familiar with the survey instrument.* Know the instrument so well that you can look at the respondent while asking questions.

7. *Ask every question in its proper sequence and exactly as written.* The interview schedule should have been carefully constructed. Questions are in the order presented because it is easier for interviewers to ask them in this order, because there is a logical flow of the topics, because the order helps respondents think through or recall material, or for similar reasons. Remember that very slight changes in the wording of items have been shown to affect the results.

8. *Do not assume the answer to any question.* A respondent may imply the answer to a question in answering a previous question but may respond differently when asked the question formally.

9. *Speak slowly in a clearly understood, well-modulated voice.* If respondents are to give reliable answers, they must understand the questions.

10. *Do not put answers in the respondent's mouth.* This is one of the most common mistakes of interviewers. If a respondent seems unsure of an answer, pause and then repeat the question exactly as worded. Do not suggest an answer or a series of answers. Not all interviewers would suggest the same responses, and therefore, respondents would not be choosing from the same suggestions. This would result in biased data.

11. *Use an appropriate, neutral probe when needed.* Probing is used when the initial response is incomplete, ambiguous, or irrelevant. A variety of probes are possible, but they

must be neutral; that is, they must stimulate a more valid response without suggesting an answer. Sometimes, as suggested in point 10, pausing or repeating the question may be sufficient to motivate the respondent to add to or clarify the response. At other times, a neutral question such as one of the following may be needed: Is there anything else? Can you tell me more? In what ways? The survey instrument designer may include on the interview schedule certain probes to use with particular items when needed.

12. *Record responses as you go along.* Do not try to recreate the interview later. Before leaving the residence, skim the instrument to be sure all questions have been answered. Later, check to be sure responses will be understandable to the coders. Add notes in parentheses if necessary.

Regarding motivation, some respondents feel irritated by the unilateral nature of a structured survey: They cannot converse with the researcher or interviewer, they cannot qualify or expand answers, and they may be forced to choose among alternative answers that they find unsatisfactory. Fowler (1995:99–102) believes that respondents' resistance to standardized survey interviewing can be overcome by initially orienting or training them to play the role of a respondent. Since interviewer–respondent interaction in a highly structured survey differs from everyday conversation, respondents should be given an explanation of the rationale and the rules of standardized surveys to prepare and motivate them for the interview task.

Standardization also may reduce validity if respondents' misinterpretations of questions are ignored or uncorrected. In a widely cited article, Lucy Suchman and Brigitte Jordan (1990) argued that standardization suppresses elements of ordinary conversation that are crucial for establishing the relevance and meaning of questions. Interviewers who are trained to read questions as written and to discourage elaboration are not prepared to listen carefully for misunderstandings and correct them. From videotapes of standardized interviews, Suchman and Jordan gave several examples of miscommunication, such as an interviewer failing to correct a respondent who interprets "alcoholic beverages" to include hard liquor but exclude wine, which led to invalid responses. Such problems could be resolved, they claimed, if interviewers were granted the freedom and responsibility to negotiate the intended meaning of questions through ordinary conversational conventions.

Although they acknowledge the communication problems identified by Suchman and Jordan, advocates of standardized interviewing tend to disagree with them about causes and remedies. Some advocates contend that problems arise chiefly because of poorly worded questions and that whether respondents interpret questions consistently and accurately depends on adequate question pretesting (Kovar and Royston, 1990). Detractors of standardization maintain that efforts to improve question wording are rarely, if ever, sufficient. Researchers need interviewers to help ensure consistent interpretations, but this is unlikely unless interviewers are given a freer hand in communicating with respondents than standardization allows.

Paul Beatty (1995) notes that advocates on both sides of this debate tend to take extreme positions that seem incompatible. He argues, following Nora Cate Schaeffer (1991), that although the problems of standardization should not be overlooked, it also is foolish to ignore its merits. The real issue for Beatty is how researchers can solve communication problems while harnessing the full benefits of standardization. One means is the development of better questions; another may involve adapting the role of the interviewer. For certain types of questions, such as requests for factual information, permitting interviewers to stray from standardized scripts to correct respondents' misunderstandings may improve data quality; but allowing interviewers too much flexibility will greatly increase interviewer error as well as interview length (Groves et al., 2009).

KEY POINT

Although standardized interviewing is intended to reduce interviewer error, it may dampen respondents' interest and inhibit interviewers from clarifying questions and correcting respondents' misinterpretations.

The standardization controversy aside, a serious weakness of surveys is their reactivity. This is especially problematic in interviews, where biases may be produced not only by the wording, order, and format of the questions but also by the interaction between interviewer and respondent. Like the subject in an experiment, the respondent's chief concern often is with gaining the interviewer's social approval, or at least with avoiding his or her disapproval. And even though an interviewer's main goal is to obtain valid responses, interviewers may unknowingly affect responses in myriad ways. In survey research, the general term for such effects, or measurement errors, is **response effects**. More precisely, a response effect is "the amount of the error in response to a question that is associated with a particular factor" (Sudman and Bradburn, 1974). Chapter 10, on survey instrument design, suggests ways in which to minimize response effects related to the interview schedule (or questionnaire), such as question wording or position. Here, we focus on effects resulting from the interaction of interviewer and respondent.

One source of response effects is the interviewer's physical characteristics. For example, several studies have shown that the race of an interviewer affects racially relevant responses (Anderson, Silver, and Abramson, 1988; Krysan and Couper, 2003; Savage, 2016). In general, blacks express fewer antiwhite sentiments to white than to black interviewers and whites give fewer antiblack answers to black than to white interviewers. A 1989 pre-election survey also found a significant race-of-interviewer effect on expressed voter preferences for a black versus white gubernatorial candidate (Finkel, Guterbock, and Borg, 1991). Respondents in the state of Virginia were more likely to support the black candidate, L. Douglas Wilder (subsequently elected the nation's first black governor), when the interviewer was black and were more likely to favor the white candidate, J. Marshall Coleman, when the interviewer was white.

Less is known about whether other demographic variables such as age, gender, and class have the same effect as race, although this seems likely when a specific interviewer trait is particularly relevant. For instance, Emily Kane and Laura Macaulay (1993) found gender-of-interviewer effects on several items measuring gender-role attitudes, with both male and female respondents tending to give more egalitarian responses to female than to male interviewers.

In a fashion similar to experimenter effects, interviewers also may inadvertently communicate their expectations to respondents about how they should respond. To illustrate, if an interviewer believes a respondent to be of limited intelligence and inarticulate, he or she may expect shorter, less articulate responses and may communicate this expectation indirectly by short pauses. Since the respondent is looking to the interviewer for clues to the appropriateness of his or her behavior, he or she will likely provide short responses, thus fulfilling the interviewer's expectations.

On the other side, a respondent's reports to an interviewer may easily be distorted by such things as poor memory, desire to impress the interviewer, dislike for the interviewer, or embarrassment. Similarly, a respondent's feelings about the topic of the study or toward the organization sponsoring it may also affect the quality of data obtained (Groves et al., 2012). Finally, settings for interviews may present problems. A housewife who is being interviewed while supervising children may not be able to focus on the tasks of the interview sufficiently to provide as full and accurate responses as she might in another situation. In the British Household Survey, the presence of a spouse during an interview led to greater agreement between husbands and wives on several attitudinal and behavioral items (Zipp and Toth, 2002). A study by Nancy Brener and associates (2006) showed that high school students were more likely to report drinking alcohol, smoking marijuana, sexual activity, and other risk behaviors when questioned at school than when questioned at home.

Supervision and Quality Control

Once the interviewing phase of the survey begins, the researcher or an interviewer supervisor oversees all aspects of the data collection. A supervisor's role involves three interrelated sets of activities: managing the work of the interviewers, monitoring their performance, and administering quality-control procedures. In their management role, supervisors provide materials, collect completed survey records, pay for work done, make themselves available to answer questions and provide help, identify and resolve problems, hold regular meetings with interviewers, and review and give feedback on the interviewers' work.

To detect problems and review interviewers' progress, supervisors monitor their performance. In virtually all surveys, part of performance monitoring involves careful record keeping and evaluation of completed interviews. Records kept on the number of hours worked, amount paid, number of eligible contacts, and number of refusals provide critical information on interviewer productivity, survey costs (e.g., time and dollars per interview), and survey quality (response and refusal rates). By reviewing completed surveys, supervisors also can screen uncoded responses and check to see whether interviewers are following instructions and recording answers appropriately. To tell whether interviewers ask questions exactly as written, use neutral probes, and record answers correctly, many survey organizations also monitor or observe the interview process. In FTF interview surveys, supervisors may observe interviewers by either accompanying them on interviews or digitally recording random interview segments on the CAPI laptops. In telephone interview surveys, special monitoring phones allow supervisors to listen to a sample of ongoing interviews without being heard by either the interviewer or the respondent.

Reviewing completed questionnaires and observing interviews are two mechanisms of controlling the quality of interviewers' work and thereby determining the quality of the data. Two other processes are retrieving missing data and validating interviews (E. Weinberg, 1983). When data are missing, particularly for factual items that are critical to the survey, respondents may be recontacted to retrieve the information. Also, it is standard in all well-conducted surveys to verify that the interview actually took place and that the interviewer did not fabricate some responses or deviate from prescribed procedures (see Groves et al., 2009:319–22). Validation usually is done by re-interviewing a sample of respondents for each interviewer. Respondents may be asked a subset of items, and in the case of in-person surveys, the re-interviews often are carried out by telephone.

Finally, another important aspect of the supervisory role is sustaining interviewers' motivation and enthusiasm and preventing feelings of isolation. It is easy to assume that interviewers will do better work as they gain experience; however, studies have shown that the opposite may be the case. For example, validity studies of reports of hospitalizations and physician visits found that the more interviews an interviewer had done, the greater the problem of underreporting (Cannell, Marquis, and Laurent, 1977). Thus, supervisors should meet with interviewers regularly throughout the interviewing period not only to provide continuing feedback and reinforcement of skills but also to communicate the importance of good interviewing. GSS interviewers report, mostly via e-mail, to their field supervisors at least weekly, but more often if needed, to go over the status of their assignments (T. W. Smith, personal communication, 2016).

Follow-Up Efforts

The final phase of fieldwork consists of following up on nonrespondents in an attempt to gain their cooperation. If no contact is made initially, then GSS interviewers are instructed "to try several follow-up procedures, such as (a) calling back at different times and days of the week, (b) asking neighbors when people are usually at home or how they might be contacted, (c) leaving notes, and (d) using a reverse directory to get a telephone number for the household" (Davis and Smith, 1992:51). Follow-up efforts help to raise response rates.

Besides using follow-ups, response rates may be improved (1) by appropriate efforts to gain access, discussed earlier; (2) in interview surveys, by proper interviewer training and supervision; and (3) for mailed questionnaires, by inclusion of a stamped return envelope and a token prepayment, as well as by attention to the length, difficulty, and appearance of the questionnaire (see Chapter 10).

The particular follow-up activities depend on the survey mode. For telephone and FTF surveys, the major problem is dealing with refusals. In many surveys, more experienced interviewers or supervisors are used to try to gain the respondent's cooperation on the second try. The NHSLS dealt with some initial refusals by employing follow-up interviewers who specialize in converting reluctant respondents and by sending out "conversion letters" that answered special concerns that potential respondents were raising (Laumann et al., 1994). In response to a clear refusal, however, one follow-up call or visit should be the limit to avoid respondent feelings of harassment.

Because the NHSLS investigators were worried about reaching their target response rate (75 percent), they started offering incentive completion fees to reluctant respondents on a selective basis in low-response areas (Laumann et al., 1994:56–57). Although incentive fees ranging from $10 to $100 were offered for interviews, the fees were viewed as cost-efficient given the high cost of interviewer wages and travel costs (the cost of completed interviews averaged $450). The fees and other techniques for converting reluctant respondents eventually paid off with a final 79 percent response rate.

Since response rates are typically lower for mailed questionnaires, follow-up efforts are especially important with this mode. Typically, three follow-up mailings are used. For example, in Henry Wechsler and associates' (1994) initial college alcohol survey, respondents received four separate mailings, approximately 10 days apart: the initial mailing of the questionnaire, a postcard thanking those who had completed the questionnaire and urging those who had not to do so, a mailing with another copy of the questionnaire again appealing for its return, and a second reminder postcard. Given that this survey was truly anonymous, all persons in the sample had to be sent the subsequent mailings. If questionnaires have been coded so that a researcher knows who has responded, there can be a savings in postage and paper because only nonrespondents need to receive the follow-up mailings.[5]

In the Tailored Design Method, Don Dillman (2007) recommends three more widely spaced follow-ups, each of which entails new and more persuasive appeals. The first follow-up, sent out about 2 weeks after the original mailing, consists of a postcard thank you/reminder as in the Wechsler et al. alcohol survey. The second follow-up, mailed 2 weeks later, is sent only to nonrespondents and contains a replacement questionnaire; the cover letter for this mailing communicates that the respondent is receiving individual attention, emphasizes their importance for the success of the survey, and notes that others have responded as a means of encouraging response. The third follow-up, mailed 4 weeks later, invokes special procedures, such as special mail or contact by telephone, to emphasize the importance of the respondent's cooperation. When Dillman (2007:185) used certified mail for this final request in five statewide surveys of the general public, he raised the response rates from an average of 59 to 72 percent. These follow-up efforts should yield adequate response rates, but pushing rates higher is expensive and difficult; therefore, additional follow-up mailings are seldom used.

KEY POINT
Researchers attempt to increase survey participation by reducing respondents' perceived costs and increasing the perceived importance and benefits of the survey.

These follow-up efforts are intended to raise response rates. As we note in Chapter 6, however, the common wisdom of pursuing high survey response rates to decrease nonresponse bias is being challenged (Groves, 2006; Peytchev, 2013). Instead, concern should focus on nonresponse bias for key variables within a survey. From this perspective, aggressive efforts to increase survey response rates may increase nonresponse bias in individual variables. If men are overrepresented among nonrespondents in a telephone survey, for example, additional call-backs may increase the gender bias by reaching and interviewing more women than men. Groves (2006:666) cites another example of an election exit poll experiment in which an incentive did increase response rates but also increased nonresponse bias by attracting more Democratic than Republican voters.

Strengths and Limitations of Surveys

Now that we have examined a wide range of surveys, different survey designs and modes, and the steps in planning and conducting surveys, we are in a position to consider the strengths and weaknesses of this approach. What can they tell us better than other methods of social research? And what are their major limitations?

Whereas experiments are used almost exclusively for explanatory, hypothesis-testing research, surveys are used extensively for both descriptive and explanatory purposes. Among all approaches to social research, in fact, surveys offer the most effective means of social description; they can provide extraordinarily detailed and precise information about large, heterogeneous populations. Using probability sampling, one can be certain, within known limits of sampling error, whether the responses to a sample survey accurately describe the larger target population. Furthermore, the topics covered and the questions that may be included in surveys are wide ranging. Topics of the studies we have cited ranged from academic achievement to alcohol consumption and from sexual activity to attitudes toward the police. The scope of possible survey questions is suggested by the following classification (Schuman and Kalton, 1985):

1. Social background information (e.g., What is your religious preference? What is your date of birth?)
2. Reports of past behavior (e.g., Did you vote in the last presidential election? Have you ever been the victim of a crime? On an average day, about how many hours do you personally watch television?)
3. Attitudes, beliefs, and values (e.g., Do you believe that there is a life after death? Do you think homosexual couples should have the right to marry one another?)
4. Behavior intentions (e.g., If the presidential election were held today, whom would you vote for? Would you yourself have an abortion if there were a strong chance of serious defect in the baby?)
5. Sensitive questions (e.g., Have you ever been arrested for a crime? Have you used cocaine in the past month?)

For categories 1, 2, and 5, which pertain to behavior and personal characteristics, the information may be verifiable from records or observer reports; but it is often impractical, unethical, or even illegal to obtain information from sources other than the individuals themselves. For subjective phenomena such as categories 3 and 4, the information can be directly known, if at all, only by asking the individuals themselves.

As this listing suggests, surveys can address a much broader range of research topics than experiments can. Ethical considerations preclude studying some topics experimentally—for example, the effect of emotional traumas on mental health—while practical considerations rule out many others; for instance, one normally cannot experimentally manipulate orga-nizations or nations. Surveys can also be an efficient data-gathering technique. Whereas an experiment usually will address only one research hypothesis, numerous research questions can be jammed into a single large-scale survey. Furthermore, the wealth of data typically contained in a completed survey may yield unanticipated findings or lead to new hypotheses.

The secondary analysis of surveys also affords many unique advantages. The cost of obtaining the data for analysis is usually a small fraction of the cost of collecting and coding the data. Survey data made available for secondary analysis tend to come from professional polling and research centers with the resources to obtain high-quality information from large, national samples. In addition, secondary analysis may enable one to (1) assess social trends by examining questions repeated over time and (2) increase sample size by combin-ing data from several surveys.

The major disadvantage of surveys relates to their use in explanatory research. Beyond association between variables, the criteria for inferring cause-and-effect relationships cannot be established as easily in surveys as in experiments. For example, the criterion of directionality—that a cause must influence its effect—is predetermined in experiments by first manipulating the independent (or causal) variable and then observing variation in the dependent (or effect) variable. But in most surveys this is often a matter of interpretation since variables are measured at a single point in time. Consider also the criterion of elimi-nating plausible rival explanations. Experiments do this effectively through randomization and other direct control procedures that hold extraneous variables constant. In contrast, surveys must first anticipate and measure relevant extraneous variables in the interviews or questionnaires and then exercise statistical control over these variables in the data analysis. Thus, the causal inferences from survey research generally are made with less confidence than inferences from experimental research.

Another serious weakness of surveys is one they share with laboratory experiments: They are susceptible to reactivity, which introduces systematic measurement error. A good example of this, noted in Chapter 5, is the tendency of respondents to give socially desir-able answers to sensitive questions. Another inherent weakness is that surveys rely almost exclusively on reports of behavior rather than observations of behavior. As a consequence, measurement error may be produced by respondents' lack of truthfulness, misunderstand-ing of questions, inability to recall past events accurately, and instability of opinions and attitudes. In addition, a brief encounter for the purpose of administering a survey does not provide a good understanding of the context within which behavior may be interpreted over an extended period of time. For this kind of understanding, the best approach is field research, discussed in Chapter 11.

KEY POINT

Compared with experiments, surveys provide weaker tests of causal relationships but more precise descriptions of populations; both approaches, however, are highly susceptible to reactive measurement effects.

Finally, we have identified several issues in this chapter that are making it increas-ingly difficult and costly to conduct surveys, forcing some researchers to seek alternative approaches to social research. Robert Groves (2011:866) notes several problems that have surfaced in the past quarter-century, including access impediments such as "walled subdivision, locked apartment buildings, telephone answering machines, [and] telephone caller ID," declining response rates, increasing costs due to "increased effort to contact and interview the public," and telephone survey coverage issues created by the increase in mobile phones.

Summary

- Social surveys have three common features: a relatively large number of respondents generally chosen by some form of probability sampling, formal observation procedures involving interviews and/or questionnaires, and computerized statistical analysis of data.
- The units of analysis in sample surveys are typically individuals selected from a single community or nation; however, surveys of social units other than individuals are also done and samples from different countries are sometimes combined, as in comparative studies.
- Although standardization is the norm, data-collection procedures vary along a continuum from highly formal and structured to less formal and structured, the choice of which depends on the researcher's objectives.
- Survey research designs are divided into two broad categories: (1) cross-sectional studies, in which data are gathered from a sample of a community or larger grouping at essentially one point in time, and (2) longitudinal studies, in which data are gathered at two or more points in time from either the same sample of respondents (panel study) or independently selected samples of the same population (trend studies).
- Two variants of the cross-sectional design have been developed to study social structural influences: (1) contextual studies, in which different groups are sampled to examine the effects of the group or context on individuals, and (2) social network studies, in which every individual in a group is studied to delineate networks of personal relationships.
- Cohort studies, a special instance of trend studies, trace changes across cohorts to separate the effects of age, cohort or generation, and historical period.
- The initial stages in planning a survey depart from other research strategies primarily in the construction of the survey instrument (interview schedule or questionnaire), which we discuss at length in the next chapter, and the development of the sampling plan.
- Survey data may be conducted through personal FTF interviews, telephone interviews, self-administered questionnaires, various computer methods, or a combination of these modes (mixed-mode survey).
- Interviews, in comparison with questionnaires, offer greater flexibility in the type and format of questions, provide the opportunity to clarify questions and elicit fuller responses, and tend to have higher response rates.
- FTF interviews also permit lengthy interviews with complex questions, although they may introduce greater bias through interviewer–respondent interaction, and they tend to be expensive.
- By comparison, telephone interviews offer a substantial savings in time and money and are easier to administer, although they require simpler questions and may elicit less complete responses.
- Mailed self-administered questionnaires are the least expensive survey mode, but they tend to have lower response rates, result in more nonresponse to individual questions, and must contain simpler questions for reliable responses.
- New electronic self-administered methods, which are rapidly gaining acceptance, may reduce time and cost and allow for more varied and user-friendly questionnaire design; however, Internet surveys in particular suffer from coverage error, and their most productive use in the short run may be as a complement to interviews in mixed-mode surveys.
- Field administration in survey research begins with interviewer selection and training and instrument pretesting, continues with interviews and staff supervision, and ends with follow-up efforts to reach initial nonrespondents.

- Interviewers must be able simultaneously to put an interviewee at ease, to ask questions and guide the interview to its completion, and to record responses. Accomplishing these objectives requires careful interviewer selection and training.
- Before data are gathered from respondents, the survey instrument should be pretested and access to respondents should be gained by contacting appropriate community officials and mailing a cover letter.
- During the course of interviewing, interviewers must (1) be wary of introducing bias; (2) be courteous and tactful, dress appropriately, and guard the confidentiality of respondents' replies; (3) be relaxed but businesslike; and (4) be thoroughly familiar with the instrument so as to maintain rapport, use probes when necessary, and record answers as they go along.
- Supervision of interviewees—keeping a record of each interviewer, checking completed interview schedules, and so forth—is essential for quality control, whereas follow-up efforts to contact initial nonrespondents are essential to obtain an adequate response rate, especially in mail surveys.
- Relative to other research strategies, surveys generally are more flexible in that they can be used with equal facility for both descriptive and explanatory research and can address a wider range of research topics.
- On the other hand, surveys present greater problems for inferring causal relationships, are limited to reports of behavior rather than observations of behavior, and, like laboratory experiments, are subject to reactive effects.

Key Terms

cross-national surveys	panel study
structured interview	interview schedule
unstructured interview	face-to-face interview
semistructured interview	computer-assisted personal interviewing
descriptive and explanatory surveys	telephone interview
secondary analysis	random-digit dialing
cross-sectional design	computer-assisted telephone interviewing
contextual design	paper-and-pencil questionnaire
social network design	computer-assisted self-interviewing
longitudinal design	mixed-mode survey
trend study	pretesting
cohort	cover letter
cohort study	response effect

Exercises

1. In December 1994, Henry Wechsler and associates reported the results of their first college alcohol survey in the prestigious *Journal of the American Medical Association* (vol. 272, pp. 1672–77). This study raised awareness of the extent and harmful consequences of binge drinking and stimulated considerable research on drinking among college students. Read the article and answer the following questions.
    a. What was the researchers' target population in this study?
    b. Fully describe the sampling design.
    c. To draw the sample, the researchers used two sampling frames. What were they?
    d. Which school—a 20,000-student public university or a private liberal arts college with 2000 students—had a better chance of being selected for the study? Explain.
    e. This study consisted of a mailed questionnaire survey. What principal advantages of this survey mode are likely to have prompted its use?
    f. What inducement was offered to encourage students to return their questionnaires?

g. What follow-up procedures were used to increase the response rate?

h. How did the researchers attempt to rule out biases resulting from nonresponse?

2. A week before the 2008 presidential election, with Barack Obama comfortably ahead of John McCain in most polls, an article in the *Washington Post* asked, "Could the polls be wrong?" The article claimed that there was an undercurrent of concern among polling professionals, in part because of the wide variation in Obama leads: from 2 to 15 percentage points. Suppose someone asks you how there can be so much variation in poll results. Assuming that all the polls were telephone surveys that used probability sampling, identify and briefly describe four possible sources of error.

3. Suppose that you are planning to conduct a campus survey of voluntarism. In addition to accurately documenting the extent of formal volunteering, you intend to describe the types of volunteer service that students perform and the relationship between volunteering and background factors such as gender, religion, and academic major. From a "total error perspective," discuss the relative advantages and disadvantages of doing an FTF survey, telephone survey, mail questionnaire survey, and Web-based survey.

Notes

1. Social network analysis is an interdisciplinary paradigm that developed primarily from earlier work in American sociology and social psychology (sociometry) and British anthropology (Wasserman and Faust, 1994).

2. Whereas the flowchart in Figure 9.1 shows the top-to-bottom and sideways influences, later decisions may result in modifications of earlier decisions. For example, sampling-plan cost considerations may bring about a change in the research objectives.

3. See Shosteck and Fairweather (1979) for a study comparing physician response rates to mailed and personal interview surveys.

4. Fieldwork is not always carried out exactly in this order. Pretesting, for example, may occur before, during, or after the training of interviewers. Efforts to gain access to respondents may well begin earlier than depicted.

5. Another strategy is to enclose a postage-paid postcard that identifies the respondent (name or identification number) in the first mailing (Mangione, 1995). Respondents are asked to mail the postcard separately from the anonymous questionnaire, and they are told that the postcard indicates that the questionnaire has been returned and they will receive no reminder notices.

10

Survey Instrumentation

The two most critical features for successful survey research are the sample and the survey instrument. Accurate generalizations about populations of interest depend on the quality of the sample. But no matter how carefully the sample is selected, a sample survey is only as good as the design of the questionnaire or interview schedule.

Survey instrument design is a creative process, partly art and partly science (Payne, 1951). Like an artist, a survey designer selects "raw materials" and combines them creatively within certain principles of design. For an artist, raw materials may consist of paper or canvas; pencil, charcoal, chalks, watercolors, acrylics, or oils; brushes; and so forth. A survey designer's raw materials are such things as free-response and fixed-choice questions, direct and indirect questions, question-and-response formats, overall physical layout, and instructions.

However, a survey designer is unlike an artist in at least one important way: An artist is mainly concerned with expressing his or her own personal ideas, emotions, or other subjective experience, whereas a designer of a survey instrument must be concerned ultimately with obtaining reliable and valid reports about other people. This concern is what makes a survey designer a scientist rather than an artist. The reports may be of subjective experiences, such as values, opinions, fears, and beliefs; or they may be of overt experiences, such as job history, salary, political behavior, place of residence, consumer behavior, or leisure activities. The verbal reports obtained in surveys are answers to questions; survey instrumentation is thus the science of asking questions.

In this chapter we focus on standardized instruments, in which the wording and order of questions are the same for all respondents. Yet many of the principles discussed here apply to less structured interview approaches. Also, we generally do not treat separately the primary modes of asking questions (face-to-face [FTF] interviews, telephone interviews, paper-and-pencil questionnaires, and computer-assisted self-interviews), although these may require different questions and formats. We do consider mixed-mode instrument designs, in which different respondents are surveyed by different data-collection modes.

We begin by discussing cognitive and communication theories of how people answer survey questions. Then we examine "materials" available to the survey designer—types of questions and response formats. Next we consider the overall design or "sketch" of the survey instrument. Then we look at practical guides for "filling in the sketch"—writing items to arrive at a first draft. Finally, we discuss methods of evaluating and pretesting questions that are necessary to transform a draft instrument into a finished product.

The Survey as a Social Occasion

Until recently, the science of asking questions was based largely on two sources of information: the experience of professional survey researchers and empirical evidence from experiments on question wording. For example, experience has shown that it is best for question crafters to use simple, plain-spoken language (Converse and Presser, 1986); research has shown that respondents are more likely to give a "no opinion" response if it is explicitly offered as a response alternative (Schuman and Presser, 1981). Such wisdom has resulted in important guidelines for questionnaire design, but these guidelines are ad hoc and often not clearly understood. What has been needed is a solid theoretical understanding of how people go about answering survey questions. Fortunately, over the past 3 decades survey methodologists have drawn heavily on work in cognitive and social psychology (for detailed discussions, see Schwarz, 1996; Sudman, Bradburn, and Schwarz, 1996; Sirken et al., 1999; Tourangeau, Rips, and Rasinski, 2000; Tourangeau and Bradburn, 2010) to develop theoretical models of the response process.

Scientifically, a survey interview is an occasion to obtain valid responses to a series of questions; however, it also is a social occasion subject to the influences of the social world. Being interviewed is an uncommon, sometimes anxiety-provoking experience for many respondents. Unfamiliar with the canons of structured interviewing, respondents turn to the social and linguistic rules governing everyday conversation for guidance on how they should behave. In answering each question, they also attend to a sequence of cognitive tasks with certain levels of ability and motivation. What can each of these perspectives tell us about designing a survey instrument?

From the perspective of cognitive processing, answering survey questions requires that respondents (1) comprehend the question, (2) retrieve the information requested from memory, (3) formulate a response in accord with the question and the information retrieved, and (4) communicate a response deemed appropriate (Sudman, Bradburn, and Schwarz, 1996:58–75; see also Tourangeau, Rips, and Rasinski, 2000; Tourangeau and Bradburn, 2010). Each of these steps involves mental tasks that can give rise to response errors. For example, to comprehend a question according to what the researcher had in mind, a respondent must understand both its literal and its intended meanings. Therefore, the question–answer task breaks down not only when the question wording is vague but also when the purpose of the question is misunderstood. Consider the question, "What have you done today?" Although the literal meaning of the words may be clear, it may not be sufficient to answer the question because the respondent still needs to know what sort of activities are of interest to the researcher. Would this include, for example, mundane activities such as brushing one's teeth and taking a shower (Schwarz, Groves, and Schuman, 1998)? Analyses of the other cognitive steps in the response process indicate that response errors are likely to occur when there is insufficient time to access relevant information from memory, when the accessed information does not fit the response options provided in the question, and when the respondent modifies the information to project a favorable image to the interviewer. We discuss ways to minimize these problems later in this chapter.

Another perspective, conversational analysis, suggests that respondents make sense out of structured interviews and self-administered questionnaires by relying on tacit assumptions underlying ordinary conversations. This perspective draws on the work of Paul Grice (1989), a philosopher of language. According to Grice, conversations generally run smoothly because speakers and listeners follow four maxims:

1. Speakers should not say things that they believe to be false. [Truthfulness]
2. Speakers should make comments that are relevant to the purposes of the conversation. [Relevance]
3. Speakers should make their contributions as informative as possible and not repeat themselves. [Nonredundancy]
4. Speakers should express themselves as clearly as possible. [Clarity]

As respondents follow these conversational maxims to infer the intended meaning of questions, they may be unintentionally influenced by subtle aspects of the survey instrument and administration, such as prior questions, response formats, and other cues irrelevant to the intended purpose of the current question. The principle of relevance, for example, implies that respondents will see everything about the survey as relevant to a given question, including seemingly irrelevant design features such as the numeric values on a rating scale. Norbert Schwarz and associates (1991) demonstrated this by asking respondents to answer the question, "How successful would you say you have been in life?" on an 11-point scale with end points labeled "not at all successful" and "extremely successful." The answers, as it turned out, depended on the numeric values assigned to these end points. When the end points ranged from 0 (not at all successful) to 10 (extremely successful), 34 percent endorsed a value from 0 to 5, whereas when the end points ranged from −5 (not at all successful) to +5 (extremely successful), only 13 percent endorsed a formally equivalent value of −5 to 0. Follow-up questions revealed that the numeric values affected how respondents interpreted the end points. When accompanied by a value of 0, they interpreted "not at all successful" to mean the absence of success, but when accompanied by a value of −5, they interpreted it to mean explicit failure.

KEY POINT

Seemingly innocuous features of a survey instrument, such as numerical labeling of rating scales, may serve as cues by which respondents interpret the meaning of questions.

Similarly, the experimental inclusion of a picture of either a healthy woman exercising or a sick woman in a hospital bed in a Web survey affected respondents' health self-assessment ratings. Those respondents seeing the picture of the fit woman reported themselves to be in poorer health than those exposed to the picture of the sick woman (Couper, Conrad, and Tourangeau, 2007). Thus, the pictures were relevant to respondents' interpretation of the intended meaning of a health self-rating question.

Another study shows how the methodological strategy of exploring complex topics by asking a series of related questions runs counter to the conversational principle of non-redundancy. Fritz Strack, Norbert Schwarz, and Michaela Wänke (1991) asked German students to answer two questions about their lives: One question asked them to rate their happiness, and another asked them to rate their satisfaction with life as a whole. Both questions had 11-point rating scales with similar end points (11 = very happy and 11 = very satisfied). "Happiness" and "life satisfaction" are nearly identical concepts. Not surprisingly, when both questions were asked in ostensibly unrelated questionnaires, the two measures were highly correlated; however, when the questions were introduced in the same questionnaire with the sentence "Now, we have two questions about your life" and then were asked one after the other, the correlation was much lower. Apparently, asking both questions in the same conversational context implied that they were intended to convey a different meaning; after all, asking the same question twice would not make sense.

Finally, a third theoretical perspective, rational choice theory, focuses on how respondents' *motivation* to provide acceptable answers to survey questions can affect their responses (Krosnick, 1991, 1999). Answering survey questions requires considerable mental effort. At the least, respondents must go through the four cognitive steps outlined previously. Some questions, such as those that require memory recall or thoughtful opinions on controversial issues, require more work than others; and lengthy interviews require more effort than shorter ones. When respondents exert the maximum effort to generate a complete and unbiased answer, they are said to be "optimizing"; when they do not expend the necessary effort but take shortcuts, such as not searching their memories thoroughly, they are said to be "satisficing." Satisficing may explain why some respondents tend to give "no opinion" or "don't know" responses; it requires less effort to express no opinion than to think through one's position. On attitude questions that ask respondents whether they agree or disagree with a series of statements, satisficing also may account for the tendency to agree more often than disagree because it is easier to politely agree with reasonable assertions than to generate reasons why they may not be true.

Theoretically, the likelihood of satisficing behavior increases with question difficulty and decreases with a respondent's motivation and ability to answer the question. One study (Holbrook, Green, and Krosnick, 2003) compared evidence of satisficing responses in telephone versus FTF interview surveys. As evidence of their lesser motivation to provide optimal answers, telephone respondents were judged to be less cooperative and engaged in the interview and expressed more dissatisfaction with the length of the interview. Consistent with the theory, they also evidenced more satisficing behavior. For example, they were more likely to give "no opinion" answers on several attitudinal items and were more likely to express agreement on yes/no and agree/disagree questions.

The methodological implications of these theories are clear. To identify likely problems when designing survey instruments, researchers must understand the conversational, cognitive, and motivational processes that underlie question asking and answering (Sudman, Bradburn, and Schwarz, 1996:258). As we examine the options available to question designers, we will consider these perspectives on the response task. Given the complexity of this task, however, decisions about questionnaire design are best worked out in a thorough process of pretesting. Indeed, one of the most important products of this theoretical movement is the development of rigorous diagnostic procedures for pretesting survey instruments, which we discuss at the end of the chapter.

Materials Available to Survey Designers

Like an artist, a survey designer has many choices of raw materials. We now offer some guides regarding choices among certain types of question and response formats and regarding the use of visual aids and questions from previous research.

Open-Ended and Closed-Ended Questions

A major choice among materials concerns open-ended and closed-ended questions. An **open-ended** (also called "free-response") **question** requires respondents to answer in their own words (in written form on a questionnaire or aloud to an interviewer). A **closed-ended** (or "fixed-choice") **question** requires respondents to choose a response from those provided. Here are examples of two questions written in both open and closed forms.

1. How would you rate the president's performance in office so far? (OPEN)
1. How would you rate the president's performance in office so far? (CLOSED)
    ( ) Poor
    ( ) Below average
    ( ) Average
    ( ) Above average
    ( ) Excellent

2. What do you think is the number one domestic issue the president should be concerned with? (OPEN)
2. Which one of the domestic issues listed below should the president be most concerned with? (CLOSED)
    ( ) Unemployment
    ( ) Inflation
    ( ) Reform of the welfare system
    ( ) Balancing the budget
    ( ) The energy crisis
    ( ) Other

The choice between open- and closed-ended questions is complex because each has a number of advantages and disadvantages. The greatest advantage of open questions is the freedom respondents have in answering. The resulting material may be a veritable gold mine of information, revealing respondents' logic or thought processes, the amount of information they possess, and the strength of their opinions or feelings. Frequently, a researcher's understanding of the topic is clarified and even completely changed by unexpected responses to open questions. But, alas, this very quality of open questions, the wealth of information, has a drawback: the "coding" problem of summarizing and analyzing rich and varied (and often irrelevant and vague) responses. Coding such material is a time-consuming and costly process that invariably results in some degree of error. (See Chapter 15 for a further discussion of coding.)

Open questions also require interviewers skilled in "recognizing ambiguities of response and in probing and drawing respondents out . . . to make sure they give codable answers" (Sudman and Bradburn, 1982:151). The following interviewer–respondent exchange illustrates the importance of probing to give respondents encouragement and time to think and to clarify their responses (Sudman and Bradburn, 1982:150):

Interviewer: What are the most important problems facing the nation today?
Respondent: I don't know, there are so many.
Interviewer: That's right, I'd just like to know what you think are the most important problems.
Respondent: Well, there's certainly inflation, and then government spending.
Interviewer: Government spending . . . how do you mean? Could you explain that a little? What do you have in mind when you say "government spending"?
Respondent: There's no end to it. We have to cut down federal spending somehow.
Interviewer: Any others?
Respondent: No. I think those are the most important ones.

Other problems with open questions include (1) the varying length of responses (some people are verbose; others are reticent), (2) the difficulty with inarticulate or semiliterate respondents, (3) the difficulty interviewers have in getting it all down accurately, and (4) the reluctance of many persons to reveal detailed information or socially unacceptable opinions or behavior. Open-ended questions also entail more work, not only for researchers but also for respondents. Indeed, open questions should be used sparingly, if at all, in self-administered questionnaires or Web surveys, where respondents must write or type rather than speak.

Closed-ended questions are easier on respondents because they require less effort and less facility with words. The presence of response options also enhances standardization by creating the same frame of reference for all respondents. When used in an interview, closed questions require less work and training to administer, and the interview may be shortened considerably.

On the other hand, good closed questions are difficult to develop. It is easy to omit important responses, leading respondents to choose among alternatives that do not correspond to their true feelings or attitudes. Research shows that respondents tend to confine themselves to the alternatives offered, even if they are explicitly given a choice such as "Other _____ (please explain)" (Schuman and Presser, 1981). This is consistent with Grice's relevance principle because respondents are likely to view the list of response options as indicative of the researcher's interests. To provide a list of response options that are meaningful to respondents, the recommended procedure is to use open questions in preliminary interviews or pretests to determine what members of the study population say spontaneously; this information then may be used to construct meaningful closed alternatives for the final instrument. Unfortunately, this procedure is not always followed; time and financial limitations may prevent pretesting of sufficient scope to yield adequate information on the population's responses.

Even when the range of possible responses is known, they may be too numerous to list in a closed question, especially in a telephone interview. It is better to ask the open question, "In what state or foreign country were you born?" than to list all states and foreign countries. Similarly, questions about occupations, medical conditions, favorite television shows, and the like are best asked open ended (Fowler, 1995).

Given these advantages and disadvantages, when should one choose open or closed questions? Robert Kahn and Charles Cannell (1957) suggest these five considerations: (1) the objectives of the survey, (2) the level of information possessed by respondents in regard to the topic, (3) how well respondents' opinions are thought out or structured, (4) motivation of respondents to communicate, and (5) the extent of the researcher's knowledge of respondents' characteristics.

KEY POINT

Compared to open-ended questions, effective closed-ended questions are easier on respondents but harder on survey designers.

1. Consider first the study's objectives. If you simply want to classify respondents with respect to some well-understood attitude or behavior, a closed question would probably be appropriate and most efficient. However, an open question is usually preferable when the survey objectives are broader and you are seeking such information as the basis on which opinions are founded, the depth of respondent knowledge, or the intensity with which respondents hold opinions.

2. A second consideration is the amount of information that respondents already have on the topics of interest. If you believe that the majority will have sufficient information regarding the survey's topics, a closed question may be acceptable. But if you are uncertain as to the level of information of the respondents or if you anticipate a wide range in the amount of knowledge, an open question is more appropriate. With closed questions, uninformed respondents may conceal their ignorance by making arbitrary choices, yielding invalid reports. And even adding the response option "don't know" may not resolve the problem since this option is unlikely to be popular with respondents who are sensitive about appearing ill-informed.[1] It is easier, for example, to respond "approve" or "disapprove" of the Supreme Court decision *Roe v. Wade* than to admit not knowing what it is.

3. A related consideration is the structuring of respondent thought or opinion. Are respondents likely to have thought about the issue before? Can they take a position or express

a definite attitude? If respondents are likely to have given previous thought to the matter *and* the range of typical responses is known to the researcher, a closed question may be satisfactory. This might be the case, for example, with a survey designed to measure the attitudes of registered voters toward the performance of the president. However, if respondents' ideas are less likely to be structured, open questions may be preferable. Suppose you wanted to ascertain why college students chose XYZ University or why couples desired a certain number of children; for such questions, the reasons may be numerous and not always immediately accessible to respondents. A series of open questions would allow respondents time to recall, think through, and talk about various aspects of their decisions, rather than hastily selecting a possibly incomplete or inappropriate response provided by a closed question.

4. Motivation of respondents to communicate their experiences and thoughts is a further consideration. In general, open questions will be successful only when the respondent is highly motivated because this question type is more demanding in terms of effort, time, and self-disclosure. Therefore, with less motivated respondents, closed questions may lead to better-quality data. On the other hand, closed questions sometimes dampen respondent motivation, in that some people prefer to express their views in their own words and find being forced to choose among limited fixed-choice responses irritating.

5. A fifth important consideration in choosing between open and closed questions is the extent of a researcher's previous knowledge of respondent characteristics. That is, how well does the researcher understand the vocabulary and amount of information possessed by the respondents, the degree of structure of respondents' views, and their level of motivation? Unless the researcher has done similar studies previously or has done extensive preliminary interviewing, the most likely answer is "not very well." If this is the case, open questions should yield more valid (albeit more difficult to summarize and analyze) data.

One approach is to use the different types of questions at different stages of research, first utilizing open questions in preliminary interviewing and using the information provided by these early interviews to develop closed questions or a combination of open and closed questions on the final instrument. Or you may decide from the start on some combination of open and closed questions appropriate to your purposes. (For a further comparison of open and closed questions, see Box 10.1.)

Direct and Indirect Questions

Another choice of materials concerns the use of direct and indirect questions. A **direct question** is one in which there is a direct, clear relationship between the question that is asked and what the researcher wants to know. The bulk of questions used in survey research are direct. "What is your total family income?" and "What do you think is the ideal number of children for your family?" are examples of direct questions.

With **indirect questions**, the link between a researcher's objectives and the question asked is less obvious. An investigator interested in studying the sex-role attitudes of male factory workers, for example, might ask the indirect question, "Do you believe your co-workers would mind having a woman as supervisor?" instead of the direct question, "Would you mind having a woman as supervisor?" Although the investigator really wants

BOX 10.1 An Experimental Comparison of Open and Closed Questions

Discussions of the advantages and disadvantages of open and closed questions are based largely on common sense and the unsystematic experiences of survey researchers. One of the few exceptions is Howard Schuman and associates' (Schuman and Presser, 1981; Schuman, Ludwig, and Krosnick, 1986; Schuman and Scott, 1987) use of an experimental design within large-scale sample surveys to compare systematically responses elicited by parallel open and closed questions. The table in this box shows the outcome of one of these experiments (Schuman and Scott, 1987), in which half of the respondents in a national telephone survey were randomly assigned to an open version and half were assigned to a closed version of the same question about the most important problem facing the country.

The open question has been used repeatedly in national surveys. This particular closed version listed four problems, each of which had been mentioned rarely in recent uses of the open question. As expected, only 2.4 percent of the sample mentioned any of these four problems in response to the open question. The categories most frequently mentioned were "unemployment" and "general economic problems." In response to the closed question, however, 60 percent of the respondents chose among the alternatives offered to them, even though the question explicitly instructed them to consider other alternatives. Furthermore, unemployment, mentioned by 17 percent of respondents on the open version, was named by only 6.2 percent of respondents on the closed version. As Schuman and Scott (1987:957) point out, "the issues mentioned on the open question give the better overall picture of American concerns and : . . the findings on the closed question are distorted by the constraint or inertia produced by listing the four problems as part of the question."

Open question		Closed question
What do you think is the most important problem facing this country today?		Which of the following do you think is the most important problem facing this country today—the energy shortage, the quality of public schools, legalized abortion, or pollution—or if you prefer, you may name a different problem as most important?
1. The energy shortage	0.0%	5.6%
2. The quality of public schools	1.2	32.0
3. Legalized abortion	0.0	8.4
4. Pollution	1.2	14.0
Subtotal	2.4	60.0
5. All other responses	93.0	39.3
6. Don't know	4.7	0.6
	100.0%	100.0%
Number of respondents	(171)	(178)

Source: Reprinted with permission from Schuman and Scott, 1987. Copyright 1987 American Association for the Advancement of Science.

(continued)

(continued)

This experiment clearly demonstrates how differences in the form of a question can produce quite different results. Although these data suggest the superiority of the open version, other evidence indicates that open and closed questions will ordinarily lead to the same conclusion, so long as the closed form includes as alternatives the most frequently mentioned issues in response to the open form (Schuman and Presser, 1981). When in doubt about response alternatives, investigators should be careful not to impose their own frames of reference on respondents but should begin with open questions and then use the "free" responses to construct a set of "fixed" alternatives. In addition, open questions may be necessary as "why" follow-ups to closed questions, when alternatives are too complex or too many to present easily in a closed version, and when rapidly changing events undermine the adequacy of closed alternatives (Schuman and Presser, 1981).

---

to determine the respondents' own sex-role attitudes, he or she may suspect that they will be unwilling to admit personal sexist sentiments to an interviewer. Knowing, however, that individuals' attitudes and beliefs shape the way they perceive the world about them, the researcher assumes that respondents will impute their own attitudes to their co-workers.

Indirect questions may be appropriate when a researcher is interested in characteristics or experiences that respondents are unwilling or unable to reveal in direct terms. Respondents may be unwilling because the behavior in question is considered socially undesirable or unacceptable; they may be unable because the characteristics—motives, needs, fears—are below their level of conscious awareness.

Most indirect measurement is based on the notion of projection: that individuals tend to attribute their own inner needs, feelings, opinions, and values to the outer world. Thus, an individual presented with ambiguous stimuli will tend to interpret the material in ways that reflect his or her own needs and values. Some of the more common projective techniques are word association, sentence completion, and storytelling. In word association, respondents say the first thing that comes to mind in response to each of a list of words read by an interviewer. Sentence completion requires respondents to finish incomplete sentences, such as "When I think of cities, I think of _____." Storytelling involves asking respondents to interpret such ambiguous stimuli as inkblots and pictures.[2]

Most indirect measures were developed for clinical use and designed to aid in the diagnosis of emotional disorders by revealing an individual's personality and needs. This remains their principal use, although they also have been used in attitude and motivation research, especially in marketing. To illustrate the indirect approach, let us examine a classic study from marketing research, conducted in 1950.

Mason Haire (1950) was interested in attitudes toward instant coffee, one of the early instant-food preparations. Using direct questioning, Haire found that when women who reported not using instant coffee were asked "What do you dislike about it?" most of them said that they did not like the flavor. Suspecting, however, that this was a stereotypic response that concealed other motives, Haire developed an indirect approach to measure consumers' attitudes. He prepared two grocery shopping lists that were identical, except that one contained "Nescafé instant coffee" and the other contained "1 lb Maxwell House coffee (drip ground)." He then asked subjects to read one or the other shopping list and to describe the personality and character of the woman who made it out. As it turned out, Nescafé and Maxwell House coffee users were perceived quite differently. For example, nearly half of the subjects described the Nescafé user as lazy and failing to plan household purchases, whereas the Maxwell House purchaser was rarely described in these terms. The evidence from the indirect approach thus suggested that the decision to buy instant coffee was influenced as much by prevailing attitudes about what constitutes good housekeeping as by the flavor of instant coffee. Early replications of the study produced similar results and subsequent replications show changes consistent with changes in attitudes toward gender roles and housework (Fram and Cibotti, 1991).

Although one should be aware of the possibility of indirect questioning, it is used relatively infrequently in survey research today. One likely reason is that its use often requires intensive training in the administration, scoring, and interpretation of responses. Some researchers also question the validity of such measures. On the infrequent occasions that tests of validity and reliability have been done, the results have not been encouraging (Kidder and Campbell, 1970). Furthermore, the use of indirect questions comes with serious ethical concerns. To what extent are respondents giving their informed consent? To what extent is deception being used, and is its use justifiable?

Response Formats

In addition to making decisions about the broad categories of open and closed questions and direct and indirect questions, a creative survey designer will consider the possibilities offered by various **response formats** for closed-ended questions. The simplest response option is a simple "yes" or "no." This format would be appropriate for such questions as "Do you belong to a labor union?" and "Have you ever been threatened with a gun?" However, even though many types of information form natural dichotomies, this kind of question appears less frequently than you might think. With many apparently dichotomous items, respondents may prefer to answer "don't know," "uncertain," or "both." About 10 percent of General Social Survey (GSS) national samples, for instance, respond "don't know" to the question "Do you believe in life after death?" (T. W. Smith, Marsden, and Hout, 2016).

The decision to encourage or discourage "don't know," "no opinion," or "refuse" responses is complex, depending on the question subject and whether the mode is interviewer assisted or self-administered (Fowler, 1995:164–65; Krosnick and Presser, 2010). When respondents are truly uninformed or lack firsthand experiences with the subject of the question, the researcher must learn this by explicitly providing "don't know" options and, in some circumstances, including a statement that sanctions a know-nothing response. Otherwise, respondents may haphazardly pick a response to conform to normative expectations that they should answer the question (Grice's relevance principle). When measuring feelings or subjective states, in contrast, respondents who are ambivalent, indifferent, or even lazy are likely to choose an explicit "don't know" option rather than attempt to express their feelings (satisficing strategy). In such situations, it may be more appropriate to omit "don't know" response categories, thus limiting no opinions to volunteered responses. In interviewer surveys, "don't know" options may be omitted from the question and left to the interviewer's discretion. If they are omitted from the set of responses in a Web survey, respondents should be allowed to skip the question and not be forced to choose an answer to continue the survey.[3]

Ordinal response scales are commonly used to measure the strength or intensity of respondents' feelings. One of the most popular formats, the **Likert response format** used in Likert scaling (see Chapter 13), consists of a series of responses ranging from "strongly agree" to "strongly disagree." This is a common way of measuring attitudes. A respondent is presented with a statement and asked to indicate the extent of his or her agreement. For example,

> It is sometimes necessary to discipline a child with a good, hard spanking.
> ( ) Strongly agree
> ( ) Agree
> ( ) Uncertain
> ( ) Disagree
> ( ) Strongly disagree

In addition to degrees of agreement, a variety of other rating scales exist for assessing attitudes and opinions. To evaluate objects ranging from consumer products to personal attributes to government policies, respondents could be given the categories "excellent," "very good," "good," "fair," and "poor," as in the following question.

> Compared with the jobs that your friends have, would you say that your job is excellent, very good, good, fair, or poor?
> ( ) Excellent
> ( ) Very good
> ( ) Good
> ( ) Fair
> ( ) Poor

One can also create scales by asking respondents "how" they feel and then using a series of adverbs to modify the intensity of opinion. The following item from the GSS measures job satisfaction in this way.

> On the whole, how satisfied are you with the work you do—would you say you are very satisfied, moderately satisfied, a little dissatisfied, or very dissatisfied?
> ( ) Very satisfied
> ( ) Moderately satisfied
> ( ) A little dissatisfied
> ( ) Very dissatisfied

It is also common to use numerical rating scales, with verbal ratings provided for the numerical end points, as in the GSS item below (Smith, Marsden, and Hout, 2016).

I am going to name some institutions in this country. Some people have complete confidence in the *people running* these institutions. Suppose these people are at one end of the scale at point number 1. Other people have no confidence at all in the *people running* these institutions. Suppose these people are at the other end, at point 7. And, of course, other people have opinions somewhere in between at point 2, 3, 4, 5, or 6. Where would you place yourself on this scale for banks and financial institutions?

Complete confidence						No confidence at all
1	2	3	4	5	6	7

Another popular rating approach measures people's reactions to stimulus words or statements on a 7-point scale with end points anchored by opposing adjectives (e.g., "good" and "bad," "fast" and "slow").[4] Respondents are asked to rate the stimulus word or statement as it relates to each pair of adjectives. For example,

President Trump

Fun	:	:	:	x	:	:	:	:	:	Boring
Real	:	:	:	:	:	x	:	:	:	Fake
Strong	:	x	:	:	:	:	:	:	:	Weak
Cold	:	:	:	:	x	:	:	:	:	Warm

Here, a hypothetical respondent evaluated President Trump to be slightly fun and fake and extremely strong and was neutral or undecided on the cold–warm dimension.

A particular advantage with this format is that it is easily adapted for people from different backgrounds using words appropriate to their vocabulary. Robert Gordon and colleagues (1963) adopted this format to test predictions from several delinquency theories regarding the values of gang, nongang lower-class, and nongang middle-class boys. With use of such adjective pairs as "clean–dirty," "good–bad," "brave–cowardly," and "smart–sucker," the boys studied were asked to rate various stimulus descriptions (e.g., "someone who works for good grades at school," "someone who shares his money with his friends," "someone who knows where to sell what he steals," "someone who stays cool and keeps to himself"). The gang boys were found to endorse middle-class norms to a much greater extent than predicted.

In creating a rating scale, two important considerations are the number of categories to use and whether the scale should be defined primarily by numerical or adjectival labeling (Fowler and Cosenza, 2008; Krosnick and Presser, 2010). Should the response format comprise two categories (e.g., "yes," "no"), five categories (e.g., Likert), seven categories (e.g., the preceding two examples), or even more? Unless respondents' views are limited to a few categories, seven categories seem best for measuring the full range of their attitudes, beliefs, or feelings. An exception to the principle of using longer scales to obtain more precise information is a telephone survey, in which respondents may not retain all of the scaling instructions because, unlike other survey modes, they cannot be handed a visual aid or questionnaire portraying the scale. When scales are administered by telephone, it is best to keep them short and provide a description that is easy to remember.

Adjectival labeling of each response category conveys less ambiguity to a reader than numerical values alone or numerical values with verbal labeling of end points (Fowler and Cosenza, 2008; Krosnick and Presser, 2010). Suppose that respondents are asked to rate the honesty of a particular politician, either on scale A from 0 ("Not at all honest") to 6 ("Extremely honest") or on scale B from −3 ("Not at all honest") to +3 ("Extremely honest"). Although both scales have seven categories and the same end-point labels, as we discussed earlier, respondents will actively use the numerical information in determining an appropriate answer (Schwarz et al., 1991). Thus, they are likely to interpret scale B as bipolar, with categories ranging from degrees of dishonesty (negative values) to degrees of honesty (positive values). In contrast, scale A may be construed as unipolar categories representing degrees of honesty ranging from its absence (0) to its highest presence (6). Also, the "0" category of version B better conveys a middle or neutral position than the somewhat ambiguous "3" of version A. If the intended scale was conceptualized as bipolar, the following adjectival labeling format might be used instead of numerical values:

Extremely dishonest	Moderately dishonest	Slightly dishonest	Neither dishonest nor honest	Slightly honest	Moderately honest	Extremely honest

Ranking questions present another possibility to survey designers, as in this example.

> A number of factors influence people's career choices. Rank the factors listed below from 1 to 5, according to their importance to you in choosing a career:
> _____ Making a lot of money
> _____ Being creative
> _____ Being free from supervision
> _____ Having opportunities for advancement
> _____ Avoiding a high-pressure job

Although ranking questions frequently are handy and appropriate to use, we have chosen this example to illustrate several potential problems. First, unless pretesting with an open-ended question has been done, who can say these five factors are the most salient to the respondents? You can probably think of other important factors, especially if you are interested in working with people and helping others. (This is a general problem with closed questions.) Even if these factors have been shown to be the most important ones, further questions of validity may be raised. Do people really *know* why they choose certain careers? If so, will they tell you? How many respondents would freely admit that, to them, "making a lot of money" is the most important factor? Would "being creative" tend to get a spuriously high ranking? (For several additional examples of ranking questions, see Sudman and Bradburn, 1982:158–65.)

Visual and Media Aids

An effective survey instrument also may include miscellaneous aids such as illustrations, photographs, films, and cards that contain written material. The use of illustrations in a self-administered questionnaire may improve clarity and appeal, increasing respondent motivation and perhaps improving the completion rate. In interviewing, photographs and films sometimes are used to acquire data not obtainable through questioning alone. In a study of early socialization practices, for example, photographs of mothers with their young babies might be taken to stimulate the mothers to discuss their child-rearing attitudes and behavior, especially if the mothers have difficulty answering highly abstract questions.

Other aids used in FTF interviewing may speed up the interview or make it easier for respondents to answer accurately. A common practice in FTF surveys is to present respondents a card containing the responses to a fixed-choice question so that the respondent can view the choices while answering the question. As a rule, cards are used whenever the response categories are lengthy or more than five or six in number. For example, GSS interviewers hand respondents a card similar to the one shown here when they ask, "Which of the categories on this card come closest to the type of place you were living in when you were 16 years old?" (Smith, Marsden, and Hout, 2016).

1. In open country but not on a farm
2. On a farm
3. In a small city or town (under 50,000)
4. In a medium-size city (50,000–250,000)
5. In a suburb near a large city
6. In a large city (over 250,000)

Compared with other survey modes, Web surveys permit richer visual and media presentation, including pop-up menus, sounds, animation, slider bars, automatic skipping over nonrelevant questions, and so forth. The limited empirical research on Web design indicates that potential Web features are not well understood and may have unintentional outcomes. Just as respondents pick up clues from numerical values assigned to rating scales, they use visual stimuli to interpret and answer survey questions. Research on visual design in Web surveys, however, shows how good design can improve survey effectiveness (Christian, Dillman, and Smyth, 2007; Tourangeau, Conrad, and Couper, 2013). For a discussion of how effective visual design in a questionnaire can guide respondents and partly substitute for the role interviewers play, see Dillman (2007:462–93).

Existing Questions

Of all the raw materials available to survey researchers, perhaps the most important are questions that have been used in previous research. Most survey instruments contain existing questions, at least in adapted form, and it is easy to understand why. The use of existing questions shortcuts the measurement and testing processes. It also enables researchers to compare results across studies, to estimate trends, and, under certain conditions, to estimate response reliability (Sudman and Bradburn, 1982:14). Lest one be concerned about the ethics of using another person's questions, Seymour Sudman and Norman Bradburn (1982:14) note that "the mores of social science in general and survey research in particular not only permit but encourage the repetition of questions." Unless questionnaire items have been copyrighted, no permission is required.

Many sources of questions are available on most topics. Literature reviews on the research topic should uncover references with pertinent questions. One may also consult more general sources of questions such as PollingReport.com and the polls section of *Public Opinion Quarterly*, or data archives, such as the Roper Center and National Opinion Research Center. Finally, every survey contains demographic questions on age, gender, marital status, and so forth. Floyd Fowler provides an excellent critical discussion of alternative ways to word these basic questions about respondent characteristics (1995:166–76).

KEY POINT

To the extent possible, survey researchers should use existing questions developed by reputable sources.

Sketches or Preliminaries

Having considered likely raw materials, a survey designer, like an artist, will go on to make a sketch. The sketch for survey designers essentially is an outline of the question topics to be covered in the interview or questionnaire.

The most general principle to follow is to formulate your research objectives clearly before you begin. We could not agree more with Sudman and Bradburn's recommendation (1982:41), especially for beginning researchers, "that—before you write any questions—you put down on paper the aims of the study, hypotheses, table formats, and proposed analyses." This material then "should not become a straightjacket for you" (41), but should guide you in writing items, clarifying their meaning to respondents, and organizing them into a meaningful sequence.

Beyond a formal statement of objectives, certain practices in survey design have been shown to enhance the effectiveness of the research instrument. For instance, when a topic is abstract, using many items or questions results in better-quality data. In general, the more abstract the topic, the more items are required; however, this principle must be balanced by the need to keep the instrument reasonably short. The principle may be illustrated by a hypothetical interview schedule investigating job satisfaction. Topics might include wages, hours or shift worked, opportunities for learning and advancement, whether the work is interesting, supervisor–worker relations, and other working conditions. The topic concerning hours or shift worked might well be covered by a couple of questions, whereas "supervisor–worker relations" is more abstract; several distinct questions probably would be needed to get an accurate picture of a worker's satisfaction or dissatisfaction in this area.

Finally, the instrument design should reflect the perspectives of the target population as well as that of the survey designer. The job satisfaction survey outlined previously, for example, could be ineffective if it excludes topics important to workers. **Focus group** discussions, which are unstructured discussions among a small group of participants led by a skilled interviewer, are often used to learn how people think about a survey topic (Fowler, 1995:105–10; Krueger and Casey, 2000). In planning a survey of sexual practices among teenagers, for example, teen focus groups could provide insight into how teens cognitively organize, label (vocabulary), and retrieve sexual information.

The Opening

At this point, one should decide what the opening topic will be and draft the opening questions. It is best to have an interesting and nonthreatening topic at the beginning that will get respondents involved and motivate them to cooperate in completing the interview or questionnaire. The first question should be congruent with respondents' expectations: It should be a question they might reasonably expect to be asked on the basis of what they have been told by the interviewer about the study. This sometimes involves using a question that has no research purpose other than motivating respondents by conforming to their preconceptions about what should occur in a competent survey. The first question also should be relatively easy to answer, thus preventing respondents from becoming discouraged or feeling inadequate to fulfill their role as respondents.

In an interview survey, the beginning is a good place to have an open-ended question.[5] Most people like to express their views and to have someone listen and take them seriously. An interesting opening question is a good way to meet this need of respondents and to get them to open up and warm to the respondent role. Here are two examples:

> As far as you're concerned, what are the advantages of living in this neighborhood? What do you like about living here?

> Let's talk first about medical care. What would you say are the main differences between the services provided by doctors and hospitals nowadays compared with what they were like when you were a child?

The Placement of Sensitive and Routine Questions

It would be prudent to avoid both boring, routine questions and sensitive, personal questions in the beginning; build up interest, trust, and rapport before risking these types of questions. Uninteresting routine questions such as background information (e.g., age, gender, marital status) are often placed toward the end of a survey instrument. Asking personal questions (e.g., racial prejudices, income, sexual activity, alcohol or drug use, religious beliefs) prematurely may embarrass or otherwise upset respondents and possibly cause them to terminate the interview or question the researcher's motives.

Some researchers place sensitive or personal topics at the end of an interview, arguing that if the respondent fails to cooperate at that point, not much information will be lost. However, this may leave respondents with a bad taste in their mouths and may promote negative feelings toward survey research. Probably it is best to introduce such questions after the interview is well under way because the respondent will have invested time and effort by then and possibly will have developed trust toward the research and/or interviewer. In addition, sensitive questions should fit into the question sequence logically; they should be preceded when possible by related but less sensitive questions or topics so that the relationship of the personal questions to the topic and to the research is clear to the respondent. It also may be helpful to precede the most sensitive questions with a direct explanation of their importance to the research and to repeat an assurance of confidentiality.

Order, Flow, and Transition

After decisions have been made regarding the first topic and questions and you have a general idea of how you plan to introduce both sensitive and routine questions, the next task is to put the remaining topics in some reasonable order. What additional considerations go into the organization of topics?

The respondent's point of view must be considered as a researcher attempts to order the topics. The order must seem logical to respondents if their thinking about the questions is to be facilitated and motivation enhanced. In general, questions on the same topic should be grouped together. Early topics should be easy to answer and of interest to respondents; subsequent topics should seem to flow naturally from the early ones. The survey instrument may even begin with topics of little or no interest to the researcher but that will facilitate the introduction at a later point of topics more pertinent to the research objectives. If there are to be questions that demand hard work on the part of respondents, these should be included not at the beginning but sometime later, when commitment and momentum have been developed but before respondents could become tired.

An excellent example of topic flow is provided by the University of Michigan Surveys of Consumers (see Institute for Social Research, 2016). Each monthly survey contains about 50 core questions that measure consumer expectations with respect to their personal financial situation and the general economy. From the first survey in 1946 to the present, the survey has begun with a broad question on how respondents feel about current economic conditions: "We are interested in how people are getting along financially these days. Would you say that you are better off or worse off financially than you were a year ago?" (Curtin, 2004). The survey then flows logically from questions about likely business conditions for the next 12 months and next 5 years (e.g., Will unemployment increase? Will prices go up?) to questions about prospects for making major purchases (e.g., Is it a good time to purchase a house, major household item, car?) to more specific personal questions about personal assets (e.g., What is the current market value of your home? Is the value likely to increase in the next 12 months and next 5 years?). Finally, it flows naturally from personal assets to future plans, including financial readiness for retirement and investment in the stock market.

Researchers also must be sensitive to the problem of question-order effects (Schwarz et al., 2008). A topic or question appearing early in an interview may start respondents thinking in a way that will affect later responses by activating or changing the information readily accessible in memory. Since respondents tend to truncate memory searches as soon as they have enough information for an acceptable answer, the most accessible information is likely to be that used recently to answer previous questions (Sudman, Bradburn, and Schwarz, 1996). For example, questioning cigarette smokers early in an interview about their beliefs in a link between cancer and smoking could influence their responses to later questions about perceived benefits and drawbacks of continued smoking. Even questions appearing later in self-administered questionnaires can influence responses to earlier questions since respondents may skip ahead and then return to the earlier questions (Sudman, Bradburn, and Schwarz, 1996:82).

Research indicates that questions vary in their susceptibility to order effects (S. G. McFarland, 1981; Schuman and Presser, 1981). In particular, general questions are more susceptible than questions with more specific content. When, for example, a general question about abortion followed a specific question (abortion in the case of a defect in the unborn child), respondents were less likely to support abortion than when the general question preceded the specific (Schuman and Presser, 1981:37). Responses to the specific question, however, were unaffected by its placement. This pattern of findings is consistent with Grice's nonredundancy principle. After responding to the specific question, respondents interpreted the subsequent general question as excluding birth defects to avoid reiterating information already provided.

On the other hand, respondents sometimes include, rather than exclude, information previously given to specific questions in responding to a general question (Sudman, Bradburn, and Schwarz, 1996). That is, they assimilate the old information, which is readily accessible in memory from answering previous questions, into their response to the general question. For example, in an experiment with college students, the correlation between a specific question on dating frequency and a general question on life satisfaction dramatically increased when the specific question preceded the general question (Strack, Martin, and Schwarz, 1988). When respondents perceive specific and general questions as belonging together, however, they may exclude the information already given to specific questions from the general question to avoid being redundant (Schwarz, Strack, and Mai, 1991). Thus, whether responses from previous questions are included or excluded from subsequent general questions is difficult to predict in advance. Careful instrument pretesting may clarify how respondents are influenced by question ordering.

A number of strategies mitigate unintended influences of earlier questions on later questions: Eliminate the earlier questions, reword the later questions to make them more specific and less ambiguous, increase the separation between the earlier and later questions by adding intervening "buffer" questions, use separate boxes or pages to visually separate them in a questionnaire, and provide explicit instructions to include or exclude certain information in answering the later questions (Sudman, Bradburn, and Schwarz, 1996).

KEY POINT

Although complex topics are best explored with multiple, overlapping questions, order effects can occur when respondents invoke the conversation principle of nonredundancy to answer similar questions differently.

After the researcher has made an outline of the topics, considered the location of routine and sensitive questions and the problem of question-order effects, and written the opening questions (and perhaps a few others), transitions between major topics should be considered. Transitions indicate that one topic is completed and another topic is to be discussed; the main objective is to focus a respondent's attention on the new topic. Transitions also may be used to explain briefly why the new topic will be discussed or how it relates to the research purposes. Although they are not needed between every change in topic, transitions can improve the flow of an interview or questionnaire as well as respondent understanding and motivation. The following are examples of topic transitions:

> "Now I would like to ask some questions about your family. As you were growing up, let's say when you were around 16, how much influence do you remember having . . . ?"

> "Okay, now I'd like to change the subject slightly to one part of campus life that we're particularly interested in. As you may know . . . "

> "I would like to shift the subject slightly and get some of your opinions about . . ."

> "Fine. Now we have just a few background questions."

The sketch of the instrument will be completed by drafting an introduction. The introduction should explain briefly the general purpose of the study, assure respondents of confidentiality, and provide basic instructions for responding to the interview or questionnaire. Of course, a researcher never divulges specific hypotheses or relationships of interest during the introduction because to do so would be an invitation to respondents to give the desired or expected responses.

Filling in the Sketch: Writing the Items

Drawing on the raw materials outlined earlier, a survey designer is now ready to fill in the sketch by writing the individual items. An artist has elements such as line, perspective, light effects, and color to aid in filling in a sketch. Are there principles or "elements of design" by which a survey designer likewise may be guided? We now consider useful principles for wording questions, for grouping questions to achieve greater effectiveness, and for avoiding common problems.

Using Language Effectively

Even slight altering of the wording of a question can greatly affect responses, whether the question is open ended or closed ended. For example, a question might be written, "What is your annual income?" or "What is your total annual income from all sources?" A person answering the first item might neglect to consider income from such sources as interest on stocks or savings, sale of stocks, and rental income.

In general, research findings on question wording indicate that it is potentially important but difficult to predict whether a wording change will have an effect (Converse and Presser, 1986). For this reason, it is essential to pretest new questions adequately. Furthermore, it is generally a good idea not to base conclusions on results from a single item. Approaches to the problem of wording effects include asking multiple questions on a topic; using two forms of the question, each with a different, randomly selected subset of respondents; and using open-ended questions as follow-ups to closed-ended questions to probe for a respondent's meaning (Converse and Presser, 1986). Edward Laumann and associates

(1994:292–301), for example, used six different sets of questions in the National Health and Social Life Survey (NHSLS) to examine components of homosexuality (self-identification, homoerotic fantasies, and actual practice).

Additional guidelines for using language to obtain better data have been developed on the basis of survey researchers' experiences and of validity and reliability testing. Although some of these guidelines seem to be self-evident or common-sense suggestions, the plethora of poorly worded items continually being produced would seem to indicate a need for more attention to the language of items. The following questions provide a framework for examining the language of the items.

1. Are the items unambiguous, easily read, and sufficiently brief? Clarity and precision are essential qualities of well-worded items. At times, an item that appears perfectly clear to the designer may be confusing or carry a different meaning to someone with a different background and point of view. The point is easily illustrated by the question, "How many years have you been living here?" To one respondent, "here" may mean the present house or apartment; to another, the city; and to another, the United States.

Especially troublesome are indefinite words such as "usually," "seldom," "many," "few," "here," "there"; these will have different meanings to different respondents. Following are two alternative items illustrating the problem; the second is an improvement over the first because the responses are specific and thereby have the same precise meaning for both researchers and respondents.

1. How often do you attend religious services?
   ( ) Seldom or never
   ( ) Often
   ( ) Very often
   ( ) Every day

2. How often do you attend religious services?
   ( ) Never
   ( ) Less than once a year
   ( ) About once or twice a year
   ( ) Several times a year
   ( ) About once a month
   ( ) Two or three times a month
   ( ) Nearly every week
   ( ) Every week
   ( ) Several times a week

Items also should be easy to read or hear accurately. Succinct wording of items will enhance the accuracy of responses, as will avoiding the use of negative words such as "not." Some respondents will skip over or tune out the negative word in an item and respond the opposite of the way the question is intended. If negative words must be used, it is wise to print them in all capitals, underline them, or verbally emphasize them.

If key terms are subject to multiple meanings, definitions should be provided before they are used in a question. In a self-administered section of the NHSLS, for example, the respondents were asked about sexual partners after the following definition of "sex" was provided:

> People mean different things by sex or sexual activity, but in answering these questions, we need everyone to use the same definition. Here, by "sex" or "sexual activity," we mean any mutually voluntary activity with another person that involves genital contact and sexual excitement or arousal. That is, feeling really turned on, even if intercourse or orgasm did not occur.

> . . . please include all persons or times . . . where you had direct physical contact with the genitals (the sex organs) of someone else and sexual excitement or arousal occurred. Certain activities such as close dancing or kissing without genital contact should NOT be included. (Laumann et al., 1994:622)

If a key term is defined within a question, the definition should precede the actual question. Otherwise, respondents may skip or tune out the definition after hearing the question (Fowler, 1995). In the following question, for example, female respondents might report only pregnancies that resulted in live births *if* the definition of "pregnancy" had followed the actual question:

> Now I would like to ask you about *any* pregnancies you might have had. I'm interested in all your pregnancies, whether they resulted in a live birth, stillbirth, abortion, or miscarriage, even those which ended very early. How many pregnancies have you ever had, NOT including a current pregnancy? (Laumann et al., 1994:619)

2. Is the instrument's vocabulary appropriate for the respondents you intend to interview? If the target population is highly heterogeneous, the vocabulary must be kept extremely simple, and survey designers should be aware of regional and other group differences in the meanings of words. To exemplify the problem of translating social science concepts into language understandable by nearly everyone, let us assume for a moment that you are studying "socialization" among a random sample of American parents. You decide to start the interview with a broad, open question. Although any of the three examples that follow could be used, the third would doubtless be most effective.

> What do you consider to be the most important factors in the socialization of children?

> What child-rearing practices do you think are most important?

> What things do you think are most important for parents to do if they want to bring up their children right?

On the other hand, with some surveys, "talking down" may be a potential problem. When sampling a more homogeneous or specialized group (say, city managers, doctors, or nuclear engineers), use vocabulary that is appropriately sophisticated and technical for that group.

In choosing an appropriate vocabulary to characterize sexual practices, Laumann and associates (1994) steered a middle course between language that would be too technical (e.g., "fellatio") or too colloquial or slangy (e.g., "blow job") to be widely understood in a national survey. Their solution was to use simple, standard English (e.g., "oral sex") and to provide definitions when terms were first introduced.

3. Do the questions contain a single idea, or are any of them addressing two or more issues at once? A **double-barreled question** is one in which two separate ideas are presented together as a unit. An example (perhaps from the socialization study) might be, "What factors contributed to your decision to marry and have children?" The researcher seems to assume that marrying and having children is a single act or decision, whereas in fact there are two questions being asked here. It is a good idea for survey designers to examine all questions with the word "and" or "or" in them to be sure that they are not double-barreled.

Consider the following question that was included in a "questionnaire" distributed by a political interest group:

> Do you believe that for every dollar of tax increase there should be two dollars in spending cuts with the savings earmarked for deficit and debt reduction?
> ( ) Yes
> ( ) No

About four ideas are hidden within this "quadruple-barreled" question. Should taxes be increased? Should every tax increase dollar be matched by two dollars in spending cuts? Should spending cut savings be applied to deficit reduction? Should savings be applied to debt reduction?

The single-idea principle may also be violated in response formats as illustrated by asking workers to describe their boss using such fixed-choice categories as "Very professional and friendly," "Generally professional and friendly," "Somewhat unprofessional and unfriendly," and "Very unprofessional and unfriendly." Even the popular Likert response categories combine two ideas, as in the following example.

> A preschool child is likely to suffer if his or her mother works outside the home.
> ( ) Strongly agree
> ( ) Agree
> ( ) Disagree
> ( ) Strongly disagree

The respondent is given response choices that combine two different dimensions: agreement and strength of feelings (Fowler, 1995). The first response might be selected because a respondent is in complete agreement *or* has a strong emotional conviction about how to raise young children. Fowler (1995) suggests an alternative wording to avoid such double-barreled response categories:

> ( ) Completely agree
> ( ) Generally agree

( ) Generally disagree
( ) Completely disagree

4. Are the items free of emotionally loaded words and other sources of bias? Emotionally loaded words and phrases, such as "communists," "racial preferences," "pro-life," "cops," or even "the president's statement," may evoke cognitive responses that have little to do with the real attitudes or opinion of the respondent regarding the issue the researcher is attempting to study.[6] In general, try to word questions in a neutral way, and avoid identifying a statement or position with any controversial or prestigious person or group. Note the loaded words ("union czars," "forcing," "knuckle under") in the following question (Sudman and Bradburn, 1982:2):

> Are you in favor of allowing construction union czars the power to shut down an entire construction site because of a dispute with a single contractor, thus forcing even more workers to knuckle under to union agencies?

This question was part of a questionnaire distributed by a political lobbying group for fundraising purposes, a practice that social scientists consider deceptive and unethical.

Another source of bias is **leading questions**. Leading questions suggest a possible answer or make some responses seem more acceptable than others. The question "How often do you smoke marijuana?" may seem to imply that everyone indulges at least occasionally. A question that begins "Do you agree . . ." may suggest to some persons that they ought to agree. The generally accepted practice is to balance attitudinal questions using such phrases as "agree or disagree," "favor or oppose," and "satisfied or dissatisfied" (Sudman and Bradburn, 1982).[7]

An incomplete listing of alternatives either in the question or in the response options given is another common error. An example of the former is the question, "When you discipline your children, do you spank them, take away privileges, or what?" It would be better to either give a complete listing of alternatives or give none. The problem of making sure the responses to a closed question are exhaustive was discussed earlier in the chapter; it is also important that the responses be balanced. For example, if the responses represent attitudes toward same-sex marriage, it would be judicious to have an equal number of positive and negative statements, as well as a neutral statement. Furthermore, you would want to represent both extreme and moderate attitudes in each direction. Otherwise, respondents interpret an unbalanced set of response options as relevant to question intent and indicative of the range of typical or normal responses.

Consider the following question, which was used in a mail questionnaire to gauge University of California employee satisfaction with their health maintenance organizations (HMOs).

Based on the experience of everyone in your family, how satisfied was your family with your HMO plan in 1995?

1. Very satisfied   3. Neither satisfied nor dissatisfied   5. Very dissatisfied
2. Satisfied   4. Dissatisfied   6. Don't know or doesn't apply

Both the question and the formatting of the response categories skew the responses in the direction of satisfaction. A more neutral wording such as "How would you rate your HMO?" is likely to produce more critical responses than asking "How satisfied . . . ?" Note also that the two "satisfied" categories (1 and 2) are spatially grouped together in such a way as to be seen next after reading the end of the question. The scale end point printed first tends to draw more responses than if the categories are reversed and it is printed last (Sudman, Bradburn, and Schwarz, 1996:157). It is not surprising, then, that some HMOs received 80 percent or higher satisfaction ratings (combining "very satisfied" and "satisfied" responses) on this leading question.

5. On personal and sensitive questions, is the wording as tactful, diplomatic, and face-saving as possible? The topic of sensitive questions was discussed earlier in reference to their placement in the instrument. It was pointed out that motivation could be enhanced not only by logical placement of the item but also by showing the relevance of the question to the research purpose, reassuring the respondent of confidentiality, and including a wide range of response options. In addition to these efforts, careful diplomatic wording of the items may boost motivation and facilitate more candid responses. A housewife may feel irritated or defensive if asked "Do you work?" but perhaps not if asked "Do you work outside the home?"

A sensitive question might also be preceded by a statement that in effect sanctions the less socially desirable response, such as "Some people feel that smoking marijuana is pleasant and harmless, while others feel that it is harmful. What do you think?" or "Many people have taken an item from a store without paying for some reason. Have you ever done this?"

Finally, to make the best use of language, survey designers will usually need to make, test, and revise several successive drafts of the questions. Early drafts should be subjected to careful scrutiny by both the researcher and colleagues with the aforementioned wording issues in mind. Then, cognitive interviewing techniques, discussed later in this chapter, should be used to identify further problems by probing the thought processes employed to answer the questions. Finally, a semifinal draft should be field pretested under realistic conditions with a population similar to the one for which the survey instrument is designed.

KEY POINT
A survey designer starts with a topic outline, drafts and refines questions, and then pretests the survey instrument.

The "Frame of Reference" Problem

Often, the questions we ask people seem clear in meaning to us but can be answered from several perspectives or frames of reference. For example, suppose a survey of second-semester college students asked, "Generally speaking, how satisfied are you with your decision to attend State University?" Students giving the same response, such as "relatively satisfied," could have different reasons for doing so. One may feel relatively satisfied because she has a generous scholarship and feels the school is as good as most others from an academic standpoint. Another may be thinking of the social life and a third of intramural sports activities. Yet, from their answers, a researcher would not know what the respondents' reasons were for their satisfaction or dissatisfaction.

There are many ways to determine or to control a respondent's frame of reference. A straightforward way to determine the frame of reference is to follow the question with a probe such as "Can you tell me why you feel that way?" or "What things specifically do you feel are satisfactory (or unsatisfactory) about State University?" Another simple means of controlling the frame of reference for individual questions is to specify the frame of reference within the question, such as "Compared with other universities in the state system, how do you feel about the intellectual life at Caufield State?"

By particular arrangements of questions, researchers also can direct respondents to the investigator's frame of reference. A **funnel sequence** moves from a general question to progressively more specific questions. Suppose one wanted to study the impact of inflation on people's attitudes about the performance of the president. Research on question-order effects, reported earlier, suggests that asking specific questions about inflation first might impose this frame of reference on respondents so that later general questions about the president's performance are judged with reference to the president's inflation efforts. Instead, a funnel sequence could start out with general questions about achievements ("What do you think about the president's performance in office?" and "Why do you feel this way?"), which will likely disclose the respondents' frame of reference. These questions then could be followed by questions on inflation ("Do you think we have a serious inflation problem?" or "Has it had much effect on you?") and, finally, specific questions about the president's activity in this area ("Do you believe the president is doing a good job of fighting inflation?").

The previous example illustrates the effectiveness of a funnel sequence in avoiding the possibility that asking more specific questions first will influence responses to more general questions. This sequence also offers the advantage of beginning with the respondent's ideas and perspectives, which may increase interest and motivation. Funnel sequences may consist entirely of open-ended questions or of an open-ended question (or questions) followed by closed-ended questions.

A common frame of reference also may be established through an **inverted-funnel sequence** of related questions. Here, one begins with the most specific questions and ends with the most general. Although this approach lacks the advantages of the funnel sequence, it is useful in some situations. First, it may be used to ensure that all respondents are considering the same points or circumstances before expressing their general opinions. For example, if we wanted to make sure that respondents were judging the president's performance in office on similar bases, an inverted-funnel sequence would enable us to bring up and question performance in specific areas (inflation, unemployment, foreign policy) before asking for a general evaluation. A second advantage of the inverted funnel sequence is that, whether or not respondents have previously formed an opinion regarding the final question in the sequence, all will have time to think through certain aspects of a complex issue before giving their opinion. Instead of asking respondents to express immediately their attitude toward liberalizing laws on abortions, for example, one might ask about approval of abortion in various specific circumstances (if there is a strong chance of a birth deformity, if the woman became pregnant as a result of rape, if the woman's own health is seriously endangered, if the woman is married and does not want the child, if the family cannot afford any more children), at the end of which the respondents' general opinion would be sought. (See Box 10.2 for additional examples of a funnel sequence and inverted-funnel sequence.)

Will an inverted-funnel sequence be susceptible to order effects, since respondents may avoid being redundant by excluding previously given information from the final general question? There is limited evidence (Schwarz, Strack, and Mai, 1991) that another conversational norm, a request for a summary judgment, may operate when a general question follows a block of specific questions as in the second example of Box 10.2.

BOX 10.2 Examples of Funnel and Inverted-Funnel Sequences of Questions

Here is a sample funnel sequence from a study of union printers (Lipset, Trow, and Coleman, 1956:493–94).

7. (a) All things considered, how do you like printing as an occupation?
   Do you dislike it?
   Are you indifferent?
   Do you like it fairly well?
   Do you like it very much?
   (b) Why do you feel this way?
8. (a) Is there any occupation you would like to have other than the one you now have— either in or outside the printing trade?
   (If so) Which one?
9. Let's look at it another way: If you were starting all over again, what occupation would you want to get into?
10. (a) How would you rate printing as an occupation? For example:
   (1) Would you rate the *pay* as excellent, good, fair, or poor?
   (2) How about *job security* in the printing trade? Would you rate it as excellent, good, fair, or poor?
   (3) How about the *prestige* printing receives from people outside the trade?

A brief inverted-funnel sequence used to measure perceptions of well-being (Andrews and Withey, 1976:376) is reproduced here.

13. Here are some faces expressing various feelings. Below each is a letter.

(continued)

(continued)

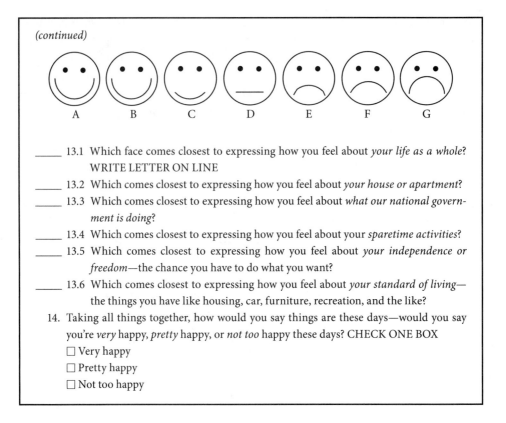

A   B   C   D   E   F   G

_____ 13.1 Which face comes closest to expressing how you feel about *your life as a whole*? WRITE LETTER ON LINE

_____ 13.2 Which comes closest to expressing how you feel about *your house or apartment*?

_____ 13.3 Which comes closest to expressing how you feel about *what our national government is doing*?

_____ 13.4 Which comes closest to expressing how you feel about your *sparetime activities*?

_____ 13.5 Which comes closest to expressing how you feel about *your independence or freedom*—the chance you have to do what you want?

_____ 13.6 Which comes closest to expressing how you feel about *your standard of living*—the things you have like housing, car, furniture, recreation, and the like?

14. Taking all things together, how would you say things are these days—would you say you're *very* happy, *pretty* happy, or *not too* happy these days? CHECK ONE BOX
    ☐ Very happy
    ☐ Pretty happy
    ☐ Not too happy

Reason Analysis

The funnel sequence illustrates the benefits of using a sequence of questions to explore complex issues. Similarly, a well-devised series of questions is invariably more effective than the simple question "Why?" in finding out the reasons for people's behavior. Suppose we ask undergraduates why they decided to attend UCLA, and we receive the following responses: Mary—"My parents convinced me"; Sam—"Because I live in LA"; Pascual—"For a scholarship"; Irma—"To be with my boyfriend"; Reuben—"It's a fun school and I wasn't accepted at the other schools I applied to." These reasons are not only brief and diverse but also likely incomplete; surely these students selected UCLA for more than one reason (only Reuben mentioned two reasons). Perhaps Mary and Sam also were influenced by scholarships; maybe Irma was not alone in having a close friend at UCLA or Reuben was not the only one turned down by other schools. Also, other determinants of the respondents' choice of UCLA may have been overlooked, such as the recommendations of high school teachers, the academic reputation of UCLA, and the climate of southern California.

The simple "why?" question implies that a simple, prompt answer is desired. Consequently, respondents may expend minimum effort (satisficing) to generate quickly a plausible answer that is easy to verbalize. How, then, can we go about discovering the main factors that influenced our respondents to attend UCLA? Fortunately, Hans Zeisel (1968) systematized the process of asking why. The key idea in Zeisel's **reason analysis** is the development of an "accounting scheme" outlining the general categories of reasons, or dimensions of the decision, which in turn provides a model or structure for formulating a comprehensive series of questions.

The accounting scheme is based on the research objectives (not all reasons may be of interest), on the researcher's creativity, and usually on informal exploratory interviewing or focus group discussions with members of the group under study. Unless one is reasonably well informed about the various categories of reasons for an action (perhaps from previous research or experience), these are sought through exploratory interviewing. The information from these preliminary interviews is culled for reasons not pertinent to the research objectives,[8] and the remaining responses are creatively grouped into an integrated model of relevant categories to form the accounting scheme.

Often, an accounting scheme is structured in terms of the typical stages in a decision process. To return to our example, for many students the decision to attend UCLA involved (1) a decision to attend college, (2) the selection of schools to apply to for admission, and (3) the final choice of UCLA. At each of these stages the respondent's behavior may be influenced by sources of information (knowledge, gossip, rumors learned from the media, friends, and strangers), advice from significant others (recommendations of friends, parents, teachers), constraints or limitations (financial needs, health requirements, need to live with or near a friend or relative), the respondent's particular needs (academic interests, vocational objectives, social and recreational interests), perceived characteristics of the schools considered (reputation or image, strengths and weaknesses, location and climate, housing availability, costs), and responses by the schools (offers of aid or scholarships, athletic awards, special recruitment efforts, rejection of admission application).

After a systematic outline of the accounting scheme just sketched out is made, the final step in our reason analysis would be to write a series of questions to assist the respondents in reviewing the stages of their decisions to attend UCLA: "When did you first seriously consider going to college?" "How did you reach this decision?" "Did you apply to any other colleges or universities? Which ones?" "What were the characteristics of UCLA that you particularly liked?" "Did your parents, friends, teachers, or any other persons help you come to your decision? Who?" "How much influence did this have on you?" Although the process of reason analysis in this situation calls for intense mental labor, we would end up knowing immensely more about the college decisions of Mary, Sam, Pascual, Irma, and Reuben than had we simply asked, "Why UCLA?"

The sequence of stages of a decision process is not the only basis for accounting schemes. Zeisel (1968) discusses in detail several common schemes. In studies of why people move from place A to place B (or shift jobs or, in general, change preferences from A to B), the reason analysis focuses particularly on the negative aspects of A and the positive aspects of B. This is called the "push–pull scheme" in migration studies since the decision to move may be precipitated by factors that push one out of the old location (e.g., an increase in rent, a change in neighborhood character, the loss of a job) and/or that pull or attract one to a new habitat (e.g., the anticipation of employment, a better wage, a better environment). Another common accounting scheme used in studies of consumer behavior has three major dimensions: the perceived attributes of the consumer product (its effects, price, etc.), the motives or needs of the respondent to be satisfied by the product, and the influences that affect the purchase decision (advertising, recommendations of friends, etc.).[9]

Reason analysis thus is a useful and general technique for guiding questionnaire construction and for avoiding superficial and incomplete answers to important questions. The researcher basically is asking many specific whys rather than a general why question. Compared with a general question, a comprehensive series of specific questions better conveys to a respondent the information sought by the researcher, as well as facilitating information retrieval by triggering different memory associations.

Memory Problems

There are two kinds of memory problems. First, respondents may be unable to retrieve information the researcher is seeking about life events. According to Cannell and Kahn (1968), the ease with which material may be recalled depends on three factors: how long ago the event occurred, how significant the event was when it occurred, and how relevant the event is to the respondent's life currently. Generally, respondents will have a longer memory for significant rare and costly events in their lives, such as getting married or having major surgery, than for more trivial habitual occurrences, such as losing a small amount at gambling or the content of the previous evening's television programs. Furthermore, they will remember more effectively events of continuing importance in their lives. The presence of an unsightly scar, for example, is a reminder of the accident that produced it.

A second difficulty arises from memory distortion. People do not uniformly recall events objectively; rather, memories seem to be distorted either in the process of organizing one's past and making it consistent or in an unconscious effort to maintain a positive self-image. One common type of memory distortion in responses to survey questions is called "telescoping" (Sudman and Bradburn, 1974). This occurs when a respondent erroneously recalls the timing of an event as having occurred more recently than it did. When respondents are asked about events that occurred within a specific reference period, such as visits to doctors in the past 6 months, telescoping leads to overreporting because some events that happened before the reference period (e.g., a doctor visit 7 months ago) are remembered as occurring during the reference period. Another type of memory distortion involves respondents reconstructing the past by projecting their present experiences and views backward (Groves et al., 2009:233). For example, respondents may draw on their current attitude toward capital punishment to infer their attitude 10 years ago.

What can be done to stimulate accurate recall? Here are some suggestions (see Converse and Presser, 1986; Sudman, Bradburn, and Schwarz, 1996; Krosnick and Presser, 2010):

1. Shorten the reference period. As a rule, the shorter the recall period, the more accurate the report. Sudman and Bradburn (1982) emphasize the appropriateness of the time period—with memory of a year or more for high-salience events (e.g., major accidents or illnesses) and a few weeks to a month for low-salience events. For example, the NHSLS (Laumann et al., 1994) asked about sexual partners during the past 12 months, whereas the National Health Interview Survey, 1992: Youth Risk Behavior Supplement (Willard and Schoenborn, 1995) used a shorter reference period of 30 days to ask youth about episodes

of heavy drinking. Jean Converse and Stanley Presser (1986) recommend that, for certain events, the time period be narrowed to the immediate past, such as yesterday or last week. For example, to obtain an estimate of the amount of time students spend studying, it would be better to ask "How much time did you spend studying on weekdays during the past week?" than to ask "How much time per day do you spend studying?"

2. Give respondents more time to search their memories for a response. This may be accomplished by lengthening the question (e.g., by adding redundant phrases and sentences), by instructing the respondents that the question may take some time to answer, and by training interviewers to allow adequate time for a response (Sudman, Bradburn, and Schwarz, 1996:225).

3. Use retrieval cues by providing a helpful context and question sequence as in "reason analysis." Rather than asking a respondent, for example, "At what addresses have you resided in the last 10 years?" begin with the present, asking "How long have you lived in Atlanta?" A second question might ask whether the respondent had lived at other addresses in Atlanta, and a later question might ask about residences before moving to Atlanta. Or one might ask the respondent to recall an important past event, such as completing school or leaving the parental home, and then guide the respondent to recall subsequent events (marriage, first job, etc.) in a forward time sequence.

4. Some questions demanding accurate memory may be best asked by means of closed questions utilizing lists. Doctors sometimes present new patients with a list of illnesses and ask them which they have had. Social researchers likewise may present lists for aiding recall of such things as magazines read, television programs watched, and organizational memberships.

5. Conduct a household inventory with the respondent. Studies of consumer behavior have revealed that even the current day's grocery purchases (type, brand, size) are best documented by examining with respondents their refrigerator and pantry provisions.

6. Where appropriate, ask respondents to check their records (birth and marriage certificates, school records, financial information, scrapbooks, photographs, etc.). In panel surveys, respondents may be encouraged to keep records available to answer certain questions (e.g., doctor bills to answer questions about doctor visits and medical costs) (Groves et al., 2009:217–18), or they may be asked to enter information in a diary that may be collected later (Krosnick and Presser, 2010).

The first suggestion as well as suggestions 3 through 5, which involve the use of "aided-recall" procedures, deal directly with the problem of forgetting but also may contribute to some memory distortion. A shorter reference period, for example, decreases omission errors but increases dating errors (telescoping).[10] The use of records deals most effectively with both kinds of memory problems, although this information is often difficult to acquire.

All of these suggestions are geared toward conventional standardized interviewing, which has been the focus of this chapter. By contrast, a relatively new method, the event history calendar (EHC), employs "flexible" semistructured interviewing to enhance recall (Belli et al., 2007; Belli, Stafford, and Alwin, 2009). In EHC interviewing, information is collected according to a calendar of salient life events (e.g., residence, schooling, employment, marriage) that extend across a predetermined time period (e.g., 2 years, 30 years) and serve as a common reference point during the interview. As interviewers follow a timeline in collecting information on major life events, questions about these events serve as retrieval cues that enable respondents to recall other events of interest in the survey. For example, someone may recall that he or she started smoking a week after he or she graduated from college. Unlike standardized interviewing, interviewers may construct their own wording of questions and may decide how to use information from one life domain to help respondents recall events in another.[11]

Finally, researchers have begun to explore ways of augmenting surveys with information from administrative records, which effectively avoids recall problems. In the Health and Retirement Survey, respondents are now asked for their social security numbers so that their survey responses may be linked to the Social Security Administration's Earnings and Benefits file (Lane, 2010). And the Add Health Survey now uses GPS data to link respondents' household location to contextual information about the person's neighborhood (Lane, 2010).

KEY POINT

Reason analysis accounting schemes and *event history calendars* use cuing techniques to facilitate respondents' information retrieval.

Response Bias Problems

Other instrumentation problems arise from the social situation surrounding the administration of interviews and questionnaires. Just as experimenters must be concerned about how a laboratory setting may produce disingenuous subject behavior, survey researchers must be alert to how the social situation in surveys may produce responses irrelevant to the object of measurement. We discussed this problem briefly in Chapter 9 in relation to response effects introduced by the interaction between interviewers and respondents and extensively in this chapter from the perspective of cognitive, conversational, and motivational theories. Here, we focus on biases produced by respondent tendencies to answer in certain ways as a function of the content or form of survey questions.

One frequent **response bias tendency** is to answer in the direction of **social desirability** (see DeMaio, 1984). We all have our private self-image to maintain; in addition, many respondents will want to make a good impression on the researcher by appearing sensible, healthy, happy, mentally sound, free of racial prejudice, and the like. Some individuals and groups demonstrate this tendency more than others. Indeed, Derek L. Phillips (1971:87–88) suggests that the consistent finding of greater happiness, better mental health, and lower racial prejudice among middle-class compared with lower-class respondents may not reflect true class differences in these variables but instead a greater concern among the middle class to give socially desirable responses. Some common techniques for minimizing social desirability bias have been mentioned previously: use of indirect questions, careful placement and wording of sensitive questions, assurances of anonymity and scientific importance, statements sanctioning less socially desirable responses, building of rapport between interviewer and respondent, and collection of sensitive information within FTF interviews with self-administered forms or other modes that provide privacy to the interviewees.

A second response bias is the **acquiescence response set**. This is the tendency for respondents to be very agreeable: Presented with a question having options such as "yes/no" or "agree/disagree," they are more apt to agree or say yes than to disagree or say no. This tendency also extends to such formats as the Likert scale, where there are gradations of agreeing or disagreeing. One way of circumventing the problem is to give specific content to the response options. For example, one may construct the second item below to avoid a possible acquiescence effect in response to the first item.

1. Rent control is necessary in order for many of the people of River City to obtain adequate housing.
   ( ) Completely agree
   ( ) Generally agree
   ( ) Uncertain
   ( ) Generally disagree
   ( ) Completely disagree

2. From the following statements, select the one that most closely represents your opinion about the need for rent control in River City.
   a. Rent control is necessary in order for many of the people of River City to obtain adequate housing.
   b. Rent control is necessary in order for some of the people of River City to obtain adequate housing.
   c. I am uncertain whether rent control is necessary or not.
   d. Very few people are really helped by rent control.
   e. Rent control is unnecessary.

Research has shown that reliability and validity are higher with questions that explicitly array the full attitude dimension than with agree/disagree and yes/no questions (Krosnick and Presser, 2010). One problem with this approach, however, is that it requires much greater effort on the part of survey designers.

Another way to control as well as check for an acquiescence response set when a researcher wishes to retain a yes/no or an agree/disagree format is to include within the instrument two items measuring the same concept that are roughly opposite in meaning. The items should be located at different points in the instrument. The following item pair from the F scale, a measure of authoritarianism, illustrates this approach (Bass, 1955:619):

1. Human nature being what it is, there will always be war and conflict.
2. Human nature being what it is, universal peace will come about eventually.

Responses to the two conflicting statements may be compared to see whether a significant number of persons answered both statements affirmatively. The major problem with this approach is the difficulty in constructing truly contradictory items. It would not necessarily be inconsistent, for example, to reject both of the above statements.

Ordinal or **position response bias** represents a third response tendency. In visual modes of data collection, some respondents are more likely to pick response options listed earlier—a primacy effect—such as the first choice in a multiple-choice question. In auditory modes, the opposite—a recency effect—may happen, as when options presented later are chosen more frequently. In 548 telephone experiments, in which two response categories were randomly ordered, recency effects occurred predominantly in questions or answers that were difficult to comprehend and in those that were asked after many prior questions (Holbrook et al., 2007). Because these recency biases may reflect satisficing behavior, Allyson Holbrook and associates (2007) recommend simple wording for questions and for response categories, short questionnaires, and rotating the order of response choices in telephone surveys. In visual modes, ways of addressing position biases, as well as the tendency to acquiesce, include varying the arrangement of questions and the manner in which they are asked as well as avoidance of "check-all-that-apply" blocks of questions (Dillman, 2007).

Format Considerations

Finally, the format or physical organization of the survey instrument must be planned. There are many possibilities, but a few main points should be considered (for Web and computer-assisted telephone interviewing [CATI] surveys, see Dillman, Smyth, and Christian [2009] and Gwartney [2007], respectively).

Probably most important, the physical form of the instrument should be appealing to respondents and interviewers. In addition, the design should facilitate the tasks of reading, completing, and coding. Numbering items consecutively throughout, using clear type, and allowing sufficient space between items and between response options can help greatly. With interview schedules, different type styles (or capitalization and underlining) should be used to differentiate instructions to the interviewer from material to be read aloud to interviewees.

While planning the physical organization, it would be appropriate to consider whether using "filter" and "contingency questions" would improve the instrument. **Contingency questions** are intended for only a part of the sample of respondents. By addressing only those persons for whom the questions are clearly relevant, contingency questions avoid the waste of time and possible decline in respondent motivation that may occur when the same questions are asked of all respondents. Responses to a **filter question** determine who is to answer which subsequent contingency question(s). One format is illustrated below from a hypothetical survey of adolescent sexual attitudes and practices.

19. Have you ever had sexual intercourse? (FILTER QUESTION)
    ( ) Yes (Please answer questions 20–29.) (CONTINGENCY QUESTIONS)
    ( ) No (Go to question 30. Please skip questions 20–29.)

(Box 10.3 presents a series of filter and contingency questions from a GSS interview schedule.)

BOX 10.3 Examples of Filter and Contingency Questions

The following is one page from an interview schedule for the General Social Survey. The physical layout is designed to facilitate interviewing and computer processing.

29. Last week were you working full time, part time, going to school, keeping house, or what?

CIRCLE ONE CODE ONLY. IF MORE THAN ONE RESPONSE, GIVE PREFERENCE TO SMALLEST CODE NUMBER THAT APPLIES.

HAND CARD C

Working full time ....(ASK A) 01 09-10/
Working part time ....(ASK A) 02
With a job, but not at work because
   of temporary illness, vacation,
   strike ....(ASK B) 03
Unemployed, laid off, looking for
   work ....(GO TO Q.30)...................... 04
Retired...(ASK C)................................. 05
In school ....(ASK C)................................. 06
Keeping house..(ASK C)................................. 07
OTHER (SPECIFY AND ASK C) _____08

A. **IF WORKING, FULL OR PART TIME:** How many hours did you work last week, at all jobs?

Hours:☐☐   11–12/

NOW GO TO Q.30

B. **IF WITH A JOB, BUT NOT AT WORK:** How many hours a week do you usually work, at all jobs?

Hours:☐☐   13–14/

NOW GO TO Q.30

C. **IF RETIRED, IN SCHOOL, KEEPING HOUSE, OR OTHER:** Did you ever work for as long as one year?

Yes............. (ASK Q.30) 1   15/
No............. (SKIP TO INSTRUCTIONS BEFORE Q.33) 2

Mixed-Mode Instrument Designs

Instruments optimized for particular modes are not easily mixed in respondent-specific mixed-mode designs in which different modes are used to survey different respondents. Motivating respondents, clarifying questions, probing, and other functions performed by interviewers are difficult to incorporate in paper-and-pencil forms or to program into computer-assisted self-interviewing and Web surveys. The absence of visual contact implies that optimal telephone surveys must be short with simple questions. Questions and/or response choices may be randomly rotated in CATI but not in paper-and-pencil questionnaires. Several strategies are recommended to address these problems. One approach is to optimize the instrument for a preferred or main mode (Biemer and Lyberg, 2003). In a mail survey, for example, telephone interviewing might be used only to follow up with the mail nonrespondents. If the mail survey instrument is then optimized for visual self-administration, it will be less than optimal for CATI follow-up efforts.

When one mode is not preferred over the others, the instrument may be optimized for each mode separately (mode-specific design) or constructed the same for each mode (unified-mode design) (Dillman, Smyth, and Christian, 2009). In a mode-specific design, for example, FTF interviewers might hand out response cards for lengthy response choices, whereas visual cards could not be used in telephone interviews. Although the rationale for a mode-specific design is to use the best data-collection approach for each mode, the effort may be undermined by the incomparability of the data. A unified-mode design, in contrast, aims to achieve comparability by using the same instrument in each mode. For example, if self-administered survey questions include explicit "don't know" options, they also should be read with the questions in an interviewer-administered mode. (For mixed-mode design principles, see Dillman, 2007:232–40).

Evaluating and Pretesting

Throughout the chapter, we have outlined principles for writing good survey questions. Still, no matter how well informed one is about proper question wording, structure, and order, drafts of survey questions should be evaluated and pretested to determine whether respondents clearly understand and are able to answer them. Failure to do so can result in a meaningless study. For once the study has been conducted, it is too late to benefit from the information, for example, that in one item 99 percent of the respondents chose the same option or that many respondents misunderstood the meaning of a question. Experience has shown that the amount of effort expended on study planning and pretesting is related directly to the ease with which data may be analyzed and to the quality of results.

Initially, researchers may use evaluative methods that do not involve data collection. **Expert reviews** may be carried out by experts in survey design or in the survey topic, who either independently or as a group evaluate a draft questionnaire or subset of questions. Experts or researchers also may employ checklists that identify problems. In the Questionnaire Appraisal System (QAS), users complete a form in which they evaluate each question on a 26-item checklist of problems (Lessler and Forsyth, 1996; Willis and Lessler, 1999); for example, "Question is lengthy, awkward, ungrammatical, or contains complicated syntax," "Reference periods are missing, not well specified, or in conflict," and so on. Alternatively, Arthur Graesser and colleagues (2000, 2006) have developed a computer program called Questionnaire Understanding Aid, which provides an automated question appraisal. The researcher enters a question into a Web facility and receives "a list of potential problems with question comprehension, including unfamiliar technical terms . . . vague or ambiguous noun phrases, complex syntax, and working memory overload" (Graesser et al., 2006:3).

Limited evidence suggests that such ex ante methods can be effective in evaluating questions (e.g., Rothgeb, Willis, and Forsyth, 2001); however, these methods indicate what *could* go wrong with the questionnaire, whereas pretesting reveals what actually *does* go wrong (van der Zouwen and Smit, 2004).

Traditionally, pretesting has been done solely "in the field," that is, in the homes of respondents drawn from the target population. However, sparked by the study of cognitive aspects of surveys, researchers now often test questions in the laboratory. We first review procedures developed in the laboratory, which have proven to be effective in identifying potential wording, ordering, and formatting problems. The information gained through these procedures gives direction to further revision efforts. Often, several pretests and revisions of a questionnaire may be necessary to arrive at a good semifinal draft. Once the questionnaire is in this form, it is routinely tested in the field; therefore, we also discuss various techniques used in field pretesting.

KEY POINT

All questions should be evaluated and pretested, including those that seem clear to the survey designer.

Cognitive Laboratory Interviews

The goal of **cognitive interviewing** is to understand the thought processes involved in answering survey questions. Verbal reports from respondents, collected during or after their response to pretest questions, are used to identify problems and revise questions. The cognitive laboratories established at the Census Bureau and other federal statistical agencies typically use paid subjects who are recruited for intensive sessions lasting 1 to 2 hours; however, cognitive interviewing also may take place outside a laboratory facility (e.g., in subjects' homes) and involve only a tape or video recorder (Fowler, 1995; DeMaio and Rothgeb, 1996). In either case, the primary methods are "thinkaloud" interviews, probing questions, and paraphrasing follow-ups (for a more complete review, see Presser et al., 2004; Beatty and Willis, 2007; Collins, 2015).

"Thinkaloud" Interviews

The respondents are asked to think out loud, reporting everything that comes to mind, while arriving at answers to the questions. They verbalize their thought processes either concurrently as they work out an answer to each question or retrospectively after they answer each question or complete the survey (Dillman, 2007:142–46). Here is an example of an improved question resulting from cognitive interviewing:

> One question asked, "How many times during the past twelve months have you stopped smoking for one day or longer?" The intent of this question was to measure attempts to quit smoking. However, the question was not always interpreted this way. Several respondents included instances when they had not smoked for at least one day because of illness, excessive drinking the previous day, or other extraneous circumstances. The revised version makes the intent clearer, asking specifically, "How many times during the past twelve months have you stopped smoking for one day or longer because you were trying to quit smoking?" (DeMaio and Rothgeb, 1996:182–83).

Probing Questions

A weakness of the thinkaloud technique is that some respondents have great difficulty verbally describing their thought processes (Schaeffer and Presser, 2003). Instead, an interviewer can focus on particular aspects of the cognitive processes by special probes, such as "What did you think I meant by 'stopping smoking'?" Probes may directly follow each question (when the information used to answer the question is freshest in memory) or may come at the end of the survey (to avoid reactivity associated with the probing). Here is an example of probes used to pretest a question intended for elderly people (Jobe, Keller, and Smith, 1996:201):

> By yourself and without using special equipment, how much difficulty do you have bathing or showering: some, a lot, or are you unable to do it?

> Probes: "I said without using special equipment. What sort of things do you think would be special equipment?" "Do you use anything to help you bathe or shower?"

Paraphrasing Follow-ups

Another technique is to ask respondents to summarize or repeat the question in their own words. This not only provides a good test of whether respondents understand the literal and intended meaning of the question, but also may reveal better ways to word the question.

Cognitive diagnostic procedures are only a partial solution to good instrument development. First, they are better at diagnosing problems than providing solutions. Second, since they are usually based on small, unrepresentative samples of paid subjects, they may not detect problems that will occur in subgroups of larger, more diverse populations. Third, different problems may occur in the field under more realistic interviewing conditions. We now examine techniques to field test survey instruments.

Field Pretesting

Field pretesting a survey instrument consists of trying it out on a small sample of persons (usually 25 to 50) having characteristics similar to those of the target group of respondents. The pretest group is normally not a probability sample since you are not planning to publish your pretest findings. However, it should be as heterogeneous as the target population. For example, if your target group is a national sample of college and university students, the pretest group should include college students at all levels (first-year through graduate students) and from different types of institutions (large, small, religious, secular, liberal arts, technical, etc.).

Field pretesting should provide answers to questions such as these:

> Does the level of language match the sophistication of the target population? Are instructions to respondents and to interviewers clear? Are transitions smooth and informative?
> Are the questions and question format varied enough to retain respondents' interest and attention?

Are responses to open questions so diverse as to be impossible to analyze?

Are the choice options to closed questions clear and exhaustive?

Are interviewing aids such as cards or photographs effective and practical?

Are there questions that respondents resist answering?

How long, generally, does the interview take to complete?

For some time, field pretesting to identify such problems has consisted of having either experienced interviewers or interviewers in training both administer the draft questionnaire and observe the process. The interviewers might take notes during the interviews or file reports afterward, but their observations generally are conveyed in a group oral debriefing (Converse and Presser, 1986). However, this process has several limitations (Fowler, 1995; Fowler and Cannell, 1996). Playing the role of interviewer may interfere with the task of observing the process; each interviewer's observations are based on a small number of interviews, which may not be adequate for reliably assessing question problems; the standards for evaluation may not be well articulated or may be applied inconsistently, resulting in a lack of agreement about problem questions; and the recognition of question-comprehension problems is limited to items in which respondents ask for clarification or give inappropriate answers. Some of these problems may be addressed by cognitive laboratory interviewing. Recently, however, several strategies have been applied to make field pretesting more systematic and reliable. These include behavior coding, respondent debriefings, interviewing ratings, split-ballot tests, and response analysis.

Behavioral Coding

Systematically coding live or taped interviewer–respondent interactions is an effective technique for identifying instrument problems under realistic field conditions. Coding consists of categorizing responses and counting the number in each category (see Chapter 15). In **behavioral coding** of pretest interviews, interactions with respect to each question are coded to identify the frequency of problematic respondent and interviewer behaviors, such as interviewers incorrectly reading or skipping questions, respondents interrupting interviewers before the question is completely read, respondents requesting that the question be repeated or clarified, and interviewers probing to follow up on inadequate answers (Holbrook, Cho, and Johnson, 2006; Fowler, 2011). For example, behavioral coding revealed that a question commonly used in governmental health studies—"When was the last time you had a general physical examination or checkup?"—elicited a high proportion (87 percent) of inadequate answers because respondents did not understand the meaning of "general physical examination or checkup" and if the "when" requested a date, elapsed time, or their age (Fowler and Cannell, 1996). Behavioral coding is designed to identify potential problems. The next two pretest techniques, which involve the active participation of respondents and interviewers, are better at identifying the nature of the problem.

Respondent Debriefings

In Chapter 7 we discussed how debriefing sessions following experiments provide valuable insights into subjects' understanding and motivation during the experiment. Similarly,

respondent debriefings, which are structured follow-up questions at the end of pretest interviews, may reveal question-and-answer problems as well as the sources of the problems (for procedural details, see DeMaio and Rothgeb, 1996:188–94; Martin, 2004). Since the results of cognitive interviews tend to be limited in generalizability due to very small, unrepresentative samples, respondent debriefing provides a way to assess the external validity of cognitive testing results.

Interviewer Debriefings

Another perspective on question-and-answer problems may be sought from the pretest interviewers. For example, interviewers reported that a relentless sequence of Current Population Survey labor force questions angered retirees and women working at home by giving the impression that the "government believes persons should either be working or looking for work" (Campanelli, Martin, and Rothgeb, 1991:255). Although **interviewer debriefings** customarily entail informal group discussions with the interviewers, Fowler (1995:121–24) recommends that more systematic information be collected by having the interviewers fill out standardized ratings of each question prior to the debriefing session.

Split-Ballot Tests

Experimental manipulations of question ordering, wording, and formats, which survey designers commonly call "randomized" or **split-ballot** tests, are a costly but effective way to check out suspected problems or weaknesses under field conditions (see discussion of survey experimental designs in Chapter 7 and Box 10.1). Split-ballot tests require random assignment of adequate-size samples of pretest respondents to the versions being tested. For example, the results of cognitive interviewing might suggest a serious problem of question-order effects. This suspicion could be experimentally tested by randomly assigning pretest respondents to two forms of the instrument in which the order of related questions differs and then comparing the responses on the two forms.

Response Analysis

The responses of the pretest respondents also can be tabulated and examined for such problems as a low response rate to sensitive questions, the incidence of "don't know" responses, items where nearly everyone makes the same response, the adequacy of responses to open-ended questions, or confusion as to the meaning of questions. The generalizability of a **response analysis** is dependent on the pretest sample size and the degree to which the pretest respondents resemble the target population.

Each of these pretesting techniques offers a slightly different window on the question-and-answer process: Behavior coding allows researchers to see interviewer–respondent interaction under actual field conditions, respondent debriefings and other cognitive interviewing methods reveal problems from the respondent's perspective, interviewer debriefings expose problems from the interviewer's perspective, response analysis reveals problems from the researcher's perspective, and split-ballot tests show differences among instrument versions. This suggests that some pretest methods are better than others at identifying particular types of question problems.

A few studies have systematically compared various methods for evaluating and testing survey items. Stanley Presser and Johnny Blair (1994) compared four methods: conventional field pretesting with oral group debriefings, behavior coding of live pretest interviews, cognitive interviewing combining follow-up probes with concurrent and retrospective thinkalouds, and panels of experts. Each method was applied to a single questionnaire in repeated trials. Results indicated that behavior coding was the most reliable and conventional pretesting was the least reliable, expert reviews identified the largest number of problems and were the least costly, experts and cognitive interviewing were the only methods likely to spot problems affecting the data analysis, and conventional pretesting and behavior coding were the only effective methods for spotting problems involving the interviewer.

Another study found that appraisal forms (specifically QAS) tend to detect a higher number of question problems than either experts or cognitive interviewing (Rothgeb, Willis, and Forsyth, 2001). A third study limited to the evaluation of eight income items showed a strong correlation between experts and QAS in identifying problematic questions, but a relatively low correlation between the latter methods and behavior coding (van der Zouwen and Smit, 2004).

In general, these comparisons imply that questionnaires should be subjected to more than one form of evaluation and testing. After reviewing an evaluation of the Current Population Survey, James Esposito and Jennifer Rothgeb (1997) concluded that the use of multiple techniques is critical to any comprehensive program of evaluation because it capitalizes on the strengths of individual techniques while compensating for the unique weaknesses associated with each one. More specifically, according to Johannes van der Zouwen and Johannes H. Smit (2004:128), "The best practice . . . would seem to be first to use ex-ante methods [e.g., expert review, QAS] for testing early versions of the questionnaire, and after necessary improvements are made, to evaluate the draft questionnaire using field-testing methods."

Summary

- Survey design is an art as well as an evolving science that draws on communication, cognitive, and behavioral theories.
- The design of the survey instrument must (1) ensure effective two-way communication between the respondents and the researcher; (2) assist respondents in recalling and clarifying their experiences, attitudes, and thoughts; and (3) keep the respondents interested and motivated.
- In gathering raw materials, survey designers choose among open and closed questions, direct and indirect questions, and a wide variety of response formats.
- A researcher may also select visual aids and will almost certainly draw on questions developed in previous research.
- Open questions are most appropriate in FTF interviews when a researcher is unsure of response categories or is dealing with complex issues that require an in-depth understanding. They often are used effectively in preliminary interviewing to determine appropriate closed questions and response alternatives.

- Closed questions are best used when both researcher and respondent have ample information on the topic. Although they are easier for researchers to analyze and for respondents to complete, closed questions are more difficult to develop, may bias results by structuring responses, and may dampen respondents' interest in the survey.
- Most questions in surveys are linked apparently or directly to what the researcher wants to know. However, when examining characteristics that respondents are unable or unwilling to report directly, researchers may use indirect questions that disguise the researcher's intent.
- After considering raw materials, a survey designer makes a sketch of the instrument—an outline of topics to be included.
- Focus group discussions may be used to learn how people think and talk about a survey topic.
- Opening questions are critical for motivating respondents to complete the survey; therefore, they should be interesting, relatively easy to answer, and consistent with respondents' expectations.
- Sensitive questions are best placed somewhere between the middle and end of the instrument; routine background items are usually placed at the end.
- All questions should be ordered in a way that seems natural and logical to the respondent and that does not produce unintended order effects. Transitions may improve the flow from topic to topic.
- Properly worded items are clear and precise, are written in a vocabulary appropriate for the respondents, contain a single idea, are free of emotionally loaded words and phrases, and are tactfully worded.
- To control the respondent's frame of reference in investigating complex topics, one can arrange questions in a funnel sequence, moving from general to progressively more specific questions, or in an inverted-funnel sequence, moving from the most specific to the most general questions.
- Complex issues also can be examined through reason analysis. This involves the development of an accounting scheme, based on preliminary interviewing, that identifies the key dimensions of reasons for an action and integrates them into a model of the action.
- Recall accuracy may be improved by shortening the recall period, by giving respondents more time to respond, by aided-recall procedures (e.g., providing a helpful context or list), or by encouraging the use of records.
- Among the ways to minimize the social desirability bias are careful placement and wording of questions as well as assurances of anonymity. Response set biases are best handled by varying the type of questions and response format.
- It is also important for the format of the instrument to be neat and appealing. To save time and prevent adverse reactions, the format might include filter questions that direct respondents to appropriate contingency questions.
- Question evaluation and revision begins early with first drafts of questions and continues until the survey is successfully field pretested on a group of respondents similar to those in the target population.
- Initially, researchers may use panels of experts, question appraisal forms, and/or computer programs to identify question wording and comprehension problems.
- Pretesting with cognitive interviewing techniques (thinkaloud interviews, probing questions, and paraphrasing follow-ups) may then be used to further diagnose question problems.
- Field-pretesting techniques, including behavior coding, respondent debriefings, interviewer debriefings, response analysis, and split-ballot tests, are then used to evaluate the survey instrument under realistic field conditions.

Key Terms

open-ended (free-response) question
closed-ended (fixed-choice) question
direct question
indirect question

response format
Likert response format
focus group
double-barreled question

leading question

funnel sequence

inverted-funnel sequence

reason analysis

response bias tendency

   social desirability bias

   acquiescence response set

   position response bias

contingency question

filter question

expert review

cognitive interviewing

field pretesting

   behavioral coding

   respondent debriefings

   interviewer debriefings

   split-ballot tests

   response analysis

Exercises

1. Suppose you are constructing a questionnaire for the purpose of conducting a survey of sex-role attitudes. What would be the best placement (beginning, middle, end) of the following questions?
    a. How many sisters do you have?
    b. Does your mother work outside the home?
    c. Mothers should put their children before themselves.
        ( ) Strongly agree
        ( ) Agree
        ( ) Disagree
        ( ) Strongly disagree
    d. Would you say that women nowadays are more likely to work outside the home than they were when you were growing up?
2. The text identifies five common wording problems in constructing survey questions: (1) lack of clarity or precision, (2) inappropriate vocabulary, (3) double-barreled question, (4) loaded word or leading question, and (5) insensitive wording. Identify the wording problem(s) in each of the following questions and then rewrite the questions to make them more satisfactory.
    a. How many siblings do you have? ( ) 0–2 ( ) 3–7 ( ) 8 or more.
    b. Do you think the man should initiate and pay for the first date?
    c. In divorce or separation cases, the man has just as much right as the woman to have custody of the children.
        ( ) Strongly agree
        ( ) Agree
        ( ) Disagree
        ( ) Strongly disagree
    d. Because women are less aggressive than men, a woman's place is in the home.
        ( ) Strongly agree
        ( ) Agree
        ( ) Disagree
        ( ) Strongly disagree
    e. Do you hold traditional sex-role attitudes?
    f. Does your mother work?
    g. Is the leadership in your family matriarchal, patriarchal, or egalitarian?
3. Suppose you want to know why students choose a specific major (e.g., sociology). Applying reason analysis, construct a series of questions to find out the reasons for students' choice of major.
4. Imagine that you want to conduct a campus survey on voluntarism. Specifically, you are interested in who volunteers, why they choose to volunteer, where they volunteer, how often they volunteer, and what kind of volunteer work they do. To reduce costs, assume you choose to do either a mail questionnaire survey or Web survey and you need to construct a survey instrument.
    a. Outline the question topics to be covered.
    b. Write at least one question or find an existing question for each topic.
    c. Give an example of a good opening question.

    d.   Identify possible sensitive questions. Where will you place them in the questionnaire?

    e.   Give examples of a contingency question and a filter question that you will include.

5.   Once you have developed questions for your campus survey (exercise 4), pretest your questions on a small sample of potential respondents using thinkaloud and probing questions.

Notes

1.   For experimental investigations of the effects of including "don't know" options in opinion questions, see Howard Schuman and Stanley Presser (1981).

2.   Indirect questioning should not be confused with proxy reporting, which involves asking respondents information about others in their households or social environments (spouses, relatives, co-workers, neighbors, etc.). Proxy reporting reduces interviewing costs because information about several persons (e.g., all household members) may be collected during a single interview. In the November 1984 Current Population Survey, for example, about 40 percent of the reported presidential election participation (voting turnout) figures were based on proxy reports (U.S. Census Bureau, 1986:Table 18). The rationale underlying indirect questioning, that respondents will perceive others to be like themselves, is a potential source of error in proxy reporting.

3.   Forcing a response is likely to dampen respondent motivation and to violate typical institutional review board requirements that responses are voluntary. Instead, a Web survey could branch to a follow-up screen query to ascertain that the respondent intended to leave the previous question blank.

4.   This response format is used in, but not limited to, the semantic-differential scaling technique. For details see Charles Osgood, George Suci, and Percy Tannenbaum (1957).

5.   This rule applies to interviews only. As indicated earlier, open-ended questions are usually inappropriate in mail surveys and, if placed at the beginning of a self-administered questionnaire, may discourage respondents from completing the survey.

6.   A test of question wording shows how the word "communist" can alter the tone of the question. Schuman and Presser (1981:284–86) compared the responses to two questions regarding support for American military intervention: "If a situation like Vietnam were to develop in another part of the world, do you think the United States should or should not send troops?" and "If a situation like Vietnam were to develop in another part of the world, do you think the United States should or should not send troops to stop a communist takeover?" When these questions were asked in separate but comparable national sample surveys in 1974, 1976, and 1978, an average of 15 percent more people favored sending troops when the communist-takeover phrase was added.

7.   Research supports this practice. A famous study by Donald Rugg (1941), replicated by Schuman and Presser (1981:276–78), compared responses to two freedom-of-speech questions, one using the word "forbid" and the other the antonym "allow": "Do you think the United States should allow public speeches against democracy?" and "Do you think the United States should forbid public speeches against democracy?" When these questions were asked in three separate but comparable national sample surveys in the 1970s, more than 22 percent fewer people, on average, were willing to forbid than to not allow such speeches.

8.   If the UCLA administration had hired us to study the impact of financial aid programs on the quality of undergraduate admissions, for example, our accounting scheme would definitely incorporate financial considerations; and the sample under study also should include UCLA applicants who are accepted but choose to go elsewhere to school. If, instead, our client were the UCLA student government, which wanted to improve programs serving the needs of first-year students, our accounting scheme would focus on these needs and would likely omit information about other schools considered.

9.   Sometimes an accounting scheme guides the entire research design, not just the wording of a few questions. Nine years after the first major announcement in 1953 of a possible link between cigarette smoking and lung cancer, Bruce Straits (1967) conducted a survey to study why the health reports

were apparently having only slight effects on cigarette smokers. His study was designed around the accounting scheme that this anxiety-arousing information was having negligible impact on smokers because they (1) were unaware of the reports, (2) disbelieved them, (3) were not motivated to give up smoking, or (4) were unable to translate their motivation into action.

10. In some panel surveys interviewers reduce telescoping errors by having the respondents compare reference-period recalled events with those given during the previous wave to avoid duplications (Groves et al., 2009:234).

11. Like many recent methodological advances in survey research, the EHC method is informed by theoretical knowledge in cognitive psychology, specifically on autobiographical memory. Such knowledge indicates that memory is structured in a hierarchy, with salient life events at the top and other events indexed within this hierarchy. Retrieval cues embedded within EHC interviewing take advantage of this to optimize recall (Belli, Shay, and Stafford, 2001).

11

Field Research

When we introduced experiments and surveys, we appealed to the reader's casual familiarity with these approaches—from either having read about or participated in actual studies. In this chapter, we appeal to a different sense of familiarity. The field research approach resembles the natural inquisitiveness that is part of everyday life. At one time or another you have joined a group or organization or entered an unfamiliar setting (e.g., your first time in a bar, your first rock concert, the first day in your research methods class), where you have watched and listened closely to others to learn what is going on and how you should act. You also have reflected occasionally on the actions, thoughts, and feelings of others in situations you encounter every day—at work, in class, at meals, in the library. Each of these examples captures the essence of field research: to render our daily lives socially intelligible and meaningful by keenly observing others as well as reflecting on our own experience.

This is not to say that everyone is a field researcher or that common sense is all there is to it. The major point of similarity between field research and other forms of common-sense inquiry is "the observation of naturally occurring everyday events" (J. M. Johnson, 1975:21). The ultimate goal of field research, however, is not personal but scientific—to build a general, abstract understanding of social phenomena. Among social scientists, field researchers are "distinctively committed to displaying social realities as they are lived, experienced, understood, and familiar to the people being studied" (J. Katz, 1997:391). To observe, describe, and understand everyday life, they have developed special skills and techniques.

Although we have chosen the label **field research**, the methodological approach examined in this chapter generally corresponds to what others have called "qualitative" (as opposed to "quantitative") research (see H. Schwartz and Jacobs, 1979; S. J. Taylor, Bogdan, and DeVault, 2016). We avoid this term, however, for two reasons. First, it implies that there is no place for counting or assigning numbers to observations. Although field research "data" typically consist of written, verbal descriptions, researchers may, in fact, generate data on the frequency of certain behaviors and events and may use accounting schemes for recording behavior. Second, the label qualitative research generally applies to a variety of methods, including life histories, visual methods, and unstructured interviews, which are thought to represent a fundamentally different way of doing research and understanding social life from the so-called quantitative research espoused in this textbook (see Gubrium and Holstein, 1997; Denzin and Lincoln, 2005; S. J. Taylor, Bogdan, and DeVault, 2016). By contrast, we see these methods as complementing field observation and overlapping other basic approaches to social research.

Two other terms are also associated with this approach. Because much of field research examines a single social phenomenon or unit of analysis—for example, a particular community, organization, or small informal group—it becomes a *case study* (see Feagin, Orum, and Sjoberg, 1991). However, although many case studies involve field research, not all field research is restricted to the holistic analysis of a single setting or unit of analysis. Similarly, many field studies are called "ethnographies," a label derived from cultural anthropology. Ethnography refers to the description of a culture. In anthropology, it is assumed that this description is based on an extended stay in the field, where the investigator's aim is "to understand another way of life from the native point of view" (Spradley, 1980:3). Although this clearly falls within the purview of field research, ethnography is a less inclusive category.

Outside anthropology, field research has tended to focus substantively on community or ethnic groups, deviance and powerlessness, occupations and professions, and, more recently, aspects of everyday life. Some field studies of elites have been done (e.g., Ostrander, 1993; Morrill, 1995), but field research generally has entailed "studying down"—focusing on the poor, the powerless, and the marginal members of society.[1] Perhaps it is more difficult to gain access to the rich and powerful than it is to gain access to the "common person." Similarly, everyday aspects of social life are easier to locate than sporadic and uncommon events.

As you might imagine, there are an extraordinarily large number of "fields" in which to do field research. Consider, for example, some of the topics of studies that have been conducted in this tradition: becoming a doctor (H. S. Becker et al., 1961), "cooling out" men in singles bars and nightclubs (Snow, Robinson, and McCall, 1991), selling used cars (Browne, 1976b), doing undercover police work (Marx, 1988), playing Little League baseball (Fine, 1987), drug dealing and smuggling (Adler, 1993), waitressing (Paules, 1991), surviving with jobs that don't pay a living wage (Newman, 1999), becoming a boxer (Wacquant, 2004), and performing mountain search-and-rescue operations (Lois, 2003).

General Features of Field Research

To varying degrees, field research involves the following features:

1. Broad research questions dictate rudimentary and emergent decisions about research design.
2. Primary data collection is by means of direct observation in natural settings.

3. Unstructured and semistructured interviewing complement direct observation.
4. Most data analysis is qualitative.

Next we introduce several examples of field research as we flesh out the meaning of and variation in each of these features.

Rudimentary, Emergent Research Design

Unlike experiments and surveys, in which the elements of research design—hypothesis formation, measurement, sampling—are specified before data collection, design elements in field research usually are worked out during the course of the study.[2] Typically, field researchers begin with (1) broad substantive and theoretical questions and (2) a methodological approach based primarily on observation in natural settings. Neither of these desiderata permits a rigid research design. Because preconceived images may be misleading, researchers avoid preset hypotheses and instead let their observations in the field guide the formulation of hypotheses, the asking of questions, and sampling. And because the observed setting is not under the researcher's control and the social life of the setting typically is not known before the researcher enters the field, research design is necessarily emergent rather than predetermined. Let us examine sampling in field research to see the special design problems that this approach presents.

KEY POINT
Research design in field research is largely emergent rather than preplanned as sampling units, choosing topics, and deciding what questions to ask evolve during the course of research.

Initially, field research almost always involves the nonrandom selection of a small number of settings and subjects. The nature of field research generally focuses attention on interactive social units such as encounters, social relationships, organizations, and communities. These units are much less amenable to probability sampling techniques than the discrete individuals typically sampled in experiments and surveys. Smaller interactive units seldom can be enumerated before their occurrence; and studies of larger units—for example, a community, an area of the city, an organization—usually are restricted to the one case under investigation. The delicate operation of entering the field—of locating suitable observation sites and making fruitful contacts—also necessitates nonrandom selection. Convenience, accessibility, and happenstance by and large determine where researchers can begin to make observations, whom they will meet there, and whom they will find most informative. Finally, the time required to conduct field observations tends to restrict the possible sample size to a very small number of cases.

A field study of elementary school students illustrates these sampling restrictions. Jessica Calarco (2011) was interested in whether children's social class background encourages classroom behavior that creates different learning opportunities. Time and resources (she could not afford assistants) restricted her to a single research site that would allow her to observe middle- and working-class students interacting together in the same school setting. This requirement eliminated the vast majority of U.S. elementary schools, which have little class diversity. Eventually, she located a school in which a majority of students were middle class but a substantial minority (approximately 25 percent) came from working-class families. She was familiar with the school because one of her relatives was a district employee. Within this setting, again because of limited resources, she restricted her observations to 12 classrooms from the 3rd to the 5th grade.

Nonprobability sampling is also the norm once a researcher enters the field. The determination of a sampling frame, a necessary ingredient of probability sampling, presupposes a detailed knowledge of the field setting that researchers seldom have. Furthermore, the usual purposes of field research—to get an insider's view, to describe a particular social setting holistically, and to develop working hypotheses—do not require considerations of statistical generalization that underlie probability sampling. Sampling in field research, therefore, ordinarily is designed to enhance the informational value of one's observations by maximizing variation (Lincoln and Guba, 1985).

Maximizing variation may sound similar to purposive sampling for heterogeneity, described in Chapter 6, but there are some crucial differences. In purposive sampling for heterogeneity, which occurs before data collection, units of analysis are carefully selected on the basis of a priori assumptions and knowledge about the population to enhance generalizability. In field research, however, sampling plans emerge during the course of research for the purpose of extending the information already obtained. One way this is accomplished is by "serial selection of sample units" (Lincoln and Guba, 1985). Each unit (e.g., a person or setting) is selected and analyzed one at a time. Other units are then selected to extend, fill in gaps, or test the information obtained so far. This might be accomplished by asking initial contacts to identify others, as in snowball sampling. Since the purpose is to maximize information, sampling ceases when no new information is forthcoming.

Another way to maximize variability is to identify and sample relevant dimensions of units. Typical dimensions include time and space; variations in either can serve to protect against bias as well as increase the scope of the observations. For example, during her more than 2 years in the field, Calarco visited the school two times a week for about 3 hours per visit. To maximize her exposure to various activities, she divided her "time equally between four classes in each grade and rotated days and times [she] observed each class." During this time, she observed "regular classes, enrichment classes, lunch, recess, and other school activities (e.g., assemblies and field-days)" (Calarco, 2011:866).

Research questions that emerge in the field can help to focus data collection and identify relevant dimensions for sampling. In a study of police work, for example, one might ask, "How do police officers interpret laws when arresting and booking suspects?" (Miles and Huberman, 1994:30). This research question suggests the dimensions of setting (e.g., precinct station, squad car, crime scene), actors (police officers and suspects with different characteristics), events (e.g., arrests and bookings), and processes (e.g., making the arrest, relating to suspects, interpreting laws) (Miles and Huberman, 1994).

A related strategy, called **theoretical sampling** (Glaser and Strauss, 1967), is to sample broad analytical categories that will facilitate the development of theoretical insights. In other words, sampling is directed toward gathering information relevant to a specific working hypothesis or theory. For example, in a field study of altruism, you may decide that the time required to perform an altruistic act and the amount of physical risk or suffering incurred are important factors in your developing theory of altruism. To incorporate such variability in your study, you might investigate acts that involve different time commitments (e.g., cash contributions versus volunteer work) and acts that cause different levels of hardship (e.g., donating blood versus donating a kidney).

Although it is rarely possible, rigorous sampling can occur in the field. Murray Melbin's research (1969) on behavioral disturbances in mental hospitals provides an example of the use of probability sampling techniques in a field study. Melbin found that among patients in a small private mental hospital, far more unusual disturbances (e.g., walking around naked, making animal-like noises, lying stiffly in front of a doorway) occurred on weekdays than on evenings and weekends but that this pattern did not appear in a large state institution nearby. In making his observations, Melbin chose times and places according to a probability sampling design. First, he listed all sites in each hospital where patients could be found, and he apportioned the waking hours of the day into 2-hour units. Then, he randomly selected combinations of site, time, and day of the week for observation. Melbin concluded that patients tended to behave crazily when they could get the attention of professional treatment personnel—psychiatrists, social workers, and psychologists. The private hospital had an ample professional staff, which was present on weekdays and Saturday mornings, whereas the state hospital had far fewer professionals available at any time.

Melbin's study notwithstanding, probability sampling is rarely used in field research. Melbin had the luxury of three other trained observers to help record observations. And even though he did not use pre-established observational categories, his observations were much more restricted—specifically to the conduct of aides and patients—than in most field studies.

The sampling methods and philosophy of field research are in some ways similar to experimental research. The primary objective of experiments is to achieve a rigorous test of a hypothesis. This focuses attention on the internal validity of the research design; generalizability, a secondary issue, is achieved by varying the operationalizations and experimental context in subsequent studies. Field research similarly emphasizes the internal validity of the study, albeit with a different objective, to understand naturally occurring social events and processes; generalizability to other populations and settings is secondary to clarifying one's theoretical understanding by means of dimensional and theoretical sampling.

Direct Observation in Natural Settings

The primary method of data collection in field research is observation. Field researchers nearly always begin with field observations; even when they turn to other data sources such as interviewing "informants" or analyzing personal documents, these data generally serve as supplemental evidence or cross-checks on their observations.

The kind of observation conducted by field researchers differs from both casual, everyday observation and generic "scientific observation." George McCall (1984:264) noted that "while nearly everyone who goes to a zoo *sees* the animals there, and many even *watch* some of those animals, very few can be said to *observe* their behavior." In contrast to casual watching, field observation is planned, methodically carried out, and intended to extract meaningful interpretations of the social world. This differs from other forms of scientific observation in two important ways. First, whereas the latter can be both direct and indirect, field observation involves *direct observation*, usually with the naked eye, rather than the sort of indirect observation that characterizes respondents' reports in questionnaires or interviews. Second, field observation takes place in a *natural setting*, not in a laboratory or other contrived situation. Observations made in the field also tend to be less structured than those made in the laboratory, although this is not an essential difference. Field research varies in structure, but it differs primarily in terms of the extent to which the researcher actively participates in the social setting being observed. At one extreme is a passive and intentionally unobtrusive nonparticipant observer; at the other is an active and intentionally involved participant observer.

Nonparticipant Observation

A nonparticipant observer is, in effect, an eavesdropper, someone who attempts to observe people without interacting with them and, typically, without their knowing that they are being observed. This form of observation often is used in conjunction with participant observation, especially in the early stages of research when one is reconnoitering a social setting as preparation for more intensive study (R. L. Gold, 1958). As a separate, inclusive method, however, **nonparticipant observation** is comparatively little used, despite its amenability to studies of social phenomena. It has been applied most routinely in the field by psychologists studying children and animals.

Direct scientific observation involves the selection, recording, and encoding of behavior and events. *Selection* refers to the fact that scientific observers make intentional and unintentional choices about what to observe and record (Weick, 1968). *Recording* consists of making records of events (e.g., by taking field notes), and *encoding* involves the simplification of records (e.g., by categorizing or counting the frequency of different behaviors) (Weick, 1968). All of these processes may be more or less structured. Observation is **structured** when it uses explicit and preset plans for selection, recording, and encoding of data; it is **unstructured** to the extent that these processes are implicit and emergent (McCall, 1984).

A good example of unstructured, nonparticipant observation is Lyn Lofland's study (1971, 1973) of how people in cities—strangers in public places—relate to one another in terms of appearance and spatial location. Although Lofland drew on other materials, her study was based largely on hundreds of hours of observations. She made the observations in and around Ann Arbor and Detroit, Michigan, in bus depots, airports, libraries, stores, restaurants, bars, theaters, and parks; aboard buses; and on the streets. In most of these settings, she was able to "blend into the scenery," even for periods of several hours. Imagining herself viewing others through a one-way mirror, Lofland attempted to record everything within her line of vision. She did not systematically sample observation sites or resort to checklists for recording behavior. As the study progressed, she concentrated at times on certain kinds of behavior—for example, seating patterns and entrance behavior—but in general she simply recorded as much as she could.

One of Lofland's observation sites was a glass-walled hallway, called the "Fishbowl," between two buildings on the University of Michigan campus. Here, she became sensitized to the "grooming" actions people go through as they are about to enter a public setting. Lofland (1971:303) describes how she made this discovery:

> One wall of the Fishbowl, the one which contains the doors, is solid glass, so that whenever I happened to be observing from a bench close to the doors, I could not fail to be struck by the preparation behavior that occurred over and over again as student after student neared the door, stopped, groomed himself [or herself], and then entered. There were many instances of this behavior recorded in my notes before I ever "recognized" it as a pattern, but once I did, I was led to look for similar activities in other settings and eventually to "see" the full entrance sequence.

Lofland maintains that some of her discoveries were made possible by her prolonged periods of observation in only a few sites. This provided sufficient familiarity with the settings to enable her to recognize faces and to make important distinctions among the different inhabitants, such as residents, patrons, customers, and newcomers. If her observations had been more structured, it seems unlikely that she would have discovered many of the patterns she reports. However, more structured observation could have provided other important kinds of sociological information, such as the duration and frequency of occurrence of the behavior patterns Lofland observed.

KEY POINT

Unstructured observation allows for the discovery of behavioral patterns; *structured observation* can be used to measure the duration and frequency of those patterns.

The early phase of most field research involves relatively unstructured observation. As a researcher gains a greater understanding of the setting, his or her observations may become more selective and structured. For example, an investigator may become increasingly specific about when and where to observe; what specific aspects of the setting or behavior to observe; and how to make and record the observations. As the research is delimited in this way, even more structure may be introduced in the form of area and time sampling of observation sites and checklists or other more elaborate schemes for categorizing behavior.

A good example of the progression from unstructured to structured observation is Calarco's field study of social class and help-seeking behavior among elementary school children. Initially, Calarco observed and recorded as much as possible that was happening within the classroom, including interactions between students and their peers as well as between students and teachers. After collecting data on students' class backgrounds (from surveys of their families), she noticed an interesting divergence in student–teacher interactions along class lines in terms of students' seeking help. This led her to systematically count student's help seeking during her last 6 months in the field. First, she created observational categories of help seeking based on her previous observations: requests for assistance, clarification, information, and checking of work. Then she counted students' requests for help during 16 four-hour sessions in four classrooms. Results showed that middle-class children sought help from teachers far more often than their working-class peers.

The advantage of structured observation lies in its greater control of sampling and measurement error, which permits stronger generalizations and checks on reliability and validity. We can see how this is possible in one of the relatively few sociological studies of this type, an investigation of crime and law enforcement by Albert Reiss (1967). Among other things, Reiss observed police–citizen transactions in eight high-crime areas of three large cities. To do so, he assigned 12 observers and a supervisor to each city. Because he wished to generalize about transactions with citizens, Reiss (1968:358) sampled several units: "days of the week, watches of the day, and the officer based unit of the beat within precincts." He also used standardized procedures for recording observations. Following each 8-hour period of observation, observers completed booklets for each encounter of 2 minutes or longer. Each booklet contained a sequence of questions about the transaction. By systematically recording observations and using multiple observers, Reiss was able to show that the race of the observer was related to differences in reporting of officer deviance: White observers were less likely than black observers to report the undue use of force among black officers. Thus, he was able to uncover a source of error that in all likelihood would have gone undetected in a solo unstructured observation study.

With highly structured observation, it is assumed that the categories of observation established by a researcher reflect the meaning of events to those who are studied. Because field researchers tend to challenge this assumption, most fieldwork develops "relevant categories and analytical distinctions over the course of the study" and does not use pre-established, standardized schedules for recording observations (Emerson, 1981:352).[3] In the remainder of the chapter, therefore, we will concentrate on field research that is less structured than the Reiss (1967) study.

Participant Observation

Historically, field research has been associated most closely with **participant observation**. In ideal descriptions of this method, the observer is said to participate actively, for an extended period of time, in the daily lives of the people and situations under study. This may require that the observer live or work in an area; it clearly assumes that the observer will become an accepted member of the group or community, able to speak informally with the people—to "joke with them, empathize with them, and share their concerns and experiences" (Bogdan and Taylor, 1975:5).

Despite the tidiness of this description, however, there is a fine line between nonparticipant and participant observation. As with the dimension of structure in observational studies, participation is a matter of degree. Some would argue that even a relatively unobtrusive observer sitting at a table in a restaurant taking notes influences the situation by virtue of his or her mere presence; thus, however unwittingly, such an observer is also a participant. Calarco was primarily an observer, but she also participated by freely interacting with teachers and students in the classroom and occasionally assisting teachers with organizational tasks.

It is more accurate, therefore, to think of the two types of field observation as poles of a continuum. At one extreme is a participant observer who becomes completely absorbed in the group under observation; at the other is a nonparticipant observer who tries to remain aloof from it. Because field research is rarely either detached observation, on the one hand, or embroiled participation, on the other, participation often becomes a question of "how much." To fully immerse oneself in the situation is to risk altering the events one observes and perhaps even losing sight of one's role as researcher. But field researchers argue that these risks are small compared with the benefits to be gained from being a participant. A stranger to a situation may easily take a word, a sigh, or other gesture or a relationship for something wholly different from what it means to a participant.

The kind of understanding fieldworkers hope to gain is based on shared meanings. As the anthropologist Rosalie Wax (1971:11) points out,

> A fieldworker who approaches a strange people soon perceives that these people are saying and doing things which *they* understand but he [or she] does not understand. One of the strangers may make a particular gesture, whereupon all the other strangers laugh. They share in the understanding of what the gesture means, but the fieldworker does not. When he [or she] does share it, he [or she] begins to "understand." He [or she] possesses part of the "insider's" view.

To appreciate the importance of obtaining an insider's view, imagine that you are one of the subjects of someone else's field research. Assume for a moment that your place of work, a club you belong to, the church you attend, a class you are taking, or a favorite tavern you visit is the setting for the researcher's observations. Now think of all the things that the researcher would have to learn to make appropriate judgments about the activities of the group. What do you know so well that you take for granted about the job (e.g., how the places where people take their coffee breaks serve to reinforce territorial influence and status in the workplace), the conduct of the club's business (e.g., how the president influences the opinions of certain members), the symbols of your church (e.g., how the theology of your religion makes these symbols meaningful), the daily affairs of the class (e.g., what seating patterns mean in terms of social cliques), or the differences among customers at the tavern (e.g., differences among regulars and casual visitors in terms of where they sit and how they are served)?

Even if this same researcher used you as an informant to help him or her understand the situation, there will be features that you are likely to forget, not convey accurately and completely, or omit because their understanding is assumed. In short, it is difficult to imagine full comprehension without a heavy dose of participation. Everything that you know about these various settings you learned because of your activity as a participant.

Thus, to fully understand the shared meanings of a group, the first step is to become a participant or insider. In time, participant observers must be able to think and act within the perspective of two different social worlds—the one in which they were reared and the one they are studying. But eventually they hope to be able to step outside both these worlds, for social scientists must realize "that while the outsider simply does not know the meanings of patterns, the insider is so immersed that he may be oblivious to the fact that patterns exist" (Wax, 1971:3).

Becoming a participant observer carries with it some risks. It can be an emotionally stressful experience for a researcher (see J. Lofland et al., 2006). William Shaffir, Robert

Stebbins, and Allan Turowetz (1980:3) describe fieldwork as "usually inconvenient, to say the least, sometimes physically uncomfortable, frequently embarrassing, and, to a degree, always tense." In the early days in the field, before learning the ropes, researchers are likely to experience awkward and embarrassing encounters; after a while they may become sensitive to hostile and suspicious challenges to their intentions and "observer" role. Eventually, researchers may come to loathe the people under observation and wish to withdraw or may identify so strongly with the group that they cease their research. Finally, after being in the field for so long and developing deep attachments, researchers often find it difficult to leave.

Balancing the requirements of both participating and observing can be challenging. To gain an insider's view, you must gain the acceptance of those you are studying; to be accepted, you must become actively involved in others' activities. However, it often is difficult to know where to draw the line. It is not unusual for fieldworkers to witness and to be pressured to participate in physically dangerous or morally or legally questionable activities (Taylor, Bogdan, and DeVault, 2016). For example, Albert Reiss (1968:362–63) described an observer who had the role of plainclothes detective thrust on him by the police officer he was observing:

> The officer arrested two citizens, and one began to flee. The officer in this case turned to the observer, handed him his nightstick, and said: "Hold him." He then chased the fleeing man. The observer obeyed and, what is more, as he held the man against the patrol car, the man resisted and attempted to flee. And then . . . the observer threatened the citizen with the nightstick.

Reiss contended that his assistant in this case clearly went too far, that he should have responded as Reiss himself had in a similar situation—by refusing the nightstick and reminding the officer that he was an observer. However, subjects usually come to treat participant observers as at least "quasi"-members of the team or group and expect them to participate, such as by assisting a police officer in holding a suspect. Refusal to participate may jeopardize the observer's relations with subjects and his or her continued presence in the field.

To make the issue even more complicated, there may be sins of omission involved in maintaining observer distance. The sociologist Don Zimmerman (personal communication, 1986) once found himself in a situation where a social worker he was observing discovered a very young child abandoned by her caretaker. Leaving the child alone, the worker returned to the office to report the situation. Her supervisor responded by immediately calling the police and reprimanding the worker. For not assuming custody of the child, she and Zimmerman could have been held criminally culpable. Zimmerman was uncomfortable about leaving the child, but his research plan called for strict nonintervention in the work activities of the social workers. Thus, he faced a difficult ethical dilemma in which his research plan conflicted with his personal values and civic duty. It also could be said, by the way, that Reiss's assistant performed a civic duty by assisting the officer in holding the suspect. As these examples show, the issues in balancing participant and observer roles are seldom as easy or clear-cut as they seem.

Unstructured and Semistructured Interviewing

Besides observing and nearly always participating in the social worlds they study, field researchers converse with the people in those worlds. Sometimes these conversations involve mere chitchat, part of being a participant, but often they take the form of formal interviews. In either case, interviews are unstructured or semistructured.

Interviewing in field research may serve many purposes. It is impossible to observe everything in a setting or scene; many relevant events will occur in the researcher's absence, and there may be other revealing information to which the researcher is not privy. Therefore, field researchers typically rely on the careful questioning of other participants, called **informants**, to gain information. Another important purpose of interviewing is to question members or participants about their feelings, motives, and interpretations of events. These reactions not only are likely to be of direct interest to researchers but also often serve as critical validity checks on the researcher's inferences.

There are two basic forms of interviewing in the field. Most interviewing occurs informally, in ordinary conversations and as a natural extension of participant observation. Initially, such casual interviewing may entail orientation questions, as researchers get acclimated in a setting. For example, "Where can I find this?" "Who is she?" or "What does she do?" Eventually, the questions are aimed at expanding information about specific actions and events and probing their deeper meaning. John Lofland and Lyn Lofland (1995:70) note that field researchers devote much of their time to asking questions such as these:

> What do you think she meant by that?
> What are they supposed to do?
> Why did she do that?
> Why is that done?
> What happens after _____?
> What would happen if _____?
> What do you think about _____?
> Who is responsible if _____?

KEY POINT

To get an insider's view of reality, field researchers participate in the settings they observe and interview participants in those settings.

After researchers have been in the field for a while and have begun to develop an understanding of the setting, they may conduct formal interviews with informants to secure more detailed information on individuals, to get different perspectives on events, and to round out and check information already obtained. This was an important source of data in the help-seeking study. Calarco had numerous informal conversations with teachers. But in addition, she formally interviewed teachers from each of the 12 classrooms she was observing, "asking about their expectations for students and about students' home lives, academic strengths and weaknesses, and progress over time" (Calarco, 2011:866).

Formal **in-depth**, or intensive, **interviews** are scheduled in advance, are much less structured than those in surveys, and take much longer, often requiring several sessions. Indeed, in-depth interviews with one or more subjects can become a major source of data in the field. For studying phenomena that lack a geographical base or transcend particular settings, intensive interviewing may be the best way to proceed (Kleinman, Stenross, and McMahon, 1994; J. Lofland et al., 2006). This method, sometimes with limited field observation, has been applied effectively, for example, in studies of chronic illness (Charmaz, 1991), divorce (Kohler Riessman, 1990), poor single mothers (Edin and Lein, 1997), and assimilation and ethnic identity among first- and second-generation Mexican Americans (Vasquez, 2011).

Intensive interviews do not proceed without significant preparation and always are guided by specific topics and themes that the researcher wants to pursue. Rather than create the sort of standardized interview schedule found in surveys, however, field interviewers develop what is known as an **interview guide** (J. Lofland et al., 2006; Kvale, 1996). Interview guides stem from the general topic of investigation and from ideas and hypotheses that emerge in the field. They may consist merely of an outline of topics in some logical order or they may contain many specific questions, arranged thematically. In either case, the interview generally progresses from questions about concrete situations to more abstract and interpretive questions that probe an informant's experience and interpretation of events. Furthermore, the order of the questions and their exact wording will depend on the background of the informant and the general course of the conversation. Rather than rigidly follow a series of questions worked out in advance, an interviewee's answers shape "what the researcher subsequently asks," as in a normal conversation. And "the researcher customizes questions for each interviewee, accommodating both to what the person knows and to the topics that [he or she] is most comfortable discussing" (H. J. Rubin and Rubin, 2012:7).

Calvin Morrill's (1995) field study of conflict management among corporate executives offers a good example of field interviewing. Morrill spent 2 years doing intensive fieldwork that included individual and group observation as well as informal and formal interviews. The informal interviews with executives and their staff were carried out during their daily routines. Many of these interviews consisted of "nothing more than a few conversational turns," whereas others stretched for an hour or more as Morrill and his informant "shot the breeze" (243). Usually, Morrill asked direct questions to elicit information, but he also used a procedure called "interviewing by comment" (see Snow, Zurcher, and Sjoberg, 1982). For example, to prompt the informant to say more, he repeated an informant's statement or acted puzzled by making comments such as "I don't quite follow you" or "I don't understand." In the same manner, he also got informants' views by trying out hypotheses about particular situations.

Morrill conducted the formal interviews, lasting from 30 minutes to nearly 6 hours, in various locales—"in executives' private offices, favorite eating and drinking establishments, and homes" (241). For these semistructured interviews, he developed an interview guide, based on his first 30 interviews, that contained clusters of questions. Initial questions asked about the nature of the informants' position and the organizational context.

For example, "How many employees does _____ have?" "How many executives are at the executive levels?" or "What are your responsibilities here at _____?" (245). As the executives described their work, Morrill focused the questions on communications, and then he turned to issues that someone studying managers would be expected to want to know. For example, "What characteristics do you believe make an executive effective?" or "How is performance measured at the executive level?" (246). These questions led to more personal questions about the informants themselves, for example, about their educational background, work history, and the strengths they brought to their current position. Finally, later in single interviews or in follow-up interviews, Morrill asked questions designed to produce information on trouble cases within the corporation. Once he identified these cases, he probed further to learn "the basis of the conflict, its management, and its participants and their relationships and backgrounds" (244).

To maintain as much consistency as possible, Morrill attempted to ask this repertoire of questions of every executive. But typical of field interviewing, the questions served mainly as a skeletal outline as he varied their wording and order as the situation required. For example, whenever he detected information on organizational conflicts, he immediately plied the informant for more details. Some informants were reluctant and uneasy about answering questions; others were quickly drawn into the conversation and gave detailed information about their corporations that in effect anticipated the questions on Morrill's interview guide. Morrill also noted that he always "attempted to maintain an even emotional balance—not too excited, but interested" (244). As his time in the field progressed, he became adept at reading verbal and nonverbal cues that communicated reluctance or rapport. Finally, if an executive appeared anxious toward the end of the interview, especially after disclosing conflicts, Morrill ended with wrap-up, noncontroversial questions to put the informant at ease; for example, "What are the company's goals at present?" or "What do you look forward to in your job in the near and long term?" (248).

Qualitative Data Analysis

The principal data in field research consist of words and text generated by recorded observations and transcribed verbatim statements of informants and interviewees. In other words, the data are inherently qualitative; they cannot be transformed easily into numerical values and subjected to statistical analysis. Still, like quantitative analyses in surveys, the analysis of qualitative data is both descriptive and explanatory.

Field researchers aim to describe the people and settings they are investigating from the viewpoint of participants. One way they do this is using direct quotations; another way is to impart details of the social context. Both of these elements are apparent in Calarco's examples of help seeking. In one instance, as she describes:

> Students were working on practice problems using protractors to draw angles. While Ms. Dunham was writing the homework assignment on the board, Anna, an athletic middle-class girl with long, dark hair called out for assistance:
>
>> Anna looks up at Dunham and calls out loudly: "Ms. Dunham! I need help! Ms. Dunham!"

Ms. Dunham glances over at Anna, who is sitting on the rug at the back of the room, struggling to draw angles. Ms. Dunham nods, noting distractedly: "I'll be there soon."

Anna, however, does not give up, adding: "I can't get it to stay so I can do 170 degrees."

At this, Ms. Dunham immediately moved toward Anna, squatting down and showing her how to hold the protractor. (Calarco, 2011:869)

In qualitative analysis, *explanation* is arrived at through a process of coding words or fragments of text into meaningful units, identifying themes and patterns, and then developing theoretical interpretations. We discuss this process later in the chapter as we flesh out the stages of field research. In addition to reading and rereading field notes and transcripts, field researchers often use computer software programs as analytic aids. Calarco (2011:866–67) used ATLAS.ti software to code and link different data sources, including recorded observations, interview transcripts, and other documents, which "allowed [her] to identify common themes in the data (e.g., seeking assistance, seeking clarification, raising hands, and interrupting) and to assess how themes occurred in relation to situations and participants."

Stages of Field Research

As we have noted before, scientific investigations rarely proceed smoothly in a neat sequence of steps. This is especially true of field research. Nevertheless, we can identify a series of essential problems faced by all field researchers, even if they do not always occur in a prescribed sequence. Figure 11.1 shows the overlapping stages in conducting a field study. The major problems, considered in the following sections, are (1) selecting a research setting, (2) gaining access to the setting, (3) presenting oneself, (4) gathering information in the field, and (5) analyzing the information and developing a theoretical scheme for interpretation. To provide an overview, we first summarize a field study.

A Field Study of the Homeless

Beginning in the mid-1970s, evidence of increasing homelessness in America generated much public interest and debate. Correspondingly, social researchers began conducting studies of homelessness in communities throughout the country. Most of these studies shared two characteristics: (1) they were based on questionnaire surveys and (2) they were concerned primarily with describing personal characteristics and disabilities of the homeless, such as mental illness and alcoholism (Snow and Anderson, 1991:150). Peter Rossi's 1989 study, the sampling design for which was discussed in Chapter 6, typifies this approach. Rossi used 15- to 20-minute interviews with randomly selected homeless individuals to estimate the number and characteristics of the homeless population of Chicago.

For nearly a year and a half in the mid-1980s, David Snow and Leon Anderson (1987, 1991) conducted a field study of homeless individuals living in or passing through Austin, Texas. In contrast to most other studies of homelessness, they were interested in understanding

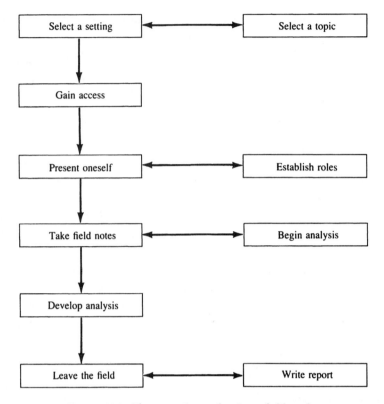

FIGURE 11.1. The stages in conducting a field study.

the nature of street life as experienced by the homeless themselves. In particular, they wanted to examine how homeless individuals managed their daily existence—the routines and strategies they used to subsist and survive and the factors that shaped these routines and strategies.

Field observations of the homeless were made over a period of 1 year, from September 1, 1984, to August 31, 1985, with Anderson as the principal ethnographer. His strategy was to "hang out" with as many homeless "individuals as possible on a daily basis, spending time with them in varied settings (e.g., meal and shelter lines, under bridges, in parks, at day-labor pickup sites), over the course of the twelve-month period" (1987:1342). In the end, he spent more than 400 hours in 24 different settings with 168 homeless individuals. In addition, Snow spent another 200 hours negotiating access to records and interviewing police officers, local political officials, and personnel of agencies serving the homeless.

The principal data were based on direct observation of and interaction with homeless people, especially listening to their conversations. Although Anderson asked questions and probed from time to time, mostly he engaged in relatively unobtrusive listening that took two basic forms: (1) eavesdropping (e.g., listening to others while waiting in meal lines) and (2) ordinary conversational listening when interacting with two or more homeless individuals. Some of these persons were apprised of Anderson's researcher status and some were not. Yet the nature of the encounters maintained the naturalness of the setting and of people's reactions. Even when the homeless people knew Anderson's true status, they typically lost sight of it "as he continued to spend time on the street with them, dressed in old clothes, and more or less walked in their shoes" (1987:1343).

Data from observations and conversations were recorded in two steps. First, while in the field, Anderson took mental notes and jotted down key phrases and words to aid his recall of particular events. Second, as soon as possible after leaving the field, he elaborated this information into a detailed narrative account. As an aid to this process, Anderson routinely met with Snow to review his field experiences, discuss their methodological and theoretical implications, and make plans for subsequent observations.

As the study unfolded, Snow and Anderson attempted to identify the range of relevant social settings and types of homeless persons who existed on the streets of Austin. This informed their sampling strategy of maximizing variation, which involved spending "time with as many homeless as possible in the range of settings most relevant to their daily lives" (1991:155).

Initially, they organized their daily recordings into three major coding categories: single focal settings (e.g., the Salvation Army, plasma centers, parks, bars), cultural domains (e.g., drinking and alcohol, sleeping and shelter, work, social relationships), and homeless individuals. Each piece of information was assigned to one or more of these categories. They soon discovered, however, that some "settings and domains were more central than others to the lives and daily routines of the homeless" (1987:1345). One of these, which was unanticipated, was the identity and self-concept domain. Snow and Anderson were surprised by the amount of talk among the people who attempted to generate personal identities that provided them with a measure of self-worth and dignity.

Different patterns of "identity talk" were identified. One of these was called "associational distancing," such as disassociating oneself from homeless persons as a social category. For example, one individual who had been on the streets for less than 2 weeks said, "I'm not like the other guys who hang out down at the 'Sally' [Salvation Army]. If you want to know about street people, I can tell you about them; but you can't really learn about street people from studying me, because I'm different" (1987:1349). Another pattern was labeled "fictive storytelling." This involves stories about one's experiences and accomplishments that are clearly embellished to some degree, such as (1) exaggerated claims regarding past or current wages and (2) fantasies about the future. For example, some homeless persons fantasized about becoming rich. As one said, "You might laugh and think I'm crazy, but I'm going to be rich. I know it. I just have this feeling. I can't explain it, but I am" (1987:1361).

There were many other important findings as well, but a consideration of these would go well beyond the purpose of this example: to convey the process of conducting a field study. In the remainder of the chapter we will make reference to and elaborate on other features of Snow and Anderson's research.

Selecting a Research Setting

One must begin somewhere; and for a field researcher, the first problem is deciding *where* to begin. How do you select an appropriate site in which to conduct your study? With regard to participant observation, Steven Taylor, Robert Bogdan, and Marjorie DeVault (2016) describe the ideal setting as one that is directly related to the researcher's interests, is easily accessible, and allows for the development of immediate rapport with informants. This ideal is seldom realized, however. The homeless study satisfied the first two criteria. The site of the study—Austin, Texas—was also the location of the University of Texas, where Snow and Anderson were, respectively, a professor and a graduate student. Austin served their purposes well not only because of its proximity but also because of the relatively large and rapidly increasing number of homeless individuals living there in the mid-1980s. Immediate rapport, however, is difficult in any setting where a researcher enters as a stranger. Furthermore, broad research questions that guide field research rarely point to a particular setting. It is not uncommon, in fact, for investigators to end up in settings that are ill-suited to their interests (Geer, 1964). Consequently, the setting itself may dictate research interests because it is only after entering the field and beginning to make observations that a researcher comes to know exactly what theoretical issues may be explored.

Regardless of the extent of a researcher's participation, the setting should permit clear observation. To nonparticipants, it is also important not to alter the naturalness of the setting by making participants aware that they are being observed. The counterpart of this rule for participant observers is to select a setting where they can participate naturally and easily become an accepted and familiar part of the surroundings. Finally, given the time required for this type of research, the setting should be as accessible as possible.

Together, these criteria suggest that novice field researchers might do well to select a setting close at hand where they can readily fit in. This does not necessarily mean a setting with which they are intimately familiar. In familiar settings, especially where they have a direct personal or professional stake, researchers often experience problems in overcoming their own views of reality and of holding their feelings in abeyance (Taylor, Bogdan, and DeVault, 2016). It is extremely difficult to be able to treat the familiar as new and to observe more as a researcher in a familiar setting than you observe as a natural participant. Still, John Lofland and associates (2006:9) suggest that the best starting place for field research may be "where you are." Noting that a good deal of field research is born out of accidents of the "current biography" of the researcher, they say, "A job; a physical mishap; the development, loss or maintenance of an intimate relationship; an illness; an enjoyed activity; a living arrangement—all these and many other possible circumstances may provide you with a topic you can care about enough to study" (9–10). Thus, for Lofland and associates, starting where you are is a matter of interest as well as access to a social setting.

This approach has a long history dating to the 1920s and 1930s at the University of Chicago, where students were encouraged to build on their experience and to use the city as their "lab" (see Box 11.1). An example of this tradition is Mitchell Duneier's (1992) description of the men who frequented "Slim's table" at a cafeteria where he ate meals as a graduate student at the University of Chicago. Other examples of starting where you are (see also J. Lofland et al., 2006:11) include Julius Roth's study (1963) of the passage of time in a hospital, based on his experience as a tuberculosis patient; Lawrence Ouellet's study (1994) of truckers, developed from his job as a truck driver which he took to support himself while in graduate school; and a study called *Synagogue Life* by Samuel Heilman (1976), who as an Orthodox Jew had joined the synagogue before the conception of his study. In each of these cases, the researcher "naturally" belonged in the setting but was new to it, so his degree of familiarity did not encumber his observations.

BOX 11.1 Origins of Field Research

Modern field research traces its origins to two related traditions, one in anthropology and one in sociology.* Ethnographic fieldwork, the study of native cultures by learning the native language and observing and taking part in native life, originated with the founders of modern anthropology: the German-trained Franz Boas (1858–1942) and the Polish-born British social anthropologist Bronislaw Malinowski (1884–1942). Before the work of these two men, anthropology was largely an armchair discipline relying on the testimonies of explorers, missionaries, and colonial officials for its data.

Boas, who did research on Native Americans, was particularly concerned about how the biases of Western culture affected understanding of native life. He believed that only by living among native peoples and learning the language of native thought could one come to see the world as natives saw it. Malinowski, whose major field studies took him to the Pacific islands, was the first anthropologist to provide a detailed account of how he carried out his fieldwork. These two field researchers reoriented the whole field of cultural anthropology. They and their students (e.g., Margaret Mead, Ruth Benedict, Alfred Kroeber) made it possible by their methodology to get an insider's view of the culture. This goal of understanding the subject's point of view remains a central feature of field research.

Another major source of modern field research is the social reform tradition of sociology. This tradition is as old as sociology itself. However, it became more empirically oriented toward the end of the nineteenth century as social reformers and sociologists turned first to social surveys and then to a more varied methodology based primarily on field observation. In the United States, the latter approach became identified with the so-called Chicago school of sociology. One of the key figures was W. I. Thomas (1863–1947), who, with his collaborator Florian Znaniecki, published a monumental study, *The Polish Peasant in Europe and America* (1918). This work contributed to the field approach by its use of a variety of techniques, including the examination of letters and life histories. Thomas also advocated the importance of understanding the individual's own "definition of the situation" as part of a more self-conscious theoretical analysis.

More than Thomas, however, it was Robert Park (1864–1944) who established the place of field research in modern sociology. Educated in Germany and trained as a journalist, Park was for many years the chairperson of the sociology department at the University of Chicago. Park and his associates at Chicago inspired a generation of researchers who used the city as their social laboratory. There they investigated pickpockets, police, juvenile gangs, the Jewish ghetto, hobos, taxi-hall dancers, and other assorted groups and areas of the city. They were guided by the desire to ameliorate the problems of city living, which they saw as the natural outcome of urban crowding. One might say that Park's participant observers contributed to our understanding of different urban subcultures in much the same way that Boas- and Malinowski-inspired ethnographers promoted our understanding of different cultures.

*Although it was not until the late nineteenth and early twentieth centuries that this became a self-conscious method of social research, some aspects of field research are as old as recorded history. (See Hughes [1960] and Wax [1971] for historical sketches of "fieldwork.")

Starting where you are also is likely to facilitate a researcher's efforts in other ways. Field research is not easy work. A good field researcher must be able to feel comfortable in the presence of informants who are almost always, at least at the outset, strangers and must be able to make these informants feel comfortable as well. The ability to develop rapport is not a skill that each of us possesses to the same degree. An optimal site, therefore, may be one that encourages ease in the researcher.

Gaining Access

How do you go about getting into a group that you wish to study? The answer to this question depends first on the nature of the group or setting. If the setting is a formal organization, one should seek permission from those in charge, referred to as **gatekeepers** in field research. Obtaining permission may be facilitated by having a friend vouch for the researcher or by getting one's foot in the door, as by first visiting or volunteering to serve the organization in some way.

If the setting is public (e.g., park, street corner, public restroom), you may not need to negotiate access as an observer, although we recommend informing the police or other proper authority about what you are doing. In the homeless study, Snow negotiated and legitimated access to several settings for his partner Anderson. If the setting is semipublic (e.g., bar, theater, store), it is generally a good idea to speak to the manager or owner before you begin your research. It is almost impossible to spend long periods in public places without having to give a proper account of oneself. Observers can be arrested for loitering and may be suspected of shoplifting when hanging around a store. Anderson was arrested and jailed for violation of an open-container ordinance with two homeless men one evening. He was bailed out the same night, and as a result of prior negotiations with the local police, "his arrest record was subsequently expunged from the police file and the arresting officer was reprimanded" (Snow, Benford, and Anderson, 1986:395). The best practice, therefore, is to seek the cooperation of those who are likely to question what you are doing.

As a participant, you also will have to figure out ways of interacting with people and, if necessary, of becoming an accepted member of the group (Taylor, Bogdan, and DeVault, 2016). The usual recommendation is simply to station yourself at an active spot and try to engage people in casual conversation. Anderson began by hanging out at the Salvation Army facility, Austin's only public shelter for the homeless, where he simply struck up conversations with strangers. Yet, there can be problems with this seemingly innocuous approach. Since people are wary of strangers, researchers must be careful that their intentions are not misconstrued. Consider a classic field study conducted by William Foote Whyte (1993) in an Italian neighborhood in Boston. Having been advised that he could learn a great deal by visiting a tavern, striking up a conversation with a woman, and buying her a drink, Whyte decided to try this approach. As he recounts,

> With some trepidation I climbed the stairs to the bar and entertainment area and looked around. . . . There were women present all right, but none of them was alone. Some were there in couples, and there were two or three pairs of women together.

I pondered this situation briefly. I had little confidence in my skill at picking up one female, and it seemed inadvisable to tackle two at the same time. Still, I was determined not to admit defeat without a struggle. I looked around me again and now noticed a threesome: one man and two women. It occurred to me that here was a maldistribution of females which I might be able to rectify. I approached the group and opened with something like this: Pardon me. Would you mind if I joined you? There was a moment of silence while the man stared at me. He then offered to throw me downstairs. (1993:289)

Later, Whyte had the good fortune to be introduced by a social worker to someone, referred to as "Doc," who would be instrumental in his gaining entry into "Cornerville." Doc became Whyte's closest friend, sponsor, and major source of information. The key to opening doors in the community, such persons are called **key informants** by field researchers. Not only was Doc able to introduce Whyte to many people from the neighborhood, but also Doc himself was well regarded in the community. Being introduced as Doc's friend thus gained Whyte immediate acceptance by people who were willing to accept any friend of Doc. Still, just as Whyte was able to bask in Doc's light, so too would he have been cast into Doc's shadow if Doc had been held in low regard by the community.

One of the problems with relying on contacts in a strange group is that one cannot always be certain how well regarded the contact may be. Martin Weinberg and Colin Williams (1972) note that frequently it is easier to meet those who are more peripheral to the group than it is to meet those more central. At the outset of field research, most investigators will feel ill at ease and alone in a new setting. Marginal members of the group may have similar feelings and thus be easier to contact. Weinberg and Williams tell the story of the first day in the field doing a study of nudists (172): "The first day . . . the researcher ended up spending too much time with an unmarried male who, it was later learned, was held in disrepute. The motive imputed to this nudist as well as to other single nudists was of being there to look at other members' wives." Such situations present a dilemma for field researchers. One must be careful about whom to accept as a friend. At the same time, as an outsider one cannot afford to offend others by rejecting their friendship.

KEY POINT
Field researchers select accessible sites that fit their interests; they gain entry to organizations and communities through friends and sponsors.

Finding out how informants stand vis-à-vis the setting or community they "inform" is also critical because of its impact on research findings. William Labov (1973) discusses this issue in terms of what he calls the "linguistic consequences of being a lame." In his study of the linguistic habits of a group of young black men, Labov found that the men most accessible and willing to serve as informants were those who were marginal to their groups—in a word, "lames." Thus, inferences concerning linguistic patterns among blacks might reflect the habits of informants on the periphery and thereby be limited in generalizability.

Many of the settings and situations into which Whyte ventured in the community were private: homes, social clubs, political campaign meetings, and places of illegal business operations. His means of gaining entry to these settings can be traced to his contact with the social worker who introduced him to Doc, who in turn introduced him to other "street corner boys," politicians, and racketeers, who introduced him to still others. Thus, snowball sampling is the basic approach to obtaining access to private settings. The key to its implementation is knowing where to start. Some successful strategies include checking with friends to see if they can arrange personal introductions; involving oneself in the community using local stores and facilities and attending public meetings; going to agencies that serve the community such as churches, day-care centers, and neighborhood centers (where Whyte began); and advertising one's research interests in the local newspaper (Taylor, Bogdan, and DeVault, 2016:48).

Presenting Oneself

Related to the problem of gaining entry is deciding how to present oneself to those in the field. Certain aspects of this problem must be resolved before a researcher attempts to gain access to a setting, whereas other aspects cannot be anticipated fully and must be worked out during the course of the study.

As you consider how to gain access to a research setting, you must determine how to present yourself in the context of the research and how to relate to others in the setting. This issue boils down to deciding what role or roles to play. Roles are strategic because they greatly affect what a researcher is able to learn. The role you assume will determine where you can go, what you can do, with whom you can interact, and what you can inquire about and be told.

The Observer/Participant Roles

The four "master roles" from which other role relationships develop stem from the positions of scientific observer and participant (R. L. Gold, 1958; Junker, 1960). At one extreme is a *complete observer*, represented by our earlier description of nonparticipant observation. At the other is a *complete participant*, who conceals the observer role while becoming a fully accepted member of the in-group. In both of these cases, a researcher hides his or her true identity from those being observed. This avoids the problem of reactivity and has other advantages: For a complete observer, it is easier to play one role than to try to balance two; for a complete participant, access may be gained to information that would escape or be withheld from an observer. But such concealment has major disadvantages: A complete observer may wish to clarify points by questioning those being observed, and, most important, such covert research invariably raises ethical questions.

Covert research generally does not present serious ethical problems when the setting is public and open, where anyone has a right to be present (J. Lofland et al., 2006). In this situation, no harm can come to the people observed, the researcher is likely to be a passive observer, and concealing one's status as a researcher is considered a mild form of deception. However, as we noted in Chapter 3, many social scientists believe that concealment can become a serious problem when a researcher enters a private or closed setting, especially when his or her identity is purposely misrepresented to gain entry (see Erikson, 1967). Others defend covert research by maintaining that the scientific knowledge and social benefits of research may justify deceptive practices. Some research questions probably could not be investigated without complete cover for one's actions. In fact, some important, albeit controversial, studies have been conducted using a covert approach.

You may recall Laud Humphreys's study (1975) of impersonal sex in public places mentioned briefly in Chapter 3. In this study the author, posing as a voyeur and lookout, loitered around public restrooms waiting for opportunities to study brief sexual encounters among anonymous men. While engaging in this action, Humphreys made note of participants' license plate numbers and had them traced. A year later he conducted interviews at the men's homes to find out more about them than he could learn during the covert observation of their homosexual behaviors. Humphreys's research created a heated controversy. Some applauded him for his courage in undertaking such pioneering research, for his scrupulous care in protecting the identity of the people he observed, and for contributing to the understanding of a sensitive and private aspect of social life. Others denigrated him for his vivid descriptions of homosexual activities and, more important, for the blatant deception involved and the dangers posed, especially during the follow-up phase of his research (Glazer, 1972).

The other two master roles that a field researcher can play combine observation and participation. The *participant as observer* role emphasizes participation. The researcher's "observer activities are *not* wholly concealed, but are 'kept under wraps' as it were, or subordinated to activities as a participant" (Junker, 1960:36). Thus, others in the field generally relate to the researcher in his or her informal participant role, and the researcher is likely to spend more time participating than observing. This master role probably occurs most frequently in community studies, where relationships with informants develop over an extended period (R. L. Gold, 1958).

Finally, a field researcher can assume the role of *observer as participant*. In this role, observer activities are overriding as the researcher intentionally draws attention to his or her status as an observer and may even be publicly sponsored by people in the situation studied (Junker, 1960:37). Relationships with informants are thus more formal. This master role is likely to be invoked in brief encounters that do not allow relationships with informants to develop to the point of personal friendship. The observer role would be dominant, for example, in accompanying professionals such as physicians or police officers as they perform their routine daily activities.

Being able to relate to the people studied as a participant is likely to help one gain access to information hidden from an observer and a better understanding of the "native" point of view. Using one's professional observer/researcher identity, however, often is necessary to legitimate one's presence in the field to public officials. It also may be useful to call on this status to gather information—for example, to schedule formal interviews and secure access to institutional and agency records. Most participant observation, therefore, involves both of these master roles, albeit at different times and in relation to different informants. Almost always the roles are assumed by the same researcher, in what is called the "lone ranger" approach. However, because the roles are often difficult to balance, some researchers (e.g., Douglas, 1976; Snow, Benford, and Anderson, 1986) recommend a team approach, with different members of the team assuming different, complementary roles. This is what occurred in the homeless study. Snow acted primarily in the role of researcher and outside observer, whereas Anderson was a participant observer who interacted daily with homeless persons and witnessed, if not totally shared, their experiences.

Membership Roles

Given some degree of participation, field researchers face crucial choices about what **membership role** to adopt and how to relate to others in the setting. One "may become involved in either *peripheral, active,* or *complete* membership roles" (Adler and Adler, 1987:33). Each role affects the level of trust and rapport that can be developed with others, the extent and type of information that can be gathered, and the personal consequences of the fieldwork experience.

Peripheral members are only marginally part of the settings they observe; they limit their involvement in the group's activities, do not strive for full member status, or may be blocked from more central membership because of their personal characteristics. In her study of a Chicano youth gang, for example, Ruth Horowitz (1986) did not participate in the group's illegal activities, and she was distinguished from the gang members by her different appearance, social background, gender, and age. Gang members at first identified her as a "lady" and eventually as a "lady reporter." This identity gained her acceptance and enabled her to develop trust and respect so that she could ask questions about fights, school, and work as well as participate in some ongoing activities. Her reporter identity also inhibited others from treating her as a sexual object, suppressing sexual teasing and advances. However, it did not allow her to gather personal information about family, girlfriends, hopes, and aspirations.

Another common type of peripheral membership is that of the "buddy-researcher," a "blending of the roles of researcher and friend" (Snow, Benford, and Anderson, 1986). Anderson assumed this dual role in the homeless study. In so doing, he

> made daily institutional rounds with homeless individuals and small groups, provided individuals with minor necessities, small loans (which weren't expected to be repaid), clothes, rides, and a sympathetic ear for their hopes, troubles, and fears. (Snow, Benford, and Anderson, 1986:384)

As a buddy, Anderson received as well as gave (e.g., accepting offers of beer and marijuana), and he avoided being too distinctive in dress and speech. This generated trust and good will, and his being forthright about his researcher status lent credibility to his inquiries into personal matters.

Active membership means that researchers assume a functional role in the setting but retain sight of its temporary nature and do not fully commit themselves to the organization or group. In his study of a college basketball team, for example, Peter Adler (Adler and Adler, 1987:50) became an assistant coach, "serving as the team's interpersonal counselor, career counselor, and academic advisor." This made him an integral cog in the program, which allowed him to relate to others in a businesslike as well as personal way. Peripheral and active members may be either covert or overt about their researcher status. In Humphreys's study of homosexual encounters in public bathrooms, he performed the active membership role of "lookout" who watches for police or other unfriendly strangers.

Complete membership means becoming fully immersed in the setting and attaining full-member status. In his 2-year study of the peace movement, for example, Robert Benford became an "ardent activist," an active, loyal, and enthusiastic participant who "unquestioningly embraced the movement's ideology, goals, and rhetoric" (Snow, Benford, and Anderson, 1986:383). Complete membership gains researchers the greatest acceptance by other members, which affords the opportunity to gather data on the most personal and intimate matters. In addition, researchers are "able to supplement the data they gather with the greatest degree of their own subjective insight" (Adler and Adler, 1987:81). On the other hand, complete membership is intense and time-consuming, may have profound personal consequences, and often creates a conflict between the member and researcher roles.

Once researchers assume a particular membership role, they must decide how to present themselves in that role. Suppose, for example, that you are considering doing a study of medical technicians. You apply for a position as a laboratory assistant so that you will be able to observe the interactions of people in a medical research setting. How, then, will you present yourself? Will you allow people to teach you to do tasks that you might already know how to do? Will you pretend to be more naive than you are so that you can see how people will explain things to a know-nothing? Or will you flaunt your expertise so that you might become a valued member of the staff? Perhaps you think that people will tell you more if they have confidence in your abilities.

These are difficult choices, each with its particular consequences. Some field researchers recommend presenting oneself as naive or as an "acceptable incompetent" (J. Lofland et al., 2006; Taylor, Bogdan, and DeVault, 2016). This can be an effective way of gaining information, because it gives the impression of someone who is ignorant, needs to be taught, and therefore is expected to ask questions. On the other hand, in some settings—for example, in studies of higher-status people and "deviants"—it is clearly better to show competence (see Gorden, 1975:227–28). Informants are likely to judge researchers on their knowledge as well as interest in areas in which the informant is expert. Asking people about their occupation from a starting point of total ignorance usually just irritates them. Moreover, criminals may con you unless you make it clear that you are in the know.

KEY POINT
Field researchers must decide how much to accentuate their observer and participant roles and, as participants, how they will relate to others in the setting.

Ultimately, the best guideline for deciding what to do is to consider how one's behavior will affect the naturalness of the setting and how it will affect the development of trust and rapport with people in the setting. This appears to be the strategy that Calarco used in her help-seeking study. Presenting herself as a researcher and graduate student, she explained to students, "I am a student like you, but instead of studying math and language, I study how kids interact at school." And to gain the students' trust, she told them that she "would not 'tattle' or 'tell on' them unless someone's life was in danger" (personal communication, 2013).

Finally, assuming that an observer's identity as a social researcher is revealed, how much should others be told about the research? It is generally not a good idea—in fact, it is rarely necessary—to reveal the details of a study. One reason is that this may make people more self-conscious of the researcher's presence (Taylor, Bogdan, and DeVault, 2016). It is also unnecessary to volunteer information; however, people will want to know what you are up to, and it is important to develop a careful account of yourself. J. Lofland and associates (2006:43–44) offer several rules of thumb: (1) be as brief and direct as possible; (2) avoid jargon and make your interests clear, comprehensible, and appropriate to the audience; (3) avoid identifying yourself in ways that arouse suspicion or accentuate status differences (e.g., it is better to say you are a student or teacher than to say you are a criminologist); (4) be prepared to tell your informants how your research might benefit them (e.g., by giving voice to their story); and (5) be as candid as possible. Often, accounts are delivered orally and are staged and tailored to the audience; however, institutional review boards nowadays may require signed informed consent forms or a prepared script to be read to informants.

Gathering Information

Gathering information in the field presents several complex problems. To gain insight into the nature of these problems, let us imagine a hypothetical field study.

Suppose that you are going to do some field research. You have solved the problem of site selection by deciding to study the class you are currently taking in research methods; therefore, the classroom in which it meets and the surrounding campus constitute the site. Choosing this setting also simplifies the problem of self-presentation; after all, you are a *student* in the class. Given what you already know about the class and its participants, you also know that you want to do a participant observation study. You are ready, as Robert Park is reported to have encouraged his students at the University of Chicago, to "go get the seat of your pants dirty in *real* research" (McKinney, 1966:71). Or are you ready?

Before you begin your study, you should consider the nature of your participant–observer role in the class and the limitations that this places on what you can find out. As a student, it is extremely likely that your behavior and your perceptions of the instructor's behavior will be affected by your ego involvement in the class. You will, after all, be graded; you might even be graded on your class participation. Professional ethics will prevent the instructor from giving an honest account of his or her opinions about class members and the quality and significance of their participation. Thus, you are probably in the best position to study the way a student culture develops in a class, as long as you do not play too central a role in it.[4]

With this objective in mind, how do you proceed? Immediately you face the dilemma of every other participant observer: How do you perform your student (participant) role, such as listening and taking class notes, at the same time that you observe all the other activities in the classroom? Initially you will be most keenly aware of your observer role. In fact, you will probably find so much going on that you will have to forego note taking and borrow someone else's notes! How will you observe and remember the following:

where people sit; who asks questions; how people address one another and interact with one another; who speaks to whom before, after, and during class; who attends regularly; who is absent or late; what people say about assignments, exams, the instructor, and so forth? If you just think about everything that goes on in a class, you will see the enormity of the problem. The vast amount of information afloat in any social setting seems especially overwhelming at the beginning of a study when you are uncertain about what is relevant or important and what is not.

There are two crucial issues here:

1. How, when, and where will you record your observations?
2. What do you observe and record?

Recording Observations

While observing in the field, you have three choices for managing and recording data: an audiotape or videotape recorder, a notebook and pencil, and your memory. Consider some of the implications of each of these choices. A tape recorder has the advantage of allowing you to record everything that is said. But there may be nonverbal behavior to observe, so you cannot rely solely on audiotaping. Both audiotape and videotape recorders also have the distinct disadvantage of being highly obtrusive. Taping a conversation with someone is the surest way to get that person to be careful about his or her choice of words, at least at the outset.

The advantage of *getting* everything on tape also carries with it the problem of getting *everything* off the tape. Tape-recording formal interviews is often recommended (J. Lofland et al., 2006). This allows a researcher to take sparse notes while attending to the interviewee and the flow of the conversation. It may prove useful as a backup to the written record. And in cases where talk in the setting is the major focus of observation, a verbatim record furnishes a primary source of data to which the researcher (and others) might return again and again. But for many purposes, taped recordings of group interactions produce useless overload. Since it takes about 6 to 8 hours to transcribe 1 hour of a taped dialogue, you can quickly find yourself overwhelmed with transcriptions. The tendency to be swamped with data in field research is already great, so most people shun the use of tape recorders except for dictating notes in the field.

What about the second strategy of note taking at the scene? Although generally less obtrusive than mechanical devices, extensive note taking can be a distraction to subjects and researchers alike. This technique probably would prove easy for recording classroom observations. In interviews outside the class, however, many people would find it annoying to be talking to someone who constantly looks away to take notes. Writing things down also is conspicuous in many settings and is inconsistent with many participant roles, and it is likely to interrupt the normal flow of activities. Imagine taking notes in a bar or church or while interacting with drug dealers.

The third choice for "recording" observations is to rely on your memory. Given the caveats about taped recordings and note taking, it is easy to understand why it is important for field researchers to develop their ability to remember. Nonetheless, practitioners of field research warn against relying heavily on one's memory: "memory is a very poor recording device" (Bernard, 2013:346); "the human mind tends to forget much that has occurred and to do so rather quickly" (J. Lofland et al., 2006:108). So what do you do?

First, nearly all field researchers take **field jottings**—"little phrases, quotes, key words, and the like that you put down during the observation" (J. Lofland et al., 2006:109). The rule of thumb is to make the jottings as inconspicuous as possible. Also, a field researcher must be alert to the opportunities naturally afforded for jotting. In her study of behavior in bars, Sherri Cavan (1966) went to the bathroom, an easily accountable act, to jot down notes. In the homeless study, Anderson often jotted down key phrases and longer quotes immediately after the end of a conversation. If such opportunities do not present themselves, a researcher must rely on mental notes and quick jottings to help trigger the later recall of important details.

KEY POINT

Field notes, the basic data of field research, may be facilitated by on-the-scene *field jottings* and should be recorded daily as soon after a researcher leaves the field as possible.

Second, to guard against forgetting, field researchers should write up **field notes** at the end of each day or as soon after the observations as possible, just as Anderson did in the homeless study. Based on field jottings and memory, field notes provide an extensive, detailed record of events. They are the crucial data of field research, analogous to a survey researcher's completed interviews or questionnaires. Field researchers, therefore, must be extremely disciplined and rigorous about recording notes. Indeed, the actual writing of notes may take as much time as the observation.

Determining What to Observe and Record

In field research, the "primary sources of data are the *words and actions* of the people you are interviewing or observing" (J. Lofland et al., 2006:85). A complete observer will have to rely on listening and observing, whereas a participant has access to the broadest range of data. In either case, field notes should provide as detailed and complete a *description* of events as possible. J. Lofland et al. (2006:112) point out that field notes

> are a more or less chronological log of what is happening . . . a running description of settings, events, people, things heard and overheard, and interactions among and with people, including conversations. Each new physical setting, person, interactional episode, and event observed merits a description. You should also record changes in what you are observing. Since you are likely to encounter many of the same settings, people, and other phenomena again and again, you need not repeat such descriptions, but only augment them as changes occur.

When recording field notes, the first rule is to be concrete, take note of specific behavioral details, and avoid attaching your own abstract labels to things. As Joy Browne (1976a:77) advises, "it is crucial . . . to collect only data, not analysis. Don't interpolate or integrate—just remember. What is important or trivial is usually not evident until much later. So don't sift, just collect." In other words, force yourself to see first and conceptualize later. Earlier we alluded to Lyn Lofland's study, in which she observed the grooming behavior of people about to enter public places. Grooming was the conceptual category Lofland arrived at on the basis of more specific, concrete observations. Here are two examples of her observations of people preparing to enter a building:

> A young man approaches the door. He carries a briefcase in one hand; the other hangs free. As he nears the door he uses his free hand to brush the hair back from his forehead, then opens the door with that hand and enters.

> Two girls come toward the entrance. About three yards from the door, each begins to pass her hand over her hair, as though brushing it. They continue this until they reach the door. Apparently finished, they stop for a few seconds in front of the door while continuing the process. (L. Lofland, 1973:141)

As the research progresses, you might want to intersperse your record of what happens with your own feelings and ideas. For example, you might observe in the classroom that two students are looking intently and steadily out the window during the instructor's lecture; at the same time, you feel bored and sense that others are also. You should not, however, confuse or confound your impression of "boredom" with your factual observation of students "gazing" out the window. Both kinds of observations are important, but should be kept separate (Browne, 1976a). One way to separate different kinds of notes is to assign codes (e.g., "O" for observation, "P" for personal reaction, "A" for analytical idea, "M" for methodological aside).[5]

In addition to firsthand observation, a field researcher's primary source of data, you will undoubtedly obtain much information by questioning the professor and other students in the class. In the homeless study, Anderson frequently elicited information in casual field encounters by making intentional comments such as "I don't get it," "I don't understand," or "I didn't think you were a regular Sally [Salvation Army] user" (Snow and Anderson, 1987:1343). Snow and Anderson (1987:1344) also supplemented their field observations with in-depth interviews of "six homeless individuals who had been on the streets for various lengths of time, ranging from two months to 14 years."

Finally, field researchers frequently supplement observations and conversations with other sources of information, such as official records (e.g., agency records, census data, court transcriptions) and personal documents (e.g., diaries, letters, scrapbooks). Documentary data may prove especially useful in the early stages of field research, as a means of learning about the history and the physical and social characteristics of a setting. For example, Snow and Anderson examined pamphlets, records, and reports of various agencies serving homeless people. This was helpful in orienting their study, for example, providing information on the growth of homelessness in Austin and indicating how agencies (e.g., the police) dealt with the homeless. Documentary data also can serve the same purposes as interviewing—that is, to gather and cross-check factual information.

Institutional data also were collected in the homeless study to complement fieldwork findings. After several months in the field, Snow and Anderson decided to track a random sample of homeless people through selected institutions (see Snow et al., 1986; Snow, Baker, and Anderson, 1989). Because the Salvation Army operated Austin's only public shelter and was also the only facility in the city that provided free breakfast and dinner, nearly all of the Austin homeless population had utilized the Salvation Army services at least once. In addition, all first-time users were required to fill out a brief questionnaire that asked for name and social security number as well as other background information. After receiving permission to use this identifying information, Snow and Anderson drew a random sample of 800 names. They then negotiated access to the records of six other local and state agencies (e.g., the city police department, the state department of mental health and mental retardation), and they tracked their sample through these institutions. An important finding related to the mental health of homeless persons: Only 10 percent of their sample had been institutionalized one or more times, and the greatest proportion of these institutionalizations was for substance abuse rather than purely psychiatric problems. This and related findings contradicted many estimates and claims regarding the prevalence of profound psychiatric illness among the homeless population.

One of the features of field research that makes describing it difficult is that it "is not a single method gathering a single kind of information" (Zelditch, 1962:567) but a blend of methods and techniques. The ways of collecting data we have outlined constitute a short list of the means for understanding the social world used by field researchers. For example, in her study of behavior in public places, Lyn Lofland drew on a broad range of materials, including not only field observations but also personal experiences, anecdotes, interviews, and historical and anthropological studies. Anything that promotes understanding is grist for the field researcher's mill.

Analyzing the Data

This brings us to the data-analysis phase of field research. Unlike in other research approaches, data analysis occurs throughout the period of data collection. The act of recording field notes itself is the beginning of analyzing and making sense of field data.

A major goal of field research, as we have often noted, is to get an insider's view of reality. The data collected by field researchers should render, therefore, a richly detailed picture of social life that describes the people on their own terms, graphically capturing their language and letting them speak for themselves. Descriptions in field research thus often involve the presentation of selected anecdotes and quotes from informants. They also provide concrete details about the setting and the actions and incidents that occur there.

Like any other form of data, however, such descriptions cannot speak for themselves. Rather, they must be integrated with concepts and ideas that help to order and explain an insider's view of reality. Description alone, in other words, is not enough. Investigators also must formulate a theoretical understanding that lends coherence to their data. This does not mean that field researchers enter the field with preset hypotheses and theoretical formulations. Many field researchers believe, in fact, that fieldwork should be directed toward the development or "discovery" of theory. Barney Glaser and Anselm Strauss (1967) refer to theory that is generated from the data as **grounded theory**, as distinguished from theory logically derived from a priori assumptions. The "grounded" approach advocates loosely structured research designs that allow theoretical ideas to "emerge from the field in the course of the study" (Miles and Huberman, 1994:17). Some field researchers contend that field studies can be used both to develop and to verify theory (see Burawoy, 1991). Others point out that field researchers invariably bring *some* orienting ideas and general research questions to fieldwork that direct their data-gathering efforts (Miles and Huberman, 1994). Irrespective of these positions, the field approach to data analysis generally entails some attempt to summarize and order the data by identifying themes, concepts, propositions, and theories. How, then, does one go about doing this?

In the broadest sense, data analysis consists of "the search for patterns in data and for ideas that help explain the existence of those patterns" (Bernard, 2013:394). This process can be broken down into three interrelated tasks: (1) organizing information and identifying patterns, (2) developing ideas, and (3) drawing and verifying conclusions.

Organizing Information

The raw data of a field researcher—field notes—present several problems for a data analyst. Words are harder to process than numbers, field notes can contain a massive amount of words, and there is usually little inherent structure in field notes other than a sequential and narrative account of one's observations and experiences. In the homeless study, Snow and Anderson ended up with more than 600 double-spaced typed pages of field notes. Their initial task was to reduce this bulk of information into meaningful and analyzable units. To do this, they used the field researcher's most common method of organizing field notes—coding.

Coding, which is a common aspect of all social research (see Chapter 15), consists of assigning symbols or numbers to categories. In survey research, numerical codes are assigned to response categories to facilitate data processing and analysis. The codes can be and usually are established before data collection, when the survey instrument is complete. In field research, codes are applied to transcribed field notes to categorize words or "chunks" of words, such as a sentence or paragraph, into units of meaning (Miles and Huberman, 1994). Because one is often working toward theory rather than from theory, the codes are usually developed from field observations. In fact, from the grounded theory standpoint, it is inappropriate to approach the field with preconceived notions or *pre*coded protocols detailing how the world is to be understood. Instead, codes (*post*codes, if you will) are developed as part of making sense of the world.

To organize their field notes, Snow and Anderson used a two-step process: (1) they extracted from their field notes "data entries" that varied from a single sentence to several pages in length and (2) they assigned these entries to one or more of three broad categories that emerged over time: focal settings, cultural domains, and homeless individuals. The 24 focal settings consisted of institutions and sites relevant to the daily lives of homeless people. The 30 cultural domains pertained "to categories of meaning, events, and problems that constitute the social world and life-style of the homeless (e.g., drinking and alcohol, drugs, food and eating, sleeping and shelter, social relationships, and work)" (Snow and Anderson, 1987:1345). Through this coding scheme, Snow and Anderson discovered the importance of self and identity issues in the lives of the homeless, as indicated by the number of data entries in this domain.

Developing Ideas

Beyond coding, there are few guidelines and procedures for analyzing field data. In part, this is because it is hard to catalog the sources of creative insight. When an insight does occur, during coding or the process of going over field notes and reviewing the day's observations, it is important to get it down immediately in writing. To do this, field researchers recommend writing memos. **Memos** are small pieces of analysis, usually a paragraph or two, that capture emergent ideas that help make sense of the reality one is encountering (Glaser, 1978).

One way to focus your thinking in the field is to continually ask questions about the data. J. Lofland et al. (2006:144–67) identified several questions that can help orient field researchers' thinking. Following is a paraphrasing of some of these questions:

What type of unit (e.g., encounter, relationship, group, organization) is this?
What is the unit's structure and characteristics?
What are its causes?
What are its consequences?
How frequently does this action or event occur?
What social processes are occurring in this setting?
What is the situation people face and what strategies do they use to deal with it?

In the homeless study, recall, Snow and Anderson (1991) were interested in how homeless people adapted to their environment and the factors that shaped this adaptation. This research question led them to identify three main types of adaptation and orientation among the homeless and five distinct types of organizational response. The types of organizational response ranged from "accommodative," as exemplified by the sustenance-oriented caretaking of the Salvation Army, to "containment," as represented by the harassment of the city police.

Another, often overlooked, strategy for analyzing field data is counting. Matthew Miles and A. Michael Huberman (1994:253) note that "there is a lot of counting going on when judgments of qualities are being made. When we identify a theme or pattern, we're isolating something that (a) happens a number of times and (b) consistently happens in a specific way. The 'number of times' and 'consistency' judgments are based on counting." Counts and comparisons are also implied, they point out, whenever we make generalizations or use words such as "important" and "recurring." Resorting to counts can serve not only to verify specific hypotheses and protect against bias but also to help see the data more clearly.

One working hypothesis that emerged in the homeless study was that types of identity talk among the homeless varied according to how long the individual had been on the streets. For example, Snow and Anderson (1987) identified three types of "distancing" statements: (1) categoric distancing, which involved dissociation from the general street role identity; (2) specific or situational distancing, which included dissociation from specific groupings of homeless individuals, such as "novices" and those who are institutionally dependent; and (3) institutional distancing, indicated by expressions of disdain for

TABLE 11.1. Types of Distancing by Time on the Streets

Time on the streets	Type of distancing			
	CATEGORIC	SPECIFIC	INSTITUTIONAL	TOTAL (N)
Less than 6 months	80.0%	6.7	13.3	100.0% (15)
6 months to 2 years	10.0%	60.0	30.0	100.0% (10)
2 years to 4 years	4.3%	56.5	39.1	99.9% (23)
More than 4 years	15.4%	23.1	61.5	100.0% (13)

Source: Snow and Anderson (1987:1353). Used by permission of the authors and University of Chicago Press.

street institutions, such as the Salvation Army and soup kitchens. Categoric distancing was thought to be more prevalent among those who had spent the least amount of time on the streets, whereas the other forms of distancing would be more likely to be used by those more entrenched in street life. To examine this relationship, Snow and Anderson divided homeless people into groups with varying amounts of time on the street and then counted the number of categoric, specific, and institutional distancing statements made by individuals in each group. Table 11.1 presents these data. Note that categoric distancing statements were made by 80 percent of the individuals who had been on the streets less than 6 months, compared with 15.4 percent or less of those who had been on the streets for 6 months or more.

Drawing and Verifying Conclusions

In the end, field researchers generally seek to identify the larger meaning of their findings, especially as they relate to existing theoretical frameworks. In Snow and Anderson's research, this meant explaining the patterned identity talk that they had identified. Why did it occur? How were the patterns they observed related to existing role-identity theory? One of their conclusions pertained to the importance of distancing behavior and other identity talk among the homeless. They questioned the assumption that the need for self-esteem is secondary to the satisfaction of physiological survival needs. Maintaining a sense of meaning and self-worth, they contend, may be especially critical for the survival of homeless people and other marginal members of society because it enables them to "retain a sense of self and thus their humanity" (Snow and Anderson, 1987:1365).

To check the validity of such interpretations, it is always a good idea to entertain alternative explanations. Explanations should be generated early and often and checked repeatedly against observations. One might seek out alternative explanations from others, for example, colleagues. A time-honored tradition in field research is to get feedback from respondents. Finally, as a further validity check on conclusions, a researcher could look for negative evidence, that is, data that oppose or are inconsistent with a particular conclusion (Miles and Huberman, 1994).

KEY POINT
Data analysis in field research occurs throughout the period of observation as researchers organize information and identify and interpret patterns of social life.

Because of the relatively unstructured nature of field research, it is critically important to consider ways of avoiding bias and enhancing validity. For a participant observer, this process begins early, when he or she attempts to establish rapport and trust with those in the field setting, to reduce the problem of reactivity. It continues throughout fieldwork in other ways. Researchers should constantly seek corroborating feedback for their observations from others in the setting. They should check for inconsistencies between informants and find out why they disagree (Bernard, 2013:395). And when possible, they should check informants' reports against other sources of data, such as institutional records. The rule of thumb, which we discuss further in Chapter 13, is to seek out a variety of evidence to support one's conclusions—the greater the variety and the more abundant the evidence, the stronger the conclusions.

Strengths and Limitations of Field Research

Field research may complement other approaches both by providing suggestive leads for explanatory research and by adding depth and meaning to survey and experimental results. It is more often the research approach of choice simply because it is more appropriate for a particular research purpose.

As we have discussed, a major reason for doing field research, especially participant observation, is to get an insider's view of reality. By observing and participating in the activities of the people being studied, field researchers can capture participants' definition of the situation. And in so doing, they can see processes that might otherwise be hidden and understand the coherence and maintenance of views that may seem implausible to outsiders. Indeed, insofar as field research is descriptive, it may have little more than this as its goal.

By observing social life in *natural settings*, field research is preferable to other approaches: (1) when it is essential to preserve "whole" events in all their detail and immediacy (Weick, 1968); (2) when a situation is complex, involving interrelated phenomena that must be studied simultaneously and as a whole—for example, the study of a prison as an institution (R. S. Weiss, 1966); and (3) when the focus is on the relationship between the person *and* the setting so that it is important not to separate one from the other (Weick, 1968).

Preserving the natural order of things not only provides a holistic and contextual understanding of social actions; it also reduces the problem of reactivity prevalent in experiments and surveys. Reactivity and other measurement issues often make self-reports poor indicators of behavior. This is why some scholars contend that field research, by observing behavior directly under real-world conditions, provides more valid inferences about social actions than other approaches (Jerolmack and Khan, 2014). As discussed in Box 11.2, field research also may be more effective than other approaches for understanding the disparity between what people actually do and what they say they do.

Additionally, field research may be used when methodological problems preclude other research strategies—for example, when subjects are unable (young children) or unwilling (gang members) to participate in a formal survey—and when one knows relatively

BOX 11.2 FIELD RESEARCH AND THE ATTITUDINAL FALLACY

A long-standing "methodological challenge" in the social sciences is that what people say is often inconsistent with what they do. It is a challenge because researchers routinely use self-reported behavior and verbalized attitudes (feelings or sentiments) as proxies for actual behavior. Recently, Colin Jerolmack and Shamus Khan (2014:181) argued "that ethnography [synonymous with "field research" as described in this chapter] is one of the most effective methods for addressing this challenge." To understand their argument, let's first examine evidence of a lack of attitude–behavior consistency. Then, we will discuss the methodological implications of what Jerolmack and Khan call "the *attitudinal fallacy*—the error of inferring situated behavior from verbal accounts" (179).

One of the many areas of research on the attitude–behavior consistency problem is the relationship between racial attitudes and behavior. Richard LaPiere (1934) conducted a landmark study in which he traveled around the United States in the early 1930s with a young Chinese student and his wife. Keeping detailed records of how the couple was received at 251 hotels, auto camps, restaurants, and cafes, LaPiere reported that they were denied service only once. Six months after patronizing these establishments, he mailed a questionnaire to each one in which he asked, "Will you accept members of the Chinese race as guests in your establishment?" Among the 128 who responded, more than 90 percent replied "no."

Fast-forward to a study conducted in 2001 by Devah Pager and Lincoln Quillian (2005), which compared the results of a field experiment on hiring discrimination with a survey conducted several months after the experiment. The field experiment was an audit study (see Box 8.1) in which black and white men, half with and half without criminal records, applied for the same jobs. Several months later, each of the employers who had been contacted was asked to participate in a telephone interview on hiring preferences and practices. During the interview, the employers responded to a vignette describing a hypothetical job applicant who closely matched the auditor with the criminal record who had applied in person for the job. In the survey, 61.7 percent of the respondents reported that they were "very likely" or "somewhat likely" to hire the black ex-offender; however, in the audit study, only 14.7 percent had received a callback for an interview.

Both of these studies reveal considerable disparity between attitudes, or what people said they would do, and behavior, or what they actually did. This disparity does not always occur; for example, research shows a high correlation between voting intentions and voting behavior and between fear of violent crime and behaviors intended to alleviate this fear, such as installing extra locks and alarm systems and purchasing guns (cited by Cerulo, 2014). However, the general finding is one of great variability in the relationship between self-reports and behavior; for example, a meta-analysis of 57 studies investigating the relationship between racial attitudes (prejudice) and behavior (discrimination) showed correlations ranging from −.38 to .69, with a relatively low average of .26 (Talaska, Fiske, and Chaiken, 2008). Thus, it is clearly a fallacy to presume a correspondence between attitudes and behavior. And for several reasons, Jerolmack and Khan contend that the most useful approach to resolving this fallacy is field research.

First, field research observes behavior directly; therefore, it reveals what people actually do in specific situations. Second, field researchers observe behavior in a variety of interactional contexts, whereas surveys merely indicate what people think and feel and are willing to

(continued)

(continued)

say in one context—an interview or questionnaire. As Jerolmack and Khan point out, survey data "prioritize the representativeness of individuals." However,

> the unique context of the interview/survey situation means that the findings produced cannot be assumed to be generalizable to everyday life—we can infer that individuals not sampled would provide a similar distribution of self-reports as those in the sample, but we cannot infer that these self-reports are indicative of how people will act under social situations not sampled. . . . Ethnography's epistemology is different: It does not select representative samples of individuals, rather it samples everyday situations and interactions. (Jerolmack and Khan, 2014:202)

Third, in addition to being able to *observe* inconsistencies between saying and doing across various situations, field researchers can directly compare self-reports in field interviews with "what actors do on a day-to-day basis" (Jerolmack and Khan, 2014:195). Although what people say is important in understanding actors' definitions of the situation, the *meaning* of what they say is constructed through a process of interaction and should take into account what they are doing "in relation to other people and in particular situations" (200).

"At its best," Jerolmack and Khan conclude, "ethnography carefully adjudicates between what actors say—in interviews or in conversations with each other—and what they actually do in the contexts of their everyday lives; and it exploits such comparisons to uncover motivation" (196). They point out research that shows Americans overreport how often they attend church by twofold, whereas Europeans give unbiased reports of church attendance. According to Jerolmack and Kahn, "This suggests that Americans have a deep desirability to identify as religious persons, but that their actions are not in accordance with their sentiments" (190). In a similar fashion, the vast majority of Americans endorse the principle of racial equality,[6] even though they may violate this principle in their everyday lives. Pager and Quillian found that "hearing a description of a hypothetical black offender is quite different from seeing a young black man approach one's business in search of employment" (2005:371). When being asked about the applicant in the abstract vignette, the employer gives an honest answer that reflects an endorsement of the principle of equal opportunity. But confronting this situation in real life "may trigger feelings of fear, anxiety, and threat" and bring into play "contingencies of the hiring process [that] render hypothetical scenarios irrelevant" (371).

little about the topic under investigation. The less you know about something, the less you can afford to limit data collection. Experiments and surveys generally require substantial prior knowledge about the topic being investigated. Such knowledge is essential for deciding what to manipulate and control or what to ask about and what to ignore. Once these decisions are made, however, experimentalists and survey researchers are fairly locked into their design, whereas field researchers are more flexible, often changing design elements after they enter the field and as they analyze their data.

Finally, the decision to adopt a field approach may depend on one's resources. Research can be costly. All research strategies require time, space, money, and personnel. Conducting interviews with a large sample of individuals can be expensive in terms of sampling, interviewer training, data collection, and so forth. Similarly, experiments, although generally on a smaller scale than surveys, can be complex and expensive to conduct. Field research, if it is to be conducted at a nearby location, can be the least expensive approach. It does not require elaborate tools or equipment and, since it is typically conducted entirely by a single investigator, requires no additional personnel or training period beyond the preparation of the investigator. On the other hand, field research can be labor-intensive. Investigators have been known to spend years in the field. Thus, the most important resource to field researchers is field researchers themselves.

Field research thus lends itself best to investigating settings in which it is important to preserve the natural order of things and settings in which a researcher's minimal understanding makes it crucial to understand the subjects' interpretation of reality. Field research takes time, however, and may not be an efficient way of gathering certain kinds of information. For enumerating the distribution of certain demographic characteristics (e.g., age, gender, occupation) or beliefs and attitudes within a certain population, surveys are much quicker and more reliable. For testing causal hypotheses, experiments are far superior because of their greater control.

Because field research typically is carried out by a single observer who interacts with a limited number of people in a limited number of settings, it is highly dependent on the observational and interpretive skills of the researcher, is difficult to replicate and compare, and may lack generalizability. The usual outcome is a richly detailed description of a segment of the social world; however, the segment is not only necessarily small but also often selected on an ad hoc basis, for reasons of availability and convenience. This pattern tends to undermine the ability of field studies to contribute to a body of knowledge addressing theoretically formulated problems (P. K. Manning, 1987:22–23).

Summary

- Traditionally, field research has tended to focus on the downtrodden and, more recently, on aspects of everyday life.
- Field research entails a rudimentary, emergent research design, direct observation in natural settings, unstructured and semistructured interviewing, and qualitative data analysis.
- Field researchers are flexible about research design, working out the specifics of their approach during the course of the study. In sampling, for example, a flexible approach is necessitated by the nature of the social units studied and by the delicate problems of entering the field and establishing field relations.
- Small, nonrandom samples typify the selection of subjects and settings. In the field, the general approach to sampling is to enhance the informational value of evidence by maximizing variation. Specific strategies include the serial selection of units and sampling analytical dimensions relevant to the study.
- The foundational method of data collection in field research is firsthand observation. Field observation varies in terms of structure, with less structured observation characterizing the early phases of research.

- Highly structured observation entails formalized rules for extracting information specifying when and where observations will take place, who will make the observations, and what will be observed.
- Field observation also varies according to the researcher's degree of participation in the setting being investigated. At one extreme is an intentionally unobtrusive, nonparticipant observer; at the other is an engaged participant observer.
- Participant observation is far more common than nonparticipant observation as an inclusive method, perhaps because being a participant is seen as crucial to gaining an insider's view of the world. However, the marginal position of a participant observer makes this a difficult and often stressful role to play.
- Interviewing supplements field observations by eliciting information about unobserved events, different perspectives on events, and informants' thoughts and feelings.
- Interviewing may occur through casual questioning that flows from ordinary participation in a setting or by means of interviews formally arranged with informants.
- Interview guides consisting of question topics and questions direct formal interviews, although the order and precise wording of questions depend on what is said, as in any normal conversation.
- Data in field research are often limited to text that is subjected to qualitative analysis to describe and develop a theoretical understanding of social life.
- The first stage of fieldwork is electing an appropriate setting. For reasons of accessibility and interest, some researchers recommend "starting where you are," which has a strong tradition in field research.
- Gaining access to a setting is the second stage. In a formal organization, this is usually a matter of getting the permission of those in charge. Public settings are more readily accessible but require ingenuity in interacting with people and finding informants. In private settings, the principal means of gaining entry is the development of relations with key informants, followed by snowball sampling.
- The third stage of field research, which begins with the task of gaining entry, is presenting oneself to those in the setting. Researchers must decide, first, on the extent to which they will reveal themselves as scientific observers and the extent to which they will participate in the setting.
- Although not uncommon, covert field research presents ethical problems and is frowned on by some investigators. More commonly, field researchers combine undisguised observation and participation, while varying the enactment of these two roles during the course of a single study.
- Participant or membership roles also must be developed by researchers, who may become a peripheral, active, or complete member in the field setting. Finally, in presenting oneself, it is important to consider how one's behavior will affect the development of trust and rapport with those in the setting.
- The final two stages of field research, gathering and analyzing information, are concurrent. To collect data, field researchers rely on field jottings and mental notes to record detailed field notes as soon after their observations as possible.
- In addition to using firsthand observation, they also may question participants and consult records and personal documents. From this information, researchers develop a rich description of events that conveys the experience of someone who "was there."
- Furthermore, throughout the process of gathering information, researchers develop concepts and tentative hypotheses to make sense of the data. Aids to identifying patterns and gaining insights include coding field notes, writing memos, asking questions, and counting.
- It is also important to entertain alternative explanations and perform various validity checks, for example, by seeking corroborative evidence.
- Field research implies an attempt to develop an understanding of human behavior as defined by the subjects themselves and/or as related to the situation in which the behavior occurs.
- Field research is recommended under the following conditions: (1) when it is essential to preserve the interrelatedness of the person and situation, (2) when methodological problems, resources, or ethics preclude the adoption of other research strategies, and (3) when little is known about the topic under investigation.
- However, field research is an inferior way of testing specific causal hypotheses, a time-consuming and sometimes inefficient method of gathering data, necessarily limited to a few settings, and highly dependent on the observational skills of the researcher.

Key Terms

<table>
<tr><td>field research</td><td>covert research</td></tr>
<tr><td>theoretical sampling</td><td>membership role</td></tr>
<tr><td>nonparticipant observation</td><td>peripheral membership</td></tr>
<tr><td>structured observation</td><td>active membership</td></tr>
<tr><td>unstructured observation</td><td>complete membership</td></tr>
<tr><td>participant observation</td><td>field jottings</td></tr>
<tr><td>informant</td><td>field notes</td></tr>
<tr><td>in-depth (intensive) interviewing</td><td>grounded theory</td></tr>
<tr><td>interview guide</td><td>coding</td></tr>
<tr><td>gatekeepers</td><td>memos</td></tr>
<tr><td>key informants</td><td></td></tr>
</table>

Exercises

1. In the January 1991 issue of the *Journal of Contemporary Ethnography* (vol. 19, p. 423–49), David Snow, Cherylon Robinson, and Patricia McCall report a participant observation study of the strategies that women use to "fend off men and parry their advances" in public places. Read this article and answer the following questions.

   a. What are the two interconnected research questions that the researchers addressed?

   b. Why did the researchers select singles bars, cocktail lounges, and other night spots to study the "cooling-out process"?

   c. What three means of data collection did the researchers use?

   d. Explain how they used "interviewing by comment" to learn about specific cooling-out episodes.

   e. What purpose did the semistructured interviews serve? (That is, how did they complement the information obtained from observation and informal conversations?)

   f. How did the researchers validate "flight" to the women's restroom as a form of avoiding encounters with men?

   g. What do the researchers claim about the generalizability of their findings to the cooling-out process in other public settings?

2. Most researchers, field researchers included, report the bare details of their methodology. Rarely do they provide a detailed, realistic description of "the process by which the research was actually done," including the "traps, delays, and frustrations which inevitably accompany field work" (Lareau, 2000:197). However, a few monographs based on field research have provided insightful accounts of the methods of study and the researcher's field experience. To broaden your understanding of fieldwork, read one or more of the following accounts:

   • William Foote Whyte, "Appendix A: On the Evolution of Street Corner Society," pp. 278–373 in *Street Corner Society: The Social Structure of an Italian Slum*, 4th ed. (1993). A sociological classic; Appendix A also is available in earlier editions.

   • Gary Alan Fine, "Appendix 2: Participant Observation with Children," pp. 222–42 in *With the Boys: Little League Baseball and Preadolescent Culture* (1987).

   • Gary Alan Fine, "Appendix: Ethnography in the Kitchen, Issues and Cases," pp. 233–53 in *Kitchens: The Culture of Restaurant Work* (1996).

   • Charles L. Bosk, "Appendix: The Field Worker and the Surgeon," pp. 193–213 in *Forgive and Remember: Managing Medical Failure* (1979).

   • Annette Lareau, "Appendix: Common Problems in Field Work: A Personal Essay," pp. 197–233 in *Home Advantage: Social Class and Parental Intervention in Elementary Education* (2000).

3. In Chapter 1, we described Rebecca Allahyari's (2000) field research at two charities that provided food to the poor. She found that volunteers saw caring for the poor as part of a personal search for moral betterment that was expressed in both their relationship to the poor and their own sense of

virtue. Suppose you want to understand how such "moral selving" plays out in other volunteer settings and organizations and you decide to do a participant observation study. Choose a specific setting or organization, perhaps a volunteer program on a college campus. How might you gain access? Would you emphasize the observer or participant role? What membership role might you play as a participant? Besides field notes based on your observations, what other data would you collect?

4. To give you experience in observing and taking field jottings and field notes, select a public place such as a cafeteria, coffee shop, library, or student lounge where you can unobtrusively observe others without anyone questioning your presence. Your research objective is to describe as fully as possible how people use this space. Are they there alone or with others? In what sort of activities are they engaged? How long are they in the setting? Before entering the field, you should consider what to observe and record. Plan to observe for at least an hour during a relatively busy time of the day and focus on a clearly delimited area such as a set of tables. Record your field notes as soon after leaving the field as possible, and then go over your notes and develop a coding scheme for organizing the information.

Notes

1. Robert Park (see Box 11.2) was instrumental in establishing this focus. Trained as a journalist, Park was the press agent for the famous black educator Booker T. Washington when they coauthored a book entitled *The Man Farthest Down*. This book attracted the attention of the sociologist W. I. Thomas, who invited Park to leave the Tuskegee Institute in Alabama, where he had worked with Washington, to come to the University of Chicago. Park did so in 1913, ultimately becoming the chair of the sociology department and establishing the intellectual tradition of studying "those farthest down."

2. The one exception to this is structured observation, which relies on a well-developed scheme for coding behavior. A researcher observing children at play, for example, may record specific features of the play that are designed to test clearly stated hypotheses. Perhaps the hypothesis is that boys' games are more complex than girls' games. This would require pre-established observational categories based on such characteristics as the size of the play group, the rules of the games, the nature of the different task roles performed by players, and so forth (see Lever, 1978).

3. Robert Emerson (1981) likens structured observation studies to surveys insofar as each employs designs with prespecified procedures for when, where, and what to observe and sample. The only difference is the mode of data collection: asking questions versus direct observation.

4. By contrast, a student making the same kind of observations in a course in a different college, after getting the instructor's permission to observe, would face a different set of constraints. This setting probably would provide more access to the instructor's opinions but less access to the student network outside the class. It also presents the problem of whether a student researcher should conceal his or her status in the class from other students.

5. H. Russell Bernard (2013:347–48) recommends keeping a separate personal diary to help one "deal with loneliness, fear, and other emotions that make fieldwork difficult" and provide "an outlet for writing things that you don't want to become part of a public record."

6. Several questions from national surveys show strong support for racial equality in principle, so much so that many of these questions are no longer asked. For example, the 1972 GSS showed that 97 percent of Americans thought blacks should have as good a chance as whites to get any kind of job; as of the 2002 GSS, 90 percent thought there should not be laws against marriages between blacks and whites; and as of the 2010 GSS, 96.6 percent said they would vote for a qualified black candidate for president if nominated by their party (T. W. Smith, Marsden, and Hout, 2016).

12

Research Using Available Data

As different as experiments, surveys, and field studies may seem, they do have one common feature that distinguishes them from the methodological approach described in this chapter: Each involves the firsthand collection of data. Doing any of these three kinds of research entails gathering information, by either questioning or direct observation, from the people and groups who are the objects of study. Thus, the data originate with the research; they are not there before the research is undertaken.

By contrast, the fourth general strategy for doing social research is to make use of available data. Sometimes a researcher uses data that were produced by another investigator for a completely different research purpose. At other times, one may use available data that were not produced for any research purpose at all. The variety of such data is tremendous; it is limited only by the researcher's imagination. As you will see in this chapter, that imagination has found sources of data in letters and diaries, government and court records, newspapers, and magazines. Even tombstones and graffiti have been used as the raw material for social research.

We begin this chapter by considering several studies that suggest the sources of and possibilities for using available data. With reference to these studies, we discuss common methodological issues related to this approach. The diverse data sources give rise to different forms of analysis, with distinctive research purposes. Therefore, we also take a closer look at two types of available-data research: historical analysis and content analysis.

Sources of Available Data

The sources of available data may be placed in six broad categories: (1) public documents and official records, including the extensive archives of the Census Bureau; (2) private documents; (3) mass media; (4) physical, nonverbal materials; (5) social science data archives; and (6) big data. These categories provide a useful summary of data sources, although they do not constitute a mutually exclusive typology. Any given data source may be placed in one or more of these categories. Also, analysts may draw on more than one data source in any given study.

Public Documents and Official Records

Exemplifying the available-data approach is a historian who searches for traces of events and processes from the past. More than any other source of evidence, historians rely on the written record. Writing, or the physical manifestation of the spoken language, is regarded as a mark of civilization. Its presence denotes the beginning of history, as we know it. Records refer to accounts of the past kept in writing or some other form.

Much of the written record is public. Documents created to ensure the normal functioning of offices and departments are maintained at every level of government (not to mention by virtually every private business and organization) in every society throughout the world. These include the proceedings of government bodies, court records, state laws, and city ordinances. Many government agencies, most notably the Census Bureau, also maintain numerous volumes of official statistics. Add to this birth and death certificates, directories, almanacs, and publication indexes such as the *New York Times Index* and *Reader's Guide to Periodical Literature* and one can imagine the massive amount of information available from public records.

An especially rich data source is **vital statistics**: data on births, deaths, marriages, divorces, and the like. By state law, all births must be recorded, and death records must be filed before burial permits can be obtained. Birth records provide information not only on the child born but also on the parents, including the father's full name, address, age, and usual occupation. These data make possible research ranging from a study of social class and fertility to a study of maternal age and the incidence of twin births. Similarly, death records may contain, in addition to the usual biographical information, data on cause of death; length of illness (where applicable); whether injuries were accidental, homicidal, or self-inflicted; and the time and place of death. With such data, all sorts of demographic and epidemiological studies (studies dealing with the incidence or prevalence of disease) are possible. Indeed, much of what we know about death has come from the analysis of death records. Ordinarily, researchers obtain these records from an agency such as the Centers for Disease Control and Prevention, which compiles data for the nation as a whole, or from international organizations such as the United Nations, which compile such statistics for the world.

One of the earliest sociological studies to make use of official records—in this case, death records—was Emile Durkheim's classic study *Suicide* (1951), which we discussed at length in Chapter 2. In the late eighteenth century, many European nations began to compile data from death certificates, including cause of death as well as personal characteristics of the deceased such as sex, age, and marital status. Several scholars before Durkheim focused on suicide as a specific cause and further compiled and published data relating suicide rates to such variables as religion, season of the year, gender, and marital status. Using these data, Durkheim rejected several hypotheses popular at the time, such as that suicide was the result of mental illness, and ultimately arrived at his influential theory that a lack of social integration contributes to suicides. Supporting his theory were data showing that suicide rates were lowest when social ties were strong (as among persons who are married and members of religions that emphasize social cohesion) and highest when social ties were weak (as among the divorced and members of religions that emphasize individualism).

Kai Erikson (1966) used several public documents to study deviance in Puritan New England. As a way of examining how the community defined deviance and, in so doing, defined its moral boundaries, Erikson examined three "crime waves" among the Puritans over a 60-year period. The first wave, called the antinomian controversy of 1636–38, developed over a conflict concerning who was qualified to preach the Gospel in Boston and culminated in a civil trial for sedition and the banishing of two prominent citizens from the colony. The second wave involved violent, court-ordered persecutions of the Quakers from the 1650s to the 1660s, and the third wave consisted of the famous witchcraft hysteria centered in Salem in 1692. To analyze these events, Erikson relied on the extensive records of the Essex County Court and on the writings of some principals in these conflicts, such as Anne Hutchinson and the Puritan ministers John Winthrop and Cotton Mather. He concluded, in support of his hypothesis, that these historical events were in effect created by the community to establish its moral boundaries.

Stephen Sales (1973) also made use of multiple sources of available data, including official statistics, in his study of threat and authoritarianism. *Authoritarianism* is a personality pattern characterized by a tendency to be unduly respectful of those in positions of authority. Authoritarians tend to admire power and toughness; to be superstitious, cynical, and opposed to introspection; and to believe in harsh treatment of those who violate group norms. Sales tested the hypothesis that these tendencies would be especially likely to occur in response to a threatening environment, such as exists in a period of economic depression. He compared existing data from the 1920s, a period of low economic threat in the United States, with data from the 1930s, the time of the Great Depression. For example, given that authoritarians wish to condemn and punish violators of in-group values, Sales expected an increase in support for police forces during the 1930s. He therefore examined the city budgets of two cities, New York and Pittsburgh. When he calculated the proportions of the budget devoted to the police force and the fire department (which he used as a control), he found that appropriations were higher for the police and lower for the fire department in the 1930s than in the 1920s. Moreover, this increase in budgeting for the police did not result from an increase in crime; when Sales consulted the *Uniform Crime Reports for the United States* he found a decline in crime from the 1920s to the 1930s.

Sales also found a variety of other data from public records consistent with the hypothesis that authoritarianism increased in the 1930s. For example, as indicated by the *United States Catalog, Cumulative Book Index*, and *Reader's Guide to Periodical Literature*, there were more books and articles published on astrology (authoritarians are superstitious) and fewer books and articles on psychoanalysis and psychotherapy (authoritarians are opposed to introspection).

Perhaps the most widely used public storehouse of data is that collected and maintained by the U.S. Bureau of the Census. The bureau gathers an enormous amount of information. According to the Constitution, every person in the nation must be counted at least once every 10 years. Data from these decennial censuses, which began in 1790, are made available in two different forms: aggregate and individual. Aggregate data are released within months of their collection and describe various characteristics of the population of the states, counties, metropolitan areas, cities and towns, neighborhood tracts, and blocks.

The censuses of population and housing gather detailed information on the composition of every household in the country. The information gathered has varied over time, but it generally includes data on the age, gender, race, and marital status of each person and numerous household characteristics, such as home value or monthly rent and number of rooms. From 1940 to 2000, the U.S. Census Bureau used two questionnaires: a short form, which most people received, and a long form that was sent to a sample of the population. In 2010, the bureau went to a single short form consisting of 10 questions, and questions asked in previous long forms are now included in the annual American Community Survey.[1] Social scientists have used census data to study everything from the ecology of cities to residential mobility to racial segregation.

In Chapter 5, we mentioned John Logan and Brian Stults's (2011) use of the 1960 through 2010 censuses of the population to trace changes in minority segregation in the past half-century. Based on the index of dissimilarity, a popular measure of residential segregation, these researchers found that beginning in 1980 black–white segregation has slowly declined but that the segregation of Hispanics and Asians from whites has either increased or remained the same in the majority of metropolises. However, blacks remained far more segregated from whites than Hispanics or Asians.

The unit of analysis in the study of residential segregation is the census track. By aggregating data to describe geographic units rather than individuals, the Census Bureau protects the privacy of individual persons, which it is sworn to do. However, after a period of 72 years, individual census records—known as the **manuscript census**—are released to the general public. (See Box 12.1 for an example of research using the manuscript census.)

Beginning with the 1960 Census, the bureau also has made available individual-level data (actual responses) on samples of the decennial census, called the **Public Use Microdata Sample** (PUMS). A 1 percent PUMS sample is available for the 1940 through 1970 censuses; both 1 percent and 5 percent samples are available online for the 1980, 1990, and 2000 censuses. In addition, PUMS files are available since 2005 for the complete American Community Survey. To ensure confidentiality, the bureau removes names, addresses, and all other personal identifying information from these sample files. A project called IPUMS (the "I" is for "Integrated") is extending this series to other years and integrating the data over time by creating uniform codes for variables (Minnesota Population Center, 2016).[2]

In addition, once a month the bureau conducts the Current Population Survey (CPS), which we have described briefly in earlier chapters. The CPS is administered to approximately 60,000 households in nearly 800 areas throughout the 50 states and the District of

BOX 12.1 Using the Manuscript Census in Social Research: Nineteenth-Century Shaker Demographics

Social scientists have been interested for many years in a religious group that has almost disappeared. The Shakers developed in England as a branch of the Quakers around the middle of the eighteenth century. In 1774 the group's prophetess, Ann Lee, came to America with eight others to start one of the most interesting chapters in the history of American religion. The Shakers lived a rigidly communitarian life, requiring that new members give up all personal property. They also did not believe in marriage, cohabitation, sex, or procreation. Men and women lived in different houses, and members of the opposite sex were prohibited from talking to one another in the halls or crossing one another's paths.

As celibates, the Shakers' principal means of gathering new members was voluntary joining. Yet, despite their austere living conditions, the sect survived for more than 200 years and even thrived for a time, growing from the 9 members who immigrated to America to a population that standard reference works estimate at 17,000 at the height of the movement. Some believe that this is an underestimate; indeed, the director of the Shaker Museum and Library at Sabbathday Lake, Maine, estimates that "total membership ran to about sixty-four thousand" (Kephart, 1982:208). Other estimates are more modest; Mark Holloway (1966:70) claims that in 1830, 5000 members were scattered among 18 different Shaker communities. What was the actual popular success of the Shaker experiment? How many Shakers were there? The fragmentary and scattered nature of the data make all of the foregoing estimates rough guesses. However, William Sims Bainbridge (1982) put the original enumeration schedules of the U.S. Census to good use in estimating the Shaker population in the latter half of the nineteenth century. In so doing, he also provides insight into the nature of recruitment, defection, and the gradual decline of this sect.

Seventy-two years after each census, the original schedules on which census enumerators recorded their data are released to the general public. These data are available on microfilm at the National Archives in Washington and in 13 regional archives around the country. The organization of the data files facilitates the location of individuals by persons interested in learning more about their ancestors. In fact, the 1900 census files have a "soundex" system that allows genealogists to trace the location of heads of households by identifying their names phonetically. Social scientists face several problems in using these data. For the first six censuses, 1790–1840, relatively little information was collected on individuals, because only heads of households were identified by name. For later censuses the sheer volume of data presents a barrier to many researchers. Methods have been developed for sampling census records (see R. C. Johnson, 1978). But the small population of Shakers made sampling inappropriate.

From historical accounts, Bainbridge first identified 22 colonies of Shakers in the period 1840–1900. These colonies were located in eight states (five in Massachusetts, four each in New York and Ohio, three in Maine, two each in New Hampshire and Kentucky, and one each in Connecticut and Florida). Since Bainbridge could not know in advance the last names of Shakers, he was forced to search through some 150 rolls of microfilm reporting data for these eight states. And because the manuscript schedules for 1890 do not exist, having been destroyed in a fire, he decided to examine the data for every other census in the

(continued)

(continued)

period 1840–1900. Describing the difficulties in researching the census of 1840, Bainbridge (1982:354) says that

> when one is scanning through a town which is supposed to contain a Shaker colony, and finds a household with 215 members, one may guess the Shakers have been located. But this presumption is not good enough. For one thing, Shaker colonies were divided into "families," sometimes as many as six of these subunits composing a colony, and some of the smaller families could be mistaken for other kinds of groups, and vice versa. Some families in 1840 were labeled "Shakers," but most were not. Many could be identified because the "head of household" whose name was recorded was a prominent Shaker mentioned in published histories.

Through painstaking cross-checking (e.g., using the 1850 census to identify some names listed in 1840), Bainbridge estimated the Shaker population at 3489 in 1840 and 855 in 1900. By analyzing the age and sex distributions of Shakers, he also showed that the proportion of females always was greater than in the general population and increased substantially over time, from 58 percent in 1840 to 72 percent at the turn of the century. Contributing to this transformation to a female society was "the defection of males, recruitment of destitute young mothers with children, and intentional differential acceptance of female children" (363).

Columbia. It is the primary source of information on labor force statistics such as unemployment rates and provides information on numerous other population characteristics. For the past 30 years, the CPS and individual-level census data have been the most widely used data sources cited in *Demography*, the leading journal for the study of structure and changes in human populations (Ruggles, 2014). Finally, there are regular censuses of business, manufacturers, agriculture, and other institutions.[3]

KEY POINT

Census data are commonly available in three forms: aggregate data on social units such as states, towns, and census tracts; 1 percent and 5 percent samples of individual-level data; and individual records, released 72 years after each census.

Christine Schwartz and Robert Mare (2005) used both the IPUMS and the CPS to examine trends in *educational homogamy*, the tendency for husbands and wives to have the same level of education, from 1940 to 2003. Classifying each spouse into five categories of highest year of schooling (<10, 10–11, 12, 13–15, ≥16), they found first a decline and then a steady increase in homogamy over this period. The percentage of couples having the same level of education fell from 50–60 percent in 1940 (depending on whether the couple was recently married) to 45 percent in 1960 and then rose to 55 percent in 2003. Interestingly, much of the increase in educational homogamy after 1960 came from an increase in the tendency of college graduates to marry one another rather than persons of lower education.

An interesting application of census data is suggested by Marcus Felson (1983), who recommends using diverse available-data sets, including the Census of Manufacturers, to measure social and cultural change. The *1977 Census of Manufacturers*, for example, shows that during the 1970s increases in sales of electronic musical instruments did not result in reduced sales of traditional acoustical instruments; the shipment of neckties sharply declined, whereas shipments of baseballs, softballs, and baseball mitts increased; and shipments of girdles declined, whereas shipments of women's and girl's athletic shoes increased.

Private Documents

A less accessible but no less important data source is private documents: information produced by individuals or organizations about their own activities that is not intended for public consumption. Diaries and letters long have been a favorite data source for historians; other examples include businesses' personnel and sales records, inventories, and tax reports; hospital patient records; and college transcripts.

Perhaps the best known research using letters is W. I. Thomas and Florian Znaniecki's classic 1918 study *The Polish Peasant in Europe and America*. The study dealt broadly with problems of immigration and assimilation into American society. The authors drew on several sources of information, including newspaper accounts, autobiographies, and the records of social agencies such as the Legal Aid Society. But by far their largest single data source was a collection of more than 750 personal letters exchanged between Polish immigrants in America and their relatives and friends in Poland. Thomas and Znaniecki's analysis of these materials was mainly descriptive. It consisted largely of introductions to sets of letters, commentaries on individual letters, and the letters themselves, nearly all of which were published as part of their study.

A second example of research using personal documents is Jerry Jacobs's analysis of suicide notes (1967). To understand how individuals justify their actions to themselves and others, Jacobs analyzed 112 notes left by persons who committed suicide in the Los Angeles area. He was able to place nearly all of the notes in six general categories: "first form notes," "sorry illness notes," "not sorry illness notes," "direct accusation notes," "will and testament notes," and "notes of instruction." The largest category, first form notes, pertains to accounts in which the person faced an intolerable problem for which death was seen as the only possible resolution.

Julie Kmec's (2007) study of the role of race and social networks in job turnover drew on personnel records from a U.S. branch of a private, multisite business. The company maintained a database of job applicants and hires over 32 months, which was long enough for Kmec to observe routine turnover. In addition, the database contained information on the sex and race of applicants and, most important for examining network effects, on how applicants contacted the company. Examining persons hired for one entry-level position, Kmec found that, irrespective of race, workers recruited by a current employee of the company were less likely to leave voluntarily than workers recruited in other ways. Apparently, informal ties with a current employee provide social support and enrichment that bind workers to the company.

Institutional records also have been used to supplement survey data. After the fourth wave of the National Educational Longitudinal Survey (NELS) (see Chapters 4 and 6), transcripts were requested from more than 3000 postsecondary institutions that respondents in the third (1994) and fourth (2000) waves reported attending. Adding transcript data on attendance patterns, fields of study, specific courses taken, and grades and credits earned supplements the database of factors that may explain educational and economic outcomes. For example, using the NELS transcript data, Sara Goldrick-Rab (2006) found that students' socioeconomic background affected their pathway through college; students of lower socioeconomic status were four times more likely than more advantaged students to experience discontinuous enrollment by taking more than 6 months off from college. Students who lack financial resources are more apt to take this nontraditional path, which lowers the likelihood of earning a degree. Thus, the route that students take through college contributes to stratification in higher education.

Mass Media

Also constituting part of the written record (as well as an oral and nonverbal record) are the mass media—newspapers, magazines, television, radio, films, the Internet. By analyzing the content of these sources, social researchers have addressed a variety of issues.

In the aforementioned study of threat and authoritarianism, Sales (1973) also did a simple analysis of comic strips. Because authoritarians tend to admire power and strength, Sales expected that popular fictional protagonists would become stronger and more powerful in the threatening 1930s than they had been in the relatively nonthreatening 1920s. Searching through Stephen Becker's *Comic Art in America*, Sales identified 20 comic strips that first appeared in the 1920s and 21 comic strips introduced in the 1930s. He and two other coders then judged whether the main character in each strip was either (1) "physically powerful or controlled great power or (2) not particularly powerful" (46). Supporting his hypothesis, Sales found that only two of the strips started in the 1920s emphasized the power of the main character (*Buck Rogers* and *Tarzan*), whereas 12 of the strips started in the 1930s were about powerful men (e.g., *Joe Palooka*, *Dick Tracy*, and *Superman*).

Although most research on the media has analyzed verbal content, one can also analyze visual content. Erving Goffman (1979) looked at hundreds of pictures from advertisements in newspapers and magazines to see what they revealed about the meaning of gender in American society. One image he identified was that of women as subordinate and dependent, which he called "ritualization of subordination." This was evidenced by pictures consistently showing women bowing or otherwise on a lower plane than men, in a recumbent or reclining position, displaying a "bashful knee bend," canting (lowering) the head or upper part of the body, being victimized by men in playful games of "mocked assault," and in childlike, playful, or unserious poses. Goffman provided a provocative description of "gender displays," but the purpose of his study was to identify different ways that women are portrayed in advertisements. Thus, he developed a set of categories to describe gender stereotyping and chose examples to illustrate the categories, but he did not randomly select or systematically analyze advertisements.

To examine the generalizability of Goffman's depictions, several studies have systematically applied his coding scheme to carefully drawn samples. Katharina Lindner (2004) analyzed advertisements in selected issues of *Time* (a general interest magazine) and *Vogue* (a women's fashion magazine) from 1955 to 2002. Her sample consisted of issues from January and June of both magazines in the years 1955, 1965, 1975, 1985, 1995, and 2002. For each selected issue, she analyzed all advertisements showing one or more women by coding the presence or absence of nine different categories. The category "feminine touch," for example, was coded as present when:

> The woman touches herself (e.g., hair, face, lips) or her clothes in an unnatural way or uses her fingers and hands to trace the outline of an object, cradle it, or caress its surface. This type of touching is to be distinguished from the utilitarian kind, which involves grasping, manipulating, or holding objects. (Lindner, 2004:414)

At least one of the nine coding categories was present in 78 percent of the 1374 advertisements that Lindner analyzed; three categories were present in one-third or more of the ads; and except for decreases in ritualization of subordination, feminine touch, and one other category, few significant changes occurred over time. Thus, there is little question that advertisements in these two mass circulation magazines portray women stereotypically.

In addition to the foregoing studies that measured mass media content as an indicator of cultural change, numerous studies have examined media influence. For example, researchers have investigated whether capital punishment deters homicide by examining the effects of execution publicity on murder rates. William Bailey examined this issue in two separate studies (W. C. Bailey and Peterson, 1989; W. C. Bailey, 1990). Both studies used monthly homicide figures issued by the U.S. Department of Health, Bureau of Vital Statistics. In the first study, Bailey and Peterson (1989) measured the effects of execution publicity, as found in newspapers, on the homicide rate between 1940 and 1986. Executions were classified as high in publicity if they appeared in *Facts on File* (a national index of major news stories) and the *New York Times*, as moderate in publicity if they appeared in the *Times* but not in *Facts on File*, and as low in publicity if they did not receive coverage in either of these sources. In the second study, Bailey (1990) examined the effects of televised execution publicity on homicide rates from 1976 to 1987. In this case, both the extent of television coverage and the type of publicity (e.g., artist drawings, witness accounts) were measured after viewing ABC, CBS, and NBC evening news programs located in the Vanderbilt Television News Archives. The findings of both studies failed to support the deterrence hypothesis as the publicity surrounding executions had no discernible effect on murder rates over time.

Finally, the Internet has become an increasingly popular data source. Andreas Wimmer and Kevin Lewis (2010), for example, created a rich data set from Facebook profile pages for the first-year class at a private college where more than 97 percent of the class maintained profiles. With the permission of Facebook and the college, they downloaded the profiles. Then, they inferred each student's race/ethnicity from uploaded photos and other information; merged these data with other profile data; and, again with the college's permission, linked the profile data with college major and roommate and dormmate information. Restricting themselves to social ties within the college, they found a preference for associating with others of the same race or ethnicity, but they also found that factors such as friendship reciprocity, residential propinquity, and being from the same state had a greater influence on friendship formation.

Physical, Nonverbal Evidence

Although seldom used in the social sciences, nonverbal materials such as works of art, clothing, household items, and various artifacts constitute a rich source of evidence. Cave paintings, tools, and other artifacts are important data to archaeologists studying past civilizations, and historians find invaluable evidence in sculpture and other works of art. A study of tombstones is another example.

Between 1690 and 1765 the Puritans, in the words of the historian Richard Bushman (1967), became Yankees. This historic transformation is evident in changes in attitudes toward death, available for all to see in the tombstones of New England's colonial cemeteries. Observing engravings on gravestones, David Stannard (1977) found that throughout the late seventeenth and early eighteenth centuries, stones invariably bore some version of the "death's-head" carving of a winged skull, representing the Puritans' grim vision of death. This visage dominated until the 1730s, when the death's-head motif and accompanying epitaphs steadily gave way to more romantic and optimistic designs of cherubs and angels. As this shift occurred, Stannard notes (1977:157), "the cemeteries in which those gravestones were placed began to become overcrowded while simultaneously falling into neglect and disarray. The Puritan community was becoming a relic of history."

Social Science Data Archives

Over the past 50 years, the social sciences have seen a tremendous proliferation of **data archives**, repositories of data collected by various agencies and researchers that are accessible to the public. Most of these archives contain survey data, but archives also exist for collections of ethnographies, in which the whole society is the unit of analysis. Thus, the use of data archives is an extension of both survey research and field research. As such, each archival data source has advantages and disadvantages associated with two different approaches to social research.

We have already discussed and provided examples of the analysis of available survey data, called "secondary analysis," in Chapter 9. A noteworthy example, you may recall, is the General Social Survey (GSS), whose data are deposited in several archives, including the Inter-University Consortium for Political and Social Research, the Roper Center for Public Opinion Research, and the Survey Documentation and Analysis Archive. Social scientists also analyze data derived from studies of whole societies. One valuable archive of such data, called the Human Relations Area Files, contains information recorded on microfiche and/or electronically on more than 350 societies. These files, fully indexed with many available online, are in "raw data" form, with pages from ethnographic reports organized by topic. Analysts have indexed every paragraph in the collection with subject codes denoting aspects of cultural belief and practice. Two other sources of cross-cultural data available in "coded" form, with numeric codes on several variables for each society, are the *Ethnographic Atlas* (Murdock, 1967) and the Standard Cross-Cultural Sample (Murdock and White, 1969). The *Atlas* contains codes on approximately 40 variables for more than 1100 societies; the Standard Cross-Cultural Sample contains more extensive data on a smaller sample of 186 societies. The following study used all three of these sources.

Obtaining data from a sample of 48 tribal societies, Willie Pearson and Lewellyn Hendrix (1979) tested the hypothesis that divorce increases as the status of women increases. This follows from the reasoning that as women gain economic resources, they become more autonomous and less dependent on their husbands. Pearson and Hendrix's findings showed that divorce rates were moderately correlated with female status even when theoretically relevant variables such as community size, marital residence, and descent rules were controlled.

Big Data

The final category of available data is a recent product of the digital age. Ten years ago, "very few people were using the term 'big data'" (Kitchin, 2014:67). In short order, however, the term became a buzzword in industry and academia. One search of the Web of Science database showed that the term first appeared in academic publications in 2011 and that by 2014, the number of publications exceeded 1600 (Jenkins, Slomczynski, and Dubrow, 2016). Its presence in the social sciences is even more recent, with the majority of publications in sociology and political science, according to the same search, appearing since 2014 (Jenkins, Slomczynski, and Dubrow, 2016).

Big data are the outcome of "a shift in data collection toward digital records" (D. A. McFarland, Lewis, and Goldberg, 2016:15), which was facilitated by technological advances in computer processing, networking, and data storage (Kitchin, 2014). As Daniel McFarland, Kevin Lewis, and Amir Goldberg (2016:15) point out, "Today, a growing number of organizations retain digital data on millions of persons . . . and much of social life is mediated by technology that retains a digital record of every action." As examples of the remarkable variety of such data, they mention "robotic medical devices that retain data on every movement; insurance and hospital records of patient health and treatment; credit card records of every transaction; online social media retaining every click, communication, and timestamp; internet protocol (IP) addresses registered on every cell tower . . ." (16). Of particular interest to social scientists, much of these data concern activities, interactions, and relationships in everyday life.

Thus far there is no agreed-on definition of big data. Kevin Lewis (2015:1) associates big data with three concepts that are often conflated: (1) unusually large data sets that (2) are collected digitally and (3) require sophisticated computational methods. Three frequently cited characteristics of big data are volume, velocity, and variety (Laney, 2001):

1. *Volume.* In the computer industry, the term big data has been applied to data sets so large that they could not be processed or analyzed with standard computer software (Manovich, 2011). One can get a sense of what "volume" means from two of Bernard Marr's (2015) 20 facts about big data: "In August 2015, over 1 billion people

used Facebook in a single day," and "Facebook users send an average of 31.25 million messages and view 2.77 million videos every minute."

2. *Velocity*. In contrast to "small data" studies, in which the data are "freeze-framed at a particular time and place" or, in the case of longitudinal studies, the data are captured periodically (e.g., every month or year), big data are generated continuously (Kitchin, 2014:76), capturing activities dynamically in "real-time, over time" (Tinati et al. 2014). The Facebook activities just mentioned are examples.

3. *Variety*. As we have shown, there is a great variety of data; however, with big data, "different kinds of data are more likely to be combined and linked" (Kitchin, 2014:77). Consider Facebook again: "posts consist of text that is often linked to photos, or video files, or other websites, and they attract comments by other Facebook users" (77).

At this early stage, a primary source of big data for social scientists is social media. More than 100 studies have drawn on the microblogging website Twitter (Tinati et al., 2014), which allows users to "tweet" 140-character messages to followers and anyone else having access to the Twitter website. For example, researchers have studied the role of Twitter in election campaigning (Murthy, 2015) and in mobilizing social movements (Tremayne, 2014) and have drawn on Twitter to measure happiness (Curini, Iacus, and Canova, 2015), teen interest in birth control and abortion (Kearney and Levine, 2014), and mood as a predictor of the stock market (Bollen, Mao, and Zeng, 2011).

The analysis of big data presents methodological challenges. Ramine Tinati and colleagues (2014) contend that analyses of Twitter data often are restricted by traditional social science methods that do not take advantage of the scale or flow (velocity) of big data. For example, to make the data manageable, analysts have applied small-scale content analyses of users and/or samples of tweets. Similarly, Wimmer and Lewis's Facebook study, cited above, was restricted to a single first-year class of students, which bypasses the scale of Facebook data. More consistent with the concept of big data is research on Facebook that used the entire network of approximately 721 million users and 69 billion friendship links to show an average of 3.74 degrees of separation between friendships (Backstrom et al., 2012).

Another challenge is the varied and complex structure of the data (variety). Unlike a simple subject × variable matrix of data (see Chapter 15), which can be analyzed with standard computer software and statistics, big data often have a different structure (e.g. with Facebook data, subject × subject) or format (narrative text and photos) that are not easily combined or analyzed. The analysis of data of such variety (and scale) requires advanced technical training, which is why "the first wave of studies" of big data "has been dominated by physical, computer, and information scientists" (Golder and Macy, 2014:145).

In the long run, Scott Golder and Michael Macy (2014:144–46) believe that graduate programs in the social sciences must provide training in skills needed to analyze big data. Their list of skills includes learning to use programming interfaces (which is how one downloads Twitter data), manipulate unstructured data and nested data structures (forms of big data "that cannot be directly imported into standard statistical packages" [145]), and store large data sets (which may exceed the capacity of a single computer).

General Methodological Issues in Available-Data Research

The four basic approaches to social research differ according to the stages that require the greatest labor and creativity on the part of the researcher. In experimentation, experimental design (e.g., number of conditions, measurement of key variables, instructions to subjects) is crucial; therefore, much of the effort goes into perfecting the design and preparing for its implementation (pretesting), and the data analysis is simple and straightforward. When the design is not experimental, the data analysis requires great effort and skill. And when the data were collected for another purpose and investigators cannot directly oversee the procedures producing the data, a search for appropriate measures and the evaluation of data quality are extremely important research phases.

Searching for and Procuring Available Data

As the aforementioned studies reveal, the use of available data is a flexible and powerful approach to social research. Still, a major problem with this approach is finding and procuring relevant information. Although the material to study a given topic may exist, how do you know what to look for? And how do you find it, acquire it, and/or gain permission to use it?

Perhaps the best advice is to let the research problem or hypothesis serve as a guide to appropriate sources. In one sense, this is obvious. For example, researchers like Kmec who are interested in job turnover will readily entertain the possibility of using company personnel records. But this advice holds true in another way. Aimlessly searching through records or dredging up data from survey archives is unlikely to yield anything of value. Even though the data pre-exist, that does not mean researchers should reverse the research process by analyzing the data and then developing some post hoc rationale for the analysis. More than likely, the outcome of such an approach will be a trivial and flawed study. It is far better to let your research problem dictate your methodology than to let your method override the substantive and theoretical focus of your research.

A second guide to locating pertinent data is to search the literature for studies by previous investigators. No doubt Erikson's study of deviance in Puritan New England was aided by the mounds of data already uncovered by earlier historians who investigated that era. It also helps to know where to go for tips on locating available data. You can learn about the location of many data sources by consulting a librarian. Several libraries as well as the Reference and User Services Association of the American Library Association have created websites with useful guides and lists of primary sources for historical research.[4] Another valuable resource is the Library of Congress's online catalog. For a variety of quantitative data, the Inter-University Consortium for Political and Social Research and the Roper Center for Public Opinion Research provide numerous social science data archives.

Access to public sources varies among the archives and agencies holding the data. Many of these data, such as those compiled by the Census Bureau and other government agencies, are mandated for public use without restrictions. The greatest access problems pertain to private documents and confidential records. Obtaining such data may require a little ingenuity, such as Thomas and Znaniecki (1918) used in their study of letters written to and from Polish immigrants. They acquired the letters through advertisements in a Polish-language newspaper that offered to pay 10 to 20 cents per letter. Gaining access also may depend on the permission and cooperation of others. Jacobs, for example, collected his suicide notes with the aid of an acquaintance who was a deputy coroner in the Los Angeles County Coroner's Office. Kmec (personal communication, 2008) learned about the personnel records she used through a friend who happened to be a vice president at the company. She was allowed to use the records provided that she conceal the company's identity in reporting the results of her study. To obtain respondents' transcripts, NELS administrators took great pains in contacting more than 3000 different colleges and universities and carefully explaining requirements of the Family Educational Rights and Privacy Act of 1974, which authorized these institutions to release the transcripts.

Measurement of Key Concepts

Using available data is a bit like wearing someone else's shoes. They may fit perfectly well. But more likely they will either be too small, pinching your toes, or too large, causing you to stumble. Seldom will available data be ideally suited to the purposes a researcher has in mind. At best, the data may require the creative construction of measures that provide indirect evidence of a given variable. At worst, the data may be inadequate to address the research question.

In much available-data research, an investigator must develop creative measures that approximate variables of interest. Many of the measures in Sales's (1973) research on authoritarianism are indirect. Unable to question individuals directly about their attraction to powerful people, Sales relied on the popularity of comic strip characters as an indicator of such attraction. And when no reference work covering new comic strips was available for the later periods he investigated, he speculated that individuals "attracted to strength and power in times of stress . . . might be more inclined to purchase strong and powerful dogs" (1973:52). Sure enough, an examination of American Kennel Club registrations of some 116 breeds showed that 9.8 percent of all dogs registered by the club in the low-threat period (1959–1964) were in the attack-dog classes (German shepherds, Doberman pinschers, Great Danes), whereas these dogs accounted for 13.5 percent of the registrations in the relatively threatening period (1967–1970).

Sales's measurement of threat also is somewhat indirect since it depends on the tenor of the times rather than on the measurable feelings of individuals. More direct measures of threat can be found in experiments where individuals have been "threatened" by being told that they have failed tests of intelligence (see Sales and Friend, 1973) or by being led to anticipate receiving electrical shocks. Sales, on the other hand, identified contiguous historical periods that appeared to pose contrasting environmental threats for the population as a whole. He ended up comparing periods marked primarily by differences in economic prosperity: the 1920s versus the 1930s and 1959–1964 versus 1967–1970. These contrasts do not unambiguously represent low- versus high-threat conditions. For example, as Sales (1973:51) himself noted, the presumed "low-threat" period of 1959–1964 "included the abortive Bay of Pigs invasion, the Cuban missile crisis, and the assassination of J. F. Kennedy."

But the facts that he used two sets of contrasting historical periods and that the relationship between threat and authoritarianism was so consistently demonstrated lend considerable credibility to his measurement of "threat." Indeed, Sales's historical measure would appear to provide a much more powerful test of his hypothesis than weak and short-lived, albeit direct, experimental manipulations of threat.

As we argue in the next chapter, the use of several different measures of a given variable is always a good practice in social research. This is even more imperative in available-data research that uses indirect and approximate indicators. The use of multiple indicators, however, is not a panacea for inappropriate measures. One problem with available data is that their mere availability may lead researchers to use measures that are inadequate for research purposes. This is especially apparent in secondary analyses of survey data. For example, a question first asked in 1973 and now repeated each year in the GSS is, "Is there an area right around here—that is, within a mile—where you would be afraid to walk alone at night?" This has been identified in many studies as a measure of fear of crime. Yet the item makes no reference to crime or any other object of the fear, and it is entirely hypothetical, which may overestimate an individual's actual experience of fear in day-to-day situations (Ferraro and LaGrange, 1987). The point is that available data, like any tool, should be appropriate for the task at hand.

Data Evaluation and Adjustment

Perhaps the most important general rule that applies to the use of available data, irrespective of the source, is that researchers must reconstruct the process by which the data were originally assembled (Riley, 1963:252). If you gather the data yourself, you generally are aware of their limitations, possible errors, and biases and you can adapt your analyses accordingly. But such adaptations also may be required of available data. Therefore, it is crucial to try to determine, as far as possible, how, when, where, and by whom the data were collected. Only then can you begin to assess the validity of the data.

Researchers using historical documents must be especially concerned about their authenticity. Authentication is a highly technical matter that requires a thorough knowledge of the historical period from which the documents are purported to originate. In addition to checking the logical consistency of the content, one must examine handwriting, writing style, and even the chemical composition of ink and paper. The historian Louis Gottschalk (1969) notes that doubts about authenticity arise frequently, and if they seem not to, it is only because a skilled historian has already authenticated the sources. For this reason, social researchers like Kai Erikson usually are spared the task of authentication. Assuming authenticity, however, one must still ask how the data were collected. Is the available evidence accurate, complete, and reliable? A series of studies of colonial Boston illustrate how easy it is to be misled if you do not have a thorough knowledge of the conditions of data collection.

According to the historian G. B. Warden (1976), the traditionally accepted view of colonial Boston was that of an egalitarian community with a town-meeting democracy and a relatively equitable distribution of wealth. These egalitarian conditions, moreover, are believed to have made the city a center of radical political agitation before the Revolution.

In the 1960s a group of scholars (see, e.g., Henretta [1965]) challenged this position, claiming that Boston experienced dramatic increases in social and economic inequality in the eighteenth century. Indeed, these scholars alleged that it was the resulting socioeconomic tensions that contributed to radical political agitation. The extensive arguments supporting the latter view are based largely on evidence from tax assessments in 1687 and 1771 (unfortunately, tax records for the intervening years are not available).

For example, one of the propositions put forth was that Boston experienced extraordinarily rapid economic growth in the eighteenth century, which increased stratification and the maldistribution of wealth. Evidence of this came from an observed increase in the total assessed wealth of Boston from 16,591 pounds in 1687 to 460,493 pounds in 1771, which translates into an annual growth rate of 33 percent. As Warden points out, however, these figures do not take into account how property was estimated for tax purposes. In 1687 all property was estimated for tax purposes at about one-twentieth of its true market value, whereas in 1771 real property (land and house) was estimated at about one-twelfth of its market value and personal property (e.g., stock in trade) was estimated at close to its actual value. If appropriate adjustments are made, the estimated "simple annual growth rate is only about 2.3 percent, which is relatively low compared with other colonial communities" (Warden, 1976:589).

Warden shows how similar problems exist with other interpretations of these data. Another proposition was that the richest Bostonians possessed an increasingly disproportionate share of the wealth. But once again, the data purported to support this proposition are flawed by inconsistencies. The different assessments of real and personal property in 1771, for example, magnify the difference between the actual taxable wealth of property holders in the bottom and top halves of the distribution. As a consequence,

> there appears to be a heavy concentration of wealth in the upper half of the group; the apparent concentration occurred, however, not because the retailers and merchants were all that much richer than those in the bottom half but because the wealth of those in the top was estimated at a much higher rate than the wealth of those in the bottom half. (Warden, 1976:604)

Even for more recent data sources, the same general rule of carefully assessing the accuracy and consistency of the data applies. Consider, for example, an unwary user of crime statistics. There are two major sources of crime data: (1) self-report data from the National Crime Victimization Survey, in which people are asked to indicate crimes in which they have been personally victimized, and (2) data from official reports of crimes known to the police, which are compiled in the *Uniform Crime Reports* by the Federal Bureau of Investigation. These two sources clearly offer different operational definitions of crime; one focuses on the victim and the other on the offense. And, as it turns out, there is no simple relationship between the two measures. A single offense (e.g., a robbery of several persons in an establishment) may have more than one victim. Some offenses (murder) have no victims who can be interviewed, and other offenses (e.g., prostitution and gambling) have no victims in that the "victims" are also the offenders. Each of these measures also suffers from other methodological problems. Victimizations are limited to persons over the age of 12. Not all crimes are brought to the attention of the police (e.g., burglaries of uninsured items); also, the police themselves may fail to record incidents.

Such problems do not render crime statistics useless or totally invalid. They do, however, force researchers to focus on a particular definition of crime—either offenses or victimizations—and to consider the implications of using data with a relatively large measurement error (Jacob, 1984). More generally, the flawed nature of these data points to the need for every researcher using available data to become acquainted with the process by which the information was gathered. How did the data collectors define categories (e.g., "crime" and "tax assessments")? If the data were collected repeatedly over time, have there been changes in record-keeping or data-collection procedures? In the case of the media and first-person documents, how might the writer's ideological position have affected his or her interpretation of events? Without recourse to the usual checks on validity, knowing how the data were collected is often the only way to determine the authenticity and accuracy of available data.

Another procedure that is especially useful for evaluating reliability is the use of several different sources of evidence. As a rule, historians do not accept an account of an event as reliable unless it is confirmed by two or more independent sources. Demographers, who analyze population statistics, often use several data sources and different estimation procedures. C. R. Schwartz and Mare used two data sources, IPUMS and CPS, which produced highly similar estimates of educational homogamy. The only difference was slightly lower estimates for the census data, which the researchers attributed to greater measurement error in the census.

Once the data have been evaluated, it may become necessary to refine measures. If measurement errors or changes in definitions are detected, researchers must make the necessary adjustments to allow for proper interpretation. Warden's reanalysis of tax assessments in Boston offers one example. Two other examples involve changes in the wording of questions. In the 2000 Census, the question about race allowed respondents for the first time to select more than one racial category. To compare racial segregation in 2000 and 2010 with segregation in earlier censuses, Logan and Stults therefore had to recombine the 2000 and 2010 racial categories; for example, the combination of black with any other race was operationally defined as black. Similarly, changes in the wording of the educational attainment question by the CPS in 1992 and the census in 1990 forced C. W. Schwartz and Mare to establish a new set of categories that maximized comparability between the old and new questions.

Assessment of Data Completeness

In addition to evaluating the quality of existing measures, it is essential to assess the adequacy of the existing sample of information. Consider, for example, the U.S. Census. Despite the effort and cost of conducting the U.S. Census, the population is nearly always undercounted. Analyses indicate that the overall undercount is quite low—only about 1.4 percent in 2000—but that it varies by race, gender, and age. Even in 2010, when the census produced an overall overcount, blacks were more likely than whites, males more likely than females, and young children (aged 0–4) more likely than adults to be omitted (Hogan et al., 2013). Kirsten West and David Fein (1990) claim that the effects of such undercount are rarely considered by census data users. One possible effect, for example, is that the number of female-headed households among blacks is overestimated as a result of the census undercount of black males. However, analyses adjusting for undercount seem to make little difference, as Kelly Raley (2002) showed with respect to race differences in marital status.

In contrast to the generally high quality of census and survey archival data, cross-cultural data banks constitute nothing more than availability samples; they do not contain data on modern industrialized societies or even a representative sample of nonindustrial societies. This limits generalizations as well as the types of research that can be undertaken. Cross-cultural researchers using these data cannot make predictions or estimate worldwide societal characteristics. But they can provide limited tests of hypotheses (Lee, 1984). In their study of divorce and the status of women, Pearson and Hendrix were forced to use only those societies—48 in all—for which they could obtain adequate measures on key variables. Their rationale for this data set was that it included societies from all continents except Australia and contained sufficient variation in the key variables.

The representativeness of the data is even more problematic for researchers studying the more remote past, who must rely on whatever traces of information they can find. These data are certain to be incomplete and are probably biased. This is especially true of physical evidence, which invariably is subject to selective survival and selective deposit. **Selective survival** refers to the fact that some objects survive longer than others. The fact that pottery and bone survive the elements better than wood and paper has long been a problem for archaeologists. A graver problem for users of the written record is **selective deposit**— systematic biases in the content of the evidence that is available. Records may be selectively destroyed; other information may be edited.

Eugene Webb and associates (2000) note that members of Congress are allowed to edit proofs of the *Congressional Record*, a transcript of the speeches and activities of the U.S. Congress, which means that this document hardly serves as a spontaneous account of events. As another example, these authors cite a study of the longevity of the ancient Romans based on evidence from tombstones. Wives who died after their husbands may have been underrepresented insofar as they were less likely to get a tombstone than wives who died before their husbands. Also, middle-class and upper-class Romans were probably more likely to have tombstones than the lower classes of Roman society. And the fact that mortality rates are likely to have varied across classes could bias estimates of longevity.

KEY POINT

When data are produced by someone else, it is important to understand how they were originally assembled and to assess their limitations and completeness.

Similar problems may exist in studies of the written record. Only about 10 to 20 percent of those individuals who commit suicide leave notes. The question that must be asked of the Jacobs study, therefore, is whether the rational and coherent character of the notes he observed describes the mental condition of suicide victims *not* leaving notes. In other words, are persons who leave notes representative of the entire population of persons who commit suicide? More generally, Kenneth Bailey (1982:305–06) observes that documents may be biased by educational level. Not only are poorly educated people much less likely to write documents, but also the mass media are likely to be aimed at and to be more representative of well-educated people.

Similarly, one of the fallacies of big data is that they provide complete coverage of populations. In reality, "certain kinds of people are more likely than others to turn up in certain digital data sets"; even if the data set contains "every phone call, every message, or every friendship," not everyone owns a cell phone, is on Twitter, or has a Facebook account (Lewis, 2015:1–2). Furthermore, the activity levels of social media participants may bias inferences. For example, a small fraction of highly active users produce most Twitter content, and more than 40 percent of Twitter accounts "did not create a single tweet in the previous year" (reported in Park and Macy, 2015:10).

For many sources of available data, there is no choice in the selection of information. Researchers simply use all the data they can obtain, and then they attempt to account for sample selection bias. However, for studies of the more recent past, probability sampling of time and space are not only feasible but also often necessary because of the massive amount of information. For example, the task of analyzing all advertisements in all issues of even one magazine over a 50-year period, roughly the time frame of K. Lindner's study, would be monumental. Many data sources lend themselves to probability sampling: Actuarial, political, and judicial records usually may be sampled over time; voting records may be sampled across precincts (Webb et al., 2000); and documents and the mass media may be sampled in various ways (see the discussion of content analysis below).

Historical Analysis

The analysis of available data takes as many forms as the data themselves. In part, the type of analysis is a function of research purposes and research design. Descriptive accounts of a single event or historical period differ from tests of general hypotheses, which differ from trend studies. The analysis also depends on data sources. Researchers use different techniques for analyzing population statistics, mass media communications, and historical documents. In this section and the next, we briefly discuss aspects of two sharply different approaches to the analysis of available data: historical analysis and content analysis.

Descriptive and Analytical History

The word "history" has several meanings. It refers, for example, to (1) actual events or happenings of the past, from the recent past, such as the 2016 presidential election, to the remote past, such as the assassination of President Lincoln; (2) a record or account of what has or might have happened; and (3) a discipline or field of study (Shafer, 1980:2). One type of historical analysis refers to the set of methods that historians apply when they gather and evaluate evidence to describe specific moments of the past. This form of analysis, which we call **descriptive history**, stresses the accuracy and completeness of the *description* of unique, complex events. Outside the discipline of history, however, historical analysis moves beyond description to the use of historical events and evidence to develop a generalized understanding of the social world. Although this characterizes much of the field of historical sociology, we prefer the generic term **analytical history** to denote this type of historical analysis.

Surprisingly, analytical history is a relatively recent redevelopment. Despite the historical orientation of such founding fathers of modern-day social science as Karl Marx, Emile Durkheim, and Max Weber, much of social research during the past half-century has lacked a historical focus. Only in the past 40 years has there been a revived interest in the historical perspective. Erikson's study of deviance in Puritan New England is representative of this work.

Erikson was careful to reconstruct events with documents of the time, much as a historian might do. But the reconstruction was not an end in itself. Rather, he attempted to use a particular historical case as a way of demonstrating and elaborating Durkheim's general theory of deviant behavior—that deviance provides a mechanism for defining community boundaries and demonstrating shared values and norms. This sort of analysis, Theda Skocpol (1984:365) points out, is valuable "because it prompts the theorist to specify and operationalize . . . abstract concepts and theoretical propositions." Thus,

> Erikson must pin down historically such ideas as "community boundaries" and "group norms" and he must show us how, in terms of the symbols and social practices of the Massachusetts Puritans, deviant persons and their acts supplied "needed services to society by marking the outer limits of group experience and providing a point of contrast which gives . . . [social norms] some scope and dimension."

Erikson started with a general theory and used the specific case to explicate the theory. Another strategy for integrating social theory and history is to start with a particular historical event or pattern and then develop and test one or more explanations to account for it. For example, John Sutton (1991) attempted to explain the rapid growth of asylums in the United States between 1880 and 1920. To many observers of this period, Sutton notes, "asylum expansion was a sign that America was undergoing an epidemic of madness" (666), which they attributed to a range of evils, including rapid urbanization and uncontrolled immigration. Using quantitative data from the states (e.g., the number of persons living in urban areas, the number of persons over age 65, the number of asylum and almshouse inmates), Sutton tested several explanations of asylum expansion: (1) as reformers succeeded in shutting down almshouses, asylums were forced to absorb the aged poor individuals who were expelled; (2) urbanization enhanced the development of specialized and formally organized means of treatment, such as asylums; (3) asylum expansion depended on the revenues of state governments; (4) the need for asylum placements was inversely related to the distribution of direct benefits (e.g., pensions) to dependent groups; and (5) patronage politics may have supported expansion insofar as asylums were sources of jobs, contracts, and services that parties could use to reward supporters. Sutton's findings showed that all these factors, among others, contributed to asylum expansion.

Still another strategy, called **comparative-historical analysis**, is to search for general causal explanations of well-defined historical outcomes or patterns (Skocpol, 1984). In this case, an investigator does not focus on a particular historical event but rather on two or more similar events or cases, which are then compared systematically to identify causal regularities. For example, the sociologist Theda Skocpol (1979) analyzed the causes of social revolutions by comparing the revolutions of France in 1789, Russia in 1917, and China from 1911 to 1949. Given the broad scope of her study, she did not consult original documents; instead, she drew on the work of historians of each period and place to identify patterns of political conflict and development. Among the common factors that Skocpol identified as precipitating revolution were that each society (1) had strong peasant communities and (2) faced foreign pressures and entanglements that made it difficult to meet the needs of economic development.

Finally, historical analysts may also treat history itself as an independent variable in their analyses. That is, they may examine sequences of past events as a way of understanding the present. Used in this way, history represents the temporal dimension of social life rather than a particular outcome to be explained (as in Sutton's research) or a manifestation of large-scale social change (as in Skocpol's work).[5]

Representative of this type of analytical history is the economist Paul David's (1985) analysis of the establishment of the "QWERTY" keyboard layout as a standard of the typewriter industry. David showed that the influence of temporally remote events accounts for the persistence of this awkward layout on current typewriters and computer keyboards. The QWERTY format first appeared in 1873, as a result of an early effort to find an arrangement that would reduce the frequency of typebar jamming. The format was then modified into a sales gimmick. That is, E. Remington and Sons "assembled into one row all the letters that their salesmen would need" to rapidly type the brand name TYPE WRITER without lifting their fingers from the keyboard. The future of QWERTY was not protected by technological necessities as competitive designs introduced in the 1880s eliminated the jamming problem and a keyboard arrangement patented by Dvorak and Dealey in 1932 was demonstrably more efficient. Rather, a key event occurred late in the 1880s that locked in the QWERTY standard. The advent of "touch" typing was adapted to Remington's keyboard so that typists began learning this design rather than others. Employers then found it less expensive to buy machines with the QWERTY arrangement than to retrain typists. Finally, non-QWERTY typewriter manufacturers adapted their machines to the QWERTY-trained typists.

Historical analysis thus consists of the following:

1. Reconstructions of past events, which emphasize the accurate description of *what* happened;
2. Applications of a general theory to a particular historical case(s), which focus on *how* the theory applies;
3. Tests of explanations of historical events, which examine *why* a specific event occurred;
4. The development of causal explanations of historical patterns, which also analyzes *why* events occurred but seeks a more general understanding of social phenomena; and
5. The use of history to understand the present or explain *how* and *why* particular phenomena came to be.

Each of these genres of historical research represents a slightly different level of abstraction and analysis. Descriptive historians (1) are interested in presenting sequences of specific, concrete events, whereas analytical historians (2), especially those applying abstract theories, may apply highly general concepts and propositions. Quantitatively oriented analysts engaged in testing hypotheses of a particular historical instance (3) tend to follow the traditional scientific model of investigation and are more explicit about operationalizing concepts. Comparative-historical analysts (4), in contrast, typically take an inductive approach similar to that of field researchers.[6] Finally, those who examine long-term temporal sequences and connections among events (5) may combine a historian's narrative approach with the quantitative analyses of sociologists. Regardless of these differences, however, all historical research involves, first, the use of written residues of the past to describe the past and, second, an interpretation of past events.

Handling Documentary Evidence

Although historical researchers may use any source of available data, they tend to rely mostly on documents. The historian Vernon Dibble (1963) classifies documents into two main categories: **testimony** and **social bookkeeping**. Historians traditionally have been especially fond of direct testimony by major actors as contained in autobiographies, depositions, private letters, and the like (Tilly, 1981). Through the testimony of witnesses, historians attempt to reconstruct where, when, and what happened. Testimony, however, tends to focus the analysis on the activities and motivations of individuals, especially "major actors."

Social bookkeeping refers to documents containing recorded information produced by groups or organizations, such as bankbooks, court records, transcripts of congressional debates, vital statistics, and the list of graduates of Yale University. As the product of social systems, social bookkeeping is more likely than testimony to be used to draw inferences about social structural variables. Charles Tilly (1981:32) also points out that the numbers and abstractions that social scientists glean from such evidence have facilitated

> the bringing of ordinary people back into the historical record. . . . Ordinary people leave few diaries, letters, and novels, but their experiences leave documentary evidence nonetheless. The documentary evidence shows up in birth certificates, marriage contracts, notarized transactions, conscription registers, tax rolls, rent books, censuses, catechetical records, and other routine sources.

When drawing inferences from documents to events of the past, historians are primarily concerned with the authenticity and credibility of the evidence. Judgments of authenticity, as we mentioned earlier, involve highly technical techniques that are best left to professional historians or archivists. Once the evidence is authenticated, a researcher must evaluate how credible the evidence is. The best checks on the credibility of testimony are corroboration and the absence of contradiction. Consistent independent sources of testimony enhance the probability that a particular account is accurate. However, because corroboration is often impossible, historians use a variety of other checks to assess credibility. Robert Shafer's (1980:166–67) checklist includes the following suggestions:

KEY POINT

As historical evidence, testimony such as private letters and diaries emphasizes the roles of individual major actors, whereas public documents such as court records and vital statistics focus attention on social structure and ordinary people.

1. Is the real meaning of the statement different from its literal meaning? Are words used in senses not employed today?
2. How well could the author *observe* the thing he [or she] reports? Were his [or her] senses equal to the observation? Was his [or her] physical location suitable to sight, hearing, touch? Did he [or she] have the proper social ability to observe: did he [or she] understand the language . . . ?
3. . . . Regarding the author's *ability* to report, was he [or she] biased? Did he [or she] have proper time for reporting? Proper place for reporting? Adequate recording instrumentation? . . . When did he [or she] report in relation to [the] observation? Sooner? Much later? [Reports written soon after an event are more likely to be accurate than reports recorded long afterward; disinterested, incidental, or casual testimony is more likely to be accurate than testimony that is ideologically relevant or intended for a particular audience.]
4. Are there inner contradictions in the document?

With their emphasis on credible testimony and the accurate description of past events, historians put much stock in the use of primary as opposed to secondary sources. **Primary sources** are eyewitness accounts of the events described, whereas **secondary sources** consist of indirect evidence obtained from primary sources. Kai Erikson used both types of evidence in his study of deviance in Puritan New England: (1) court records and the journals of those witnessing the events of the time (primary) and (2) the writings of numerous historians (secondary). Theda Skocpol relied on secondary sources for her study of revolutions. "As a general rule," Louis Gottschalk (1969:116) claims, "the careful historian will be suspicious of secondary works in history, even the best ones." Gottschalk therefore recommends that these works should be used for limited purposes, such as to get general information about the setting of the historical period under investigation, to obtain bibliographic leads, and to derive tentative interpretations and hypotheses. However, it is difficult to imagine how broad-based historical analyses such as Skocpol's could ever be undertaken if she first reconstructed past events with primary sources.

Social bookkeeping requires a different kind of evaluation than does testimony. Because the documents are produced by groups or organizations, they must be read in the light of the social systems that produced them (Dibble, 1963:207). One might ask and try to discern, for example, the following: What processes intervened between the observing and recording? Was the record subject to editing (recall our example of selective deposit in the *Congressional Record*)? For whom was the record intended? For whom might it have been valuable, and who might have been hurt by it?

In general, then, when the evidence is secondhand and the subject matter remote, an investigator must be all the more thoughtful about the evidence and skeptical of his or her relationship to it (Erikson, 1970:335). Even when a researcher is confident of the authenticity and credibility of the documents, he or she must also wonder how they came to be preserved. With regard to the rich and varied documents available for the study of seventeenth-century Massachusetts, Erikson (1970:335) points out that

> one cannot spend more than a few hours in their company without wondering whose history they speak of. Not only were they originally composed by men with a vested interest in the events they were reporting, they have been passed along to us by a succession of other men, each of whom has taken a turn sifting, rearranging, and even rewriting those materials. The surviving records, then, register not only what impressed John Winthrop in the early years of settlement, but what Cotton Mather regarded as worth remembering in the second half of the seventeenth century, what Thomas Hutchinson considered "historic" in the eighteenth century, and what whole generations of chroniclers and antiquarians decided to place on the shelves in the nineteenth century.

Beyond providing more or less direct evidence of historic events, documents are an important source of indicators or measures of large-scale social structural variables and processes. In his study of asylum expansion, for example, Sutton (1991) measured urbanization, the aging of the population, and changes in the number of inmates of asylums and almshouses with data from various U.S. census publications; he used reports to the U.S. Congress by the commissioner of pensions to determine the number of pensioners in each state; and from gubernatorial voting data published in the *Congressional Quarterly's Guide to U.S. Elections*, he measured party patronage by the closeness of the votes for Republican and Democratic gubernatorial candidates. The quality of such indicators depends not only on the credibility of the bookkeeping sources, but also on the reliability and validity of the data as measures of particular variables. Since multiple indicators and independent sources of validation are rarely available in historical research, validity assessment is largely a matter of face validation. This was not a problem for most variables in Sutton's study because of the directness of the measures; for example, data on the number of persons over age 65 have palpable validity as a measure of the age of the population. However, for less direct measures, such as the difference in votes for party gubernatorial candidates as an indicator of patronage, face validity is less than satisfactory, albeit often the only means of validation.

Historical Interpretation

Historical analysts are interested in understanding the past. For descriptive historians, this implies establishing what happened in a factual way. During the Salem witchcraft hysteria, for example, who was accused by whom? Who was executed? But analysis never stops here. To arrive at some *understanding* of what happened, even if the goal is merely to describe a sequence of events as accurately as possible, a researcher must order the facts according to some interpretation of the materials. As we repeatedly have noted, a tenet of social research is that facts do not speak for themselves. The search for evidence itself, however haphazard or rigorous, is always guided by a broad theory or interpretation relevant to the researcher's interest. Tilly (1981:10), for example, notes that "the American historian who examines the treatment of slaves by undertaking a detailed study of slaveholders' diaries, while neglecting the records of slave auctions, makes an implicit choice favoring a theory in which slaveholders' attitudes are significant determinants of slave experience." To examine the role of historical interpretation of particular past events and the importance of entertaining alternative explanations, we discuss different studies of the Salem witchcraft episode, including Kai Erikson's aforementioned study of deviance in Puritan New England.

One of the three crises that Erikson analyzed was the Salem witchcraft hysteria. The events of this well-known episode have been well established through court depositions and writings of that period, and readers may be familiar with them through popular accounts such as Arthur Miller's play *The Crucible*. In 1692 two daughters of the local minister Samuel Parris became ill, or at least they began to exhibit rather bizarre behavior. They would scream unaccountably and go into convulsions, their bodies would become contorted, and they would crawl around on all fours and bark like dogs. Possibly the girls suffered from hysteria, although nobody knew then or knows now precisely what afflicted them. Whatever it was spread quickly to other girls in the community, who began to manifest similar symptoms. In the wake of this panic, unable to bring this strange behavior under control, someone offered a diagnosis of witchcraft. And when the girls were pressed into identifying who was tormenting them, they implicated three women. One of the women was Parris's slave Tituba, who was from the West Indies and known for her practice of voodoo magic. She confessed and conveniently identified, among others, the two other women named by the girls as agents of the devil. Other confessions and accusations followed, supposed witches were arrested and put on trial, and before it was over, 19 people were hanged and 1 was pressed to death.

Why did this unfortunate episode occur? Erikson, you will recall, saw this as one of three crime waves in the seventeenth century that served to reinforce the moral boundaries of the community. The need to reaffirm moral boundaries and community solidarity arises, according to Erikson, when the sense of community control and consensus is threatened. The threat to Salem Village, however, was not posed by the alleged witches; they were conveniently chosen deviants. Rather, it was the uncertain political status of the community. In the 1670s, Erikson points out, the colony was beset by strife between clergy and magistrates, whose alliance "had been the very cornerstone of the New England Way" (1966:138), and by a costly war with a confederacy of Indian tribes. Then, in the 1680s King Charles II of England imposed the establishment of an Anglican church in Boston and revoked the charter that had legally protected the colony for more than half a century. At the onset of the witchcraft hysteria, colonial agents were visiting England in an attempt to restore the charter. Finally, there were many land disputes and feuds at the time, which undermined the harmony on which the community had depended. All of this, according to Erikson's interpretation, evoked a need to reaffirm the Puritan way of life.

Although Erikson's analysis of these events is thorough and persuasive, it has been challenged by other sociologists and by subsequent historical research. William Chambliss (1976) contrasts Erikson's "functionalist" explanation with "conflict" theory, siding firmly with the latter. He sees the witchcraft hysteria, in addition to the other two crime waves, as "indeed created for the consequences it had. But the consequences were not 'to establish moral boundaries'; rather, they aided those in power to maintain their position" (15). Chambliss points out in support of this interpretation that the actions of court assistants were followed and criminal sanctions imposed so long as members of the ruling elite were not accused. However, when the witch finders began to overstep this bound, the witchcraft trials came to an end.

The historians Paul Boyer and Stephen Nissenbaum (1974) offer still another interpretation of these events. Using many of the same references as Erikson as well as some previously neglected sources of data (e.g., community votes, tax assessments, petitions), they noticed a split between accusers and accused that coincided with whether people supported or opposed Samuel Parris, the minister in whose home the girls first experienced their afflictions. As it turned out, this split between pro-Parris and anti-Parris factions existed before the witchcraft outbreak and went well beyond support for the local minister. Compared with supporters, for example, opponents of Parris tended to be wealthier and to live and own land close to the adjacent commercial town of Salem and were less likely to be members of the Salem Village church. Thus, in part, Boyer and Nissenbaum contend "that the accusations of 1692 represented a direct and conscious continuation of factional conflict" (186).

All of this points to a major difficulty and an important caveat regarding historical analysis. Historical events invariably are subject to a variety of interpretations. It is possible for more than one interpretation to be valid, especially if the interpretations represent different levels (e.g., psychological versus sociological) or focus on different aspects of an event. For example, in explaining the witchcraft mania, one may account for not only why it took place at this point in time in the Massachusetts colony (which is what Erikson was attempting to explain) but also why it was focused in the community of Salem Village (which Boyer and Nissenbaum explained), why it began among these particular girls, why the citizens of the community actually could believe that there were witches in their midst (which the historian Chadwick Hansen [1969] has attempted to explain), and so forth.

On the other hand, if researchers assume that some explanations may be valid and others are not, it becomes important to entertain plausible rival interpretations and to evaluate them critically in light of the evidence. How well does a given interpretation account for the evidence? What does the interpretation assume and what consequences follow from it? Chambliss assumes a singularly valid explanation in raising such questions about Erikson's hypothesis: If Erikson is right, then it follows that the witchcraft mania (as well as the other crime waves) should have increased community solidarity. Did this occur? If each crime wave increased solidarity, why did the community experience three major crime waves in a period of 60 years? These are precisely the kinds of critical issues that must be raised about *any* historical interpretation. Better yet, historical analysts should entertain and critically evaluate multiple interpretations and hypotheses and compare the relative plausibility of each one. Only then can we reach an understanding of events in the scientific sense.

KEY POINT

Researchers who interpret historical events should consider alternative interpretations and the theoretical assumptions on which each is based.

Content Analysis

William Chambliss and Kai Erikson have divergent perspectives on the functions of crime in society. So it is not surprising that they would arrive at different interpretations of the events in Salem Village. This difference points to one of the problems with the mere *reading* of written documents—the lack of agreement or reliability. One way to overcome this problem is to be explicit about how one should read the text. In fact, it is possible to develop objective criteria for systematically transforming written text into quantifiable data. That is the goal of content analysis.

More than just a single technique, **content analysis** is a set of methods for analyzing the symbolic content of any communication. The idea is to reduce the total content of a communication (e.g., all of the words or all of the visual imagery) to a set of categories that represent some characteristic of research interest. Thus, content analysis may involve the systematic description of either verbal or nonverbal materials. It also may involve either quantitative or qualitative analysis, although we focus here on the former.

Sales's analysis (1973) of comic strips and K. Lindner's (2004) analysis of gender stereotyping in magazine advertisements are examples of content analysis. K. Lindner carefully selected a sample of advertisements in two magazines and then proceeded to (1) identify the categories into which the ads were to be coded (e.g., relative size of men and women present in the ads, feminine touch, ritualization of subordination, and so forth), (2) define the categories according to objective criteria that could be applied by anyone, (3) code the advertisements in terms of these objective criteria, and (4) report the frequency of the categories into which the ads had been coded.

The process just described is exactly the same as that found in systematic observation studies. It is also the same process that one would use in analyzing responses to open-ended questions (see Box 15.1). Sociologists have used content analysis to analyze field notes and unstructured interviews, and psychologists have applied it to verbal responses to assess the psychological states of persons. So, as you can see, its application is not limited to the analysis of existing data. Still, its most common application is to the available printed or spoken word. Content analysis has been applied to written documents with varied and complex content, including political party platforms (R. P. Weber, 1990), novels (Griswold, 1981), letters of recommendation (Schmader, Whitehead, and Wysocki, 2007), newspaper articles (A. M. Lindner, 2009), and song lyrics (Christiansen, Roberts, and Bjork, 2012). Let us take a closer look at the steps in carrying out such an analysis: select and define content categories, define the unit of analysis, decide on a system of enumeration, and carry out the analysis (Holsti, 1969).

Select and Define Content Categories

To the extent that human coders are used, selecting and defining the categories for content analysis is analogous to deciding on a set of closed-ended questions in survey research. Instead of giving the questions to respondents who provide the answers, a content analyst applies them to a document and codes the appropriate category. The "questions" applied to the document should be adequate for the research purpose, and the categories should be clearly defined, exhaustive, and mutually exclusive.

Recall that Sales asked one question of the comic strips he analyzed: Is the central character strong and powerful? Wendy Griswold (1981), who analyzed a random sample of 130 novels published in the late nineteenth and early twentieth centuries, was interested in how the American novel might reflect unique properties of American character and experience. Accordingly, she asked several questions pertaining to characteristics of the protagonist (e.g., gender? age? social class at the beginning of the novel? social class at the end?) and to the plot (e.g., What is the setting of the main action? What is the time period? Is adult heterosexual love important to the plot? Is money important in the novel?).

Both Sales and Griswold used human coders, who recorded "answers" based on a *codebook* of questions and answer categories (the use of codebooks in quantitative analysis is discussed in Chapter 15). In fact, Griswold's study is unusual because of her large sample of novels, which required 10 readers/coders. Many content analysts do computer text analyses. In an analysis of sex bias in letters of recommendation for faculty positions, Toni Schmader, Jessica Whitehead, and Vicki Wysocki (2007) used a computer program to count the number of words in several categories, including achievement words (e.g., goal), tentative words (e.g., perhaps), certainty words (e.g., always), and standout adjectives (e.g., superb). First, they created an electronic file of 886 letters written on behalf of 277 applicants. Then they provided the computer with a "dictionary" similar in structure to a thesaurus. One of the dictionary entries was the following list of words representing the use of "standout adjectives" (the asterisk is a stand-in for different forms of the word): excellen*, superb, outstanding, unique, exceptional, unparalleled, *est, most, wonderful, terrific*, fabulous, magnificent, remarkable, extraordinar*, amazing, supreme*, unmatched (127).

Regardless of whether one uses a human coder or a computer, the reliability and overall value of the content analysis depend on the clear formulation of content categories and of definitions or rules for assigning units to categories. It is common for content analysts to report tests for intercoder reliability. For example, K. Lindner and an assistant separately coded 70 advertisements in two issues randomly selected from her sample of magazines. When their codes were compared, the percentage agreements for the nine coding categories ranged from 86 to 97 percent, with a mean of 91.7 percent.

Define the Unit of Analysis

Content analysts refer to their units of analysis as **recording units**. A recording unit is that element of the text or visual image that is described by the content categories. It could be the single word or symbol; the sentence, paragraph, or other grammatical unit; the whole text; or some other aspect of the text such as the character or plot. Schmader and colleagues' recording unit was the word, whereas Griswold used three different units—character, plot, and whole novel. K. Lindner's unit was the whole advertisement; Sales's unit, however, was the character within the comic strip.

In general, smaller units may be coded more reliably than larger units because they contain less information (R. P. Weber, 1990). However, smaller units such as words may not be sufficient to extract the meaning of the message, and there may be too many such units for a researcher to manage. Imagine, for example, using the word as the recording unit in Griswold's analysis of 130 novels! These limitations apply to the use of computers in content analysis because, at this time, the only units programmable for computer analysis are words, word senses, and phrases such as idioms and proper nouns.

Because it may not be possible to place the recording unit in a particular category without considering the context in which it appears, content analysts also distinguish **context units** (Holsti, 1969). Sales's coders would need to be familiar with the comic strip to make judgments about the power of the main character; thus, his recording unit is the character, and his context unit is the comic strip.

Decide on a System of Enumeration

There are many ways of quantifying the data in content analysis. The most basic systems of quantification are listed here.

1. *Time–space measures.* Early content analysts of newspapers often measured the space devoted to certain topics. Using column inches as their measure, for example, Janet Lever and Stan Wheeler (1984) found that sports coverage in the *Chicago Tribune* increased from 9 percent of the newsprint in 1900 to 17 percent in 1975. Analogously, television content has been measured in time (e.g., the number of hours of televised violence).

2. *Appearance.* Sometimes it is sufficient simply to record whether a given category appears in a recording unit. Sales's measurement consisted of classifying the central character in a given comic strip as powerful or not. Many of Griswold's categories were measured in this way: Is the main character a male? Is religion important to the plot?

3. *Frequency.* The most common method of measuring content is in terms of the frequency with which a given category appears in the contextual unit. Schmader and colleagues counted the number of times categories appeared in each letter of recommendation. In an analysis of the Democratic and Republican party platforms, Robert Philip Weber (1990) calculated the proportion of words in the category "wealth" (e.g., "capital," "inflation," "unemployment").[7]

4. *Intensity.* When attitudes and values are the objects of the research, content analysts may resort to measures of intensity. For example, rather than ask whether money is important to the novel's plot, one might ask *how* important it is. Devising mechanisms for making judgments of intensity is essentially the same as in the construction of indexes and scales, which we discuss in Chapter 13.

How a researcher decides to enumerate the data depends on the requirements of the problem under investigation. However, the choice of a system of enumeration carries with it certain assumptions regarding the nature of the data and the inferences that one can draw from the data (Holsti, 1969). Space–time measures may appropriately describe certain gross characteristics of the mass media, but they are too imprecise to serve as indicators of most verbal content. Appearance measures also tend to be imprecise, although they are more flexible and can be applied to a larger range of content than space–time measures. Frequency measures are better still but involve two crucial assumptions that should be examined: first, they assume that the frequency of a word or category is a valid indicator of its importance, value, or intensity; second, they assume that each individual count is of *equal* importance, value, or intensity. It may be that some categories or some recording units should be weighted more heavily than others. It has been suggested, for example, that front-page articles might be more important and therefore weighted more than articles appearing elsewhere in a newspaper (Holsti, 1969). (Box 12.2 also discusses the problem of making inferences from frequencies of the "manifest" content of materials.)

BOX 12.2 Perspectives on Gender Differences in Graffiti

The grist for content analysts—recorded language and visual representations—is essentially messages in a communication process. The object of content analysis is to uncover the *meanings* of the message. Among the many possible meanings, at least one will be manifestly understood by the source as well as the receiver of the message, but a great many more meanings may be latent to one or both parties. Thus, the message may reveal something about the characteristics or unconscious intent of the source or about the beliefs and values of a group or culture. But how one comes to understand these meanings depends on the theoretical orientation that informs the analysis. Nowhere is this better illustrated than in research on restroom graffiti.

Research on restroom graffiti consistently shows that the inscriptions written by men differ from those written by women. Edward Bruner and Jane Paige Kelso (1980) divide this research into two types. One type establishes categories of manifest observations (e.g., sexual humor, racial insults, romantic, political) and then assigns each graffito to one of these categories. These studies show where gender differences lie (e.g., men use more insults, women are more romantic) but leave unclear the meanings of these differences. In this research, according to Bruner and Kelso, "there is an implicit theory of text which assumes that the meaning is the message, and that significance will be revealed by counting the frequency with which items of manifest content appear. The graffiti mean what the graffiti say, without any attempt to interpret the text" (240).

The second type of research goes beyond the manifest meaning to a deeper level of interpretation. These studies interpret graffiti in terms of such Freudian imagery as unconscious impulses, infantile sexuality, and primitive thoughts. As Bruner and Kelso point out, however, the "connection between the data and the Freudian meaning is not readily apparent," and this approach suffers from "an over-attribution of meaning compared to the under-attribution" characteristic of the first approach (240).

By contrast, Bruner and Kelso offer a "semiotic perspective." Noting that graffiti are never found where others will not be able to see them, they argue that restroom graffiti constitute communication among anonymous partners. "The writing of graffiti," they say, "is an essentially social act that cannot be understood in terms of the expressive functions performed for an isolated individual. To write graffiti is to communicate; one never finds graffiti where they cannot be seen by others" (241). Moreover, given the segregation of restrooms in American culture, restroom graffiti must be understood as same-sex communication—men writing for other men and women writing for other women.

Approaching the data from this perspective, Bruner and Kelso find that, on the surface, women's graffiti are more interpersonal and interactive than those written by men. Men tend to write egocentric and competitive inscriptions about sexual conquests and sexual prowess and derogatory inscriptions that attack, insult, or put down; women tend to raise serious questions about love, sexual relations, and commitment, often soliciting or giving advice regarding women's relationships with men. Going beyond this surface text, Bruner and Kelso conclude that "the underlying message in both male and female graffiti is fundamentally political. . . . Graffiti reflect the power positions of men and women in the social structure" (250). Accordingly, "men write graffiti to tell themselves and other men that they have maintained their superior position and are still in control," whereas women write graffiti that "express the cooperation of the dominated and reflect the strategy of mutual help employed by those in a subordinate status" (249–50).

Carry Out the Analysis

To carry out the analysis, one first obtains a sample of material. As in survey sampling, researchers should always be mindful of the population to which inferences are made. Three populations are relevant to content analysis: communication sources (e.g., types of newspapers, novels, speeches), documents (e.g., specific newspaper issues), and text within documents (e.g., pages). Often, a sample of documents is drawn from a single source; for example, Griswold took a random sample of all novels published in the United States between 1876 and 1910. K. Lindner purposefully sampled communication sources. She chose one general interest magazine (*Time*) and one women's fashion magazine (*Vogue*); then she selected issues from two months (January and June) for six different years between 1955 and 2002. Although researchers also have sampled text, R. P. Weber (1990:43) recommends that the entire text be analyzed when possible because this preserves its semantic coherence. If it is necessary to sample text, then meanings are best preserved by sampling paragraphs rather than sentences.

Having selected the sample, one proceeds to code the material according to the coding categories and system of enumeration. This gives an analyst a description of the communication content. Finally, content analysts truly engage in *analysis* by relating content categories to one another or by relating the characteristics of the content to some other variable. Griswold compared the content of novels written by American and foreign authors, finding many similarities but also some interesting differences. For instance, American authors were likely to place protagonists in the middle class; foreign authors favored the upper class. American authors also were more likely to set their novels in small towns and less likely to set the action in the home. When Schmader and colleagues compared letters written for male and female candidates for a faculty position, they found that the letters were similar with one major exception: recommenders used significantly more standout adjectives to describe male candidates.

R. P. Weber's content analysis of party platforms (1990) showed how Democrats and Republicans have varied over time in their concerns. Figure 12.1 shows the pattern of change

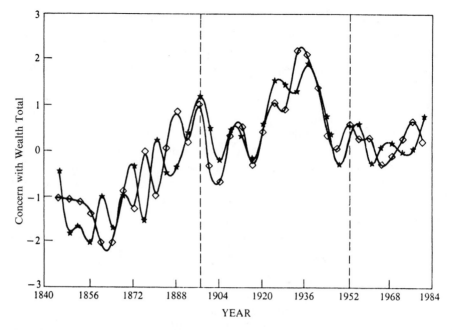

FIGURE 12.1. Democratic and Republican concern with wealth, 1840–1984. Diamonds, Republican platforms; stars, Democratic platforms.

Source: R. P. Weber, "Computer-Aided Content Analysis: A Short Primer," *Qualitative Sociology*, vol. 7, p. 139, 1984. Used by permission of Human Sciences Press.

with respect to the percentage of each platform devoted to economic matters. The vertical axis is based on the percentage of words in the platform that fall into the category wealth.

KEY POINT

The content analyst must decide what communications to code and how to code them and then must sample and analyze the content.

R. P. Weber points out several features of Figure 12.1: (1) the general rise between 1844 and about 1952 in the level of concern about economic matters, perhaps reflecting the increasing importance of the federal government in the management of economic affairs; (2) the relatively constant level of concern from 1952 to 1984; and (3) the change over time in the relationship between the two parties' concern with economic matters as the parties manifested similar levels of concern between 1896 and 1952 and moved opposite to one another before and after this period.

Strengths and Limitations of Research Using Available Data

The strengths and limitation of research using available data depend on the data source; however, we can safely make several generalizations that pertain to most forms of secondhand data analysis. The first two strengths that we discuss pertain to sources other than survey data archives. The remaining five benefits originally were outlined by Herbert Hyman (1972) with reference to the secondary analysis of survey data but also apply to most other available-data research.

First, an important strength of many available-data sources is that they are **non-reactive**. Much social research, as we have seen, is susceptible to *reactive measurement*: changes in behavior that occur because of subjects' awareness that they are being studied or observed. Research with available data also encounters this problem to the extent that the data sources are surveys or documents like autobiographies in which the author is clearly aware that what is said will be in the public domain. But with physical evidence and many other available-data sources, there is simply no reasonable connection between a researcher's use of the material and a producer's knowledge of such use. By analyzing census data, Schwartz and Mare's analysis of educational homogamy was nonreactive. Imagine, however, the kind of self-censorship that might have occurred if they had asked respondents in an interview survey whether they preferred to marry someone with the same educational level. If respondents were married, their spouse's educational level would be likely to dictate their answer; if not, their answer may reflect normative expectations and, in any event, would measure preferences rather than actual choices.

The risk of reactivity is so high in some areas of study that available data may provide the only credible evidence. Consider, for example, studies of illegal activities such as consumption of illegal drugs. Survey evidence is likely to be contaminated by concealment and underreporting; police records such as number of arrests for controlled substances may be distorted by differential efforts at law enforcement. An ingenious use of available data, however, can provide nonreactive evidence on drug use. Noting that the federal government imposes a tax and keeps a record of taxes collected on cigarette papers and tubes, Marcus Felson (1983) observed that federal taxes collected on these items changed little during the 1950s and 1960s but jumped about 70 percent compared to 1960s levels in 1972. Meanwhile, loose tobacco sales declined during this same period. The conclusion Felson reached is that a new market had been created for cigarette papers in the production of marijuana "joints." That market, it would appear, opened in 1972.

KEY POINT

Available-data research often avoids reactive measurement error because the data are used without the knowledge or participation of those who produced it.

Second, available data can be used to analyze properties and changes in social structure. Despite the avowed focus of the social sciences on social structure, much of social research examines individual attitudes and behavior. Surveys are of individuals, and few surveys utilize contextual or social network designs, which provide direct measures of social relations; experiments rarely study the group as the unit of analysis; and field studies are based on the observation of individual behavior. Available data, however, often enable researchers to analyze larger social units. In many of the studies described in this chapter, the unit of analysis was not the individual nor was the focus on individual behavior. For Durkheim as well as Pearson and Hendrix, the unit was the whole society; for Erikson, the community; for Logan and Stults, the metropolitan area; and for Schwartz and Mare, the married couple. Even the studies by Sales and W. C. Bailey on individual propensities toward authoritarianism and homicidal behavior, respectively, investigated these phenomena with societal-level data in terms of large-scale social processes.

Third, available data provide social researchers with the best and often the only opportunity to study the past. To study some aspect of American society 50 or more years ago, it might be possible to conduct a survey of people who were alive at the time. But to do so presents several methodological problems, from the inaccuracy of respondents' memories to survivor bias in the sample. A study of periods before the twentieth century necessitates the search for available data. Documentary records and other archival evidence have therefore been a favorite source of data for historians, as we saw in Erikson's and Stannard's studies of the Puritans. More recent events also can be investigated with the aid of survey data archives. Finally, studies of the past are not limited merely to understanding the past. They also can be done to test general propositions about social life, as we saw in Erikson's study, W. C. Bailey's research on the deterrent effect of capital punishment, and Sales's research on threat and authoritarianism.

Fourth, whereas both experiments and field research have limited time spans and longitudinal surveys rarely were undertaken until the last quarter of the twentieth century, the analysis of available data is well suited to studies of social and cultural change. Trend studies, such as Logan and Stults's analysis of racial segregation and Schwartz and Mare's study of educational homogamy, have a long tradition among social demographers who rely on the census and other demographic data. K. Lindner's analysis of gender stereotyping in advertisements and Stannard's analysis of the carvings on gravestones illustrate other sources of evidence on social change. Moreover, the establishment of data archives has resulted in a marked increase in the number of studies that trace relatively recent changes in various attitudes, opinions, and behaviors. Indeed, the GSS was designed partly to measure trends in social conditions.

Fifth, the analysis of available data may be used to study problems cross-culturally. One important development that has made this possible is the development of the International Social Survey Program,(ISSP) described briefly in Chapter 9. The ISSP was formed in 1984 to provide cross-national survey data similar to that from the GSS (T. W. Smith, 1990). By 2016, more than 50 collaborating nations were supplementing regular national surveys with a common core of questions, with these data pooled and made available to the social science community. In addition to the ISSP, other sources of available data—for example, national censuses and vital statistics as well as ethnographies—will continue to be a major data source for cross-national studies. Pearson and Hendrix's investigation of the relationship between divorce and the status of women is but one of numerous examples.

Sixth, available data can enhance study quality through increased sample size and replication. Experiments and field studies use samples of very limited size, and most surveys of local populations are relatively small. Similarly, historical document analysis often focuses on a small number of cases. The use of available data, however, may afford the opportunity to generate unusually large samples. Drawing on two data sources, Schwartz and Mare analyzed data on nearly 2 million marriages; K. Lindner coded a total of 1374 magazine advertisements. Sample size is important for two reasons. First, large samples generally enhance our confidence in study results; with random sampling, increases in sample size increase the reliability of findings, as we saw in Chapter 6. Second, by increasing sample size we may gain access to specialized problems and smaller populations that otherwise could not be studied. One reason for using census data, including sample-based data, is that the huge samples provide reliable estimates for small segments of the population. Consider *intermarriage*—marriage between partners of a different race or ethnicity. Because of generally low rates of intermarriage (less than 7 percent of whites in 2013), only a data set as large as PUMS would enable researchers to examine intermarriage across various racial/ethnic groups.

Increasing sample size in effect replicates observations. Although replications are relatively rare in the social sciences, they often may be carried out easily with available data. A good example is Sales's research on threat and authoritarianism. Sales used diverse sources. We mentioned his use of municipal budgets, listings of books on astrology and psychotherapy, and comic strips. But he used several other sources that we did not mention and analyzed changes in similar indicators for two later periods in the United States: 1959–1964 and 1967–1970. And that is not all. Other researchers, using comparable data sources, have replicated Sales's work for Germany in the 1920s and 1930s (Padgett and Jorgenson, 1982) and for later periods in the United States (Doty, Peterson, and Winter, 1991; B. E. Peterson and Gerstein, 2005). One study (Perrin, 2005) used letters to the editors of 17 newspapers to examine increases in authoritarianism in the wake of the September 11, 2001, terrorist attacks, a major national threat.

Finally, insofar as research using available data bypasses the stage of data collection, it can economize greatly on cost, time, and personnel. Whereas this is especially true of the secondary analysis of surveys, other sources of available data also tend to be less costly than experiments, surveys, and field studies. These costs vary depending on the nature of the data source and the time, money, and personnel required to obtain and to analyze the data. The tasks of researchers using available data, such as searching for and coding relevant information, often are tedious and time-consuming. Imagine, for example, the efforts of K. Lindner and her assistants in acquiring 60 periodicals, identifying eligible advertisements, and coding nine categories in 1374 ads. Yet, the cost per case in such studies is generally quite small compared with the cost of interviewing a respondent or running a single subject through an experiment.

Alas, despite its numerous advantages, research using available data has some limitations. Although the amount of existing data is massive and has increased exponentially in the digital age, these data only become useful and meaningful when users can "[bring] questions to the data and [find] their answers in the data" (Groves, 2011:868). To make available data useful, analysts must either find data that can answer a prespecified research question or mine data to discover patterns that suggest questions and hypotheses. The problem with the former approach is that existing data with valid measures of key variables are often hard to find; the problem with the latter is that false discoveries are likely.

A second issue with available data is access. One likely reason for the relatively widespread use of Twitter is that its data have been made available to the public (via Twitter's Application Programming Interface). However, much of the written and digital record, including valuable big data, is often inaccessible "for reasons of privacy and/or commercial sensitivity" (Tinati et al., 2014:664).

A third issue concerns data quality and completeness. To avoid biases and errors of interpretation, as we noted earlier, analysts of available data must carefully assess the authenticity of historical records and must account for how the data were generated in the first place. As we also noted, available data may be subject to selective deposit or in other ways unrepresentative of the relevant population. After gauging data quality, analysts often must repair or adjust the data before analysis.

Summary

- Available data consist of secondhand information. Sources of such information include the written public record, ranging from court proceedings to vital statistics to the voluminous data files of the Census Bureau; private documents such as diaries, letters, and business records; the mass media; nonverbal physical evidence such as works of art, clothing, and other artifacts; social science data archives generated from surveys and ethnographies; and big data.
- When one uses data collected for another purpose, the search for appropriate data and the evaluation and refinement of the data become extremely important research phases.
- In general, the research problem should guide the search for sources of available data. The research literature also may provide useful leads for locating sources, which may be augmented by consulting a librarian or various listings of publicly accessible data sets.
- Some sources of information may require the creative construction of substitute or indirect measures of key variables or the use of multiple indicators.
- It is also essential to assess the validity of the data—to determine their authenticity, whether definitions used in compiling records have changed over time, whether the meaning of words and phrases in written documents has changed, and so forth. Following such evaluation, it is often necessary to refine or make adjustments to allow for proper interpretation.
- Finally, one should consider the adequacy of the data as a sample of information. Written records from the more remote past invariably suffer from selective deposit, and physical materials are subject to selective survival. For voluminous data sets, probability sampling based on time and/or space is often possible and necessary.
- The analysis of available-data research depends on research purposes and the nature of the source of information.
- Historical analysis may involve attempts to reconstruct past events (descriptive history) as well as the use of historical evidence to generate and test social theories (analytical history).
- The most basic historical evidence consists of documents—testimony and social bookkeeping. Historical researchers judge testimony with respect to authenticity and credibility; they evaluate bookkeeping in the light of the organizations and groups that produced the documents.
- Descriptive historians emphasize primary sources, whereas analytical historians often rely on secondary sources.
- Because the understanding of the past invariably is open to interpretation, historical researchers should critically evaluate and compare the relative plausibility of alternative explanations.
- Researchers use content analysis to analyze the symbolic content of communication, which may include words and/or visual imagery.
- The steps in content analysis are selecting and defining a set of content categories, defining and then sampling the elements described by the categories, quantifying the categories such as by counting their frequency of occurrence, and then relating category frequencies to one another or to other variables.
- Compared with other research strategies, available-data research is better suited to the analysis of social structural variables, to cross-cultural research, and to studies of the past and of social change.

- Advantages of available-data research include nonreactive measurement, the ability to increase sample size and to replicate research, and reduced cost and time.
- Use of available data is limited in terms of the kinds of questions that it may address; some valuable data may be inaccessible; and the data must be carefully evaluated for biases and errors of interpretation.

Key Terms

vital statistics	comparative-historical analysis
manuscript census	testimony
Public Use Microdata Sample	social bookkeeping
data archives	primary sources
big data	secondary sources
selective survival	content analysis
selective deposit	recording units
descriptive history	context units
analytical history	nonreactive measurement

Exercises

1. To familiarize yourself more broadly with the data sources and tools available online from the U.S. Census Bureau, visit the home page http://www.census.gov. Using this site as a point of departure, find the table or data that will answer the following questions:
   a. What percentage of the U.S. population has income below the poverty line? (Provide the most recent estimate.)
   b. What percentage of the U.S. population is foreign born?
   c. Which states have the highest and lowest median family incomes? (Provide the most recent estimate.)
   d. What was the average price of new single-family homes sold in 2017?
   e. What percentage of the U.S. population who commute to work drive alone? (Hint: Look up "commuting.")
   f. What percentage of the population in your state are college graduates? (Provide the most recent estimate.)
   g. What was the growth rate of the world population in 1970? What is it estimated to be in 2020?
2. In the December 2000 issue of *Social Psychology Quarterly* (vol. 63, pp. 352–64) Matthew Hunt and associates report a content analysis of the attention given to race and ethnicity in a leading social psychology journal. Read the article and answer the following questions.
   a. What general assumption of social psychological theory and research is called into question by the researchers, as reflected in the main title of the article, "Color Blind"?
   b. What is the researchers' unit of analysis (i.e., the recording unit)?
   c. One aspect of attention to race/ethnicity is whether race/ethnicity was "seriously considered" in the analysis. How is this operationally defined?
   d. What evidence is given regarding the reliability of the coding scheme?
   e. As indicated in Table 1, what changes occurred between 1970–74 and 1995–99 with respect to each type of attention to race/ethnicity?
   f. When a similar coding scheme was applied to the attention given to gender in the same journal, what did the researchers find? Compare changes in attention to *gender* between 1970–74 and 1995–99 with changes in attention to *race/ethnicity*.
   g. Were certain methodological approaches (e.g., surveys, experiments) more conducive to the examination of race/ethnicity than others? Briefly explain.

3. Two advantages of much available data mentioned in the text are the abilities to measure social change and to replicate previous research. Older content analyses in particular are well suited to both these goals. Find a study using content analysis that was published in the 1970s or 1980s and replicate it by extending the period of observation from the end date in the original study until the present time. Examples of studies that could be replicated are Leslie Zebrowitz McArthur and Beth Gabrielle Resko's (1975) study of the portrayal of men and women in television advertisements, Neil Malamuth and Barry Spinner's (1980) analysis of sexual violence in best-selling erotic magazines (*Playboy* and *Penthouse*), and Ruth Thibodeau's (1989) analysis of the depiction of blacks in *New Yorker* cartoons.

Notes

1. Michael Lavin's (1996) *Understanding the Census* provides an overview of the decennial census and describes some of the many uses of census data. For a brief history of each census that includes questionnaires and instructions given to enumerators, see *Measuring America: The Decennial Censuses from 1790 to 2000* (https://www.census.gov/prod/2002pubs/pol02-ma.pdf). For an overview of the 2010 Census, including a copy of the questionnaire, available data sets, and where to go for assistance, visit the website of the U.S. Census Bureau: http://www.census.gov.
2. IPUMS also has compiled microlevel data on censuses in other countries. According to Steven Ruggles (2014:289), by 2018, IPUMS "expects to have released data . . . from 300 censuses of about 100 countries."
3. The U.S. Bureau of the Census "Factfinder for the Nation" series is an excellent guide to census products. Also consult the "American Factfinder" on its website (http://factfinder.census.gov/faces/nav/jsf/pages/index.xhtml).
4. See, for example, http://lib.colostate.edu/research/history/primarysources.html, http://guides.lib.berkeley.edu/subject-guide/163-Finding-Historical-Primary-Sources, and http://www.ala.org/rusa/sections/history/resources/pubs/usingprimarysources.
5. For a discussion of this approach, see the special May 1992 issue (volume 20, number 4) of *Sociological Methods and Research*.
6. For a critique of the inductivist approach to comparative-historical sociology, see Edgar Kiser and Michael Hechter (1991); for a critique of the application of a general theoretical model to particular historical instances, see Theda Skocpol (1984:365–68).
7. Word counts have proven especially useful in content analyses designed to determine who wrote a certain document. A study of the disputed authorship of several of *The Federalist* papers showed, for example, that the disputed authors James Madison and Alexander Hamilton differed in known writings in their rate of use of noncontextual words like "by" and "to." When the papers were analyzed, the rate of use of these words corresponded closely in all but one paper to Madison's rather than Hamilton's writing (Mosteller and Wallace, 1964).

13

Multiple Methods

The preceding chapters described four principal research strategies for understanding the social world: experiments, surveys, field research, and research using available data. By studying these approaches separately, you may have gotten the idea that these are entirely separate ways to proceed, that decisions about methods are necessarily of the either/or variety. However, given the limitations and biases inherent in each of the main approaches—indeed, inherent in all research procedures—the best way to study most research topics is to combine methodological approaches. This chapter begins with a discussion of a central principle called "triangulation." Next, we examine various "multiple-methods" combinations, ranging from multiple measures of concepts within the same study to multiple tests of hypotheses across different studies. Then, we compare the relative strengths and weaknesses of the four basic approaches to social research. Finally, we discuss meta-analysis, the use of systematic procedures for summarizing the results of multiple studies.

Triangulation

In their everyday lives, people frequently use more than one means to solve a problem. Consider, for example, the simple problem of arising earlier than usual to catch a flight. Let us say a woman presented with this problem normally awakens by means of an electric clock radio set for 7:00 AM. To make sure that she awakened by 6:00, she might employ several methods. She might set the clock radio for 5:55, set a cell phone alarm for 6:00, and ask an early-rising friend to phone her at 6:05. She would then have three independent and somewhat dissimilar methods for solving the problem. If the electricity should go off, the cell phone alarm would work. If the cell phone battery dies, the friend should come through. If

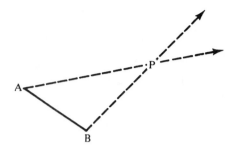

FIGURE 13.1. Triangulating a pirate radio station (P) from two points (A and B).

the friend proves unreliable, one of the other methods should work. Using multiple methods that do not share the same inherent weaknesses, we enhance our chances of solving the problem.

Social scientists have borrowed the term **triangulation** from the field of navigation to help describe how the use of multiple, independent approaches to a research question can enable an investigator to "zero in" on the answers or information sought (Campbell and Fiske, 1959). To understand the conventional meaning of triangulation, imagine that you are an employee of the Federal Communications Commission assigned the task of determining the location of a pirate (unlicensed) radio station (P). First, using a Federal Communications Commission mobile receiver with directional-finder antenna, you measure the direction (compass bearing) to the pirate radio station from a certain point, point A, and again from a second point, point B. Knowing the distance between points A and B, you can now determine the distance AP or BP, using trigonometry, and thus the position of P (Figure 13.1).

The process of triangulation in navigation requires accurate measuring instruments. Suppose, for example, that your directional-finder antenna was off calibration (biased) so that it always gave a figure that was 15 degrees below the true figure. In that case you would fail to locate the pirate station (Figure 13.2). After failing to find the station, you might suspect that the measuring instrument (the directional antenna) was inaccurate, or you might entertain the possibility that the "concept" being measured changed between the first and second measurements (i.e., the pirate is a mobile radio station).

In social research, the logic of triangulation applies to situations in which two or more dissimilar measuring instruments or approaches are used. These approaches are analogous to the different vantage points, A and B, in the figures. The key to triangulation is

FIGURE 13.2. Triangulating a pirate radio station (P) from two points (A and B), with directional antenna off calibration by 15 degrees.

the use of *dissimilar* methods or measures, which do not share the same methodological weaknesses—that is, errors and biases. The observations or "scores" produced by each method will ordinarily contain some error. But if the pattern of error varies, as it should with different methods, and if these methods independently produce or zero in on the same findings, then our confidence in the result increases.

Unfortunately, social researchers rely altogether too frequently on a single method or measure when multiple approaches could be brought to bear on the research question (Webb et al., 2000). Suppose, for example, you are investigating the hypothesis that airline crashes increase the anxiety of air travelers. Rather than rely on a single measure of anxiety, it would be better to use several. Eugene Webb and colleagues (2000) suggested the following indicators of anxiety: increased sales of alcoholic beverages at airport bars, increased sales of flight-insurance policies, and decreased sales of air-travel tickets following a crash. Any one of these indicators, by itself, represents a relatively weak measure of anxiety. But note that the three measures do not share the same weaknesses: A downturn in the economy might decrease sales of tickets but would probably not affect the sales of inexpensive trip-insurance policies to a great extent; publicity on insurance policy rip-offs could decrease policy sales but would not be expected to affect bar sales or ticket sales; an increase in the price of drinks might affect bar sales but would not be expected to affect the other measures; and so forth. Thus, if all three indicators of anxiety point to a relationship between airline crashes and travelers' anxiety, we can be relatively confident that such a relationship exists. As the number of dissimilar indicators increases, the likelihood that the relationship is an artifact of measurement error or spuriously created by an uncontrolled extraneous variable (such as a downturn in the economy) decreases.

Previously, we encountered the triangulation principle in terms of convergent validity assessment (Chapter 5). It also applies to varied testing to eliminate rival hypotheses, as illustrated by a study of cultural differences in "susceptibility to optical illusion" (Campbell, 1969:363–64). To rule out differences among anthropologists in the administration of visual tasks (instrumentation) as an alternative explanation for the observed cross-cultural differences, half of the researchers in one sample were purposely instructed to administer the tests in a manner deviating sharply from the standard instructions given to the remaining data collectors. By injecting this additional instrumentation variation, the investigators were able to demonstrate that differences-in-administration effects were very small compared with the observed cultural differences.

Multiple methods refers here to "methods" in the broadest sense. In addition to the use of multiple indicators of a single concept and varied testing, the logic of triangulation applies to such research activities as the use of multiple investigators in field research, cross-cultural archival research, and replications.

KEY POINT
Using multiple methods, each subject to different sources of error, increases confidence in research findings because the strengths of one method offset the weaknesses of another.

Jack Douglas (1976) advocates the use of a team approach in field research to obtain multiple perspectives on the setting. This is especially important when the setting contains several conflicting groups so that it is impossible for one person simultaneously to be a member and gain the trust of more than one group. In a study of drug-crisis intervention, for example, different members of an investigative team might become observers of the police, hospital staff, and drug users. Team members also might play different roles, such as we saw in David Snow and Leon Anderson's research on homelessness (Chapter 11), where Anderson became an insider, or participant-observer, of the homeless street scene, whereas Snow for the most part remained an outsider. Similarly, mixed-gender research teams may gain access to more valid information by capitalizing on their gender identity. In a field study of a nude beach, for example, female and male team members discovered that people told them different things about the sexual dimensions of the scene (C. A. B. Warren and Rasmussen, 1977). Single men told the male researcher about their sexual interests but provided the female researcher only with "the rhetoric of 'naturalism'" (355). Likewise, single women revealed their real sexual interests only to the female researcher and invoked the naturalism rhetoric with the male researcher.

William Crano (1981) also holds that the principle of triangulation is implicit in studies that utilize cross-cultural archives, such as the *Ethnographic Atlas* described in Chapter 12. Each society in the *Atlas* provides a different observational setting for the measurement of variables, and each ethnographer who contributed to the *Atlas* represents a different method, subject to distinctive biases and error. Triangulation occurs when multiple methods are applied to the same setting (i.e., when a given society is investigated by two or more researchers). Since each ethnography constitutes an independent investigation, systematic biases should not accumulate in measures of the social reality experienced in any given society.

The final type of triangulation, replication, involves multiple tests of hypotheses. Each test may use a separate sample of subjects and different measures of key variables. Multiple tests also may entail either the same research strategy or a combination of strategies, such as when a researcher uses both experimentation and the analysis of available data to test the same hypothesis. In this chapter we examine replications using the same and different approaches to social research. We begin, however, with a discussion of the most common form of triangulation: the use of multiple indicators in the same study.

Multiple Measures of Concepts within the Same Study

Suppose we want to test the hypothesis that a mother's expression of love toward her infant is directly related to the mother having a positive self-concept. In Figure 13.3, an arrow pointing from the independent variable ("self-esteem") to the dependent variable ("mother love") represents the hypothesis. Mother love is measured by the indicators L1 (amount of *time* a mother spends with the child), L2 (frequency of *physical contact* such as lifting, holding, kissing, and stroking the child), and L3 (duration of *verbalizations* such as talking, singing, and cooing to the child); self-esteem is also measured by three distinct indicators: P1, P2, and P3. There are two general ways to analyze the results of a study such as this that uses multiple measures: (1) reduce the complexity of the data by combining all measures

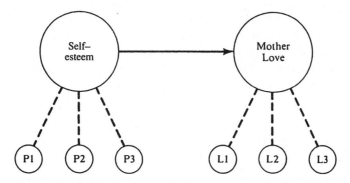

FIGURE 13.3. Diagram of the relationship between self-esteem and mother love, with three indicators per concept.

of each concept into a composite measure (an index or scale) and then determine whether the composite measures are related in the way hypothesized or (2) formulate a model to represent the relationships among concepts as well as the measures of those concepts and then test the model to see how well it fits the data. Let us examine each of these approaches in some detail.

Composite Measures: Indexes and Scales

Multiple measures are often combined into an index or scale. As we pointed out in Chapter 5, it is difficult to measure a concept well with a single indicator or question. Not only do single indicators rarely capture all the meaning of a concept, but also each indicator is likely to have distinctive sources of error or bias. By combining several indicators into a composite measure, we generally get a better overall representation of the concept and the errors tend to cancel each other out, yielding a more reliable measure.

An example is provided by the questions on abortion included in the General Social Survey (GSS) (T. W. Smith, Marsden, and Hout, 2016):

> Please tell me whether or not you think it should be possible for a pregnant woman to obtain a legal abortion. . . . [The interviewer then reads each of the following statements.]
> A. If there is a strong chance of serious defect in the baby?
> B. If she is married and does not want any more children?
> C. If the woman's own health is seriously endangered by the pregnancy?
> D. If the family has a very low income and cannot afford any more children?
> E. If she became pregnant as a result of rape?
> F. If she is not married and does not want to marry the man?

Responses to these questions may reflect attitudes unrelated to abortion per se, such as attitudes toward handicaps (A), large families (B), growing up in poverty (D), rape (E), or premarital sex (F). However, by combining these items into an index, we avoid the biases inherent in any single item. For example, if only question A, C, or E were used as our measure, the overwhelming majority of the U.S. population in 2014 would be pro-abortion. If only question B, D, or F were used, then the majority in 2014 would be anti-abortion (T. W. Smith, Marsden, and Hout, 2016). In either case we would have a biased estimate of the general attitude toward abortion in the United States. However, if all six items were used, we would get a better overall estimate, one that is less likely than any single item to underestimate or overestimate the strength of individuals' attitudes.

How are separate measures combined or "aggregated"? The simplest and most common procedure is to add or to take an average of the scores of the separate items; this is what we generally mean by an **index**. For example, public attitudes toward racial integration have been surveyed repeatedly with the use of the following five-question index developed by Donald J. Treiman (cited in D. G. Taylor, Sheatsley, and Greeley, 1978).

1. Do you think white students and black students should go to the same schools or to separate schools?
2. How strongly would you object if a member of your family wanted to bring a black friend home to dinner?
3. White people have a right to keep blacks out of their neighborhoods if they want to, and blacks should respect that right. (Do you strongly agree, agree . . . or strongly disagree?)
4. Do you think there should be laws against marriages between blacks and whites?
5. Blacks shouldn't push themselves where they're not wanted. (Do you strongly agree, agree . . . or strongly disagree?)

The index consists of the number of pro-integration responses to these five questions; thus, scores may range from 0 (strongly anti-integrationist) to 5 (strongly pro-integrationist). Interestingly, between 1963 and 1976 the average score for the U.S. white population increased steadily, with the sharpest rise from 1970 to 1972.

Nathan Keyfitz (1976) provides another example of an index, one that is constructed from available data rather than questionnaire items. To study the relationship between use of natural resources and global growth of the middle class, he needed some way to estimate the size of the world middle class in different years. He obtained this estimate by developing an index based on four separate indicators: the number of passenger cars in use, the number of telephones, the amount of electric energy produced, and the consumption of crude oil. (Each of these indicators required mathematical operations that we will not describe here.) The values yielded by the four separate estimates of the world middle class were then averaged. One of the conclusions of the study was that if more of the poor are to enter the high-consumption middle class, ways must be found to support the middle-class standard of living with less energy and fewer natural resources.

In both of these examples, each of the multiple measures (questionnaire items or separate population estimates) was assumed to be of equal value in determining the index score. In other words, each indicator was given the same "weight" in computing the index. One could, however, assign different weights by multiplying the separate indicators by different values (weights). Measures of socioeconomic status, for example, typically combine indicators of occupational prestige, education, and income. Because occupational prestige is thought to contribute more to socioeconomic status, it is generally weighted more heavily. Thus, in August Hollingshead's (1971) two-factor Index of Social Position, an occupation score is given a weight of 7 and an education score is given a weight of 4. To compute the index, one would first determine an individual's occupation and education scores on separate 7-point measures, multiply each score by its respective weight, and then add the score–weight products.

The advantage of indexing may be illustrated as follows. Suppose the value of each observed measure (X) is equal to a true score corresponding to the concept being measured (C) and an error score (e); thus, $X = C + e$. Now suppose that we have four different measures and pretend we know the true and error scores for a particular respondent (see the following tabulation).

Measure	Observed score (X)	True score (C)	Error score (e)
Item 1	2	4	−2
Item 2	3	2	+1
Item 3	7	5	+2
Item 4	5	8	−3
Total	17	19	−2

For each separate item, about one-third or more of the observed score represents error. If the error tends to be random (or if it is systematic but in different directions for the separate items), the error scores tend to cancel out when we sum over the items. Consequently, if we form an index by summing the four items, we obtain a greatly improved measure. For the respondent shown above, the index score would be 17 units, only a small fraction of which represents error (2 units).

Although most composite measures constitute indexes, multiple indicators may also be combined to form **scales**. The distinction between an index and a scale is fuzzy, and some social scientists use the terms interchangeably. But we think it is a distinction worth making. An index usually refers to the arbitrary combination of indicators, such as when we simply add together the responses to separate items without regard to what each actually contributes to the measurement of the underlying concept. The chief problem with an index is ensuring **unidimensionality** since it may be measuring more than the intended concept (e.g., "political liberalism" as well as "attitude toward racial integration"). A scale, in contrast, combines indicators according to nonarbitrary rules that are ordinarily designed to reflect only a single dimension of a concept.

Some scales differ from indexes by assigning scores to patterns of responses to a set of items. To illustrate the idea of patterns of responses, let us return to the Treiman index of attitudes toward racial integration referred to earlier (cited in D. G. Taylor, Sheatsley, and Greeley, 1978:43). Suppose that two respondents, Earl and Rudolph, gave the responses shown here to the five questions (see tabulation). If the items were scored as an index and we counted pro-integration responses, Earl and Rudolph would receive the same score, even though they have very different response patterns. Can one say which of the two is more racially liberal?

Question number	Earl	Rudolph
1	Pro-integration	Anti-integration
2	Pro-integration	Anti-integration
3	Anti-integration	Anti-integration
4	Anti-integration	Pro-integration
5	Anti-integration	Pro-integration

This contrived example points out a problem with index construction, namely, an issue of validity. If the same score may be achieved with very different responses, the possibility exists that the items are measuring more than one dimension or concept. In addition to attitudes toward racial integration, Earl's and Rudolph's responses may reflect other concepts, such as a concern to give socially desirable responses.

The construction of scales assumes that a concept can be understood in terms of an underlying continuum; in the case of an attitude, the continuum may range from favorable to unfavorable or positive to negative. It is further assumed that scores on individual items and composite measures represent specific points along the relevant continuum (or "scale"). Each score, in other words, should uniquely reflect the strength or degree of something—for example, an individual's degree of prejudice or a nation's level of modernization. But whereas these assumptions are implicit in an index, scaling procedures make them explicit and are designed to test their validity.

To illustrate a scaling technique, we will describe the approach developed by Louis Guttman (1950). Suppose we measure people's reading ability by testing their reading comprehension of items *ordered* in terms of difficulty, such as portions of a 3rd-grade reader, a 9th-grade textbook, and a college textbook. Subjects would be tested on each item starting with the easiest, and the item at which someone changed from "passing" to "failing" the reading tests would indicate the subject's position on a scale of reading ability. Four response patterns are expected if the items form a perfect Guttman scale: (1) flunk each item, (2) pass only at the 3rd-grade level, (3) pass all but the college text, and (4) pass all reading tests. Other response patterns, such as passing the 9th-grade test and flunking the other two, are called "nonscale" or "mixed types." By selecting a set of items that minimize the proportion of nonscale response patterns, the Guttman approach attempts to ensure a unidimensional scale.

KEY POINT

Indexes combine indicators more or less arbitrarily; *scales* combine indicators based on response patterns that represent the dimensions of a concept.

The actual process of **Guttman scaling** is sometimes quite elaborate. A researcher may start with a large battery of items thought to measure a concept. Then, subsets of these items are tested, often with a computer program, to determine whether they satisfy the expectations of a Guttman scale. Let us illustrate part of this process using the six GSS abortion items referred to earlier. Based on the proportion of 1975 GSS respondents answering yes to each question, Clifford Clogg and Darwin Sawyer (1981) ordered the items from the "easiest" condition under which to approve of abortion (woman's health is seriously endangered by the pregnancy) to the "most difficult" condition (woman does not want more children). Table 13.1 shows this question ordering and the seven response patterns possible if the items form a perfect Guttman scale. Each column in Table 13.1 displays a different response pattern ("Y" and "N" denote yes and no answers, respectively), and the yes responses are totaled to obtain a scale score for each response pattern.

In contrast to an index, a respondent's score on a *perfect* Guttman scale uniquely identifies the person's response pattern. In Table 13.1, for example, a score of 2 is always the pattern "Y Y N N N N." Note also that a score on a perfect Guttman scale indicates the point at which the respondent shifts from one response to another (e.g., those who score 3 approve of an abortion in the three easiest conditions and then shift to disapproval). Whether a set of items is reasonably close to the ideal of a perfect Guttman scale is an empirical question. We found that 19.5 percent of the 2014 GSS respondents had nonscale response patterns (e.g., "Y N Y N N N"). Using conventional measures of scalability, this indicates that the six questions form an acceptable Guttman scale for the 2014 GSS sample. The employment of Guttman scaling to ensure unidimensionality, however, is sample dependent. A set of items may be unidimensional for one sample of respondents but not for another. Differences in scalability across samples reflect sampling and measurement error as well as population differences (see Clogg and Sawyer [1981] for details and alternatives to the Guttman approach).

Various scaling procedures have been developed. Some capitalize on the inherent pattern among a set of items, whereas others capitalize on each item's placement with regard to an underlying continuum. The construction of scales is a topic beyond the scope of the current text. For a good overview of the subject of index and scale construction, see R. Michael Furr (2011). (Also see Box 13.1 for a description of another popular scaling technique.)

Although we have presented composite measures from the standpoint of triangulation, there are other good reasons for building indexes and scales. One is ease of analysis: The number of variables that must be considered is reduced. Another has to do with the variability in respondents' scores provided by the measure. Sometimes items provide very little information because of low variability (e.g., 90 percent of the respondents make the same response). By combining several items with low variability, it is possible to obtain an index with much greater variability, hence a more informative measure.

TABLE 13.1. **Response Pattern of a Perfect Guttman Scale**

Approve of an abortion if:	Response pattern						
The woman's own health is seriously endangered by the pregnancy.	Y	Y	Y	Y	Y	Y	N
There is a strong change of serious defect in the baby.	Y	Y	Y	Y	Y	N	N
She became pregnant as a result of rape.	Y	Y	Y	Y	N	N	N
The family has a very low income and can't afford any more children.	Y	Y	Y	N	N	N	N
She is not married and does not want to marry the man.	Y	Y	N	N	N	N	N
She is married and does not want any more children.	Y	N	N	N	N	N	N
Scale score	6	5	4	3	2	1	0

BOX 13.1 An Example of Likert Scaling: The Development of the FEM Scale

Guttman scales are designed so that each item represents a particular point on the underlying dimension. Because the set of items is ordered and cumulative, an individual's total scale score not only denotes a place on the underlying dimension but also reveals his or her responses to each item. Thus, both the items and the individuals are scaled with respect to the underlying concept. Another scaling technique, called **Likert** or summated ratings, assumes that each scale item reflects the entire range of the underlying continuum to the same degree. In a measure of attitude toward feminism, for example, each item may have response categories that vary from strongly antifeminist to strongly profeminist. Each item thus constitutes a separate rating, and an individual's score consists of the sum of his or her ratings (hence, the label "summated ratings"). Unlike a Guttman scale, the items of a Likert scale are not ordered or scaled; consequently, individual scores indicate a place on the underlying continuum but do not indicate a pattern of responses to particular items.

In developing a Likert scale, the object is to create a set of items whose combination provides the best measure of differences among respondents on the underlying concept. The construction of the FEM Scale, the validation of which we described in Chapter 5 (see Box 5.2), illustrates the steps in developing a Likert scale, including the criteria for selecting constituent items.

Step 1. Eliot Smith, Myra Marx Ferree, and Frederick Miller (1975) initially developed 57 items, each stating either the acceptance or the rejection of a feminist belief. The sources of ideas for specific items in the Likert scale are limited only by the researcher's imagination. In this case the researchers drew many items from an earlier study by Clifford Kirkpatrick (1936); for other items, they may have considered the published statements of avowed feminists and antifeminists. Below are five sample items that eventually were included in the scale.

1. Women have the right to compete with men in every sphere of activity.
2. As head of the household, the father should have final authority over his children.
3. The unmarried mother is morally a greater failure than the unmarried father.
4. A woman who refuses to give up her job to move with her husband would be to blame if the marriage broke up.
5. A woman who refuses to bear children has failed in her duty to her husband.

Step 2. The researchers asked 39 students to indicate whether they agreed or disagreed with each item as they role-played a "strong profeminist" or a "strong antifeminist." The purpose of this step, not always a part of scale construction, was to eliminate items that were ambiguous—that is, items that were not clearly perceived as representing either a profeminist or an antifeminist position. When there was sizeable disagreement over the direction of an item, the item was discarded. This process left 48 items.

Step 3. The next step is to select a subset of items that best discriminate among persons who hold different attitudes. To make this selection, researchers administer an initial item set to a group of respondents who are similar to those for whom the scale is intended. Smith, Ferree, and Miller shortened their scale in two stages. First, they asked the same students who role-played to give their own opinions. From an analysis of these responses, they selected 27 items. The basis of their selection was the items' variability. Greater variability generally indicates better discriminability (the ability to discriminate among individuals with different attitudes); if an item shows low variability, meaning that it elicits similar responses from all individuals, then it does not reveal how individuals differ in their attitudes.

Next, the researchers administered the preliminary 27-item scale to 100 Harvard summer-school students. Again, they assessed the items' ability to discriminate among respondents, this time using a technique called "factor analysis." Factor analysis is one of several ways to assess an item's discriminability. A simpler approach is to calculate each individual's scale score, determine the highest and lowest 25 percent of the scores, and then identify those items that best differentiate between the high and low scores. For example, if both high and low scorers are equally likely to endorse a particular statement, that statement would have poor discriminability. On the basis of the factor analysis, E. Smith, Ferree, and Miller selected the 20 items with highest discriminability.

Step 4. In its final form, a Likert scale consists of a series of statements with which respondents are asked to indicate their level of agreement or disagreement. The response format permits several categories of response. For the FEM Scale there are five: "strongly agree," "agree," "undecided," "disagree," and "strongly disagree." To arrive at a scale score, these categories are assigned numbers from 1 to 5, with the highest number representing strong agreement with a profeminist statement (or, conversely, strong disagreement with an antifeminist statement). Adding item responses, we get a possible range of 20 to 100 for the 20-item scale. This range corresponds to a dimension that at the low end indicates a very unfavorable attitude toward feminism and at the high end indicates a very favorable attitude toward feminism.

Step 5. At this point, the scale is ready to test for reliability and validity, a process that we have described in Box 5.2.

Structural Equation Modeling

At one time, indexes and scales were almost always constructed when one had multiple measures of concepts. In part this was because most social scientists were unfamiliar with procedures for analyzing multiple measures simultaneously. However, as social researchers became more knowledgeable about a technique called **structural equation modeling** and computer software was developed to apply such modeling, researchers increasingly turned to simultaneous testing. The term "structural modeling" refers to the systematic identification of the possible relationships among a set of concepts and their indicators. Each distinctive model describes a different "structure" of relationships that can be represented with a unique system of mathematical "equations." When applying this technique, one essentially checks to see how well the data fit various models. The mathematics required to do this are advanced. Still, one can get a sense of the value of structural equation modeling by considering the following example.

Recall the hypothetical study described earlier in this section involving the relationship between mother love and self-esteem. All the mothers in the study would have to be measured on each of the six indicators. Since measurement may be reactive, there is the possibility that measuring L1 may influence L2, L3, or even P1 or self-esteem. For example, the presence of an observer might affect the extent to which the mother touches the infant or perhaps even the mother's self-esteem. Consequently, an adequate representation of the relationships among the variables might be considerably more complicated than indicated in Figure 13.3.

Consider Figure 13.4. Note the arrows leading from mother love and self-esteem to each of their respective indicators; these represent the assumption that the unobserved concepts mother love and self-esteem cause their measured indicators. This model also shows that P1 and P2 partly share the same methodological weaknesses (diagrammed by the curved arrow between them denoting this common bias) and that the measurement of P3 influences mother love. There are many possible models depicting the variables in Figure 13.4. For example, deleting the arrow from P3 to mother love or adding a curved arrow between L1 and L3 produces a different model. It is the job of the researcher to consider the more plausible models and to test each to determine which "fit" the data.

Structural equation modeling differs from composite measurement in that it maintains the separate identity of each indicator throughout the analysis. This requires that a researcher specify how each indicator is related to the underlying concept it measures. An advantage of this approach is that it makes it possible to test for certain kinds of measurement error. One disadvantage is that it becomes extremely difficult to consider all possible combinations of relationships as the number of indicators and concepts increases. Modeling is discussed further in Chapter 16. For an excellent introduction to structural equation modeling concepts and techniques, see Rex Kline (2016).

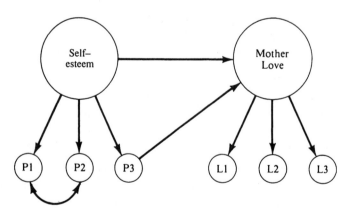

FIGURE 13.4. Diagram of a structural equation model of the relationship between self-esteem and mother love.

KEY POINT

Structural equation modeling provides evidence of each indicator's contribution to the underlying concept.

Multiple Tests of Hypotheses across Different Studies

One of the best ways to increase our confidence in a particular finding is to repeat a study to see whether we can obtain the same result. Indeed, the ability to replicate research findings is a foundation of science. If it were not, findings would merely be historical facts. Despite the value placed on replicability, however, studies that attempt to literally replicate earlier research are rarely published (Nickerson, 2000). "Exactly" duplicating the procedures of a study is seen as less challenging and interesting and is valued much less by the scientific community than performing an original study. Still, scientists do value the validation and extension of hypotheses and theories; therefore, it is common to investigate the same relationship as an original study but to change one or more aspects of the study. For this reason, the term **replication** is best applied to any attempt to repeat the findings of another study. All replications are inherently dissimilar. Even an attempt to strictly reproduce the methods of a study will be conducted at a different time and generally will involve a different sample of subjects. In general, the greater the dissimilarity between a replication and an original study in terms of methods, time, place, and so forth, the greater the confidence that the findings support the research hypothesis rather than being artifacts of particular research conditions and procedures.

Although social scientists often replicate findings in the process of pursuing a related research question, they infrequently carry out research solely for the purpose of replication. The one exception to this pattern is experimental research. Not only are small-scale experiments less costly to replicate than other kinds of research, but also replication is the principal method of increasing the external validity of experimental results.[1] In the following example, a team of investigators carried out several experiments to test the same hypothesis. The experiments used different manipulations and measures of the hypothesis-linked concepts.

KEY POINT

A *replication* is inherently dissimilar to an original study; the more dissimilar, the greater the confidence in a replicated finding.

Replications Using the Same Research Strategy: Social Exclusion and Helping

Why do people choose to help others? In Chapter 1, we described an experiment by Jean Twenge and associates (2007) that tested one possible answer to this question. These researchers hypothesized that helping depends on a sense of belongingness—of believing that one is a part of a mutually supportive community. People who have this sense will view helping as a way of reaping the rewards of belonging to the group. People who feel excluded will be wary of being taken advantage of and will not see helping as being repaid with belongingness. Hence, social exclusion will reduce helping behavior.

To test this hypothesis, the researchers carried out seven experiments. All of the subjects in these experiments were psychology students who participated for partial course credit. Social exclusion was manipulated in three ways. In the experiment described in Chapter 1, subjects met together in groups of four to six to get to know one another. Following the discussion, they filled out forms that asked them to name the two people in their group with whom they would most like to work. Then, after collecting this information, the experimenter told each subject that either everyone or no one in their group had chosen them as someone they'd like to work with. In this way, half the subjects felt accepted and the other half felt rejected. For the other six experiments, subjects were given false feedback after completing a personality questionnaire. Those in the social exclusion condition were told that, based on the questionnaire results, "they were likely to be alone later in life"; two other groups were told either that "they would enjoy a future rich in personal relationships (future belonging)" or that "they would be accident prone (misfortune control)." In five experiments, the participants heard this feedback directly from the experimenter, whereas in the sixth experiment, they received the feedback in a sealed envelope so that the experimenter was blind to the subjects' condition.

Across the seven experiments, the researchers also varied the measure of helping behavior. Following the group-discussion manipulation, subjects were asked if they would be willing to volunteer to participate in additional experiments for which they would not receive extra credit. The operational definition of helping by volunteering consisted of the number of extra experiments for which each subject volunteered. Three additional forms of helping were paired with the false-feedback manipulation. In two experiments, subjects were given $2 in quarters for participating and then were asked to donate some of their payment to a student emergency fund. The donations were placed in a box while the experimenter was in another room, and helping was operationalized as the amount donated. In one experiment, following the manipulation of exclusion, the experimenter accidentally knocked a cup of pencils off a shelf and onto the floor; the number of pencils the subject helped to pick up operationalized helping.

The measure of helping in the remaining three experiments consisted of cooperative responses in the Prisoner's Dilemma Game. In this game, players must choose between two options: cooperating with their partner for their mutual gain or competing with their partner to maximize personal gain. The dilemma is that when both players choose the competing response, they both lose, whereas if they both cooperate, they win less individually than if one partner competed and the other cooperated. Although subjects believed they were playing the game with another student, in reality they played with a computer programmed to mimic the subjects' response on the preceding turn. In two of the three prisoner-dilemma experiments, subjects played for points and were encouraged to earn as many points as they could for themselves; in the other experiment, they played for real money. Given that cooperating benefited another person, the measure of helping was defined as the number of cooperating responses.

Finally, the investigators incorporated measures of possible mediators of the exclusion–helping relationship in several of the experiments. For example, in one donating-money experiment, after the exclusion manipulation but before the request to donate to the student emergency fund, subjects completed a measure of empathic concern, ostensibly as part of an unrelated study. In one prisoner-dilemma experiment, after the manipulation but before they played the game, subjects completed a questionnaire measuring trust in others, feelings of belongingness, sense of control, and feelings of self-awareness. In still other experiments, mood and self-esteem were measured.

The results were consistent across the seven experiments. For every measure of helping, subjects who were made to feel excluded or to believe that they faced a future alone helped significantly less than subjects in the control condition and than subjects who felt accepted or who faced a future of belonging. For example, in the volunteering experiment, only 20 percent of the "rejected" subjects volunteered to help by doing at least one experiment compared with 90 percent of the "accepted" subjects; in the two donating-money experiments, those in the future-alone condition donated on average one-quarter to one-third as much money as those in the future-belonging condition.

Altogether these systematic replications provide strong support for the hypothesized relationship between social exclusion and helping. Consider the repeated tests of statistical significance. When tested at the .05 level of significance, a finding that is significant in one experiment could occur by chance 1 in 20 times; however, if the finding is replicated 7 times at this level, the likelihood that chance accounts for the finding is extremely small. The variations in operational definitions also increase our confidence that the finding is not the product of reactive effects or limited to a particular way of manipulating exclusion or measuring helping. In the Prisoner's Dilemma Game, for example, another student was the recipient of the prosocial behavior, whereas in the volunteer experiment the experimenter was the beneficiary. Also, the false-feedback manipulation was not dependent on hearing the feedback from the experimenter because it also affected helping when the feedback was given in a sealed envelope. At the same time, the consistent findings enhance external validity as they suggest that social exclusion affects a range of prosocial behavior, from donating money and volunteering to spontaneous helping and cooperating to benefit another. Finally, the experiments yield important evidence of a theoretical link between exclusion and helping. Although several auxiliary measures were related to the social exclusion manipulation, only one— empathic concern—mediated the link between exclusion and helping. Apparently, feelings of exclusion reduce the ability to empathize with others, an ability that inclines people to provide help.

The results of the experiments "establish that laboratory-administered exclusion causes a reduction in prosocial behavior" (Twenge et al., 2007:64). As the researchers note, however, practical and ethical considerations limit the manner in which exclusion can be manipulated in the laboratory; their manipulations were "merely threatening, compared with actual harm or loss" (64), such as the loss of a loved one. Another limitation, typical of experiments, is that all the subjects were students enrolled in psychology courses who were participating for course credit. To gain further confidence in this relationship, we need to combine these experimental results with findings from studies that use a different basic approach, as in the next two examples.

Replications Using Different Research Strategies
Deterrent Effects of Arrest

Two studies on the deterrent effects of arrest for domestic violence may be used to illustrate further the application of multiple methods to test hypotheses across different studies. Unlike the set of experiments just described, which entailed the same basic approach, the following two studies were carried out in different settings with different approaches.

The first study, called the Minneapolis Domestic Violence Experiment, was designed to test the relative merits of two alternative theories of punishment. The deterrence doctrine holds that the "pains of punishment deter people from repeating the crimes for which they are punished." Labeling theory, alternatively, holds that "punishment often makes individuals more likely to commit crimes" because it changes their self-image and social interaction patterns and forecloses certain life options (Sherman and Berk, 1984:261). To test these theories, Lawrence Sherman and Richard Berk (1984) carried out a field experiment in the city of Minneapolis over an 18-month period, between March 1981 and August 1982. The experimental design called for police to apply randomly one of three intervention strategies when confronting incidents of simple (misdemeanor) domestic assault: arrest the offender, force the offender to leave the premises, or give advice and/or mediate the dispute.[2] The effects of these three responses were assessed by determining whether an offender repeated an incident of domestic assault within a 6-month follow-up period. The investigators measured this outcome in two ways: (1) through police records indicating whether an offense or arrest report had been filed and (2) through interviews with victims, who were asked to indicate if there had been an actual or threatened assault or property damage. On both measures, the results showed that arrested offenders were least likely to commit another act of domestic violence.[3] Thus, the study tends to support the efficacy of deterrence.

Sherman and Berk considered several potential sources of error or bias that might have influenced their findings. For example, the official outcome measure—police reports—might be affected by the reluctance of victims to call the police. This effect would be confounded with the arrest intervention strategy if the arrest were seen as "an undesirable intervention, and rather than face the prospect of another arrest from a new incident, these victims [decided] not to invoke police sanctions" (269). Sherman and Berk note, however, that identical results were obtained with the interview self-report data, which should not have been subject to the same source of bias. Hence, a triangulation of the dependent measure effectively eliminated this interpretation. In a similar fashion, the researchers considered other potentially problematic features of the study, and they argued in each case against the likelihood of a contaminating effect. The one limitation that they did not minimize was the external validity of the study. It is possible that special features of the site, the police department, and the officers who volunteered to take part in the study might have affected the findings. The effects of arrest, in other words, might not be the same in other jurisdictions with different characteristics.

Despite this qualification, the Minneapolis Domestic Violence Experiment received enormous publicity and apparently began to affect police policy around the country (Berk and Newton, 1985). It became especially important, therefore, to test the generalizability of the findings. To this end, Richard Berk and Phyllis Newton (1985) conducted a second study in which they tested the same hypothesis, with the same official outcome measure but in a different setting with a different research approach involving the analysis of existing data.

The data consisted of "783 wife-battery incidents coming to the attention of police over a 28-month period in a county in California" (Berk and Newton, 1985:253). More than one-fourth of the incidents had resulted in arrest, and it was possible from police records to identify subsequent cases of police intervention as well as when the new incidents occurred. Unlike the previous study, however, where cases were randomly assigned to intervention strategies, differences between arrested and nonarrested offenders were not randomized. Therefore, the investigators statistically controlled for these differences by using other information from police records about offender characteristics (e.g., age, number of previous convictions, employment status) and situational features of the incident (e.g., time of day, presence of a witness). The control amounted to a measure of the propensity of the police to arrest. With this control, the most general finding was consistent with the Minneapolis results: Arrests deter new incidents of domestic assault. Berk and Newton also found that arrests were most effective with batterers whom police would ordinarily be inclined to arrest. That is, there was a direct relationship between propensity to arrest and the deterrent effect of arrest. Although the investigators were cautious about the study's implications for policy recommendations (they noted, for example, that little is known about how the arrest process deters domestic assault), they concluded that "our study places the burden of proof heavily on those who believe that wife batterers should not be arrested" (262).

Separately, each of these studies has major limitations that undermine the credibility of the findings. The setting and other unique features of the Minneapolis experiment limit its external validity. Without random assignment of offenders to treatments, the second study has relatively low internal validity. Together, however, they greatly increase our confidence in the principal finding. Not only do they represent independent confirmations of the same hypothesis, but also the strengths in one study offset the weaknesses in the other. The second study enhances the generalizability of the experimental results insofar as it involves a different police department in a different setting, with a natural rather than manipulated measure of the independent variable. By the same token, we gain confidence in the findings of the second study by virtue of obtaining the same basic result in another study with high internal validity.

Although the two studies, taken together, increased the credibility of the arrest intervention strategy, research conclusions are always tentative and subject to change or reinterpretation as new evidence accumulates. Indeed, subsequent replications of the Minneapolis Domestic Violence Experiment failed to consistently replicate the original findings (Berk et al., 1992; Pate and Hamilton, 1992; Sherman and Smith, 1992; Sherman, 1992, 1993). These replications indicated that the effect of arrest varied across jurisdictions, with a deterrent effect in some areas, no discernible effect in others, and an escalating effect in still others. Furthermore, the deterrent effects of arrest appear to depend on the length of the follow-up period, the length of detention, the background of the offender, and whether the offender perceives that he or she has been treated fairly (Paternoster et al., 1997). For example, arrest seems to be more effective for those who are employed than for those who are unemployed; it also is more effective when an arrested suspect perceives that he or she has been treated in a procedurally fair manner.

Effect of Abuse on Marriage and Cohabitation

An excellent example of research combining survey and field research is Andrew Cherlin and associates' (2004) study of the influence of physical and sexual abuse on marriage and cohabitation among low-income women. Whereas in many multiple-methods studies separate approaches are applied independently to investigate the same relationships, these investigators used an iterative process of gathering and analyzing data that integrated the two approaches. Thus, they began with analyses of basic associations in the survey data; these associations provided useful leads for identifying and exploring more detailed patterns of abuse and intimate relations through the field research. Then, they used their deepened understanding from the fieldwork to develop hypotheses that could be tested with the survey data.

The investigators carried out their two-pronged study in low-income neighborhoods in Boston, Chicago, and San Antonio. The survey sample was randomly selected from households with children in which a female was the primary caregiver and the income was below 200 percent of the federal poverty line. In all, 2402 women were interviewed, with questions about sensitive topics such as abuse and sexual activity asked using audio computer-assisted self-interviews to ensure confidentiality. Families in the field research, who were not in the survey, were recruited nonrandomly from the same neighborhoods as the survey. Data from these 256 families were drawn from a combination of in-depth interviews and participant observation that took place over a 4-year period. For the first 18 months, the families were visited once or twice a month as researchers interviewed caregivers and accompanied them and their children "to the welfare office, doctor, grocery store, or workplace" (Cherlin et al., 2004:773). Thereafter, they were seen every 6 months.

Previous theory and research as well as preliminary analyses led the investigators to expect parallel sets of associations in the field and survey data. For example, one association involved women who had withdrawn from serious relationships with men altogether. The investigators discovered this pattern, which they called "abated unions," from their field research. Reasoning that experiences with abusive men might lead women to avoid intimate relationships, they expected the fieldwork data to show that women who have been abused as adults but not as children will be more likely to have withdrawn from serious relationships than other women. The cross-sectional survey could measure only union status at the time of the survey—whether the woman was married, cohabiting, or single. Unlike the field research data, it did not contain enough information to construct the history of the unions. Cherlin and associates reasoned, however, that these status categories should correspond to fieldwork expectations in predictable ways. Women classified as having abated unions, for example, should be more likely to be single than married or cohabiting at the time of the survey; therefore, they hypothesized that women who have experienced abuse as adults are more likely to be currently single than married or cohabiting compared with women who have not been abused as adults.

In a similar fashion, the investigators developed other expectations and hypotheses about the impact of a history of childhood abuse or no history of abuse on marriage and cohabitation. In every instance, both fieldwork expectations and survey hypotheses were supported by the data. Each approach lends a different perspective to the relationship between abuse and the formation of intimate relationships, and each has distinctive strengths and weaknesses. The survey measured abuse with a series of specific questions that respondents answered in confidence, whereas in the field, participants disclosed that they had been abused at various points—when they trusted the researcher enough to share such sensitive information. The survey data presented a cross-sectional view of respondents' union status; by contrast, the field research provided detailed observations on union histories. For example, about one-sixth of the women in the field study who were classified as having abated unions had not been married or cohabiting for at least 1 year prior to the research, were not in such a relationship during the fieldwork period, and indicated that they had no interest in forming such a relationship. Based on a relatively small, nonrandom sample, the field research also provided concrete examples of abuse–union patterns. By comparison, the survey was based on a large random sample and contained measures of several variables that were controlled in the statistical analysis. Thus, the fieldwork and survey complemented one another well, cross-validating measures of abuse and providing a multilayered understanding of the impact of abuse on unions among low-income men and women.

A Comparison of the Four Basic Approaches to Social Research

The principle of triangulation emphasizes the value of testing hypotheses with different methods that do not share the same methodological weaknesses. In this way, we build confidence in our assertions about the social world. This position has two related implications. First, as Joel Smith (1991:2) asserts in an article entitled "A Methodology for Twenty-First Century Sociology," social research "should be shaped by the nature of the question, the phenomena being considered, and the sort of answer that will satisfy us." Too often in social research, methods are not chosen or created to fit the task but "have become ideologies that define what to study and how" (2). Qualitative research is valued over quantitative research (or vice versa); comparative historical methods are valued over survey research; field research is valued over experimentation. These dogmatic positions, however, obscure the fact that all conclusions in social research rest on the resolution of the same basic issues. According to Smith (11–13), these are encompassed by the following five questions:

1. What does one want to know and why? (Any study should have a clear and specific purpose guided by a clear theoretical interest.)
2. What is to be observed? (Choices must be made about time and place, unit of analysis, relevant characteristics, and the processes in which units are embedded.)
3. Which and how many objects are to be examined? (Because any study provides a limited set of observations, one should be aware of what the observations represent and

how many cases should be selected in light of theory, desired reliability of estimates, and available resources.)

4. How are the phenomena of interest to be observed? (The method of observing—asking questions, noting appearance and behavior, recording physical traces, and so forth—should depend on theory and the relative advantages and disadvantages of each approach.)

5. How are answers to be decided? (The analysis should indicate what can be asserted with what certainty about what has been found.)

In short, the focus of social research should be on what one wants to know and why rather than on how to apply a particular approach. We must be capable of applying particular techniques and methods, to be sure; but these should not be treated dogmatically lest their application become an end in itself.

The second implication of triangulation is that social researchers need to know the relative strengths and weaknesses of each approach to decide which methods to select and how best to combine them when possible. Table 13.2 summarizes the strengths and weaknesses of the four main approaches. To simplify the comparisons, the table focuses attention on particular ideal forms of these four strategies: laboratory experiments, structured

TABLE 13.2. **Strengths and Weaknesses of Approaches on Eight Dimensions**

Dimensions of assessment	Relative Strength*			
	LABORATORY EXPERIMENT	SURVEY**	FIELD RESEARCH†	ARCHIVAL RECORDS‡
Content restrictions: What is and is not feasible or practical to study	W	M	M	W
Internal validity: Control over extraneous variables	S	M	W	M
Ease of measurement: Ability to measure or perform checks on reliability and validity	S	S	W	M
Nonreactive measurement: Control for effects of awareness of being tested or observed	W	W	M	S
Control for investigator bias: Control for effects of researcher characteristics and behavior	W	W	M	S
Contextual understanding: Ability to study actions in relation to the social context	W	W	S	M
External validity: Ability to generalize from sample results	W	S	W	M
Ability to replicate	S	S	W	M

*W, weak; M, medium; S, strong.
**Structured questionnaire or interview with probability sampling.
†Participant observation.
‡Available-data research excluding private documents and survey and ethnographic archives.

surveys, participant observation, and documentary evidence. However, it is important to recall the variations within each basic strategy. Experiments may be conducted in the field as well as in the laboratory; surveys vary in mode (e.g., telephone interviews and mail questionnaires); field research may involve in-depth interviewing and varying degrees of participation in the research setting; and available data come in myriad forms subject to distinctive methodological problems. Furthermore, there are other research strategies that do not fit neatly into this fourfold typology, which we have ignored or touched on only lightly in this book, such as structured observation, ethnomethodology, and life histories.

KEY POINT
Researchers should select the methodological approach or combination of approaches that best addresses the research question.

The entries in Table 13.2 summarize the relative strength of each approach on eight dimensions. "W" means that the approach is relatively weak, "M" means that it is of medium strength or weakness, and "S" indicates that the dimension is a strength of this approach. As the table shows, none of the basic strategies is highly flexible with regard to the topics or research questions that it may address. The relative inflexibility of experiments and archival records stems from analogous limitations: Experimentation depends on what it is practically and ethically possible to manipulate; available-data research depends on the availability of the data. Beyond their general accessibility to research problems, each approach is uniquely suited to obtaining particular kinds of information. Thus, surveys are best for estimating population characteristics and describing the distribution of attitudes and opinions; field research affords access to actors' definitions of complex situations and events; and the analysis of available data often provides the best and/or only means of studying the past and larger social units.

Experiments are strong in establishing internal validity because they provide the strongest inferences about cause and effect. Statistical controls possible in surveys and some available-data research allow for partial control of extraneous variables (hence the "M" in the table); however, the absence of such formal controls generally makes field research least acceptable for testing causal hypotheses.

Although it is easier to replicate measures and assess reliability and validity in experiments and surveys, these approaches are most vulnerable to methodological artifacts stemming from subjects' awareness of being tested and experimenter or interviewer effects. Nonreactive measurement is a major strength of much available-data research. However, the extent to which field research is vulnerable to these artifacts depends on how well the investigator becomes accepted by others in the field setting and on how well he or she is able to perform simultaneously the roles of participant and observer. The greater the trust the investigator is able to develop, the less the likelihood of reactive measurement; the more adept he or she is at managing the participant and observer roles, the less the likelihood of investigator bias.

By observing social life in naturalistic settings, field research is best able to provide a holistic and contextual understanding of social actions. By comparison, experiments— whether in the laboratory or the field—isolate one or a few variables at a time, making it difficult to study complex interactions; surveys study what people say in the unique context of an interview or questionnaire, which may not indicate how they will act and feel in everyday life; and available data may provide limited contextual information.

Survey research affords the greatest control over error and bias associated with sampling and therefore provides strong sample generalization. The susceptibility of documents to selective deposit makes the available-data approach moderate on sampling limitations. By contrast, this is a major deficiency of experiments insofar as they typically take place in highly restricted settings with small, nonrandom samples of subjects. And although the quality of sampling is generally better in field research than in experiments, field studies are nonetheless based on isolated settings and nonrandom sampling procedures.

Experiments and survey studies are the easiest to replicate. Indeed, replication is fairly common in experiments, and surveys such as the GSS and various polls repeatedly ask the same questions to measure trends. The time-consuming nature of and lack of standardization in field research make this approach very difficult to replicate. Replication with alternative measures or with respect to different time periods is sometimes possible with available-data research, but this depends again on the availability of the data.

As Table 13.2 shows, the pattern of vulnerability varies across the four main approaches; that is, no two research strategies share the same strengths and weaknesses. As our replication examples showed, this is what makes the approaches complementary and strengthens inferences based on a triangulation of methods.

In addition to triangulation (*multiple* approaches to a research question), a variety of strategies and measures may be combined within a *single* approach to exploit the relative strengths and weaknesses of complementary methods. For example, compared with face-to-face interviews, mail questionnaires are relatively inexpensive but tend to have relatively large nonresponse rates. The advantages of both survey methods may be attained within one study by (1) mailing questionnaires to a probability sample of the target population and (2) conducting face-to-face interviews with a smaller sample of those not responding to the mail questionnaire to estimate the nonresponse bias. Other examples of harmonious combinations of methods within single studies include face-to-face interviewing in pretesting and debriefing experimental subjects, vignette experimental designs in survey research, preliminary interviews with open-ended questions to develop closed questions, use of archival records to identify groups for field research, field research to determine survey instrument content and to resolve ambiguous survey findings, and probability sampling in field and available-data research.

Meta-analysis

A logical extension of triangulation is a method of research synthesis called **meta-analysis**. Coined by Gene Glass (1976), meta-analysis refers to the application of statistical techniques to summarize the results of multiple studies that address the same research question. Prior to its development, literature reviews in the social sciences consisted of verbal descriptions of previous research in which investigators relied on their personal judgments to summarize and synthesize the basic findings. Investigators still conduct such reviews, but if the studies in an area have quantitative outcome measures, meta-analysis offers a more systematic assessment of the literature.

Performing a meta-analysis is somewhat like doing a content analysis (Chapter 12), except that the observations (units of analysis) are primary research reports rather than communications produced for purposes other than research. After investigators identify reports of empirical studies in a particular area, they code their basic findings and other study features. Then they calculate summary statistics to estimate the overall strength of the relationship between the independent and dependent variables as well as the effect of other features of the study on this relationship.

Meta-analyses offer several advantages. In contrast to traditional literature reviews, which tend to provide general impressions of the strength and reliability of findings, a meta-analysis produces summary statistics that estimate the size and significance of effects. By combining (or triangulating) the results of several studies, they also provide evidence of the reliability and external validity of a research finding. Meta-analysis is particularly useful and powerful in the experimental literature, where internal validity is strong and external validity is weak. Demonstrating that an effect is consistent across experiments with varying procedures, research settings, and samples greatly increases its generalizability. Finally, meta-analysis can be applied to test hypotheses about research findings. This was the object of an interesting analysis of teacher-expectancy effects by Stephen Raudenbush (1984).

KEY POINT
Traditional literature reviews rely on the subjective judgment of the reviewer; *meta-analysis* systematically summarizes quantitative studies on a topic with precise statistical estimates of effects.

Raudenbush reasoned that the mixed results of experiments testing the effects of teacher expectancy on elementary students' IQ gains might be explained by between-study differences in how well the teachers knew the pupils before the expectancy manipulation. The basic teacher-expectancy design (see Rosenthal and Jacobson, 1968) involves manipulating teacher expectations about their pupils' intellectual development. Typically, teachers are given bogus IQ "aptitude" test results that randomly selected pupils—the experimental group—will "bloom" during the school year. This manipulation is followed by retesting IQ at year end to determine whether the "bloomers" gained more than the control group. Raudenbush hypothesized that the impact of the bogus information is inversely related to the length of teacher–pupil contact before the expectancy manipulation. Testing his hypothesis in a factorial design (manipulation of prior teacher–pupil contact as well as expectancy) would be logistically difficult in a school setting. Instead, by doing a meta-analysis of 18 experiments that naturally varied in prior teacher–pupil contact time, Raudenbush was able to demonstrate strong support for his hypothesis.

Let us now take a closer look at the steps in carrying out a meta-analysis: defining a research problem, searching for relevant research studies, coding the studies, carrying out the analysis, and presenting the results (Cooper and Hedges, 2009).[4]

Problem Formulation

Whether the impetus for a meta-analytic study is to assess the reliability and generality of a finding or to test a new hypothesis, the starting point is to identify a research question that can be answered by examining previous studies. Consider, for example, the questions addressed in the following studies and the meta-analytic results:

1. Do juvenile delinquency programs prevent recidivism? Mark Lipsey (1994) found, on average, a small positive effect in 443 delinquency treatment studies.

2. Why do boys and girls differ in science achievement? Betsy Jane Becker and associates (1994) tested a complex causal model of the relationship of gender and achievement. One important policy-related finding was that the same factors were relevant for predicting science achievement for males and for females, which suggests that programs to foster science achievement should be the same for both sexes.

3. How much do door-to-door canvassing, phone canvassing, and direct mail increase voter turnout? Separate meta-analyses of each of these get-out-the-vote tactics by Donald Green and Alan Gerber (2008) confirmed the results of a single experiment, reported in Box 7.2: The more personal the method of contact, the greater the impact on voter turnout. Face-to-face contact works best, followed by volunteer phone calls, calls from commercial phone banks, and direct mail.

4. Is there a positive association between the quality of marital relations and the quality of parent–child relations? In a meta-analytic review of 68 studies, Osnat Erel and Bonnie Burman (1995) found a moderately positive relationship. Their findings support the spillover hypothesis (the mood of the marriage spills over to parent–child relations) in contrast to the compensatory hypothesis (parents seek satisfaction in either parent–child or marital relationships to compensate for deficiencies in the other).

5. What are the strongest predictors of college students' academic performance? Michelle Richardson, Charles Abraham, and Rod Bond (2012) examined 50 predictors of college grade-point average in more than 1100 independent studies. They found the largest correlation ($r = .59$) for performance self-efficacy (perception of capability of performing well academically), followed by high school grade-point average (.40), ACT test score (.40), and grade goal (.35) (self-assigned minimum goal).

A research question that is amenable to meta-analysis is one that can be answered from previous studies. Raudenbush (1984) could not have tested his hypothesis if the teacher–pupil contact time before the expectancy manipulation had not varied (0–24 weeks) in the 18 experiments. As in other available-data research, an investigator may settle for a less than satisfactory research question because of data limitations. Suppose, for example, we are interested in the criterion-related validity of the ACT test for predicting aptitude for higher education. Alas, the available studies generally exclude those students with lower ACT scores who are not admitted to or do not enroll in college. Consequently, we settle for a research question for which data are available: How well does the ACT test predict the grades of enrolled college students?

Data Collection

The research question leads directly to consideration of the target population to which the meta-analytic results are to be generalized. Ideally, we would like to include, or sample, all studies bearing on the research question. In practice, however, the data obtained will be a biased sample of the targeted research. Raudenbush (1984), for example, used published literature reviews and a computerized database to locate teacher-expectancy studies using children in grades 1 through 7 and IQ as the outcome. His sample is biased to the extent that it underrepresents unpublished research and studies too recent to be included in literature reviews or databases.

The absence of unpublished research in literature searches is called the "file drawer" problem (Rosenthal, 1991:103). Because journals are reluctant to publish studies that produce nonsignificant results, such research is likely to be hidden away in file drawers. Consequently, published studies may be a biased sample of all studies ever conducted.

The best approach to data collection in meta-analysis is to use multiple, complementary information channels (triangulation) that do not share the same biases (Cooper and Hedges, 2009; White, 2009). Contacting researchers working in the field, for example, is a means of locating new and unpublished studies that are unavailable through literature reviews and databases. Thomas Cook and associates (1994:289–94) suggest starting with key word computerized literature searches (for books, articles, unpublished dissertations, research and technical reports, and conference papers), followed by cross-checking the references in each item, and finally contacting scholars who have been identified as working in the field.

A thorough search, however, may produce too many candidate studies, which then must be pared through probability sampling or culled using eligibility criteria. Lipsey (1994:87–88) employed detailed criteria to cull more than 8000 delinquency studies to 443 for his meta-analysis. Included in his eligibility criteria were requirements that the study was conducted in an English-speaking country after World War II, that a majority of the subjects were age 21 or younger, that at least one outcome variable measured delinquency for treatment and control groups, and that random assignment or other means was used to assess the similarity of treatment and control groups before treatment.

Data Evaluation

The evaluation and coding of each study are similar to the defining and coding of categories for content analysis. The investigator determines relevant questions to ask about the studies and ways to extract answers (measures and codes) from each study. For example, in addition to outcome measures of marital and parent–child relationships, Erel and Burman (1995) abstracted such information as the study design (cross-sectional or longitudinal) and source (journal article, book chapter, or dissertation), sample size and type (families dealing with stressful life circumstances, clinical, community, or other), the child's age and birth order, and the sex of parent and child. For each juvenile delinquency study, Lipsey (1994:101–12) coded 92 variables about the methodological design, subjects, treatments, outcomes, and context (author's discipline, affiliation, funding source, type, and year of publication).

Decisions on what to code may emerge from the research literature, relevant theory, or the researcher's insights. Raudenbush's (1984:87) hypothesis that previous teacher–pupil contact time is inversely related to experimentally induced teacher-expectancy effects was derived from cognitive dissonance theory. He also coded information relevant to published critiques of methodological shortcomings in teacher-expectancy studies, and he was able to demonstrate analytically a lack of support for rival hypotheses that variations in study findings were a result of uncontrolled measurement (individual- versus group-administered IQ tests) or tester bias (blind versus aware of bogus bloomer information).

T. D. Cook and associates (1994:297) mention that critics have assailed meta-analysis for "camouflaging a 'garbage in garbage out' process by using fancy statistical techniques" and allowing the more numerous poorer studies to crowd out the results of exemplary studies. Actually, variation in study quality can be used to advantage in meta-analysis because it may explain differences in study results. Some very poor studies, of course, are unusable. Lipsey (1994) rejected many delinquency treatment studies for design shortcomings (e.g., the absence of a control group). By coding various methodological design features and technical quality ratings of the remaining 443 studies, Lipsey found that slightly more than one-fourth of the variability in the delinquency study outcomes was methodologically related.

Analysis and Interpretation

To compare outcomes across studies, meta-analyses calculate a quantitative measure of the size of the relationship between two variables called an **effect size** (Borenstein, 2009). Relationships can be quantified in various ways, depending on the level of measurement and study design (e.g., survey versus experiment), and so there are various statistical indices of effect size. Erel and Burman (1995) and Green and Gerber (2008) used a standardized measure of the mean difference between groups; Richardson, Abraham, and Bond (2012) used the correlation coefficient.[5]

Two general statistical frameworks are used to account for study-to-study variability in the effect size. The **fixed-effects model** assumes that the included studies are essentially identical except for the sampling of cases. Hence, between-study variability is treated as arising from sampling and other chance processes. In the **random-effects model**, outcome results may be shaped by between-study variability in methods, conditions, and settings as well as by sampling. The issues involved in choosing between fixed- and random-effects frameworks are complex and beyond the scope of this book (see Konstantopoulos and Hedges [2009] and Raudenbush [2009]).

As an illustration of the main distinction between the two frameworks, let us reconsider the teacher-expectancy experiments. If one posits that the expectancy manipulation will produce the same (fixed) effect for all teachers in all studies, the variation in results from study to study is attributed to randomization and other chance processes. Meta-analysis may then be used to estimate the common (fixed) effect apart from the chance disturbances (noise). Now suppose, instead, that the teacher-expectancy effect is expected to vary by teacher's sex. This would still yield a fixed-effects formulation since the expectancy effects are assumed to be the same for all male teachers and for all female teachers.

The effectiveness of the expectancy manipulation depends on both successful deception of the teachers and teachers behaving toward the bloomers in such a manner as to fulfill their expectancy for unusual intellectual development. It seems unlikely that both circumstances (deception and conveyance of expectancy) would be identical for all teachers. Therefore, using a random-effects framework would allow the expectancy effect to vary across teachers (low for some, higher for others). Within a classroom, however, the expectancy effect of a particular teacher would be the same (fixed) for all pupils. The random-effects analysis would then be used to estimate the average and the variability of expectancy effects among the teachers. A similar random-effects approach was used by Lipsey (1994) because the delinquency studies were too diverse (treatment program, subjects, methodological design, and outcomes) to justify the assumption of identical (fixed) program effects.

Public Presentation

Preparing a meta-analytic review is similar to writing a research report, which is discussed in Chapter 17 (for specific meta-analysis advice, see Clarke [2009]). The author must inform the reader of the purpose (research question), the data collection (literature search, eligibility criteria), the data evaluation (measures and coding, handling of incomplete or missing data), the analysis (statistical methods and framework, presentation of findings), and the author's interpretation of the results.

The audience must be given specific details on procedures (operational definitions, training of coders, and so forth), the handling of difficult problems (e.g., missing data), and checks on quality (reliability and validity assessments) so that they can understand and judge the merit of the meta-analysis. Erel and Burman (1995:115), for example, inform their readers that their eligibility criteria included the restriction that the marital and parent–child relations studies had to be available in a Los Angeles university library. By clearly spelling out their eligibility criteria, Erel and Burman allow the audience to evaluate the extent to which generalizations may be drawn from their meta-analysis.

Since meta-analysis is research on top of research, sometimes there is confusion about the methodological underpinnings of a conclusion. When the primary studies are true experimental designs and the research purpose is to summarize the average effect of the experimental variable, the meta-analytic results share the advantages of an experimental design (Table 13.2) plus a likely, substantial boost in external validity. However, if coded features of experiments are used to explain variations in study results, the design becomes "correlational" and more vulnerable to problems of internal validity. Hence, the evidence for Raudenbush's hypothesis that prior teacher–pupil contact reduces or mutes the teacher-expectancy manipulation is weaker than if it had been derived from an experimental design.

Summary

- Triangulation in social research is the selection of different research strategies and measures that do not share the same methodological weaknesses. If different methods produce similar findings, our confidence in the results increases.
- Triangulation in social research may occur through such activities as the use of multiple measures of concepts, the deployment of investigator teams in field research, the use of cross-cultural data archives, and replications of studies.
- Traditionally, the use of multiple indicators has involved the construction of indexes and scales. Indexes combine indicators more or less arbitrarily in the absence of checks to see how well the indicators correspond to the underlying concept; scales combine indicators according to procedures designed to determine the degree of correspondence between indicators and a single underlying dimension. The primary benefit of indexes and scales is the reduction of measurement error.
- An alternative approach, structural equation modeling, retains the identity of each indicator by incorporating all variables—observed indicators and their underlying unobserved concepts—into causal models. Unlike index measurement, this approach allows one to test for certain kinds of measurement error.
- The most frequent replications in social research are of small-scale, low-cost experiments. Rather than duplicating an experiment exactly, investigators usually vary certain features, such as the subject population, the manipulation of the independent variable, and the measurement of the dependent variable.
- Replications involving different research strategies render even more confidence in research findings.
- The principle of triangulation implies that (1) methods should be selected to fit the particular research problem and (2) the relative strengths and weaknesses of alternative research strategies should be weighed in selecting an approach and in combining approaches.
- Meta-analysis is a systematic procedure for synthesizing the results of replications or of multiple, related studies. Researchers often use meta-analysis to determine whether the variability in the results of previous studies is associated with between-study differences in sampling (size and design), in methods (inherent biases), or in conditions and settings (external validity).
- Conducting a meta-analysis involves defining a suitable research problem, searching for and then selecting relevant research studies, coding pertinent aspects of the studies, carrying out a statistical analysis, and presenting an interpretation of the results.

Key Terms

triangulation
index
scale
unidimensionality
Guttman scaling
Likert scaling

structural equation modeling
replication
meta-analysis
effect size
fixed-effects model
random-effects model

Exercises

1. The GSS contains many sets of items that may be combined to create an index. To give you practice and understanding in preparing an index from a set of indicators, visit the GSS Data Explorer website (https://gssdataexplorer.norc.org/). First, decide on the concept you would like to measure (e.g., abortion, empathy, participation in the arts). Next click "Explore GSS data" and enter your concept in the Keyword box on the left side. Now click on each variable for details including question wording, years included in the survey, and related variables. Decide on the variables you wish to include and construct your index.

2. The five items in the Treiman index of attitude toward racial integration have been included numerous times in the GSS. Seven times between 1972 and 1985, all five items were included in the survey. Below are the GSS labels for the five items, with pro- and anti-integration response codes in parentheses:

   RACSCHOL Do you think white students and black students should go to the same schools or to separate schools? (1 = pro; 2 = anti)

   RACDIN How strongly would you object if a member of your family wanted to bring a black friend home to dinner? (3 = pro; 1, 2 = anti)

   RACSEG White people have a right to keep blacks out of their neighborhoods if they want to, and blacks should respect that right. (3, 4 = pro; 1, 2 = anti)

   RACMAR Do you think there should be laws against marriages between blacks and whites? (2 = pro; 1 = anti)

   RACPUSH Blacks shouldn't push themselves where they're not wanted. (3, 4 = pro; 1, 2 = anti)
   To observe trends in scores on the index from 1972 to 1985, go to the website http://sda.berkeley.edu/sdaweb/analysis/?dataset=gss14. At this site, click "create variables" at the top of the page and use this link to create an index based on the above five items.

   First, recode each of the items so that a value of "1" is assigned to pro-integration responses and a value of "0" is assigned to anti-integration responses. Use the same name for the "new variable" as for the existing variable, ignore labels, and check "replace that variable, if it already exists"; then click "Start Recoding."

   After recoding all five items, click the "compute" command and enter the expression "RACINDEX = RACSCHOL + RACDIN + RACSEG + RACMAR + RACPUSH"; then click "Start Computing."

   Finally, click "Analysis" at the top of the page, then click "Means"; enter "RACINDEX" as the dependent variable, "RACE(1)" as the row variable, and "YEAR" as the column variable; now click "Run the Table."

   What is the average value of the index for all seven surveys? Attitudes toward integration became more favorable over time. When did the greatest change occur: between 1972 and 1977 or between 1977 and 1982?

3. Although we describe the use of Guttman scaling to measure individual attitudes, social scientists also have used Guttman scaling to measure characteristics of social units such as groups, communities, and whole societies. While doing field research in a small coastal village in Ecuador, the anthropologist Greg Guest (2000) constructed a quantitative measure of the wealth of each household. Fieldwork indicated that a family's wealth was measured in terms of material possessions. From interviews and observations, for example, he learned "that the really poor do not have a gas stove and that the really, really poor cannot even afford mosquito nets" (Guest, 2000:348). On the basis of testing, Guest constructed a Guttman scale that consisted of the following seven items in order of wealth: (1) mosquito net; (2) mattress; (3) gas stove; (4) television; (5) refrigerator; (6) stereo; and (7) savings account.
   a. Create a table that shows the response patterns of a perfect Guttman scale.
   b. Give an example of a nonscale response pattern.

4. What basic approach to social research would you use to address each of the following research objectives? In each case, explain the advantages of this approach over others.
   a. Suppose you want to test role-identity theory, which has been used to explain acts of altruism. According to this theory, the more important a role is to a person, the more likely that he or she will act out that role identity. For example, the more important the role identity of blood donor, the more likely the person will actually give blood if given the opportunity (Callero, 1985).
   b. Suppose a student task force is asked to document the current state of formal volunteering on a college campus: How many students volunteer? Where do current students volunteer? What kinds of volunteer work do they do?
   c. In a comparative study of 15 European nations, Kieran Healy (2000) showed that how blood is collected and distributed in a society affects who gives blood and how much or how often they donate. Suppose you decide to investigate the relationship between blood-collection practices and blood donation in the United States from World War II to the present day.

5. An excellent example of meta-analysis is Thomas Pettigrew and Linda Tropp's meta-analytic test of intergroup contact theory in the May 2006 issue (vol. 90, pp. 751–83) of the *Journal of Personality and Social Psychology*. To familiarize yourself with meta-analysis, read this article and answer the following questions.

    a. How does a meta-analysis resolve the major shortcomings with previous reviews of research on intergroup contact theory?

    b. Pettigrew and Tropp attempted to rule out alternative explanations of the contact–prejudice effect. How did they examine the possibility of a reverse causal sequence—that prejudice reduces intergroup contact?

    c. How did they address the file-drawer question?

    d. Specify their criteria for including studies in the meta-analysis.

    e. How did they locate relevant studies?

    f. How did they take into account the methodological rigor of studies?

    g. Recent studies have expanded intergroup contact theory to include target groups other than racial and ethnic minorities, such as homosexuals and individuals who are physically and mentally disabled. According to the meta-analysis, does the theory apply equally well to these two subsets?

Notes

1. According to Howard Bahr, Theodore Caplow, and Bruce Chadwick's analysis (1983) of 300 replicative studies between 1973 and 1981, more than half of the studies appeared in psychology journals. We suspect, however, that this substantially underestimates the proportion of experimental replications. Their analysis was based on a search of the *Social Sciences Citation Index* "for journal articles whose titles included the words 'replication,' 'replicating,' 'replicated,' or 'replicate.'" Yet the word "replication" is seldom used in article titles reporting experiments because of the common practice of reporting two or more experiments, often involving some form of replication, in a single article. This indeed was true of the experimental replication reported below.

2. In simple (misdemeanor) assault, both the suspect and the victim are present when the police arrive. According to Sherman and Berk (1984:262), "the experiment included only those cases in which police were empowered (but not required) to make arrests under . . . Minnesota state law." For ethical reasons, the investigators excluded "cases of life-threatening or severe injury, usually labeled as a felony (aggravated assault)" (262).

3. The ordering of the three intervention strategies differed on the two dependent measures: Arrested suspects differed significantly from those who were forced to leave based on the official data and from those given advice based on the victim report data.

4. For a thorough discussion of meta-analytic research practices, see Cooper, Hedges, and Valentine (2009).

5. See Michael Borenstein (2009) and Joseph Fleiss and Jesse Berlin (2009) for reviews of effect sizes for continuous (interval/ratio) variables and dichotomous variables.

14

Evaluation Research

A distinction is made between two types of social research: basic and applied. The goal of **basic social research** is to develop a theoretical understanding of the social world; therefore, it is (or should be) guided by theoretical interests, and it is directed to and evaluated by an audience of peers within a scientific discipline. In contrast, the immediate purpose of **applied social research** is to provide information for solving an existing problem; the primary audience is a client who ordinarily finances the work in the hope of gaining valued information (Rossi and Whyte, 1983). (Box 14.1 outlines other differences between these two research traditions.)

In this chapter we are concerned with a specific form of applied social research called **evaluation research**. Evaluation research consists of the application of social research methods for the purpose of assessing social intervention programs and policies. Evaluation researchers apply the same repertoire of methods as basic researchers do to address the same fundamental issues. Thus, we discuss familiar issues of research design, internal validity, measurement, and external validity. What differentiates evaluation research from basic social research is the social context in which the methods are applied. As you will see, the political agenda and administrative realities to which evaluation studies are linked present unique methodological problems.

Framework and Sample Studies

Evaluation is a crucial phase in the process of rational decision making or problem solving (T. D. Cook, Leviton, and Shadish, 1985:700). First, a problem is identified; second, options for its solution are considered; third, one or more options is implemented; fourth, the implemented option is evaluated; and finally, a decision is made about whether the option is worth adopting. All sorts of problems may be identified and evaluated. In the private sector, companies enlist management consultants, research and development specialists, and marketing professionals to study policies, personnel, and products. As the term is used in social research, however, evaluation research usually pertains to the analysis of social programs instituted by federal, state, and local governments to help solve social problems.

BOX 14.1 Characteristics of Basic and Applied Research

The table in this box contrasts the characteristics of the basic and applied research traditions. As the table shows, the impetus for basic research comes from an individual investigator's intellectual curiosity and desire to advance theoretical knowledge, whereas applied researchers take their lead from a sponsor's need to test the efficacy of some program in addressing a particular problem. The public's role, therefore, is very different; basic researchers tend to regard the public as patrons, while applied researchers are more likely to envision their work as directed toward improving the general public welfare. Basic researchers adhere, as far as possible, to absolute norms regarding rigor and scholarship that emphasize laboratory-type control and internal validity; applied researchers do what is necessary to address the sponsor's needs, and the utility of their research depends crucially on its applicability in the field. Finally, basic researchers succeed insofar as they publish their work in learned journals, but the success of applied researchers depends on their ability to communicate their findings clearly to sponsors so as to facilitate rational decision making.

	Basic research	Applied research
Problem selection determined by:	Individual researcher	Employer or sponsor
Researcher intrinsically motivated by:	Intellectual curiosity and satisfaction in advancing knowledge	Commitment to promote the public welfare
The goal is:	Generalized theoretical understanding	Cost-effective reduction of social problems
Rigor of methods based on:	Disciplinary norms of scholarship	Uses to which results may be put
Preoccupied with:	Internal validity	External validity
Research arena tends to be the:	Laboratory	Real-world setting
Dissemination of knowledge by:	Publication in learned, technical journals	Communication with lay decision makers

Source: Adapted from Fishman and Neigher (1982) and Freeman and Rossi (1984).

The application of scientific procedures to the solution of social problems is hardly new. Measures to assess social conditions and social experiments to test interventions can be traced to the beginnings of modern science in the 1600s (Rossi, Lipsey, and Freeman, 2004).[1] Moreover, the establishment of American sociology in the late nineteenth and early twentieth centuries is associated with the Progressive and social reform movements (Oberschall, 1972). Many early sociologists envisioned the discipline as a means of bettering society and promoting social justice; applying the scientific method to social problems and social policy interventions was thus central to the discipline's mission.

From the beginnings of the discipline, however, there were tensions between "academic" and applied sociologists. By the second and third decades of the twentieth century, many academic sociologists began to distance themselves from the social reform tradition in an effort to legitimate the scientific status of sociology (Gollin, 1983). Eventually they created a professional ideology that at first rejected the objective of social amelioration in favor of value neutrality and, over time, assigned lower status to all forms of applied work. Consequently, although there always have been some social scientists engaged in applied research, evaluation research did not flourish—indeed, the term was not even invented—until the federal War on Poverty and Great Society programs of the 1960s (Haveman, 1987; C. H. Weiss, 1987). Written into virtually all this social legislation was the requirement for program evaluation. As the demand for evaluation grew at an enormous rate in the 1960s and 1970s, evaluation research emerged as a distinct field of study. Numerous articles and books on the practice of evaluation research were published, journals were established, and professional associations were formed (Rossi, Lipsey, and Freeman, 2004:9).

Evaluation studies have been used to investigate literally thousands of problems and intervention strategies: for example, the extent of homelessness, child and spouse abuse, and racial discrimination in the availability of educational opportunities; the effects of increased police presence on crime rates, financial aid on ex-prisoners' adjustment to civilian life, and compensatory educational programs such as Head Start on cognitive development. Evaluation studies mentioned in previous chapters include the Chicago Homeless Survey (Rossi, 1989; Chapter 6), field experiments on the television series *Sesame Street* (Ball and Bogatz, 1970; Chapter 7) and on police patrol staffing in San Diego (Boydstun, Sherry, and Moelter, 1978; Chapter 7), the time-series analysis of the Connecticut crackdown on speeding (Campbell and Ross, 1968; Chapter 8), the Great Books and Small Groups study (Davis, 1964; Chapter 9), and the Minneapolis Domestic Violence Experiment (Sherman and Berk, 1984; Chapter 13). We now summarize three studies to illustrate the types and special problems of evaluation research.

Example 1: Aid to Released Prisoners

The first evaluation study we consider evaluated a policy designed to reduce *recidivism*, the tendency of convicted felons to return to a life of crime after release from prison. Data from the U.S. Department of Justice (Durose, Cooper, and Snyder, 2014), which followed more than 400,000 prisoners released in 2005, showed that 76.6 percent were arrested and 55.1 percent returned to prison within 5 years of release. Two factors that seem to reduce recidivism are age and employment: "Older men and ex-felons who find jobs and retain them are less likely to be returned to prison" (Rossi, Berk, and Lenihan, 1980:6). Whereas little in the way of social policy can be done about the aging process, various social programs have been tried to improve the employment chances of ex-felons. Peter Rossi, Richard Berk, and Kenneth Lenihan (1980) investigated the effects of one such program in a $3.4 million, large-scale field experiment sponsored by the Department of Labor.

Over the years the Department of Labor has supported several different efforts to help prisoners find productive employment. Without much success, the department has tried skills training, special job-placement services, and small amounts of financial aid. Government officials were encouraged, however, when an experiment conducted in Maryland in the early 1970s showed that modest payments in the form of unemployment insurance benefits lowered arrest rates for property crimes. On the basis of these findings, the Department of Labor commissioned a larger study, called the Transitional Aid Research Project (TARP), to test the external validity of the policy.

The TARP experiment was carried out in two states, Georgia and Texas, beginning in January 1976. Over a 6-month period, approximately 2000 released prisoners were randomly assigned to one of six conditions: three treatment groups that varied in the number of weeks financial aid was offered and the amount the benefit was taxed when the recipient was employed, a treatment group that consisted of special job-placement services, and two control groups. Payments were made through the state unemployment-benefit system at minimum benefit levels, $63 per week in Georgia and $70 per week in Texas. Except for one control group, all participants were interviewed before release from prison and periodically throughout the first year after release. Finally, all participants were tracked through computer files for information on arrests and earnings.

The main purpose of the TARP experiment was to test whether modest financial support would lower recidivism rates for released prisoners. When the investigators examined arrest rates, they found no overall differences between those who were receiving payments and the controls; hence, the payments clearly failed as administered. Additional bad news was that the payments acted as a disincentive to work since those in the payment groups generally worked fewer weeks and earned less than those in the control conditions.

To understand why the experiment ostensibly failed, Rossi, Berk, and Lenihan re-examined the theoretical model underlying the experiment. As they note (101),

> TARP assumes that for released felons property crimes are an important source of income, a source that competes quite favorably with legitimate jobs, in the sense of being more available than such jobs and more attractive than many available jobs. Hence, the provision of funds may help released felons to get through a period of postrelease unemployment without resorting to property theft.

The designers of the experiment failed to anticipate, however, that modest payments could compete easily with the kinds of jobs typically available, thereby creating a strong work-disincentive effect. Furthermore, the theoretical model underlying TARP ignores the full impact of employment on recidivism. TARP assumes that employment is a source of income that eliminates the need to resort to crime. But employment also "occupies time and reduces opportunities to commit crimes" (Rossi, Berk, and Lenihan, 1980:101).

On the basis of such reasoning, Rossi, Berk, and Lenhihan proposed a "counterbalancing model" of TARP effects: TARP payments reduced arrests by lowering financial need but increased arrests by increasing unemployment. This explains, at once, why there was no difference between treatment groups and controls in arrest rates but there was a significant difference in employment. When this more complex model was tested, essentially examining the effect of TARP payments on arrests while controlling for length of employment, it was found that payments did indeed reduce recidivism. Rossi, Berk, and Lenihan concluded that modest financial aid to released prisoners, by lowering arrests and thereby reducing the costs of crime, is likely to be cost-effective, provided that work disincentives are somehow detached from the payments.

Example 2: Curbing Drunk Driving

According to Peter Rossi (1989:14), "a societal condition becomes a social problem when it draws the attention of a significant portion of the public." By this definition, drunk driving became a social problem in the United States in the 1980s, because "national press coverage of drunk driving increased more than tenfold between 1980 and 1983, and television networks ran stories about it on an average of more than one every three weeks in the mid-1980s" (Ross, 1994:2). This attention was accompanied nationwide by numerous police crackdowns, new drunk driving laws and other countermeasures to reduce drunk driving, and ultimately evaluation studies of these innovative policies.

Several countermeasures have targeted young persons who drink. Traffic accidents are the leading cause of death of young people, and in about half these cases alcohol is involved (Ross, 1992:82). Concern about this age group was heightened during the early 1970s when crash-related fatalities among young people increased after the legal drinking age was lowered in many states.[2] Indeed, evidence of this relationship from early evaluation studies led to the Federal Uniform Drinking Act of 1984, which effectively established a 21-year national minimum drinking age.

The 21-year minimum drinking age has been studied extensively over the past 30 years; by the early 1990s, H. Laurence Ross (1992:83) described it as "one of the most thoroughly evaluated social interventions of our time." Almost uniformly, these studies found that raising the drinking age reduced alcohol-related traffic accidents (for reviews, see General Accounting Office, 1987; Shults et al., 2001; Wagenaar and Toomey, 2002). Many of these studies used interrupted time-series or multiple time-series designs (see Chapter 8) that traced motor-vehicle accident rates before and after changes in the state drinking-age law. Assuming the minimum drinking age was raised to 21 in a given state, automotive crashes among the affected age group—18- to 20-year-olds—were compared with other age groups, such as 16- to 17- and 21- to 45-year-olds. Also, crash data for the affected group were compared with data for the same age group in states that did *not* change the drinking age during the same time period. For example, one early study by Alexander Wagenaar (1983), whose research was partially funded by the U.S. National Institute on Alcohol Abuse and

Alcoholism, examined crash data in four states: Michigan and Maine, which raised the drinking age in the late 1970s, and New York and Pennsylvania, where the drinking age remained the same (18 and 21, respectively). He found a sudden decline in the number of 18- to 20-year-old drivers involved in injury crashes in Michigan and Maine after these states raised the drinking age to 21 but no change in injury crashes among this age group in New York and Pennsylvania.

Example 3: Immunizing against Gang Membership and Delinquency

In the last quarter of the twentieth century, there was an unprecedented growth in youth gangs in the United States. In 1970, 19 states reported the presence of youth gangs, but by 1995, all 50 states reported gang problems. During this same period, the number of cities with youth gangs grew from 201 to 1487, a 640 percent increase (Miller, 2001). What makes these trends a cause for concern is that research consistently shows that gang membership increases juvenile delinquency, especially violent offenses (Krohn and Thornberry, 2014).

One policy response to the problem of youth gangs was the development of programs designed to teach students how to avoid gang membership. Our third evaluation study assessed one such program, the Gang Resistance Education and Training (G.R.E.A.T.) program, originally developed in Phoenix, Arizona, in 1991. The goal of the program is to provide students with the information and skills necessary "to say no to gangs" and "avoid involvement in youth violence" (Winfree, Peterson Lynskey, and Maupin, 1999). Its main component is a middle school lecture-based curriculum delivered by a law enforcement officer. The original program consisted of eight lessons. Students learned about crime and drugs and their impact on their neighborhood and school; cultural differences; how to peacefully resolve conflicts; how to meet their needs without joining a gang; how to be responsible members of the community; and how to set goals (Winfree, Peterson Lynskey, and Maupin, 1999). To participate in the program, G.R.E.A.T. instructors or representatives may contact school officials or vice versa.

As the program quickly spread, in 1994 and again in 2006, the National Institute of Justice (NIJ) solicited grant proposals to conduct a national evaluation. The NIJ awarded both grants to the criminologist Finn-Aage Esbensen and a research team that he assembled (Esbensen, 2015). Our focus here is on the second evaluation, but we begin with a brief description of the first.

The first evaluation of G.R.E.A.T. involved two studies: a cross-sectional survey of 8th-graders attending public schools in 11 U.S. cities (Esbensen and Osgood, 1999) and a quasi-experimental longitudinal design that repeatedly surveyed students from the 7th through 11th grades in six U.S. school districts (Esbensen et al., 2001). The first study found many positive effects; for example, G.R.E.A.T. participants had lower rates of gang membership and committed fewer minor juvenile offenses than nonparticipants. However, the more rigorous second study failed to replicate the results of the first study.

Based in part on these evaluations, G.R.E.A.T. underwent a substantial curriculum review and revision that was implemented in 2004.[3] The second evaluation of the revised curriculum had two components: an evaluation of program fidelity, or how well the program was carried out as planned, and an evaluation of how well the program met its stated goals. The latter evaluation is contingent on the former; without knowing whether a program has been implemented as intended, one cannot attribute measured effects—successful or not—to the program.

Esbensen and his colleagues (Esbensen, Matsuda, Taylor, and Peterson, 2011) assessed program fidelity in three areas where it was possible for implementation to break down: (1) officer preparedness and commitment; (2) teacher support and involvement; and (3) program delivery. To assess these areas, they used multiple methods and data. These included the following:

- Observations of G.R.E.A.T. Officer Trainings to assess the quality of the training that officers receive;
- Surveys and interviews of G.R.E.A.T.-trained officers and supervisors to determine their own perceptions of preparedness and level of commitment to delivering the program;
- Surveys of school personnel to evaluate officers' abilities as instructors and educators' involvement in the program; and
- Onsite, direct observations of officers to determine the quality of program delivery (Esbensen et al., 2011:17).

Observations of officer training were carried out at eight sessions, with at least one in each of five regions of the country. Surveys, interviews, and classroom observations were conducted at four or five schools within seven cities selected to vary in size, region, and level of gang activity. Results showed that G.R.E.A.T. officers were sufficiently trained and prepared to deliver the program; school personnel generally supported it; and, with few exceptions, officers delivered the program with "average" to "excellent" fidelity. Although officers' enthusiasm for being in the program varied, teacher involvement was minimal, and time management issues undermined the quality of program delivery, the investigators concluded that G.R.E.A.T. "was implemented with sufficient fidelity to reasonably attribute" observed effects to the program (Esbensen et al., 2011:31).

The investigators assessed program effects by means of an *experimental longitudinal panel design* or, in other words, an experiment with long-term follow-up (Esbensen et al., 2013). First, they selected a purposive sample of 31 schools from seven cities (the same cities and schools in the assessment of program fidelity). Second, they randomly assigned classrooms within each school to the treatment (i.e., G.R.E.A.T.) or control condition. Then, all students completed a pretest, a posttest, and four follow-up confidential questionnaires. The questionnaires contained multiple measures of the program's three primary goals: (1) to help youth avoid gang membership; (2) to reduce violence and criminal activity; and (3) to help youth develop a positive relationship with law enforcement. Analysis of the posttest through the 4-year follow-up showed that the odds of belonging to a gang were 24 percent lower for the G.R.E.A.T. students and that these students had more positive attitudes toward the police than non-G.R.E.A.T. students. There was no statistically signifi-cant difference in delinquency.

Types of Evaluation Research

These three studies illustrate a range of evaluation activities. We can clarify these activities by considering how each phase of policymaking requires answers to different evaluative questions. Figure 14.1 illustrates this linkage in two columns: The first column presents a heuristic model of the policymaking process (adapted from Mark and Shotland, 1985; also see Pancer and Westhues, 1989); the second column identifies key evaluation activi-ties at each stage of the process. The word "heuristic" emphasizes that this is a useful, albeit simplified, idealized model. Policymaking seldom proceeds precisely along these lines, and policies rarely involve all possible forms of evaluation. Even the development of new policies and programs seldom entails a comprehensive, staged evaluation; and evalu-ation research often analyzes long-established programs and past interventions.

Figure 14.1 identifies six phases of policymaking: (1) identification of a problem that requires amelioration; (2) policy planning—the consideration of alternative intervention strategies for addressing the problem; (3) development of a specific policy action or pro-gram; (4) implementation of the policy or program; (5) analysis of the program's impact; and (6) feedback on the problem and policy and administrative action. Although evalua-tion research is identified most often with the fifth stage, social research can contribute at all stages.

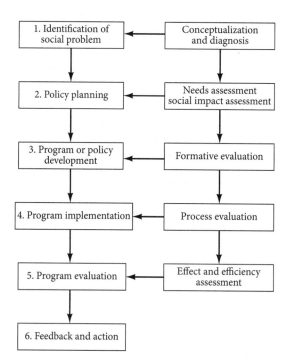

FIGURE 14.1. Stages of policymaking and associated evaluation activities.

Problem Identification: Conceptualization and Diagnosis

Social programs and policies address social problems. This begs the question, How does a social condition become identified as a social problem? It is partly a matter of objective criteria and, as Peter Rossi, Martin Lipsey, and Howard Freeman (2004:107) point out, partly a social construction. Consider homelessness. There always have been homeless people in the United States, but they have not always been considered a social problem. During the Great Depression, homelessness became an object of concern when the number of homeless people swelled to roughly 1 percent of the population (Burt, 1992). For the next 4 decades, however, the homeless population did not receive much media attention. In 1975, not a single article about the homeless was listed in the *Readers' Guide to Periodical Literature* (Rossi, 1989:14). In the early 1980s, homeless people became more visible on the streets of major cities, and emergency shelters and soup kitchens experienced an increased demand for their services. Still, although the homeless population increased, the best estimates of its size—about 0.2 percent of the population (Burt, 1992:4)—indicated that homelessness in the 1980s was nowhere near the problem it was in the 1930s. Suddenly, however, the plight of the homeless began to receive a great deal of media attention. Public consciousness was raised by the appearance of numerous articles and several television documentaries on the homeless and by the creation of the National Coalition for the Homeless.

In short, problems are not revealed directly by statistical patterns and trends. Rather, problem identification depends on how data are interpreted and whether the interpretation becomes a matter of public concern, which depends on the values and influence of various parties, especially political elites. Social scientists may contribute to problem definition, but they generally have played a lesser role than investigative reporters, advocacy groups, and political and moral leaders in bringing problems to public attention.

Once a problem has been identified, government officials often use social research to inform their decisions. Social science input may begin with conceptualization and analysis, indicating what is known and unknown about the problem and providing insights into its nature and causes. For example, when called upon by the superintendent to help solve racial problems in the Austin, Texas, schools, the social psychologist Elliot Aronson (Aronson et al., 1975, 1978) drew on his knowledge of the scientific literature for clues about why desegregation was increasing rather than decreasing racial tension. Research and theory suggested that equal-status contact—presumably created by desegregation—should increase interracial interaction and reduce prejudice. This should occur, however, only when members of different racial groups were in pursuit of common goals. The problem, as Aronson saw it, was that children in a typical American classroom rarely rely on one another to pursue common goals. Systematic observations of numerous elementary school classrooms led him to conclude that the educational process is highly competitive, with children vying with one another for the attention of the teacher and the respect of their classmates. And this competitive environment accentuates prejudices and differences in ability that existed prior to desegregation. For desegregation to work, therefore, we must change the process of education so that children will learn to use one another as resources.

Social science data also may be used to document the extent of the problem: to specify when and where the problem takes place and who is affected. The federal government sponsors numerous surveys that serve this purpose. For example, since 1996, the National Gang Center, funded by two agencies within the U.S. Department of Justice, has conducted an annual survey of local law enforcement agencies to track the size and scope of gang activity nationwide. Contrary to popular belief, recent data indicate that gang activity is not spreading to less densely populated areas; however, the number of gangs and gang members has increased in larger cities (Egley, Howell, and Harris, 2014).

In many instances, social scientists use existing data to estimate the extent of and historical trends in social problems. A particularly useful type of data for identifying trends is a **social indicator**. Social indicators are broad, aggregate measures of important social conditions that are relevant to policy decisions. Examples include measures of crime, family life, health, job satisfaction, satisfaction with government services, and schools and public transportation; these indicators may be contrasted with familiar economic indicators such as the consumer price index, the gross national product, and the unemployment rate.

Like economic indicators, social indicators may be measured at repeated intervals to identify societal trends. The Current Population Survey, briefly described in earlier chapters, is the primary source of information on labor force characteristics of the U.S. population. The interview survey includes questions on employment, earnings, hours of work, and other characteristics. The Bureau of Labor Statistics uses these data to compile statistics, chart trends, and make projections, which serve as important indicators of the nation's economic situation for government policymakers and legislators. From the Current Population Survey, for example, we know that the labor force participation of married women with children under 6 years old increased from 30.3 percent in 1970 to 62.3 percent in 2011 (U.S. Census Bureau, 2008:380; U.S. Bureau of Labor Statistics, 2013) and that between 2014 and 2024 the three occupations projected to have the highest number of jobs are personal care aides, registered nurses, and home health aides (U.S. Bureau of Labor Statistics, 2016b).

Social indicators can greatly facilitate problem identification and policy planning (Rossi, Lipsey, and Freeman, 2004:110). Trends may reveal whether particular problems are improving, remaining the same, or getting worse. The data also may provide information on the size of the problem and its geographic and social distribution. For many social problems, however, no social indicators exist. For others, the national data are of little or no use in tracking the problem at the state or local level. When the data do not exist, local sample surveys usually provide the most accurate information on the extent and distribution of social problems, although they often require considerable resources.

Policy Planning: Needs and Social Impact Assessments

Having defined the problem, the second stage in rational decision making is to conceive alternative solutions. Rational decision making also implies that numerous feasible options will be considered. Policymakers, however, tend to examine a restricted range of alternatives, often dictated by ideological and pragmatic considerations. Richard Berk and Peter Rossi (1976) point out, for example, that policymakers are conservative, and new policies rarely amount to bold reforms. Moreover, the urgency of a problem and the pace at which new programs are sometimes legislated simply may not allow enough time for empirical evaluation. Consequently, social scientists typically have had little input into policy formulation prior to the proposal of a new program (Chelimsky, 1987).

Still, two forms of evaluation research have proven useful at the stage of policy formation and program planning: needs assessment and social impact assessment. **Needs assessment** refers to several different kinds of appraisals. It may be undertaken to identify and forecast problems that need attention, to establish perceived priorities among problem areas in communities and organizations, to study the scope of a problem, and to estimate the extent to which a program will be used or otherwise address appropriate needs. A good example of this latter form of needs assessment is Rossi's survey of the Chicago homeless population (1989), described in Chapter 6. The survey was sponsored by the Robert Wood Johnson Foundation and the Pew Memorial Trust, which were financing medical clinics for the homeless in 19 U.S. cities. To assess the coverage and adequacy of these clinics, the foundations needed precise, reliable estimates of the size of the homeless population and the nature and extent of their medical problems.

Another example of needs assessment is Royce Singleton's (unpublished report, 1994) Senior Center Survey of Worcester, Massachusetts, residents 60 years of age and older. Despite its relatively large older population at the time, Worcester did not have a senior center, although many surrounding, much smaller towns did. The telephone survey was designed to aid a committee of the Commission on Elder Affairs as it sought to establish a senior center. Among the questions addressed were whether residents would be likely to use a center, what locations they favored for the center, and what kinds of programs and services they preferred.

A second aid to program planning is impact assessment. Once policy alternatives have been proposed, social research may be conducted to assess the potential consequences, or impact, of the alternatives. Since 1969, federal law has required **environmental impact studies** (EISs) for all public works projects receiving federal funds except minor projects that are deemed to have no significant impact on the environment. An important component of EISs is a **social impact assessment**: an assessment of the consequences of a policy or project for the social environment. A policy or project could have an impact on the social environment insofar as it alters "the ways in which people live, work, play, relate to one another, organize to meet their needs and generally cope as members of society" (Burdge and Vanclay, 1996).

Projects for which social impact assessments would be appropriate include the expansion or relocation of a hospital, various forms of urban renewal, the construction of alternative highway routes, and the closing of military bases. Such projects may have myriad consequences. They can affect individuals biologically (e.g., putting them more or less at risk to health and safety hazards), psychologically (e.g., increasing levels of stress), economically (e.g., increasing or decreasing the availability of jobs, goods, and services), and socially and personally (e.g., affecting people's social networks or accessibility to social institutions)

(Finsterbusch and Motz, 1980:94–110). Although a major concern is potential negative consequences, EISs ideally should present a balanced picture so that conflicting interests as well as costs and benefits can be weighed in judging alternatives. Kurt Finsterbusch and Annabelle Bende Motz (1980) cite an EIS of the proposed expansion of New York's Kennedy Airport as an example. The study pointed out costs of the expansion, such as damage to the natural environment of Jamaica Bay, the negative effect on the recreational use of the bay, and the pervasive problem of aircraft noise; but it also detailed the benefits of airport convenience and recommended alternative means of expanding airport service.

Program Development: Formative Evaluation

After a specific program or policy intervention has been proposed, the next step is development and preparation of the intervention for implementation. As this occurs, a **formative evaluation** may be conducted to help improve the program design. Formative evaluation is much like experimental pretesting. Experimental pretests provide feedback on how well the components of the experiment—the cover story, randomization process, manipulation, and so forth—are working. Similarly, formative studies provide feedback on specific program components to determine whether they are consistent with program objectives.

One of the best examples of a successful formative evaluation occurred during the creation of the children's television program *Sesame Street* (Reeves, 1970). The planners of the program did 18 months of formative research before they went on the air. The research staff first translated the general goals of the program into highly specific objectives. They also tested the general level of competence of the targeted audience—economically disadvantaged children. Then, they developed technical strategies for achieving objectives and reaching this audience. Filmed segments under development were tested repeatedly in relatively simple experiments. Since audience appeal was vital to the program's success, a key dependent variable was level of attention, which was measured by the distractor method. As children watched the program on a television monitor, slides were projected on a wall at an angle to the child. Attention was operationalized as the proportion of time a child viewed the program instead of the slide. Through this method, program content was related to attention, and generalizations about the relative effectiveness of various filmed segments and their elements (e.g., animation, animals, children, adults) were developed.

Like experimental pretests, formative studies are less rigorous and sophisticated than tests of effects after the program has been fully implemented. The emphasis is on speed of feedback rather than on generalizability or precise estimates of effects. Therefore, formative research typically uses unstructured interviews and observation with small non-random samples of the target population, observed at one or a few sites. Data of this sort can be especially important in the design of educational programs. Catherine Matthews and colleagues (1995), for example, used semistructured and unstructured interviewing techniques with students and teachers to help develop an AIDS education program for secondary students in South Africa. By providing an in-depth understanding of students' sexual experiences and sexual health needs and teachers' concerns and by exploring the impact of cultural values and religious beliefs on AIDS education, the researchers could develop a culturally appropriate educational program. And, as important, through the interview process the researchers were able to gain the trust and support of the teachers who would implement it.

Program Implementation: Process Evaluation

When it comes time to assess the impact of a program, it is essential to know whether the program was carried out as designed. If implemented fully and appropriately, observed outcomes can be attributed confidently to the program; but if the implementation is incomplete or faulty, interpretations are ambiguous. To assess the fit between the design and implementation of a program, evaluation researchers resort to **process evaluation**. Also called "implementation research" and "program monitoring," process evaluation consists of the systematic evaluation of (1) program coverage, or the extent to which the program is reaching its target population; (2) program delivery, or whether the services provided by the program are, in fact, consistent with design specifications; and (3) the resources expended to conduct the program (Rossi, Lipsey, and Freeman, 2004:171). Process evaluation may be as basic as checking to see that a particular service or program was implemented as planned or as elaborate as a detailed description of program activities, administrative staff, and program participants.

Our first and third sample evaluation studies involved extensive process evaluations. A major part of the G.R.E.A.T. evaluation assessed officers' preparedness and commitment to teach the program, teachers' support and involvement, and the quality of program delivery. Finding that the program "was implemented with fidelity in the vast majority of classrooms" provided confidence in the evaluation of program effects (Esbensen et al., 2011:33).

The investigation of the implementation process also was a critical feature of the TARP evaluation study. To assess whether the experimental design was carried out properly, the experimenters gathered evidence on the success of the randomization procedure, the delivery of payment benefits, and TARP participants' understanding of the terms of their eligibility. If random assignment were successful, experimental and control groups should differ only within the range of chance variation. Consistent with this expectation, in each state where the experiment was conducted the experimenters found no significant differences across the treatment and control groups on a dozen variables (e.g., age, percentage female, years of education, length of sentence).

When they inspected agency records to audit payment delivery, TARP investigators found that the substantial majority of subjects used all their payment eligibility by the end of the postrelease year. However, interviews with TARP participants indicated a less than satisfactory understanding of the details of the benefit plans. Almost all participants knew the amounts of the weekly payments for which they were eligible, but only one-third to one-half knew the number of weeks of eligibility. Even more problematic was knowledge of benefit loss due to earned income. Two treatment groups were "taxed" at 100 percent—their benefit was reduced $1 for each dollar earned. A third treatment group had a 25 percent tax rate, with benefits reduced 25 cents for each dollar earned. The purpose of this generous tax rate was to encourage participants to work; however, most participants in this treatment group either were unaware of the favorable tax rate or did not understand how it operated. Thus, the program's failure to reduce recidivism appears to have been masked not only by conceptual limitations of the experimental design, noted earlier, but also by deficiencies in its implementation. Because participants did not understand the terms of their eligibility for benefits in the event of employment, a clear work incentive (the favorable tax rate) had no chance of offsetting the work disincentive created by the benefit payment.

As these studies illustrate, when evaluating social programs it is vitally important to know whether the program or treatment is delivered appropriately and is attracting or reaching its target population. Ineffectiveness of a program may not be a result of the nature of the program or treatment as planned but of how well the plan was implemented. Implementation problems, unfortunately, are common. Rossi, Lipsey, and Freeman (2004:183–95) document cases in which services or treatments were never delivered, most eligible participants were never reached, and program delivery was incomplete or inconsistent across sites. By the same token, when a program achieves positive results, a detailed knowledge of how it was implemented can enable the researcher to explain more fully why it worked.

In addition to complementing the evaluation of program effects, process evaluations can provide useful feedback regarding the effectiveness of program delivery. Although Esbensen and colleagues concluded that G.R.E.A.T. was implemented with fidelity, they also identified problems with time and classroom management and teacher involvement that needed to be addressed for optimum program delivery. Similarly, a program may be monitored to determine whether it is or why it is not reaching an appropriate target population. For example, to understand why homeless youth tend to underutilize shelters compared to other services, one study conducted focus group interviews with 49 homeless youth in the Houston area (Ha, Narendorf, Santa Maria, and Bezette-Flores, 2015). Barriers to shelter use included pride and wanting to be self-reliant, inaccessibility, adverse shelter conditions, and restrictive shelter rules. To address the problem of inaccessibility, the investigators recommended multiple shelter locations and transportation to shelters from access points such as public libraries.

KEY POINT

Evaluating how a program is implemented (*process evaluation*) may help to interpret whether a program succeeds or fails to achieve its desired outcome (*effect assessment*).

Program Evaluation: Effect and Efficiency Assessment

For new or ongoing programs or any sort of social intervention, the ultimate issue is whether they are effective. Has the program achieved the desired outcomes, goals, and objectives? Is it worth continuing in light of benefits and costs? The type of evaluation study that addresses these questions is called a **summative**, or outcome, **evaluation**. Outcome evaluations focus on two issues: Has the program produced its intended effects? What are its benefits in relation to its costs? We will refer to the former as **effect assessment** and to the latter as **efficiency assessment**.

Effect assessment was the primary objective of all three sample evaluations. The TARP experimenters assessed effects by applying statistical tests to determine whether the TARP payments lowered recidivism. As noted previously, TARP payments did lower arrest rates but only when the effect of the payments on employment was removed. Many studies analyzed differences among age groups in traffic accidents before and after the raising of the legal drinking age. On the basis of his research, Wagenaar (1983) estimated that raising the minimum drinking age reduced the number of alcohol-related automobile crashes involving young drivers by approximately 20 percent. A recent study examined the effects of 20 laws aimed at preventing underage drinking in the United States (e.g., illegal to possess, illegal to purchase, license suspension for alcohol citation). Based on an analysis of youth alcohol-related traffic fatalities, the study found that the nine most effective laws "are currently saving an estimated 1,135 lives each year in the states that have these laws" (Fell, Scherer, Thomas, and Voas, 2016:257).

As we reported previously, the effects of the G.R.E.A.T. program varied. A major outcome was that the odds of belonging to a gang were 24 percent lower for program participants than for nonparticipants 48 months postprogram. Other results, however, were less easily quantified: G.R.E.A.T. students had significantly more positive attitudes toward the police, but there was no statistically significant difference in delinquency.

The principal method of assessing effects in basic research is a test of statistical significance, which determines the probability that research findings are due to chance factors. Statistical tests assume, however, either random sampling or random assignment of subjects, both of which may be missing in an evaluation study. Although social statisticians disagree over the use and meaning of significance tests (see Morrison and Henkel, 1970), we share David Gold's position (1969) that results that easily could have occurred by a chance process (i.e., "nonsignificant" results) should not be taken seriously. Consequently, as a minimal but not sufficient condition for attributing importance to a program, the results should be statistically significant.

However, discovery that a program has had a statistically significant effect does not have the same meaning or importance in evaluation research that it would have in basic hypothesis-testing research. Whereas in basic research a researcher is most interested in whether a predicted effect is present, an evaluation researcher is more interested in the magnitude of the effect and its practical significance. Quantitative measures of effect size (see Chapter 13) include correlation and regression coefficients, the mean difference between groups, and risk of occurrence such as the aforementioned odds that G.R.E.A.T. participants would join a gang. In their evaluation of G.R.E.A.T., Esbensen and colleagues (2013) used Cohen's d to report effect sizes for most outcomes. Technically, this statistic expresses the magnitude of effects as the difference between treatment and control groups in standard deviation units (see Chapter 15). Unfortunately, the interpretation of Cohen's d is not straightforward; sizes of .2 are considered small, .5 medium, and .8 large; however, a "small" effect can be of great practical significance (Durlak, 2009). Although several outcome measures of the G.R.E.A.T. program were statistically significant, the effect sizes were small, with Cohen's d ranging from .05 to .14 over 48 months posttreatment (Esbensen et al., 2013:404).

In addition to estimating a program's impact on targets, evaluation researchers are interested in the program's efficiency. If a program is ineffective, it makes no sense to undertake an efficiency analysis. But if a program has estimable effects, an efficiency assessment can reveal whether it is worth the cost to continue or to fund on a larger scale. Efficiency assessment generally takes two forms: **cost–effectiveness analysis** and **cost–benefit analysis**. The difference lies in how the outcomes of a program are measured: in cost–effectiveness analyses, outcomes are measured in substantive terms; in cost–benefit analyses, outcomes are measured in monetary terms (Rossi, Lipsey, and Freeman, 2004:333). Cost–effectiveness analysis may be used to compare interventions with common goals, such as different gang prevention programs, whereas cost–benefit analysis may be applied to compare economic efficiency irrespective of program goals.

The TARP experiment was designed to reduce recidivism; therefore, the relevant outcome was the percentage of released felons who returned to prison. A cost–effectiveness analysis of TARP might have calculated the costs of payments to released prisoners per 1 percent reduction in the percentage of released prisoners who were reincarcerated. Or one could carry out a cost–benefit analysis by comparing the costs of the payments with the costs of imprisonment and processing persons through the criminal justice system. When the TARP investigators did this, they found that "it is cheaper to provide payments of between $800 and $1200 to 100 released prisoners than to process about five additional persons through the criminal justice system, provide prison space for them for periods of 2 and 3 years, and cover other associated costs of imprisonment as well as welfare payments for dependents" (Rossi, Berk, and Lenihan, 1980:112).

According to Esbensen and colleagues (2013:399), reviewers have criticized G.R.E.A.T., and rating schemes have declined to classify the program as "effective" because of the evaluation's small effect sizes. As Greg Duncan and Katherine Magnuson (2007:46) point out, however, any assessment of program effectiveness "must compare the value of a program's effects with the costs incurred in achieving them. An inexpensive program that produces small but economically valuable outcomes may make for good policy, whereas a very expensive program that produces larger but not proportionately larger effects may not." In the cost–benefit equation, it also is important to consider the cumulative benefits of an intervention, including benefits accruing to the large community and society. For example, interventions that reduce juvenile crime can benefit crime victims (Duncan and Magnuson, 2007). Given the relatively low cost of G.R.E.A.T. as well as the finding of 10 statistically significant outcome measures 4 years after participation in the program, it is reasonable to argue that the small effects justify the program (Esbensen et al., 2013).

Methodological Issues in Evaluation Research

Each type of evaluation presents distinct methodological problems that require different research procedures. In-depth interviews and participant observation, for example, can be particularly effective in formative evaluation. Being chiefly concerned with *describing* the operation of a program, process evaluations use questionnaires and interviews, field observation, and the analysis of program records—in short, every major approach except experimentation. Evaluation researchers have devised many useful guidelines for determining when, how, and in what combination to use these approaches in implementation studies (see, e.g., King, Morris, and Fitz-Gibbon [1987]). Space does not allow us to examine the application of methods in all types of evaluation. In the remainder of the chapter, therefore, we focus on methodological issues pertinent to effect assessment.

Theory as a Guide to Research

Like basic explanatory research, effect assessments are concerned with cause and effect. A useful paradigm for thinking about cause and effect is the "black box model." The black box consists of organisms or situations; inputs to and outputs from the black box can be observed, but the connecting processes within the box are not readily visible. According to Martin Lipsey (1993), this model aptly depicts the research paradigm in most evaluation studies. The black box is the situation in which a social program is applied; the input is the program, treatment, or intervention; and the output is its effects. Thus, in the TARP experiments, benefit payments (the input) were given to released prisoners (the black box of interest) to try to reduce their postrelease arrest rates (the output of interest).

Lipsey uses the black box model to draw attention to a major shortcoming of many evaluation studies: the lack of an adequate "treatment" theory of program effects. Although theory building is the primary objective in basic research, the value of theory in applied research has not always been appreciated. Thus, evaluation researchers, like behaviorists who treat the mind as a black box, often ignore what goes on inside the black box; that is, they fail to describe the causal process through which a program or intervention is expected to affect a specified target population. Without a theory of this process, effect assessment amounts to a trial-and-error, "let's try this and see if it works" approach (Lipsey, 1993:7). This may prove useful at times, but often it oversimplifies a complex reality. The TARP experiment illustrates this problem. The anticipated effects and research design were based on the relatively simple principle that financial aid to released prisoners would reduce their need to resort to property crime as a source of income. A more complete description of the causal process, however, would have accounted fully for the work disincentive of the payment benefit and the impact of employment on recidivism.

The problem of unspecified or oversimplified theories of the causal process applies to input and output as well as to the forces operating within the black box. On the input side, intervention programs often are treated as singular "molar" categories when in fact they are complex and multidimensional. Moreover, contextual and environmental factors may interact with and significantly affect the impact of a program. On the output side, effects frequently are assessed in terms of "a narrow range of dependent variables to the neglect of unexpected side effects, the interrelationships among effects, and the timing, magnitude, and durability of those effects" (Lipsey, 1993:8).

It is not unusual for gang and delinquency prevention programs to lack an explicit theoretical basis. In fact, as originally developed, G.R.E.A.T. was "essentially based on common sense and the perceptions of law enforcement officers" (Curry, 2010). Esbensen and his colleagues believed, however, that "a thorough evaluation of G.R.E.A.T." was possible only if they could establish links between program elements and criminological theory (Winfree, Esbensen, and Osgood, 1996:182–83). Fortuitously, their analysis identified connections between the G.R.E.A.T. curriculum and a combination of self-control theory and social learning theory. These theories enabled them to delineate "key concepts and . . . the variables selected for measurement" and, ultimately, to explain precisely why the program should achieve specific results (Winfree, Esbensen, and Osgood, 1996:183).

According to self-control theory, for example, crime or delinquency is a result of low self-control, which leads individuals to take advantage of opportunities for self-gratification that involve criminal activities. Weak social control and opportunities to commit crime and violence are associated with youth gangs. Lesson 5 ("Meeting Basic Needs") offers strategies for meeting social and emotional needs without joining gangs; Lessons 7 ("Responsibility") and 8 ("Goal Setting") examine the concepts of responsibility and deferred gratification (Winfree, Esbensen, and Osgood, 1996). Reflective of these theoretical links, attitudinal measures in the student questionnaires included altruism, collective efficacy, and the values of doing things for others and making a difference in the community.

Lipsey's critique of the atheoretical nature of much evaluation research echoes a familiar theme in social research: the mutual dependence of theory and research. For effect assessment to be most fruitful, its methods must be integrated with a treatment theory, which will determine the research design capable of detecting effects, the operationalization of the treatment, and the selection of appropriate output measures. Having identified this general problem, we now address problems of research design and internal validity, measurement validity, and external validity.

KEY POINT

The more clearly articulated the underlying causal process that produces program effects, the easier it will be to evaluate the program.

Research Design and Internal Validity

As in basic hypothesis-testing research, the ideal design strategy in effect assessment is a true experiment, with units of analysis randomly assigned to at least two conditions, one with the intervention present and the other with the intervention absent. Whether this strategy may be implemented depends on whether the intervention is (1) existing or new and (2) delivered to all or only some members of a target population. Indeed, the crucial distinction for determining available design strategies is among programs or interventions that (1) provide full coverage, whether existing or new; (2) are existing and provide partial coverage; and (3) are new and provide partial coverage. Only with this last type of program is it possible to use a true or randomized experimental design.

Existing and New Programs/Interventions That Provide Full Coverage

For ongoing and new programs that reach or are designed to reach virtually all of the population (called "full-coverage" programs), the primary research design is a time-series analysis. This consists of repeated measures of effects before and after the time when the program or intervention was introduced. Rossi, Freeman, and Lipsey (1999:268) point out that although time-series analyses are technically complex, the underlying logic is simple:

The researcher analyzes the trend before a treatment was enacted in order to obtain a projection of what would have happened without the intervention. This projection is then compared with the actual trend after the intervention. Statistical tests are used to determine whether or not the observed postintervention trend is sufficiently different from the projection to justify the conclusion that the treatment had an effect.

For example, Wagenaar (1983) used a time-series analysis to study the effects of raising the legal drinking age to 21 in the state of Michigan. On the basis of an analysis of alcohol-related crashes before the age was raised in 1978, he projected the number of such accidents in 1979 and then compared this figure with the actual number. The comparison showed that 18- to 20-year-old drivers in Michigan had 22 percent fewer alcohol-related crashes in 1979 than were predicted.

Wagenaar's (1983) time-series analysis used aggregate archival data. When full-coverage interventions and programs are not delivered uniformly, it may be possible to assess effects by conducting a panel study, a survey design with repeated measurements of the same *individuals*. For example, whereas exposure to television is almost universal among young children, there is variation from child to child and over time in exposure to programs containing episodes of violence and aggression. Therefore, by repeatedly measuring aggressiveness and the viewing of violent television programs, one could determine whether aggressiveness at one time is a function of viewing patterns at an earlier time. Several studies incorporating this design have found a modest over-time correlation between exposure to television violence (measured by viewing frequency weighted for program violence) and interpersonal aggression (generally measured by peer ratings) (Comstock and Paik, 1991:253).

Time-series and panel designs have their limitations. Panel studies are rarely feasible; they cannot be used to analyze existing programs, and they are also expensive and time-consuming. The feasibility of time-series designs depends on the availability of appropriate statistics; and a serious limitation is that they require a relatively large number of measurements before the program or intervention went into effect (at least 30 points in time are recommended) to model preintervention trends accurately. In addition, history may be a major threat to internal validity. In the Michigan drinking-age study, for example, any reduction in the number of accidents after the drinking age was raised may have been a result of other forces acting at that time, such as highway improvements, less hazardous weather conditions, or a police crackdown on speeding.

Existing Programs/Interventions That Provide Partial Coverage

When evaluating programs that are delivered to part of the population and are in place before the evaluation is undertaken, the general approach is to compare those who are exposed to or participate in the program (participants) with those who are not or do not (nonparticipants). Because random assignment is not possible, the evaluator must find alternative means of creating equivalent groups. Two general strategies are used, often in combination: statistical control and matching.

Statistical control, discussed at length in Chapter 16, is the method of establishing causality (or nonspuriousness) in cross-sectional survey designs. Suppose, for example, you were asked to evaluate the impact of a study-skills training program for first-year college students in which half of the first-year class participated. The object of the program was to improve academic performance. Thus, if it worked, participants should have achieved higher grades than nonparticipants at the end of their first year. Any difference in grades between these two groups might, however, be a result of initial differences in their verbal aptitude. To make the two groups equivalent on this variable, you could analyze the program's effect on grades while holding verbal aptitude constant; for example, you could examine this relationship separately for students with verbal SAT scores below 500 and for students with verbal SAT scores above 500. Now, if program participants in each case have higher first-year grades than nonparticipants, you have strengthened the inference that it is the program and not verbal aptitude that accounts for participants' higher grades.

An example of statistical control is a study that asked, Does attendance at Alcoholics Anonymous (AA) meetings reduce the level of drinking among individuals with drinking problems? AA was founded in the 1930s as a mutual-help group whose primary purpose is to help alcoholics stay sober. Making a voluntary commitment to participate is an important part of the AA approach. Therefore, not only is random assignment to AA and a control group not possible, but also self-selection factors are likely to distinguish these two groups.

To assess the effect of attendance at AA meetings, Keith Humphreys, Ciaran Phibbs, and Rudolf Moos (1996) recruited 218 individuals with drinking problems. All participants completed a survey when recruited and again 1 year later. Included in the surveys were measures of the dependent variable level of drinking problem, whether a participant attended AA meetings in the first 6 months, and four control variables that prior research indicated were related to participation in AA or drinking behavior. The latter variables were a participant's sex, marital status, perceived seriousness of drinking problem, and tendency to seek information when coping with problems. Results indicated that when these variables were controlled, individuals who attended AA meetings had less severe drinking problems at follow-up than those who did not attend.[4]

Another method of control is to construct or find a comparison group that is similar to the treatment group in crucial respects. This may be achieved through either individual or aggregate matching (Rossi, Lipsey, and Freeman, 2004:276). Individual matching, described in Chapter 7, pairs each participant with a nonparticipant who is the same on one or more variables. Aggregate matching consists of finding treatment and control groups that correspond to one another in the overall distribution of matching variables. For example, if one is evaluating a secondary school multiculturalism program, one may select nonparticipant schools for comparison that are similar to the participant schools in the proportion of minority students.

An interesting example of a quasi-experimental design that used aggregate matching was a study of interracial housing conducted more than 60 years ago. As a result of a housing shortage, public housing expanded rapidly after World War II. At this time, racial segregation was still the rule in the United States, and most of the newly constructed housing projects either were racially segregated or contained a very low percentage of blacks. In this context, Morton Deutsch and Mary Evans Collins (1951) studied the impact of integrated versus segregated housing on interracial attitudes. More specifically, they decided to compare tenants' attitudes in projects with two different occupancy patterns: an integrated interracial occupancy pattern (families were assigned to apartments without consideration of race) and a segregated biracial pattern (black and white families resided in the same project but were assigned to different buildings). The study design was thus a static group comparison. To control for selection bias, the principal source of invalidity in this design, Deutsch and Collins matched the projects on key variables. First, they obtained the cooperation of two neighboring cities, one (New York) with an integrated and the other (Newark) with a segregated housing policy. Next, they carefully matched housing projects in terms of their racial ratio, selecting one project in each city that was about two-thirds black and one project in each city with a 50:50 black:white ratio. Finally, they noted that approximate matching occurred on several other variables. For example, the two cities were similar in important ways, such as in their racial and ethnic composition; residents of the two cities were exposed to similar cultural influences, such as the same media; all the housing projects began at about the same time, were subject to the same federal regulations, had similar administrative setups, and were located in similar neighborhoods.

In addition to matching, Deutsch and Collins controlled statistically for some variables; they also argued against selection on the basis of racial attitudes because of the desperate need for housing and the low rate of refusals. Still, the principal weakness of this quasi-experimental design as well as cross-sectional surveys is their vulnerability to selection bias. Since statistical control is logically equivalent to matching but usually easier to carry out, the use of cross-sectional surveys with statistical controls has supplanted quasi-experimental matching designs to a considerable extent in recent years (Rossi, Lipsey, and Freeman, 2004:279). Cross-sectional surveys can provide quick, cost-effective estimates of program effects; however, the validity of such assessments depends heavily on how well the investigator has conceptualized possible selection effects and has measured characteristics of participants and nonparticipants that permit the statistical control of these potential effects. In the AA study, for example, the validity of the inference that AA attendance affected the outcome depends on how well the control variables account for selection factors that differentiate individuals who attend AA meetings from those who do not.

One other quasi-experimental design, the multiple time series, combines statistical control and matching with the analysis of available data to enable particularly strong causal inferences about program effects. The major validity threat to the single time-series design is history. Adding a control group time series permits tests for the threat of history (as well as other validity threats such as instrumentation). Recall, for example, Wagenaar's study of the impact of raising the legal drinking age in Michigan. We described this study as testing a full-coverage program since *all* 18- to 20-year-olds in the state were affected. With a single time-series design, Wagenaar showed that alcohol-related accidents among 18- to 20-year-olds in the state of Michigan decreased after the drinking age was raised. That was only part of the study, however. The Michigan law also could be construed as a partial-coverage intervention insofar as it did not affect all age groups, nor did it apply in other states. In fact, as we described earlier in the chapter, Wagenaar analyzed time-series data in two kinds of control groups. First, he compared accident trends for older age groups in Michigan who were unaffected by the law; second, he compared accident trends among 18- to 20-year-olds in two other states, New York and Pennsylvania, where the drinking age remained the same during the same time period. Neither the older age groups nor the control states showed the same decrease in alcohol-related accidents, thereby strengthening the causal inference that raising the drinking age reduced accidents among 18- to 20-year-olds.

New Programs/Interventions That Provide Partial Coverage

Any of the designs mentioned may be used to assess new, partial-coverage programs. Studies of such programs permit far greater control, however, than studies of ongoing and/or full-coverage programs. Indeed, it may be possible to meet the requirements of a true experiment, with random assignment to treatment and control groups whose experiences are comparable except for exposure to the new program or intervention. As scientific opinion has shifted more strongly in favor of randomized experiments and away from quasi-experimental and nonexperimental designs (T. D. Cook and Shadish, 1994; Gueron and Rolston, 2013), evaluation researchers have sought ways to circumvent the obstacles to conducting true experiments. The implementation problem that has received the most attention is how to plan and carry out random assignment (Boruch and Wothke, 1985).

If we assume that random assignment is feasible, the decision to implement it usually boils down to matters of practicality and ethics. Randomized experiments are time-consuming and often costly. The second G.R.E.A.T. evaluation cost $2.5 million and took more than 5 years to plan and carry out; experiments of other government programs have cost upward of $100 million at today's dollar value and have taken even longer to complete (Rossi, Lipsey, and Freeman, 2004:261).

KEY POINT

A true experiment is the ideal approach for assessing program effects, but it may be applied only to a new program that is delivered to part of the target population.

Project sponsors, administrators, and staff also may resist randomization for ethical reasons. They may argue that it is unfair, harmful, or illegal to deprive some people of a treatment or program that is believed to be beneficial. To counter this objection, evaluation researchers offer two principal arguments. First, they point out that the effectiveness of the program is unknown and will remain so until a scientific test of it is performed. Second, they argue that since the effects of the program are unproven and since there might even be undesirable effects in some cases, randomization is the only fair way to assign persons to treatment and control groups.

Ultimately, such costs and objections must be weighed against the cost of weaker causal inferences that are likely to be drawn from nonexperimental studies (Shadish, Cook, and Campbell, 2002). Evaluation researchers who investigate the effects of social programs may draw support from scientists who have studied medical experiments. John Gilbert, Bucknam McPeek, and Frederick Mosteller (1977), for example, have concluded that the social costs of being wrong about the effectiveness of a treatment or drug outweigh the costs of randomization. Imagine the social costs, for example, of continuing for years to use a less desirable treatment or program.

Even when program administrators are convinced of the value of random assignment and it is incorporated into the research design, other problems frequently arise. Commonly, researchers design the randomization process but must depend on various other officials to make the actual assignments. In the TARP experiments, for example, the state Department of Corrections was responsible for subject selection and random assignment (Rossi, Berk, and Lenihan, 1980:50). Problems occur when staff misunderstand what they are supposed to do or when they let professional judgment override random assignment because of a client's perceived need or merit. To prevent this from occurring, researchers must clearly explain the necessity of random assignment, carefully monitor the selection process, and offer to discuss special cases that service professionals think should be excluded from the process (T. D. Cook and Shadish, 1994:559).

Finally, the randomization process is far more likely to break down in an evalua-tion study than in basic research once the study has begun. The biggest problem here is treatment-related loss of participants, which would lead to dissimilarity of the treatment and control groups. This may occur either when individuals who have been assigned to a treat-ment or control group refuse to participate in the assigned group (selection bias) or when individuals drop out of the treatment and control groups at different rates (differential attri-tion). Treatment-related refusals to participate may be minimized by restricting the subject population to persons who agree at the outset to participate in any condition to which they are assigned. Solutions for minimizing treatment-related attrition include paying subjects to remain in the experiment or paying controls to provide outcome data that can be compared with those who participated, monitoring attrition cases to determine their causes and reduce their occurrence, and omitting the control group and creating different treatment groups that are approximately equal in attractiveness (T. D. Cook and Shadish, 1994:560–61). (See Box 14.2 for a case study of randomization in an evaluation experiment.)

The concerted efforts of the G.R.E.A.T. investigators to minimize attrition illustrate the challenges in implementing a randomized control study in a school setting. The initial sample consisted of 4905 students on the active rosters of 195 classrooms in 31 schools. Attrition occurred at two stages. Some sampled students were lost initially in the process of acquiring parental consent for participation, which was required by federal regulations. Then, following completion of the program, additional students were lost when they were asked to complete a posttest and four follow-up surveys (Esbensen et al., 2013).

In the end, the investigators produced relatively high response rates that are associated with low selection bias. To obtain a high rate of parental consent, they met in person with school principals and, when possible, with teachers; asked teachers to assist in the collec-tion of consent forms; and offered monetary and other incentives to students and teachers for returns. Consent was obtained for 79 percent of the students, with 11 percent of parents refusing and 10 percent of students failing to return the consent forms (Esbensen et al., 2008). To sustain students' participation, the investigators tracked highly mobile partici-pants as they transitioned from middle school to high school. From the initial enrollment

BOX 14.2 Randomization in the Minneapolis Spouse Abuse Experiment

Evaluation researchers rarely present detailed information on the practical problems of implementing and maintaining randomization. One instructive exception is Lawrence Sherman and Richard Berk's (Sherman and Berk, 1985; Berk and Sherman, 1988; Berk, Smyth, and Sherman, 1988) discussion of randomization in the Minneapolis Spouse Abuse Experiment. Planning for this study began with a research design submitted to the National Institute of Justice (NIJ) by Lawrence Sherman. The design called for random assignment of some 300 misdemeanor domestic assault cases to one of three interventions: arrest, mediation, or separation. Before Sherman could implement this design, he had to gain the cooperation of the chief of police of a major city, convince the NIJ of the ethical and legal justifications for randomization, and persuade a group of officers to "voluntarily give up their discretion in domestic assault cases for a year or more" (Sherman and Berk, 1985:19). To the NIJ, Sherman argued that because there was no empirical evidence on the deterrent effects of arrest, the study would provide important information to help police effectively reduce repeat violence; moreover, police were making few arrests in domestic assault cases and were doing so on "an arbitrary and capricious basis" (Sherman and Berk,1985:17). Having obtained the cooperation of a "freethinking police chief" (Sherman and Berk, 1985;17), Sherman met some resistance from officers in the upper echelons of the chain of command; however, after a 3-day conference with 34 patrol officers, he was able to convince all but one of them to volunteer for the experiment.

To minimize implementation problems, the investigators used several strategies. They gave the officers extensive information and training, including role-playing exercises and practice in applying the experimental procedures; met monthly with officers during the course of the experiment; had research staff periodically ride along when the officers were on patrol; and devised a randomization procedure that was easy to implement and to monitor (Berk, Smyth, and Sherman, 1988). According to this procedure, police officers participating in the experiment carried

a special pad of report forms, color coded for the three treatments. Each time officers encountered a situation meeting the experimental criteria, they were to apply the treatment indicated by the color of the report form on the top of the pad. . . .

All of the color-coded forms were arranged in random order, stapled together in sets of 25, and numbered sequentially. The colors were meant to assist officers who might have to apply a random treatment rapidly under difficult circumstances. The stapling and numbering were meant to discourage even well-intentioned efforts by officers to match particular treatments to particular incidents. The numbering also provided [a] check on whether the treatments were being implemented as designed. (Berk and Sherman, 1988:71)

Because the police faced potentially volatile situations, the researchers knew there would be circumstances where random assignment could and should be avoided. Consequently, they anticipated and clearly defined those situations in which "upgrading" to arrest from the mediation and separation interventions would be permitted (e.g., if the officers were assaulted or the offender would not leave the premises when ordered).

Still, despite their efforts to ensure proper implementation, the investigators knew that random assignment would not be perfectly executed. There would be occasions when police would make errors, forget their forms, or "place law enforcement concerns ahead of the research design" (Berk, Smyth, and Sherman, 1988:213). The low volume of cases of domestic assault made it impossible to monitor through observation whether the officers were following the randomization procedure. This not only placed a premium on the officers' cooperation and commitment to the study but also made it necessary to analyze the assignment process.

To analyze randomization, the investigators relied on information the police were instructed to record as part of the experiment. The first important evidence that the experiment was implemented validly was that there were no significant differences in the characteristics of the treatment groups (Sherman and Berk, 1985). Moreover, when the investigators compared the designed treatments with the treatment delivered in the field, they found that treatments were the same in 82 percent of the cases; virtually all of the discrepant cases consisted of the assignment of arrest when the advice or separation treatment was called for, a pattern readily explicable in terms of the special allowances for upgrading.

Although the investigators were satisfied that compliance with the randomization procedure was high, they performed one final analysis. They analyzed the results of the experiment on the basis of both design and actual assignment of treatments, and they also attempted "to adjust for potential biases that could result from the nonrandom assignment of arrest" (Berk, Smyth, and Sherman, 1988:217). These analyses all pointed to the same positive effect of arrest in cases of misdemeanor assault.

in 31 middle schools, "students were surveyed in more than 200 different [high] schools in Waves 5 and 6" (Esbensen et al., 2013:383). Contacting students in school involved locating students, gaining access from principals, and multiple visits to survey students. From the first through the fourth follow-up, retention rates declined from 87.3 to 71.9 percent.

Randomization, in short, is far more problematic in evaluation experiments than in laboratory experiments. In the laboratory, a researcher usually assigns subjects to conditions, and the success of the randomization procedure is taken for granted. Similarly, a laboratory experimenter has a high degree of control over the knowledge that subjects have about various treatment conditions, including the ability of subjects to communicate information to one another about treatments. Not so in evaluation studies. In fact, Thomas Cook and Donald Campbell (1979:54–55) have outlined four novel threats to validity that derive from the **treatment diffusion of information** from one treatment to another. All four threats have been observed in evaluation studies (T. D. Cook and Shadish, 1994:555).

The validity threat of *resentful demoralization* occurs when members of control groups become resentful and demoralized upon learning that they are receiving a less desirable treatment. As a consequence, they lower their performance or productivity so that their resentful reaction rather than the putative cause—the treatment or program—accounts for the difference between treatment and control groups. Upon learning of their less desirable treatment, members of control groups also may react with *compensatory rivalry*. This occurs when the control group, perceiving itself as an underdog in a social competition, is motivated to reduce or reverse the expected difference. The expected difference between unequally treated groups also may be lowered when administrators engage in *compensatory equalization*. In this case, administrators may try to reduce treatment–control inequities, such as by providing equal funds to control groups not receiving a new program. The problem is that this additional resource may generate effects that equal the effects of the new program. Finally, *treatment imitation* or *diffusion* "occurs when treatment providers or recipients learn what other treatment groups are doing and, impressed by the new practices, copy them" (T. D. Cook and Shadish, 1994:555).

Elliot Aronson (Aronson et al., 1975) discovered treatment diffusion in his evaluation of a cooperative learning technique. Earlier in the chapter we described how Aronson was asked to evaluate and propose solutions for reducing racial tensions in the Austin, Texas, schools. Having concluded that the competitive classroom was the root of the problem, Aronson devised a new structured method of interdependent learning called the "jigsaw method."[5] His first experimental evaluation of this method showed several significant differences between children in classrooms with jigsaw-learning groups and children in traditional classrooms. After a 6-week period, children in the jigsaw groups liked their peers more, showed more positive attitudes toward school, had more positive self-concepts, and showed an improvement in grades. When Aronson and his associates attempted to replicate this study, however, they failed to obtain the expected, significant differences between experimental and traditional classrooms. Instead, children in both conditions showed the same increase in liking for peers, satisfaction with school, and so forth. The reason for the failure was a classic case of treatment diffusion. During the course of the experiment, Aronson's trained observers discovered that

> the control classrooms were anything but traditional. Virtually all of the control teachers were using some form of group interaction with their students—not as systematically or as extensively as the experimental teachers, but enough to have an impact on the children. These control groups produced changes in the kids' liking for school and each other that were greater than the original control groups, but not so large as the experimental ones.
>
> . . . part of the reason for [the contaminated controls] was that many of the teachers, pleased and enthused over the earlier studies, told their colleagues about the new method, and word-of-mouth reports traveled across the school system. (Aronson et al., 1975:50)

Measurement Validity

The utility of evaluation research depends not only on an adequate design strategy but also on the conceptualization and the reliability and validity of the measures of cause (the treatment or program) and effect (the expected outcome). Special measurement problems arise, however, because of the political context of evaluation research. Social programs and program objectives are political statements. "They are not meant to be precise explications of how a program might reduce the severity of a social problem or to provide evaluators with explicit program rationales that can be easily translated into evaluation objectives or criteria" (T. D. Cook, Leviton, and Shadish, 1985:703). Consequently, measurement may be made more difficult in several ways: Policymakers and program administrators may present vague conceptual and operational definitions of both the treatment and the desired goals; the treatment program may be nonuniform; the treatment program may be relatively clear but the goals are stated broadly for political reasons (e.g., to attract or keep support of a government agency or sponsor); different interest groups (e.g., administrators, staff, clients) may have conflicting or unrelated goals for the program.

In the case of nonuniform treatment programs, the best means of determining the nature of the "cause" is a thorough implementation study of the program as it operates at various sites and times. With regard to ill-defined and multiple program goals, the adequacy of evaluation research depends on the evaluator's ability to perform the delicate task of translating politically acceptable goals into measurable outcomes without losing the support of the program administrators and other interested parties.

KEY POINT
Unlike basic researchers, program evaluators face unique challenges involving ethical resistance to randomization, information diffusion across treatments, and practical constraints that can compromise the research design.

Assuming a well-defined program with clear objectives, the measurement problem amounts to finding or creating valid indicators of program outcomes. For research on existing programs or past interventions, evaluation researchers often use government statistics, as in the drinking-age studies. But these statistics may be inadequate or nonexistent. The G.R.E.A.T. program had clear objectives; however, as we noted above, the evaluators believed that a thorough evaluation was possible only if it was theory based. Therefore, to develop a conceptual model and identify key outcome measures, the evaluators conducted a thorough assessment of the G.R.E.A.T. curriculum (Esbensen, 2015). This enabled them to identify not only stated goals but also potential risk factors and theoretical perspectives that the police officers did not have in mind when they developed the program. As a result, they created 33 different outcome measures, which included 5 behavioral outcomes (e.g., gang affiliation, general delinquency) and 28 attitudinal measures (e.g., attitude toward police, self-efficacy, risk taking) (Esbensen et al., 2013).

Another measurement problem relates to the timing of outcome measurement. Social research has shown that the effects of a treatment may be immediate or may occur later in time and that effects may be gradual and continuous or occur all at once (Bernstein, Bohrnstedt, and Borgatta, 1975). The problem this presents in evaluation studies is that the time between program implementation and measurement might not correspond to the time it takes for the program to manifest its effects. Indeed, the time frame of evaluation studies may restrict a researcher's ability to assess potentially more important or relevant long-term effects. Had the first G.R.E.A.T. evaluation been restricted to the immediate follow-up, the investigators would have uncovered less positive results because the evidence showed delayed effects (Esbensen et al., 2001).

In the long run, perhaps the best solution to all these problems is multiple measurement. As we argued in Chapter 13, the use of multiple indicators can increase reliability and validity insofar as they contain offsetting biases and errors. If independent measures produce convergent findings, we become even more confident when the indicators derive from different sources, such as archival records, questionnaire surveys, and observation. And if different indicators produce conflicting results, this may lead policymakers appropriately to exercise caution and recognize the complexity of an issue.[6] In addition, diverse measures of outcomes will permit the analysis of possible unplanned and unanticipated effects, the assessment of program goals held by different constituencies, and, if outcomes are measured at different points in time, the assessment of longer-term as well as short-term effects.

External Validity

Basic researchers tend to believe that internal validity should take precedence over external validity. Before one explores the generalizability of a causal connection, they reason, one should establish the validity of the connection. Some evaluation researchers maintain, however, that more emphasis should be placed on external validity (Cronbach, 1982). In either case, the issue of external validity is particularly important in evaluation research. The purpose of undertaking evaluation studies is to make informed decisions about whether to extend a program to other participants or beneficiaries. "An externally valid evaluation," Larry Orr (2015:169) states, "provides unbiased estimates of the impact of an intervention on . . . the population that would be affected if the intervention were adopted as policy (or, in the case of an ongoing program, the population currently served by the program)."

In many evaluation studies, the issue of external validity boils down to how well the sampling units represent the target population. Probability sampling provides unbiased estimates of intervention effects; however, for various reasons, evaluations rarely test interventions on probability samples (Orr, 2015). The target population often is too difficult or too expensive to enumerate. If enumeration is possible, there often are "enormous practical difficulties" in drawing a random sample, especially of widely dispersed populations (T. D. Cook and Shadish, 1994:571). Experiments also may be restricted to those individuals who agree to be randomly assigned, a group that may not be representative of the whole target population, and attrition can make the sample less representative.

When evaluation researchers must rely on nonprobability samples, several selection biases may threaten external validity. Sometimes subjects select themselves into a treatment, sometimes program participants are selected because they are most likely to generate positive results, and sometimes units are chosen because of their availability (Bernstein, Bohrnstedt, and Borgatta, 1975). As long as a program is designed only for volunteers who seek treatment, self-selection should permit reasonable generalizations to the target population. Otherwise, self-selection, as well as selection for availability and presumed excellence, is likely to produce samples that differ systematically from the target population.

External validity pertains not only to the representativeness of the sample but also to the generalizability of other aspects of the program that is the object of the evaluation, including program components, staff, setting, and time. All of these aspects may threaten external validity in various ways (Bernstein, Bohrnstedt, and Borgatta, 1977:119–25; Mertens and Wilson, 2012:311–12).

1. Programs often are described with generic labels such as "youth services" and "social skills training" that belie the complexity and multidimensionality of the treatment. Therefore, interventions should be described in sufficient detail that others can implement the same intervention in another setting (Mertens and Wilson, 2012).

2. The effectiveness of a social program may depend on the personal qualities of the staff who administer it. Thus, results would not be generalizable to later, widespread implementation by staff who are less able, committed, or enthusiastic about the program's success.

3. Knowledge that one is a participant in the evaluation of a social program can affect results. The Hawthorne effect, described in Box 2.1, suggests that program participants may increase their effort when they know that they are being evaluated. Or, they may perform better because of the excitement of participating in a new program. Such effects raise the question of whether findings are generalizable to settings where the program is no longer experimental or being evaluated.

4. The program may be effective only at the historical time in which it takes place and/or in the particular geographic setting where it takes place. This seems especially likely when an experimental program takes place at a location far removed from the setting where it ultimately will be administered.

There are no easy solutions to these external validity problems. To begin, one should draw a probability sample of the target population if possible. Whether or not this is done, one should also attempt to vary those factors—time, setting, staff, and so on—that are likely to limit the generality of study results. One approach is to attempt to make the conditions of the experimental program (e.g., sample, setting, staff) representative of the conditions under which the program ultimately would be implemented. Robert St. Pierre and Thomas Cook (1984) refer to this as **modal instance sampling**. It requires first that one describe the manner in which the program would be carried out if it became formal policy (the modal setting). Then, one selects or creates a research setting in which the program is implemented in a manner similar to that of the modal setting. If, for example, a modal program involved health education services directed to the urban poor, then the test program should involve urban poor. In this instance, one would not choose to evaluate a program located in a small town or one directed to a wider range of socioeconomic groups.

Typically, evaluations are carried out at multiple sites. If the sites were drawn randomly, this would provide an unbiased impact of the program or policy. As in the G.R.E.A.T. study, however, most evaluations select sites purposively. And if impacts vary across sites, overall sample estimates can be misleading (Olsen, Orr, Bell, and Stuart, 2013). Esbensen and colleagues (2013) did find variation in program effects across the seven cities in their evaluation, which may have reflected chance variation or differences in program effectiveness.

KEY POINT
With the goal of assessing the applicability of program effects, evaluation research places a premium on external validity.

Finally, because a delivered intervention can rarely be separated from its context, Rossi, Lipsey, and Freeman (2004:58) see program monitoring evaluations as an "indispensable adjunct" to effect assessments. Through monitoring, one can carefully identify aspects of the program or intervention, such as the geographic setting, physical plant, rules and regulations, characteristics and training of staff, and so forth, that might affect the outcome of the intervention.

The Social and Political Context of Evaluation Research

As we have seen, issues of design, measurement, and sampling are as germane to evaluation research as they are to basic research. The particular social context of evaluation research, however, creates unique problems in resolving these technical issues. Thus, we have alluded to the validity threat posed by the diffusion of information across treatments; the difficulties in applying randomization procedures when program staff must be enlisted to carry them out and participants drop out; the measurement problems created by ambiguous program means and goals; and the impact of staff, locale, and time on the generalizability of program effects. Let us take a closer look now at the social and political contexts of evaluation research.

In contrast to basic researchers who exercise considerable freedom in selecting research topics and in conducting their research, evaluation researchers are constrained by and beholden to various stakeholders. **Stakeholders** are "the individuals, groups, or organizations that have a significant interest in how well a program functions" (Rossi, Lipsey, and Freeman, 2004:18). In any evaluation study, there are numerous potential stakeholders. The most obvious is the program sponsor—the government agency, private organization, or community group—that initiates and funds the program, which may or may not be the same as the evaluation sponsor who mandates and funds the study. The NIJ funded the G.R.E.A.T. evaluation. Another stakeholder is the policymaker or decision maker who ultimately determines the fate of the program. For G.R.E.A.T., this included the program governing body, the National Policy Board; the U.S. Office of Juvenile Justice and Delinquency Prevention, which currently provides funds to support the training of instructors and costs of instructional materials; and, ultimately, the U.S. Congress, which appropriates funds to federal agencies. Then there are program participants, program management and staff, the evaluators, and other interested parties. For G.R.E.A.T., such stakeholders included the children and parents of children who participated in the program, the officers who delivered the instruction, and the school principals and teachers in whose classrooms the program was taught. Finally, Rossi, Lipsey, and Freeman (2004:374) note that, "in an abstract sense, every citizen who should be concerned with the efficacy and efficiency of efforts to improve social conditions has a stake in the outcome of an evaluation."

Evaluation researchers must be aware of the various stakeholders as they design and conduct their research and communicate their findings. Because stakeholders have conflicting interests, researchers should clearly identify the perspective from which the research is being undertaken, while acknowledging the legitimacy of other perspectives. Sometimes the policymaking stage (see Figure 14.1) will dictate the relevant perspective; for example, program staff will have the primary stake in formative research designed to fine-tune programs, whereas policymakers would be primarily interested in needs assessment.

Evaluation researchers also should be aware of possible difficulties in communicating with different stakeholders. This applies both to the intelligibility of the communication, which must eschew technical vocabulary, and to the form of the communication. Although most evaluation studies culminate in a detailed, technical report that describes the research design, methods, and results, Rossi, Lipsey, and Freeman (2004:380) point out that these are "rarely read by the stakeholders who count. Many of these stakeholders simply are not accustomed to reading voluminous documents, do not have the time to do so, and might not be able to understand them." Therefore, evaluation researchers must be prepared to issue executive summaries, memos, and especially oral reports geared to the needs of specific stakeholders.

Because evaluation research takes place in the context of policymaking, with different types of evaluation linked to each policymaking phase, it is part of a political process. To be effective, therefore, an evaluation researcher must understand his or her role in this process. Speaking of program evaluation at the federal level, Eleanor Chelimsky (1987) maintains that evaluation research is likely to be maximally useful when the purpose of evaluation is to provide the highest-quality information in addressing policy questions determined by the policymaker. The researcher undertaking an evaluation thus should not act as an advocate but rather should serve as a handmaiden of the policymaker. Similarly, Rossi, Lipsey, and Freeman (2004:382) liken the

> evaluator's role to that of expert witness, testifying to the degree of a program's effectiveness and bolstering that testimony with empirically based information. A jury of decisionmakers and other stakeholders may give such testimony more weight than uninformed opinion or shrewd guessing, but they, not the witness, are the ones who must reach a verdict.[7]

So, how much use is made of an evaluator's expert testimony? Unfortunately, there is little systematic evidence and general disappointment regarding the extent of the use of evaluation studies (Rossi, Lipsey, and Freeman, 2004; Sechrest and Figueredo, 1993). Much of the time the information is simply ignored by policymakers. This seems to have been the case, for example, with regard to the TARP experiments on the effect of short-term financial support on reducing recidivism. Still, Chelimsky (1991) cites several instances in which evaluation research provided critical knowledge for policy development in the federal government, including forecasting the likely impact of new immigration policy and obtaining precise counts of homeless populations. She contends that the use of evaluation in policymaking "is real, measurable, and growing dramatically" Chelimsky (1987:32).

Others (C. H. Weiss, 1987; Rossi, Lipsey, and Freeman, 2004) contend that although few evaluation studies lead to direct and immediate changes in policy and practice, they do influence thinking in a more indirect, general way. According to C. H. Weiss (1987:44), "The generalizations and ideas that [these studies] produce percolate into the consciousness of informed publics, and over time they can alter the terms of policy discourse." Given the expansion of the evaluation enterprise, the steady development of technical knowledge, and the increasing awareness of the political context in which evaluation takes place, we expect the partnership between research and policymaking to continue to grow.

Summary

- Evaluation research is a form of applied social research whose basic aim is to apply social research methods to the assessment of social intervention programs.
- Evaluation is integral to rational decision making and can be linked to the various stages of policymaking.
- At the stage of problem identification, evaluation researchers draw on existing social scientific knowledge to help conceptualize problems and solutions; and they use social indicators to estimate the prevalence of and trends in social problems.
- To aid in policy formulation and program planning, evaluation researchers assess perceived priorities among problem areas, called "needs assessment," and assess the impact of proposed programs on the social environment.
- Evaluation researchers also conduct formative evaluations to assist in the development of programs, do process evaluations to determine how well the implementation of a program matches its design, and conduct summative or outcome evaluations to determine the impact and efficiency of a program.
- Although each type of evaluation encounters different methodological problems, this chapter focused on the application of methods to summative evaluations of program effects.
- A general problem with summative evaluations is the absence of an adequate theory that specifies the relationship between program elements and presumed outcomes.
- For existing and new programs and interventions that affect the entire population, time-series analyses work best, although their feasibility depends on the existence of appropriate data. Without such data, surveys may suffice.
- For existing programs that reach part of the population, the design usually involves a survey and comparison of affected and unaffected groups, with some form of control for selection bias.
- In the case of partial-coverage new programs, the ideal design is a true experiment. However, implementing experiments may be problematic as stakeholders must be convinced of the value and ethics of randomization, which must be carefully monitored, participants may drop out of the study, and diffusion of information from one treatment to another may threaten internal validity.
- The political context of evaluation research creates special measurement problems, such as vaguely defined program means and ends, nonuniform programs across sites, and an indeterminate time lag between treatments and effects. An implementation study may help to identify causes, but multiple measurement offers the best overall solution to these problems.
- Because the usefulness of evaluation findings depends on their applicability to real-world settings, evaluation researchers place a premium on external validity, which may be threatened by self-selection, the Hawthorne effect, the special qualities of the staff, and the limited locales and times in which a program is tested.
- Throughout the research process, evaluation researchers must be aware of relevant stakeholders. Ultimately, the utility of evaluation studies depends on the researcher's ability to address the needs and interests of stakeholders and to successfully carry out his or her role in the political process to which evaluation is linked.

Key Terms

basic social research
applied social research
evaluation research
social indicator
needs assessment
environmental impact studies
social impact assessment
formative evaluation
process evaluation

summative evaluation
effect assessment
efficiency assessment
  cost–effectiveness analysis
  cost–benefit analysis
treatment diffusion of information
modal instance sampling
stakeholders

Exercises

1. Initially, the G.R.E.A.T. program was, to a considerable degree, modeled after Drug Abuse Resistance Education (DARE), a widely used program to prevent drug use (Esbensen, 2015). Exercise 4 in Chapter 8 describes a hypothetical study to evaluate the impact of DARE. The story behind DARE's continuing public support is an interesting case study of the political context of evaluation research. According to Dennis Rosenbaum (2007:815), this "program receives over $200 million annually in public funding despite overwhelming evidence of its ineffectiveness." Visit the official website of DARE (http://www.dare.com/home/default.asp) to learn more about this program. Does this site articulate a "treatment" theory on which the program is based? Who are the stakeholders in an assessment of this program? Why do you suppose that DARE continues to be widely used?

2. One major study of DARE tracked drug use from 1 to 10 years after its implementation. Richard Clayton, Anne Cattarello, and Bryan Johnstone fully describe the research design and 5-year follow-up results of this study in a 1996 article published in *Preventive Medicine* (vol. 25, pp. 307–18). Read this article and answer the following questions.

    a. Although the authors state that they used a "longitudinal design," this refers mainly to the 5-year follow-up measurement of DARE effects. Explain why the basic approach is experimental. (Hint: How were the comparison groups formed?)

    b. What outcome measures were used to assess the effects of DARE?

    c. How did the researchers address the internal validity threat of differential attrition? What did they conclude?

    d. What do Figures 2–4 reveal about the difference between the comparison and intervention groups in terms of annual use of marijuana, change in attitudes toward drugs, and estimated number of peers who use cigarettes?

    e. Evaluate this study from the standpoint of external validity.

3. Suppose your college is initiating a new policy of assigning first-year students to the same residence halls, thereby segregating the residence halls into first year versus upper class. By making this change, the administration hopes to ease first-year students' adjustment to college life and to engender a greater sense of community and intellectual engagement among the first-year class. You have been asked to advise them on how to evaluate the impact of this policy.

    a. Who are the relevant stakeholders in this study?

    b. Suppose that, as an experimental program, the administration plans to assign one-third of incoming students to all-first-year residence halls, with the remaining first-year students integrated into other multiclass residence halls. What basic research design would you use to assess program effects? What are the obstacles to effectively implementing this design?

    c. Now suppose that the entire incoming class will be segregated in a few all-first-year residence halls. How would you assess the effects of the new living arrangement? What are potential threats to internal validity?

    d. Devise possible measures of the intended effects of this new policy.

Notes

1. Frederick Mosteller (1981) describes a "nutrition experiment" carried out in 1601 to test the effects of lemon juice on scurvy among sailors on four British ships sailing from England to India. Among those on the largest ship in the fleet, who drank 3 teaspoons of lemon juice every day, few became ill. But more than a third of those on the three smaller ships died before they reached the Cape of Good Hope. Despite this evidence and another successful experiment done 150 years later, it was not until 1795 that "the British Navy began using citrus juice on a regular basis and wiped out scurvy in the service" (Mosteller, 1981:882).
2. Throughout the first half of the twentieth century, individuals in most states did not gain either the right to vote or the right to purchase alcoholic beverages until they reached the age of 21. During the late 1960s, however, popular support for lowering the voting age grew as large numbers of 18- to 20-year-olds were sent to Vietnam. "The central argument was that someone old enough to die for his country should be old enough to vote" (Clark, 1992:228). This reasoning led ultimately to a constitutional amendment in 1971 that gave 18-year-olds the right to vote in federal elections. When most states followed suit by lowering the local and state voting age to 18, they adopted the same rationale for lowering the legal drinking age. In fact, between 1970 and 1975, 29 states lowered their drinking ages, usually from 21 to 18 or 19 (Saffer and Grossman, 1989).
3. The program was expanded from 8 to 13 lessons; the management style encouraged more communication and collaboration between program administrators and teachers; the curriculum was linked to known risk factors associated with joining gangs; and the instructional approach emphasized the development of social competency skills through cooperative learning and role playing rather than assimilating information (Esbensen et al., 2002).
4. A related statistical approach that, according to Rossi, Lipsey, and Freeman (2004), is becoming more commonplace is a two-stage analysis called "selection modeling." The first stage of the analysis uses control variables to calculate "propensity scores" that predict selection into treatment and control groups; the second stage incorporates these scores into an analysis of program effects. Using selection factors to predict selection and not simply as additional outcome predictors, this method more effectively controls for selection effects. When Humphreys, Phibbs, and Moos (1996) applied selection modeling to their data, they found that attendance at AA meetings had a statistically significant effect size that was almost twice as large as that derived from the one-stage analysis.
5. The jigsaw method begins by placing students in six-person learning groups. Each group is given a lesson that is divided into six paragraphs, and each paragraph is assigned to one member of the group. To learn the entire lesson, group members must put together the six paragraphs, like the pieces of a jigsaw puzzle, to get the whole picture. But to do so, each individual group member must learn his or her own segment and teach it to the other members of the group. (See Aronson et al. [1978], for a more complete description.)
6. According to Mark and Shotland (1985:354), however, divergent results may induce less salutary reactions. Instead of producing uncertainty, contradictory findings may strengthen the beliefs of partisans on both sides, or they may reduce policymakers' confidence in social scientists' ability to provide useful information.
7. Alternatively, Irwin Deutscher and Margaret Gold (1979:109) argue that maintaining a position of scientific objectivity may limit the usefulness of evaluation research. They believe that the proper role of evaluators is that of a "sympathetic skeptic," whose "partisanship . . . is essential for a sympathetic grasp of the intentions and the problems posed by the program."

PART IV

Data Processing, Analysis, and Interpretation

As with other facets of research, data analysis is very much tied to the researcher's basic methodological approach. In the chapters on field and available-data research, we discussed certain data-analytic techniques at length, but in the case of experiments and surveys we alluded only briefly to this stage of research. The first two chapters in this section take up where our discussions in Chapters 7 and 9 left off. Having collected data in a study, a researcher must quantify them, put them in computer-readable form, and analyze them statistically. Chapter 15 charts this process for survey research, outlining the key steps in processing data prior to analysis and describing elementary statistical analyses. Chapter 16 then considers some more advanced statistical techniques for assessing the causal relations among sets of variables.

Although our attention in these two chapters is focused mostly on the analysis of survey data, the underlying logic and flow of the analysis described are basically the same as in other approaches. For example, there is always a constant interplay between theory and data. The stage for data analysis is set by the researcher's theoretical model of antici- pated relationships, which limits and guides the kinds of analyses that can be carried out. The analysis, in turn, assays and elaborates this model and invariably suggests new models for further analysis. The first rule in all this is that facts (data) never speak for themselves. Rather, they must be interpreted. That interpretation will be influenced by prior research and ultimately will be communicated in the form of a research report, book, or article that will be read and interpreted by others. Thus, in Chapter 17, we examine the reading and writing of research.

15

Data Processing and Elementary Data Analysis

As we consider the later stages of research, it is valuable to recall the broader process of scientific inquiry. Science is a means to understanding that involves a repetitive interplay between theoretical ideas and empirical evidence. Data analysis takes place whenever theory and data are compared. This comparison occurs in field research and in some analyses of existing data when an investigator attempts to bring order to, or to make sense of, his or her observations. In surveys and experiments, a researcher typically brings theory and data together when testing a hypothesis once the data have been gathered and processed. In any case, initial data analyses set the stage for a continued interaction between theory and data.

This chapter and the next chapter focus on data processing, analysis, and interpretation. Together the two chapters follow the typical development of a survey study following data collection: from handling the data and putting them in computer-readable form to preliminary analyses involving one and two variables (Chapter 15) to more advanced statistical analyses (Chapter 16). Both chapters are oriented toward readers more as consumers than as producers of research and in no way can substitute for a course in statistics. In fact, we eschew computational formulas in favor of verbal presentations. What we want to do is give readers a sense of the *process* of data analysis—a learning process achieved through comparing empirical evidence with theoretical expectations.

Preview of Analysis Steps

In a sense, data analysis begins with a statement of hypotheses, the construction of a theoretical model, or, at the very least, implicitly anticipated relationships among a set of variables; these models guide the collection of data and thereby determine the alternative relationships or models that may be analyzed. In Chapter 4, for example, we discussed Beckett Broh's (2002) study of the impact of extracurricular involvement on academic achievement. In examining this relationship, Broh considered the impact of gender, race–ethnicity, parents' educational attainment, family income, and other antecedent variables. Each of these variables, she reasoned, could either independently affect academic achievement or possibly create a spurious causal relationship between extracurricular involvement and academic achievement. She also identified various intervening variables intended to capture theoretical links between sports participation and educational achievement, which she derived from developmental theory, the leading crowd hypothesis, and social capital theory. As in all social research, these theoretical expectations guided Broh's selection and measurement of variables and ultimately her analysis of the data.

Chapter 16 focuses on statistical techniques for assessing the causal relations among sets of variables. This is where we see how Broh tested her various theoretical models. Following data collection, however, several steps are necessary to prepare for this final stage of hypothesis testing. Let us preview the basic analysis steps that we cover in this chapter: (1) placing relevant information in computer-readable form, (2) inspecting and transforming the data for the intended statistical analyses, and (3) preliminary hypothesis testing.

In survey research, the first step includes editing and summarizing the responses (coding), data entry, and error checking (cleaning). Some of this **data processing** occurs during data collection in computer-assisted surveys. Researchers performing secondary analysis, as in Broh's analysis of data from the National Educational Longitudinal Survey (NELS), begin their analysis at the second step, data inspection and data modification. The goal of inspection is to get a clear picture of the data to determine appropriate statistical analyses and necessary data modifications. Usually, one examines each variable singly (univariate analysis), especially for insufficient variation in responses, missing information, abnormalities, and other weaknesses that may be mitigated prior to the analysis. The reasons for **data modification** are many: For example, a researcher may want to combine the responses to several items to create an index or scale, change one or more of the values for a variable, or collapse categories for purposes of analysis. In Chapter 5 we described how Beckett Broh created measures of interscholastic sports participation and time spent on homework by combining variables in the NELS data set.

The analysis then turns to empirical testing of the theorized relationships. For simple two-variable (bivariate) hypotheses, an analyst determines whether the association between the independent and dependent variables confirms theoretical expectations. Broh, for example, found that participation in interscholastic sports was positively associated with students' math and English grades, as predicted. In a true experiment, assessing the relationship between the independent and dependent variables is the final analysis step because an adequate design effectively controls extraneous variables. But in nonexperimental designs, extraneous variables may pose serious rival explanations that require statistical control. Broh had to explore the possibility, for example, that higher-performing students were more likely than their peers to play interscholastic sports.

Some researchers skip the previous step (preliminary hypothesis testing) in favor of a full-blown multivariate model containing all relevant independent, dependent, antecedent, intervening, and other variables. We prefer to conceptually describe the process as having two interrelated stages. If preliminary hypothesis testing supports theoretical expectations, an analyst formulates multivariate models to rule out, to the extent possible, that the initial results were a spurious consequence of uncontrolled antecedent variables. Conversely, if hypothesized relationships are not supported in preliminary testing, a researcher designs multivariate models to determine whether uncontrolled extraneous variables are blocking or distorting the initial results. The preliminary testing step also may reveal unanticipated (serendipitous) findings that suggest alternative multivariate models.

Data Processing

According to James Davis and Tom Smith (1992:60), data preparation (or processing) is "the least glamorous aspect of survey research." Yet, as they also point out, "probably at no other stage . . . is there a greater chance of a really horrible error being made. . . . To avoid such errors, many checks and safeguards must be built into the system" (60). In survey data processing, four essential steps constitute the process of checking the data and making them serviceable for analysis: editing, coding, data entry, and cleaning. Some of these procedures are performed by software in computer-assisted telephone interviewing (CATI), computer-assisted personal interviewing (CAPI), and computer-assisted self-interviewing (CASI).

Editing

Editing is a quality-control process applied mostly to paper-and-pencil surveys. Its purpose is to ensure that the information on a questionnaire or interview schedule is ready to be transferred to the computer for analysis. "Ready" means that the data are as complete, error-free, and readable as possible.

Editing is carried out both during and after the process of data collection, and much of it occurs simultaneously with coding (see the next section). In interview studies, the editing process begins in the field. Interviewers should check over their completed forms for errors and omissions soon after each interview is conducted. Respondents should be recontacted if necessary, or corrections should be made from memory. Field supervisors may also do some editing at this point, such as determining whether the interviews have been properly conducted from the standpoint of using the correct forms, legibly recording answers, and interviewing the correct respondents.

Most of the editing in large-scale surveys is done in a central office. Here, an editor or coder, who serves much the same function as a copy editor for a writer, goes over each completed form (1) to evaluate interviewers and detect interviewing problems (e.g., inadequate use of probes to obtain answers to open-ended questions); (2) to check for multiple answers to single items, vague answers, response inconsistencies (e.g., reporting 0 hours of television watched in one section and the viewing of a specific television program in another section), and the like; and (3) to make sure that the interview schedule or questionnaire is complete—that all items, especially those with "missing" responses, have coded values. The editor may bring glaring errors to the attention of the principal investigator or the field supervisor, who provides feedback to interviewers; but mostly he or she simply will make corrections directly on the form.

The NELS involved both on-site and centralized follow-up editing and data retrieval. Students, teachers, and parents completed questionnaires, which were supplemented with data from school officials. Field interviewers checked the student questionnaires at the schools, giving special attention to items designated as "critical," such as a student's sex, race, date of birth, household composition, and parents' employment status and education. If they found missing or undecipherable responses to these critical items, they privately contacted the respondents. For the other questionnaires and data, similarly designated critical items were checked in the central office and retrieval took place by telephone.

Some editing activities can be programmed into computer-assisted interviewing (CAI) and CASI software. CAI or CASI programs can prompt an interviewer or respondent to answer certain questions, to skip others, to use appropriate response codes, and to review obviously inconsistent responses to related questions. But lacking the intelligence of a human editor, CAI and CASI software cannot determine fully whether interviewers and respondents are recording consistent and adequate answers. A Web-based or laptop CASI program, for example, may accept "none of your business" as an adequate answer to an open-ended question.

Coding

Coding for computer analysis consists of assigning numbers or symbols to variable categories. In surveys such as the NELS, the categories are answers to questions; and the common practice, which simplifies data entry and analysis, is to use numerical codes only. For the variable gender or sex in the NELS, a code of 1 was used for males and 2 for females. The numbers used are arbitrary; a code of 2 might just as well have been used for males and a code of 1 for females. These numerical codes generally are specified directly on the questionnaire or interview schedule. For example, in the NELS second follow-up survey, students were asked if they had participated in (1) a team sport (baseball, basketball, football, soccer, hockey, etc.), (2) an individual sport (cross-country, gymnastics, golf, tennis, track, wrestling, etc.), or (3) cheerleading, pompom, or drill team. For each question, they circled the highest number that applied among five response alternatives: (1) school does not have, (2) did not participate, (3) participated on a junior varsity team, (4) participated on a varsity team, and (5) participated as a captain/co-captain on any team.

For closed-ended questions, coding is straightforward: There are relatively few categories, and you simply must assign a different code to each category. For open-ended questions, however, the number of unique responses may number in the hundreds. Coding for this type of question is very much like coding in content analysis (see Chapter 12). Researchers try to develop a coding scheme that does not require a separate code for every respondent or case but that adequately reflects the full range of responses. The idea is to put the data in manageable form while retaining as much information as is practical. (See Box 15.1 for an example of coding open-ended questions.)

BOX 15.1 Reasons for Giving up Cigarette Smoking: An Example of Coding Responses to Open-Ended Questions

Developing coding categories for open-ended questions, like many other research activities, involves an interplay between theory and data. Let us follow the procedure used by Bruce Straits (1967) in a study based on personal interviews of ex-smokers ("quitters"), current smokers who tried but were unable to quit smoking ("unables"), and current smokers who have never made a serious attempt to stop smoking ("smokers"). Hypothesizing that specific factors precipitate and support smoking cessation, Straits asked quitters and unables the open-ended question, Why did you want to stop smoking? (Smokers were asked, What reasons might you have for giving up smoking?) Individual responses to the question were too diverse and numerous to manage and analyze without grouping them into a smaller number of categories.

Both theory and data guided Straits's development of coding categories. Theoretical considerations included the hypothesis that current physical ailments (especially those easily connected with smoking) play a more important role in the discontinuation of smoking than health fears for the future (e.g., incurring lung cancer). The coding procedure involved first listing each reason given by the 200 respondents. (Typically, studies use a sample of about 50 to 100 respondents to build codes.) Tally marks were used to note identical reasons. Here is part of the listing:

"I couldn't get over a bad cough" ||||| ||||| ||||
"Job requirements" ||||| |
"Not good for health" ||||| ||||| ||||| |||
"It is too expensive" ||||| ||||| |||
"Live longer" ||||| |
"Sore throat" ||||| ||||| |
"To see if I could" ||||| |||||
"Heart attack" |
"Quit for Lent and didn't return" |
"Doctor's advice" ||||| ||||| |||
"Sinus condition" ||||| ||||| |
"Causes lung cancer" ||||| ||||| ||||| |||
"My wife hates it" |||

Next, coding categories were formed by grouping together reasons that seemed similar from the research perspective. For example, people with bad coughs were placed in the same

(continued)

(continued)

category as those reporting sore throats. Although the distinction between a cough and a sore throat is important from a medical standpoint, it was not pertinent to Straits's hypothesis.

Empirical considerations also influenced construction of the coding categories. Some reasons had to be lumped together in "other" categories because they occurred too infrequently. An unanticipated category had to be established for quitters who had not made a conscious decision to quit but instead found themselves in situations where they were unable to smoke for a temporary period, such as while recovering from an operation.

The final coding scheme, which was used to code *each* reason given, was as follows.

Current health reasons

1. Didn't feel well (unspecified illness)
2. Nasal congestion (bad cold, sinus, etc.)
3. Cough, sore throat (smoker's cough, dry throat, etc.)
4. Shortness of breath (cutting down on wind, etc.)
5. Poor appetite, loss of weight
6. Other ailments (headaches, nervous condition, nausea, dizziness, etc.)

Advised by doctor

7. Unspecified (ordered by doctor, etc.)
8. Because of specific ailment (heart trouble, palsy, etc.)
9. Doctor said smoking harmful

Future health reasons

10. Smoking is harmful (unspecified)
11. Live longer
12. Fear of cancer (lung cancer, etc.)

Other

13. Sensory dislike (bad taste in mouth, smell, dirty house, etc.)
14. Pressure from close associates (wife, co-worker, etc.)
15. Financial reasons (waste of money, etc.)
16. Test of willpower (to see if could, control life, etc.)
17. Work requirement (smoking not allowed)
18. Quit temporarily (because of operation, illness, Lent, etc., and didn't return to smoking)
19. Other reasons
20. Don't know
21. No answer

The coding scheme represents a balance between too much and too little detail. The classification preserves possibly relevant distinctions such as identifying those who specifically mentioned cancer. The detailed categories are easily collapsed (recoded) when the analysis requires broader groupings. For example, Straits (1967:75) reports that a higher proportion (82 percent) of quitters mentioned current health ailments and/or advice from a doctor than did the unables (60 percent) or smokers (37 percent), who mentioned less immediate health threats or weaker reasons such as "waste of money" or "test of willpower" more frequently.

If anything, the tendency for novice researchers is to use too few categories, which gloss over potentially meaningful differences. Once the data are coded and data analysis is under way, it is easy to combine code categories for purposes of analysis, but it is impossible to recover lost detail. Consider a questionnaire study that needed a count of respondents' siblings: Instead of asking for that number, respondents were asked to list the ages of any brothers and sisters. Now, one could code only the number of siblings. But consider what happens when all the available information is retained—when the age and gender of each sibling are coded and entered separately into the database. Doing this makes it possible, by computer manipulation, not only to count the number of siblings but also to generate measures of number of brothers, sisters, older brothers, younger sisters, respondent's spacing from next sibling, and so on.

Entering the Data

One can think of the data as a matrix or spreadsheet, with observations as rows and variables as columns, which have been entered into a computer file and stored on a disk, tape, CD, or other media.[1] In a data matrix for a survey, the coded responses to each question occupy a designated column in the rows for each respondent. There are several options for data entry. One can enter information from paper-and-pencil surveys into a computer file using data-entry software programmed to detect some kinds of erroneous entries, called computer-assisted data entry. The NELS used this method to enter data obtained from school administrators and school records. An optical scanner or reader is another option. One device reads pencil-marked "bubbles" adjacent to question response categories on survey instruments or on response sheets, such as the answer forms to the SAT, and then enters this information into a computer file. The NELS optically scanned the questionnaire data from students, parents, and teachers. Finally, in computer-assisted surveys, interviewers (CATI and CAPI) or respondents (CASI) simply enter the answers directly into a computer laptop or terminal.

Before the development of CAI and CASI direct data entry, optical scanners, and data entry–monitoring software, clerical staff would enter the data by hand using a computer terminal or keypunch machine. This introduced various errors because entry operators misread edits and codes on the survey forms, skipped over or repeated responses to questions, transposed numbers, and so on. The standard procedure for minimizing such data-entry errors is to enter the information on each survey twice (ideally by a different person each time) and then compare the two entries for errors. When punched cards were the means of recording and storing data, this was done on a machine called a "verifier." Nowadays, two persons can independently enter the data into separate computer files, and a software program then compares the two files for noncomparable entries. The same verification strategy can reduce coding errors if each file is independently coded by a different person.

Cleaning

After the data have been entered into a computer file, the researcher should check them over thoroughly for errors. Detecting and resolving errors in coding and in transmitting the data to the computer is referred to as **data cleaning**. This is an essential process that may also identify respondent-related errors. Researchers who have invested a great deal of time and energy in collecting their data do not want their work undermined by avoidable mistakes made at the stage of data processing because, unlike sampling error and certain kinds of measurement error, data-processing errors *are* avoidable. The way to avoid them is to be exceedingly careful about entering the data and to use every possible method of checking for mistakes. Here are a few ways to clean your data.

First, data entry should be verified whenever feasible. When verification is not possible, as in CAI or CASI direct data entry, the error rate may be minimized by careful training and monitoring of the data-entry persons (interviewers or respondents) and extensive field pretesting of the computer-assisted survey procedure.

Beyond training, monitoring, and verification, two cleaning techniques generally are applied. The first of these is sometimes called **wild-code checking**. Every variable has a specified set of legitimate codes. The aforementioned NELS questions on sport participation, for example, had possible codes of 1 (for "school does not have") to 5 ("participated as a captain/co-captain"); in addition, a code of 6 was used for "multiple response" and 8 for "missing." Wild codes are any codes that are not legitimate. Wild-code checking consists of examining the values recorded for each item to see whether there are any out-of-range codes, such as 7, 9, and 0 for the sport participation questions. Some CAI, CASI, and data-entry software can be programmed to do this kind of cleaning automatically by refusing to accept wild-code values. Alternatively, one can run a frequency distribution for the variable, check to see whether there are any erroneous codes, and then computer search the data file to find the errors. One should keep in mind that wild-code checking does not detect typographical or other errors involving legitimate codes.

Third, most large-scale surveys use a process called **consistency checking**. The idea here is to see whether responses to certain questions are related in reasonable ways to responses to other specific questions. For example, it would be unreasonable, and therefore an indication of coding error, to find a respondent who is married and age 5 or a medical doctor with 3 years of formal schooling.

One common type of consistency checking involves contingency questions. As you may recall from Chapter 10, these are questions designed for a subset of the respondents. The General Social Survey (GSS), for example, first asks people about their employment status last week. If the respondent is working full or part time, he or she is asked the following contingency question: How many hours did you work last week, at all jobs? Consistency checking determines whether a question such as this was answered only by those for whom the question was intended. We would not expect an answer to this question if the respondent was unemployed, retired, or in school. To identify such erroneous responses, one must break down the frequency distribution for the contingency question by pertinent subsamples of the population. One might check to see, for example, whether any of the subsample of nonworking respondents answered the question on number of hours worked last week.

KEY POINT

Most data-processing errors are avoided with computer-assisted interviewing; to eliminate errors with paper survey forms, data entries should be verified and checked for illegitimate (*wild*) codes and for consistency.

Ideally, a suspected error can be resolved by retracing the process from the survey interview through to the dubious data entry. One may resolve errors by examining the original questionnaires or survey schedules, by listening to taped telephone interviews, or by contacting the original respondents. When this is not possible, researchers may flag the dubious entries as suspicious or reclassify them as missing data.

One can get an idea of the importance of editing and data cleaning by considering the measures taken to edit and clean the GSS data before the GSS implemented CAI in 2002 (Davis and Smith, 1992). Before the data were entered, interviewers in the field went over their interview schedules after each interview to check for errors; field supervisors reviewed the first two forms submitted by each interviewer to check for completeness, clarity, and following of proper coding procedures and then checked a sample of forms submitted thereafter; and coders or editors at the National Opinion Research Center's central office carried out various checks and prepared the completed forms for data entry. The latter included coding responses to open-ended questions and other responses that were not precoded (e.g., "not applicable" or "no answer") on the form, attempting to obtain missing data on crucial questions, and selecting random cases for validation checks. The data were entered into the computer with the aid of a data-entry program, which automatically alerted the investigator to wild-code errors at the time of entry. Once data from all of the forms had been entered, data from a proportion of the forms were entered a second time to ensure that data-entry errors were minimal. Next, cleaning programs were run, first to check again for wild-code errors and then to do consistency checking for certain questions. When errors were detected, corrections were made and the cleaning process was "repeated until all questions on all cases come up as 'clean.'" Finally, the coders turned the clean file over to the researchers, who generated frequency distributions for another round of consistency checking.

Data Matrices and Documentation

Once you have entered all the data into a computer file, you are ready to inspect, modify, and analyze them. Before we discuss these steps, however, let us examine the typical form of data storage, the technical terms, and the documentation required to describe a data set. Imagine that you are preparing the data for secondary analysis. What would others need to know to analyze your data? What documentation accompanies the NELS and other processed archived data?

Two types of information are necessary to adequately describe study data: a matrix of variable values or codes for each observation and supporting documentation. The spreadsheet view in Figure 15.1 illustrates a partial **data matrix** of selected variables (columns) for more than 200 countries of the world (rows) gathered from *The World Factbook 2002* and other online sources. The countries are in alphabetical order, and only the first 14 observations (the As) are shown. The number in each cell of the data matrix represents the value of a particular variable (column) for a particular country (row). The first coded cell value of "27.8" indicates that the 2002 population size (first column) of Afghanistan (first row) is estimated as approximately 27,800,000 persons. One can read down a column to inspect the

Country	Population Mid-2002 (millions)	Total Fertility Rate	Life Expectancy at Birth (years)			Percent Urban	Literacy Rate (% ages 15 and above)		
			Total	Male	Female		Total	Male	Female
Afghanistan	27.8	5.7	46.6	47.3	45.9	22	36	51	21
Albania	3.5	2.3	72.1	69.3	75.1	43	93	NA	NA
Algeria	32.3	2.6	70.2	68.9	71.7	58	62	74	49
America Samoa	0.1	3.4	75.5	71.1	80.2	53	97	98	97
Andorra	0.1	1.3	83.5	80.6	86.6	92	100	NA	NA
Angola	10.6	6.4	38.9	37.6	40.2	35	42	56	28
Anguilla	0.01	1.8	76.5	73.6	79.5	100	95	95	95
Antigua, Barbuda	0.1	2.3	71.0	68.7	73.4	37	89	90	88
Argentina	37.8	2.4	75.5	72.1	79.0	88	96	96	96
Armenia	3.3	1.5	66.6	62.3	71.1	67	99	99	98
Aruba	0.1	1.8	78.7	75.3	82.2	51	97	NA	NA
Australia	19.6	1.8	80.0	77.2	83.0	91	100	100	100
Austria	8.2	1.4	78.0	74.8	81.3	67	98	NA	NA
Azerbaijan	7.8	2.3	63.1	58.8	67.5	52	97	99	96

FIGURE 15.1. **Partial data matrix for countries.**

Sources: The World Factbook 2002 (Washington, DC: Central Intelligence Agency, 2003); Population Division of the Department of Economic and Social Affairs of the United Nations, *World Population Prospects: The 2002 Revision* (New York: United Nations, 2003) and *World Urbanization Prospects: The 2001 Revision* (New York, United Nations, 2002).

distribution of values for each variable. The literacy rate in the 14 countries, for example, ranges from 100 percent (Andorra and Australia) to 36 percent (Afghanistan).

The accompanying online documentation explains variable definitions and important data limitations. The total fertility rate (second column), for example, is defined as "a figure for the average number of children that would be born per woman if all women lived to the end of their childbearing years and bore children according to [current birth rates] at each age" (*World Factbook 2002*). Thus, if Angola's 2002 age-specific birth rates do not change over time, women will average 6.4 children during their lifetime. Andorra and Austria, in contrast, currently have very low fertility rates. Perusal of the data for the first 14 countries suggests research questions for exploring the full data set: Do high-fertility countries tend to have low female literacy? Is there a positive relationship between country literacy levels and life expectancy at birth? Do more urbanized countries have lower birth rates?

Before one tests hypotheses, however, it is important to carefully examine the documentation ("the fine print") for data inconsistencies and other limitations. Although the *World Factbook 2002* is based on information available on January 1, 2002, some of the data were collected much earlier in time. The literacy rate for Algerian females, for example, is based on a 1995 estimate. In addition to data-collection dates, variable definitions may vary by country. The *Factbook* reports that there "are no universal definitions and standards of literacy. Unless otherwise specified, all rates are based on the most common definition— the ability to read and write at a specified age." For the first 14 countries the specific age was 15, except for Albania (age 9) and Anguilla (age 12). Finally, invariably some of the information is unavailable (missing). For the country data, the missing cells are coded NA (not available) in Figure 15.1.

Figure 15.2 presents a partial data matrix for 10 of the 12,578 NELS student respondents in Broh's study. The rows represent respondents, who are identified by unique ID codes (first column). The remaining columns represent variables, whose names may identify time frames (e.g., "by" = base year) and question numbers (e.g., "36a" = question 36a) or abbreviated variable names (e.g., "pared" = parental education). Numerical codes in the matrix cells identify question responses or summary variable categories. For respondent's sex (fifth column), recall that a code of 1 was used for males and 2 for females. Thus, the first two listed respondents are males, and the next two are females. For race, a code of 1 was used for "Asian or Pacific Islander," 2 for "Hispanic, regardless of race," 3 for "black, not of Hispanic origin," 4 for "white, not of Hispanic origin," 5 for "American Indian or Alaskan Native," and 8 for "missing" (no answer or multiple-race categories were chosen by the respondents). Although Figure 15.2 lists only whites (sixth column), about a third of the students were members of the other race–ethnicity categories.

Once study results are entered into a data matrix or equivalent computer-readable format, the researcher should prepare the **codebook** documentation. A codebook is like a dictionary in that it defines the meaning of the numerical codes for each named variable, such as the NELS codes for sex and race. Codebooks also may contain question wording, interviewer directions, and coding and editing decision rules, such as how to handle two answers circled to a single-response question. Originally, survey codebooks were single physical documents, but now this information may be scattered across various sources and media. In addition to an electronic codebook accompanying NELS data sets, numerous technical and methodological reports are available online from the National Center for Education Statistics (http://nces.ed.gov/surveys/NELS88/). The NELS electronic codebook reports, for example, that sex was coded from the "Your Background" section of the base-year student questionnaire or, when unavailable from this source, from school rosters. If sex was missing from both the student questionnaire and the school roster, it was imputed from the student's name if it could be done unambiguously. Extremely complex coding rules are given for parental education (seventh column of Figure 15.2) and family composition

Id	bys36a	bys36b	bys36c	sex	race	bypared	byfcomp
124902	3	2	2	1	4	3	1
124915	3	2	2	1	4	3	1
124916	2	3	3	2	4	3	1
124932	2	3	3	2	4	3	1
124939	3	2	2	1	4	3	4
124944	3	3	3	2	4	2	1
124947	2	3	2	2	4	2	1
124966	3	3	3	2	4	3	1
124968	3	3	3	1	4	3	1
124970	1	2	3	1	4	4	1

FIGURE 15.2. Partial data matrix for NELS:88.

(eighth column), which are composite variables based on relevant responses from student and parent questionnaires.

When variables are coded directly from a questionnaire, the codebook entries look very much like the survey instrument with the addition of response and nonresponse codes. The entry for Broh's parent–child social capital variables (columns 2–4 of Figure 15.2) includes the following:

36. Since the beginning of the school year, how often have you discussed the following with either or both of your parents or guardians?

{bys36a} Selecting courses or programs at school
{bys36b} School activities or events of particular interest to you
{bys36c} Things you studied in class

Code	Label
1	NOT AT ALL
2	ONCE OR TWICE
3	THREE OR MORE TIMES
6	{MULTIPLE RESPONSE}
8	{MISSING}

A code of 6 indicates students who marked more than one response on the optical scan questionnaire. If they failed to respond at all, a code of 8 was used to indicate missing information. In many surveys, missing data for a variable are divided into three categories of those who "don't know" (DK), who provide "no answer" (NA), or for whom the question is not applicable (NAP or IAP).

An excellent online site for viewing codebook documentation for the GSS is maintained by the National Opinion Research Center (http://gss.norc.org/Get-Documentation). The GSS, which we described in Chapter 9, consists of interviews administered to national samples using a standard interview schedule. Among the items covered are (1) requests for standard background information on gender, race, occupation, religion, and so on; (2) questions about the quality of the respondent's life in various areas (e.g., health, family, social relations); (3) requests for evaluations of government programs; and (4) questions covering opinions and attitudes about a wide range of issues, such as drug usage, abortion, religious freedom, and racial equality. The online codebook contains information for each question, including wording, response codes, and frequency distributions for each year in which the question was included, and numerous appendices with information about sampling design and weighting, coding instructions, recodes, and so forth.

The Functions of Statistics in Social Research

Starting with a cleaned data set, the next analysis step is to inspect the data to decide on subsequent statistical analyses. But how do you decide what kind of analysis to do? Naturally, that decision depends on what you want to know. Broh wanted to know whether playing interscholastic sports (the independent variable) promotes academic achievement (the dependent variable). To establish a causal relation such as this, she would need to show that the two variables are associated (that changes in one variable accompany changes in the other), that the direction of influence is from the independent variable to the dependent variable, and that the association between the variables is nonspurious. To begin her analysis, Broh could have examined the NELS data respondent by respondent to see whether playing interscholastic sports was associated with academic achievement. But with more than 12,000 respondents, this task would be incredibly tedious and probably not very reliable. Therefore, what she needed was a fast and efficient means of summarizing the association between these variables for the entire sample of respondents. This is precisely where statistics (and computers) enters in. A *statistic* is a summary statement about a set of data; statistics as a discipline provides techniques for organizing and analyzing data.

Traditionally, statistics has been divided according to two functions—descriptive and inferential. **Descriptive statistics** is concerned with organizing and summarizing the data at hand to make them more intelligible. The high and low scores and average score on an exam are descriptive statistics that readily summarize a class's performance. Broh needed a descriptive statistic that would summarize the degree of association between playing interscholastic sports and academic achievement in the NELS sample. **Inferential statistics** deals with the kinds of inferences that can be made when generalizing from data, as from sample data to the entire population. Broh needed this form of analysis as a means of determining what the NELS sample of observations indicated about the effects of playing interscholastic sports on academic achievement in the target population of American secondary students.

Based on probability theory, inferential statistics may be used for two distinct purposes: to estimate population characteristics from sample data (discussed in Chapter 6) and to test hypotheses.[2] Traditionally, hypothesis testing is employed to rule out the rival explanation that observed data patterns, relationships, or differences are due to chance processes arising from random assignment (in the case of experiments), sampling error (in the case of probability sampling), random measurement error, or other sources.[3] In experiments, such testing determines whether the differences between experimental conditions are "statistically significant"—that is, not attributable to random assignment. In surveys with probability sampling, significance tests determine whether sample results may be generalized to a specified population. The appropriate role of significance tests is a long-standing controversy (see Morrison and Henkel, 1970; Hagen, 1997; Harlow, Mulaik, and Steiger, 1997). Following David Gold's argument (1969) regarding nonexperimental data that results that easily could have occurred by a chance process should not be taken seriously, we view tests of significance as an effective means of screening out trivialities and chance mishaps.

Inspecting and Modifying the Data

At this stage, a researcher is ready to give the computer instructions for inspecting and transforming the data.[4] Some of these operations may occur during earlier data-cleaning and coding processes. The goal of inspection is to get a clear picture of the data by examining one variable at a time. The data "pictures" generated by **univariate analysis** come in various forms—tables, graphs, charts, and statistical measures. The nature of the techniques depends on whether one is analyzing variables measured at the nominal/ordinal level or variables measured at the interval/ratio level (discussed in Chapter 5). Following data inspection, a researcher may want to change one or more variable codes, rearrange the numerical order of variable codes, collapse variable categories, impute estimated values for missing data, add together the codes for several variables to create an index or scale, and otherwise modify the data for analysis.

Nominal- and Ordinal-Scale Variables

Broh might have done univariate analyses simply to get a sense of the nature of the variation in the variables to be analyzed. It is generally a good idea, for example, to see whether there is sufficient variation in responses to warrant including the variable in the analysis. As a rule, the less variation, the more difficult it is to detect how differences in one variable are related to differences in another variable. To take the extreme case, if all students scored the same on self-esteem, then it would be impossible to determine how *differences* in this variable were related to differences in academic achievement. Fortunately, there was sufficient variation in Broh's main independent variable as nearly a third of the students reported participating in interscholastic sports during both the 10th and the 12th grades.

A core GSS question asks, "Generally speaking, would you say that most people can be trusted or that you can't be too careful in dealing with people?" Suppose that we wanted to inspect the responses to this question in the 2014 GSS. One means is to organize responses into a table called a **frequency distribution**. A frequency distribution is created by first listing all the response categories and then adding up the number of cases that occur in each category. If we instruct the computer to do this, our output might look like that in Table 15.1, which gives the 2014 distribution of responses to the trust question. This presents a clearer picture than does a case-by-case listing of responses. However, this sort of table generally would serve as a preliminary organization of the data because more readable formats can be derived from it. In particular, researchers often compute the percentage of respondents in each category. To see how this might create a still clearer picture, examine the raw figures in Table 15.1.

TABLE 15.1. **Frequency Distribution of Trust in People,* 2014 General Social Survey**

Code	Label	Frequency
1	Most people can be trusted	519
2	Can't be too careful	1076
3	Depends (volunteered)	88
7	Don't know	3
8	No answer	1
9	Not applicable	851
Total		2538

*Question: "Generally speaking, would you say that most people can be trusted or that you can't be too careful in dealing with people?"

Note that the number of "most people can be trusted" responses in the sample is 519. This number by itself is meaningless unless we provide a standard or reference point with which to interpret it. More than likely as you peruse Table 15.1 you will see the figures in relation to one another, invoking implicit points of comparison. You may note, for example, that there are more "can't be too careful" than "most people can be trusted" answers or that 88 respondents volunteered a qualified response ("it depends"). **Percentage distributions** provide an explicit comparative framework for interpreting distributions. They tell you the size of a category relative to the size of the sample. To create a percentage distribution, you divide the number of cases in each category by the total number of cases and multiply by 100. This is what we have done in Table 15.2. Now you can see more clearly the relative difference in responses. Now we see, for example, that a little more than 5 percent of the respondents volunteered a qualified response.

It should be noted that the percentages in Table 15.2 are based on the total number of responses, excluding "missing data"—those in the "no answer" and "not applicable" categories. About one-third (851) of the respondents were in a random subsample that were not asked the trust question, and one other (the "no answer") either was not asked the question (interviewer error) or did not respond. Since these are not meaningful variable categories (i.e., they say nothing about trust in people), it would be misleading to include them in the percentage distribution. The total number of missing responses is important information. If this information is not placed in the main body of a table, then it at least should be reported in a footnote to the relevant table or in the text of the research report. Also note that the base on which percentages are computed (1686) is given in parentheses below the percentage total of 100 percent. It is customary to indicate in tables the total number of observations from which the statistics are computed. This information may be found elsewhere—at the end of the table title or in a headnote or footnote to the table; often it is signified with the letter *N*.

Univariate analysis is seldom conducted as an end in itself, especially in explanatory research. One important function mentioned earlier is to determine how to collapse or recode categories for further analysis. For the trust in people variable, one might limit the analysis to those who directly answered the question (codes 1 and 2 in Table 15.1), but this would result in the loss of 91 "depends" and "don't know" responses that then would be recoded as missing for analysis purposes. Instead, one might retain the "depends"

TABLE 15.2. **Percentage Distribution of Trust in People for the Distribution in Table 15.1**

Response	%
Most people can be trusted	30.8
Can't be too careful	63.8
Depends (volunteered)	5.2
Don't know	0.2
Total	100.0
(Number of responses)	(1686)
(Missing data)	(852)

and "don't know" responses by recoding them as middle responses in a three-category ordinal scale:

1 Most people can be trusted
2 Depends, Don't know
3 Can't be too careful

Alternatively, one could collapse the responses into a dichotomy by comparing either of the extreme categories with all others. Respondents definitely expressing low trust in people, for example, could be contrasted with the less pessimistic or uncertain responses:

1 Can't be too careful
2 Depends, Don't know, Most people can be trusted

Either of the above recodes achieves the practical objective of minimizing the missing observations. The choice of one of these, or an alternative recoding, should be guided primarily by theoretical considerations.

A univariate inspection also can inform decisions about how to collapse the categories of a variable for further analysis. Collapsing decisions may be based on theoretical criteria and/or may hinge on the empirical variation in responses. Thus, years of education might be collapsed into "theoretically" meaningful categories (grade 8 or lower, some high school, high school graduate, some college, college graduate) on the basis of the years of schooling deemed appropriate over time in the United States for leaving school and qualifying for certain occupations. Alternatively, one might collapse categories according to how many respondents fall into each category. If the sample contains only a handful of respondents with less than a college education, these respondents may be placed in one category for purposes of analysis.

In the absence of theoretical criteria for collapsing, the best strategy is to try to obtain an approximately equal proportion of cases in each category. If the distribution is to be dichotomized, this would mean a 50:50 split. Achieving such a split for a nominal variable is a matter of combining conceptually similar categories. For example, if we wanted to compare students with different majors on some relevant variable and we found that 50 percent majored in mathematics or natural science, 30 percent in sociology, and 20 percent in psychology, then we might combine the latter two categories. At the ordinal, interval, and ratio levels, a variable is typically collapsed into about five to eight categories to preserve essential information from the original distribution.

KEY POINT

A *frequency distribution* can indicate whether there is enough variation to include a variable in the analysis and how to recode or collapse categories for further analysis.

Information is invariably lost when the original categories of a variable are collapsed. Ideally, the information lost should not be pertinent to the intended research. For example, respondents with 9, 10, or 11 years of education may be viewed as essentially equivalent ("some high school") in studying occupational attainment. But for other purposes, such as health conditions and practices, collapsing education into a few categories would result in a serious loss of vital information.

Interval- and Ratio-Scale Variables

Creating frequency or percentage distributions is about as far as the univariate analysis of nominal- and ordinal-scale variables usually goes. However, data on interval and ratio variables may be summarized not only in tables (or graphs) but also in terms of various statistics. Consider a core GSS question measuring television viewing, which asks respondents, "On the average day, about how many hours do you personally watch television?" Since respondents' answers were recorded in number of hours (the range was 0–24), this variable may be considered a ratio-scale measure. We could get a picture of the number of hours watched, as we did with the trust in people variable, by generating a distribution of the responses. Table 15.3 presents a computer-like output for this variable for the 2014 GSS. Although it is not a problem here, the relatively large number of values for most interval

TABLE 15.3. **Number of Hours of Television Watched on Average Day, 2014 General Social Survey**

Code	Label	Frequency	Percentage
00	0 HOURS	120	7.2
01	1 HOURS	310	18.6
02	2 HOURS	437	26.2
03	3 HOURS	293	17.6
04	4 HOURS	227	13.6
05	5 HOURS	113	6.8
06	6 HOURS	75	4.5
07	7 HOURS	11	.7
08	8 HOURS	37	2.2
09	9 HOURS	1	.1
10	10 HOURS	17	1.0
12	12 HOURS	14	.8
14	14 HOURS	2	.1
16	16 HOURS	3	.2
17	17 HOURS	1	.1
18	18 HOURS	1	.1
20	20 HOURS	2	.1
24	24 HOURS	5	.3
98	DON'T KNOW	6	MISSING
99	NOT APPLICABLE	863	MISSING
TOTAL		2538	100.0
(VALID CASES) (1669)		(MISSING CASES)	(6)

and ratio variables makes it necessary to collapse categories to get a compact, readable table. Had we generated the distribution for the variable of age, for example, we would have had so many values—more than 70—that they might not have fit on a single page of computer output. In this case, we might lump together respondents according to the first age digit— those under 20, between 20 and 29, 30 and 39, and so on.

Note that Table 15.3 presents two kinds of distributions: frequency and percentage. Can you tell from the table what percentage of respondents report that they do not watch any television at all on the average day? We also could get a picture of a distribution by looking at its various statistical properties. Three properties may be examined. The first consists of measures of central tendency—the mean, median, and mode. These indicate various "averages" or points of concentration in a set of values. The **mean** is the arithmetical average, calculated by adding up all of the responses and dividing by the total number of respondents. It is the "balancing" point in a distribution because the sum of the differences of all values from the mean is exactly equal to zero. The **median** is the midpoint in a distribution—the value of the middle response; half of the responses are above it and half are below. You find the median by ordering the values from low to high and then counting up until you find the middle value. The **mode** is the value or category with the highest frequency. The modal value in Table 15.3 is 2 hours. By comparison, the mean is 2.98 hours and the median is 2.93 hours.

A second property that we can summarize statistically is the degree of variability or dispersion among a set of values. The simplest dispersion measure is the **range**. Statistically, this is the difference between the lowest and highest values, but it is usually reported by identifying these end points, such as "the number of hours of television watched ranged from 0 to 24 hours." Of several other measures of dispersion, the most commonly reported is the **standard deviation**. As we saw in Chapter 6, this is a measure of the "average" spread of observations around the mean. One of its important uses in statistics involves the calculation of "standard scores." A standard score is calculated by dividing the standard deviation into the difference between a given value and the mean of the distribution. This converts the value from a "nonstandard" measurement (e.g., hours, years) specific to the variable and sample to a "standardized" measure expressed in terms of standard deviations from the mean. Similar in some ways to "percentaging" a table, standardizing provides a reference point for comparing individual responses in the same or different distributions.

With respect to the variable of television viewing, the standard deviation is perhaps best interpreted as an index of heterogeneity, which could be used to compare the degree of variability in hours watched among different subsamples or in samples from different populations. The standard deviation of the foregoing distribution of all GSS respondents is 2.59. Among respondents with less than a high school education, the standard deviation in hours watched is 2.87, revealing more variability in this group than among those respondents with a graduate degree, for whom the standard deviation is 1.35. As a further example, the ages of GSS respondents in 2014 range from 18 to 89, with a standard deviation of 17.41 years. By comparison, the standard deviation for age in a sample of college undergraduates would be around 1.5 years.

A third statistical property of univariate distributions is their shape. This property is most readily apparent from a graphic presentation called a **frequency** or **percentage polygon**. Figure 15.3 presents the percentage polygon for the data in Table 15.3. The figure reveals that the distribution has a single high point (or mode), with the data lopsided or "skewed" mostly to the right (or positive side) of this point. This shape also is typical of income distributions. Many variables in social research have "bell-shape" distributions, so called because they form the general shape of a bell. In a bell-shape distribution, the three measures of central tendency are identical, whereas in a positively skewed distribution like Figure 15.3 the mode has the lowest value (2), followed by the median and then the mean. One particular type of bell-shape distribution, called the **normal distribution**, describes the shape of many variables and statistics, such as the sampling distribution of the mean. The normal distribution is an important concept in inferential statistics.

Collectively, these three statistical properties—central tendency, dispersion, and shape—provide such a good picture of quantitative data that they often obviate the need for tabular presentations. Many investigators, in fact, describe their data simply in terms of a mean or median, an index of dispersion, and occasionally the overall form (for which there are also statistical indices). Other researchers prefer to be as "close" as possible to the data and use various graphical procedures to inspect the data for unexpected patterns and other anomalies (see Box 15.2). If a researcher, for example, computes only the mean and standard deviation of reported television viewing and fails to inspect the entire distribution (Table 15.3), he or she would miss the exaggerated report of 24-hour and possibly 16- to 20-hour daily television watching. It is important to spot extreme values or **outliers** as they can adversely affect some statistical procedures and may have to be excluded from the data analysis.

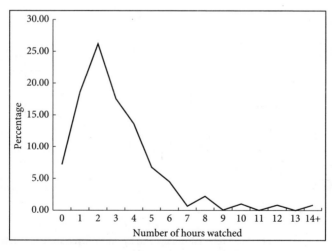

FIGURE 15.3. Percentage polygon for the distribution in Table 15.3.

BOX 15.2 Television Viewing and Labor Force Status: An Example of Graphing Data

Graphic procedures for data analysis (Cleveland, 1985:1), when implemented in computer software, offer an attractive alternative to strictly numerical analysis of data. One useful tool is the *box-and-whisker* or *box plot* (Tukey, 1977:39–41). Figure A presents box plots that summarize television viewing reported by the 1985 GSS female respondents grouped according to their current labor force status. (The computer program Stata produced these examples.)

The box plots aptly display key aspects of each frequency distribution. The top and bottom of each box indicates, respectively, the 75th and 25th percentiles of television viewing, and the crossbar within each box shows the median (50th percentile). The height of a box is one measure of dispersion, showing the spread of television viewing among the middle 50 percent of the respondents (e.g., 1–3 hours for full-time female workers). An off-center position of the crossbar (median) within the box reflects skewness in the central 50 percent of the distribution (e.g., positive skewness for part-time workers). The width of each box is proportional to the number of respondents; this serves to flag patterns in the data that must be ignored or cautiously interpreted because of small sample sizes (e.g., the unemployed).

The vertical lines (or "whiskers") extending above and below each box include all but the most extreme data values, which are plotted separately as circles.* The whiskers serve to fence out stray values, which are possibly *outliers* requiring special attention. Sometimes outliers result from measurement error, which seems likely here for the full-time worker who watches television 20 hours a day. Conversely, the reports of watching television 8 hours daily by a few full-time workers are not overly suspicious. Extreme outliers are usually excluded from the

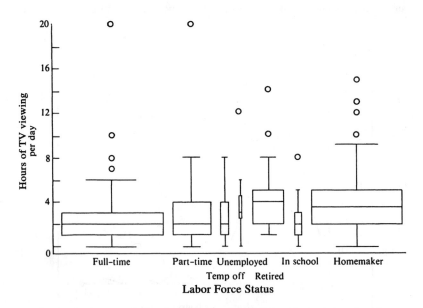

FIGURE A. **Average daily television viewing by labor force status, female, 1985 General Social Survey.**

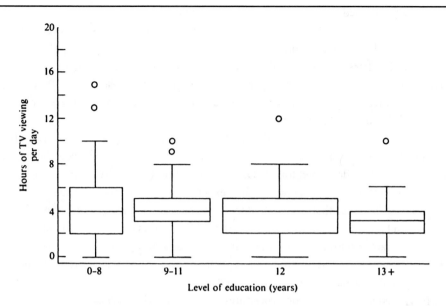

FIGURE B. **Average daily television viewing by education, female homemakers, 1985 General Social Survey.**

data analysis (especially if measurement error is suspected) or analyzed separately from the main data since some statistical procedures may be adversely affected by a few unusual values.

Now you should be able to interpret the box plots in Figure A. Which groups report the lowest median television viewing? Which has the lowest variation (dispersion) in viewing habits? How do retired individuals differ from those keeping house?

Box plots are one of a set of tools designed for exploratory data analysis, which has applications ranging from preparing data for testing prior hypotheses to dredging data for theoretically unexpected patterns. Because of their exploratory purpose, these techniques are relatively resistant to outliers and other data anomalies. And with an appropriate computer program it is easy to explore a data domain. When you studied the box plots in Figure A for example, you may have wondered about the large variation in television viewing among women working at home. Perhaps the viewing differences among the homemakers reflect, in part, educational differences. This hunch is easily checked by requesting the computer program to draw box plots for various educational groups (8 years or fewer of completed schooling, 9–11, 12, and 13 years or more), which is shown in Figure B. What do these box plots show?

*Each whisker extends 1.5 times the height of the box or to the most extreme value if that distance is shorter.

KEY POINT

The distributions of interval/ratio variables can be described in terms of their central tendency, variation, and shape.

One important function of data inspection is to determine the prevalence of missing values. The simplest way to handle cases with missing values, which we did in percentaging Table 15.2, is to remove them from the statistical calculations. This method, called **listwise**

deletion, often is used when there are relatively few missing cases. Excluding cases with missing data on *any* of the variables in a planned multivariate analysis, however, can lead to a much smaller, biased sample that is unrepresentative of the target population. Paul Allison (2002) relates a hypothetical illustration of a sample of 1000 that shrinks to only 360 respondents after excluding the 5 percent of missing values on each of the 20 variables.[5] Consequently, researchers typically use various ad hoc or formal procedures for replacing or otherwise handling missing data.

When missing data result from the respondents' uncertainty ("don't know") or refusal to answer the question ("no answer"), a recoding operation may eliminate the missing values, as previously described for the GSS trust question. Alternatively, researchers with in-depth knowledge of the data may use their expertise to replace missing values with "educated guesses." Suppose that one wanted to study the male literacy rates for the countries illustrated in Figure 15.1. One might replace the missing values for males with the country's total literacy rate or with a corresponding male rate for a similar, neighboring country. In like manner, other responses within a survey interview, or from a similar respondent, may be used on an ad hoc basis to replace missing data.

In addition to these ad hoc procedures, formal statistical solutions, called **imputation**, have been devised to replace missing values with a typical value calculated from the available ("nonmissing") data. Broh simply replaced her NELS missing values with variable sample means. According to Allison (2002), however, this method often produces biased statistics and generally should be avoided. Consider, for example, replacing missing data on respondents' ages with the sample mean for the available data. Although the replacements will not change the calculated mean age, they will bias downward the estimated standard deviation because all imputed values are zero distance from the mean. The most sophisticated imputation procedures for handling missing data predict missing values from the known values of other variables. These computer-intensive methods, which are beyond the scope of this textbook, are difficult to learn and implement and are underutilized in survey research; nonetheless, they offer the best solutions for the missing data problem.

Another important function of data modification is to reduce data complexity by combining variables into indexes, scales, or other composite measures. We discussed this process in relation to both measurement and the use of multiple methods in earlier chapters. The simplest composite measure would consist of combining two "yes/no" questions. This would produce four distinct response categories: (1) yes, yes; (2) yes, no; (3) no, yes; and (4) no, no. An index based on the number of yes responses reduces the category total from 4 to 3 (0, 1, or 2 yes's). Similarly, the 16 possible response patterns for four yes/no questions reduces to 5 by indexing the affirmative responses (0, 1, 2, 3, or 4 yes's). Paul Lazarsfeld (1972) describes this data-reduction approach as "arbitrary numerical" because formerly distinct categories (e.g., "yes, no" and "no, yes") are combined.

Beckett Broh used this approach to create measures of several concepts. For example, she measured social capital between students and parents by combining responses to three questions (see p. 500), which asked how frequently students talked with their parents about course selection, school activities, and studies. Possible responses included "not at all," "once or twice," and "three or more times," which she coded as 0, 1, and 2, respectively.

Thus, when these questions were summed, the composite measure of "student–parent talk" had a possible range of 0 to 6.

Finally, the assignment of numerical values to the categories of nominal-scale variables may be used to transform them into ordinal or interval scales for some purposes. In the GSS, for example, the occupations of respondents and their relatives (mother, father, spouse) are coded into 503 U.S. Census occupational categories. Numerical values representing occupational characteristics, such as prestige ratings or gender composition, may be used to convert the 503 nominal categories into simpler, continuous variables for studying, say, occupational mobility or gender segregation. Each coded occupation in the GSS is assigned a prestige score, which ranges from 86 (physicians) to 17 (miscellaneous food preparation occupations).[6] Occupational complexity is substantially reduced as formerly distinct occupations receive the same prestige ratings, such as prestige scores of 73 (architects, chemical engineers, and chemists), 49 (funeral directors, real estate sales occupations), and 22 (messengers, janitors and cleaners, hand packers and packagers). Similarly, the percentage female in each census occupational category may be used to transform the 503 categories into a continuum ranging from about 2 percent (e.g., mechanical engineers) to 96 percent (kindergarten teachers) for studying gender-based occupational segregation (Straits, 1998).

Preliminary Hypothesis Testing

Following data inspection and necessary modifications, researchers turn to empirical testing of bivariate relationships. The object of **bivariate analysis** is to assess the relationship between two variables, such as that between extracurricular involvement and academic performance. In general, this amounts to determining, first, whether the relationship is likely to exist (or whether it might be a product of random error) and, second, how much effect or influence one variable has on the other. As with univariate analysis, the way in which this is done depends on the level of measurement.

Nominal- and Ordinal-Scale Variables

When the variables analyzed have only a few categories, as in most nominal- and ordinal-scale measurement, bivariate data are presented in tables. The tables constructed are known as cross-tabulations, cross-classifications, or contingency tables. A cross-tabulation requires a table with rows representing the categories of one variable and columns representing the categories of another. When a dependent variable can be identified, it is customary to make this the row variable and to treat the independent variable as the column variable, although this arbitrary convention is often broken for formatting considerations.

Let us first consider the cross-tabulation of the two nominal-scale variables from the 2014 GSS shown in Table 15.4. The row variable consists of "attitude toward capital punishment" or, more precisely, whether the respondent favors or opposes the death penalty for persons convicted of murder. The column variable is "sex," male or female. Sex is the independent variable simply because, in one's lifetime, one's sex is determined earlier than one's attitude toward capital punishment. What sort of information does Table 15.4 convey?

TABLE 15.4. Attitude toward Capital Punishment
by Sex, 2014 General Social Survey

Attitude toward capital punishment*	Sex		
	MALE	FEMALE	TOTAL
Favor	752	778	1530
Oppose	338	511	849
Total	1090	1289	2379

*Question: "Do you favor or oppose the death penalty for persons convicted of murder?"

First, note that the last column and the bottom row, each labeled "Total," show the total number of respondents with each single characteristic, for example, 1090 men. Because these four numbers (1530, 849, 1090, 1289) are along the right side and the bottom margin of the table, they are called **marginal frequencies**, or *marginals*. The row marginals (1530, 849) are the univariate frequency distribution for the variable "attitude toward capital punishment"; the column marginals (1090, 1289) are the univariate frequency distribution for the variable "sex." Also, the number at the lower right-hand corner (2379) is N, the total sample size excluding missing cases. N equals either the sum of the row or column marginals or the sum of the four numbers (752 + 778 + 338 + 511) in the body of Table 15.4.

The body of Table 15.4 where the categories of the two variables intersect contains the bivariate frequency distribution. Each intersection is called a *cell* and the number in each cell is called a **cell frequency**. Cell frequencies in a *bi*variate table indicate the numbers of cases with each possible combination of *two* characteristics; for example, there were 752 *males* who *favored capital punishment*. Because Table 15.4 has two rows and two columns, it is referred to as a *2 × 2 table*.

Now that we know the meaning of the numbers in a cross-tabulation, how do we analyze these numbers to assess the relationship between the variables? What comparisons should we make? With sex as the independent variable in Table 15.4, the relevant substantive questions are as follows: Does sex influence attitude toward capital punishment? If so, how much influence does it have? If a relationship exists, then a change in sex should produce a change of "favor"/"oppose" responses in the distribution on the dependent variable. Either males will be more likely to favor and less likely to oppose than females or females will be more likely to favor and less likely to oppose than males. Note, however, that when we compare cell frequencies there are more females than males who both favor (778 versus 752) and oppose (511 versus 338).

Obviously, there is a problem here. Although we are comparing the proper cells, the comparison is invalid because the cell frequencies for males and females are based on different total frequencies. To be valid, the cell numbers compared must be expressed as parts of the same total. This is accomplished by creating separate percentage distributions for males and females, thereby converting each total to 100 percent. The result is a bivariate percentage distribution, presented as Table 15.5. Now when we compare responses across sex, we see clearly that males are more likely to favor capital punishment by a percentage of 69.0 to 60.4 and, conversely, less likely to oppose (31.0 percent to 39.6 percent).

TABLE 15.5. Attitude toward
Capital Punishment by Sex (%),
2014 General Social Survey

Attitude toward capital punishment	Sex	
	MALE	FEMALE
Favor	69.0%	60.4%
Oppose	31.0	39.6
Total	100.0%	100.0%
(N)	(1090)	(1289)

A bivariate percentage distribution enables one to compare the distribution of one variable across the categories of the other. In Table 15.5, we created such a distribution by percentaging *down* so that the column totals, corresponding to the categories of the independent variable, equaled 100 percent. The rule that we followed in deriving Table 15.5 is to *compute percentages in the direction of the independent variable* (i.e., based on the categories of the independent variable). If sex had been the row variable and attitude toward capital punishment the column variable, we would have run the percentages in the other direction—across rather than down. To interpret the relationship in Table 15.5, we compared percentages by reading *across* the table. In so doing, we followed a second rule: *Make comparisons in the opposite direction from the way percentages are run.* Having percentaged down, we compared across; had we percentaged across, we would have compared down.

These are extremely important rules to follow, because cross-tabulations may be percentaged in either direction and are easily misinterpreted.[7]

KEY POINT

The rule for interpreting a cross-tabulation is to compare percentages across the variable categories on which the percentages are based; therefore, percentage across, read down or, conversely, percentage down, read across.

Broh might have done bivariate analyses to see whether there were sex differences on her key variables. Table 15.6 presents the percentage distribution of student reports of school discussions with their parents by sex.[8] What does this table reveal about the relationship between these variables? It clearly shows that in this sample of students females report more school discussions with their parents than do males. But does this necessarily mean that the relationship holds for the population from which the sample was drawn?

As you read across Table 15.6, you see that there is a small difference of 9.9 (46.4 − 36.5) in the percentage of females as opposed to males who report three or more school discussions with their parents. This "percentage difference" indicates that a relationship exists for these data; if there were no difference between the percentages, we would conclude that no relationship exists. Remember, however, that these are *sample* data. The important question is not whether a relationship exists in these data; rather, do the observed cell frequencies reveal a true relationship between the variables in the *population*, or are they simply the result of sampling and other random error?

TABLE 15.6. **Discuss Programs at School* with Parents by Sex (%), NELS:88 Base Year**

Discuss selecting courses or programs at school with parents	Sex	
	MALE	FEMALE
Not at all	14.8%	8.7%
Once or twice	48.7	44.9
Three or more times	36.5	46.4
Total	100.0%	100.0%
(N)	(5661)	(5819)

*Question 36a: "Since the beginning of the school year, how often have you discussed the following with either or both of your parents or guardians?—Selecting courses or programs at school."

To determine whether a relationship exists or whether it is due to chance factors, researchers use *tests of statistical significance*. For cross-tabulations, the most commonly used statistic is the **chi-square** (or χ^2) **test for independence**. The chi-square test is based on a comparison of the observed cell frequencies with the cell frequencies one would expect if there were no relationship between the variables. Table 15.7 shows the expected cell frequencies, assuming no relationship, and the derived bivariate percentage distribution. Note that the cell percentages in Table 15.7 (reading across) are the same as the marginals; this indicates that knowing whether a respondent is male or female is of no help in predicting school discussions with parents, precisely the meaning of "no relationship" between variables. The larger the differences between the actual cell frequencies and those expected assuming no relationship, the larger the value of chi-square and the more likely that the relationship exists in the population. Chi-square values for the data in Tables 15.5 (19.18) and 15.6 (167.78) are both statistically significant at $p < .001$. This suggests that in the American population, females are less likely than males to favor capital punishment (Table 15.5) and high school girls are more likely than high school boys to discuss school courses or programs with their parents (Table 15.6).

Knowing that these relationships exist in the population, however, does not tell us how much effect the independent variable has on the dependent variable. It is possible for a relationship to exist when changes in one variable correspond only slightly to changes in the other. The degree of this correspondence is a second measurable property of bivariate

TABLE 15.7. **Discuss Programs at School with Parents by Sex, Assuming No Relationship**

Discuss selecting courses or programs at school with parents	Frequencies			Percentages		
	MALE	FEMALE	TOTAL	MALE	FEMALE	TOTAL
Not at all	663	682	1345	11.7%	11.7%	11.7%
Once or twice	2647	2720	5367	46.8	46.8	46.8
Three or more times	2351	2417	4768	41.5	41.5	41.5
Total	5661	5819	11,480	100.0%	100.0%	100.0%
(N)				(5661)	(5819)	(11,480)

distributions. In a 2 × 2 table, the percentage difference provides one indicator, albeit a poor one, of the strength of the relationship: The larger the difference, the stronger the relationship. However, researchers prefer to use one of several other statistics to measure the size of this effect. These **measures of association** are standardized to vary between 0 (no association) and plus or minus 1.0 (perfect association). One such measure, commonly used for 2 × 2 tables, is *phi*, which equals .09 for the data in Table 15.4. Although the choice of labels is somewhat arbitrary, the magnitude of phi suggests a "low" association between sex and attitude toward capital punishment (see Davis, 1971:49).

A third property—the direction of the relationship—may be measured when the categories of both variables can be ordered, that is, when both have at least ordinal-level measurement. *Direction* refers to the tendency for increases in the values of one variable to be associated with systematic increases or decreases in the values of another variable. Both variables may change in the same direction (a positive relationship) or in opposite directions (a negative relationship). In a positive relationship, lower values of one variable tend to be associated with lower values of the other variable, and higher values of one variable tend to go along with higher values of the other. The categories of the variables of education and income, for example, can be ordered from low to high. When we examine the association between these variables we expect it to be positive, with less educated persons tending to have lower incomes and persons of higher education tending to have higher incomes.

Table 15.8 shows a positive relationship between two 2014 GSS ordinal variables, level of education (highest degree obtained) and self-reported happiness. Carefully examine Table 15.8 before reading further. We will consider happiness and highest degree dependent and independent variables, respectively, since educational attainment occurs earlier in time and is a much more permanent condition than the expression of happiness given during the interview. Note that, as in the previous examples, Table 15.8 is percentaged down for each category of the independent variable, highest degree; thus, comparisons should be made across. The percentage of persons "not too happy" (first row) generally falls with increasing education: 24.8 to 14.5 to 10.8 to 7.5 to 7.5 percent. Similarly, the percentage claiming that they are "very happy" (third row) generally rises as educational attainment increases: 26.4 to 27.8 to 31.4 to 38.8 to 38.1 percent. It is this sort of pattern (greater happiness associated with higher education) that suggests a clearly positive relationship.

TABLE 15.8. **General Happiness by Highest Degree Received, 2014 General Social Survey**

| | *Highest degree* | | | | |
| | LESS THAN HIGH SCHOOL | HIGH SCHOOL | ASSOCIATE/JUNIOR COLLEGE | BACHELOR'S DEGREE | GRADUATE DEGREE |
*Happiness**					
Not too happy	24.8%	14.5%	10.8%	7.5%	7.5%
Pretty happy	48.8	57.7	57.8	53.7	54.4
Very happy	26.4	27.8	31.4	38.8	38.1
Total	100.0%	100.0%	100.0%	100.0%	100.0%
(*N*)	(330)	(1265)	(185)	(469)	(281)

*Question: "Taken all together, how would you say things are these days—would you say that you are very happy, pretty happy, or not too happy?"

In a negative (inverse) relationship, there is a tendency for *lower* values of one variable to be associated with *higher* values of the other variable. Table 15.9 reveals such a relationship between education and the number of hours of television watched on an average day: As education increases, television viewing time decreases. (There are many possible explanations here: Perhaps higher-income persons are more apt to be exposed to and can better afford other, more expensive forms of entertainment or perhaps higher-educated people have less leisure time or maybe they read more.)

The statistical significance of a relationship between two ordinal-scale variables also may be tested with the chi-square statistic. Ordinal measures of the strength of association, although they differ in name from nominal measures of association, are similar in concept. The magnitude of such statistics, ignoring the sign, indicates the strength of the relationship; and the sign (+ or −) indicates the direction of the association (positive or negative). (For variables with nominal categories, the sign, + or −, does not reveal anything meaningful about the nature of the relationship.) One such statistic, gamma, equals .20 for the data in Table 15.8 and −.33 for the data in Table 15.9. Thus, there is a low positive association between happiness and educational attainment and a moderate negative association between television hours and years of schooling.

Armed with the knowledge of how to interpret cross-tabulations, you are ready to test a bivariate hypothesis. We will illustrate hypothesis testing first with the results from a split-ballot wording experiment from the 2014 GSS. The GSS uses a series of questions about spending priorities in key policy areas to track trends in public support for various government spending programs. Respondents are asked whether they think "we're spending too much money on it, too little money, or about the right amount" on various labeled problems (crime, welfare, national defense, education, etc.). Since the "welfare" label may convey unfavorable connotations, it was paired with an alternative "assistance to the poor" label in one of several wording experiments. Respondents were randomly assigned to either the welfare or the assistance to the poor question version. Table 15.10 reveals that the wording manipulation (independent variable) produced dramatic differences in support for government spending (dependent variable). Only 19.6 percent in the welfare condition thought too little money was being spent compared to 62.3 percent in the assistance to the poor condition. Similarly, the percentage responding that government spending was too much

TABLE 15.9. **Number of Hours per Day Watching Television by Highest Degree Received, 2014 General Social Survey**

Number of television hours	Highest degree				
	LESS THAN HIGH SCHOOL	HIGH SCHOOL	ASSOCIATE/JUNIOR COLLEGE	BACHELOR DEGREE	GRADUATE DEGREE
0–1	15.2%	22.6%	27.1%	32.8%	39.5%
2–3	35.7	41.3	51.1	48.4	50.8
4 or more	49.0	36.2	21.8	18.8	9.6
Total*	99.9%	100.1%	100.0%	100.0%	99.9%
(N)	(210)	(829)	(133)	(320)	(177)

*May not add to 100 due to rounding error.

TABLE 15.10. Split-Ballot Wording Experiment,
2014 General Social Survey

Response	Experimental wording*	
	"ASSISTANCE TO THE POOR"	"WELFARE"
Too little	62.3%	19.6%
About right	23.8	29.2
Too much	11.5	47.3
Don't know	2.5	3.8
Total**	100.1%	99.9%
(N)	(1264)	(1273)

*Question: "We are faced with many problems in this country, none of which
can be solved easily or inexpensively. I'm going to name some of these
problems, and for each one I'd like you to tell me whether you think we're
spending too much money on it, too little money, or about the right amount.
Are we spending too much money, too little money, or about the right amount
on [assistance to the poor/welfare]?"
**Does not add to 100 due to rounding error.

increased from 11.5 percent for the poor to 47.3 percent for the welfare label. Since the split-ballot was a true experimental design, the only rival explanation for the wording results is that they were created by prior subject differences uncontrolled by random assignment. This is ruled out by a statistically significant chi-square test result.[9]

KEY POINT

Measures of association indicate how strongly variables are related; *tests of statistical significance* indicate the likelihood that the relationship occurred by chance.

In a true experiment, the analysis usually begins and ends with an empirical examination of the hypothesized relationship between the dependent variable and the independent variable (experimental treatment). In surveys and other nonexperimental designs, the bivariate association between the dependent and independent variables is only the first step toward a multivariate analysis as extraneous variables may pose rival explanations for the results. Next, we present two nonexperimental examples of preliminary hypothesis testing, and we introduce statistical techniques that are the foundation for the advanced multivariate techniques discussed in Chapter 16.

So far we have restricted ourselves to variables having only 2 to 5 categories and to tables with 4 to 15 cells. This is not unusual because most cross-tabulation analyses in social research are limited to variables with relatively few categories. There are three important reasons for this. First, the size of the table increases geometrically as the number of categories for each variable increases. And the larger the table, the more difficult it is to discern the pattern of the relationship, which can be much more complex than the positive or negative relationships we have described. Second, as we pointed out in our discussion of sampling, the finer the breakdown of one's sample into various categories, the fewer cases there will be for any given breakdown (or cell of the table). Hence, larger tables may require impractically large samples for reliable assessments. Finally, variables with a relatively large number of categories either constitute or tend to approximate interval-scale measurement. With interval-scale variables, we can use a more precise and more powerful form of statistical analysis known as "correlation" and "regression."

Interval- and Ratio-Scale Variables

In Chapter 4 we showed how relationships between two quantitative variables are depicted by plotting the values of each variable in a graphic coordinate system. In conjunction with this form of presentation, social researchers use a statistical method called **regression analysis** to analyze the effect of one interval/ratio variable on another. This is done by finding the mathematical equation that most closely describes the data.

We will use previously described variables from the country data set (Figure 15.1) to explore the hypothesis that countries with low rates of female literacy tend to have high rates of fertility. Let us begin our analysis by looking at a **scatterplot** of total fertility rates and female literacy rates for 178 countries (Figure 15.4). Each plot or point in the graph represents the values of one of the 178 countries on two variables. With the vertical axis as our reference, we can read the value of the dependent variable (total fertility rate); and with the horizontal axis as our reference, we can read the value of the independent variable (female literacy rate). The country of Niger, for example, has the highest fertility rate (7.1) and the lowest female literacy rate (10%). The lowest total fertility rates belong to Hong Kong (1.0) and Georgia (1.1), which have high female literacy rates (90% and 98%, respectively).

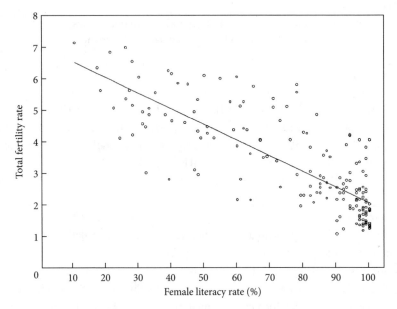

FIGURE 15.4. **Scatterplot of total fertility rate by female literacy, 178 countries. Missing female literacy values for 15 high-literacy countries were replaced with the country's total literacy rates. Countries with missing values for total literacy and/or fertility were excluded from the analysis.**

Sources: The World Factbook 2002 (Washington, DC: Central Intelligence Agency, 2003); The World Bank Developmental Indicators, *WDI Database Archives* (beta) (http://databank.worldbank.org/data/reports. aspx?source=wdi-database-archives-%28beta%29).

The scatterplot gives a researcher a rough sense of the form of the relationship: whether it is positive or negative and whether it is best characterized with a straight or a curved line. This is crucial information because regression analysis assumes that the data have a particular form. If a straight line provides the best fit with the data, one should do linear regression; if a curve provides the best fit, one should use special techniques for fitting curvilinear relationships (which are beyond the scope of this book). As a first step in our analysis, we will examine the scatterplot to make a judgment about form. The overall form of the data in Figure 15.4 is somewhat difficult to discern; however, since the relationship does not appear to be sharply curvilinear, we can assume that a straight line offers as good a fit as a curved line. The trend of the data also suggests that fertility decreases as literacy increases.

Having decided to fit a straight line to the data, and therefore to do *linear* regression analysis, we must know two things: (1) the mathematical equation for a straight line and (2) the criterion for selecting a line to represent the data.

The general form of the equation for a straight line is $Y = a + bX$, where Y is the predicted value of the dependent variable and X is the corresponding value of the independent variable. Thus, an equation for a straight line relating female fertility and literacy is

$$\text{Total fertility rate} = a + b \text{ (Female literacy rate)}$$

The value a, called the **Y-intercept**, is the point where the line crosses the vertical axis (where literacy = 0). The value b, called the **slope** or **regression coefficient**, indicates how much Y increases (or decreases) for every change of one unit in X—in other words, how much increase (or decrease) occurs in the total fertility rate (number of children) for every change of 1 percent in female literacy. To get the line of best fit, then, we could simply draw a line on the scatterplot that seems to reflect best the trend in the data and then determine the values of a and b from the graph. Of course, there are many lines that we could draw—a and b can take on an infinite number of values. How, then, do we know when we have obtained the best fit?

Regression analysis uses the method of least squares as the criterion for selecting the line that best describes the data. According to this method, the best-fitting line minimizes the sum of the squared vertical distances from the data points to the line. We have drawn the **regression line**, also called the "**least squares line**," on the scatterplot. Now imagine a dashed line showing the vertical distance, as measured by the fertility number of children, between a specific data point, say Niger, and the regression line. The regression line represents the equation for predicting Y from X; the vertical distances between data points and this line represent prediction errors (also called **residuals**). Thus, by finding the line that minimizes the sum of the squared distances from it, we are, in effect, finding the best linear predictor of the fertility rate from knowledge of a country's rate of female literacy.

The precise equation generated by the method of least squares can be found via a mathematical formula with the aid of a computer program. When we applied this formula to the data in Figure 15.4, we got the following equation:

$$\text{Total fertility rate} = 6.98 - .05 \text{ (Female literacy rate)}$$

In other words, women in a hypothetical country with 0 percent literacy would be predicted to average about seven children during their lifetime; and, for every 10-unit increase in literacy (10 percent), a decrease of about a half a child (.50) is expected in birth rates. The regression equation gives the best linear prediction of the dependent variable based on the data at hand. Niger, for example, has a predicted fertility rate of 6.48 (6.98 − .05 × 10), which is .62 less (the residual) than its current 7.1 fertility rate. Can you spot the largest residuals in Figure 15.4? They belong to the Republic of Congo (5.76 fertility, 78% literacy) and Bangladesh (2.95 fertility, 32% literacy).

The strength of the association between two variables measured at the interval/ratio level is frequently measured by the **correlation coefficient** (symbolized as r), which may vary between −1 and +1. The sign of the coefficient, which is always the same as the sign of the regression coefficient, indicates the direction of the relationship. The magnitude of its value depends on two factors: (1) the steepness of the regression line and (2) the variation or scatter of the data points around this line. If the line is not very steep, so that it is nearly parallel to the X-axis, then we might as well predict the same value of Y for every unit change in X because there is little change in our prediction (as indicated by b in the equation) for every unit change in the independent variable. By the same token, the greater the spread of values about the regression line (regardless of the steepness of the slope), the less accurate are predictions based on the linear regression. The scatterplot for the regression of fertility on literacy shows that the line is fairly steep in relation to the horizontal axis and that the data points (countries) cluster fairly close to the line. Not surprisingly, therefore, the correlation coefficient indicates a strong negative association of −.80. Statistics also exist for testing whether the correlation coefficient and the regression coefficient are significantly different from zero. These may be found in most statistics textbooks. Both of these coefficients are significant ($p < .001$) for the data in Figure 15.4.

The strong negative association between countries' fertility and female literacy rates by itself, however, does not tell us whether there is a causal connection between the two. To establish this, we must show that the direction of influence is from literacy to fertility (the presumed independent and dependent variables, respectively) and that the association between the variables is not spurious. This, in turn, requires a country-level theoretical model of fertility determinants, along with a multivariate analysis to rule out rival explanations of the negative association. At the country (aggregate data) level, both high fertility and low female literacy may reflect discrimination against women in traditional societies, as well as low income levels, high infant mortality rates, government opposition to family planning, poor health care, and so forth.

KEY POINT

Regression coefficients indicate the direction and amount of change in the dependent variable for each change of one unit in the independent variable. *Correlation coefficients* add information about the strength of the relationship or how well a linear regression predicts the dependent variable.

Our second example of regression analysis is from Broh's (2002) study of extracurricular activities and academic achievement. In a preliminary analysis, she explored the hypothesis that playing high school interscholastic sports (independent variable) improves students' math grades (dependent variable). Since the NELS longitudinal (panel) study collected information from 8th-graders in 1988 (baseline) with follow-ups when most were in the 10th (1990) and 12th (1992) grades, she examined if the interscholastic sports participants during both the 10th and the 12th grades ("athletes") had higher 12th-grade math grades than those who did not participate in the 10th and 12th grades ("nonathletes").

Regression analysis can be applied to independent variables with only two categories, such as Broh's comparison of athletes and nonathletes, by creating what is called a **dummy variable**. This is a variable that has been recoded so that one of its categories has a value of 1 and the other category has a value of 0. Dummy coding enables a researcher to manipulate the variable numerically and to use certain kinds of statistical analysis that would not be possible otherwise. We could, for example, code women as 1 and men as 0 and proceed to regress an interval/ratio-level variable, such as number of television hours watched, on gender. The horizontal axis would have only two values, 0 and 1, and the regression coefficient would indicate the difference between men and women in the mean number of television hours watched. Broh used dummy coding to measure interscholastic sports performance during both the 10th and the 12th grades (1 = participated in both years, 0 = did not participate in both years).

Because the scaling of some NELS measures differed in baseline and follow-up years, Broh put them on equal footing by re-expressing them in standard score form (mean = 0, standard deviation = 1).[10] A student with math grades right at the mean for all NELS students in 1990 and 1.5 standard deviation below the mean in 1992, for example, would have standardized scores of 0 and −1.5, respectively. When Broh regressed interscholastic sports participation on 12th-grade (1992) math grades for 10,379 students, she got the following equation:

$$\text{1992 math grades} = .005 + .230 \text{ (athlete in 10th \& 12th grade)}$$

In other words, the regression equation estimates that athletes in both the 10th and the 12th grades will have math grades in 1992 about one-quarter (.230) of a standard deviation higher than students not playing interscholastic sports.[11] Although the higher math grade for interscholastic athletes was statistically significant ($p < .001$), the observed association between playing sports and math grades may be spurious. Smarter students, for example, might be more likely than their peers to play interscholastic sports and to do well in math. In the next chapter we describe how Broh used multivariate statistical techniques to test for spuriousness and to model theorized causal links between high school sports participation and educational achievement.

Summary

- Data analysis involves an iterative comparison of theory and data. Data analysis begins and ends with a researcher's hypotheses or theoretical model, which guides the collection and analysis of data.
- Before quantitative analysis can begin, the data are processed and put in computer-readable form. In survey research, this entails four steps: editing, coding, data entry, and cleaning. Some of these procedures occur during data collection in computer-assisted surveys.

- Editing is designed to ensure that the data to be entered into the computer are as complete, error free, and readable as possible.
- Coding consists of assigning numbers to the categories of each variable. In survey research, coding for fixed-choice questions is done before data collection, and codes for open-ended questions are developed after the data are collected.
- After editing is complete, the data are entered into the computer and stored in a data file. Typically, a data set is organized as a matrix or spreadsheet, with observations as rows and variables as columns.
- After entry, the data are cleaned for errors in coding and transmission to the computer. This is a multistep process, sometimes beginning with a verification procedure, followed by wild-code checking for "illegal" codes among the values recorded for each variable and consistency checking for reasonable patterns of responses.
- With the data cleaned, researchers usually prepare a codebook, which gives the answers that correspond to each numerical code, the location of each variable in the data file, and coding and decision rules.
- The primary functions of statistics are descriptive and inferential. Descriptive statistics are designed to summarize the data at hand; inferential statistics indicate the extent to which one may generalize beyond the data at hand.
- To inspect and modify the data for the planned analysis, researchers get a clear picture of the data by examining each variable singly (univariate analysis).
- Data modifications include changing one or more variable codes, rearranging the numerical order of variable codes, collapsing variable categories, imputing estimated values for missing data, and adding together the codes for several variables to create an index or scale.
- In univariate analysis the categories or values of each variable first are organized into frequency and percentage distributions. If the data constitute interval-level measurement, researchers will also compute statistics that define various properties of the distribution.
- Statistical measures of central tendency reveal various points of concentration: the most typical value (mode), the middle value (median), and the average (mean). Common measures of dispersion are the difference between the lowest and highest values (range) and an index of the spread of the values around the mean (standard deviation). Distributions also may be described in terms of their shape, such as their skewness.
- Bivariate analysis examines the nature of the relationship between two variables. For relationships involving exclusively nominal- or ordinal-scale variables, such analysis begins with the construction of cross-tabulations, with table cells containing the bivariate distribution.
- The rule for percentaging cross-tabulations is to percentage in the direction of the independent variable; the rule for reading such tables is to make comparisons in the direction opposite the way the percentages are run.
- For relationships involving interval- or ratio-scale variables, the data are plotted in a scatterplot and characterized in terms of a mathematical function. Linear regression analysis identifies the straight-line function that provides the best fit with the data by virtue of minimizing the sum of the squared deviations from the line. The slope of the line reveals the predicted change in the dependent variable per unit change in the independent variable.
- Nominal/ordinal-scale variables may be included in regression analyses as independent variables by dummy-coding categories 0 and 1, in which case the slope indicates the mean difference between categories on the dependent variable.
- Bivariate analysis assesses both the likelihood that the observed relationship is the product of random error and the strength of the association between the variables. The first task usually is accomplished by tests of statistical significance such as chi-square for cross-tabulations. Statistical measures of association generally vary from +1 to −1, with the sign indicating the direction of the relationship and the magnitude indicating the strength of the association.
- Bivariate analysis may be used to test simple two-variable hypotheses, which is the final analysis step in true experiments since an adequate design effectively controls extraneous variables as rival explanations for the results. But in nonexperimental designs, extraneous variables may pose serious rival explanations that require statistical control in a multivariate model, which we will discuss in the next chapter.

Key Terms

data processing	standard deviation
data modification	frequency/percentage polygon
editing	normal distribution
coding	outliers
data cleaning	listwise deletion
wild-code checking	imputation
consistency checking	bivariate analysis
data matrix	marginal frequencies
codebook	cell frequencies
descriptive statistics	chi-square test for independence
inferential statistics	measures of association
univariate analysis	regression analysis
frequency distribution	scatterplot
percentage distribution	Y-intercept
N	slope/regression coefficient
mean	regression (least squares) line
median	residuals
mode	correlation coefficient
range	dummy variable

Exercises

1. To become familiar with data documentation, coding, and data modification, access the GSS Codebook online (http://gss.norc.org/Get-Documentation). The codebook has three indexes: (1) an index to the data set with mnemonic labels listed by data order, (2) an alphabetized list of variable names (mnemonic labels) by survey year (Appendix U), and (3) a subject index to the questions (Appendix V). With this in mind, answer the following questions.
   a. Find the GSS questions on respondents' labor force status, number of siblings, attendance at religious services, knowledge of science, alcohol use, and job satisfaction.
   b. The codebook indicates if questions were recoded, and Appendix D describes the recodes. Go to Appendix D. What question is asked in the GSS to measure age? According to Appendix D, why is this question asked and how are responses to the question recoded? Now find the variable MOBILE16 in the codebook. What does it measure? What are the response categories, and how were they created?
   c. The 2000 GSS asked two open-ended questions on the meaning of freedom. Find these in the codebook. How many coding categories were created for the first freedom question: When you think about freedom, what comes to mind? How was this question coded when a respondent gave more than one answer?
   d. The 2002 and 2004 GSS contained a module on altruism that included seven questions that measured empathy. Find "empathy" in the subject index under the heading "Feelings." Examine these questions in the codebook and decide how you will combine them to create an index.
2. This exercise asks you to test a bivariate hypothesis using GSS data. First, formulate a hypothesis by selecting one independent variable and one dependent variable from the following lists.

Independent Variables	Mnemonic Label
Sex (male/female)	SEX
Race (white/black)	RACE(1,2)
Level of education	DEGREE(r:0-1;2-4)

Dependent Variables	Mnemonic Label
Support for legalization of marijuana (should/should not be legal)	GRASS
Attitude toward homosexuality (sexual relations between adults of same sex is always wrong or not wrong at all)	HOMOSEX(r:1-2;3-4)
Whether or not one has seen an X-rated movie	XMOVIE

GSS data are available online and may be analyzed easily by visiting a website maintained by the University of California, Berkeley: http://sda.berkeley.edu/sdaweb/analysis/?dataset=gss14. To test your hypothesis, you will need to "run" a cross-tabulation as follows: To the right of the page, below "SDA Frequencies/Crosstabulation Program," enter the mnemonic for your dependent variable as your Row variable; enter the mnemonic for your independent variable as your Column variable; then enter "YEAR(2014)" as your Selection Filter(s). Click "Output Options," select "Column" for Percentaging, "Summary statistics," and "Question text"; finally, click on "Run the table" in the shaded box to perform the analysis.

a. Do these data support your hypothesis? Briefly explain.

b. Is the value of chi-square significant? What is the value of gamma? What do these statistics tell you about the relationship?

3. Consider the following values of phi for three different sets of variables: −.82, +.04, +.35. Which association is strongest? Which association is negligible?

4. Dummy code the following variables: gender, attitude toward capital punishment (favor/oppose), and race (white/black, treating "other" as missing). What does the mean value of a dummy variable indicate?

5. Consider the following equation based on 2014 GSS data:

Respondent's years of education = 10.08 + .328 (Father's years of education)

Describe the predicted relationship in this equation. How much change in respondent's education is associated with each increase of 1 year in father's education? What are the predicted years of education of a respondent whose father has completed 16 years of education? (This will require some calculation.)

Notes

1. There are other database options for organizing complex data sets. In contextual analysis, a single data file may contain, for example, both student-level and school-level variables. Or there could be a hierarchical arrangement of separate data files (e.g., neighborhoods, schools, classrooms, and students) with links identifying the students in a particular classroom, the classrooms in a particular school, and the schools in a particular neighborhood. In one social network design, the social actors are listed in both the rows and the columns of a data matrix, with the cell entries representing relationships or connections among pairs of actors.

2. The distinction between descriptive and inferential statistics should not be confused with the scientific goals of description and explanation. Both forms of statistical analysis may be used to accomplish both goals. The first purpose of inferential statistics identified here is description, and the second purpose is explanation. Similarly, descriptive statistics may provide a summary measure of some characteristic of the sample data (description) or may indicate the strength of a hypothesized association between two variables (explanation).

3. Chance may enter into theoretical explanations, which has important implications for popular statistical techniques (Berk, 1983).

4. Social scientists today rarely write their own programs of instructions to the computer. Instead, they rely on "canned" or "packaged" programs stored in the computer and specially written to perform statistical analyses of social science data. To use these programs, you must (1) give the computer a command that accesses the particular package; (2) using the rules for that package, describe the format and location of the data file; and (3) indicate the specific analyses you want done. Thorough discussions of these procedures can be found in the manuals for SPSS, Stata, SAS, or any other packages available for your computer.

5. Allison (2002) assumes that the chance of missing data on one variable is independent of the chance of missing data on any other variable.

6. See GSS Codebook (http://gss.norc.org/documents/codebook/GSS_Codebook.pdf) Appendices F (Occupational Classification Distributions) and G (Prestige Scores Distributions).

7. Sometimes these rules are broken for descriptive reasons (e.g., to ascertain the educational background of different income groups) or because the data are unrepresentative of the population with respect to the dependent variable (see Zeisel, 1968:30–36).

8. Statistical analyses ordinarily require adjustments for complex sampling designs such as those used in the GSS and NELS. The NELS, for example, used disproportionate stratified cluster sampling, with students clustered by schools. For pedagogical reasons, all tables are based on unweighted frequencies.

9. For Table 15.10, excluding the "don't know" responses, chi-square $= 565.13$, $df = 2$ ($p < .001$).

10. Variables are standardized by subtracting the variable mean from each original score and then dividing by the standard deviation of the original scores.

11. The equation for athletes is $.005 + .230(1) = .235$; for nonathletes, it is $.005 + .230(0) = .005$.

16

Multivariate Analysis

In the last chapter we examined bivariate relationships; statistically, this amounted to calculating the degree of association or correlation between two variables. Bivariate analysis provides a basis, as exemplified by regression slope coefficients, for predicting the values of one variable from values of another. However, if our goal goes beyond prediction to testing causal hypotheses, then calculating bivariate associations is never sufficient. As we have emphasized repeatedly, causal inferences are based not only on association but also on theoretical assumptions and empirical evidence about direction of influence and nonspuriousness.

In a cross-sectional survey, for example, a correlation between X and Y may imply that X causes Y, that Y causes X, that X and Y mutually cause each other, or that X and Y are causally unrelated (spurious association). The statistical techniques introduced in this chapter help researchers to choose among such possible interpretations. But it is important to realize that statistical analyses by themselves do not provide a basis for inferring causal relationships. Instead, a researcher starts with a theoretical model of the causal process linking X and Y and then determines whether the data are consistent with the theory.

Direction of influence, in particular, is usually based on theoretical or practical knowledge. In experiments, the direction is set by the manipulation of the independent variable, which always precedes measurement of the dependent variable. Similarly, the natural time order of many nonexperimental variables indisputably determines causal direction. In relating high school students' occupational aspirations to their parents' education, for example, the latter occurs earlier in time and may be a cause but not an effect of students' aspirations. When time order is indeterminate, causal direction often is determined on the basis that one variable is more fixed, more permanent, or less alterable than the other

(M. Rosenberg, 1968:11–12; Davis, 1985:14–15). Sex, a fixed variable, may influence sports participation but not vice versa. Religious affiliation may influence happiness if we theorize that the former is relatively unchangeable compared with the latter.

Theoretical knowledge sometimes dictates treating direction of influence as mutual or reciprocal. Reviewing explanations of the inverse correlation between American women's employment and childbearing, Linda Waite and Ross Stolzenberg (1976) found strong arguments for mutual causation. Young women may be having fewer children because they want to work more outside the home (career aspirations influence fertility). And women may be working more because they want fewer children (fertility plans influence employment). Using a statistical method appropriate for studying mutual causation, Waite and Stolzenberg concluded that employment plans dominate fertility expectations.[1]

The misguided self-esteem enhancement movement underscores the importance of causal direction. Acting on the "obvious" supposition that low self-esteem (independent variable) is a cause of poor performance (dependent variable) in school and elsewhere, a flourishing cottage industry in the past 45 years has been churning out intervention programs to raise the self-esteem of students, workers, cigarette smokers, underage drinkers, drug addicts, and even taxpayers.[2] An extensive review of the self-esteem literature by the psychologist Roy Baumeister and his colleagues (2003), however, found little evidence for the efficacy of self-esteem interventions. Indeed, some experiments and longitudinal studies with objective measures of school performance suggest that self-esteem is an effect (dependent variable) rather than a cause (independent variable) of good school performance. Doing well in school may make students feel good about themselves (i.e., boost self-esteem).

Theory also guides tests for spuriousness. Through theory, we identify antecedent variables that might produce spurious statistical associations. Utilizing such theoretical knowledge, we can apply statistical techniques that go a long way toward demonstrating nonspuriousness. In principle, these techniques have the same effect as randomization in experiments. The main difference is that whereas randomization is assumed to control for *all* antecedent variables, statistical control in nonexperimental studies can be applied only to measured variables. This places a premium on identifying and measuring relevant variables and on specifying their causal relations. Thus, it is easy to see why modeling has become so important because modeling is a way of specifying various possible causal relations among a set of variables. It is now time to take a closer look at a data analyst's conception of a model.

KEY POINT

Guided by theoretical knowledge, statistical analysis examines the fit between theory (models) and data.

Modeling Relationships

A statistical model is a simplified picture of reality, a representation of the theorized relations among the variables that generated the observed data. The translation of a theory into a statistical model ordinarily takes the form of one or more mathematical equations.

FIGURE 16.1 **Arrow diagrams for different causal relationships.**

However, to convey the logic of **modeling** and analysis, we will use easily understood arrow diagrams, which often serve as a modeling visualization aid.

Arrow Diagrams

Arrow diagrams represent the causal ordering of a set of variables. Each arrow indicates causal direction. Thus, the arrow pointing from X to Y in Figure 16.1A means that X is hypothesized to be a cause of Y. Two arrows pointing in opposite directions (Figure 16.1B) indicate **reciprocal causation**—that X and Y are thought to influence each other. A single line (often curved) with arrows on both ends (Figure 16.1C) indicates that there may be a statistical association between the variables, but that a causal explanation of the association is not part of the model (**noncausal association**). Finally, the absence of an arrow connecting two variables means that no causal relationship is hypothesized.

In addition to causal order, arrow diagrams can indicate the direction of a relationship. This is generally signified with a sign, + or −, above the arrow. A plus sign indicates a presumed positive relationship: As X increases in value, Y increases. A minus sign indicates a presumed negative (inverse) relationship: As X increases in value, Y decreases.[3] Thus the arrows in Figure 16.2 pointing from X to Y in models A and B indicate predicted

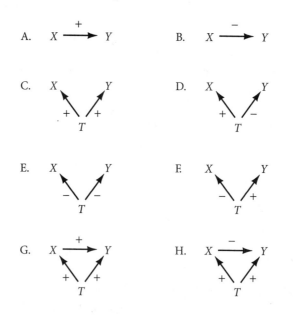

FIGURE 16.2. **Two-variable relationships and alternative antecedent variable models.**

positive and negative relationships, respectively. Adding an antecedent variable, T, to the picture creates alternative theoretical models positing that the original relationship is spurious. Models C and E also predict a positive association between X and Y as antecedent T causes both variables to move in the same direction even though there is no direct causal link (arrow) between X and Y. As T increases in model C (or model E), both X and Y increase (or decrease), thus creating a spurious positive association. Similarly, a decrease in T causes both X and Y to move in the same direction (downward for model C, upward for model E).

Note that models C and E represent rival explanations for model A but not for model B because they predict a positive rather than a negative statistical association between X and Y. Antecedent variable T in models D and F generates a spurious negative relationship (X and Y move in opposite directions), which is a rival explanation for the negative association predicted by model B. Finally, model G illustrates another theoretical possibility in which both X and T causally produce a positive association between X and Y. In Beckett Broh's study (2002), for example, a positive association between students' extracurricular involvement (X) and academic achievement (Y) may be spurious, or partially spurious, if antecedent parents' income (T) positively influenced both variables (models C or G). However, if parents' income is inversely related to extracurricular involvement (model F), parental income could not produce a spurious *positive* association between extracurricular involvement and academic achievement.

Figure 16.3 shows arrow diagrams of an intervening variable (T) causally positioned between an independent (X) and a dependent (Y) variable. Model I predicts a positive association between X and Y: When X increases, T decreases; when T decreases, Y increases— thus X and Y move in the same direction (positive relationship). The intervening variable in model K produces a negative relationship: When X goes up, T goes up; when T goes up, Y goes down. The predicted relationship between X and Y can be determined by simply multiplying the signs of the arrows along the path connecting the two variables (Davis, 1985:29). The predicted relationship will be positive (models I and J) unless there is an odd number of negative arrows (models K, L, and M) intervening between X and Y. In Broh's study, an intervening mechanism producing a positive association between students' extracurricular involvement (X) and academic achievement (Y) might be time spent on homework (T) if both causal arrows are positive (model J). But if extracurricular involvement (X) decreases time spent on homework (T), as in model L, then homework could not represent the intervening causal process by which extracurricular involvement promotes academic achievement.

Model N in Figure 16.3 posits that an independent variable (X) positively affects the dependent variable (Y) by having a **direct effect** (the positive arrow from X to Y) and an **indirect effect** via a positive path involving a causally intervening variable (T). That is, theoretical model N identifies part of the causal process, the indirect effect, by which X affects Y. Model J, in contrast, theorizes that the only causal mechanism linking X and Y is intervening variable T. For the previous Broh example, model N proposes that homework (T) is responsible for only part of the positive association between extracurricular involvement (X) and academic achievement (Y).

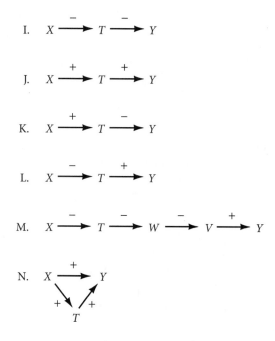

I. $X \xrightarrow{-} T \xrightarrow{-} Y$

J. $X \xrightarrow{+} T \xrightarrow{+} Y$

K. $X \xrightarrow{+} T \xrightarrow{-} Y$

L. $X \xrightarrow{-} T \xrightarrow{+} Y$

M. $X \xrightarrow{-} T \xrightarrow{-} W \xrightarrow{-} V \xrightarrow{+} Y$

N. $X \xrightarrow{+} Y$

FIGURE 16.3. Alternative intervening variable models.

These alternative models have different implications for the original hypothesis of a *positive* relationship between academic achievement and extracurricular involvement: Models A and G support it; models B, C, D, E, F, H, K, L, and M do not support it; and models I, J, and N, in addition to supporting the basic hypothesis, provide a more thorough understanding of the causal sequence. And these three-variable models do not exhaust the possibilities. For example, time spent on homework and extracurricular activities may interact in promoting academic achievement.

Stochastic and Systematic Components

In addition to specifying hypothesized relationships among the explanatory variables, statistical models posit that some variability in phenomena occurs randomly or by chance. Thus models contain both **systematic** (theorized relationships as represented by arrow diagrams) and **stochastic** (chance processes) **components** (King, 1989:8–12). To clarify this distinction, we will consider a simple example.

Suppose that the midterm exam (50 true–false questions) for a social research class was given to a physics class by mistake. The physics students duly completed the test without raising any questions about the content, but some scored better than others. How can we explain this distribution (variability) of exam scores? One simple hypothesis is that the students merely guessed the answers, which could be translated into a statistical model corresponding to flipping a fair coin 50 times and marking the question as true for "heads" outcomes (statistically this would be modeled as a binomial distribution). The model (and its underlying theory) would then be judged by comparing the model-predicted distribution of exam scores with the actual class results. A good fit between the model and the observed data would provide support for the hypothesis that the physics students were merely guessing the answers.

The model contains only a stochastic component: The only theorized basis for differences in exam scores is a chance process. Systematic components could be included in the model by adding independent variables. For example, we might hypothesize that (1) men would guess more often than women and (2) lower-division students would guess more frequently than upper-class students on the midterm. This would translate into a model that explains the exam scores as a combination of stochastic (chance) and systematic (hypothesized sex and class-standing differences) components.

Earlier we discussed simple models containing stochastic and systematic components in conjunction with experimental designs and probability sampling. In the former, the stochastic component is introduced by random assignment of subjects to experimental conditions. A test of statistical significance is then used to rule out the rival hypothesis that the experimental outcome is due to chance (stochastic component produced by randomization) rather than by the experimental manipulation (systematic component). Similarly, a stochastic component is introduced by probability sampling. Significance tests or confidence intervals are then used to distinguish sample results due to systematic differences in the population from those due to chance (sampling error).

In addition to being produced by randomization, probability sampling, and measurement errors, the stochastic or chance component may be produced during the process theorized to have generated the data, as in the midterm example of guessing answers (Berk, 1983; King, 1989:3–13). For example, a theory might specify that actions by nations, voting decisions of the electorate, or people's friendship ties may be explained by stochastic (chance) as well as by systematic components.

The Process of Modeling

Since they are derived from tentative theories, models are never "correct" about social processes. Instead, they serve as an economical and informed means of getting on with the data analysis. Research then becomes a learning process as the analysis reveals discrepancies between model predictions and the data; these discrepancies, in turn, lead analysts to modify or replace the model that will be used for further or new data analysis; and so forth (Box, 1976). To illustrate this learning process, suppose you hypothesize that cynicism (dependent variable) is positively related to educational attainment (independent variable). The data, unfortunately, reveal a negative correlation between education and cynicism, an explanation of which requires a new theoretical model. One possibility is that better-educated people are more trusting of human nature because they have experienced a better life (jobs, health, etc.) and have been less victimized than those with less schooling—a new model that yields multiple testable predictions.

How does one determine if the data support a model? In the last chapter we did a bivariate analysis of the effect of interscholastic sports participation on math grades, finding a statistically significant positive relationship consistent with Broh's original hypothesis (model A in Figure 16.2). But as you can see, to draw conclusions from this analysis alone could be misleading. The question now is, how do we analyze the data to estimate effects represented by other, more complex models involving three or more variables, such as models C, E, G, I, J, and N in Figures 16.2 and 16.3?

Multivariate analysis of nonexperimental data is basically a matter of statistical control. Statistical control is analogous to randomization in experiments; both procedures are designed to eliminate the possibility that prior (antecedent) variables have created a spurious association. Randomization does this by creating random variation across experimental conditions in all extraneous variables; statistical control does it by examining the relationship between an independent and a dependent variable with specified antecedent variables held constant. As we have noted, statistical controls cannot be applied to unmeasured antecedent variables. Also, the presence of measurement error in control variables reduces the effectiveness of statistical control procedures. Despite these limitations, however, this form of analysis does have one major advantage over experimental randomization: It enables us to test for indirect as well as direct effects and to analyze much more complex models than is possible with experimental designs.

KEY POINT

Nonexperimental studies control statistically for antecedent variables that could create spurious relationships, but only variables identified and measured can be controlled.

Among the several strategies for multivariate analysis, we now introduce elaboration of contingency tables and multiple-regression analysis.

Elaboration: Tables and Beyond

Throughout the 1950s and 1960s, **multivariate analysis** with contingency tables usually involved a simple technique known as **elaboration** (Lazarsfeld, 1955). This technique introduces a third (and sometimes additional) control variable into the analysis to enhance or "elaborate" our understanding of a bivariate relationship. We start with an illustration of elaboration using contingency tables. Then we discuss the logic of three-variable elaboration and describe various meaningful outcomes. Our main purpose is to introduce a general modeling strategy, focusing on antecedent and intervening variables, that may be used with simple, three-variable tables as well as with the more complex, multivariate procedures that we introduce later in this chapter.

To illustrate the logic of elaboration, we will examine the relationship between two variables of particular interest to educators: collegiate alcohol consumption and academic performance. Royce Singleton (2007) gathered data on these variables in a series of campus surveys at the College of the Holy Cross. Each semester from fall 2003 to spring 2005 students enrolled in his research methods course conducted face-to-face interviews with randomly selected fellow students. Among the measures of alcohol consumption included in the surveys, we will focus on the amount of alcohol—specifically the number of drinks—that students reported consuming "on a typical weekend night." To measure academic performance, respondents were asked at the conclusion of the interview for permission to obtain grade information from the college registrar.

TABLE 16.1. Cumulative Grade-Point Average
(GPA) by Number of Drinks Consumed
on a Typical Weekend Night (%)

| Cumulative GPA | Number of drinks consumed | |
	FIVE OR LESS	SIX OR MORE
Less than 3.2	39.9%	58.6%
3.2 or greater	60.1	41.4
Total	100.0%	100.0%
(N)	(356)	(324)

Although we cannot be certain about direction of influence, we will assume that number of drinks consumed is the cause, or independent variable, and cumulative grade-point average (GPA) is the effect, or dependent variable. Table 16.1 shows the bivariate association between number of drinks consumed and cumulative GPA. The data indicate that there is an association: By a difference of 18.7 percent, students who consume six or more drinks on a typical weekend night are more likely to have a cumulative GPA less than 3.2 than students who consume five or fewer drinks. Moreover, the chi-square test = 21.61, which is significant at $p < .001$; so, an association is likely to exist among all students at the college from which this sample was drawn.

The object of elaboration is to examine the impact of additional "third" variables on an observed relationship. We are especially interested in understanding the impact of antecedent variables that might create a spurious relationship and intervening variables that might reveal how one variable affects another. For example, researchers have speculated that the association between drinking and GPA might be spurious because of precollege factors such as academic aptitude. That is, students with a relatively low aptitude might be likely to drink more and to do less well academically than students with a relatively high aptitude. To explore this possibility, we introduce a measure of respondents' aptitude—SAT total score—into the analysis by holding it constant. In contingency table elaboration, third variables are held constant by means of subgroup classification. Each category of the third variable constitutes a distinct subgroup, and the original two-variable relationship is recomputed separately for each subgroup. Table 16.2 does this for the variables of cumulative GPA, number of drinks consumed, and SAT total score. The table gives hypothetical marginal frequencies and percentages.

TABLE 16.2. Cumulative Grade-Point Average (GPA) by Number
of Drinks Consumed on a Typical Weekend Night and SAT
Total Score (%), Hypothetical Data

| Cumulative GPA | SAT total score less than 1270 | | SAT total score 1270 or greater | |
	FIVE OR LESS DRINKS	SIX OR MORE DRINKS	FIVE OR LESS DRINKS	SIX OR MORE DRINKS
Less than 3.2	62.5%	62.5%	32.0%	32.0%
3.2 or greater	37.5	37.5	68.0	68.0
Total	100.0%	100.0%	100.0%	100.0%
(N)	(92)	(283)	(264)	(41)

Note that we now have two "tables," one for each category of the variable "SAT total score." These are called **partial tables** or **partials**, because each shows the association between alcohol consumption and GPA for part of the total number of observations. SAT total score is held constant, because in each partial table all respondents are alike with respect to their SAT scores. Look over the partial tables carefully. What do they reveal about the relationship between alcohol consumption and GPA when SAT score is controlled?

Reading across each partial table, we find virtually no association between alcohol consumption and GPA. In other words, the original relationship (shown in Table 16.1), which indicated that heavier drinkers had lower GPAs than lighter drinkers, has disappeared when SAT score is controlled. These hypothetical data, therefore, support model F in Figure 16.2. The relationship is spurious, produced by a common association with SAT score, an indicator of academic aptitude. We draw this inference not only on the basis of the data, however, but also on the basis of prior theoretical assumptions about the causal ordering of these variables. These same data are also consistent with the following model:

$$\text{Number of drinks} \longrightarrow \text{SAT total score} \longrightarrow \text{Cumulative GPA}$$

Here "SAT total score" is an *intervening* variable between "drinks consumed" and "cumulative GPA," whereas in model F, SAT total score is an *antecedent* variable with respect to these variables. We prefer model F as an interpretation because it is unreasonable to believe that the number of drinks that students reported consuming at the time of the survey determined the scores they obtained on the SAT while in high school. But it is crucial to realize that this interpretation rests on theory; the data in Table 16.2 are consistent with either model.

The outcomes of elaboration analysis are seldom this tidy. Recall that the data in Table 16.2 are hypothetical. As the real data in Table 16.3 show, the relationship between number of drinks consumed and cumulative GPA does not reduce to zero in either partial. Rather, it exists in both partial tables, although it is somewhat stronger in one than in the other. Students who consume greater amounts of alcohol are more likely to have a cumulative GPA less than 3.2, but the percentage difference is 13.5 among those with relatively low SAT scores (less than 1270), compared with 22.9 percent among those with relatively high SAT scores (1270 or greater). So, alcohol consumption appears to have a somewhat greater effect on GPA among those with high SAT scores.

TABLE 16.3. **Cumulative Grade-Point Average (GPA) by Number of Drinks Consumed on a Typical Weekend Night and SAT Total Score (%)**

Cumulative GPA	SAT total score less than 1270		SAT total score 1270 or greater	
	FIVE OR LESS DRINKS	SIX OR MORE DRINKS	FIVE OR LESS DRINKS	SIX OR MORE DRINKS
Less than 3.2	55.9%	69.4%	25.3%	48.2%
3.2 or greater	44.1	30.6	74.7	51.8
Total	100.0%	100.0%	100.0%	100.0%
(N)	(170)	(160)	(186)	(164)

Showing that the relationship between drinking and GPA is maintained when controlling for SAT total score eliminates the possibility that academic aptitude produced a spurious relationship. This conclusion is limited, however, and it is subject to three criticisms that pertain to much analysis of contingency tables: (1) Collapsing variables such as amount of alcohol consumed, GPA, and SAT scores into two categories may eliminate important information and distort the results; (2) several other variables (e.g., sex, race, parents' income) might produce a spurious association between alcohol consumption and GPA; and (3) controlling for one variable at a time ignores the possibility that spuriousness may be created by the simultaneous action of two or more extraneous variables.

We can never be certain that alcohol consumption lowers grades. Ultimately, our confidence in this causal relationship depends on our holding constant all antecedent variables that might reasonably be expected to produce a spurious relationship. In addition to SAT total score, Singleton (2007) controlled for parents' education and income, high school class rank, gender, race, class year, and whether a student was an intercollegiate athlete. And unlike contingency table elaboration, he did not introduce these controls one at a time. Instead, he used multiple regression, a technique described in the next section. Multiple regression is generally better when we want to analyze the simultaneous effects of several independent variables on a dependent variable. Still, because of its simplicity and clarity, elaboration of contingency tables will continue to be used when there are a limited number of control variables and the variables have relatively few categories.

Although the elaboration scheme was originally developed for analyzing contingency tables, the general logic of three-variable elaboration is easily extended to multiple regression and other forms of multivariate analysis involving many variables. Figure 16.4 presents a logical guide to using a third variable (T) to elaborate the relationship between an independent variable (X) and a dependent variable (Y) (adapted from Lazarsfeld, 1955; M. Rosenberg, 1968). The original association between X and Y is called a **zero-order relationship** because there are zero variables being controlled. If T is introduced as a control variable, then the association between X and Y becomes a **first-order relationship** or simply a "partial."[4] The columns of Figure 16.4 are arranged in the logical order of elaboration steps: (1) formulate a three-variable theoretical model, (2) confirm that the three-variable model is consistent with the initial zero-order association, (3) control for the third variable, and (4) interpret the results. The first step requires a theoretical decision on the causal position of the third variable: Should T be antecedent to, intervening after, or unrelated to variable X? In the preceding example, academic aptitude was modeled to be antecedent to alcohol consumption and academic performance.

In the following steps, brackets denote the statistical association between two variables. For example, $[XT] = -$ (or +, or 0, or $\neq 0$) indicates a negative (or positive, or zero, or nonzero) association between variables X and T. The necessary empirical prerequisites for the three-variable models are outlined in column 2 of Figure 16.4. For example, if $[XT] = -$, then $[TX]$ would have to be negatively associated and $[TY]$ positively associated (or $[TX]$ positive and $[TY]$ negative) for an antecedent model to predict a negative, albeit spurious, zero-order association between X and Y. In our earlier discussion of Figure 16.2 arrow diagrams, models D and F, but not C and E, are consistent with a negative association

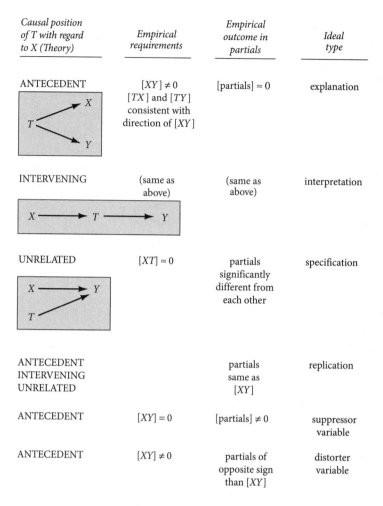

Causal position of T with regard to X (Theory)	Empirical requirements	Empirical outcome in partials	Ideal type
ANTECEDENT	$[XY] \neq 0$ $[TX]$ and $[TY]$ consistent with direction of $[XY]$	[partials] ≈ 0	explanation
INTERVENING	(same as above)	(same as above)	interpretation
UNRELATED	$[XT] \approx 0$	partials significantly different from each other	specification
ANTECEDENT INTERVENING UNRELATED		partials same as $[XY]$	replication
ANTECEDENT	$[XY] = 0$	[partials] ≠ 0	suppressor variable
ANTECEDENT	$[XY] \neq 0$	partials of opposite sign than $[XY]$	distorter variable

FIGURE 16.4. Ideal types of elaboration.

between X and Y. Thus, for SAT score to qualify as a possible explanation for a spurious relationship between alcohol consumption and GPA, it must have a negative association with one variable (as SAT score increases, alcohol consumption decreases) and a positive association with the other (as SAT score increases, GPA increases).

Provided that the empirical requirements (column 2) are satisfied, the next step is to examine the relationship between X and Y when the third variable (T) is controlled. If the data are consistent with the first model in Figure 16.4, for example, then the association between X and Y in the partials should vanish or become very small (≈ 0) since only variable T produces the zero-order association. This ideal type of outcome is called **explanation** because the third variable "explains" away the zero-order association. Conversely, if the zero-order relationship is also being produced by other antecedent variables besides T, or by a causal link between X and Y (model G in Figure 16.2), the first-order partials may be smaller than the zero-order relationship but not vanish. The hypothetical data in Table 16.2 provide an example of explanation.

The second ideal elaboration outcome, **interpretation**, has the same empirical requirements and outcomes as explanation. The only difference between the two is the causal position of the third variable. If the partials vanish when an intervening variable T is controlled, the model provides an "interpretation" of the causal process or mechanism by which X influences Y (Lazarsfeld, 1955). However, if T does not completely account for the causal process linking X and Y (e.g., model N in Figure 16.3), the zero-order partials will not completely disappear. Mollie Orshansky and Judith Bretz (1976) provide an interesting example of an intervening variable that interprets the relationship between family size and poverty. First, they show that the prevalence of poverty increases as the household head's number of siblings increases. Then, they show that this relationship disappears when the household head's level of education is controlled. Thus, the larger one's family of origin, the lower one's level of education and, as a consequence, the more likely that one will experience poverty (model I in Figure 16.3).

Even when T is causally unrelated to X, the first-order partials may be significantly different from each other if T and X interact in affecting Y. Although Paul Lazarsfeld (1955) reserved the term **specification** for a strong form of interaction when T was unrelated to X, generally the term is applied whenever an antecedent or intervening control variable specifies the conditions under which the initial zero-order relationship varies (our previous interpretation of Table 16.3). In a 1952 study of college students' values, Morris Rosenberg (1968:140–42) found that students with low faith in people placed more emphasis on the importance of getting ahead in life (success orientation). When sex was controlled, Rosenberg discovered that the initial relationship between faith in people and success orientation became stronger in the partial table for females and weaker in the partial table for males. He concluded that the initial relationship is weaker among males because males at that time were under more "general social pressure" to be successful, irrespective of their faith in people, than were females.

Replication is the opposite of specification: The partials are not significantly different from the initial zero-order relationship (Hirschi and Selvin, 1967:99). The causal position of the control variable in replication may be antecedent, intervening, or unrelated to the original independent variable. Although at first glance replications appear to be undesirable or boring outcomes, they often represent favorable evidence in support of the initial zero-order hypothesis. Showing that the initial relationship holds when critical antecedent variables are controlled or that it remains essentially unchanged within categories of various control variables (gender, race, education, age, and so forth) strengthens one's confidence that the relationship is nonspurious and has high external validity.

The final ideal types of elaboration shown in Figure 16.4, **suppressor** and **distorter variables**, are really the mirror image of explanation. In the latter, the zero-order association supports the initial hypothesis and an antecedent variable is introduced to test for a possible spurious relationship. In the former, the hypothesis is not supported and an antecedent variable is controlled to determine whether it is suppressing or distorting the direction of the zero-order association. An uncontrolled suppressor variable may reduce or cancel out the true relationship between two variables, whereas an uncontrolled distorter variable may reverse the true direction of the relationship (M. Rosenberg, 1968). As an illustration, let us return to our Chapter 4 example of a positive zero-order correlation between the number of firefighters at a fire (X) and the amount of damage suffered (Y). Model H (Figure 16.2) reveals how an antecedent variable, size of fire (T), can distort the apparent effectiveness of firefighters in reducing damage. As the size of the fire (T) increases, so do the number of firefighters (X) called up and the amount of fire damage (Y), thus producing a positive association between X and Y. If the positive relationship produced by T is stronger than the negative causal link between X and Y, the resultant zero-order association will be positive. When T is controlled, the first-order relationship changes to a negative direction, confirming that having more firefighters will reduce the amount of damage. A suppressor variable is similar to a distorter variable in that by operating in the opposite direction from the causal link between X and Y, it may weaken or even eliminate the zero-order association. The relationship between X and Y is revealed when the suppressor variable is controlled.

KEY POINT

Introducing a third variable to elaborate a two-variable relationship may explain away the original relationship as spurious (*explanation*), interpret the causal process linking the original two variables (*interpretation*), disclose an interaction (*specification*), or support the original relationship (*replication*).

The elaboration labels in the fourth column of Figure 16.4 describe ideal types of expected outcomes provided that (1) the social phenomenon can be adequately represented by a three-variable model and (2) the data are free of measurement error. Since these assumptions are never satisfied with real data, actual outcomes fall short of the ideal types. In a typical "explanation" outcome, for example, the partials may weaken but not disappear. Establishing spuriousness (i.e., vanishing partials) is likely to require controlling additional antecedent variables simultaneously in a multivariate model and possibly better measurement. Similarly, teasing out the intervening mechanism causally linking two variables may require a more elaborate model than a simple three-variable representation.

In a multivariate analysis, it is important to consider carefully all antecedent variables that reasonably might be expected to produce a spurious association, as well as theorized intervening variables, interaction effects, and other predictions. For example, using a representative sample of 21,204 U.S. adults from the 1987 National Health Interview Survey, the demographer Robert Hummer and associates (1999) found a strong inverse relationship between religious involvement, as measured by reported church attendance, and the risk of dying over a 9-year follow-up period. Compared to those who attend church "more than once a week," the risk of dying between 1987 and 1995 was 87 percent higher for those who "never attend," 31 percent higher for the "less than weekly" attendees, and 15 percent higher for the "weekly" churchgoers. To explore the possibility that the relationship was spuriously produced by uncontrolled antecedent variables linked to church attendance and mortality, Hummer and associates simultaneously controlled for selected background factors (age, sex, race, region, income, and education) and baseline measures of health (self-reported health status, activity limitations, and bed-sick days). Controlling for background factors or for interaction effects between background and church attendance did not explain away the initial relationship between religious involvement and the risk of dying ("replication").

Controlling for health factors, however, did slightly reduce the zero-order association between church attendance and mortality (limited "explanation").

In addition to demonstrating that likely antecedent variables were not spuriously producing the strong zero-order association, Hummer and associates identified two sets of intervening variables, social ties (marital status, social activity, friends and relatives to call on in times of need) and harmful behaviors (cigarette smoking, alcohol use, and obesity), that link religious attendance to mortality. Frequent church attendance may promote social ties and discourage harmful behaviors, which in turn may affect mortality. Social ties and harmful behaviors not only accounted for a portion of the association between religious attendance and mortality (interpretation) but also varied in a meaningful way for various causes of death. For example, controlling for social ties substantially reduced the association between religious attendance and diabetic mortality; diabetics often must rely heavily on social ties to maintain adequate care.

Now, we will introduce multiple-regression analysis and provide three illustrations of its use in multivariate modeling.

Multiple-Regression Analysis

Multiple regression is simply an extension of bivariate regression (Chapter 15) to include two or more independent variables. Like the partial tables of elaboration analysis, it provides information on the impact of an independent variable on the dependent variable while simultaneously controlling for the effects of other independent variables. Unlike the case with partial tables, control is not limited to a few variables nor is information lost from collapsing variables into fewer categories. Here, we present a cursory exposition of this powerful and popular linear-modeling technique. Our main purpose is to make it easier for you to read and understand research employing multiple-regression analysis.

Example 1: The Moral Integration of American Cities

Let us start with an early application of multiple regression in sociology—Robert Angell's 1951 study, "The Moral Integration of American Cities." Angell was interested in understanding why the populations of various cities differ in their conformity to certain social mores ("moral integration"). As an operational definition of moral integration, he constructed an elaborate index combining information on crime rates (negative integration) with local contributions to community charity funds (positive integration) for 43 cities with a population greater than 100,000. Angell theorized that moral integration is more easily maintained in homogeneous populations and in populations with a low turnover of members. Two measures were constructed to test these hypotheses: (1) a heterogeneity index based on the relative number of nonwhites and foreign-born whites in each city and (2) a mobility index based on the relative number of persons moving into and out of each city.

An arrow diagram representing Angell's model is shown in Figure 16.5. The arrows pointing from mobility and from heterogeneity to moral integration indicate the hypothesized negative relationships. The curved arrow indicates that mobility and heterogeneity

FIGURE 16.5. Angell's moral integration model.

may be correlated, which is taken as given and not to be explained in the model. An incorrect approach to testing Angell's theory would be to test each hypothesis separately using bivariate regression. The results from such an approach show that each of these variables is significantly related to moral integration in the predicted direction; for ethnic heterogeneity, $b = -.1027$, and for residential mobility, $b = -.1789$.

Thus, on the basis of bivariate regressions, Angell appears to be right: Moral integration decreases with increasing heterogeneity and with increasing mobility. Unfortunately, this is not a proper test of his model. Study Figure 16.5 again. First, since the theory signifies that both independent variables *simultaneously* influence moral integration, they should be analyzed accordingly. Second, since heterogeneity and mobility may be strongly correlated (curved arrow), some or all of the apparent contribution of one to a bivariate prediction of moral integration actually may be caused by the other. Suppose, for example, that heterogeneity but not mobility is causally related to moral integration and that mobility and heterogeneity are strongly correlated. Then, a bivariate regression of moral integration on mobility could produce a significant regression coefficient, which would be entirely a consequence of the correlation between mobility and heterogeneity. Leaving out important variables from a model, which may produce misleading results, is called a **specification error**. Therefore, bivariate regressions represent misspecification of Angell's theory.

Now that we are convinced that a multivariate test is in order, how do we proceed? The general formula for a multiple-regression equation is

$$Y = a + b_1X_1 + b_2X_2 + b_3X_3 + \ldots e$$

where Y is the dependent variable, each X represents an independent variable, the b values are **partial-regression coefficients** or **partial slopes**, a is the Y-intercept (the predicted value of Y when all of the X values are equal to zero), and e represents the prediction error or residual (the stochastic component). This, of course, is the linear equation for bivariate regression (Chapter 15), augmented to include additional independent variables. For Angell's data, the equation reduces to

$$\text{Moral integration} = a + b_1 \text{ heterogeneity} + b_2 \text{ mobility} + e$$

Estimation of the coefficients in a multiple-regression equation follows the same logic as bivariate regression. In the case of two independent variables, the approach is easy to visualize geometrically. Imagine constructing a three-dimensional scatterplot of Angell's data within a large room. The 43 cities will appear as a "swarm" of points within the room, with the location of each point determined by that city's score for moral integration (using the room height as the axis of measurement), heterogeneity (room length), and mobility (room width). The multiple-regression solution appears as a (two-dimensional) plane in this three-dimensional space. (The bivariate-regression solution was also a geometric figure, a line, in a two-dimensional space.) Now, if we mentally position the regression plane in the room so as to minimize the sum of the squared residuals (vertical distances from the city points to the regression plane), we have found the multiple-regression solution.

A computer program, of course, is a more practical approach to multiple-regression estimation. Computing estimated coefficients for Angell's data gives the following prediction equation:

$$\text{Moral integration} = 19.993 - .108 \text{ (heterogeneity)} - .193 \text{ (mobility)}$$

These results are consistent with Angell's model and are statistically significant. The multiple-regression or partial coefficients reveal the amount by which the dependent variable is expected to change with a one-unit change in the independent variable *when* the other independent variables are held constant (controlled). Thus, the moral integration index for a city is expected to fall by .193 unit for every unit increase in the residential mobility index. What is predicted when ethnic heterogeneity decreases by 10 units?

The partial coefficients address questions like the following: If several cities have the same degree of residential mobility but differ on ethnic heterogeneity, how will these differences in heterogeneity affect moral integration? A geometric interpretation of partial coefficients for the case of two independent variables is provided in Figure 16.6. As discussed, this regression equation represents a plane positioned to minimize the sum of the squared vertical distances (Y-axis) of the observations (not shown) from the plane. Now, if we construct a plane perpendicular to the X_1-axis, we are in effect holding X_1 constant since any

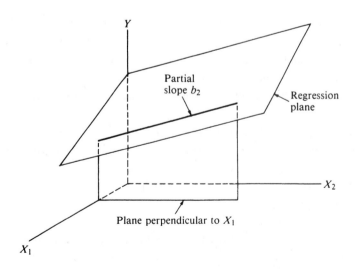

FIGURE 16.6. The multiple-regression plane.

observation lying on this plane has the same X_1 value. This plane intersects the regression plane in a straight line (bold line in Figure 16.6), the slope of which is the partial coefficient for independent variable X_2. That is, this partial slope indicates the amount by which the dependent variable (Y) is expected to change with each unit change in X_2 when the other independent variables (only X_1 in this case) are controlled.

The basic principle underlying partial coefficients and partial tables is the same as that expounded for good experimental design (Chapter 8): "doing only one thing at a time"—that is, allowing only one independent variable to vary while controlling all other variables. Sometimes this is difficult to achieve in regression analysis because of high correlations among the independent variables. Consider the extreme case of a **collinear**, or perfect, **association** between two independent variables. Suppose that we inadvertently included two collinear predictors in a regression equation: age and year of birth. Then it would be impossible to estimate the regression equation since age could not be varied while year of birth was held constant. Perfect collinearity is easily handled by dropping one of the collinear variables from the regression equation. A far more difficult problem is high **multicollinearity**, which arises when combinations of two or more independent variables are highly correlated with each other. The presence of high multicollinearity requires great care in interpreting the regression results since estimates of the coefficients will be unstable (varying greatly from sample to sample) and it will be difficult to distinguish significant from nonsignificant independent variables.

KEY POINT

Formidable statistical output tables from multivariate analyses may be simply nonsense if the model is undermined by errors of specification, measurement, and multicollinearity.

Example 2: Interscholastic Sports and Academic Achievement

Throughout the book we have been describing Broh's study of extracurricular involvement and academic achievement. We now present a series of Broh's analyses that are intended to give you a feel for the modeling enterprise and to show you how to read and interpret regression results. Our discussion will be limited to only one of her four outcome measures (math grades) and to only one of her three sets of intervening variables (the developmental model).

In the last chapter, standardized math grades in the 12th grade were regressed on interscholastic sports participation during both the 10th and the 12th grades, which supported the hypothesized positive relationship between athletic performance (independent variable) and classroom performance (dependent variable). Could the positive zero-order relationship between math grades and sports participation be a spurious result of uncontrolled antecedent variables? To explore the possibility that higher-performing students were more likely than their peers to play interscholastic sports, Broh added as controls a prior measure of the dependent variable, 10th-grade math grades, and various family and social characteristics found in previous studies to predict academic achievement.

Broh's bivariate (model 1) and multivariate (model 2) regression results are summarized in Table 16.4, which is typical of the format used in research articles. Model 1 coefficient estimates (discussed in the last chapter) for the Y-intercept (.005) and playing sports (.230) are listed in the first column. The third column displays partial-regression coefficient estimates for the additional variables included in model 2. The second and fourth columns display estimated standard errors for each regression coefficient. These are used to compute significance tests (**t-tests**), which indicate whether a regression coefficient is significantly different from zero when the other independent variables are taken into account. All **t-values** large enough to be significant at some predetermined probability level are flagged by a marker (asterisks in Table 16.4) or otherwise noted.[5] Consequently, for model 1 the likelihood is less than 1 in 1000 ($p < .001$) that the observed coefficient for playing interscholastic sports could have occurred by chance.[6]

To interpret model 2, one must start with an understanding of the variable coding, which is specified in Table 16.5. The variables described in column 3 ("Metric") as "standard units" were transformed to standard scores (mean = 0, standard deviation = 1) to facilitate comparisons of measures collected during both the 10th- and the 12th-grade follow-ups. The range, mean, and standard deviation are reported in Table 16.5 for the National Educational Longitudinal Survey (NELS)-coded variables family income, parents' education, and school size.[7]

TABLE 16.4. **Standardized 12th-Grade Math Grades Regressed on Selected Independent Variables, NELS:88**

Independent variables	Model 1 (N = 10,379)		Model 2 (N = 10,379)	
	COEFFICIENT ESTIMATE	STANDARD ERROR	COEFFICIENT ESTIMATE	STANDARD ERROR
Athlete, 10th and 12th grades	.230***	.021	.044**	.017
10th-grade math grades	—	—	.608***	.007
Female	—	—	.172***	.014
African American	—	—	−.373***	.024
Asian American	—	—	.057	.036
Hispanic	—	—	−.138***	.026
American Indian	—	—	−.339***	.077
Family income (in $10,000s)	—	—	.004*	.002
Parental education	—	—	.091***	.007
Two-parent household	—	—	.074***	.016
Public school	—	—	−.066*	.028
Suburban school	—	—	−.047*	.019
Rural school	—	—	−.010	.022
School size	—	—	−.045***	.007
Intercept	.005***		−.114	
R^2	.011***		.481	

*$p < .05$, **$p < .01$, ***$p < .001$ (two-tailed tests).
Source: Table 1 of Broh (2002). Used by permission of the author and the American Sociological Association.

TABLE 16.5. Variable Descriptions, Means, and Standard Deviations (SD)

Variable name	Description	Metric	Mean	SD
Athlete	Interscholastic sport participant in 10th and 12th grades	0 = did not participate both years	.32	.47
Math grades (10th, 12th grades)	Standardized scores of math grades	Standard units	.00	1.0
Female	Sex of student	0 = male, 1 = female	.49	.50
Black	Respondent identifies as black	0 = no, 1 = yes	.11	.31
Hispanic	Respondent identifies as Hispanic	0 = no, 1 = yes	.09	.29
Asian	Respondent identifies as Asian American	0 = no, 1 = yes	.04	.19
American Indian	Respondent identifies as American Indian	0 = no, 1 = yes	.01	.09
White	Respondent identifies as white	0 = no, 1 = yes	.75	.43
Family income	Total annual family income in $10,000s	Range: 0–29.6285	4.24	4.07
Parents' education	Highest educational level attained by either parent	1 = didn't finish high school 6 = PhD, MD, or other	3.11	1.22
Parent structure	Student lives in a dual, biological parent household	0 = no, 1 = yes	.69	.46
Public school	Student's school is public	0 = private, 1 = public	.91	.29
Urban school	School is located in an urban area	0 = no, 1 = yes	.25	.44
Suburban school	School is located in a suburban area	0 = no, 1 = yes	.41	.49
Rural school	School is located in a rural area	0 = no, 1 = yes	.34	.47
School size	Number of students in respondent's school	1 = less than 400 students 5 = more than 2000 students	3.02	1.21
Self-esteem (10th, 12th grades)	Standardized scale (lower scores represent lower self-esteem)	Standard units	.00	1.00
Locus of control (10th, 12th grades)	Standardized scale (lower scores represent less internal control)	Standard units	.00	1.00
Homework (10th, 12th grades)	Number of hours student spends on homework per week	Standard units	.00	1.00

Source: Appendix in Broh (2002). Used by permission of the author and the American Sociological Association.

The remaining variables are dummy (0/1) coded. Broh represents the five-category classification of race (discussed in Chapter 15) by four dummy variables in her regression models:

Black	=	1 if the respondent identifies his or her race as black; 0 if not.
Hispanic	=	1 if the respondent identifies his or her race as Hispanic; 0 if not.
Asian	=	1 if the respondent identifies his or her race as Asian American; 0 if not.
American Indian	=	if the respondent identifies his or her race as American Indian; 0 if not.

The key to the use of dummy variables is that one category of the original variable must be omitted from the dummy-variable set. Gender, for example, is represented by the dummy "female" and the male category is left out. The excluded race category consists of students identifying themselves as "white." What to exclude is an arbitrary decision. Broh could just as easily have included a dummy variable for whites and excluded some other racial category. Similarly, school location is represented by two dummy variables (suburban school, rural school) with urban schools as the omitted category.

Broh also constructed two dummy athlete "controls" to represent students who played interscholastic sports in the 10th but not in the 12th grade or in the 12th but not in the 10th grade. All of her regression models include three dummies for sports participation: (1) in the 10th grade only, (2) in the 12th grade only, and (3) in both years ("athletes"). The omitted category represents "nonathletes" who did not play sports in either year. Broh did not, however, report the values of the estimated coefficients for the two dummy controls (sports participant in only one year) for any of her regression models. Apparently, she used the controls to ensure a pure comparison between athletes and nonathletes that was not obscured by students who played sports in only the 10th or only the 12th grade.

Armed with an understanding of the variable coding, one next looks for significant regression coefficients. That is, the significance tests may be used to screen out results in the sample that easily could have happened by chance. Only two variables in model 2, Asian American and rural school, are not significant (Table 16.4). Since both are members of dummy sets, they must be compared to the omitted categories: That is, Asian Americans (or rural school students) are not significantly different from whites (or urban school residents) when all other variables in model 2 are held constant. The significant dummy coefficient for female students ($p < .001$), in contrast, indicates that modeled math grades are expected to be .172 standard deviation higher if the student is female rather than male (omitted category).

With such a large sample of more than 10,000 students, most coefficients are likely to be statistically significant. After screening for significance, one can examine the sign and size of the partial coefficients to determine the separate contribution of each variable in predicting 12th-grade (1992) math grades. Not surprisingly, the best predictor is math grades in the 10th grade (1990): For every unit change of 1 standard deviation in 1990 math grades, an increase of .608 standard deviation in 1992 math grade is expected according to model 2 (Table 16.4). Similarly, 1992 math grade is positively associated with being female ($b = .172$), family income ($b = .004$), parental education ($b = .091$), and living in a two-parent household ($b = .074$). Each slope coefficient should be interpreted in terms of the variable coding (metric) shown in Table 16.5. The coefficient for family income in model 2, for example, predicts a .004 standard deviation increase in 1992 math grades for every 1 unit ($10,000) increase in family income. Larger schools ($b = -.045$), public schools ($b = -.066$), suburban schools ($b = -.047$), and racial minorities (except Asian Americans) are negatively associated with math grades (i.e., associated with lower math grades) when the other variables in model 2 are held constant (controlled).

KEY POINT

Tables reporting multiple-regression results should be screened first for statistically significant relationships, which then can be interpreted in terms of partial regression coefficients.

Table 16.4 also lists for each model a popular but flawed measure of fit, R^2, which indicates approximately the proportion of the variance in the dependent variable (spread of observations around the mean) predicted or explained by the independent variable(s). R^2 is not always useful because it mechanically focuses on prediction instead of the theory under investigation and because it is subject to other weaknesses (Berk, 1983:526–27). Moreover, an unknown amount of the variance in the dependent variable is attributable to the stochastic component (King, 1989:24). Consequently, it is impossible to judge the performance of the independent variables from R^2, since it is not based exclusively on the systematic variance that may be explained. For example, an R^2 of .02 (2%) would be excellent if only 3 percent of the variance is systematic. Nevertheless, R^2 can be useful for comparing models based on the same dependent variable that differ on included independent variables, such as baseline model 1 ($R^2 = .011$) compared to model 2 ($R^2 = .481$).

A comparison of models 1 and 2 suggests that a substantial portion of the positive association between 1992 math grades and interscholastic sports performance is due to antecedent variables. The value of the regression coefficient for sports participation drops from .230 (model 1) to .044 (model 2) with the inclusion of the control variables. Taken together, the set of independent variables in model 2 explain nearly half (48%) of the variance in 12th-grade math grades. But even with this excellent set of math-performance predictors, interscholastic sports performance still showed a small positive relationship to improved math grades ($b = .044$, $p < .01$).[8] Consequently, even after controlling the available NELS:88 variables in model 2, Broh was unable to explain away the higher math grades of student athletes as a spurious relationship. Since it is impossible in a nonexperimental study to *control* for *all* antecedent variables, the possibility exists that future research, employing different model specifications, may reveal the athlete–grade relationship to be spurious.

Another way to buttress the inference that playing sports fosters academic achievement is to identify the intervening mechanism linking the two activities. According to one explanation, developmental theory, sports participation increases students' self-esteem, feeling of control over their lives, and work ethic. That is, the theory predicts a positive association between playing sports (independent variable) and the intervening developmental variables, which in turn are predicted to be positively associated with academic performance (dependent variable).

To explore the possibility that "character development" explains the positive effect of sports on grades, Broh constructed measures of self-esteem, locus of control, and time spent on homework.[9] First, to determine whether the developmental indicators *could* be intervening variables between sports participation and math achievement, she regressed each on sports participation, individual background, and school characteristics. Table 16.6 reveals that after controlling for the 10th-grade (1990) measure of each developmental variable and the background and school variables, interscholastic sports participation is

TABLE 16.6. Standardized 12th-Grade Developmental Model Variables Regressed
on Selected Independent Variables

Independent variables	Developmental model		
	SELF-ESTEEM ($N = 10{,}188$)	LOCUS OF CONTROL ($N = 10{,}177$)	HOMEWORK ($N = 9985$)
Athlete, 10th and 12th grades	.085***	.076***	.162***
	(.020)	(.021)	(.022)
10th-grade measure of dependent variable	.529***	.454***	.316***
	(.008)	(.009)	(.010)
Female	−.067***	.155***	.107***
	(.017)	(.018)	(.019)
African American	.159***	−.047	.019
	(.030)	(.031)	(.033)
Asian American	−.079	−.096*	−.018
	(.043)	(.045)	(.049)
Hispanic	.112***	.038	.156***
	(.032)	(.033)	(.036)
American Indian	−.036	−.056	.321***
	(.089)	(.094)	(.107)
Family income (in $10,000s)	.008***	.012***	.004
	(.002)	(.002)	(.003)
Parental education	.021**	.004	.053***
	(.008)	(.008)	(.009)
Two-parent household	−.009	.055**	−.000
	(.019)	(.020)	(.021)
Public school	.002	−.039	−.001
	(.033)	(.035)	(.038)
Suburban school	−.010	−.115***	−.006
	(.023)	(.024)	(.026)
Rural school	.023	−.051	.040
	(.026)	(.027)	(.030)
School size	.012	−.003	−.008
	(.008)	(.009)	(.009)
Intercept	−.162	−.088	−.305
R^2	.310	.229	.124

Standard errors are shown in parentheses. $*p < .05$, $**p < .01$, $***p < .001$ (two-tailed tests).
Source: Table 2 in Broh (2002). Used by permission of the author and the American Sociological Association.

positively associated, as hypothesized, with significant 1990–92 increases in self-esteem ($b = .085$, $p < .001$), feeling of self-control ($b = .076$, $p < .001$), and time spent on homework ($b = .162$, $p < .001$) between the 10th (1990) and 12th (1992) grades.

TABLE 16.7. **Standardized 12th-Grade Math Grades Regressed
on Developmental and Control Variables**

Independent variables	Model 3 (N = 9777)		Model 4 (N = 9777)	
	COEFFICIENT ESTIMATE	STANDARD ERROR	COEFFICIENT ESTIMATE	STANDARD ERROR
Athlete, 10th and 12th grades	.049**	.017	.031	.017
Self-esteem	—	—	−.009	.009
Locus of control	—	—	.091***	.009
Homework	—	—	.032***	.007
Intercept	−.142		−.117	
R^2	.485		.493	

Both models also include the independent variables of model 2 in Table 15.4. $*p < .05, **p < .01, ***p < .001$ (two-tailed tests).
Source: Table 3 in Broh (2002). Used by permission of the author and the American Sociological Association.

Having established that the developmental indicators are positively associated with sports participation, Broh then needed to demonstrate that they promote academic achievement in math. Her results are summarized in Table 16.7. The first regression, model 3, is essentially her previous set of independent variables from model 2 but limited to slightly fewer cases (9777 instead of 10,379 students) because of missing information for some of the developmental variables. In the second regression equation, model 4, she adds the three developmental indicators to her previous set of independent variables. A comparison of models 3 and 4 reveals that interscholastic sports participation no longer has a significant impact ($b = .031, p > .05$) when the developmental indicators are controlled. Increase in students' math grades between the 10th and 12th grades is positively associated with gains in internal control ($b = .091, p < .001$) and time spent on homework ($b = .032, p < .001$) but not self-esteem ($b = −.009, p > .05$).

Broh's findings support the developmental explanation of how sports participation promotes academic achievement in mathematics. High school athletes develop a greater work ethic and sense of control over their lives than do nonathletes, which has a positive effect on math grades. In a separate analysis that included all intervening variables (developmental, leading crowd, and social capital models), Broh identified an additional intervening variable, student discussions with teachers outside of class ($b = .202, p < .001$), which further reduced the effect of sports performance on 1992 math grades to a nonsignificant association ($b = .019, p > .05$). Consequently, the three intervening variables (locus of control, homework, and student–teacher discussions) provide an interpretation of the process linking sports participation to math achievement. The role of the self-esteem variable, however, may be misspecified in Broh's model because it may be an effect rather than a cause of student achievement.

For pedagogical purposes, we described only part of Beckett Broh's study. You might be wondering whether her findings would generalize to academic achievements other than math grades, to extracurricular activities other than interscholastic sports, and to intervening processes other than the developmental variables. Please see Box 16.1 for answers to these questions and a summary of her complete study.

BOX 16.1 Extracurricular Activities and High School Achievement

In the last two chapters we have described a part of Beckett Broh's analysis of the academic benefits of participating in high school extracurricular activities. Whereas we have restricted ourselves to the impact of playing interscholastic sports on math grades, Broh examined participation in a range of extracurricular activities, and she also included grades in English and scores on math and reading ability tests as outcome measures.

In analyses identical to the aforementioned modeling of math grade (see Table 16.4), Broh separately regressed each of the other 12th-grade outcome measures (English grades, math and reading test scores) on corresponding 10th-grade measures of the dependent variable, on interscholastic sports participation in the 10th and 12th grades, and on the same set of antecedent social, family, and school characteristics. Similar to the small positive relationship between playing sports and math grades ($b = .044, p < .01$) found after controlling for the antecedent variables, interscholastic sports participation was related to improved English grades ($b = .073, p < .001$) and to higher math test scores ($b = .034, p < .001$) but to lower reading test scores ($b = -.042, p < .01$). Thus, her finding that playing sports positively influences math grades also generalizes to English grades and math achievement scores.

The thesis that participation in interscholastic sports has real academic benefits was strengthened by Broh's analysis of theorized intervening variables. Two developmental variables, locus of control and time spent on homework, accounted for about "one-third of the effect of sports on grades and test scores" (Broh, 2002:78). The "leading crowd hypothesis" did not fare as well: Having more academically oriented peers did not appreciably improve an athlete's academic performance. Increases in social capital associated with interscholastic sports participation, in contrast, accounted for "almost half the effect of sports participation on math grades and over a third of the effect on English grades, but only one-fifth of the effect on scores on math tests" (Broh, 2002:81). The social capital effects were largely due to two variables: (1) whether students talk to teachers outside of class and (2) the frequency of talking to parents about school studies, programs, and classes. When the intervening and antecedent variables were simultaneously controlled, the effect of sports participation was substantially lower for English grades ($b = .037, p < .05$) and vanished to nonsignificant levels for math grades ($b = .019, p < .05$) and math test scores ($b = .014, p < .05$). Consequently, Broh identified much of the intervening mechanisms linking sports to academic performance in the NELS:88 data.

Do the apparent academic benefits of participating in interscholastic sports also extend to other extracurricular activities? Broh expanded her regression analyses to include variables representing 10th- and 12th-grade involvement in intramural sports, cheerleading, music groups, school drama, student council, yearbook or journalism club, and vocational clubs. When these other extracurricular activities were controlled simultaneously, the positive effects of playing interscholastic sports increased for math grades ($b = .111, p < .001$), English grades ($b = .141, p < .001$), and math tests ($b = .055, p < .001$), and the previous negative effect on reading tests changed to a nonsignificant association ($b = .005, p > .05$). Participation in music groups yielded similar, but smaller, gains in math grades, English grades, and math test scores. Student council participation was linked to improved grades

(continued)

(continued)

but not to higher test scores. In marked contrast to interscholastic athletes, students participating in intramural sports and, to a lesser extent, vocational clubs had consistently lower
grades and test scores over the 2-year period. Finally, involvement in cheerleading, school
drama, or the yearbook did not produce consistent grade and test score benefits for the student participants.

By and large, Broh presents an impressive set of analyses demonstrating the academic
benefits of playing interscholastic sports. Of all the extracurricular activities studied, playing
school sports produced the strongest and most consistent positive effects on grades and test
scores. An ostensibly similar activity, playing intramural sports, produced an even stronger, but negative, effect on academic performance. Broh then shows that the intramural athletes do not gain the developmental and social capital advantages associated with extramural
sports and linked to academic achievement. In fact, over the 2-year period, intramural athletes' sense of control over their lives significantly decreased, and their time spent on homework and relationships with teachers and parents did not differ from that of peers who did not
participate in extracurricular activities.

It is unlikely that Broh's recent research will be the conclusive study on the academic
consequences of involvement in high school extracurricular activities since her findings may
be reinterpreted or contradicted by future studies involving different model specifications,
better statistical procedures, or new data sets. One problem is her failure to use statistical software appropriate for the NELS:88 multistage sampling design: students clustered by school,
stratification, and disproportionate sampling of certain strata (e.g., oversampling of Hispanics). Although she did use NELS:88 sampling weights to adjust for disproportionate sampling,
clustering and stratification information is also needed to produce adequate standard error
estimates and significance tests.[10] Ignoring clustering and stratification will generally produce
standard error estimates that are too small.

Another potential problem is multicollinearity because the estimated academic effects
of playing interscholastic sports are quite small after simultaneously controlling for as many
as 15 or more antecedent variables.[11] Broh makes no mention of using regression diagnostic
procedures to assess whether collinearity among the control variables is adversely affecting
the estimated effects of playing sports. Also, by creating two dummy control variables for
playing interscholastic sports in only one year (10th but not 12th grade or vice versa), which
was intended to allow a pure comparison between "athletes" and "nonathletes," Broh may
have inadvertently removed some of the poorer students from the group of athletes (10th- and
12th-grade participants). That is, academic difficulties may explain why some of these students played sports in only one of the two years.[12]

Future research may support Broh's pioneering study and may provide answers to
important questions raised by her findings. Are the academic benefits of playing interscholastic sports similar for male and female students? Do the effects of participating in various
extracurricular activities vary by race–ethnicity as well as by parental education and income?
Are there school-level effects in addition to the individual effects of students' family and
social background? Does extracurricular participation reduce the time spent on recreational
reading and thus explain the absence of reading test improvement relative to math tests, math
grades, and English grades? How does talking to teachers after class and to parents about
school promote academic benefits to student athletes?

Example 3: Alcohol Consumption, Sleep, and Academic Performance

In the previous example, Broh estimated two separate regression equations by employing the developmental variables first as dependent variables (Table 16.6) and then as independent variables (Table 16.7). A useful statistical technique for pictorially representing and analyzing a complex model comprising a series of equations is **path analysis**. A major advantage of path analysis is that it forces researchers to be explicit about the cause-and-effect relationships among the study variables. One can perform a regression analysis, however, without specifying the theorized causal processes linking any of the variables. Broh performed her analyses, for example, without having to specify if there were any causal links between the developmental variables (self-esteem, locus of control, and time spent on homework) aside from their separate links to sports performance and math achievement. A second advantage of path analysis is that it provides quantitative estimates of the direct, indirect, and total effects of one variable on another.

An example of a path analysis model is an analysis of a subset of Singleton's (2007) campus survey data on alcohol use and academic performance that also included measures of sleep. Singleton and Amy Wolfson (2009) hypothesized that students who tend to drink heavily will go to bed later and get less sleep and will experience a greater delay between weekday and weekend bedtimes. These inadequate and erratic sleep patterns, in turn, lead to daytime sleepiness and reduce the alertness needed to focus on coursework and pay attention in class, which undermines academic performance. The complete model, presented in Figure 16.7, contains the same measures of alcohol consumption (number of drinks consumed on a typical weekend night), cumulative GPA, and SAT total score presented earlier, but in addition includes the variables sleep duration (average hours of daily sleep), sleep schedule (midpoint time of average bedtime and rise time), sleepiness (an index ranging from 14 to 30), male (sex dummy coded with male = 1), second year, and third year (class standing dummy coded with fourth year = 0).

The arrows in Figure 16.7, called paths, represent the theorized direct effects of one variable on another. All variables are causally prior to cumulative GPA, with five of them having direct effects: male, SAT total, amount consumed, sleep duration, and sleepiness. Both male and amount consumed also have indirect effects. Male affects cumulative GPA indirectly in two ways: via amount consumed and sleep duration and via sleepiness. Similarly, amount consumed has two indirect effects, one via sleep duration and the other via sleep schedule and sleepiness. Note also that second year and third year have one and three indirect effects, respectively. Can you find them in the model?

Singleton and Wolfson estimated path effects, called **path coefficients**, by regressing each of five dependent variables (cumulative GPA, sleepiness, sleep schedule, sleep duration, and amount consumed) on all causally antecedent variables. Thus, cumulative GPA was regressed on all other variables; sleepiness was regressed on all variables except cumulative GPA; sleep schedule and sleep duration were each regressed on amount consumed, second year, third year, male, and SAT total; and amount consumed was regressed on second year, third year, male, and SAT total. The path coefficients in the model are derived from the regression coefficients in each multiple regression. In addition, the vertical paths

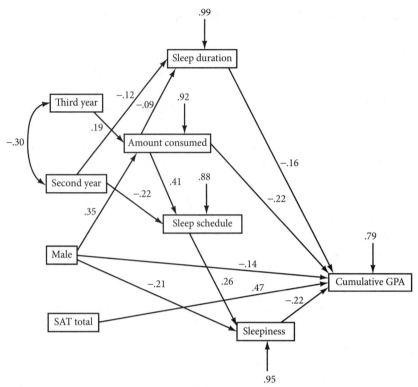

FIGURE 16.7. Path analytic model showing effects of alcohol consumption
and sleep patterns on cumulative GPA.

Source: Singleton and Wolfson (2009:361). Used by permission of Alcohol Research Documentation, Inc., Rutgers University.

to each dependent variable (e.g., .79 for cumulative GPA) represent the unexplained variation in each regression.

Singleton and Wolfson put the regression coefficients on a common footing by standardizing them.[13] A **standardized regression coefficient** may be computed by multiplying an unstandardized coefficient (which we have been using) by the ratio of the standard deviation of the independent variable to the standard deviation of the dependent variable. Standardized regression coefficients are easily interpreted as slopes in standard deviation units; a standardized coefficient of −.50, for example, indicates that the dependent variable decreases by a unit of .50 standard deviation for every standard deviation increase in the independent variable. Only statistically significant partial-regression coefficients are shown in Figure 16.7. For example, the direct effect of SAT total on cumulative GPA, a standardized coefficient of .47, indicates that GPA increases by .47 standard deviation for every standard deviation increase in SAT total.

Indirect effects are measured by taking the product of the path coefficients along a causal path and summing the products over all indirect paths (see Davis, 1985:48–64). In Figure 16.7, amount consumed has two indirect paths leading to cumulative GPA: one via sleep duration, for an indirect effect of $(−.09) \times (−.16) = .014$; and the other via sleep schedule and sleepiness, for an indirect effect of $(.41) \times (.26) \times (−.22) = −.023$. The total effect of number of drinks consumed on cumulative GPA is the sum of the direct and indirect effects: $(-.22) + (.014) + (-.023) = -.229$. Thus, cumulative GPA is estimated to decrease by about .23 standard deviation for every standard deviation increase in number of drinks consumed.

The path analysis generally supports Singleton and Wolfson's theorized model.[14] The results showed, for example, that a student's sleep habits mediate the effect of alcohol consumption on academic performance. Specifically, drinking results in a later sleep–wake schedule, which increases daytime sleepiness and negatively affects academic performance. However, the weak negative association between sleep duration and cumulative GPA was contrary to expectations insofar as sleep deprivation has been shown to diminish cognitive functioning. Singleton and Wolfson speculated that the relatively short average weekday sleep time found in their study may not amount to sleep deprivation; furthermore, other research has shown that quality rather than quantity of sleep is more strongly associated with daytime sleepiness.

KEY POINT

Standardizing by expressing values in standard deviation units facilitates the comparison of partial regression coefficients for different sets of variables and across different data sets.

Other Modeling Techniques

This discussion has just scratched the surface of multivariate modeling. There are special techniques for modeling various types of dependent variables (e.g., dichotomous, nominal, and ordinal measures), for straightening or transforming nonlinear relationships into a form suitable for linear modeling, for including interaction effects, for modeling mutual causation and measurement error, for multilevel modeling (hierarchical analysis), for social network analysis, and for modeling processes over time (longitudinal analysis) and space.[15]

Although statistically different from multiple regression, these techniques are similar in that they share the assumption that social phenomena are generated by both systematic and stochastic components. The systematic impact of the independent variables is represented by coefficient estimates of effect direction (positive or negative) and strength. However, interpretation of coefficient strength usually is not as straightforward as interpretation of regression slopes (see Stolzenberg and Land, 1983). The stochastic component in multiple regression is assumed to have a normal distribution, which may arise from the cumulative effect of a large number of unmeasured (extraneous) variables or from sampling error. When the normality assumption is unwarranted, a multiple-regression model misspecifies the data and a different stochastic component is needed.[16]

Again, we must warn that our exposition of modeling is superficial and cannot be substituted for formal course work in statistics. Our emphasis has been on interpreting modeling results to the neglect of describing the iterative process of testing various model specifications. We essentially presented the end result of modeling moral integration, academic achievement, and cumulative GPA. Before reaching a "final" model, researchers typically test a series of models of increasing or decreasing complexity, such as comparing two specifications that differ on the presence or absence of a hypothesized causal path. During this iterative process, predicted effects that are statistically insignificant or otherwise inconsistent with the data are dropped from the modeling. The resultant final model is always a tentative conclusion; subsequent research may disclose alternative models that provide just as good, if not better, fit to the data.

Summary

- Causal understanding—the goal of much social research—rests on comparisons of theory and data. Data alone cannot establish causal relationships. Rather, researchers construct theoretical models of relationships and then determine statistically the fit between data and model.
- Researchers' assumptions about direction of influence are built into their models, based on theoretical knowledge. Likewise, theory guides statistical tests for nonspuriousness by suggesting potential causes of spurious relationships (antecedent variables), and it guides tests for mediating causal processes by suggesting potential intervening variables.
- Leaving out important variables from a model is called a "specification error."
- The models for data analysis include both systematic (theorized relationships) and stochastic (chance processes) components.
- Theoretical models may be represented by arrow diagrams. Arrows indicate causal order; the signs above the arrows indicate the direction of the relationship—positive or negative.
- Model testing occurs through multivariate analysis, which enables one to (1) examine the effects of an independent variable on a dependent variable while controlling for relevant antecedent or intervening variables and (2) examine interactions among variables.
- The multivariate analysis of contingency tables, known as elaboration, begins with a two-variable relationship, and then it systematically reassesses the relationship when controls are introduced for third (and sometimes additional) variables.
- In elaboration analysis, variables are controlled, or held constant, by computing partial tables—that is, computing the original two-variable relationship separately for each category of the control variable. Several outcomes are possible:
  - If the control variable is antecedent to the other two variables and the original relationship disappears in each partial table, the original relationship is explained away as spurious (explanation).
  - If the control variable is modeled as intervening and the original relationship disappears in the partials, then the intervening causal process linking the two original variables is explicated (interpretation).
  - Other possible outcomes include specification (an interaction effect involving the increase, reduction, or disappearance of the original relationship in some partials but not in others) and replication (the partials are essentially the same as the original relationship).
  - An uncontrolled antecedent variable may suppress or distort the true causal relationship between the original two variables.
- A technique for analyzing the simultaneous effects of several independent variables on a dependent variable is multiple regression. The partial-regression coefficients in a multiple-regression equation show the effects of each independent variable on the dependent variable when all other variables in the equation are held constant.
- Multiple regression may result in unstable coefficients when some of the independent variables are highly correlated with each other, a problem known as "multicollinearity."
- Nominal- and ordinal-scale variables may be incorporated into multiple regressions by means of dummy coding.
- Partial-regression coefficients may be compared by standardizing them to the same metric of standard deviation units. Standardized coefficients indicate the number of standard deviation units the dependent variable changes for every unit change of 1 standard deviation in an independent variable.
- Standardized coefficients are used in path analysis to estimate the various indirect and direct effects between any two connected variables in a complex causal model.

Key Terms

modeling
reciprocal causation
noncausal association
direct effects
indirect effects
systematic component
stochastic component
multivariate analysis
elaboration
    partial tables, partials
    zero-order relationship
    first-order relationship
    explanation
    interpretation

specification
replication
suppressor variable
distorter variable
multiple regression
    specification error
    partial-regression coefficients/partial slopes
    collinear association
    multicollinearity
    t-tests/t values
    R^2
path analysis
path coefficients
standardized regression coefficient

Exercises

1. Surveys typically report that residents of large cities are more tolerant of deviant behavior than are residents of smaller cities and rural areas. Suppose that data are available for three variables: (1) respondent's tolerance of deviant behavior, (2) size of current place of residence, and (3) size of place in which the respondent was living at age 16. For each of the following hypotheses, draw arrow diagrams to specify a causal model incorporating the hypothesis: (a) the social environment of the current residence renders people more or less tolerant; (b) tolerance is learned during adolescence and remains relatively constant thereafter; (c) both age 16 and current residential environments affect tolerance of deviant behavior.

2. Based on data from a sample of Chinese children, Dudley Poston and Toni Falbo (1990) investigated whether only children ("onlies") differed significantly from children with siblings ("others") with respect to academic achievement. The sample consisted of 1460 schoolchildren in the 1st and 5th grades in urban and rural areas of the Changchun metropolitan area. When Poston and Falbo examined bivariate relationships, they found, as expected, that onlies performed better than others on math and verbal achievement tests. They also conducted multivariate analyses that included the following variables, in addition to only/other status: (1) parental educational achievement, (2) rural/urban residence, (3) gender, (4) parental help with homework, (5) parental expectations about the child's future, and (6) child-care arrangements prior to elementary school (either nursery school or a relative's care).
   a. Present hypothetical data showing the bivariate relationship between only/other status and academic achievement (low/high).
   b. Controlling for one of the extraneous variables identified above present hypothetical results, which indicate that the original relationship is *spurious*.
   c. Now assume that the association is not spurious and that you want to *interpret* the relationship between sibling status and academic achievement. Select one of the above extraneous variables and carefully explain how this variable mediates the relationship.

3. In a multiple-regression analysis of GPA for the first year in college, the partial coefficients for gender (dummy variable = 1 for females, 0 for males), high school GPA (range 0–4.0), and employment during the school year (range 0–50 hours) were, respectively, +0.30, +0.50, and −0.01. Given that the three partial coefficients were statistically significant, explain the meaning of each one. (Hint: Explain as partial slopes.)

4. Calculate the indirect effects and total effects of male on cumulative GPA in Singleton and Wolfson's path model (Figure 16.7).

Notes

1. There is a vast literature on the relationship between fertility and women's employment. For a meta-analysis of selected studies published between 1990 and 2006, see Matysiak and Vignoli (2008).

2. The California state assemblyman John Vasconcellos, supporting an annual $245,000 task force to increase the self-esteem of state residents, "argued that raising self-esteem would help solve many of the state's problems, including crime, teen pregnancy, drug abuse, school underachievement . . . and would help balance the state's budget because people with high self-esteem earn more money than people with low self-esteem and therefore pay more taxes" (Baumeister et al., 2003:3).

3. See Davis (1985) for a discussion of how arrow diagrams such as these apply to the logical rules for causal ordering among a set of variables.

4. A second-order partial has two control variables, a third-order relationship has three controls, and so forth.

5. These t-value statistics are computed by dividing each sample regression coefficient by its estimated standard error. In testing the null hypothesis that a coefficient has zero slope in the population (against an alternative hypothesis of a positive or negative slope [two-tailed test] or a directional alternative [one-tailed test] that the slope is positive [or negative]), the significance level (p value) is obtained from a t (sampling) distribution.

6. Strictly speaking, the probability level is a crude approximation since it depends on the extent to which the assumptions underlying the regression model are met and on proper specification of the process being modeled.

7. Apparently, Broh treats parents' education (coded 1–6) and school size (coded 1–5) as interval-scale variables in her regression analyses.

8. This was also true for English grades and math test scores.

9. Broh's measures of self-esteem and time spent on homework were discussed in Chapter 5. She reports that locus of control is also a "composite measure in the NELS data . . . comprised of multiple measures of students' . . . sense of control" (Broh, 2002:75).

10. The statistical packages STATA and SUDAAN, for example, provide estimates of standard errors for complex sampling designs.

11. For example, the interscholastic athlete coefficient for math grades (Table 16.4) is only .044 after controlling for 13 social, family, or school characteristics and for the 2 dummy variables for sports participation in only 1 year. The total count of independent variables increases by about 8 with the inclusion of all intervening variables and by about 7 when all forms of extracurricular activities are included in the regression analysis.

12. Although Broh does not report any of the estimated coefficients for the two athlete dummy controls, there is indirect evidence that one or both have negative effects in the baseline modeling of math grades (model 1, Table 16.4) since the other two coefficient estimates are positive (.230 for athletes, .005 for intercept) and the weighted total effects across all students should sum to zero (the mean of the standardized math grades).

13. Path analysis may also be performed with unstandardized coefficients.

14. Singleton and Wolfson used the model-fitting program AMOS Version 16 (SPSS, Inc., Chicago, IL) to analyze the path model. Several indexes showed that the model in Figure 16.7 provides an acceptable fit. For a good introduction to path analysis, see Kline (2016:117–63).

15. Raftery (2001) provides an excellent overview of 1950–2000 modeling developments in sociology. A good treatment of these topics may be found in Arminger, Clogg, and Sobel (1995).

16. See McCullagh and Nelder (1989) and Gill (2001) for ways to model the stochastic component with Poisson, binomial, gamma, inverse gaussian, and other probability distributions.

17

Writing Research Reports

Scientific research is a social activity, even when done by a solitary researcher. Without communication with others, one cannot participate in or contribute to the shared, cumulative body of knowledge that defines each scientific discipline. Much scientific communication takes place orally, but the advancement of science ultimately depends on writing. Through written research reports, books, and articles, researchers communicate with others who learn about, review, apply, and extend their work. The purpose of this chapter is to enhance the development of research writing skills. We will consider not only how to write about research but also how to locate materials that can inform your research and writing.

The audience and forms of research reports vary. For a professional researcher the audience is most often peers in his or her field; the vehicle is generally an article in a scholarly journal. For a student researcher, the audience may be a class and the vehicle an oral seminar presentation or a professor and a term paper. The task in each case is to communicate precisely and accurately what questions framed the research, what literature informed it, what the researcher did, what was found, and what conclusions might be drawn. When this is done well, a researcher clearly conveys what he or she has learned and others are able to make an informed evaluation of the study.

Virtually all research is grounded in an existing literature, and research reports should document the relationship of the current work to this literature. However, many students come to the tasks of doing social research and of writing a research paper with no notion of where to begin. Therefore, before discussing the mechanics of research writing, we will address this issue. Where do research ideas come from? How are topics narrowed and informed by previous research? Where does research actually begin?

Searching the Literature

When you initiate a literature search, you should have at least a general idea of what you want to study. You need not have narrowed down the topic at the outset, although eventually it will be essential to do so. To start, it is enough to know the broad area you are interested in—for example, "sex roles," "white-collar crime," "social capital," or "altruism." You will find that an information search will offer many opportunities to narrow the topic. So, where should you begin your search? Literature searches have changed dramatically since the first edition of this book. Earlier editions focused on the use of print indexes, and later editions also described searchable CD-ROM databases. Although print indexes are still available, CD-ROMs have long been replaced with electronic databases. Nowadays virtually all searches are conducted online.

Using the Internet

Suppose that, inspired by the research reported in Chapter 1, you are interested in studying "volunteerism." Entering the term in the search engine Google in July 2016, we generated a list of more than 5 million websites. Such keyword searches may yield very large lists of citations, or "hits," many of which may be irrelevant to your interests. Still, the search may be useful for brainstorming ideas. The first website listed in many searches is the popular Wikipedia, "the free encyclopedia." Although Wikipedia may provide a helpful preview of a subject, it is not a reliable source to be cited in a research report. Wikipedia and other online encyclopedias are tertiary sources that synthesize research and describe subjects more generally. We found that the entry for volunteerism (actually redirected to "volunteering") was incomplete; it discussed the etymology and history of the word as well as types and political aspects of volunteering, but did not place the term in the context of social science research and theory.

The first page of our Google search results revealed the different types of sources you may find in your Internet search. The links that followed included numerous websites, many of which were labeled "Ads," containing information on volunteer opportunities. They also included the site ServiceLeader.org and two online journals, *e-Volunteerism* and *Volunteer Today*. A review of these websites showed that they contained articles and links for those who work with, lead, or manage volunteers. Although this information may be of personal interest to you, it is not social science research. You should concentrate instead on finding primary sources, such as survey data sets and other raw data and reports of empirical research, or secondary sources, such as review articles in professional journals.

There are many excellent social science resources online, both primary and secondary, including data archives, government documents, newspaper publications, and library catalogs. Numerous social science data sets are available on the Internet. One of the largest depositories of social science data, the Inter-university Consortium for Political and Social Research, has a website. So does the General Social Survey (GSS), where you can find data files, codebooks, and other documentation available to download or order. You also can obtain census data from the website of the U.S. Census Bureau as well as data from numerous other government agencies. In fact, every major agency of the U.S. government has a website that provides extensive information about the agency and its publications. Most newspapers may be browsed on the Internet. Virtually all library catalogs can be accessed online, and the website WorldCat.org, which supports libraries worldwide, gives you the library holdings of more than 200 million bibliographic records of books, journals, and other materials.

This short list of resources suggests the scope and utility of the Internet. Some resources may not be in your library (e.g., government documents); others may be accessible only on the Internet (e.g., remote library catalogs). However, the fluid and unstructured nature of information on the Web makes it a challenge to use. Search results also must be evaluated carefully since authorship can range from grade-school students to government agencies to political interest groups. Government sites (with the .gov extension) and college or university sites (.edu) generally can be trusted to provide accurate information. But many other sites may be untrustworthy. To determine a site's credibility, you may want to consult the many university websites that contain information on evaluating online sources. (Just do an online search on "evaluating websites.") In general, these sites will ask you to consider a few important points. The credentials of the author, if indeed an author is listed, are important, as is the nature of the site, both its readership and its focus. Does it advocate a particular point of view? Is it a site for the general public, such as Wikipedia, or for professionals, such as the online journals for volunteer practitioners that we found, or is it for social scientists? If there are links and/or references, you should investigate their accuracy. You should check for the date that the item was posted and whether the links are current.

In short, the Internet is a valuable research tool but with sources that should always be examined carefully. (See Box 17.1 for further information on Internet resources.) For researchers wanting to find books and scholarly articles, where social science research is most likely to be reported, the place to search is the library.

Using the Library

Before you begin your library search, it is important to know the types of resources that are available and the kind of information each kind of resource can provide about social science research. The two major options are the online catalog and electronic databases. You can find books in the library catalog, but electronic databases allow you to search for articles and often books, book chapters, technical reports, and other written materials.

Suppose you begin with the catalog. When we searched one library catalog by typing "volunteer*" (using the wild-card asterisk to cast the widest net), we found 110 titles, including *Volunteer Tourism in the Global South*, *The Volunteer Management Handbook*, *Volunteer Slavery*, *The Volunteer Subject*, and *Volunteers: A Social Profile*. Of these, only the last, by Marc A. Musick and John Wilson, seems relevant; published in 2008, it was one of the relatively few titles with a publication date after 2000. Skimming through this book revealed that it is a thorough review of the social science literature on volunteering. Like nearly all books, however, it does not provide the most current information. In addition, all but the largest libraries will have a small proportion of available books. So, although the catalog is not a bad place to begin your search, it is limited.

In the bibliography for the Musick and Wilson book, the majority of references are articles published in professional journals, which is where most of the social science

---

BOX 17.1 Internet Resources for Social Research

Although the Internet may be of limited utility in conducting a literature search, it is an invaluable tool for social research. There is a website for this textbook (www.oup.com/us/singleton-approaches) with annotated links to Web resources for every chapter that can help you at every stage of research. Among these links are websites with the following:

- The Code of Federal Regulations and National Institutes of Health guidelines for the conduct of research involving human subjects (Chapter 3)
- Examples to clarify key methodological concepts (Chapter 4)
- Question sources and tutorials on questionnaire design (Chapter 10)
- A guide to scale construction (Chapter 5)
- Calculators for determining an appropriate sample size (Chapter 6) and response rates (Chapter 9)
- A list of questions to ask in evaluating poll results (Chapter 9)
- Learning materials for doing qualitative data analysis (Chapter 11)
- A list of public data sources for social scientists (Chapter 12)
- A content analysis guidebook (Chapter 12)
- Interactive packages for understanding statistics (Chapter 15)
- Grammar style guides for writing research papers (Chapter 17)

Of particular value as a source of evidence on volunteerism are the numerous publicly available data sets. In the first chapter, we noted that the Current Population Survey (CPS) has included an annual supplement on volunteering every September since 2002. Also, in 2002, 2004, and 2014, the GSS had modules on the related topic of altruism. Reported statistics from these and other sources will enable you to document the incidence of volunteering and its relationship to key variables. And, if available, raw data might be used to conduct a secondary analysis.

When we visited the CPS website at the Bureau of Labor Statistics (http://www.bls.gov/cps/), our search of "volunt*" led us to a link to an annual news release on the CPS volunteering data: http://www.bls.gov/news.release/pdf/volun.pdf. Following this link, we discovered CPS statistics and tables from the latest (2015) CPS volunteering survey, with breakdowns on volunteering among demographic groups, total annual hours spent volunteering, number and type of volunteer organization, and main volunteer activities. There were no links to the raw data at the CPS or other Census Bureau sites; however, these data may be downloaded from the websites of the National Bureau of Economic Research or the Inter-university Consortium for Political and Social Research, which is where we got the information on college student volunteering that we reported in Chapter 1.

---

literature can be found. To search this literature, we turn to electronic databases. Libraries generally group their databases by subject. In addition, libraries have multifield databases such as Academic Search Premier, which indexes and abstracts nearly 13,600 journals. When we searched this database for "volunteer*," we found more than 90,000 hits, many of which were unrelated to volunteerism (e.g., "The Area of Secondary Hyperalgesia following Heat Stimulation in Healthy Male Volunteers").

As with search terms, better results are generated by narrowing the choice of databases. Of particular value for social scientists are discipline-specific databases such as Sociological Abstracts, SocIndex, and PsychInfo. One or more of these are available in most college or university libraries. Each offers a somewhat different set of journals and other sources but should yield a more focused set of citations on volunteerism. To illustrate the utility of these databases and how to use them to conduct a literature review, we will use SocIndex.

SocIndex is primarily a collection of abstracts—brief summaries of articles—of journals in sociology and closely related areas of study, including criminal justice, demography, gender studies, and sociocultural anthropology. SocIndex contains abstracts of more than 2700 journals, both English language and foreign, with coverage of some journals dating back to 1895. In addition to journal articles, it indexes books, book chapters, and conference papers and other nonperiodic content sources, such as dissertations.

Our search (on July 13, 2016) of "volunteer*" in SocIndex generated nearly 14,000 results. Although this is a relatively large number of hits, searches of other topics may yield hits numbering from zero to the thousands. The number of hits is important information by itself because it indicates that the subject of volunteerism is too broad for defining a research problem. However, the citations are in reverse chronological order, which should prove useful since you generally would want to read the most recent citation first and then work backward. Also, by looking at a few of the initial screens, you can quickly see what kind of research is being done and then choose a term to add to the search to narrow the results.

The SocIndex citation list can be sorted by date or relevance or filtered by a custom field such as document type (article, book chapter, conference paper, etc.), source type (academic journals, magazines, books, etc.), or language. If you want only the most recent items, searches can be limited by year or by a range of years. Searches also can be limited to "peer-reviewed" journals, that is, journals subject to the review of fellow academics and researchers, an important distinction between scholarly and popular publications. Further, a useful feature to help you narrow the research topic is that you can filter items according to subject headings from a sociological thesaurus; among the 50 subjects into which items on our list were grouped were "volunteer service," "volunteers," "social services," and "community involvement." Finally, the list should indicate whether the article is available for download. Articles of interest can then be marked, saved, printed, and/or sent to an e-mail address.

Citations will include several types of references. To become familiar with general research and theory on volunteerism, the most useful will be reviews of the literature and meta-analyses; in fact, to find reviews, you may want to do a search with "volunteer*" and "review" in separate fields. Most articles will consist of reports of empirical research; a few will present a new theory or theoretical synthesis; a few others will consist of commentaries. Let's suppose after skimming the Musick and Wilson book or a review article on volunteerism, you decide that you might want to investigate the relationship between volunteerism and well-being. Searching for "volunteers" and "well-being" gave us a much shorter list of 426 items; however, this many hits suggest that the topic may still be too broad. To further cull the list, you might begin to read several titles and abstracts or check one of the subject headings, such as older people (55 hits), caregivers (35), or aging (24).

Among the first 10 hits in the SocIndex search, all of which appeared in academic journals, was the following article, a report of an empirical study:

Thoits, Peggy A. 2012. Role-identity salience, purpose and meaning in life, and well-being among volunteers. *Social Psychology Quarterly* 75(4):360–84.

Clicking on the article title takes us to a more detailed record that includes the abstract, as shown in Figure 17.1. To continue from this page, you can search for articles by the author or by one of the subject terms. In addition to providing an abstract, this page also includes links to 69 cited references (with hyperlinks to those included in the SocIndex database) and to 6 other references in the database in which this article has been cited (not shown in Figure 17.1). These citation lists could be useful information because they might

---

Record: 1

Title:

Role-Identity Salience, Purpose and Meaning in Life, and Well-Being among Volunteers.

Authors:

Thoits, Peggy A.[1]

Source:

Social Psychology Quarterly. Dec2012, Vol. 75 Issue 4, p360–384. 25p. 1 Diagram, 5 Charts.

Document Type:

Article

Subject Terms:

*VOLUNTEERS	*MEANINGLESSNESS (Philosophy)
*PSYCHOLOGY	*SELF-perception
*IDENTITY (Psychology)	*QUALITY of life
*WELL-being	*SOCIAL support
*VOLUNTEER service	RESEARCH
*SOCIAL psychology	PSYCHOLOGICAL aspects
*SOCIAL role	CARDIAC patients—Services for
*FRIENDLY visiting	SOCIAL aspects

Author-Supplied Keywords:

identity salience	role-identity
purpose and meaning in life	volunteer work
	well-being

FIGURE 17.1. Citation from SocIndex. Downloaded July 13, 2016.

Abstract:

Theoretically, the more important a role-identity is to a person, the more it should provide a sense of purpose and meaning in life. Believing one's life to be purposeful and meaningful should yield greater mental and physical well-being. These hypotheses are tested with respect to the volunteer role, specifically, Mended Hearts visitor, in which former heart patients visit current heart patients and their families in the hospital. Analyses of survey data from Mended Hearts visitors ($N = 458$) confirm that a sense of meaningful, purposeful life mediates the positive influences of role-identity salience on mental and physical health. The results hint at an unfolding process: the more time spent in volunteer activities, the more important the volunteer identity. The greater the identity importance, the more one perceives one matters to other people, which in turn enhances purpose and meaning. The more life seems purposeful and meaningful, the better one's well-being. [ABSTRACT FROM PUBLISHER]

Author Affiliations:

[1]Indiana University, Bloomington, IN, USA

ISSN:

0190-2725

DOI:

10.1177/0190272512459662

Accession Number:

84343225

Persistent link to this record (Permalink):

http://ezproxy.holycross.edu:2048/login?url=http://search.ebscohost.com/login.aspx?direct=true&db=sih&AN=84343225&site=ehost-live

Cut and Paste:

<A href="http://ezproxy.holycross.edu:2048/login?url=http://search.ebscohost.com/login.aspx?direct=true&db=sih&AN=84343225&site=ehost-live">Role-Identity Salience, Purpose and Meaning in Life, and Well-Being among Volunteers.</A>

Database:

SocINDEX with Full Text

FIGURE 17.1. Continued

indicate the significance of the reported study. They also enable users to examine additional articles and books for further references. By following these leads, you can quickly gain a command of the literature and think about how to narrow the topic appropriately. Finally, a list of records can be marked and collected as you go along. And by saving searches you can keep a citation list up to date by calling up and repeating the searches after the database (SocIndex in this case) has been updated.

KEY POINT

The bulk of the social science literature can be found in professional journal articles; the best way to search this literature is to use a library's online databases.

Outlining and Preparing to Write

Although we focus on the final research report in this chapter, in reality writing occurs throughout the research process. Researchers take notes as they review the literature, and once they have formulated a research question and come up with a research design to address it, they invariably write a research proposal. You may be asked to write a proposal to gain the approval of an instructor or thesis chair to carry out research, or you may submit a proposal to request funding to support your research.

A research proposal is a written description of how a researcher intends to address the research question. The outline of a proposal is essentially the same as the first three parts of a research report, which we discuss in detail below: an introduction, literature review, and description of methods and data to be used to address the research question. The difference is that a proposal describes what the researcher plans to do rather than what he or she did. In addition, it is usually shorter than the parallel parts of the final report; in fact, funding agencies usually have word and/or page limits.

In preparing to do research, you also may be required to submit a proposal to the institutional review board. This usually means completing a form that asks you to describe the aims and methods of your proposed research and to specify how participants' rights are to be protected. Although requirements vary somewhat across institutions, Chapter 3 outlines a set of issues that you will likely need to address. These include the potential risks and benefits of the research, as well as the steps you will take to gain informed consent, protect confidentiality, and otherwise secure the data.

Before you begin to write, you should have a conception of the overall organization of the research report. We recommend writing an outline that organizes the paper in terms of the following sections typically found in articles reporting empirical research.

- An *introduction* that includes a statement of the problem under investigation
- A *literature review* that summarizes and places the problem in the context of related theory and research
- A description of the *design and execution of the study* that indicates how the research was done in sufficient detail to allow a reasonable replication of it

- A presentation of the *data analysis and findings* that identifies the method of analysis and the specific results of the study
- A *discussion* of the findings that offers a broad interpretation of the results

Within each of these major headings you should list subtopics and important points. As you may discover, outlining frequently brings out the recognition of new ideas and the necessity for transition topics that lead from one point to the next. You should ask the following continually as the outline becomes detailed: How can I move logically from this point to that point? Does the organization make sense? Have I left out anything essential? A report-length paper of 15 to 20 pages requires an outline of at least 1 and possibly 2 or more single-spaced pages.

When the outline is complete, you are ready to begin the actual report. At this point it is critical for you to have a clear grasp of the audience's level of knowledge and sources of interest. This does not mean that you should "talk down" or "write down" to the consumers of your work. But you should keep in mind who is going to read it. For social science readers who are familiar with the area of study, the report may include technical language, an abbreviated presentation of previous research, and a detailed presentation of methods and findings. For lay readers it should omit technical terms and should provide a more detailed presentation of the background of the research and a more general presentation of methods and findings. Since it seems more common to err in providing too little information about research methods and using too many technical terms, we recommend that students write for intelligent and educated peers.

Only you, the researcher, are fully aware of why the study was done; how it is related to previous research; what decisions in design, operations, and measurement were made; and why. The overriding concern should be to communicate these points as accurately and clearly as possible. As in all good writing, this requires proper grammar, punctuation, and style. The principles of being concise and direct, of avoiding unnecessary jargon, of providing examples to clarify points, and so forth apply just as strongly to technical as to any other form of writing.

In addition to these considerations, we have three other recommendations as you write a draft of your proposal or report:

1. Avoid so-called "writer's block" by **free writing**—recording your thoughts quickly, without regard to grammar and punctuation and without referring to your notes, data, or other information. As experienced writers, we know how difficult it is to write. More often than we care to count, our minds have been blank as we faced a blank document on our computer screen. The sociologist Howard Becker (2007) is one of many advocates of free writing; when his students were having trouble getting started, he advised them to simply sit down and write whatever came into their heads without pausing to look at notes, books, data, or other aids. In free writing, the idea is to write continuously as quickly as you can for a time without worrying about grammar, spelling, and so forth. Although the topics in free writing may be completely open, Becker seems to suggest—and we agree—that it is important to at least stay on the research topic.

2. Related to the first point, consider your first draft a "draft" and not the final report. Too often, because of time and other constraints, students treat writing as a kind of test in which a paper is a problem that they get one shot at answering (H. S. Becker, 2007). All professionals who write fully expect to go through multiple drafts; they know that their first draft is not the finished product. Rather, they see writing as a form of thinking, in which early drafts may show some confusion and lack coherence. As Becker says, "the rough draft shows you what needs to be made clearer"; rewriting and editing "let you do it" (17). (We have more to say about revision below.)

3. Use the active voice. The use of active rather than passive verbs is standard advice in writing texts. Becker believes this practice is particularly important for sociologists. The reason, as he explains, is that

> Active verbs almost always force you to name the person who did whatever was done. . . . We seldom think that things just happen all by themselves, as passive verbs suggest, because in our daily lives people *do* things and *make them happen.* Sentences that name active agents make our representations of social life more understandable and believable. "The criminal was sentenced" hides the judge who, we know, did the sentencing and, not incidentally, thus makes the criminal's fate seem the operation of impersonal forces rather than the result of people acting together to imprison him or her. (79–80)

With these points in mind, let us consider in some detail the topical outline suggested above. It is important to note that this is only one of many possible outlines. It applies best to explanatory studies involving experimentation and survey research and least to exploratory and descriptive studies, especially field research. Moreover, considerations of length, subject matter, purpose, and audience may influence the organization and elaboration of this outline in the actual paper. A paper may emphasize measurement, sampling, or something else depending on the study. No perfect outline exists ready to be adopted for every research paper. The important point is that the outline should be functional and facilitate the writing.

Major Headings

In the social sciences, numerous professional journals report current research. The journals encountered during a literature review provide models for the research report. These models vary according to the field but in general contain the following or similar components.

The Abstract

Generally, the first portion of a scientific paper is the *abstract*, a capsule version of the full report written after the report is completed. Abstracts do not describe what takes place in the report (e.g., "after a review of the literature, we formulated and tested the hypothesis that . . .") but, rather, summarize the content, briefly describing the research question or hypothesis, methods, and key findings. They act as a prose table of contents. They typically use the same words as the report and, in fact, may be pieced together by "abstracting" phrases from the finished report.

Abstracts rarely exceed half a page and frequently are limited to 150 to 200 words. The purpose of the abstract is to help potential readers decide whether they are sufficiently interested in the topic to read the full report. Keeping this in mind will help in the formulation of a concise abstract. Authors should include only the information they themselves would want to know if they were unfamiliar with the study and wished to assess its utility for themselves. In many ways the title of a report serves the same purpose and may be regarded as an abstract of the abstract.

Introduction

This section sets up the rest of the paper. It is the place, Mark Edwards (2012:43) points out, "where you try to hook the reader with an answer to the question, 'Why should I care?'" Answering this question requires a clear statement of the problem and why it is of general interest and importance. General interest and importance may be demonstrated by relating the problem briefly to the theoretical context of the study or by pointing to its social and practical significance. For example, Bruce Straits (1985) opens his article in the *Journal of Marriage and the Family* (see Chapter 7) by briefly describing current *theoretical* explanations for low U.S. birth rates, each of which emphasizes a different set of factors influencing childbearing plans. The point of his research, he then explains, is to disentangle and determine the relative importance of these factors among a sample of young college women.

In the introduction to their article on execution publicity and homicide in the *American Sociological Review* (see Chapter 12), William Bailey and Ruth Peterson (1989:722) emphasize the social significance of the problem. They begin by noting that "the United States is the only Western nation retaining capital punishment for civil homicide" and "the death penalty is authorized in 37 of 50 states." They go on to say that the "courts have ruled that capital punishment is constitutionally acceptable as long as it is practiced properly." Furthermore, "since the mid-1970s, persons have been sentenced to death" in 34 states, with more than 2000 persons now on death row as of 1988; and "the annual number of executions has increased steadily throughout the 1980s," as 106 persons have been executed. Having established the social significance of the problem, Bailey and Peterson then point out that one empirically testable argument in favor of the death penalty is that it "discourages would-be killers." Their analysis, the introduction concludes, "examines an important deterrence and death penalty issue: the impact of execution publicity on homicides in the United States, 1940–1986."

In some ways, the introduction can be the most difficult part of the report to write. In fact, we have struggled at times to introduce chapters in this book. In these cases, we have followed some sage advice that H. S. Becker received while in graduate school: Write the introduction last, after you have a complete draft of the report. You can never be certain when you begin a report of exactly what you will write. So, it is often easier and more effective to write the introduction after you know how the paper turns out.

Literature Review

The literature review must make clear the theoretical context of the problem under investigation and how it has been studied by others. The idea is to cite relevant literature in the process of presenting the underlying theoretical and methodological rationale for the research. This means citing key studies and emphasizing major findings rather than trying to report every study ever done on the problem or providing unnecessary detail.

In studies designed to test specific hypotheses, the aim of this section should be to show, if possible, how the hypotheses derive from theory or previous research. When this is not possible—for example, because the hypothesis is based on everyday observations and experiences—one should still show the relevance of the study to previous research and theory, if only to show how it contradicts existing evidence or fills a gap in scientific knowledge. Indeed, even when there are no clearly formulated hypotheses or the research is basically descriptive or exploratory, it is still appropriate to place the research in some theoretical context.

Finally, it is a good idea, especially for lengthy literature reviews, to end this section with (1) a concise restatement of hypotheses; (2) a presentation of the theoretical model in a figure, such as an arrow diagram; and/or (3) a brief overview of the study.

Methods

In this section you should state clearly and accurately how the study was done, providing enough information to permit replication by others. The following subtopics may help you to accomplish this objective.

Design

First you must tell what type of study you have done: experiment, survey, field research, or available-data analysis. The approach determines the primary design and procedural issues that must be addressed: (1) In the case of an experiment, the key issues will include the type of experimental design and the procedures of its implementation; (2) in a survey, the survey mode and sampling design; (3) in field research, the nature of the setting(s) and the researcher's relationship to informants; (4) in research using available data, the sources of data and their completeness.

Subjects

This section should make clear who participated in the study, how many cases were sampled, how they were selected, and whom or what they represent. It is necessary to discuss sampling procedures as well as limitations of the sample data.

Measurement

Here, operational definitions are described. No matter what approach was used, you should clarify the way in which your observations were translated into variables and concepts. In an experiment, this means specifying the procedures for manipulating the independent variable and measuring the dependent variable. In a survey, this should include the specific questions that were asked as measures of each variable in the theoretical model. In field research, this means noting the kinds of observations that were made and, if relevant, other sources of information such as documents and in-depth interviewing. Longer reports may contain appendixes with some of these materials, such as copies of the complete questionnaire or transcripts of selected interviews.

Procedures

This section, which may be a part of the description of sampling and measurement, presents a summary of the various steps in the conduct of the research. This is especially important for an experiment or in field research. Experiments should include a step-by-step account of the study from the subject's point of view. Field researchers should give a chronological account of the research, telling how they selected and gained entry into the setting, how they met and developed relationships with informants, and how long they were in the setting. In fact, the research report of a field researcher often follows a narrative, from either the researcher's or the informant's point of view, which begins with a discussion of these methodological issues.

Findings

The heart of the research paper is the findings section, toward which the entire report should be aimed. This is where the problems, questions, or hypotheses that framed the research are answered. Before presenting the main results, however, a researcher should provide any evidence on reliability and validity that was not presented in the methods section. For example, it is at the beginning of the results section that one ordinarily finds the outcome of manipulation checks, survey response rates, and tests for measurement reliability and validity. Once this is done, a researcher presenting a quantitative analysis should describe what sort of statistical analyses were performed on the data. This description should be specific with regard to the kind of analysis (e.g., "three-way analysis of variance," "paired t-tests," "ordinary least squares regression"), and it may include (which we recommend for student researchers) references to descriptions of the statistical techniques or to the computer software package used to carry out the analysis.

In quantitative analyses, researchers often construct tables, charts, and graphs to facilitate the presentation of findings. Here, we have some recommendations:

1. Use tables and figures sparingly, to summarize large amounts of information. During the course of research, investigators usually generate many more tables than they can possibly present in the research report. These interim tables guide a researcher in determining the course of the analysis, but more often than not they contain single facts that can be reported in the text of the report.

2. Organize this section around the major hypotheses or theoretical questions and/or major findings. If there is a single main hypothesis, then a single table may suffice to summarize the findings.

3. Discuss the data in terms of what they show about the research problem or hypothesis. Do not let the data speak for themselves, and do not discuss the data merely in terms of

the variables or the numbers in a table. In other words, subordinate the data to your argument and use the data and tables to help tell a story.

This last point also applies to "qualitative" research. The data in such studies are usually not numbers but quotations, concrete observations, and historical events. Still, the data should be used in the same way: organized around the thesis of the report and presented to support arguments.

Discussion

This section may begin or end with a brief summary. The summary serves as a sort of "caboose abstract," reviewing the highlights of the report. This is particularly useful in cases in which the paper is long or necessarily complex. One should try not to be too repetitious here; in other words, do not lift passages from earlier parts of the paper; rather, restate the basic problem and basic findings.

The discussion section, however, generally has more lofty goals. First, it provides a place to point out the shortcomings of the research. For example, the data may be drawn from populations or under conditions that limit the generalizability of the findings. Honesty regarding such limitations is important in preventing readers from making more from the research than is warranted. Second, it provides a chance to point out inconsistencies, account for anomalies, and suggest improvements in the research design. Finally, the discussion section allows the writer an opportunity to place the whole project into broader perspective, to mention the theoretical and practical implications of the study, and to discuss possible future work.

References

Finally, some sort of bibliography must be included. Although the usual practice is to list only works cited in the body of the report, uncited works that were important in the development of the study may also be included. The format of the references varies slightly from one discipline to another. This book uses the University of Chicago Press's *The Chicago Manual of Style*.

Revision and Other Considerations

As noted earlier, many students make the mistake of treating the first draft as the only draft. Most professional writers, in contrast, assume that the first draft will be one in a series of drafts designed to sharpen and improve the final product. The purpose of a first draft is to transfer ideas, thoughts, and facts from the mind of the writer into some material form that can be reflected on by the author. We cannot put a number on how many subsequent drafts should be written; however, it is hard to imagine a polished report that is not the product of numerous drafts. Good writing requires attention to detail; it means writing as if every word and sentence should be taken seriously. And that requires extensive rewriting.

For many people the best time to revise a paper is after taking some time away from the work. Writers who wait until the last few hours or days to write a paper will not produce a good paper. Authors' judgments about the quality of their work may vary directly with the recency of the effort. The passage of time tends to bring perspective and a renewed energy to tackle a job that perhaps did not seem necessary earlier. Much revision can be of the "cut-and-paste" variety. This job usually involves the revision of what is unclear, the deletion of what is extraneous, and the addition of what had been omitted. Again, word-processing technology makes this sort of revision relatively painless.

Finally, at some point in the successive drafting of a report, a "working" draft should be shown to others who can provide critical feedback. We realize that much of the writing students do, with its rigid time constraints, does not allow for this. But there is no better way of judging the clarity of your writing than asking others if they understand what you are saying. Professionals know this and often develop a circle of friends who will read their work. We encourage students to do the same.

KEY POINT

The key to good writing is to revise and edit multiple drafts, which is done most effectively after setting aside each revision.

Length

Probably the most frequently asked question regarding student papers is, How long should it be? The most appropriate but usually unsatisfying answer is, As long as it needs to be. Many students make the mistake of underestimating the length that thoroughness demands, often through one or more serious omissions. On the other hand, some students think that the longer a report is, the better it is. The techniques of "padding" a paper through overuse of citations, excessive use of full quotations when paraphrasing would be preferable, and reliance on vocabulary and jargon intended to impress the audience are mistakes that experienced readers usually see through. Jeffrey Katzer, Kenneth Cook, and Wayne Crouch (1998:41) refer to these smoke screens as "paraphernalia of pedantry" and conclude that they are more likely to be distracting than to facilitate communication. And it is communication that is the essence of the research process.

Avoiding Plagiarism

One form of scientific misconduct that we mentioned briefly in Chapter 3 is plagiarism. *Plagiarism*, according to the U.S. Department of Health and Human Services, is "the appropriation of another person's ideas, processes, results, or words without giving appropriate credit" (Steneck, 2007:21). Plagiarism in any form, whether intentional or accidental, is a serious and often punishable offense. As you write your report, therefore, you must be careful to properly cite all work that is the source of the ideas presented.

Leonard Rosen and Laurence Behrens (1992:582) believe that much plagiarism is unintentional, occurring because of writers' carelessness or ignorance about the conventions of quotation and citation. They offer two general rules for avoiding unintentional plagiarism. First, "whenever you quote the *exact* words of others, place these words in quotation marks and properly cite the source." To quote a source is to extract a word, phrase, sentence, or passage from the original and insert it into the text. Quoted material should be enclosed within double quotation marks or, if lengthy (more than 40 words, according to the *ASA Style Guide*), indented as a block quote. Second, "whenever you *paraphrase* or *summarize* the ideas of others, do not use whole phrases, many of the same words, or sentence structures similar to the original," and be sure "to identify the source of the paraphrased or summarized material." To summarize is to condense the original into a sentence or two in your own words; to paraphrase is to follow the original statement more closely but still restate it in your own words. In general, it is better to summarize or paraphrase others' ideas than to present a stream of quotations. Your report will be easier to read and better convey your understanding of what you read. Use direct quotations when the original words are particularly well chosen—clear, incisive, and powerful.

Publishing a Research Paper

Once you have completed a report of your research, you may decide that it is worth sharing with the wider academic or social science community. You may begin, as students often do, by presenting a paper at a conference or professional meeting. But you also may want to publish your work. Assuming you would like it to appear in a scholarly journal, how do you go about submitting a manuscript for publication? And what do you need to know to increase your chances that it will be published? There are many challenges to the publishing process. A good reference for novice researchers is Philippa Benson and Susan Silver's (2013) book *What Editors Want: An Author's Guide to Scientific Journal Publishing*. Below we provide a brief overview and note some of the nuances of publishing an empirical article.

The first step in the submission process is to decide on an appropriate journal. Unfortunately, "many rejections are the result" of a mismatch between the content of the paper and the scope and mission of the journal (Hewlett, 2002:50). To begin to identify an appropriate outlet, we recommend that you carefully examine the reference list in your research report to see whether there are one or more journal titles that frequently appear. You also might seek recommendations from colleagues and mentors. As you identify possible journals, visit their websites and carefully read statements of mission and scope. Then peruse the table of contents of several issues to get a sense of the content and the methodological and theoretical thrust of articles that appear in the journal.

After you decide where to submit your manuscript, be sure read the journal's instructions for authors. This will tell you where and how to submit (almost always online) and how to prepare the manuscript for submission (e.g., format and style, headings, page limit).

When the manuscript is ready to submit, prepare a cover letter to the editor. In our experience, author instructions rarely mention cover letters or tell authors what to include. It is assumed that authors will ask the editor to "please consider the attached manuscript (title) for publication in (journal name)," but it is not clear what else, if anything, authors ought to say. However, the cover letter is the first thing that the editor will read; and so, it affords the opportunity to form a good first impression by making a case for the serious consideration of your work. In fact, it may determine whether the editor sends your manuscript out for review or rejects it outright. Therefore, we recommend that you describe the main findings of your study and why it is important and that you explain how or why it is a good fit for this journal. All of this should be done as briefly as possible, in a few sentences or perhaps two short paragraphs. Finally, it is acceptable and sometimes required for authors to suggest reviewers for your manuscript, which can expedite the review process.

After an initial screening, the editor may decide to send your manuscript out for peer review. Peer review may be blind or open, depending on the journal. Generally, the editor selects a minimum of two reviewers who have sufficient knowledge of the study area to make a fair judgment about the quality of the paper. In our experience, most journals ask reviewers to complete reviews in 3–4 weeks, but the review process can take much longer. Reviewers usually are asked to rate manuscripts on several dimensions, provide detailed comments, and recommend for or against publication. Based on reviewers' feedback, the journal editor or editorial board then arrives at a decision.

Four kinds of editorial decisions tend to be made: acceptance without revision, acceptance with minor or major revisions, revise and resubmit, and rejection. The most common decision, especially among top journals, is rejection. For example, in 2015 the *American Sociological Review* rejected about 75 percent of 719 submissions either before or after going through an initial peer review; fewer than 1 in 10 manuscripts were ultimately accepted (American Sociological Association, 2016). Of the remaining editorial decisions, the first is almost unheard of. As the psychologist Daryl Bem (1995:176) humorously described this state of affairs, "Long ago and far away, a journal editor allegedly accepted a manuscript that required no revisions. I believe the author was William James." Thus, the best you can hope for is acceptance pending minor revisions, but more likely you will be invited to make major revisions or, most commonly, revise and resubmit.

Authors receive a letter from the editor together with copies of reviewers' detailed comments. Regardless of the editor's decision, it is important to read the reviews carefully to determine why the manuscript was rejected or what you need to do to make it acceptable for publication. If your manuscript is rejected, do not despair. Every researcher is likely to experience the sting of rejection; the key to successful publishing is persistence. Our advice is to use reviewers' comments and suggestions to improve the paper and then submit it to another journal. We know of many papers, including some of our own, that have been accepted by the third, fourth, or fifth journal to which they have been submitted.

If your manuscript is accepted pending revisions, Bem (1995:176) says, "you should be deliriously happy" because publication is "under your control." And if you are invited to revise and resubmit your paper, "you should still be happy—if not deliriously so—because you still have a reasonable shot at getting it published." In 2015, for example, the *American Sociological Review* accepted the majority of papers that were revised and resubmitted (American Sociological Association, 2016).

When editors invite authors to revise and resubmit, they generally indicate the criticisms or suggestions made by reviewers that need to be addressed. Editors may or may not put a firm deadline on the revision; however, it would be a mistake either to rush to get the manuscript back in the hands of the editor or to take several months (say, more than 6 months) before you resubmit. It will take time and effort to complete a revision, and authors must thoroughly address every issue highlighted by the editor. The first step in revising is to decide how you will respond to reviewers' suggestions. This may involve making substantive changes in the manuscript; adding new material; or, if you disagree with a suggestion, developing a rationale for not incorporating the change. If reviewers make contradictory comments about what needs to change, you also may have to decide how to resolve the disagreement.

After the paper has been revised to your satisfaction, it is time to write another cover letter in which you explain to the editor how you responded to every criticism or suggestion. This letter should be a detailed point-by-point account of the changes you made in the manuscript and, if you decided not to incorporate a specific suggestion, a statement of the logic and rationale supporting that decision. Finally, either before or after you specify your revisions, we recommend that you thank the editor and reviewers for their helpful suggestions and express the hope that the editor will find the paper much improved.

In the end, you will see that publishing a paper, much like research and writing, is an iterative process. For if you have successfully revised your paper, a likely outcome is that you will receive a conditional acceptance subject to your making additional revisions.

Summary

- The World Wide Web (Internet) is a valuable resource, but it is unstable and contains a huge volume of information that must be evaluated carefully.
- The library—specifically, its online services—is the appropriate place to conduct bibliographic searches. Online library catalogs and electronic databases make it possible to search articles, books, and other written materials to review prior research and theory, which guide the development of research questions.
- Of the many options, discipline-specific databases such as SocIndex and PsychInfo offer the most effective means of locating relevant references.
- Most research reports contain the following components:
  - An abstract or short summary placed at the beginning of the paper;
  - An introduction to the problem pointing out its theoretical, practical, and/or social significance;
  - A literature review relating the research problem to previous theory and research;
  - A methods section outlining precisely how the research was done, including the overall approach and design and methods of sampling and measurement;
  - A findings section;
  - A discussion of the limitations and anomalies as well as the broader theoretical and practical implications of the research; and
  - A list of references cited in the report.
- Writing the research report is facilitated greatly by preparing an outline, keeping in mind the intended audience and how they will read the report, and writing several drafts as well as soliciting others' critical comments on early drafts.
- It is generally best, when drawing on previous publications, to summarize others' work and keep quotations to a minimum, but be sure to set off quoted material with quotation marks and to identify quoted or summarized sources.
- Publishing a research paper in a scholarly journal involves selecting an appropriate journal, following author instructions in preparing the manuscript, and writing a cover letter to the editor.
- Most papers submitted for publication are rejected; the key to success, whether in a revise-and-resubmit or submission to another journal, is effectively using critical feedback from reviewers to improve the paper.

Key Terms

free writing

Exercises

1. To familiarize yourself with library resources, log on to your college or local library website. Select a topic, and then search the library catalog for books. Next, locate the list of electronic databases. First, select a multifield database and conduct a search; second, identify and search a database for one of the social science disciplines. Finally, for comparison, use a search engine to search the same topic on the Internet.

2. Read through the first 10 citations you found when you used the discipline-specific database in Exercise 1. Identify whether each citation is (a) an article, book, book chapter, or other written document and (b) a report of empirical research, review or meta-analysis, theoretical statement, or other type of reference.

Glossary

acquiescence response set a response bias whereby respondents tend to answer in the direction of agreement, regardless of item content. (Chapter 10)

active membership role a type of participant role in field research in which the researcher assumes a functional role in the group or organization he or she is studying; *see also* complete and peripheral membership roles. (Chapter 11)

aggregate data information about one set of units that is statistically combined to describe a larger social unit. For example, information about students (gender, race, college board scores, etc.) might be aggregated to describe characteristics of their colleges (sex ratio, ethnic composition, average college board score, etc.). (Chapter 4)

analytical history the use of historical events and evidence to develop a generalized understanding of the social world; *see also* descriptive history. (Chapter 12)

anonymity an ethical safeguard against invasion of privacy; the condition wherein data cannot be identified with particular research participants. (Chapter 3)

antecedent variable a variable causally antecedent to others in a theoretical model. Two variables may be spuriously associated because both are affected by an antecedent variable. (Chapters 4, 16)

applied social research research undertaken for the explicit purpose of providing information to solve an existing social problem; *see also* basic social research. (Chapter 14)

association the strength of the observed relationship between two variables. (Chapter 4)

attrition a threat to internal validity; the loss of subjects during the course of a study (also called mortality); *see also* differential attrition. (Chapter 8)

available data existing sources of information that were not produced directly by the social researcher who uses them; this includes public and private documents, products of the mass media, physical evidence, and data archives; the use of available data is one of the four major approaches to social research. (Chapters 1, 12, 13)

basic social research research undertaken to advance a discipline's theoretical understanding, which may or may not address an existing social problem; *see also* applied social research. (Chapter 14)

behavioral coding a field pretest technique in which live or taped interviewer–respondent interactions are systematically coded to identify the frequency of problematic respondent and interviewer behaviors on each question. (Chapter 10)

between-subjects designs true experimental designs in which each subject is assigned to one of two or more conditions, such as treatment and control; *see also* within-subjects designs. (Chapter 8)

big data unusually large data sets that are collected digitally and, because of their variety and structure, may require sophisticated computational methods. (Chapter 12)

bivariate analysis statistical analysis of the relationship between two variables. (Chapter 15)

causal relationship a theoretical notion that change in one variable forces, produces, or brings about a change in another. Although the concept of "cause" is unobservable and philosophically controversial, causal theorizing is commonly and productively used in scientific investigations. (Chapters 2, 4)

cell frequency the number of cases in a cell of a cross-tabulation table. (Chapter 15)

chi-square test for independence a test of statistical significance used to assess the likelihood that an observed bivariate relationship differs significantly from that which easily could have occurred by chance. (Chapter 15)

closed-ended questions survey questions that require respondents to choose responses from those provided; also called "fixed-choice questions." (Chapter 10)

cluster sampling a probability sampling procedure in which the population is broken down into natural groupings or areas, called clusters, and a random sample of clusters is drawn. Cluster sampling may occur in a series of stages, moving from larger to smaller clusters, with individual cases sampled at the last stage; *see* multistage cluster sampling. (Chapter 6)

codebook a "dictionary" for a survey study, which lists the answers or categories that correspond to each numerical code, the location of each variable in the data file, and coding and decision rules. (Chapter 15)

coding (1) the sorting of raw data, such as field observations or responses to open-ended questions, into categories; (2) in computer analysis, assigning numbers or symbols to variable categories. (Chapters 10, 11, 15)

cognitive interviewing verbal reports from respondents, collected during ("thinkalouds") or after (follow-up probes, paraphrasing requests) responding to pretest questions, and used to diagnose question wording, ordering, and formatting problems. (Chapter 10)

cohort persons (or other units) who experience the same significant life event (e.g., birth, marriage, high school graduation) within a specified period of time; *see* cohort study. (Chapter 9)

cohort study a longitudinal research design that attempts to assess the relative effects of age (life-course changes), period (current history), and cohort ("generations" who share the same past history) on attitudes and behavior. (Chapter 9)

collinear association a perfect linear relationship between two variables. (Chapter 16)

Common Rule informal label for the set of regulations for the treatment of human research subjects that are codified under Title 45 of the Code of Federal Regulations, Part 46 (45 CFR 46). (Chapter 3)

comparative-historical analysis the development of causal explanations of social change by describing and comparing historical processes within and across a small set of cases. (Chapter 12)

complete membership role a type of participant role in field research in which the researcher assumes full-member status in the organization or group he or she is studying; *see also* active membership role and peripheral membership role. (Chapter 11)

computer-assisted personal interviewing (CAPI) a software program, usually on a laptop computer, that aids interviewers by providing appropriate instructions, question wording, and data-entry supervision. (Chapter 9)

computer-assisted self-interviewing (CASI) an electronic survey in which a questionnaire is transmitted on a computer disk mailed to the respondent or on a laptop computer provided by the researcher. (Chapter 9)

computer-assisted telephone interviewing (CATI) a set of computerized tools that aid telephone interviewers and supervisors by automating various data-collection tasks. (Chapter 9)

concept abstractions communicated by words or other signs that group together phenomena that have important things in common (e.g., the concept "extroversion" represents a broad range of specific behaviors); concepts developed for scientific purposes are sometimes called "constructs." (Chapters 2, 5)

conceptualization the development and clarification of concepts. (Chapter 5)

conditional a statement (the antecedent) introduced by an "if," followed by a second statement (the consequent) preceded by a "then." For example, "If this is a conditional proposition, then it should have an antecedent and a consequent." (Chapter 4)

confidence interval a range (interval) within which a population value is estimated to lie at a specific level of confidence; used to qualify sample estimates to take into account sampling error. For example, a researcher might report that he or she is 99 percent confident (confidence level) that the mean personal income for a population lies within plus or minus $359 of the sample mean of $18,325 (i.e., confidence interval of $18,684–$17,966). (Chapter 6)

confidentiality an ethical safeguard against invasion of privacy; the assumption that all data on research participants are not to be divulged to anyone without the participants' permission. (Chapter 3)

consistency checking a data-cleaning procedure involving checking for unreasonable patterns of responses, such as a 12-year-old who voted in the last presidential election. (Chapter 15)

construct validation measurement validation based on an accumulation of research evidence, which may include evidence that the measure in question (1) relates to other variables in a theoretically expected manner, (2) correlates highly with other measures of the same concept (convergent validity), (3) correlates not too highly with measures of other concepts (discriminant validity), and (4) varies among groups known to differ on the characteristic being measured. (Chapter 5)

content analysis systematic analysis of the symbolic content of communications in which content is reduced to a set of coded variables or categories. (Chapter 12)

content validity a subjective judgment of whether a measure adequately represents all facets (the domain) of a concept. (Chapter 5)

contextual design a survey design in which information about respondents and their social environments (contexts) is collected for the purpose of studying the separate and joint effects of personal characteristics and social contexts on individuals. (Chapter 9)

context units larger units in which the recording units of content analysis are embedded, which provide the "context" necessary to classify the recording units. For example, the meaning of words (recording units) might be determined from the sentences (context units) in which they appear; *see also* recording units. (Chapter 12)

contingency question a survey question intended for a subset of the respondents, addressing only those persons for whom the question is relevant; *see also* filter question. (Chapter 10)

control a procedure (or procedures) that eliminates, as far as possible, unwanted variation, such as sources of bias and error that may distort study results. A common approach is to control potentially confounding variables by holding them constant or preventing them from varying. (Chapters 2, 4)

control variable a variable that is held constant during the course of observation or statistical analysis. (Chapter 4)

convenience sampling a form of nonprobability sampling in which a researcher simply selects cases that are conveniently available; also called "haphazard," "fortuitous," and "accidental" sampling. (Chapter 6)

convergent validity the extent to which independent measures of the same concept correlate with each other; the higher the correlation, the greater the convergent validity. (Chapter 5)

correlation coefficient a measure of association, symbolized as *r* (Pearson's), that describes the direction and strength of a linear relationship between two variables measured at the interval or ratio level; the square of Pearson's *r* represents the proportion of variance in one variable that may be predicted from the other using linear regression. (Chapters 4, 15)

cost–benefit analysis (1) an examination of the potential costs (e.g., harm to subjects) and benefits (e.g., knowledge gained, beneficial application) of a study as a way of assessing the ethics of the study; (2) in evaluation research, an assessment of the economic efficiency of a program in terms of its monetary costs and benefits; *see also* cost–effectiveness analysis. (Chapters 3, 14)

cost–effectiveness analysis in evaluation research, an assessment of the efficiency of a program by measuring intervention outcomes in terms of program costs; *see also* cost–benefit analysis. (Chapter 14)

counterbalancing a technique used to control for order effects in within-subjects experimental designs; the sequence of treatment and control conditions is reversed, so that different groups of subjects experience each sequence. (Chapter 8)

cover letter in a survey, a letter designed to obtain cooperation from persons in the sample. The cover letter is sent before an interviewer calls on a respondent, or, in mail surveys, it accompanies the questionnaire. (Chapter 9)

cover story an introduction provided to experimental subjects to obtain their cooperation while disguising the research hypothesis. (Chapter 7)

coverage error in sampling, the error that occurs when the sampling frame does not match the intended target population. (Chapters 6, 9)

covert research a type of field research in which an investigator conducts research in private settings while concealing his or her identity as a researcher. (Chapter 11)

criterion-related validation a method of assessing the validity of a measure in terms of the degree to which it correlates with an objective current or future criterion. (Chapter 5)

cross-national surveys studies in which equivalent-sample surveys are conducted in different countries; also called "comparative studies." (Chapter 9)

cross-sectional design the most common survey design, in which data on a cross-section of respondents chosen to represent a larger population of interest are gathered at essentially one point in time; *see also* longitudinal design. (Chapter 9)

cultural relativity the principle that the cultural standards of a given society must be examined on their own terms and that researchers should be nonjudgmental regarding the society or group that is being studied. (Chapter 3)

data archives repositories of precollected survey or ethnographic data collected by various agencies and researchers that are accessible to the public. (Chapter 12)

data cleaning the detection and correction of errors that occur during data collection, coding, and data entry. (Chapter 15)

data matrix the form of a computer data file, with rows as cases and columns as variables; each cell represents the value of a particular variable (column) for a particular case (row). (Chapter 15)

data modification the process of transforming raw data for analysis, such as by collapsing the categories of a variable or imputing values for missing cases. (Chapter 15)

data processing the preparation of data for analysis; in survey research it entails five steps: coding, editing, entry, cleaning, and modification. (Chapter 15)

data sharing an ethical standard that requires researchers to share data for completed projects of published research by placing them in a public archive or making them available for a reasonable period of time. (Chapter 3)

debriefing a session at the end of an experiment in which the experimenter discusses with the subject what has taken place, the real purpose of the study, the need for confidentiality, the subject's responses and feelings, and so on. (Chapters 3, 7)

deductive reasoning a process of reasoning in which the conclusion necessarily follows if the evidence is true. (Chapter 2)

demand characteristics cues in an experiment that convey to subjects the experimenter's hypothesis or what is expected of them. (Chapter 7)

dependent variable a variable that a researcher tries to explain or predict; the presumed effect of one or more independent variables. (Chapter 4)

descriptive history type of historical analysis that emphasizes the complete and accurate description of past events; *see also* analytical history. (Chapter 12)

descriptive research studies undertaken to collect facts about a specified population or sample, for example, a public opinion poll. (Chapters 4, 9)

descriptive statistics procedures for organizing and summarizing data. (Chapter 15)

differential attrition a threat to internal validity; the existence of varying dropout rates among conditions of an experiment, which tends to make the conditions nonequivalent in composition; also called "differential mortality." (Chapter 8)

direct effects when one variable is hypothesized to affect another directly in a causal model; the total impact of one variable on another is the sum of the direct and indirect effects; *see also* indirect effects. (Chapter 16)

direct questions survey questions in which there is a direct, clear link between what is asked and what a researcher wants to know; *see also* indirect questions. (Chapter 10)

direction of influence the identification of which variable is the cause (independent) and which is the effect (dependent) in a presumed causal relationship. (Chapter 4)

discriminant validity the extent to which a measure of a particular concept differentiates that concept from other concepts from which it is intended to differ. Discriminant validity is lacking if measures of supposedly different concepts correlate too highly. (Chapter 5)

disproportionate stratified sampling a sampling procedure in which strata are sampled disproportionately to population composition. For example, a study of law enforcement might sample female police officers at a much higher rate than male police officers to ensure a sufficient number of the former for analysis purposes. (Chapter 6)

distorter variable in elaboration analysis, a test variable that reverses the direction of the original bivariate relationship, as from a positive zero-order association to a negative association in the partial tables. (Chapter 16)

double-barreled question a survey question in which two separate ideas are erroneously presented together in one question. (Chapter 10)

double-blind technique a method of preventing both subjects and research personnel from knowing the subjects' treatment conditions during the running of an experiment. (Chapter 7)

dummy variable a data-modification procedure that involves recoding the categories of nominal- or ordinal-scale variables for the purpose of regression or other numerical analysis. For example, gender categories may be represented by a single dummy variable having a value of 1 if the respondent is female and a value of 0 if male. (Chapters 15, 16)

ecological fallacy erroneous use of information pertaining to an aggregate (e.g., organizations) to draw inferences about the units of analysis that comprise the aggregate (e.g., individual members of organizations). (Chapter 4)

editing a quality-control process designed to ensure that survey or other data to be read into the computer are as complete, error free, and readable as possible. (Chapter 15)

effect assessment the most basic type of evaluation research, undertaken to assess the impact of a social program on program participants; also called "summative" or "outcome" evaluation; *see also* efficiency assessment. (Chapter 14)

effect size statistical estimate of the size of the relationship between two variables that is commonly used to compare outcomes in meta-analysis and evaluation research; includes the standardized mean difference between groups and correlation and regression coefficients. (Chapters 13, 14)

efficiency assessment a type of evaluation research in which a program's outcomes are weighed against its costs; may take the form of cost–benefit or cost–effectiveness analysis; *see also* effect assessment. (Chapter 14)

elaboration a traditional technique for the multivariate analysis of contingency tables that "elaborates" the relationship between two variables by introducing a third (and sometimes additional) variable and testing the resultant causal models. (Chapter 16)

empirical/empiricism a way of knowing or understanding the world that relies directly or indirectly on what we experience through our senses—sight, hearing, taste, smell, and touch; admissible evidence in science is limited to empirical phenomena. (Chapter 2)

empirical generalization a generalization or hypothesis inductively derived from observations. (Chapter 2)

environmental impact study a study undertaken, usually as required by law, to assess the impact of a public works project on the social and physical environment; *see also* social impact assessment. (Chapter 14)

epistemology the study or theory of the nature, source, and limits of knowledge; the epistemology of science concerns how scientists know what they know. (Chapter 2)

ethics guidelines or standards for moral conduct. In research, ethical codes prescribe principles for upholding the values of science and for resolving conflicts between scientific ideals and societal values. (Chapter 3)

evaluation apprehension subjects' anxiety about being evaluated by the experimenter, typically a psychologist, which may make them overly concerned with producing "normal" behavior. (Chapter 7)

evaluation research an area of social science research, often linked to policymaking, concerned with analyzing social policies, programs, and interventions. (Chapter 14)

exhaustive the measurement requirement that a measure includes all possible values or attributes of a variable so that every case can be classified. (Chapter 5)

expedited review an institutional review board (IRB) procedure for studies involving no more than minimal risk of harm in which a subset of IRB members, usually the chair, determines whether a study meets federal ethical guidelines; *see also* institutional review board. (Chapter 3)

experiment a major approach to social research that entails the manipulation of the independent variable and researcher control over the events to which research participants are exposed. (Chapters 1, 7, 13)

experimental realism when subjects become involved in or are affected by the procedures of an experiment rather than remaining detached. (Chapter 7)

experimenter expectancy effect effect on subject's behavior caused by the experimenter's expectations about how the experiment will turn out. (Chapter 7)

expert review an assessment of a draft survey questionnaire carried out by experts in survey design or the survey topic. (Chapter 10)

explanation (1) in science, abstract statements that relate changes in one class of events to changes in another; (2) in elaboration analysis, an outcome in which, upon controlling for an antecedent test variable, the original bivariate relationship reduces to zero or near zero in each partial table. (Chapters 2, 16)

explanatory research studies that investigate relationships between two or more variables, attempting to explain them in cause-and-effect terms. (Chapters 4, 9)

explanatory variables those variables that are the focus of the research—the independent and dependent variables in a hypothesized relationship; *see also* extraneous variables. (Chapter 4)

exploratory research studies undertaken to explore a phenomenon or topic about which little is known. (Chapter 4)

external validity the extent to which experimental findings are generalizable to other settings, subject populations, and time periods. (Chapter 7)

extraneous variables all variables other than the independent and dependent variables in a hypothesized relationship; *see also* explanatory variables. (Chapter 4)

face-to-face interview a type of interview in which the interviewer interacts face to face with the respondent; also called "in-person interview"; *see also* telephone interview. (Chapters 9, 13)

face validity a personal judgment that an operational definition appears, on the face of it, to measure the concept it is intended to measure. (Chapter 5)

factorial experimental designs an extension of the basic experimental design in which two or more independent variables (factors) are manipulated; information is provided about the separate (main) effects and joint (interaction) effects of the independent variables. (Chapter 8)

field experiment a "true" experimental design conducted in a natural setting. (Chapter 7)

field jottings short phrases, quotes, key words, and the like recorded by field researchers while in the field; *see also* field notes. (Chapter 11)

field notes thorough account of field observations recorded by field researchers as soon after each period of observation as possible, preferably at the end of each day. (Chapter 11)

field pretesting the evaluation of the survey instrument and personnel under realistic field conditions with respondents similar to those for whom the survey is designed. (Chapter 10)

field research a major approach to social research that involves directly observing and often interacting with others, usually for an extended period, in a natural setting. (Chapters 1, 11, 13)

filter question a type of survey question, the responses to which determine which subjects are to answer which subsequent contingency questions. (Chapter 10)

first-order relationship a relationship between two variables in which a third variable is controlled; *see also* zero-order relationship. (Chapter 16)

fixed-effects model a statistical framework that assumes, in meta-analysis, that between-study variability arises from sampling and other chance processes; *see also* random-effects model. (Chapter 13)

focus group a method of data collection in which an interviewer moderates a relatively unstructured discussion on a general topic among a small group of participants. (Chapter 10)

formative evaluation research undertaken in the developmental stages of a social program to guide program design; *see* evaluation research. (Chapter 14)

free writing an exercise to overcome the difficulty in beginning to write by quickly recording thoughts, without regard to grammar and punctuation or reference to notes, data, books, and other information. (Chapter 17)

frequency distribution a tabulation of the number of cases falling into each category of a variable. (Chapter 15)

frequency polygon the graphic presentation of an interval/ratio-scale variable in which the X-axis consists of the values of the variable and the Y-axis consists of the number of cases (or frequency); a line connects the frequency for each value of the variable; in a percentage polygon, the Y-axis consists of percentages. (Chapter 15)

funnel sequence a sequence of survey questions that progresses from a general question to gradually more specific questions. (Chapter 10)

gatekeepers authorities whose permission is needed to conduct research in their setting. (Chapter 11)

grounded theory theory developed inductively from firsthand observations, in contrast to theories generated by other means. (Chapter 11)

Guttman scaling a scaling procedure that attempts to ensure a unidimensional scale by selecting a set of items that, when *ordered* in terms of their "strength," will *order* individuals or other relevant units on the concept being measured. (Chapter 13)

heterogeneity the degree of dissimilarity among cases with respect to a particular characteristic. For example, the gender composition of groups might vary from 100 percent female (maximum homogeneity) to 50 percent female (maximum heterogeneity). (Chapter 6)

history a threat to internal validity; events in the subjects' environment, other than the intended experimental manipulation, that occur during the course of an experiment and that may affect the outcome. (Chapter 8)

hypothesis an expected but unconfirmed relationship among two or more variables. (Chapters 2, 4)

idiographic explanation a type of scientific explanation that describes the unique set of conditions that account for the actions of a single person or set of actors at a particular time and place. (Chapter 2)

imputation a procedure for handling missing data in which missing values are imputed from other information, such as the sample mean or known values of other variables. (Chapter 15)

independent variable a presumed cause of a dependent variable. (Chapter 4)

in-depth interviews intensive interviews that in field research are much less structured than in survey research and are much longer, often requiring several sessions. (Chapter 11)

index a composite measure of a concept constructed by adding or averaging the scores of separate indicators; differs from a scale, which uses less arbitrary procedures for combining indicators. (Chapters 5, 13)

indicator an empirical manifestation of a concept. For example, the indicator "years of schooling" often represents the concept "education." (Chapters 5, 13)

indirect effects in a causal model, when one variable is hypothesized to affect another indirectly through one or a series of intervening variables; *see also* direct effects. (Chapter 16)

indirect questions questions in which the relationship between a researcher's objectives and the questions asked is not obvious; a technique usually based on the psychological concept of "projection"; *see also* direct questions. (Chapter 10)

inductive reasoning a reasoning process in which the conclusion goes beyond the evidence; unlike in a deductive argument, the evidence may be true and the conclusion false. (Chapter 2)

inferential statistics procedures for determining the extent to which one may generalize beyond the data at hand. (Chapter 15)

informant a person from whom field researchers acquire information in the field. (Chapter 11)

informed consent an ethical practice of providing research participants with enough information about a study, especially its potential risks, to enable them to make an informed decision about whether to participate. (Chapter 3)

institutional review board (IRB) a committee formed at nearly all research institutions (e.g., universities) that is responsible for reviewing research proposals to assess provisions for the ethical treatment of human (and animal) subjects; IRB approval is required for federally funded research. (Chapter 3)

instrumentation a threat to internal validity; unwanted changes in characteristics of the measuring instrument or measurement procedure. (Chapter 8)

interaction effect an outcome in which the effect of one independent variable on the dependent variable varies according to the value or level of another independent variable. That is, the effects of the variables together differ from the effects of either alone. (Chapter 8)

intercoder reliability an "equivalence" method for assessing reliability that examines the extent to which different observers or coders get equivalent results using the same instrument or measure. (Chapter 5)

internal-consistency reliability an "equivalence" method of assessing reliability in which a statistical procedure is used to examine the consistency of "scores" across all the items of a composite measure. (Chapter 5)

internal validity sound evidence in an experiment that rules out the possibility that extraneous variables, rather than the manipulated independent variable, are responsible for the observed outcome. (Chapters 7, 8)

interpretation an outcome in elaboration analysis in which, upon controlling for an intervening test variable, the original bivariate relationship reduces to zero or near zero in each partial table. (Chapter 16)

interrupted time-series design a quasi-experimental design resembling the one-group pretest–posttest design but with a series of observations (measurements) before and after the treatment manipulation or intervention. (Chapter 8)

intersubjective testability a condition wherein two or more scientists can agree on the results of observations. (Chapter 2)

interval measurement a level of measurement that has the qualities of the ordinal level plus the requirement that equal distances (intervals) between assigned numbers represent equal distances in the variable being measured; consequently, with interval measurement it is possible to perform basic mathematical operations such as addition and subtraction. (Chapter 5)

intervening variable a variable that is intermediate between two other variables in a causal chain. For example, if the model specifies that X affects W, which in turn affects Y, then W is an intervening variable that interprets the causal process by which X affects Y. (Chapters 4, 16)

interview guide an outline of topics and questions used in in-depth interviewing; unlike the interview schedule in a structured interview, the exact wording and order of the questions may vary. (Chapter 11)

interview schedule a survey form used by interviewers that consists of instructions, the questions to be asked, and, if they are used, response options. (Chapter 9)

interviewer debriefings a field pretest technique, usually involving focus group discussions, used to identify instrument problems from an interviewer's perspective. (Chapter 10)

inverted-funnel sequence a sequence of survey questions that begins with the most specific questions on a topic and ends with the most general. (Chapter 10)

key informant a contact who helps a field researcher gain entry to, acceptance within, and information about the research setting. (Chapter 11)

law a proposition that has been repeatedly verified scientifically and is widely accepted. (Chapter 2)

leading question a survey question that suggests a possible answer or makes some responses seem more acceptable than others. (Chapter 10)

level of measurement a characteristic of measures that indicates the kind of inferences that may be drawn when comparing one variable category or value to another. The four main levels are nominal, ordinal, interval, and ratio. (Chapter 5)

Likert response format the ordered responses (usually "strongly agree," "agree," "neutral," "disagree," and "strongly disagree") to individual items; *see* Likert scaling. (Chapter 10)

Likert scaling a scaling approach commonly used to measure attitudes in which respondents choose from an ordered series of responses (e.g., ranging from "strongly approve" to "strongly disapprove") to indicate their reaction to each of a set of statements. (Chapter 13)

listwise deletion a common procedure for handling missing values in multivariate analysis that excludes cases that have missing values on any of the variables in the analysis. (Chapter 15)

longitudinal design survey design in which data are collected at more than one point in time; *see* trend study, panel study, and cohort study. (Chapter 9)

main effect in a factorial experimental design, the effect of a single independent variable (factor) by itself. (Chapter 8)

manipulation check evidence collected in an experiment that the manipulation of the independent variable was experienced or interpreted by the subject in the way intended. (Chapter 7)

manuscript census the original schedules on which census enumerators record their data, which are released to the public after a period of 72 years. (Chapter 12)

marginal frequencies row and column totals in a contingency table (cross-tabulation) that represent the univariate frequency distributions for the row and column variables. (Chapter 15)

matching a technique for assigning subjects to experimental groups so that the composition of each group matches that of the others on one or more characteristics thought to be related to the dependent variable; should be used in conjunction with, but not as a substitute for, randomization. (Chapters 7, 14)

maturation a threat to internal validity; any psychological or physiological changes taking place within subjects that occur over time, regardless of experimental manipulations. (Chapter 8)

mean a measure of central tendency that indicates the average value of a univariate distribution of interval- or ratio-scale data; calculated by adding up the individual values and dividing by the total number of cases. (Chapter 15)

measures of association descriptive statistics used to measure the strength and direction of an observed bivariate relationship. (Chapters 4, 15)

median a measure of central tendency indicating the midpoint in a univariate distribution of interval- or ratio-scale data; indicates the point below and above which 50 percent of the values fall. (Chapter 15)

membership role the participant role adopted by a researcher in participant observation studies; *see* active membership role, complete membership role, and peripheral membership role. (Chapter 11)

memos an adjunct to field notes in field research that consists of brief, recorded analyses that come to mind in going over notes and observations. (Chapter 11)

meta-analysis systematic procedures for synthesizing and summarizing the results from previous, related studies. (Chapter 13)

mixed-mode survey a survey that uses more than one mode (questionnaires, personal interviews, telephone interviews) to sample and/or collect the data. (Chapter 9)

modal instance sampling a sampling procedure recommended in evaluation research in which sites for program assessment are selected for their similarity to the setting in which the program will be implemented. (Chapter 14)

mode a measure of central tendency representing the value or category of a frequency distribution having the highest frequency; the most typical value. (Chapter 15)

modeling in statistical analysis, formal representations of hypothesized, or theoretical, relations among two or more variables. Usually alternative models are compared to determine their fit to the observed data. (Chapter 16)

multicollinearity a problem that arises in multiple regression when combinations of two or more independent variables are highly correlated with each other and that renders regression results (estimates of the coefficients) difficult to interpret. (Chapter 16)

multiple regression a statistical method for studying the simultaneous effects of several independent variables on a dependent variable. (Chapter 16)

multiple time-series design a quasi-experimental design in which a series of pretreatment and posttreatment observations (measurements) are made on a treatment group as well as on nonequivalent control groups. (Chapters 8, 14)

multistage cluster sampling a sampling procedure in which sampling occurs at two or more steps or stages (e.g., a sample of school districts, then a sample of schools from the selected school districts, and then a sample of pupils from the selected schools). (Chapter 6)

multivariate analysis statistical analysis of the simultaneous relationships among three or more variables. (Chapter 16)

mundane realism when the events in an experiment are similar to everyday experiences. (Chapter 7)

mutually exclusive the measurement requirement that each case can be placed in only one category of a variable; *see also* exhaustive. (Chapter 5)

N an abbreviation representing the number of observations on which a statistic is based (e.g., $N = 279$). (Chapter 15)

needs assessment the systematic assessment of the needs and problems of a community or agency and the ability of a program to meet appropriate needs. (Chapter 14)

negative (inverse) relationship a relationship in which an increase in the value of one variable is accompanied by a decrease in the value of the other; that is, changes in one variable are opposite in direction to changes in the other. (Chapter 4)

network sampling a sampling procedure in which respondents initially contacted in screening a probability sample are asked to identify other members of the target population who are socially linked to the respondent (e.g., relative, neighbor, co-worker). (Chapter 6)

nominal measurement the lowest level of measurement, in which numbers serve only to label category membership; categories are not ranked but must be exhaustive and mutually exclusive. (Chapter 5)

nomothetic explanation type of scientific explanation that seeks to produce a generalized understanding (e.g., common causes) of classes of events. (Chapter 2)

noncausal association when two variables are allowed to be statistically associated in a model, but a causal explanation of the association is not part of the model. (Chapter 16)

nonequivalent control group design a quasi-experimental design that resembles a true experiment (the pretest–posttest control group design), except subjects are *not* randomly assigned to treatment and control groups. (Chapter 8)

nonparticipant observation an approach to field research in which a researcher attempts to observe people without interacting with them and, typically, without their knowing that they are being observed. (Chapter 11)

nonprobability sampling processes of case selection other than random selection. (Chapter 6)

nonreactive measurement any process of measurement that by itself does not bring about changes in what is being measured. In contrast, reactive measures may produce changes in behavior because of people's awareness that they are being studied or observed. (Chapter 12)

nonresponse bias in survey sampling, when nonrespondents (sampled individuals who subsequently do not respond or cannot be contacted) differ in important ways from respondents. (Chapters 6, 9)

nonspuriousness a criterion for inferring causality that requires that an association or correlation between two variables cannot be explained away by the action of extraneous variables. (Chapter 4)

normal distribution a bell-shape distribution of data that characterizes many variables and statistics, such as the sampling distribution of the mean. (Chapter 15)

null hypothesis the hypothesis that an observed relationship is due to chance—the opposite of the research hypothesis—which is associated with tests of statistical significance; a test that is significant rejects the null hypothesis at a specified level of probability. (Chapter 4)

objectivity in science, the methodological condition that makes it possible for two or more people to agree on the results of an observation; *see also* intersubjective testability. (Chapter 2)

one-group pretest–posttest design a pre-experimental design in which a group of subjects is observed or measured (the pretest), a treatment is introduced, and the subjects are measured again (the posttest); threats to internal validity include maturation, history, testing, instrumentation, and sometimes statistical regression. (Chapter 8)

one-shot case study a pre-experimental design in which a treatment is administered to a group, after which the group is observed or tested to determine the treatment effects; threats to internal validity include attrition, maturation, and history. (Chapter 8)

open-ended questions survey questions that require respondents to answer in their own words; also called "free-response questions." (Chapter 10)

operationalization the detailed description of the research operations or procedures necessary to assign units of analysis to variable categories; produces "operational definitions" that are intended to represent conceptual properties. (Chapter 5)

ordinal measurement a level of measurement in which different numbers indicate the rank order of cases on some variable. (Chapter 5)

outliers unusual or suspicious values that are far removed from the preponderance of observations for a variable. (Chapters 15, 16)

panel study a longitudinal design in which the same individuals are surveyed more than once, permitting the study of individual and group change. (Chapter 9)

paper-and-pencil questionnaire a survey form filled out by respondents. When an interviewer records survey responses, the form usually is called an "interview schedule." (Chapter 9)

parameter a characteristic of a population, such as the percentage of women or average age. (Chapter 6)

partial-regression coefficients/partial slopes coefficients in a multiple-regression equation that estimate the effects of each independent variable on the dependent variable when all other variables in the equation are held constant. (Chapter 16)

partial tables a control procedure used in elaboration that involves recalculating the original two-variable relationship separately for each category of the control variable. Each partial table displays the association between the two original variables when the control variable is held constant. (Chapter 16)

participant observation an approach to field research in which a researcher actively participates, for an extended period of time, in the daily lives of the people and situations under study. (Chapter 11)

path analysis a form of causal modeling utilizing standardized regression coefficients that provides, among other things, quantitative estimates of the total direct and indirect effects of one variable on another. (Chapter 16)

path coefficients estimates of effects of one variable on another in a path model that are based on regression coefficients in multiple regressions; to account for all the possible paths in a path model usually requires several multiple regressions. (Chapter 16)

percentage distribution a norming operation that facilitates interpreting and comparing frequency distributions by transforming each to a common yardstick of 100 units (percentage points) in length; the number of cases in each category is divided by the total and multiplied by 100. (Chapter 15)

percentage polygon *see* frequency polygon. (Chapter 15)

peripheral membership role a type of participant role in field research in which the researcher is only marginally involved in the setting or group under study; *see also* active membership role and complete membership role. (Chapter 11)

population the total membership of a defined class of people, objects, or events; *see also* target population. (Chapter 6)

position response bias a tendency of some respondents to mark options located in a certain position, such as the first choice in a series. (Chapter 10)

positive (direct) relationship a relationship in which an increase in the value of one variable is accompanied by an increase in the value of the other or a decrease in one is accompanied by a decrease in the other; that is, the two variables consistently change in the same direction. (Chapter 4)

posttest-only control group design the simplest of the true experimental designs, which incorporates these features: random assignment to treatment and control groups, introduction of the independent variable to the treatment group, and a posttreatment measure of both groups. (Chapter 8)

pre-experimental designs designs that lack one or more features of true experiments, such as a comparison group or random assignment. (Chapter 8)

pretesting a trial run of an experiment or survey instrument with a small number of preliminary subjects or respondents to evaluate and rehearse the study procedures and personnel; *see also* field pretesting. (Chapters 7, 9, 10)

pretest–posttest control group design a true experimental design in which subjects are randomly assigned to (1) a treatment group measured before (the pretest) and after (the posttest) the experimental treatment and (2) a no-treatment control group measured at the same times. (Chapter 8)

primary sampling unit the sampling units in the first stage of a multistage sample. (Chapter 6)

primary source a historical document, such as a diary or autobiography, that contains the testimony of an eyewitness; *see also* secondary source. (Chapter 12)

probability proportionate to size sampling the selection of cases in cluster sampling so that the probability of selection is proportionate to the size of (i.e., the number of cases in) the cluster. (Chapter 6)

probability sampling sampling based on a process of random selection that gives each case in the population an equal or known chance of being included in the sample; *see* random selection. (Chapter 6)

process evaluation a type of evaluation research undertaken to determine whether a program is being carried out as designed and is reaching its intended target population; also called "program monitoring"; *see* evaluation research. (Chapter 14)

Public Use Microdata Sample a computer-based sample of individual census returns with certain information excluded to ensure confidentiality. (Chapter 12)

purposive sampling a form of nonprobability sampling that involves the careful selection of typical cases or of cases that represent relevant dimensions of the population. (Chapter 6)

qualitative research the label applied to research that produces qualitative data (e.g., text and visual images); typically involves field research, in-depth interviews, analysis of historical documents, and textual analysis. (Chapter 2)

qualitative variable a variable that has discrete categories, usually designated by words or labels, and nonnumerical differences between categories (i.e., nominal level of measurement); *see also* quantitative variable. (Chapter 4)

quantitative variable a variable that has categories that express numerical distinctions (ratio, interval, and ordinal levels of measurement); *see also* qualitative variable. (Chapter 4)

quasi-experimental designs designs that lack some features (usually randomization) of true experiments but permit stronger inferences about cause and effect than do pre-experimental designs, by means of special design features and supplementary data testing. (Chapter 8)

quota sampling a form of nonprobability sampling that involves the allocation of quotas of cases for various strata (usually proportionate to representation in the population) and the nonrandom selection of cases to fill the quotas. (Chapter 6)

R^2 a measure of fit in multiple regression that indicates approximately the proportion of the variance in the dependent variable (spread of observations about the mean) predicted or "explained" by the independent variables. (Chapter 16)

random assignment the assignment of subjects to experimental conditions by means of a random device, such as a coin toss, thus ensuring that each subject has an equal chance of being in any of the treatment and control conditions; also called "randomization." (Chapters 7, 14)

random-digit dialing a sampling-frame technique for resolving the problem in telephone surveys of missing those with unlisted numbers: dialable telephone numbers are generated (sampled) from a table of random numbers or from a computer random-number program. (Chapter 9)

random-effects model a statistical framework that assumes, in meta-analysis, that results may be shaped by between-study differences in methods (inherent biases), conditions and settings (external validity), and sampling (size and design); *see also* fixed-effects model. (Chapter 13)

random measurement error an error unrelated to the concept being measured that is the result of temporary, chance factors. Random errors are inconsistent across measurements (unpredictably varying in extent and direction) and affect reliability; *see also* systematic measurement error. (Chapter 5)

random selection a process that gives each case in the population an equal chance of being included in the sample. (Chapter 6)

range a univariate measure of variability or dispersion indicating the difference between the lowest and highest values, which is usually reported by identifying these two extreme values. (Chapter 15)

ratio measurement the highest level of measurement, which has the features of the other levels plus an absolute (nonarbitrary) zero point; consequently, it is possible to form ratios of the numbers assigned to categories. (Chapter 5)

reactive measurement effect an effect whereby the process of measurement itself, resulting from people's awareness of being studied, produces changes in what is being measured. (Chapters 5, 7)

reason analysis the development of an accounting scheme outlining the categories of reasons for decisions, which serves as a model for formulating a series of questions in survey instrumentation. (Chapter 10)

reciprocal causation when two variables are hypothesized to be causally linked in terms of their mutual influence on each other; also called "mutual causation." (Chapter 16)

recording units units of analysis in content analysis, such as words, sentences, paragraphs, television shows, or magazine ads. (Chapter 12)

regression analysis a statistical method for studying bivariate (simple-regression) and multivariate (multiple-regression) relationships among interval- or ratio-scale variables. (Chapters 15, 16)

regression line a geometric representation of a bivariate regression equation that provides the best linear fit to the observed data by virtue of minimizing the sum of the squared deviations from the line; also called the "least squares line." (Chapter 15)

relationship among variables a pattern that occurs when changes in one variable are accompanied by systematic changes in the other variable(s). (Chapter 4)

reliability the stability or consistency of an operational definition. (Chapter 5)

replication (1) a repetition of a previous study, using a different sample of cases and often different settings and methods, for the purpose of exploring the possibility that the original findings were an artifact of particular research conditions and procedures; (2) an outcome in elaboration analysis in which the original relationship is essentially repeated in each partial table. (Chapters 7, 13, 16)

research design the overall plan of an empirical study including the basic approach, sampling design, and measurement of key variables. (Chapter 4)

research ethics *see* ethics.

research misconduct as defined by federal policy, unethical actions in proposing, conducting, or reporting research involving fabrication, falsification, or plagiarism. (Chapter 3)

residuals the difference between observed values of the dependent variable and those predicted by a regression equation. (Chapters 15, 16)

respondent debriefings a field pretest technique in which structured follow-up questions at the end of pretest interviews are used to identify instrument problems from the respondent's perspective. (Chapter 10)

response analysis a field pretest technique in which the responses of pretest respondents are tabulated and examined for problematic response patterns. (Chapter 10)

response bias tendency a tendency of a respondent to answer in a certain biased direction (such as in the direction of social desirability) as a function of the content or form of survey questions. (Chapter 10)

response effect in survey research, a general term for systematic errors resulting from such factors as biased or confusing questions, response bias tendencies (e.g., social desirability effects), the effects of interviewer's physical characteristics, and so on. (Chapter 9)

response format the form of the response categories in closed-ended questions. (Chapter 10)

response rate in a survey, the proportion of people in the sample from whom completed interviews or questionnaires are obtained. (Chapters 6, 9)

sample a subset of cases selected from a population. (Chapter 6)

sample bias systematic error or bias in sample results caused by problems in executing the sampling plan, such as incomplete sampling frames and incomplete data collection (not-at-home respondents, refusals, etc.). (Chapter 6)

sampling design that part of the research plan that specifies how as well as how many cases are to be selected. (Chapter 6)

sampling distribution a theoretical distribution of sample results (means, proportions, etc.) that would result from drawing all possible samples of a fixed size from a particular population. (Chapter 6)

sampling error the difference between an actual population value (e.g., a mean) and the population value estimated from a sample. (Chapter 6)

sampling fraction the proportion of the population included in the sample. (Chapter 6)

sampling frame an operational definition of the population that provides the basis for drawing a sample; a sampling frame is constructed by either (1) listing all cases from which a sample may be selected or (2) defining population membership by a rule that provides a basis for case selection. (Chapter 6)

sampling interval the ratio of the number of cases in the population to the desired sample size, which is used to select every Kth (the interval) case in systematic sampling. (Chapter 6)

scale a composite measure of a concept constructed by combining separate indicators according to procedures designed to ensure unidimensionality or other desirable qualities. (Chapters 5, 13)

scatterplot a graph plotting the values of two variables for each observation. (Chapter 15)

secondary analysis analysis of survey or other data originally collected by another researcher, ordinarily for a different purpose. (Chapters 9, 12)

secondary source a document, such as a written history, that contains indirect evidence of past events; that is, an account of anyone who was not an eyewitness; *see also* primary source. (Chapter 12)

selection a threat to internal validity; systematic differences in the composition of control and experimental groups. (Chapter 8)

selective deposit systematic biases in the content of available historical data caused by actions such as selective destruction or editing of written records. (Chapter 12)

selective survival incompleteness of available historical data because some objects survive longer than others. (Chapter 12)

semistructured interview a type of interview that, although it has specific objectives, permits an interviewer some freedom in meeting them; *see also* structured interview and unstructured interview. (Chapter 9)

separate-sample pretest–posttest design a quasi-experimental design having two groups that receive the treatment, one group randomly selected for pretreatment measurement and the other randomly selected for posttreatment measurement. (Chapter 8)

serendipity pattern unanticipated findings that cannot be interpreted meaningfully in terms of prevailing theories and that give rise to new theories. (Chapter 2)

simple random sampling a probability sampling procedure in which every possible combination of cases has an equal chance of being included in the sample. (Chapter 6)

slope/regression coefficient a bivariate regression statistic indicating how much the dependent variable increases (or decreases) for every unit change in the independent variable; the slope of a regression line. (Chapter 15)

snowball sampling a sampling procedure that uses a process of chain referral, whereby each contact is asked to identify additional members of the target population, who are asked to name others, and so on. (Chapters 6, 11)

social bookkeeping documents, such as court records and vital statistics, that contain recorded information produced by groups or organizations. (Chapter 12)

social desirability bias/effect a tendency of some respondents to bias their answers in the direction of socially desirable traits or attitudes, thereby endeavoring to enhance their self-esteem or make a favorable impression on the interviewer or researcher. (Chapters 5, 10)

social impact assessment the systematic assessment of the consequences of a policy or project on individuals, groups, and communities; *see also* environmental impact study. (Chapter 14)

social indicators broad measures of important social conditions, such as measures of crime, family life, health, schools, or job satisfaction, applied periodically to track trends. (Chapter 14)

social network design a survey design in which data are collected on relationships or connections among social actors (people, organizations, countries, etc.) and the transaction flows (processes) occurring along the connecting links. (Chapter 9)

Solomon four-group design a true experimental design requiring four groups: a treatment and a control group that are pretested as well as a treatment and a control group that are not pretested. This design provides information regarding the effect of the treatment, the effect of pretesting alone, the possible interaction of pretesting and treatment, and the effectiveness of the randomization procedure. (Chapter 8)

specification (1) an outcome in elaboration analysis involving the increase, reduction, or disappearance of the original relationship in some partial tables but not in others (i.e., an interaction effect); (2) the formulation of a formal theoretical model. (Chapter 16)

specification error the fitting of a false model to data, such as omission of an important variable, which may produce misleading results. (Chapter 16)

split-ballot tests experimental manipulations of question ordering, wording, or formats, used occasionally in field pretests to compare instrument versions. (Chapter 10)

split-half reliability an "equivalence" method for assessing reliability in which scores on half of the items of a scale or index are correlated with scores on the other half. (Chapter 5)

spurious relationship a statistical association between two variables produced by antecedent variables rather than by a causal link between the original variables. (Chapter 4)

stakeholders of particular concern to evaluation researchers, the individuals or groups affected by the implementation and outcome of a social program; *see* evaluation research. (Chapter 14)

standard deviation a univariate measure of variability or dispersion that indicates the average "spread" of observations about the mean; the square root of the variance, which is calculated by subtracting each value from the mean and squaring the result, then taking the arithmetic average of the squared differences. (Chapters 6, 15)

standard error a statistical measure of the "average" sampling error for a particular sampling distribution; the standard deviation of a sampling distribution and thus a measure of how much sample results will vary from sample to sample. (Chapter 6)

standardized regression coefficients coefficients obtained from a norming operation that puts the various partial-regression coefficients on common footing by standardizing them to the same metric of standard deviation units; consequently, indicates the number of standard deviation units the dependent variable changes for every unit change of 1 standard deviation in an independent variable. (Chapter 16)

static group comparison a pre-experimental design in which a treatment group and a no-treatment group are both measured following the treatment; major threats to internal validity are selection and differential attrition and sometimes maturation. (Chapter 8)

statistic a characteristic of a sample; statistics estimate population parameters; *see also* parameter. (Chapter 6)

statistical regression a threat to internal validity; the tendency for extreme scorers on one measurement to move (regress) closer to the mean score on a later measurement; also known as "regression toward the mean." (Chapter 8)

statistical significance *see* test of statistical significance.

stochastic component the variability in a statistical model that is attributable to random or chance factors; *see also* systematic component. (*see* Chapter 16)

stratified random sampling a probability sampling procedure in which the population is divided into strata and independent random samples are drawn from each stratum. (Chapter 6)

stratum the variable categories (e.g., male and female) into which a population is divided in selecting a stratified random sample; *see also* stratified random sampling. (Chapter 6)

structural equation modeling a statistical technique for testing different theorized models, including "structures" of relationships among *observed* indicators and their underlying *unobserved* concepts. (Chapter 13)

structured interview a type of standardized interview in which the objectives are highly specific, all questions are written beforehand and asked in the same order for all respondents, and the interviewer's remarks are standardized; survey interviews are almost always structured; *see also* unstructured interview. (Chapter 9)

structured observation a type of direct observation with explicit and preset procedures for deciding when, where, how, and what to observe; *see also* unstructured observation. (Chapter 11)

subjective validation validity assessment based on a researcher's judgments; *see* content validity and face validity. (Chapter 5)

summative evaluation a type of evaluation research that assesses the overall outcome of a social program in terms of meeting program goals and/or efficiency; *see* effect assessment and efficiency assessment. (Chapter 14)

suppressor variable in elaboration analysis, a test variable that weakens or conceals a relationship so that when it is uncontrolled there may be little or no zero-order association. (Chapter 16)

survey a major approach to social research that involves asking a relatively large sample of people direct questions through interviews or questionnaires. (Chapters 1, 9, 13)

systematic component the variability in a statistical model that is attributable to hypothesized relations among variables; *see also* stochastic component. (Chapter 16)

systematic measurement error error from factors that systematically influence (bias) either the process of measurement or the concept being measured. Systematic errors are consistent across measurements taken at different times or are systematically related to characteristics of the cases being measured (e.g., the cultural bias of IQ tests) and thereby affect validity; *see also* random measurement error. (Chapter 5)

systematic sampling a probability sampling procedure in which cases are selected from an available list at a fixed interval after a random start. (Chapter 6)

target population in sampling, the population to which a researcher would like to generalize his or her results. (Chapter 6)

telephone interview a type of interview in which interviewers interact with respondents by telephone; *see also* face-to-face interview. (Chapter 9)

testimony documents, such as depositions and private letters, containing individual eyewitness accounts of events. (Chapter 12)

testing a threat to internal validity; changes in what is being measured that are brought about by reactions to the process of measurement; the effects of being measured once on being measured a second time. (Chapter 8)

test of statistical significance a statistical procedure used to assess the likelihood that the results of an experiment or other study could have occurred by chance. (Chapters 4, 7, 15, 16)

test–retest reliability a "stability" method for assessing reliability that involves calculating the correlation between outcomes of repeated applications of a measure. (Chapter 5)

theoretical sampling a field-research sampling strategy in which broad analytical categories are sampled to facilitate the development of theoretical insights. (Chapter 11)

theory a logically interconnected set of propositions that show how or why a relationship occurs. (Chapter 2)

threats to internal validity uncontrolled extraneous variables that pose explanations of study results that rival the hypothesized effects of the independent variable; classes of threats include history, instrumentation, statistical regression, selection, attrition, differential attrition, maturation, and testing. (Chapter 8)

treatment the manipulated conditions comprising an independent variable in an experiment. (Chapter 7)

treatment diffusion of information a threat to internal validity, most problematic in evaluation studies, in which subjects' actions are affected by their knowledge of conditions in other treatments. (Chapter 14)

trend study a longitudinal design in which a research question is investigated by repeated surveys of independently selected samples of the same population. (Chapter 9)

triangulation the addressing of a social research question with multiple methods or measures that do not share the same methodological weaknesses; if different approaches produce similar findings, confidence in the results increases. (Chapter 13)

true experimental designs an experimental design that affords strong evidence of cause and effect by means of meeting five requirements: (1) manipulation of the independent variable, (2) measurement of the dependent variable, (3) randomization, (4) at least one comparison group, and (5) constancy of conditions. (Chapters 7, 8)

t-**test** in multiple regression a test of significance that tests the hypothesis that a regression coefficient is significantly different from zero when the other independent variables are taken into account. (Chapter 16)

t **value** the outcome (statistic) computed from a *t*-test. (Chapter 16)

unidimensionality evidence that a scale or index is measuring only a single dimension of a concept. (Chapter 13)

unit of analysis the entity about whom or which a researcher gathers information; the unit may be people, social roles and relationships, groups, organizations, communities, nations, and social artifacts. (Chapter 4)

univariate analysis statistical analysis of one variable at a time; *see also* bivariate analysis and multivariate analysis. (Chapter 15)

unstructured interview a type of nonstandardized interview in which the objectives may be very general and the questions developed as the interview proceeds; preferred when the purpose is to acquire preliminary data or understandings; *see also* structured interview. (Chapter 9)

unstructured observation a type of direct observation without pre-established procedures for determining when, where, and what to observe; *see also* structured observation. (Chapter 11)

validity the congruence or "goodness of fit" between an operational definition and the concept it is purported to measure. (Chapter 5)

variance *see* standard deviation.

verbal (self-) report the form of measurement typical of survey research consisting of people's replies to direct questions. (Chapter 5)

vital statistics demographic data collected from the registration of "vital" life events, such as births, deaths, marriages, and divorces. (Chapter 12)

wild-code checking a data-cleaning procedure involving checking for out-of-range and other "illegal" codes among the values recorded for each variable. (Chapter 15)

within-subjects designs experimental designs in which each subject experiences all experimental conditions, such as both treatment and control; *see also* between-subject designs. (Chapter 8)

Y-intercept the predicted value of the dependent variable in bivariate regression when the independent variable has a value of zero; graphically, the point at which the regression line crosses the *Y*-axis. (Chapter 15)

zero-order relationship a bivariate correlation or the relationship in a bivariate table; "zero-order" means that there are no ("zero") control variables; *see also* first-order relationship. (Chapter 16)

References

Abbott, A. 2004. *Methods of Discovery: Heuristics for the Social Sciences*. New York: W. W. Norton.

Adair, J. G., T. W. Dushenko, and R. C. L. Lindsay. 1985. Ethical regulations and their impact on research practice. *American Psychologist* 40:59–72.

Adler, P. A. 1993. *Wheeling and Dealing: An Ethnography of an Upper-Level Drug Dealing and Smuggling Community*, 2nd ed. New York: Columbia University Press.

Adler, P. A., and P. Adler. 1987. *Membership Roles in Field Research*. Newbury Park, CA: Sage.

Agger, B. 1991. Critical theory, poststructuralism, postmodernism: Their sociological relevance. *Annual Review of Sociology* 17:105–31.

Ainlay, S. C., and J. D. Hunter. 1984. Religious participation among older Mennonites. *The Mennonite Quarterly Review* 58:70–79.

Ainlay, S. C., R. A. Singleton, Jr., and V. L. Swigert. 1992. Aging and religious participation: Reconsidering the effects of health. *Journal for the Scientific Study of Religion* 31:175–88.

Alexander, C. S., and H. J. Becker. 1978. The use of vignettes in survey research. *Public Opinion Quarterly* 42:93–104.

Allahyari, R. A. 2000. *Visions of Charity: Volunteer Workers and Moral Community*. Berkeley: University of California Press.

Allison, P. D. 2002. *Missing Data*. Thousand Oaks, CA: Sage.

Alwin, D. F., R. L. Cohen, and T. M. Newcomb. 1991. *Political Attitudes over the Life Span: The Bennington Women after 50 Years*. Madison: University of Wisconsin.

Allwood, C. M. 2012. The distinction between qualitative and quantitative research methods is problematic. *Quality and Quantity* 46:1417–29.

American Anthropological Association (AAA). 2009. *Code of Ethics of the American Anthropological Association*. Arlington, VA: American Anthropological Association.

American Anthropological Association. 2012. *Statement of Ethics: Principles of Professional Responsibility*. Arlington, VA: American Anthropological Association. http://ethics.americananthro.org/category/statement/ (accessed January 29, 2017).

American Psychological Association (APA). 2010. *Ethical Principles of Psychologists and Code of Conduct*. Washington, D.C.: APA. http://www.apa.org/ethics/code/principles.pdf (accessed September 22, 2014).

American Psychological Association. 2017. About APA. http://www.apa.org/about/index.aspx (accessed February 4, 2017).

American Sociological Association (ASA). 1999. *Code of Ethics and Policies and Procedures of the ASA Committee on Professional Ethics*. Washington, D.C.: ASA. http://www.asanet.org/images/asa/docs/pdf/CodeofEthics.pdf (accessed September 22, 2014).

American Sociological Association. 2016. Annual editors' reports. http://www.asanet.org/research-publications/journal-resources/annual-editors-reports#ASR (accessed July 15, 2016).

American Sociological Association. 2017. Mission statement. http://www.asanet.org/about-asa/asa-story/mission-statement (accessed February 4, 2017).

Anderson, B. A., B. D. Silver, and P. R. Abramson. 1988. The effects of the race of the interviewer on race-related attitudes of black respondents in SRC/CPS National Election Studies. *Public Opinion Quarterly* 52:289–324.

Andrews, F. M., and S. B. Withey. 1976. *Social Indicators of Well-Being*. New York: Plenum.

Angell, R. C. 1951. The moral integration of American cities. *American Journal of Sociology* 57(Part 2): 1–140.

Appelbaum, R. P. 1990. Counting the homeless. In *Homelessness in the United States*. Vol. II: *Data and Issues* (ed. J. A. Momeni), pp. 1–16. New York: Praeger.

Aquilino, W. S. 1994. Interview mode effects in surveys of drug and alcohol use. *Public Opinion Quarterly* 58:210–40.

Arceneaux, K. 2005. Using cluster randomized field experiments to study voting behavior. *Annals of the American Academy of Political and Social Science* 601:169–79.

Argyris, C. 1968. Some unintended consequences of rigorous research. *Psychological Bulletin* 70:185–97.

Arminger, G., C. C. Clogg, and M. E. Sobel (eds.). 1995. *Handbook of Statistical Modeling for the Social and Behavioral Sciences*. New York: Plenum Press.

Aronson, E., N. Blaney, J. Sikes, C. Stephan, and M. Snapp. 1975. Busing and racial tension: The jigsaw route to learning and liking. *Psychology Today* 8(February):43–50.

Aronson, E., N. Blaney, C. Stephan, J. Sikes, and M. Snapp. 1978. *The Jigsaw Classroom*. Beverly Hills, CA: Sage.

Aronson, E., M. Brewer, and J. M. Carlsmith. 1985. Experimentation in social psychology. In *The Handbook of Social Psychology*, 3rd ed., vol. I (eds. G. Lindzey and E. Aronson), pp. 441–86. New York: Random House.

Aronson, E., and J. M. Carlsmith. 1968. Experimentation in social psychology. In *The Handbook of Social Psychology*, 2nd ed., vol. II (eds. G. Lindzey and E. Aronson), pp. 1–79. Reading, MA: Addison–Wesley.

Associated Press–NORC Center for Public Affairs Research. 2015. Issue brief: Same-sex marriage and gay rights: A shift in American's attitudes. http://www.apnorc.org/PDFs/SameSexStudy/LGBT%20issues_D5_FINAL.pdf (accessed July 3, 2016).

Babbie, E. 1995. *The Practice of Social Research*, 7th ed. Belmont, CA.: Wadsworth.

Babbie, E., F. Halley, and J. Zaino. 2007. *Adventures in Social Research: Data Analysis Using SPSS 14 and 15 for Windows*, 6th ed. Thousand Oaks, CA: Pine Forge.

Backstrom, L., P. Boldi, M. Rosa, J. Ugander, and S. Vigna. 2012. Four degrees of separation. In *Proceedings of the 3rd Annual ACM Web Science Conference* (WebSci '12), pp. 33–42, Evanston, IL.

Bahr, H. M., T. Caplow, and B. A. Chadwick. 1983. Middletown III. Problems of replication, longitudinal measurement, and triangulation. *Annual Review of Sociology* 9:243–64.

Bailey, K. D. 1982. *Methods of Social Research*, 2nd ed. New York: Free Press.

Bailey, W. C. 1990. Murder, capital punishment, and television: Execution publicity and homicide rates. *American Sociological Review* 55:628–33.

Bailey, W. C., and R. D. Peterson. 1989. Murder and capital punishment: A monthly time-series analysis of execution publicity. *American Sociological Review* 54:722–43.

Bainbridge, W. S. 1982. Shaker demographics 1840–1900: An example of the use of U.S. Census enumeration schedules. *Journal for the Scientific Study of Religion* 21:352–65.

Ball, S., and G. A. Bogatz. 1970. *The First Year of Sesame Street: An Evaluation*. Princeton, NJ: Educational Testing Service.

Barrera, D., and B. Simpson. 2012. Much ado about deception: Consequences of deceiving research participants in the social sciences. *Sociological Methods and Research* 41:383–413.

Bass, B. M. 1955. Authoritarianism or acquiescence. *Journal of Abnormal and Social Psychology* 51:616–23.

Batten, T. F. 1971. *Reasoning and Research: A Guide for Social Science Methods*. Boston: Little, Brown.

Baumeister, R. F., J. D. Campbell, J. I. Krueger, and K. D. Vohs. 2003. Does high self-esteem cause better performance, interpersonal success, happiness, or healthier lifestyles? *Psychological Science in the Public Interest* 4:1–44.

Baumrind, D. 1971. Principles of ethical conduct in the treatment of subjects: Reaction to the draft report of the Committee on Ethical Standards in Psychological Research. *American Psychologist* 26:887–96.

Baumrind, D. 1985. Research using intentional deception: Ethical issues revisited. *American Psychologist* 40:165–74.

Beatty, P. 1995. Understanding the standardized/non-standardized interviewing controversy. *Journal of Official Statistics* 11:147–60.

Beatty, P. C., and G. B. Willis. 2007. Research synthesis: The practice of cognitive interviewing. *Public Opinion Quarterly* 71:287–311.

Beauchamp, T. L. 1997. Opposing views on animal experimentation: Do animals have rights? *Ethics and Behavior* 7:113–21.

Becker, B. J., C. M. Schram, L. Chang, M. M. Kino, and M. Quintieri. 1994. Models of science achievement: Forces affecting male and female performance in school science. In *Meta-Analysis for Explanation: A Casebook* (eds. T. D. Cook, H. Cooper, D. S. Cordray, H. Hartmann, L. V. Hedges, R. J. Light, T. A. Louis, and F. Mosteller), pp. 209–81. New York: Russell Sage Foundation.

Becker, H. S. 1967. Whose side are we on? *Social Problems* 14:239–47.

Becker, H. S. 2007. *Writing for Social Scientists: How to Start and Finish Your Thesis, Book, or Article*, 2nd ed. Chicago: University of Chicago Press.

Becker, H. S., B. Geer, E. C. Hughes, and A. Strauss. 1961. *Boys in White: Student Culture in Medical School*. Chicago: University of Chicago Press.

Belli, R. F., W. L. Shay, and F. P. Stafford. 2001. Event history calendars and question list surveys: A direct comparison of interviewing methods. *Public Opinion Quarterly* 65:45–74.

Belli, R. F., L. M. Smith, P. M. Andreski, and S. Agrawal. 2007. Methodological comparisons between CATI event history calendar and standardized conventional questionnaire instruments. *Public Opinion Quarterly* 71:603–22.

Belli, R. F., F. P. Stafford, and D. F. Alwin (eds.). 2009. *Calendar and Time Diary Methods in Life Course Research*. Thousand Oaks, CA: Sage.

Bem, D. J. 1995. Writing a review article for *Psychological Bulletin*. *Psychological Bulletin* 118:172–77.

Benson, P. J., and S. C. Silver. 2013. *What Editors Want: An Author's Guide to Scientific Journal Publishing*. Chicago: University of Chicago Press.

Bergan, D. E., A. S. Gerber, D. P. Green, and C. Panagopoulos. 2005. Grassroots mobilization and voter turnout in 2004. *Public Opinion Quarterly* 69:760–77.

Berglund, E., D. A. Bernstein, R. A. Eisinger, G. M. Hochbaum, E. Lichtenstein, J. L. Schwartz, and B. C. Straits. 1974. *Guideline for Research on the Effectiveness of Smoking Cessation Programs: A Committee Report*. National Interagency Council on Smoking and Health. Chicago: American Dental Association.

Berk, R. A. 1983. Applications of the general linear model to survey data. In *Handbook of Survey Research* (eds. P. H. Rossi, J. D. Wright, and A. B. Anderson), pp. 495–546. New York: Academic Press.

Berk, R. A. 1993. Policy correctness in the ASR. *American Sociological Review* 58:889–90.

Berk, R. A., A. Campbell, R. Klap, and B. Western. 1992. The deterrent effect of arrest: A Bayesian analysis of four field experiments. *American Sociological Review* 57:698–708.

Berk, R. A., and P. J. Newton. 1985. Does arrest really deter wife battery? An effort to replicate the findings of the Minneapolis Spouse Abuse Experiment. *American Sociological Review* 50:253–62.

Berk, R. A., and P. H. Rossi. 1976. Doing good or worse: Evaluation research politically reexamined. *Social Problems* 23:337–49.

Berk, R. A., and L. W. Sherman. 1988. Police responses to family violence incidents: An analysis of an experimental design with incomplete randomization. *Journal of the American Statistical Association* 83:70–76.

Berk, R. A., G. K. Smyth, and L. W. Sherman. 1988. When random assignment fails: Some lessons from the Minneapolis Spouse Abuse Experiment. *Journal of Quantitative Criminology* 4:209–23.

Bernard, H. R. 1994. *Research Methods in Anthropology: Qualitative and Quantitative Approaches*, 2nd ed. Thousand Oaks, CA: Sage.

Bernard, H. R. 2013. *Social Research Methods: Qualitative and Quantitative Approaches*. 2nd ed. Los Angeles: Sage.

Bernstein, I. N., G. W. Bohrnstedt, and E. F. Borgatta. 1975. External validity and evaluation research: A codification of problems. *Sociological Methods and Research* 4:101–28.

Berry, B. 1991. An account of a professional ethics violation in sociology. *American Sociologist* 22:261–66.

Bertrand, M., and S. Mullainathan. 2004. Are Emily and Greg more employable than Lakisha and Jamal? A field experiment on labor market discrimination. *American Economic Review* 94:991–1013.

Beveridge, W. I. B. 1957. *The Art of Scientific Investigation*, 3rd ed. London: Heinemann.

Biemer, P. P., and L. E. Lyberg. 2003. *Introduction to Survey Quality*. Hoboken, NJ: Wiley.

Biernacki, P., and D. Waldorf. 1981. Snowball sampling: Problems and techniques of chain referral sampling. *Sociological Methods and Research* 10:141–63.

Biernat, M., and C. Crandall. 2001. Two journal articles retracted, professor resigns. *Dialogue* 16(Fall):17.

Binder, A., and J. W. Meeker. 1993. Implications of the failure to replicate the Minneapolis experimental findings. *American Sociological Review* 58:886–88.

Blalock, H. M., Jr. 1964. *Causal Inferences in Nonexperimental Research*. Chapel Hill: University of North Carolina Press.

Blanton, H., and J. Jaccard. 2008. Representing versus generalizing: Two approaches to external validity and their implications for the study of prejudice. *Psychological Inquiry* 19:99–105.

Blumberg, Stephen J., and Julian V. Luke. 2015. Wireless substitution: Early release of estimates from the National Health Interview Survey, January–June 2015. U.S. Department of Health and Human Services, Centers for Disease Control and Prevention, National Center for Health Statistics (released 12/15). http://www.cdc.gov/nchs/data/nhis/earlyrelease/wireless201512.pdf (accessed May 30, 2016).

Bogdan, R., and S. J. Taylor. 1975. *Introduction to Qualitative Research Methods: A Phenomenological Approach to the Social Sciences*. New York: Wiley.

Bollen, J., H. Mao, and X. J. Zeng. 2011. Twitter mood predicts the stock market. *Journal of Computational Science* 2:1–8.

Borenstein, M. 2009. Effect sizes for continuous data. In *The Handbook of Research Synthesis and Meta-Analysis*, 2nd ed. (eds. H. Cooper, L. V. Hedges, and J. C. Valentine), pp. 221–35. New York: Russell Sage Foundation.

Boruch, R. F., and W. Wothke (eds.). 1985. *Randomization and Field Experimentation, New Directions for Program Evaluation*, No. 28. San Francisco: Jossey-Bass.

Bosk, C. L. 1979. *Forgive and Remember: Managing Medical Failure*. Chicago: University of Chicago Press.

Box, G. E. P. 1976. Science and statistics. *Journal of the American Statistical Association* 71:791–99.

Boydstun, J. E., M. E. Sherry, and N. P. Moelter. 1978. Patrol staffing in San Diego: One- or two-officer units. In *Evaluation Studies Review Annual 3* (eds. T. D. Cook, M. L. Del Rosario, K. M. Hennigan, M. M. Mark, and W. M. K. Trochim), pp. 455–72. Beverly Hills, CA: Sage.

Boyer, P., and S. Nissenbaum. 1974. *Salem Possessed: The Social Origins of Witchcraft*. Cambridge, MA: Harvard University Press.

Bradburn, N. M., and S. Sudman. 1988. *Polls and Surveys: Understanding What They Tell Us*. San Francisco: Jossey-Bass.

Brandon, L., R. M. Gritz, and M. R. Pergamit. 1995. The effect of interview length and attrition in the National Longitudinal Survey of Youth. NLS Discussion Paper, Report NLS 95-28. Washington, D.C.: U.S. Department of Labor, Bureau of Labor Statistics.

Brazziel, W. F. 1969. A letter from the South. *Harvard Educational Review* 39:348–56.

Breault, K. D. 1994. Was Durkheim right? A critical survey of the empirical literature on *Le Suicide*. In *Emile Durkheim Le Suicide: 100 Years Later* (ed. D. Lester), pp. 11–29. Philadelphia: Charles Press.

Brener, N. D., D. K. Eaton, L. Kann, J. A. Grunbaum, L. A. Gross, T. M. Kyle, and J. G. Ross. 2006. The association of survey setting and mode with self-reported health risk behaviors among high school students. *Public Opinion Quarterly* 70:354–74.

Brick, J. M. 2011. The future of survey sampling. *Public Opinion Quarterly* 75:872–88.

Brick, J. M., and D. Williams. 2013. Explaining rising nonresponse rates in cross-sectional surveys. *The Annals of the American Academy of Political and Social Science* 645:36–59.

Broh, B. A. 2002. Linking extracurricular programming and academic achievement: Who benefits and why? *Sociology of Education* 75:69–91.

Broockman, D., J. Kalla, and P. Aronow. 2015. Irregularities in LaCour (2014). https://stanford.edu/~dbroock/broockman_kalla_aronow_lg_irregularities.pdf (accessed July 10, 2016).

Brown, P. 1995. Naming and framing: The social construction of diagnosis and illness. *Journal of Health and Social Behavior* 36(Extra issue):34–52.

Browne, J. 1976a. Personal journal: Fieldwork for fun and profit. In *The Research Experience* (ed. M. P. Golden), pp. 71–84. Itasca, IL: F. E. Peacock.

Browne, J. 1976b. The used car game. In *The Research Experience* (ed. M. P. Golden), pp. 60–71. Itasca, IL: F. E. Peacock.

Bruner, E. M., and J. P. Kelso. 1980. Gender differences in graffiti: A semiotic perspective. *Women's Studies International Quarterly* 3:239–52.

Bryan, J. H., and M. A. Test. 1967. Models and helping: Naturalistic studies in aiding behavior. *Journal of Personality and Social Psychology* 6:400–407.

Burawoy, M. 1991. Reconstructing social theories. In *Ethnography Unbound: Power and Resistance in the Modern Metropolis* (eds. M. Burawoy et al.), pp. 8–27. Berkeley: University of California Press.

Burdge, R. J., and F. Vanclay. 1996. Social impact assessment: A contribution to the state of the art series. *Impact Assessment* 14:59–86.

Burt, M. R. 1992. *Over the Edge: The Growth of Homelessness in the 1980s.* New York: Russell Sage Foundation.

Bushman, R. L. 1967. *From Puritan to Yankee: Character and the Social Order in Connecticut, 1690–1765.* Cambridge, MA: Harvard University Press.

Calarco, J. M. 2011. "I need help!" Social class and children's help-seeking in elementary school. *American Sociological Review* 76:862–82.

Callero, P. L. 1985. Role-identity salience. *Social Psychology Quarterly* 48:203–15.

Campanelli, P. C., E. A. Martin, and J. M. Rothgeb. 1991. The use of respondent and interviewer debriefing studies as a way to study response error in survey data. *Statistician* 40:253–64.

Campbell, D. T. 1969. Prospective: Artifact and control. In *Artifact in Behavioral Research* (eds. R. Rosenthal and R. L. Rosnow), pp. 351–82. New York: Academic Press.

Campbell, D. T., and D. W. Fiske. 1959. Convergent and discriminant validation by the multitrait–multimethod matrix. *Psychological Bulletin* 56:81–105.

Campbell, D. T., and H. L. Ross. 1968. The Connecticut crackdown on speeding: Time series data in quasi-experimental analysis. *Law and Society Review* 3:33–53.

Campbell, D. T., and J. C. Stanley. 1963. *Experimental and Quasi-experimental Designs for Research.* Chicago: Rand McNally.

Cannell, C. F., and R. L. Kahn. 1968. Interviewing. In *The Handbook of Social Psychology*, 2nd ed., vol. II (eds. G. Lindzey and E. Aronson), pp. 526–71. Reading, MA: Addison–Wesley.

Cannell, C. F., K. H. Marquis, and A. Laurent. 1977. *A Summary of Studies of Interviewing Methodology. Vital and Health Statistics.* Series 2, Data evaluation and methods research. No. 69. DHEW Publ. No. (HRA) 77–1343, Health Resources Administration, National Center for Health Statistics, U.S. Department of Health, Education and Welfare. Washington, D.C.: U.S. Government Printing Office.

Carey, A. 1967. The Hawthorne studies: A radical criticism. *American Sociological Review* 32:403–16.

Carlsmith, J. M., P. C. Ellsworth, and E. Aronson. 1976. *Methods of Research in Social Psychology.* Reading, MA: Addison–Wesley.

Carnap, R. 1966. *Philosophical Foundations of Physics.* New York: Basic Books.

Carr, P. J., L. Napolitano, and J. Keating. 2007. We never call the cops and here is why: A qualitative examination of legal cynicism in three Philadelphia neighborhoods. *Criminology* 45:445–80.

Carter, R. E., Jr., V. C. Troldahl, and R. S. Schuneman. 1963. Interviewer bias in selecting households. *Journal of Marketing* 27:27–34.

Cavan, S. 1966. *Liquor License: An Ethnography of Bar Behavior.* Chicago: Aldine.

Ceci, S. J., D. Peters, and J. Plotkin. 1985. Human subjects review, personal values, and regulation of social science research. *American Psychologist* 40:994–1002.

Centers for Disease Control and Prevention (CDC). 2013. U.S. Public Health Service Syphilis Study at Tuskegee: The Tuskegee Timeline. http://www.cdc.gov/tuskegee/timeline.htm (accessed November 24, 2014).

Centers for Disease Control and Prevention 2015. Smoking and Cancer. Atlanta: CDC. https://www.cdc.gov/tobacco/data_statistics/sgr/50th-anniversary/pdfs/fs_smoking_cancer_508.pdf (accessed August 13, 2008).

Cerulo, K. A. 2014. Reassessing the problem: Response to Jerolmack and Khan. *Sociological Methods and Research* 43:219–26.

Chambliss, W. J. 1976. Functional and conflict theories of crime: The heritage of Emile Durkheim and Karl Marx. In *Whose Law What Order? A Conflict Approach to Criminology* (eds. W. J. Chambliss and M. Mankoff), pp. 1–28. New York: Wiley.

Charmaz, K. 1991. *Good Days, Bad Days: The Self in Chronic Illness and Time.* New Brunswick, NJ: Rutgers University.

Chein, I. 1981. An introduction to sampling. In *Research Methods in Social Relations*, 4th ed. (ed. L. H. Kidder), pp. 418–44. New York: Holt, Rinehart and Winston.

Chelimsky, E. 1987. The politics of program evaluation. *Society* 25 (November/December):24–32.

Chelimsky, E. 1991. On the social science contribution to governmental decision-making. *Science* 254:226–31.

Cherlin, A. J., L. M. Burton, T. R. Hunt, and D. M. Purvin. 2004. The influence of physical and sexual abuse on marriage and cohabitation. *American Sociological Review* 69:768–89.

Choi, I., R. E. Nisbett, and A. Norenzayan. 1999. Causal attribution across cultures: Variation and universality. *Psychological Bulletin* 125:47–63.

Christian, L. M., D. A. Dillman, and J. D. Smyth. 2007. Helping respondents get it right the first time: The influence of words, symbols, and graphics in Web surveys. *Public Opinion Quarterly* 71:113–25.

Christianson, P., D. F. Roberts, and N. Bjork. 2012. Booze, drugs, and pop music: Trends in substance portrayals in the Billboard top 100—1968–2008. *Substance Use and Abuse* 47:121–29.

Cialdini, R. B., and D. A. Schroeder. 1976. Increasing compliance by legitimizing paltry contributions: When even a penny helps. *Journal of Personality and Social Psychology* 34:599–604.

Clark, C. S. 1992. Underage drinking. *CQ Researcher* 2:219–32.

Clarke, M. 2009. Reporting format. In *The Handbook of Research Synthesis and Meta-Analysis*, 2nd ed. (eds. H. Cooper, L. V. Hedges, and J. C. Valentine), pp. 521–34. New York: Russell Sage Foundation.

Cleveland, W. S. 1985. *The Elements of Graphing Data.* Monterey, CA: Wadsworth.

Clogg, C. C., and D. O. Sawyer. 1981. A comparison of alternative models for analyzing the scalability of response patterns. In *Sociological Methodology 1981* (ed. S. Leinhardt), pp. 240–80. San Francisco: Jossey–Bass.

Clore, G. L., R. M. Bray, S. M. Itkin, and P. Murphy. 1978. Interracial attitudes and behavior at a summer camp. *Journal of Personality and Social Psychology* 35:107–16.

Code of Federal Regulations (CFR). 2009. *Title 45—Public Welfare, Part 46—Protection of Human Subjects.* Office of the Federal Register. Washington, D.C.: U.S. Government Printing Office.

Coleman, J. S. 1988. Social capital in the creation of human capital. *American Journal of Sociology* 94:S95–S120.

Coleman, J. S. 1990. *Foundations of Social Theory.* Cambridge, MA: Belknap Press of Harvard University Press.

Collins, D. (ed.). 2015. *Cognitive Interviewing Practice.* London: Sage.

Collins, R. 1989. Sociology: Proscience or antiscience? *American Sociological Review* 54:124–39.

Comstock, G., with H. Paik. 1991. *Television and the American Child.* San Diego: Academic Press.

Conrad, P., and K. K. Barker. 2010. The social construction of illness: Key insights and policy implications. *Journal of Health and Social Behavior* 51:S67–S69.

Contrada, R. J., R. D. Ashmore, M. L. Gary, E. Coups, J. D. Egeth, A. Sewell, K. Ewell, T. M. Goyal, and V. Chasse. 2001. Measures of ethnicity-related stress: Psychometric properties, ethnic group differences, and associations with well-being. *Journal of Applied Social Psychology* 31:1775–820.

Converse, J. M., and S. Presser. 1986. *Survey Questions: Handcrafting the Standardized Questionnaire.* Newbury Park, CA: Sage.

Cook, C., F. Heath, and R. L. Thompson. 2000. A meta-analysis of response rates in Web- or Internet-based surveys. *Educational and Psychological Measurement* 60:821–36.

Cook, K. S., and T. Yamagishi. 2008. A defense of deception on scientific grounds. *Social Psychology Quarterly* 71:215–21.

Cook, S. W. 1984. Cooperative interaction in multiethnic contexts. In *Groups in Contact: The Psychology of Desegregation* (eds. N. Miller and M. B. Brewer), pp. 155–85. Orlando: Academic Press.

Cook, T. D., and D. T. Campbell. 1979. *Quasi-experimentation: Design and Analysis Issues for Field Settings.* Chicago: Rand McNally.

Cook, T. D., and R. F. Conner. 1976. The educational impact. *Journal of Communication* 26(2): 155–64.

Cook, T. D., F. L. Cook, M. M. Mark. 1977. Randomized and quasi-experimental designs in evaluation research: An introduction. In *Evaluation Research Methods: A Basic Guide* (ed. L. Rutman), pp. 103–39. Beverly Hills, CA: Sage.

Cook, T. D., H. Cooper, D. S. Cordray, H. Hartmann, L. V. Hedges, R. J. Light, T. A. Louis, and F. Mosteller. 1994. *Meta-analysis for Explanation: A Casebook.* New York: Russell Sage Foundation.

Cook, T. D., L. C. Leviton, and W. R. Shadish Jr. 1985. Program evaluation. In *The Handbook of Social Psychology*, 3rd ed., vol. 1 (eds. G. Lindzey and E. Aronson), pp. 699–777. New York: Random House.

Cook, T. D., and W. R. Shadish. 1994. Social experiments: Some developments over the past fifteen years. *Annual Review of Psychology* 45:545–80.

Cooper, H., and L. V. Hedges. 2009. Research synthesis as a scientific process. In *The Handbook of Research Synthesis and Meta-Analysis*, 2nd ed. (eds. H. Cooper, L. V. Hedges, and J. C. Valentine), pp. 3–16. New York: Russell Sage Foundation.

Cooper, H., L. V. Hedges, and J. C. Valentine (eds.). 2009. *The Handbook of Research Synthesis and Meta-Analysis*, 2nd ed. New York: Russell Sage Foundation.

Corporation for National and Community Service. 2016. About Us: Who We Are. http://www.nationalservice.gov/about/who-we-are (accessed July 22, 2016).

Couper, M. P. 2011. The future of modes of data collection. *Public Opinion Quarterly* 75:889–908.

Couper, M, P., and M. Bosnjak. 2010. Internet surveys. In *Handbook of Survey Research*, 2nd ed. (eds. P. V. Marsden and J. D. Wright), pp. 527–50. Bingley, UK: Emerald Group.

Couper, M. P., F. G. Conrad, and R. Tourangeau. 2007. Visual context effects in Web surveys. *Public Opinion Quarterly* 71:623–34.

Couper, M. P., and R. M. Groves. 2002. Introductory interactions in telephone surveys and nonresponse. In *Standardization and Tacit Knowledge: Interaction and Practice in the Survey Interview* (eds. D. W. Maynard, H. Houtkoop-Steenstra, N. C. Schaeffer, and J. van der Zouwen), pp. 161–77. New York: Wiley.

Couper, M. P., M. W. Traugott, and M. J. Lamias. 2001. Web survey design and administration. *Public Opinion Quarterly* 65:230–53.

Cournand, A. 1977. The code of the scientist and its relationship to ethics. *Science* 198:699–705.

Crain, R. L., E. Katz, and D. B. Rosenthal. 1969. *The Politics of Community Conflict.* Indianapolis: Bobbs–Merrill.

Crandall, C. 2001. Scientific progress: A need for trust, a need for skepticism. *Dialogue* 16(Fall):20–21.

Crano, W. D. 1981. Triangulation and cross-cultural research. In *Scientific Inquiry in the Social Sciences* (eds. M. B. Brewer and B. E. Collins), pp. 317–44. San Francisco: Jossey–Bass.

Cronbach, L. J. 1982. *Designing Evaluations of Educational and Social Programs.* San Francisco: Jossey–Bass.

Crosby, F., S. Bromley, and L. Saxe. 1980. Recent unobtrusive studies of black and white discrimination and prejudice: A literature review. *Psychological Bulletin* 87:546–63.

Crossen, C. 1994. *Tainted Truth: The Manipulation of Face in America.* New York: Simon & Schuster.

Curini, L., S. Iacus, and L. Canova. 2015. Measuring idiosyncratic happiness through the analysis of twitter: An application to the Italian case. *Social Indicators Research* 121:525–42.

Curry, G. D. 2010. From knowledge to response and back again: Theory and Evaluation in responding to gangs. In *Youth Gangs and Community Intervention: Research, Practice, and Evidence* (ed. R. J. Chaskin), pp. 109–26. New York: Columbia University Press.

Curtin, R. T. 2004. Psychology and macroeconomics. In *A Telescope on Society: Survey Research and Social Science at the University of Michigan and Beyond* (eds. J. S. House et al.), pp. 131–55. Ann Arbor: University of Michigan.

Curtin, R., S. Presser, and E. Singer. 2005. Changes in telephone survey nonresponse over the past quarter century. *Public Opinion Quarterly* 69:87–98.

D'Amico, R. 1989. *Historicism and Knowledge.* New York: Rutledge, Chapman and Hall.

Darley, J. M., and B. Latané. 1968. Bystander intervention in emergencies: Diffusion of responsibility. *Journal of Personality and Social Psychology* 8:377–83.

Dasgupta, N., and M. Hunsinger. 2008. The opposite of a great truth is also true: When do student samples help versus hurt the scientific study of prejudice? *Psychological Inquiry* 19:90–98.

David, P. A. 1985. Clio and the economics of QWERTY. *American Economic Review* 75:332–37.

Davis, J. A. 1964. Great books and small groups: An informal history of a national survey. In *Sociologists at Work* (ed. P. E. Hammond), pp. 212–34. New York: Basic Books.

Davis, J. A. 1971. *Elementary Survey Analysis.* Englewood Cliffs, NJ: Prentice Hall.

Davis, J. A. 1985. *The Logic of Causal Order.* Beverly Hills, CA: Sage.

Davis, J. A., and T. W. Smith. 1992. *The NORC General Social Survey: A User's Guide.* Newbury Park, CA: Sage.

de Leeuw, E. D. 2005. To mix or not to mix data collection modes in surveys. *Journal of Official Statistics* 21:233-55.

de Leeuw, E. D. 2008. Choosing the method of data collection. In *International Handbook of Survey Methodology* (eds. E. D. de Leeuw, J. J. Hox, and D. A. Dillman), pp. 113–35. New York: Erlbaum.

de Leeuw, E. D., M. Callegaro, J. Hox, E. Korendijk, and G. Lensvelt-Mulders. 2007. The influence of advance letters on response in telephone surveys: A meta-analysis. *Public Opinion Quarterly* 71:413–43.

de Leeuw, E. D., and W. de Heer. 2002. Trends in household survey nonresponse: A longitudinal and international comparison. In *Survey Nonresponse* (eds. R. M. Groves, D. A. Dillman, J. L. Eltinghe, and R. J. A. Little), pp. 41–54. New York: Wiley.

de Leeuw, E. D., J. J. Hox, and D. A. Dillman. 2008. Mixed-mode surveys: When and why. In *International Handbook of Survey Methodology* (eds. E. D. de Leeuw, J. J. Hox, and D. A. Dillman), pp. 299–316. New York: Erlbaum.

Deleire, T., and A. Kalil. 2002. Good things come in threes: Single-parent multigenerational family structure and adolescent adjustment. *Demography* 39:393–413.

DeMaio, T. J. 1984. Social desirability and survey measurement: A review. In *Surveying Subjective Phenomena*, vol. 2 (eds. C. F. Turner and E. Martin), pp. 257–82. New York: Russell Sage Foundation.

DeMaio, T. J., and J. M. Rothgeb. 1996. Cognitive interviewing techniques in the lab and in the field. In *Answering Questions: Methodology for Determining Cognitive and Communicative Processes in Survey Research* (eds. N. Schwarz and S. Sudman), pp. 177–95. San Francisco: Jossey–Bass.

Demo, D. H. 1985. The measurement of self-esteem: Refining our methods. *Journal of Personality and Social Psychology* 48:1490–502.

DeNavas-Walt, C., B. D. Proctor, and C. H. Lee. 2015. *Income and Poverty in the United States: 2014.* Current Population Reports, P60–252. Washington, D.C.: U.S. Government Printing Office.

Denzin, N. K., and Y. S. Lincoln (eds.). 2005. *The Sage Handbook of Qualitative Research*, 3rd ed. Thousand Oaks, CA: Sage.

Der, G., G. D. Batty, and I. J. Deary. 2006. Effect of breast feeding on intelligence in children: Prospective study, sibling pairs analysis, and meta-analysis. *British Medical Journal* 333:945–48.

Deutsch, M., and M. E. Collins. 1951. *Interracial Housing: A Psychological Evaluation of a Social Experiment.* Minneapolis: University of Minnesota.

Deutsch, S. J., and F. B. Alt. 1977. The effects of Massachusetts' gun control law on gun-related crimes in the city of Boston. *Evaluation Quarterly* 1:543–68.

Deutscher, I., and M. Gold. 1979. Traditions and rules as obstructions to useful program evaluation. *Studies in Symbolic Interaction* 2:107–40.

Deutscher, I., F. P. Pestello, and H. F. G. Pestello. 1993. *Sentiments and Acts.* New York: Aldine De Gruyter.

DeWitt, A. L., C. M. Cready, and R. R. Seward. 2013. Parental role portrayals in twentieth century children's picture books: More egalitarian or ongoing stereotyping. *Sex Roles* 69:89–106.

Dibble, V. K. 1963. Four types of inference from documents to events. *History and Theory* 3:201–21.

Diener, E., and R. Crandall. 1978. *Ethics in Social and Behavioral Research.* Chicago: University of Chicago Press.

Dillman, D. A. 2007 *Mail and Internet Surveys: The Tailored Design Method*, 2nd ed. New York: Wiley.

Dillman, D. A., and B. L. Messer. 2010. Mixed-mode surveys. In *Handbook of Survey Research*, 2nd ed. (eds. P. V. Marsden and J. D. Wright), pp. 551–74. Bingley, UK: Emerald Group.

Dillman, D. A., J. D. Smyth, and L. M. Christian. 2009. *Internet, Mail, and Mixed-Mode Surveys: The Tailored Design Method.* Hoboken, NJ: Wiley.

Dixon, J., and C. Tucker. 2010. Survey nonresponse. In *Handbook of Survey Research*, 2nd ed. (eds. P. V. Marsden and J. D. Wright), pp. 593–630. Bingley, UK: Emerald Group.

Dobbin, F., J. R. Sutton, J. W. Meyer, and W. R. Scott. 1993. Equal opportunity law and the construction of internal labor markets. *American Journal of Sociology* 99:396–427.

Doherty, M. E., and K. M. Shemberg. 1978. *Asking Questions about Behavior: An Introduction to What Psychologists Do*, 2nd ed. Glenview, IL: Scott, Foresman.

Dorfman, D. D. 1978. The Cyril Burt question: New findings. *Science* 201:1177–86.

Doty, R. M., B. E. Peterson, and D. G. Winter. 1991. Threat and authoritarianism in the United States, 1978–1987. *Journal of Personality and Social Psychology* 61:629–40.

Douglas, J. D. 1967. *The Social Meanings of Suicide*. Princeton, NJ: Princeton University.

Douglas, J. D. 1976. *Investigative Social Research: Individual and Team Field Research*. Beverly Hills, CA: Sage.

Duncan, G. J. 2001. Panel surveys: Uses and applications. In *International Encyclopedia of the Social and Behavioral Sciences*, vol. 16, pp. 11009–15. Amsterdam: Elsevier.

Duncan, G. J., and K. Magnuson. 2007. Penny wise and effect size foolish. *Child Development Perspectives* 1:46–51.

Duneier, M. 1992. *Slim's Table: Race, Respectability, and Masculinity*. Chicago: University of Chicago.

Durkheim, E. 1951. *Suicide: A Study in Sociology* (trans. J. A. Spaulding and G. Simpson). Glencoe, IL: Free Press.

Durlak, J. A. 2009. How to select, calculate, and interpret effect sizes. *Journal of Pediatric Psychology* 34:917–28.

Durose, M. R., A. D. Cooper, and H. N. Snyder. 2014. *Recidivism of Prisoners Released in 30 States in 2005: Patterns from 2005 to 2010*. U.S. Department of Justice, Office of Justice Programs, Bureau of Justice Statistics. http://www.bjs.gov/content/pub/pdf/rprts05p0510.pdf (accessed May 12, 2016).

Edin, K., and L. Lein. 1997. *Making Ends Meet: How Single Mothers Survive Welfare and Low-Wage Work*. New York: Russell Sage Foundation.

Edson, L. 1970. Jensenism, *n.*—the theory that IQ is largely determined by the genes. In *Prejudice and Race Relations* (ed. R. W. Mack), pp. 35–55. Chicago: Quadrangle.

Edwards, M. 2012. *Writing in Sociology*. Los Angeles: Sage.

Egley, A., Jr., J. C. Howell, and M. Harris. 2014. *OJJDP Fact Sheet: Highlights of the 2012 National Youth Gang Survey*. U.S. Department of Justice, Office of Juvenile Justice and Delinquency Protection. http://www.ojjdp.gov/pubs/248025.pdf (accessed May 3, 2016).

Eichler, M. 1988. *Nonsexist Research Methods: A Practical Guide*. Boston: Allen & Unwin.

Elder, G. H., Jr. 1999. *Children of the Great Depression: Social Change in Life Experience*, 25th anniversary ed. Boulder, CO: Westview.

Ellison, C. G., and K. L. Anderson. 2001. Religious involvement and domestic violence among U.S. couples. *Journal for the Scientific Study of Religion* 40:269–86.

Emerson, R. M. 1981. Observational field work. *Annual Review of Sociology* 7:351–78.

Entwisle, D. R., K. L. Alexander, and L. S. Olson. 1994. The gender gap in math: Its possible origins in neighborhood effects. *American Sociological Review* 59:822–38.

Erel, O., and B. Burman. 1995. Interrelatedness of marital relations and parent–child relations: A meta-analytic review. *Psychological Bulletin* 118:108–32.

Erikson, K. T. 1966. *Wayward Puritans: A Study in the Sociology of Deviance*. New York: Wiley.

Erikson, K. T. 1967. A comment on disguised observation in sociology. *Social Problems* 14:366–73.

Erikson, K. T. 1970. Sociology and the historical perspective. *American Sociologist* 5:331–38.

Esbensen, F. A. 2015. The Gang Resistance Education and Training (G.R.E.A.T.) program: An evaluator's perspective. In *The Handbook of Gangs* (eds. S. H. Decker and D. C. Pyrooz), pp. 369–91. West Sussex, UK: Wiley–Blackwell.

Esbensen, F. A., A. Freng, T. J. Taylor, D. Peterson, and D. W. Osgood. 2002. National evaluation of the Gang Resistance Education and Training (G.R.E.A.T.) Program. In *Responding to Gangs: Evaluation and Research* (eds. W. L. Reed and S. H. Decker), pp. 139-67. Washington, DC: U.S. Department of Justice, National Institute of Justice.

Esbensen, F. A., K. N. Matsuda, T. J. Taylor, and D. Peterson. 2011. Multimethod strategy for assessing program fidelity: The national evaluation of the revised G.R.E.A.T. program. *Evaluation Review* 35:14–39.

Esbensen, F. A., C. Melde, T. J. Taylor, and D. Peterson. 2008. Active parental consent in school-based research: How much is enough and how do we get it? *Evaluation Review* 32:335–62.

Esbensen, F. A., and D. W. Osgood. 1999. Gang resistance education and training (G.R.E.A.T.): Results from the national evaluation. *Journal of Research in Crime and Delinquency* 36:194–225.

Esbensen, F. A., D. W. Osgood, D. Peterson, T. J. Taylor, and D. C. Carson. 2013. Short- and long-term outcome results from a multi-site evaluation of the G.R.E.A.T. program. *Criminology and Public Policy* 12:375–411.

Esbensen, F. A., D. W. Osgood, T. J. Taylor, D. Peterson, and A. Freng. 2001. How great is G.R.E.A.T.? Results from a longitudinal quasi-experimental design. *Criminology and Public Policy* 1:87–117.

Esposito, J. L., and J. M. Rothgeb. 1997. Evaluating survey data: Making the transition from pretesting to quality assessment. In *Survey Measurement and Process Quality* (eds. L. Lyberg, P. Biemer, M. Collins, E. de Leeuw, C. Dippo, N. Schwarz, and D. Trewin), pp. 541–71. New York: Wiley.

Evans, R. I. 1976. *The Making of Psychology: Discussions with Creative Contributors*. New York: Knopf.

Faulkner, J. E., and G. F. DeJong. 1966. Religiosity in 5-D: An empirical analysis. *Social Forces* 45:246–54.

Feagin, J. R. 1964. Prejudice and religious types: A focused study of Southern fundamentalists. *Journal for the Scientific Study of Religion* 4:3–13.

Feagin, J. R., A. N. Orum, and G. Sjoberg (eds.). 1991. *A Case for the Case Study*. Chapel Hill: University of North Carolina Press.

Fell, J. C., M. Scherer, S. Thomas, and R. B. Voas. 2016. Assessing the impact of twenty underage drinking laws. *Journal of Studies on Alcohol and Drugs* 77:249–60.

Felson, M. 1983. Unobtrusive indicators of cultural change: Neckties, girdles, marijuana, garbage, magazines, and urban sprawl. *American Behavioral Scientist* 26:534–42.

Ferraro, K. F., and R. LaGrange. 1987. The measurement of fear of crime. *Sociological Inquiry* 57:70–101.

Fienberg, S. E. 1971. Randomization and social affairs: The 1970 draft lottery. *Science* 171:255–61.

Fine, G. A. 1987. *With the Boys: Little League Baseball and Preadolescent Culture*. Chicago: University of Chicago Press.

Fine, G. A. 1996. *Kitchens: The Culture of Restaurant Work*. Berkeley: University of California Press.

Finkel, S. E., T. M. Guterbock, and M. J. Borg. 1991. Race-of-interviewer effects in a pre-election poll: Virginia 1989. *Public Opinion Quarterly* 55:313–30.

Finsterbusch, K., and A. B. Motz. 1980. *Social Research for Policy Decisions*. Belmont, CA: Wadsworth.

Firebaugh, G. 1978. A rule for inferring individual-level relationships from aggregate data. *American Sociological Review* 43:557–72.

Firebaugh, G. 2008. *Seven Rules for Social Research*. Princeton, NJ: Princeton University Press.

Fish, J. M. 2000. What anthropology can do for psychology: Facing physics envy, ethnocentrism, and a belief in "race." *American Anthropologist* 102:552–63.

Fischer, P., J. I. Krueger, T. Greitemeyer, C. Vogrincic, A. Kastenmüller, D. Frey, M. Heene, M. Wicher, and M. Kainbacher. 2011. The bystander-effect: A meta-analytic review on bystander intervention in dangerous and non-dangerous emergencies. *Psychological Bulletin* 137:517–37.

Fisher, C. B., and D. Fryberg. 1994. Participant partners: College students weigh the costs and benefits of deception research. *American Psychologist* 49:417–27.

Fishman, D. B., and W. D. Neigher. 1982. American psychology in the eighties. Who will buy? *American Psychologist* 37:533–46.

Fleiss, J. L., and J. A. Berlin. 2009. Effect sizes for dichotomous data. In *The Handbook of Research Synthesis and Meta-Analysis*, 2nd ed. (eds. H. Cooper, L. V. Hedges, and J. C. Valentine), pp. 237–53. New York: Russell Sage Foundation.

Fleming, J. S., and B. E. Courtney. 1984. The dimensionality of self-esteem: II. Hierarchical facet model for revised measurement scales. *Journal of Personality and Social Psychology* 46:404–21.

Ford, T. E. 1997. Effects of stereotypical television portrayals of African-Americans on person perception. *Social Psychology Quarterly* 60:266–78.

Forgas, J. P., E. Dunn, and S. Granland. 2008. Are you being served . . . ? An unobtrusive experiment of affective influences on helping in a department store. *European Journal of Social Psychology* 38:333–42.

Foucault, M. 1970. *The Order of Things: An Archaeology of the Human Sciences*. New York: Pantheon.

Fowler, F. J., Jr. 1991. Reducing interviewer-related error through interviewer training, supervision, and other means. In *Measurement Errors in Surveys* (eds. P. P. Biemer, R. M. Groves, L. E. Lyberg, N. A. Mathiowetz, and S. Sudman), pp. 259–78. New York: Wiley.

Fowler, F. J., Jr. 1993. *Survey Research Methods,* 2nd ed. Thousand Oaks, CA: Sage.

Fowler, F. J., Jr. 1995. *Improving Survey Questions.* Thousand Oaks, CA.: Sage.

Fowler, F. J., Jr. 2011. Coding the behavior of interviewers and respondents to evaluate survey questions. In *Question Evaluation Methods: Contributing to the Science of Data Quality* (eds. J. Madans, K. Miller, A. Maitland, and G. Willis), pp. 7–21. Hoboken, NJ: Wiley.

Fowler, F. J., Jr., and C. F. Cannell. 1996. Using behavioral coding to identify cognitive problems with survey questions. In *Answering Questions: Methodology for Determining Cognitive and Communicative Processes in Survey Research* (eds. N. Schwarz and S. Sudman), pp. 15–36. San Francisco: Jossey–Bass.

Fowler, F. J., Jr., and C. Cosenza. 2008. Writing effective questions. In *International Handbook of Survey Methodology* (eds. E. D. de Leeuw, J. J. Hox, and D. A. Dillman), pp. 136–60. New York: Erlbaum.

Fowler, F. J., Jr., and T. W. Mangione. 1990. *Standardized Survey Interviewing: Minimizing Interviewer-Related Error.* Newbury Park, CA: Sage.

Fram, E. H., and E. Cibotti. 1991. The shopping list studies and projective techniques: A 40-year review. *Marketing Research* 3(December):14–22.

Frankfort-Nachmias, C., and A. Leon-Guerrero. 2015. *Social Statistics for a Diverse Society*, 7th ed. Los Angeles: Sage.

Freedman, J. L., S. A. Wallington, and E. Bless. 1967. Compliance without pressure: The effect of guilt. *Journal of Personality and Social Psychology* 7:117–24.

Freeman, H. E., and P. H. Rossi. 1984. Furthering the applied side of sociology. *American Sociological Review* 49:571–80.

Fricker, S., M. Galesic, R. Tourangeau, and T. Yan. 2005. An experimental comparison of Web and telephone surveys. *Public Opinion Quarterly* 69:370–92.

Fricker, S., and R. Tourangeau. 2010. Examining the relationship between nonresponse propensity and data quality in two national household surveys. *Public Opinion Quarterly* 74:934–55.

Fridkin, K. L., P. J. Kenney, and J. Crittenden. 2006. On the margins of democratic life: The impact of race and ethnicity on the political engagement of young people. *American Politics Research* 34:605–26.

Furr, R. M. 2011. *Scale Construction and Psychometrics for Social and Personality Psychology.* Los Angeles: Sage.

Gallupe, R. B., A. R. Dennis, W. H. Cooper, J. S. Valacich, L. A. Bastianutti, and J. F. Nunamaker Jr. 1992. Electronic brainstorming and group size. *Academy of Management Journal* 35:350–69.

Geer, B. 1964. First days in the field. In *Sociologists at Work* (ed. P. E. Hammond), pp. 322–44. New York: Basic Books.

General Accounting Office. 1987. *Drinking-Age Laws: An Evaluation Synthesis of Their Impact on Highway Safety.* Report to the Chairman, Subcommittee on Investigations and Oversight, Committee on Public Works and Transportation, House of Representatives. Washington, D.C.: U.S. General Accounting Office.

Gerber, A. S., and D. P. Green. 2000. The effects of canvassing, telephone calls, and direct mail on voter turnout: A field experiment. *American Political Science Review* 94:653–63.

Gergen, K. J. 1973. Social psychology as history. *Journal of Personality and Social Psychology* 26:309–20.

Giddens, A. 1965. The suicide problem in French sociology. *British Journal of Sociology* 16:1–18.

Gilbert, J. P., B. McPeek, and F. Mosteller. 1977. Statistics and ethics in surgery and anesthesia. *Science* 198:684–89.

Gill, J. 2001. *Generalized Linear Models.* Thousand Oaks, CA: Sage.

Glaser, B. G. 1978. *Theoretical Sensitivity: Advances in the Methodology of Grounded Theory.* Mill Valley, CA: Sociology Press.

Glaser, B. G., and A. L. Strauss. 1967. *The Discovery of Grounded Theory: Strategies for Qualitative Research.* Chicago: Aldine.

Glass, G. V. 1976. Primary, secondary, and meta-analysis of research. *Educational Researcher* 5:3–8.

Glazer, M. 1972. *The Research Adventure: Promise and Problems of Field Work*. New York: Random House.

Gleick, J. 1990. The census: Why we can't count. *New York Times Magazine*, 15 July, 22–26, 54.

Glenn, N. D. 1977. *Cohort Analysis*. Beverly Hills, CA: Sage.

Glenn, N. D. 1978. The General Social Surveys: Editorial introduction to a symposium. *Contemporary Sociology* 7:532–34.

Glick, P. 2008. Restating the case: The benefits of diverse samples for theory development. *Psychological Inquiry* 19:78–83.

Glock, C. Y. 1962. On the study of religious commitment. *Religious Education* 42 (Research Suppl.):98–110.

Goette, L., and A. Stutzer. 2008. Blood donations and incentives: Evidence from a field experiment. *Research Review* 9:21–23.

Goffman, E. 1979. *Gender Advertisements*. Cambridge, MA: Harvard University Press.

Gold, D. 1969. Statistical tests and substantive significance. *American Sociologist* 4:42–46.

Gold, R. L. 1958. Roles in sociological field observations. *Social Forces* 36:217–23.

Golder, S. A., and M. W. Macy. 2014. Digital footprints: Opportunities and challenges for online social research. *Annual Review of Sociology* 4:129–52.

Goldrick-Rab, S. 2006. Following their every move: An investigation of social-class differences in college pathways. *Sociology of Education* 79:61–79.

Gollin, A. E. 1983. The course of applied sociology: Past and future. In *Applied Sociology* (eds. H. E. Freeman et al.), pp. 442–66. San Francisco: Jossey–Bass.

Goodman, L. A. 1961. Snowball sampling. *Annals of Mathematical Statistics* 32:148–70.

Gorden, R. L. 1975. *Interviewing: Strategy, Techniques, and Tactics*, rev. ed. Homewood, IL: Dorsey.

Gordon, R. A., J. F. Short, Jr., D. S. Cartwright, and F. L. Strodtbeck. 1963. Values and gang delinquency: A study of street-corner groups. *American Journal of Sociology* 69:109–28.

Gottlieb, J., and C. S. Carver. 1980. Anticipation of future interaction and the bystander effect. *Journal of Experimental Social Psychology* 16:253–60.

Gottschalk, L. 1969. *Understanding History: A Primer of Historical Method*, 2nd ed. New York: Knopf.

Graesser, A. C., K. Wiemer-Hastings, R. Kreuz, P. Wiemer-Hastings, and K. Marquis. 2000. QUAID: A questionnaire evaluation aid for survey methodologists. *Behavior Research Methods, Instruments, and Computers* 32:254–62.

Graesser, A. C., Z. Cai, M. M. Louwerse, and F. Daniel. 2006. Question Understanding Aid (AID): A web facility that tests question comprehensibility. *Public Opinion Quarterly* 70:3–22.

Gray, D. J. 1968. Value-free sociology: A doctrine of hypocrisy and irresponsibility. *Sociological Quarterly* 9:176–85.

Gray-Little, B., V. S. L. Williams, and T. D. Hancock. 1997. An item response theory analysis of the Rosenberg Self-Esteem Scale. *Personality and Social Psychology Bulletin* 23:443–51.

Green, D. P., and A. S. Gerber. 2008. *Get Out the Vote: How to Increase Voter Turnout*, 2nd ed. Washington, D.C.: Brookings Institution.

Grice, H. P. 1989. *Studies in the Way of Words*. Cambridge, MA: Harvard University Press.

Griswold, W. 1981. American character and the American novel: An expansion of reflection theory in the sociology of literature. *American Journal of Sociology* 86:740–65.

Groves, R. M. 1979. Actors and questions in telephone and personal interview surveys. *Public Opinion Quarterly* 43:190–205.

Groves, R. M. 1989. *Survey Errors and Survey Costs*. New York: Wiley.

Groves, R. M. 2006. Nonresponse rates and nonresponse bias in household surveys. *Public Opinion Quarterly* 70:646–75.

Groves, R. M. 2011. Three eras of survey research. *Public Opinion Quarterly* 75:861–71.

Groves, R. M., R. B. Cialdini, and M. P. Couper. 1992. Understanding the decision to participate in a survey. *Public Opinion Quarterly* 56:475–95.

Groves, R. M., and M. P. Couper. 1996. Contact-level influences on cooperation in face-to-face surveys. *Journal of Official Statistics* 12:63–83.

Groves, R. M., and M. P. Couper. 1998. *Nonresponse in Household Interview Surveys*. New York: Wiley.

Groves, R. M., F. J. Fowler, Jr., M. P. Couper, J. M. Lepkowski, E. Singer, and R. Tourangeau. 2009. *Survey Methodology*. 2nd ed. New York: Wiley.

Groves, R. M., and R. L. Kahn. 1979. *Surveys by Telephone: A National Comparison with Personal Interviews*. New York: Academic Press.

Groves, R. M., and K. A. McGonagle. 2001. A theory-guided interviewer training protocol regarding survey participation. *Journal of Official Statistics* 17:249–65.

Groves, R. M., S. Presser, R. Tourangeau, B. T. West, M. P. Couper, E. Singer, and C. Toppe. 2012. Support for the survey sponsor and nonresponse bias. *Public Opinion Quarterly* 76:512–24.

Gubrium, J. F., and J. A. Holstein. 1997. *The New Language of Qualitative Method*. New York: Oxford University Press.

Gueron, J. M., and H. Rolston. 2013. *Fighting for Reliable Evidence*. New York: Russel Sage Foundation.

Guest, A., and B. Schneider. 2003. Adolescents' extracurricular participation in context: The mediating effects of schools, communities, and identity. *Sociology of Education* 76:89–109.

Guest, G. 2000. Using Guttman scaling to rank wealth: Integrating quantitative and qualitative data. *Field Methods* 12:346–57.

Gurwitsch, A. 1974. *Phenomenology and the Theory of Science* (ed. L. Embree). Evanston, IL: Northwestern University Press.

Guttman, L. 1950. The basis for scalogram analysis. In *Measurement and Prediction* (eds. S. A. Stouffer, L. Guttman, E. A. Suchman, P. F. Lazarsfeld, S. A. Star, and J. A. Clausen), pp. 60–90. Princeton, NJ: Princeton University Press.

Gwartney, P. A. 2007. *The Telephone Interviewer's Handbook*. San Francisco: Jossey-Bass.

Ha, Y., S. C. Narendorf, D. Santa Maria, and N. Bezette-Flores. 2015. Barriers and facilitators to shelter utilization among homeless young adults. *Evaluation and Program Planning* 53:25–33.

Hagen, R. L. 1997. In praise of the null hypothesis test. *American Psychologist* 52:15–24.

Haire, M. 1950. Projective techniques in marketing research. *Journal of Marketing* 14:649–56.

Hall, C. S., and G. Lindzey. 1970. *Theories of Personality*, 2nd ed. New York: Wiley.

Halpern-Manners, A., J. R. Warren, and F. Torche. 2014. Panel conditioning in a longitudinal study of illicit behavior. *Public Opinion Quarterly* 78:565–90.

Hansen, C. 1969. *Witchcraft at Salem*. New York: Braziller.

Hanson, B. 2008. Wither qualitative/quantitative? Grounds for methodological convergence. *Quality and Quantity* 42:97–111.

Harding, D. J., and C. Jencks. 2003. Changing attitudes toward premarital sex. *Public Opinion Quarterly* 67:211–26.

Harlow, L. L., S. A. Mulaik, and J. H. Steiger (eds.). 1997. *What If There Were No Significance Tests?* Mahwah, NJ: Erlbaum.

Haveman, R. H. 1987. Policy analysis and evaluation research after twenty years. *Policy Studies Journal* 16:191–218.

Healy, K. 2000. Embedded altruism: Blood collection regimes and the European Union's donor population. *American Journal of Sociology* 105:1633–57.

Heilman, S. C. 1976. *Synagogue Life: A Study in Symbolic Interaction*. Chicago: University of Chicago Press.

Helmke, A., and F.-W. Schrader. 2001. School achievement: Cognitive and motivational determinants. In *International Encyclopedia of the Social and Behavioral Sciences*, vol. 20, pp. 13552–56. Amsterdam: Elsevier.

Henretta, J. A. 1965. Economic development and social structure in colonial Boston. *William and Mary Quarterly* 22:75–92.

Henrich, J., S. J. Heine, and A. Norenzayan. 2010. The weirdest people in the world? *Behavioral and Brain Sciences* 33:61–83.

Henry, P. J. 2008a. College sophomores in the laboratory redux: Influences of a narrow data base on social psychology's views of the nature of prejudice. *Psychological Inquiry* 19:49–71.

Henry, P. J. 2008b. Student sampling as a theoretical problem. *Psychological Inquiry* 19:114–26.

Hertwig, R., and A. Ortmann. 2008a. Deception in experiments: Revisiting the arguments in its defense. *Ethics and Behavior* 18:59–92.

Hertwig, R., and A. Ortmann. 2008b. Deception in social psychological experiments: Two misconceptions and a research agenda. *Social Psychology Quarterly* 71:222–27.

Hewlett, K. 2002. How to publish your journal paper. *Monitor on Psychology* 33(8):50.

Hirschi, T., and H. C. Selvin. 1967. *Delinquency Research: An Appraisal of Analytic Methods*. New York: Free Press.

Hogan, H., P. J. Cantwell, J. Devine, V. T. Mule, Jr., and V. Velkoff. 2013. Quality and the 2010 census. *Population Research and Policy Review* 32:637–62.

Holbrook, A. L., Y. I. Cho, and T. Johnson. 2006. The impact of question and respondent characteristics on comprehension and mapping difficulties. *Public Opinion Quarterly* 70:565–95.

Holbrook, A. L., M. C. Green, and J. A. Krosnick. 2003. Telephone versus face-to-face interviewing of national probability samples with long questionnaires: Comparisons of respondent satisficing and social desirability response bias. *Public Opinion Quarterly* 67:79–125.

Holbrook, A. L., J. A. Krosnick, D. Moore, and R. Tourangeau. 2007. Response order effects in dichotomous categorical questions presented orally: The impact of question and respondent attributes. *Public Opinion Quarterly* 71:325–48.

Holbrook, A. L., J. A. Krosnick, and A. Pfent. 2008. The causes and consequences of response rates in surveys by news media and government contractor survey research firms. In *Advances in Telephone Survey Methodology* (eds. J. M. Lepkowski et al.), pp. 499–528. New York: Wiley.

Holden, C. 2001. Psychologist made up sex bias results. *Science* 294:2457.

Hollingshead, A. B. 1971. Commentary on "the indiscriminate state of social class measurement." *Social Forces* 49:563–67.

Holloway, M. 1966. Shaker societies. In *Heavens on Earth: Utopian Communities in America, 1680–1880*, 2nd ed. (ed. M. Holloway), pp. 64–79. New York: Dover.

Holsti, O. R. 1969. *Content Analysis for the Social Sciences and Humanities*. Reading, MA: Addison–Wesley.

Horowitz, I. L. (ed.). 1967. *The Rise and Fall of Project Camelot: Studies in the Relationship between Social Science and Practical Politics*. Cambridge, MA: MIT Press.

Horowitz, R. 1986. Remaining an outsider: Membership as a threat to research rapport. *Urban Life* 14:409–30.

Hox, J. J., and E. D. de Leeuw. 1994. A comparison of nonresponse in mail, telephone, and face-to-face surveys. *Quality & Quantity* 28:329–44.

Huck, S. W., and H. M. Sandler. 1979. *Rival Hypotheses: Alternative Interpretations of Data Based Conclusions*. New York: HarperCollins.

Hughes, E. C. 1960. Introduction: The place of field work in social science. In *Field Work: An Introduction to the Social Sciences* (ed. B. H. Junker), pp. iii–xiii. Chicago: University of Chicago Press.

Hume, D. 1748. An inquiry concerning human understanding. In *Theory of Knowledge* (ed. D. C. Yalden-Thomson). Edinburgh: Nelson, 1951.

Hummer, R. A., R. G. Rogers, C. B. Nam, and C. G. Ellison. 1999. Religious involvement and U.S. adult mortality. *Demography* 36:273–85.

Hummon, D. H. 1990. *Commonplaces: Community Ideology and Identity in American Culture*. Albany: State University of New York Press.

Humphreys, K., C. S. Phibbs, and R. H. Moos. 1996. Addressing self-selection effects in evaluations of mutual help groups and professional mental health services: An introduction to two-stage sample selection models. *Evaluation and Program Planning* 19:301–308.

Humphreys, L. 1975. *Tearoom Trade: Impersonal Sex in Public Places*, enl. ed. Chicago: Aldine.

Hurwitz, J., and J. Peffley. 2005. Playing the race card in the post–Willie Horton era: The impact of racialized code words on support for punitive crime policy. *Public Opinion Quarterly* 69:99–112.

Hyman, H. H. 1955. *Survey Design and Analysis*. Glencoe, IL: Free Press.

Hyman, H. H. 1972. *Secondary Analysis of Sample Surveys: Principles, Procedures, and Potentialities*. New York: Wiley.

Hyman, H. H., C. R. Wright, and J. S. Reed. 1975. *The Enduring Effects of Education*. Chicago: University of Chicago Press.

Iannacchione, V. G. 2011. Research synthesis: The changing role of address-based sampling in survey research. *Public Opinion Quarterly* 75:556–75.

Ibarra, H. 1992. Homophily and differential returns: Sex differences in network structure and access in an advertising firm. *Administrative Science Quarterly* 37:422–47.

Institute for Social Research. 2016. Survey Research Center, Surveys of Consumers. Survey Information, Questionnaire. https://data.sca.isr.umich.edu/fetchdoc.php?docid=24776 (accessed June 11, 2016).

Inter-university Consortium for Political and Social Research (ICPSR). 2016. Current Population Survey, September 2015: Volunteer Supplement (ICPSR 36411).

Isen, A. M., and P. F. Levin. 1972. Effect of feeling good on helping: Cookies and kindness. *Journal of Personality and Social Psychology* 21:384–88.

Jacob, H. 1984. *Using Published Data: Errors and Remedies*. Beverly Hills, CA: Sage.

Jacobs, J. 1967. A phenomenological study of suicide notes. *Social Problems* 15:60–72.

Jenkins, J. C., K. M. Slomczynski, and J. K. Dubrow. 2016. Political behavior and big data. *International Journal of Sociology* 46:1–7.

Jensen, A. R. 1969. How much can we boost IQ and scholastic achievement? *Harvard Educational Review* 39:1–123.

Jerolmack, C., and S. Khan. 2014. Talk is cheap: Ethnography and the attitudinal fallacy. *Sociological Methods and Research* 43:178–209.

Jobe, J. B., D. M. Keller, and A. F. Smith. 1996. Cognitive techniques in interviewing older people. In *Answering Questions: Methodology for Determining Cognitive and Communicative Processes in Survey Research* (eds. N. Schwarz and S. Sudman), pp. 197–219. San Francisco: Jossey–Bass.

Johnson, J. M. 1975. *Doing Field Research*. New York: Free Press.

Johnson, R. C. 1978. A procedure for sampling the manuscript census schedules. *Journal of Interdisciplinary History* 8:515–30.

Johnstone, R. L. 1983. *Religion in Society: A Sociology of Religion*, 2nd ed. Englewood Cliffs, NJ: Prentice Hall.

Jones, J. H. 1981. *Bad Blood: The Scandalous Story of the Tuskegee Experiment—When Government Doctors Played God and Science Went Mad*. New York: Free Press.

Joy, L. A., M. M. Kimball, and M. L. Zabrack. 1986. Television and children's aggressive behavior. In *The Impact of Television: A Natural Experiment in Three Communities* (ed. T. M. Williams), pp. 303–60. Orlando: Academic Press.

Junker, B. H. 1960. *Fieldwork: An Introduction to the Social Sciences*. Chicago: University of Chicago Press.

Kahn, R. L., and C. F. Cannell. 1957. *The Dynamics of Interviewing: Theory, Technique, and Cases*. New York: Wiley.

Kalton, G. 1983. *Introduction to Survey Sampling*. Beverly Hills, CA: Sage.

Kalton, G. 2000. Developments in survey research in the past 25 years. *Survey Methodology* 26:3–10.

Kalton, G., and C. F. Citro. 1993. Panel surveys: Adding the fourth dimension. *Survey Methodology* 19:205–15.

Kamin, L. J. 1974. *The Science and Politics of IQ*. Potomac, MD: Erlbaum.

Kane, E. W., and L. J. Macaulay. 1993. Interviewer gender and gender attitudes. *Public Opinion Quarterly* 57:1–28.

Kaplowitz, M. D., T. D. Hadlock, and R. Levine. 2004. A comparison of Web and mail survey response rates. *Public Opinion Quarterly* 68:94–101.

Karpinski, A. C. 2009a. A description of Facebook use and academic performance among undergraduate and graduate students. Paper presented at the Annual Meeting of the American Educational Research Association: San Diego.

Karpinski, A. C. 2009b. A response to reconciling a media sensation with data. *First Monday* 14(5): May 4. http://www.uic.edu/htbin/cgiwrap/bin/ojs/index.php/fm/article/view/2503/2183 (accessed September 23, 2014).

Katz, D. 1949. An analysis of the 1948 polling predictions. *Journal of Applied Psychology* 33:15–28.

Katz, J. 1997. Ethnography's warrants. *Sociological Methods and Research* 25:391–423.

Katz, J. 1972. *Experimentation with Human Beings: The Authority of the Investigator, Subject, Professions, and State in the Human Experimentation Process*. New York: Russell Sage Foundation.

Katzer, J., K. H. Cook, and W. W. Crouch. 1998. *Evaluating Information: A Guide for Users of Social Science Research*, 4th ed. New York: McGraw–Hill.

Kearney, M., and P. Levine. 2014. Media influences on social outcomes: The impact of MTV's *16 and Pregnant* on teen childbearing. NBER Working Paper No. 19795. Cambridge, MA: National Bureau of Economic Research.

Kelly, E., and F. Dobbin. 1999. Civil rights law at work: Sex discrimination and the rise of maternity leave policy. *American Journal of Sociology* 105:455–92.

Kelman, H. C. 1968. *A Time to Speak: On Human Values and Social Research.* San Francisco: Jossey–Bass.

Kemeny, J. G. 1959. *A Philosopher Looks at Science.* Princeton, NJ: Van Nostrand.

Kephart, W. M. 1982. *Extraordinary Groups: The Sociology of Unconventional Lifestyles,* 2nd ed. New York: St. Martin's Press.

Kerlinger, F. N. 1973. *Foundations of Behavioral Research,* 2nd ed. New York: Holt, Rinehart and Winston.

Keyfitz, N. 1976. World resources and the world middle class. *Scientific American* 235:28–35.

Kidder, L. H., and D. T. Campbell. 1970. The indirect testing of social attitudes. In *Attitude Measurement* (ed. G. F. Summers), pp. 333–85. Chicago: Rand McNally.

Kimmel, A. J. 1996. *Ethical Issues in Behavioral Research: A Survey.* Cambridge, MA: Blackwell.

King, G. 1989. *Unifying Political Methodology: A Likelihood Theory of Statistical Inference.* Cambridge: Cambridge University Press.

King, G., R. O. Keohane, and S. Verba. 1994. *Designing Social Inquiry: Scientific Inference in Qualitative Research.* Princeton, NJ: Princeton University Press.

King, J. A., L. L. Morris, and C. T. Fitz-Gibbon. 1987. *How to Assess Program Implementation.* Newbury Park, CA: Sage.

Kirkpatrick, C. 1936. The construction of a belief-pattern scale for measuring attitudes toward feminism. *Journal of Social Psychology* 7:421–37.

Kiser, E., and M. Hechter. 1991. The role of general theory in comparative-historical sociology. *American Journal of Sociology* 97:1–30.

Kish, L. 1959. Some statistical problems in research design. *American Sociological Review* 24:328–38.

Kish, L. 1965. *Survey Sampling.* New York: Wiley.

Kitchin, R. 2014. *The Data Revolution: Big Data, Open Data, Data Infrastructures and Their Consequences.* London: Sage.

Kleinman, S., B. Stenross, and M. McMahon. 1994. Privileging fieldwork over interviews: Consequences for identity and practice. *Symbolic Interaction* 17:37–50.

Kline, R. B. 2016. *Principles and Practice of Structural Equation Modeling,* 4th ed. New York: Guilford.

Kmec, J. A. 2007. Ties that bind? Race and networks in job turnover. *Social Problems* 54:483–503.

Knoke, D. 1990. *Organizing for Collective Action: The Political Economies of Associations.* New York: Aldine De Gruyter.

Kohler Riessman, C. 1990. *Divorce Talk: Women and Men Make Sense of Personal Relationships.* New Brunswick, NJ: Rutgers University Press.

Konstantopoulos, S., and L. V. Hedges. 2009. Analyzing effect sizes: Fixed-effects models. In *The Handbook of Research Synthesis and Meta-Analysis,* 2nd ed. (eds. H. Cooper, L. V. Hedges, and J. C. Valentine), pp. 279–93. New York: Russell Sage Foundation.

Kovar, M. G., and P. Royston. 1990. Comment. *Journal of the American Statistical Association* 85:246–47.

Krohn, M. D., and T. P. Thornberry. 2014. Gang membership and offending patterns. In *The Modern Gang Reader* (eds. C. L. Maxson, A. Egley, Jr., J. Miller, and M. W. Klein), pp. 412–19. New York: Oxford University Press.

Krosnick, J. A. 1991. Response strategies for coping with the cognitive demands of attitude measures in surveys. *Applied Cognitive Psychology* 5:213–36.

Krosnick, J. A. 1999. Survey research. *Annual Review of Psychology* 50:537–67.

Krosnick, J. A., and S. Presser. 2010. Question and questionnaire design. In *Handbook of Survey Research,* 2nd ed. (eds. P. V. Marsden and J. D. Wright), pp. 263–313. Bingley, UK: Emerald Group.

Krueger, R. A., and M. A. Casey. 2000. *Focus Groups: A Practical Guide for Applied Research,* 3rd ed. Thousand Oaks, CA: Sage.

Krysan, M., and M. P. Couper. 2003. Race in the live and the virtual interview: Racial deference, social desirability, and activation effects in attitude surveys. *Social Psychology Quarterly* 66:364–83.

Krysan, M., and Farley, R. 2002. The residential preferences of blacks: Do they explain persistent segregation? *Social Forces* 80:937–80.

Kuhn, T. S. 1962. *The Structure of Scientific Revolutions*. Chicago: University of Chicago Press.

Kvale, S. 1996. *InterViews: An Introduction to Qualitative Research Interviewing*. Thousand Oaks, CA: Sage.

Labov, W. 1973. The linguistic consequences of being a lame. *Language in Society* 2:81–115.

Lane, J. 2010. Linking administrative and survey data. In *Handbook of Survey Research*, 2nd ed. (eds. P. V. Marsden and J. D. Wright), pp. 659–80. Bingley, UK: Emerald Group.

Laney, D. 2001. 3D data management: Controlling data volume, velocity, and variety. Application Delivery Strategies, META Group. https://blogs.gartner.com/doug-laney/files/2012/01/ad949-3D-Data-Management-Controlling-Data-Volume-Velocity-and-Variety.pdf (accessed July 7, 2016).

LaPiere, R. T. 1934. Attitudes vs. actions. *Social Forces* 13:230–37.

Lareau, A. 2000. *Home Advantage: Social Class and Parental Intervention in Elementary Education*, 2nd ed. Lanham, MD: Rowman & Littlefield.

Latané, B., and J. M. Dabbs, Jr. 1975. Sex, group size and helping in three cities. *Sociometry* 38:180–94.

Latané, B., and J. M. Darley. 1970. *The Unresponsive Bystander: Why Doesn't He Help?* Englewood Cliffs, NJ: Prentice Hall.

Latané, B., and S. Nida. 1981. Ten years of research on group size and helping. *Psychological Bulletin* 89:308–24.

Laumann, E. O., J. H. Gagnon, R. T. Michael, and S. Michaels. 1994. *The Social Organization of Sexuality: Sexual Practices in the United States*. Chicago: University of Chicago Press.

Lavin, M. R. 1996. *Understanding the Census: A Guide for Marketers, Planners, Grant Writers, and Other Data Users*. Kenmore, NY: Epoch Books.

Lavrakas, P. J. 1993. *Telephone Survey Methods: Sampling, Selection, and Supervision*, 2nd ed. Newbury Park, CA: Sage.

Lavrakas, P. J. 2010. Telephone surveys. In *Handbook of Survey Research*, 2nd ed. (eds. P. V. Marsden and J. D. Wright), pp. 471–98. Bingley, UK: Emerald Group.

Lavrakas, P. J., C. D. Shuttles, C. Steeh, and H. Fienberg. 2007. The state of surveying cell phone numbers in the United States: 2007 and beyond. *Public Opinion Quarterly* 71:840–54.

Lazarsfeld, P. F. 1955. Interpretation of statistical relations as a research operation. In *Language of Social Research* (eds. P. F. Lazarsfeld and M. Rosenberg), pp. 115–25. Glencoe, IL: Free Press.

Lazarsfeld, P. F. 1972. Some remarks on typological procedures in social research. In *Continuities in the Language of Social Research* (eds. P. F. Lazarsfeld, A. K. Pasanella, and M. Rosenberg), pp. 99–106. New York: Free Press.

Lazarsfeld, P. F., B. Berelson, and H. Gaudet. 1948. *The People's Choice*. New York: Columbia University Press.

Lee, G. R. 1984. The utility of cross-cultural data: Potentials and limitations for family sociology. *Journal of Family Issues* 5:519–41.

Leik, R. K. 1972. *Methods, Logic, and Research of Sociology*. Indianapolis: Bobbs–Merrill.

Lessler, J. T., J. Eyerman, and K. Wang. 2008. Interviewer training. In *International Handbook of Survey Methodology* (eds. E. D. de Leeuw, J. J. Hox, and D. A. Dillman), pp. 442–60. New York: Erlbaum.

Lessler, J. T., and B. H. Forsyth. 1996. A coding system for appraising questionnaires. In *Answering Questions: Methodology for Determining Cognitive and Communicative Processes in Survey Research* (eds. N. Schwarz and S. Sudman), pp. 259–91. San Francisco: Jossey–Bass.

Lever, J. 1978. Sex differences in the complexity of children's play and games. *American Sociological Review* 43:471–83.

Lever, J., and S. Wheeler. 1984. *The Chicago Tribune* sports page, 1900–1975. *Sociology of Sport Journal* 1:299–313.

Lewis, K. 2015. Three fallacies of digital footprints. *Big Data and Society* 2(July–December):1–4.

Lewontin, R. C., S. Rose, and L. J. Kamin. 1984. *Not in Our Genes: Biology, Ideology, and Human Nature*. New York: Pantheon.

Liebert, R. M. 1976. Evaluating the evaluators. *Journal of Communication* 26(2):165–71.

Lincoln, Y. S., and E. G. Guba. 1985. *Naturalistic Inquiry*. Beverly Hills, CA: Sage.

Lindner, A. M. 2009. Among the troops: Seeing the Iraq War through three journalistic vantage points. *Social Problems* 56:21–48.

Lindner, K. 2004. Images of women in general interest and fashion magazine advertisements from 1955 to 2002. *Sex Roles* 51:409–21.

Lindsay, D. M. 2008. Evangelicals in the power elite: Elite cohesion advancing a movement. *American Sociological Review* 73:60–82.

Link, M. W., M. P. Battaglia, M. R. Frankel, L. Osborn, and A. H. Mokdad. 2008. A comparison of address-based sampling (ABS) versus random-digit dialing (RDD) for general population surveys. *Public Opinion Quarterly* 72:6–27.

Lipset, S. M., M. Trow, and J. Coleman. 1956. *Union Democracy.* Garden City, NY: Doubleday.

Lipsey, M. W. 1993. Theory as method: Small theories of treatments. In *Understanding Causes and Generalizing about Them, New Directions for Program Evaluation*, no. 57 (eds. L. B. Sechrest and A. G. Scott), pp. 5–38. San Francisco: Jossey–Bass.

Lipsey, M. W. 1994. Juvenile delinquency treatment: A meta-analytic inquiry into the variable of effects. In *Meta-Analysis for Explanation: A Casebook* (eds. T. D. Cook, H. Cooper, D. S. Cordray, H. Hartmann, L. V. Hedges, R. J. Light, T. A. Louis, and F. Mosteller), pp. 83–127. New York: Russell Sage Foundation.

Lofland, J., and L. H. Lofland. 1995. *Analyzing Social Settings: A Guide to Qualitative Observation and Analysis*, 3rd ed. Belmont, CA: Wadsworth.

Lofland, J., D. Snow, L. Anderson, and L. H. Lofland. 2006. *Analyzing Social Settings: A Guide to Qualitative Observation and Analysis*, 4th ed. Belmont, CA: Wadsworth/Thomson.

Lofland, L. H. 1971. A world of strangers: Order and action in urban public space. PhD diss., University of California, San Francisco.

Lofland, L. H. 1973. *A World of Strangers: Order and Action in Urban Public Space.* New York: Basic Books.

Logan, J. R., and B. J. Stults. 2011. The persistence of segregation in the metropolis: New findings from the 2010 Census. Census Brief prepared for Project US2010. http://www.s4.brown.edu/us2010 (accessed July 10, 2016).

Lois, J. 2003. *Heroic Efforts: The Emotional Culture of Search and Rescue Volunteers.* New York: New York University Press.

Loomis, W. F. 1970. Rickets. *Scientific American* 223:76–82.

Lozar Manfreda, K., M. Bosnjak, J. Berzelak, I. Haas, and V. Vehovar. 2008. Web surveys versus other survey modes: A meta-analysis comparing response rates. *International Journal of Market Research* 50:79–104.

Lozar Manfreda, K. L., and V. Vehovar. 2008. Internet surveys. In *International Handbook of Survey Methodology* (eds. E. D. de Leeuw, J. J. Hox, and D. A. Dillman), pp. 264–84. New York: Erlbaum.

Lucas, J. W. 2003. Theory-testing, generalization, and the problem of external validity. *Sociological Theory* 21:236–53.

Lucy, J. A., and R. A. Shweder. 1979. Whorf and his critics: Linguistic and nonlinguistic influences on color memory. *American Anthropologist* 81:581–615.

Lundberg, G. A. 1961. *Can Science Save Us?* New York: Longmans, Green.

Lynch, M., and D. Bogen. 1997. Sociology's asociological "core": An examination of textbook sociology in light of the sociology of scientific knowledge. *American Sociological Review* 62:481–93.

Malamuth, N. M., and B. Spinner. 1980. A longitudinal content analysis of sexual violence in the best-selling erotic magazines. *Journal of Sex Research* 16:226–37.

Mangione, T. W. 1995. *Mail Surveys: Improving the Quality.* Thousand Oaks, CA: Sage.

Manning, P. K. 1987. *Semiotics and Fieldwork.* Newbury Park, CA: Sage.

Manning, R., M. Levine, and A. Collins. 2007. The Kitty Genovese murder and the social psychology of helping: The parable of the 38 witnesses. *American Psychologist* 62:555–62.

Manovich, L. 2011. Trending: The promises and the challenges of big social data. Manovich. http://manovich.net/index.php/projects/trending-the-promises-and-the-challenges-of-big-social-data (accessed July 7, 2006).

Mark, M. M., and R. L. Shotland. 1985. Toward more useful social science. In *Social Science and Social Policy* (eds. R. L. Shotland and M. M. Mark), pp. 335–70. Beverly Hills, CA: Sage.

Markowitz, F. E. 2006. Psychiatric hospital capacity, homelessness, and crime and arrest rates. *Criminology* 44:45–72.

Marr, B. 2015. Big data: 20 mind-boggling facts everyone must read. *Forbes* (September 30). http://www.forbes.com/sites/bernardmarr/2015/09/30/big-data-20-mind-boggling-facts-everyone-must-read/#7ad43fc86c1d (accessed July 7, 2016).

Marshall, E. 2000. How prevalent is fraud? That's a million-dollar question. *Science* 290:1662.

Martin, E. 2004. Vignettes and respondent debriefing for questionnaire design and evaluation. In *Methods for Testing and Evaluating Survey Questionnaires* (eds. S. Presser et al.), pp. 149–71. Hoboken, NJ: Wiley.

Martin, E. A., M. W. Traugott, and C. Kennedy. 2005. A review and proposal for a new measure of poll accuracy. *Public Opinion Quarterly* 69:342–69.

Marx, G. T. 1988. *Undercover: Police Surveillance in America*. Berkeley: University of California Press.

Massey, D. S., R. Alarcon, J. Durand, and H. Gonzalez. 1987. *Return to Aztlan: The Social Process of International Migration from Western Mexico*. Berkeley: University of California Press.

Matthews, C., K. Everett, J. Binedell, and M. Steinberg. 1995. Learning to listen: Formative research in the development of AIDS education for secondary school students. *Social Science and Medicine* 41:1715–24.

Matysiak, A., and D. Vignoli. 2008. Fertility and women's employment: A meta-analysis. *European Journal of Population* 24:363–84.

Maynard, D. W., and N. C. Schaeffer. 2002. Standardization and its discontents. In *Standardization and Tacit Knowledge: Interaction and Practice in the Survey Interview* (eds. D. W. Maynard, H. Houtkoop-Steenstra, N. C. Schaeffer, and J. van der Zouwen), pp. 3–45. New York: Wiley.

McArthur, L. Z., and B. G. Resko. 1975. The portrayal of men and women in American television commercials. *Journal of Social Psychology* 97:209–20.

McCain, G., and E. M. Segal. 1977. *The Game of Science*, 3rd ed. Belmont, CA: Brooks/Cole.

McCall, G. J. 1984. Systematic field observation. *Annual Review of Sociology* 10:263–82.

McCann, I. L., and D. S. Holmes. 1984. Influence of aerobic exercise on depression. *Journal of Personality and Social Psychology* 46:1142–47.

McConahay. J. B. 1986. Modern racism, ambivalence, and the modern racism scale. In *Prejudice, Discrimination, and Racism* (eds. J. F. Dovidio and S. L. Gaertner), pp. 91–125. Orlando: Academic Press.

McCullagh, J. A., and J. A. Nelder. 1989. *Generalized Linear Models*. London: Chapman & Hall.

McFarland, D. A., K. Lewis, and A. Goldberg. 2016. Sociology in the era of big data: The ascent of forensic social science. *American Sociologist* 47:12–35.

McFarland, S. G. 1981. Effects of question order on survey responses. *Public Opinion Quarterly* 45:208–15.

McGuigan, F. J. 1993. *Experimental Psychology: Methods of Research*, 6th ed. Englewood Cliffs, NJ: Prentice Hall.

McKinney, J. C. 1966. *Constructive Typology and Social Theory*. New York: Appleton–Century–Crofts.

Melbin, M. 1969. Behavior rhythms in mental hospitals. *American Journal of Sociology* 74:650–65.

Mendelberg, T. 2001. *The Race Card: Campaign Strategy, Implicit Messages, and the Norm of Equality*. Princeton, NJ: Princeton University Press.

Mertens, D. M., and A. T. Wilson. 2012. *Program Evaluation Theory and Practice: A Comprehensive Guide*. New York: Guilford.

Merton, R. K. 1957. *Social Theory and Social Structure*, rev. and enl. ed. Glencoe, IL: Free Press.

Miles, M. B., and A. M. Huberman. 1994. *Qualitative Data Analysis*, 2nd ed. Thousand Oaks, CA: Sage.

Milgram, S. 1974. *Obedience to Authority: An Experimental View*. New York: Harper & Row.

Millar, M. M., and D. A. Dillman. 2011. Improving response to Web and mixed-mode surveys. *Public Opinion Quarterly* 75:249–69.

Miller, W. B. 2001. *The Growth of Youth Gang Problems in the United States: 1970–98*. Washington, D.C.: U.S. Department of Justice, Office of Justice Programs, Office of Juvenile Justice and Delinquency Prevention.

Mills, J. 1976. A procedure for explaining experiments involving deception. *Personality and Social Psychology Bulletin* 2:3–13.

Minnesota Population Center. 2016. IPUMS USA, University of Minnesota. http://usa.ipums.org/usa/.

Mook, D. G. 1983. In defense of external validity. *American Psychologist* 38:379–87.

Morgan, D. L. 2007. Paradigms lost and pragmatism regained: Methodological implications of qualitative and quantitative methods. *Journal of Mixed Methods Research* 1:48–76.

Moriarty, T. 1975. Crime, commitment, and the responsive bystander: Two field experiments. *Journal of Personality and Social Psychology* 31:370–76.

Morrill, C. 1995. *The Executive Way: Conflict Management in Corporations.* Chicago: University of Chicago.

Morris, J. B., Jr. 2016. First look: Internet use in 2015. National Telecommunications and Information Administration, United States Department of Commerce. https://www.ntia.doc.gov/blog/2016/first-look-internet-use-2015 (accessed May 13, 2016).

Morrison, D. E., and R. E. Henkel (eds.). (1970). *The Significance Test Controversy.* Chicago: Aldine.

Mosteller, F. 1981. Innovation and evaluation. *Science* 211:881–86.

Mosteller, F., and D. L. Wallace. 1964. *Inference and Disputed Authorship: The Federalist.* Reading, MA: Addison–Wesley.

Murdock, G. P. 1967. Ethnographic atlas: A summary. *Ethnology* 6:109–236.

Murdock, G. P., and D. R. White. 1969. Standard cross-cultural sample. *Ethnology* 8:329–69.

Murray, B. 2002. Research fraud needn't happen at all. *Monitor on Psychology* 33(February):27–28.

Murray, D., J. Schwartz, and S. R. Lichter. 2001. *It Ain't Necessarily So: How Media Make and Unmake the Scientific Picture of Reality.* Lanham, MD: Rowman & Littlefield.

Murthy, D. 2015. Twitter and elections: Are tweets predictive, reactive, or a form of buzz? *Information, Communication and Society* 18:816–31.

Mutz, D. C. 2011. *Population-Based Survey Experiments.* Princeton, NJ: Princeton University Press.

Nagel, E. 1967. The nature and aim of science. In *Philosophy of Science Today* (ed. S. Morgenbesser), pp. 3–13. New York: Basic Books.

Nathan, G. 2001. Telesurvey methodologies for household surveys—A review and some thoughts for the future. *Survey Methodology* 27:7–31.

National Commission for the Protection of Human Subjects of Research (National Commission). 1979. Belmont Report: Ethical Principles and Guidelines for the Protection of Human Subjects of Research. Washington D.C. https://www.hhs.gov/ohrp/regulations-and-policy/belmont-report/.

National Opinion Research Center. 2016. General Social Survey, FAQs for survey participants. What were the response rates? http://gss.norc.org/Documents/other/GSS%20Response%20Period%20and%20Field%20Period.pdf (accessed June 11, 2016).

Navazio, R. 1977. An experimental approach to bandwagon research. *Public Opinion Quarterly* 41:217–25.

Neale, J. M., and R. M. Liebert. 1986. *Science and Behavior: An Introduction to Methods of Research,* 3rd ed. Englewood Cliffs, NJ: Prentice Hall.

Nettler, G. 1970. *Explanations.* New York: McGraw–Hill.

Newman, K. S. 1999. *No Shame in My Game.* New York: Alfred A. Knopf and Russell Sage Foundation.

Nickerson, R. S. 2000. Null hypothesis significance testing: A review of an old and continuing controversy. *Psychological Methods* 5:241–301.

Nunnally, J. C., Jr. 1970. *Introduction to Psychological Measurement.* New York: McGraw–Hill.

Oberschall, A. 1972. The institutionalization of American sociology. In *The Establishment of Empirical Sociology: Studies in Continuity, Discontinuity, and Institutionalization* (ed. A. Oberschall), pp. 187–251. New York: Harper & Row.

Olsen, R. B., L. L. Orr, S. H. Bell, and E. A. Stuart. 2013. External validity in policy evaluations that choose sites purposively. *Journal of Policy Analysis and Management* 32:107–21.

Orne, M. T. 1962. On the social psychology of the psychological experiment: With particular reference to demand characteristics and their implications. *American Psychologist* 17:776–83.

Orne, M. T. 1969. Demand characteristics and the concept of quasi-controls. In *Artifact in Behavioral Research* (eds. R. Rosenthal and R. L. Rosnow), pp. 147–79. New York: Academic Press.

Orne, M. T., and F. J. Evans. 1965. Social control in the psychological experiment: Antisocial behavior and hypnosis. *Journal of Personality and Social Psychology* 1:189–200.

Orr, L. L. 2015. 2014 Rossi Award Lecture: Beyond internal validity. *Evaluation Review* 39:167–78.

Orshansky, M., and J. S. Bretz. 1976. Born to be poor: Birthplace and number of brothers and sisters as factors in adult poverty. *Social Security Bulletin* 39(1):21–37.

Osgood, C. E., C. J. Suci, and P. H. Tannenbaum. 1957. *The Measurement of Meaning*. Urbana: University of Illinois Press.

Ostrander, S. 1993. "Surely you're not in this just to be helpful": Access, rapport, and interviews in three studies of elites. *Journal of Contemporary Ethnography* 22:7–27.

Ouellet, L. J. 1994. *Pedal to the Metal: The Work Lives of Truckers*. Philadelphia: Temple University Press.

Padgett, V. R., and D. O. Jorgenson. 1982. Superstition and economic threat: Germany, 1918–1940. *Personality and Social Psychology Bulletin* 8:736–41.

Page, E. B. 1958. Teacher comments and student performance: A seventy-four classroom experiment in school motivation. *Journal of Educational Psychology* 49:173–81.

Pager, D., and L. Quillian. 2005. Walking the talk? What employers say versus what they do. *American Sociological Review* 70:255–80.

Palys, T. S., and J. Lowman. 2002. Anticipating law: Research methods, ethics and the law of privilege. *Sociological Methodology* 32:1–17.

Pancer, S. M., and A. Westhues. 1989. A developmental stage approach to program planning and evaluation. *Evaluation Review* 13:56–77.

Parade Magazine. 1993. The high cost of law and order. *Parade Magazine*, June13, 12.

Park, P., and M. Macy. 2015. The paradox of active users. *Big Data and Society* 2(July–December).

Pasek, J., e. more, and E. Hargittai. 2009. Facebook and academic performance: Reconciling a media sensation with data. *First Monday* 14(5): May 4. http://www.uic.edu/htbin/cgiwrap/bin/ojs/index.php/fm/article/view/2498/2181 (accessed September 23, 2014).

Pate, A. M., and E. E. Hamilton. 1992. Formal and informal deterrents to domestic violence: The Dade County Spouse Assault Experiment. *American Sociological Review* 57:691–97.

Paternoster, R., R. Bachman, R. Brame, and L. W. Sherman. 1997. Do fair procedures matter? The effect of procedural justice on spouse assault. *Law and Society Review* 31:163–204.

Paules, G. F. 1991. *Dishing It Out: Power and Resistance among Waitresses in a New Jersey Restaurant*. Philadelphia: Temple University Press.

Payne, S. L. 1951. *The Art of Asking Questions*. Princeton, NJ: Princeton University Press.

Pearson, W., Jr., and L. Hendrix. 1979. Divorce and the status of women. *Journal of Marriage and the Family* 41:375–85.

Penner, L., M. T. Brannick, S. Webb, and P. Connell. 2005. Effects of volunteering of the September 11, 2001, attacks: An archival analysis. *Journal of Applied Social Psychology* 35:1333–60.

Perrin, A. J. 2005. National threat and political culture: Authoritarianism, antiauthoritarianism, and the September 11 attacks. *Political Psychology* 26:167–94.

Pescosolido, B. A. 1990. The social context of religious integration and suicide: Pursuing the network explanation. *Sociological Quarterly* 31:337–57.

Pescosolido, B. A., and S. Georgianna. 1989. Durkheim, suicide, and religion: Toward a network theory of suicide. *American Sociological Review* 54:33–48.

Peterson, B. E., and E. D. Gerstein. 2005. Fighting and flying: Archival analysis of threat, authoritarianism, and the North American comic book. *Political Psychology* 26:887–904.

Peterson, R. A. 2001. On the use of college students in social science research: Insights from a second-order meta-analysis. *Journal of Consumer Research* 28:450–61.

Pettigrew, T. F. 1998. Intergroup contact theory. *Annual Review of Psychology* 49:65–85.

Pettigrew, T. F., and L. R. Tropp. 2006. A meta-analytic test of intergroup conflict theory. *Journal of Personality and Social Psychology* 90:751–83.

Peytchev, A. 2013. Consequences of survey nonresponse. *The Annals of the American Academy of Political and Social Science* 645:88–111.

Peytchev, A., R. K. Baxter, and L. S. Carley-Baxter. 2009. Not all survey effort is equal: Reduction of nonresponse bias and nonresponse error. *Public Opinion Quarterly* 73:785–806.

Phillips, D. L. 1971. *Knowledge from What?* Chicago: Rand McNally.

Phillips, D. P., T. E. Ruth, and S. MacNamara. 1994. There are more things in heaven and earth: Missing features in Durkheim's theory of suicide. In *Emile Durkheim: Le Suicide One Hundred Years Later* (ed. D. Lester), pp. 90–100. Philadelphia: Charles Press.

Pierce, A. 1967. The economic cycle and the social suicide rate. *American Sociological Review* 32:457–62.

Piliavin, J. A., and I. M. Piliavin. 1972. Effect of blood on reactions to a victim. *Journal of Personality and Social Psychology* 23:353–61.

Polkinghorne, D. 1983. *Methodology for the Social Sciences: Systems of Inquiry*. Albany: State University of New York Press.

Pope, W. 1976. *Durkheim's Suicide: A Classic Analyzed*. Chicago: University of Chicago.

Porter, J. R., and E. H. Ecklund. 2012. Missing data in sociological research: An overview of recent trends and an illustration for controversial questions, active nonrespondents and target samples. *American Sociologist* 43:448–68.

Portes, A. 1998. Social capital: Its origins and applications in modern sociology. *Annual Review of Sociology* 24:1–24.

Poston, D. L., Jr., and T. Falbo. 1990. Academic performance and personality traits of Chinese children: "Onlies" versus others. *American Journal of Sociology* 96:433–51.

Presser, S., and J. Blair. 1994. Survey pretesting: Do different methods produce different results? In *Sociological Methodology 1994* (ed. P. Marsden), pp. 73–104. San Francisco: Jossey–Bass.

Presser, S., M. P. Couper, J. T. Lessler, E. Martin, J. Martin, J. M. Rothgeb, and E. Singer. 2004. Methods for testing and evaluating survey questions. *Public Opinion Quarterly* 68:109–30.

Rabinow, P., and W. M. Sullivan, eds. 1987. *Interpretive Social Science: A Second Look*. Berkeley: University of California Press.

Raftery, A. E. 2001. Statistics in sociology, 1950–2000: A selective review. *Sociological Methodology* 31:1–45.

Ragin, C. C., and L. M. Amoroso. 2011. *Constructing Social Research: The Unity and Diversity of Method*, 2nd ed. Los Angeles: Sage/Pine Forge.

Raley, R. K. 2002. The effects of the differential undercount on survey estimates of race differences in marriage. *Journal of Marriage and Family* 64:774–79.

Raudenbush, S. W. 1984. Magnitude of teacher expectancy effects on pupil IQ as a function of the credibility of expectancy induction: A synthesis of findings from 18 experiments. *Journal of Educational Psychology* 76:85–97.

Raudenbush, S. W. 2009. Analyzing effect sizes: Random-effects models. In *The Handbook of Research Synthesis and Meta-Analysis*, 2nd ed. (eds. H. Cooper, L. V. Hedges, and J. C. Valentine), pp. 295–315. New York: Russell Sage Foundation.

Reese, H. W., and W. J. Fremouw. 1984. Normal and normative ethics in behavioral science. *American Psychologist* 39:863–76.

Reeves, B. F. 1970. *The First Year of* Sesame Street: *The Formative Research*. New York: Children's Television Workshop.

Reiss, A. J., Jr. 1967. *Studies in Crime and Law Enforcement in Major Metropolitan Areas*. Field Studies III, vol. II, sec. I. Washington, D.C.: U.S. Government Printing Office.

Reiss, A. J., Jr. 1968. Stuff and nonsense about social surveys and observation. In *Institutions and the Person* (eds. H. S. Becker, B. Geer, D. Riesman, and R. S. Weiss), pp. 351–67. Chicago: Aldine.

Resnik, D. B. 1998. *The Ethics of Science: An Introduction*. London: Routledge.

Reynolds, P. D. 1971. *A Primer in Theory Construction*. Indianapolis: Bobbs–Merrill.

Richardson, M., C. Abraham, and R. Bond. 2012. Psychological correlates of university students' academic performance: A systematic review and meta-analysis. *Psychological Bulletin* 138:353–87.

Riesman, D., with N. Glazer and R. Denney. 1950. *The Lonely Crowd*. New Haven, CT: Yale University Press.

Riley, M. W. 1963. *Sociological Research I. A Case Approach*. New York: Harcourt, Brace & World.

Robinson, W. S. 1950. Ecological correlations and the behavior of individuals. *American Sociological Review* 15:351–57.

Roethlisberger, F. J., and W. J. Dickson. 1939. *Management and the Worker: An Account of a Research Program Conducted by the Western Electric Co. Hawthorne Works, Chicago*. Cambridge, MA: Harvard University Press.

Rosen, L. J., and L. Behrens. 1992. *The Allyn & Bacon Handbook*. Boston: Allyn & Bacon.

Rosenau, P. V. 1992. *Post-Modernism and the Social Sciences: Insights, Inroads, and Intrusions*. Princeton, NJ: Princeton University.

Rosenbaum, D. P. 2007. Just say no to D.A.R.E. *Criminology and Public Policy* 6:815–24.

Rosenberg, M. 1965. *Society and the Adolescent Self-Image.* Princeton, NJ: Princeton University Press.

Rosenberg, M. 1968. *The Logic of Survey Analysis.* New York: Basic Books.

Rosenberg, M. 1979. *Conceiving the Self.* New York: Basic Books.

Rosenberg, M. J. 1965. When dissonance fails: On eliminating evaluation apprehension from attitude measurement. *Journal of Personality and Social Psychology* 1:28–42.

Rosenberg, M. J. 1969. The conditions and consequences of evaluation apprehension. In *Artifact in Behavioral Research* (eds. R. Rosenthal and R. L. Rosow), pp. 279–349. New York: Academic Press.

Rosenthal, R. 1966. *Experimenter Effects in Behavioral Research.* New York: Appleton–Century–Crofts.

Rosenthal, R. 1967. Covert communication in the psychological experiment. *Psychological Bulletin* 67:356–67.

Rosenthal, R. 1969. Interpersonal expectations: Effects of the experimenter's hypothesis. In *Artifact in Behavioral Research* (eds. R. Rosenthal and R. L. Rosnow), pp. 187–227. New York: Academic Press.

Rosenthal, R. 1991. *Meta-Analytic Procedures for Social Research.* Newbury Park, CA: Sage.

Rosenthal, R. 1994. Science and ethics in conducting, analyzing, and reporting psychological research. *Psychological Science* 5:127–34.

Rosenthal, R., and K. L. Fode. 1963. Psychology of the scientist: V. Three experiments in experimenter bias. *Psychological Reports* 12:491–511.

Rosenthal, R., and L. Jacobson. 1968. *Pygmalion in the Classroom: Teacher Expectation and Pupils' Intellectual Development.* New York: Holt, Rinehart and Winston.

Ross, H. L. 1992. *Confronting Drunk Driving: Social Policy for Saving Lives.* New Haven, CT: Yale University Press.

Ross, H. L. 1994. *Drunk driving.* New York: McGraw–Hill.

Rossi, P. H. 1989. *Down and Out in America: The Origins of Homelessness.* Chicago: University of Chicago Press.

Rossi, P. H., R. A. Berk, and K. J. Lenihan. 1980. *Money, Work, and Crime: Experimental Evidence.* New York: Academic Press.

Rossi, P. H., H. W. Freeman, and M. W. Lipsey. 1999. *Evaluation: A Systematic Approach,* 6th ed. Thousand Oaks, CA: Sage.

Rossi, P. H., M. W. Lipsey, and H. E. Freeman. 2004. *Evaluation: A Systematic Approach,* 7th ed. Thousand Oaks, CA: Sage.

Rossi, P. H., and W. F. Whyte. 1983. The applied side of sociology. In *Applied Sociology* (eds. H. E. Freeman et al.), pp. 5–31. San Francisco: Jossey–Bass.

Rossi, P. H., J. D. Wright, G. A. Fisher, and G. Willis. 1987. The urban homeless: Estimating size and composition. *Science* 235:1336–41.

Roth, J. 1963. *Timetables: Structuring the Passage of Time in Hospital Treatment and Other Careers.* Indianapolis: Bobbs–Merrill.

Rothbart, G. S., M. Fine, and S. Sudman. 1982. On finding and interviewing the needles in the haystack: The use of multiplicity sampling. *Public Opinion Quarterly* 46:408–21.

Rothgeb, J., G. Willis, and B. Forsyth. 2001. Questionnaire pretesting methods: Do different techniques and different organizations produce similar results? *Proceedings of the Annual Meeting of the American Statistical Association.* Alexandria, VA: American Statistical Association.

Rowan, A. N. 1995. Scientists and animal research: Dr. Jekyll or Mr. Hyde? *Social Research* 62:787–800.

Rowe, M. 2007. Tripping over molehills: Ethics and the ethnography of police work. *International Journal of Social Research Methodology* 10:37–48.

Ruan, D., L. C. Freeman, X. Dai, Y. Pan, and W. Zhang. 1997. On the changing structure of social networks in urban China. *Social Networks* 19:75–89.

Rubin, H. J., and I. S Rubin. 2012. *Qualitative Interviewing: The Art of Hearing Data,* 3rd edition. Los Angeles: Sage.

Rubin, Z. 1970. Measurement of romantic love. *Journal of Personality and Social Psychology* 16:265–73.

Rubin, Z. 1976. On studying love: Notes on the researcher–subject relationship. In *The Research Experience* (ed. M. P. Golden), pp. 508–13. Itasca, IL: F. E. Peacock.

Ruebhausen, O. M., and O. G. Brim, Jr. 1966. Privacy and behavioral research. *American Psychologist* 21:423–37.

Rugg, D. 1941. Experiments in wording questions: II. *Public Opinion Quarterly* 5:91–92.

Ruggles, S. 2014. Big microdata for population research. *Demography* 51:287–97.

Runkle, G. 1978. *Good Thinking: An Introduction to Logic*. New York: Holt, Rinehart and Winston.

Saffer, H., and M. Grossman. 1989. Drinking age laws and highway mortality rates: Cause and effect. *Economic Inquiry* 25:403–17.

Sales, S. M. 1973. Threat as a factor in authoritarianism: An analysis of archival data. *Journal of Personality and Social Psychology* 28:44–57.

Sales, S. M., and K. E. Friend. 1973. Success and failure as determinants of level of authoritarianism. *Behavioral Science* 18:163–72.

Salmon, W. C. 1973. *Logic*, 2nd ed. Englewood Cliffs, NJ: Prentice Hall.

Savage, B. K. 2016. Race-of-interviewer effects and survey questions about police violence. *Sociological Spectrum* 36:142–57.

Savin-Williams, R. C. and G. A. Jaquish. 1981. The assessment of adolescent self-esteem: A comparison of methods. *Journal of Personality* 49:324–36.

Scarce, R. 1999. Good faith, bad ethics: When scholars go the distance and scholarly associations do not. *Law and Social Inquiry* 24:977–86.

Scarce, R. 2005. A law to protect scholars. *Chronicle of Higher Education* 51(August 12):B24–B25.

Schaeffer, N. C. 1991. Conversation with a purpose—or conversation? Interaction in the standardized interview. In *Measurement Errors in Surveys* (eds. P. P. Biemer, R. M. Groves, L. E. Lyberg, N. A. Mathiowetz, and S. Sudman), pp. 367–91. New York: Wiley.

Schaeffer, N. C., and S. Presser. 2003. The science of asking questions. *Annual Review of Sociology* 29:65–88.

Schmader, T., J. Whitehead, and V. H. Wysocki. 2007. A linguistic comparison of letters of recommendation for male and female chemistry and biochemistry job applicants. *Sex Roles* 57:509–14.

Schoenthaler, S. J. 1983. The Los Angeles Probation Department diet-behavior program: An empirical analysis of six institutional settings. *International Journal of Biosocial Research* 5:88-98.

Schuman, H., and G. Kalton. 1985. Survey methods. In *Handbook of Social Psychology*, 3rd ed., vol. I (eds. G. Lindzey and E. Aronson), pp. 635–97. New York: Random House.

Schuman, H., J. Ludwig, and J. A. Krosnick. 1986. The perceived threat of nuclear war, salience, and open questions. *Public Opinion Quarterly* 50:519–36.

Schuman, H., and S. Presser. 1981. *Questions and Answers in Attitude Surveys: Experiments on Question Form, Wording, and Context*. New York: Academic Press.

Schuman, H., and J. Scott. 1987. Problems in the use of survey questions to measure public opinion. *Science* 236:957–59.

Schwartz, C. R., and R. D. Mare. 2005. Trends in educational assortative marriage from 1940 to 2003. *Demography* 42:621–46.

Schwartz, H., and J. Jacobs. 1979. *Qualitative Methodology: A Method to the Madness*. New York: Free Press.

Schwartz, S. H., and A. Gottlieb. 1981. Participants' postexperimental reactions and the ethics of bystander research. *Journal of Experimental Social Psychology* 17:396–407.

Schwarz, N. 1996. *Cognition and Communication: Judgmental Biases, Research Methods, and the Logic of Conversation*. Mahwah, NJ: Erlbaum.

Schwarz, N., R. M. Groves, and H. Schuman. 1998. Survey methods. In *The Handbook of Social Psychology*, 4th ed., vol. I (eds. D. T. Gilbert, S. T. Fiske, and G. Lindzey) pp. 143–79. Boston: McGraw–Hill.

Schwarz, N., B. Knauper, H. J. Hippler, E. Noelle-Neumann, and L. Clark. 1991. Rating scales: Numeric values may change the meaning of scale labels. *Public Opinion Quarterly* 55:570–82.

Schwarz, N., B. Knauper, D. Oyserman, and C. Stich. 2008. The psychology of asking questions. In *International Handbook of Survey Methodology* (eds. E. D. de Leeuw, J. J. Hox, and D. A. Dillman), pp. 18–34. New York: Erlbaum.

Schwarz, N., F. Strack, and H. P. Mai. 1991. Assimilation and contrast effects in part–whole question sequences: A conversational logic analysis. *Public Opinion Quarterly* 55:3–23.

Sears, D. O. 1986. College sophomores in the laboratory: Influences of a narrow data base on social psychology's view of human nature. *Journal of Personality and Social Psychology* 51:515–30.

Sears, D. O. 1994. On separating church and lab. *Psychological Science* 5:237–39.

Sechrest, L., and A. J. Figueredo. 1993. Program evaluation. *Annual Review of Psychology* 44:645–74.

Seidman, S., and D. G. Wagner (eds.). 1992. *Postmodernism and Social Theory: The Debate over General Theory.* Cambridge, MA: Blackwell.

Sell, J. 2008. Introduction to deception debate. *Social Psychology Quarterly* 71:213–14.

Selltiz, C., L. S. Wrightsman, and S. W. Cook. 1976. *Research Methods in Social Relations,* 3rd ed. New York: Holt, Rinehart and Winston.

Selvin, H. C. 1965. Durkheim's *Suicide*: Further thoughts on a methodological classic. In *Emile Durkheim* (ed. R. A. Nisbet), pp. 113–36. Englewood Cliffs, NJ: Prentice Hall.

Shadish, W. R., T. D. Cook, and D. T. Campbell. 2002. *Experimental and Quasi-Experimental Design for Generalized Causal Inference* 2nd ed. Belmont, CA: Wadsworth Cengage Learning.

Shafer, R. J., ed. 1980. *A Guide to Historical Method,* 3rd ed. Belmont, CA: Wadsworth.

Shaffir, W. B., R. A. Stebbins, and A. Turowetz (eds.). 1980. *Fieldwork Experience: Qualitative Approaches to Social Research.* New York: St. Martin's Press.

Shapiro, A. K. 1960. A contribution to a history of the placebo effect. *Behavioral Science* 5:109–35.

Sherman, L. W. 1992. *Policing Domestic Violence: Experiments and Dilemmas.* New York: Free Press.

Sherman, L. W. 1993. Implications of a failure to read the literature. *American Sociological Review* 58:888–89.

Sherman, L. W., and R. A. Berk. 1984. The specific deterrent effects of arrest for domestic assault. *American Sociological Review* 49:261–72.

Sherman, L. W., and R. A. Berk. 1985. The randomization of arrest. In *Randomization and Field Experimentation: New Directions in Program Evaluation,* no. 28 (eds. R. F. Boruch and W. Wothke), pp. 15–25. San Francisco: Jossey–Bass.

Sherman, L. W., and D. A. Smith. 1992. Crime, punishment, and state in conformity: Legal and informal control of domestic violence. *American Sociological Review* 57:680–90.

Shih, T. H., and X. Fan. 2008. Comparing response rates from web and mail surveys: A meta-analysis. *Field Methods* 20:249–71.

Shosteck, H., and W. R. Fairweather. 1979. Physician response rates to mail and personal interview surveys. *Public Opinion Quarterly* 43:206–17.

Shotland, R. L., and C. A. Stebbins. 1983. Emergency and cost as determinants of helping behavior and the slow accumulation of social psychological knowledge. *Social Psychology Quarterly* 46:36–46.

Shuler, H. 1982. *Ethical Problems in Psychological Research* (trans. M. S. Woodruff and R. A. Wicklund). New York: Academic Press.

Shults, R. A., R. W. Elder, D. A. Sleet, J. L. Nichols, M. O. Alao, V. G. Carande-Kulis, S. Zaza, D. M. Sosin, R. S. Thompson, and Task Force on Community Preventive Services. 2001. Reviews of evidence regarding interventions to reduce alcohol-impaired driving. *American Journal of Preventive Medicine* 21:66–88.

Sieber, J. E. 1982. Ethical dilemmas in social research. In *The Ethics of Social Research: Surveys and Experiments* (ed. J. E. Sieber), pp. 1–29. New York: Springer-Verlag.

Sigall, H., E. Aronson, and T. Van Hoose. 1970. The cooperative subject: Myth or reality. *Journal of Experimental Social Psychology* 6:1–10.

Sikkel, D., and A. Hoogendoorn. 2008. Panel surveys. In *International Handbook of Survey Methodology* (eds. E. D. de Leeuw, J. J. Hox, and D. A. Dillman), pp. 479–99. New York: Erlbaum.

Silverman, I. 1968. Role-related behavior of subjects in laboratory studies of attitude change. *Journal of Personality and Social Psychology* 4:343–48.

Simon, J. L. 1978. *Basic Research Methods in Social Science: The Art of Empirical Investigation,* 2nd ed. New York: Random House.

Simpson, B., K. Irwin, and P. Lawrence. 2006. Does a "norm of self-interest" discourage prosocial behavior? Rationality and quid pro quo in charitable giving. *Social Psychology Quarterly* 69:296–306.

Singer, E. 1978. Informed consent: Consequences for response rate and response quality in social surveys. *American Sociological Review* 43:144–62.

Singer, E. 2003. Exploring the meaning of consent: Participation in research and beliefs about risks and benefits. *Journal of Official Statistics* 19:273–85.

Singer, E., and F. J. Levine. 2003. Protection of human subjects of research: Recent developments and future prospects for the social sciences. *Public Opinion Quarterly* 67:148–64.

Singer, E., and C. Ye. 2013. The use and effects of incentives in surveys. *The Annals of the American Academy of Political and Social Science* 645:112–41.

Singleton, R. A., Jr. 1998. Is sociology a science? A classroom exercise for promoting discussion. Presented at the Annual Meetings of the American Sociological Association, San Francisco.

Singleton, R. A., Jr. 2007. Collegiate alcohol consumption and academic performance. *Journal of Studies on Alcohol and Drugs* 68:548–55.

Singleton, R., Jr., and J. B. Christiansen. 1977. The construct validation of a short-form attitudes towards feminism scale. *Sociology and Social Research* 61:294–303.

Singleton, R. A., Jr., and A. R. Wolfson. 2009. Alcohol consumption, sleep, and academic performance among college students. *Journal of Studies on Alcohol and Drugs* 70:355–63.

Sirken, M. G., D. Herrmann, S. Schechter, N. Schwarz, J. M. Tanur, and R. Tourangeau (eds.). 1999. *Cognition and Survey Research.* New York: John Wiley & Sons.

Skinner, B. F. 1953. *Science and Human Behavior.* Toronto: Macmillan.

Skocpol, T. 1979. *States and Social Revolutions: A Comparative Analysis of France, Russia, and China.* Cambridge: Cambridge University Press.

Skocpol, T. 1984. Emerging agendas and recurrent strategies in historical sociology. In *Vision and Method in Historical Sociology* (ed. T. Skocpol), pp. 356–91. Cambridge: Cambridge University Press.

Slonim, M. J. 1957. Sampling in a nutshell. *Journal of the American Statistical Association* 152:143–61.

Slonim, M. J. 1960. *Sampling in a Nutshell.* New York: Simon & Schuster.

Smit, J. H., W. Dijkstra, and J. van der Zouwen. 1997. Suggestive interviewer behaviour in surveys: An experimental study. *Journal of Official Statistics* 13:19–28.

Smith, E. R., M. M. Ferree, and F. D. Miller. 1975. A short scale of attitudes toward feminism. *Representative Research in Social Psychology* 6:51–56.

Smith, J. 1991. A methodology for twenty-first century sociology. *Social Forces* 70:1–17.

Smith, S. S., and D. Richardson. 1983. Amelioration of deception and harm in psychological research: The important role of debriefing. *Journal of Personality and Social Psychology* 44:1075–82.

Smith, T. W. 1990. The International Social Survey Program. *ICPSR Bulletin* (December):1–2.

Smith, T. W., and J. M. Dennis. 2004. *Comparing the Knowledge Networks Web-Enabled Panel and the In-Person 2002 General Social Survey: Experiments with Mode, Format, and Question Wording.* GSS Methodological Report No. 99. Chicago: National Opinion Research Center.

Smith, T. W., P. Marsden, and M. Hout. 2016. *General Social Surveys, 1972–2014: Cumulative Codebook/* Principal Investigator, Tom W. Smith; Co-Principal Investigators, Peter V. Marsden and Michael Hout. Chicago: National Opinion Research Center. 3,505 pp., 28cm. (National Data Program for the Social Sciences Series, no. 23).

Sniderman, P. M., R. A. Brody, and P. E. Tetlock. 1991. *Reasoning and Choice: Explorations in Political Psychology.* New York: Cambridge University Press.

Sniderman, P. M., and D. B. Grob. 1996. Innovations in experimental design in attitude surveys. *Annual Review of Sociology* 22:377–99.

Snow, D. A., and L. Anderson. 1987. Identity work among the homeless: The verbal construction and avowal of personal identities. *American Journal of Sociology* 92:1336–71.

Snow, D. A., and L. Anderson. 1991. Researching the homeless: The characteristic features and virtues of the case study. In *A Case for the Case Study* (eds. J. R. Feagin, A. M. Orum, and G. Sjoberg), pp. 148–73. Chapel Hill: University of North Carolina Press.

Snow, D. A., and L. Anderson. 1993. *Down on Their Luck: A Study of Homeless Street People.* Berkeley: University of California Press.

Snow, D. A., S. G. Baker, and L. Anderson. 1989. Criminality and homeless men: An empirical assessment. *Social Problems* 36:532–47.

Snow, D. A., S. G. Baker, L. Anderson, and M. Martin. 1986. The myth of pervasive mental illness among the homeless. *Social Problems* 33:409–23.

Snow, D. A., R. D. Benford, and L. Anderson. 1986. Fieldwork roles and information yield: A comparison of alternative settings and roles. *Urban Life* 14:377–408.

Snow, D. A., C. Robinson, and P. L. McCall. 1991. "Cooling out" men in singles bars and nightclubs: Observations on the interpersonal survival strategies of women in public places. *Journal of Contemporary Ethnography* 19:423–49.

Snow, D. A., L. A. Zurcher, and G. Sjoberg. 1982. Interviewing by comment: An adjunct to the direct question. *Qualitative Sociology* 5:285–311.

Solomon, R. C. 1984. *Ethics: A Brief Introduction*. New York: McGraw-Hill.

Sorokin, P. A. 1937. *Social and Cultural Dynamics*, vol. II. New York: American Book Company.

Spencer, B. D., M. R. Frankel, S. J. Ingels, K. A. Rasinski, R. Tourangeau, and J. A. Owings. 1990. *National Education Longitudinal Study of 1988: Base Year Sample Design Report*. Washington, D.C.: U.S. Department of Education, Office of Educational Research and Improvement.

Spradley, J. P. 1980. *Participant Observation*. New York: Holt, Rinehart and Winston.

Sprague, J., and M. K. Zimmerman. 1989. Quality and quantity: Reconstructing feminist methodology. *American Sociologist* 20:71–86.

Squire, P. 1988. Why the 1936 *Literary Digest* poll failed. *Public Opinion Quarterly* 52:125–33.

Stacey, J., and T. J. Biblarz. 2001. (How) does the sexual orientation of parents matter? *American Sociological Review* 66:159–83.

Stangor, C. 2004. *Research Methods for the Behavioral Sciences*, 2nd ed. Boston: Houghton Mifflin.

Stannard, D. E. 1977. *The Puritan Way of Death: A Study in Religion, Culture, and Social Change*. New York: Oxford University Press.

Stark, R., and W. S. Bainbridge. 1996. *Religion, Deviance, and Social Control*. New York: Routledge.

Steeh, C. 2008. Telephone surveys. In *International Handbook of Survey Methodology* (eds. E. D. de Leeuw, J. J. Hox, and D. A. Dillman), pp. 221–38. New York: Erlbaum.

Steiger, D. M., and B. Conroy. 2008. IVR: Interactive voice response. In *International Handbook of Survey Methodology* (eds. E. D. de Leeuw, J. J. Hox, and D. A. Dillman), pp. 285–98. New York: Erlbaum.

Stein, A. 2010. Sex, truths, and audiotape: Anonymity and the ethics of exposure in public ethnography. *Journal of Contemporary Ethnography* 39:554–68.

Steneck, N. H. 2007. *ORI Introduction to the Responsible Conduct of Research*. Washington, D.C.: U.S. Government Printing Office.

Stephan, F., Jr., and P. J. McCarthy. 1958. *Sampling Opinions: An Analysis of Survey Procedure*. New York: Wiley.

Sterba, S. K. 2006. Misconduct in the analysis and reporting of data: Bridging methodological and ethical agendas for change. *Ethics and Behavior* 16:305–18.

Stevens, S. S. 1951. Mathematics, measurement, and psychophysics. In *Handbook of Experimental Psychology* (ed. S. S. Stevens), pp. 1–49. New York: Wiley.

Stinchcombe, A. L. 1968. *Constructing Social Theories*. New York: Harcourt, Brace & World.

Stolzenberg, R. M., and K. C. Land. 1983. Causal modeling and survey research. In *Handbook of Survey Research* (eds. P. H. Rossi, J. D. Wright, and A. B. Anderson), pp. 613–75. New York: Academic Press.

St. Pierre, R. G., and T. D. Cook. 1984. Sampling strategy in the design of program evaluation. *Evaluation Studies Review Annual* 9:459–84.

Strack, F., L. L. Martin, and N. Schwarz. 1988. Priming and communication: The social determinants of information use in judgments of life-satisfaction. *European Journal of Social Psychology* 18:429–42.

Strack, F., N. Schwarz, and M. Wänke. 1991. Semantic and pragmatic aspects of context effects in social and psychological research. *Social Cognition* 9:111–25.

Straits, B. C. 1967. Resume of the Chicago study of smoking behavior. In *Studies and Issues in Smoking Behavior* (ed. S. V. Zagona), pp. 73–78. Tucson: University of Arizona Press.

Straits, B. C. 1985. Factors influencing college women's responses to fertility decision-making vignettes. *Journal of Marriage and the Family* 47:585–96.

Straits, B. C. 1998. Occupational sex segregation: The role of personal ties. *Journal of Vocational Behavior* 52:191–207.

Straits, B. C., and P. L. Wuebben. 1973. College students' reactions to social scientific experimentation. *Sociological Methods and Research* 1:355–86.

Straits, B. C., P. L. Wuebben, and T. J. Majka. 1972. Influences on subjects' perceptions of experimental research situations. *Sociometry* 35:499–518.

Suchman, L., and B. Jordan. 1990. Interactional troubles in face-to-face survey interviews. *Journal of the American Statistical Association* 85:232–41.

Sudman, S. 1976. *Applied Sampling.* New York: Academic Press.

Sudman, S., and N. M. Bradburn. 1974. *Response Effects in Surveys: A Review and Synthesis.* Chicago: Aldine.

Sudman, S., and N. M. Bradburn. 1982. *Asking Questions: A Practical Guide to Questionnaire Design.* San Francisco: Jossey–Bass.

Sudman, S., N. M. Bradburn, and N. Schwarz. 1996. *Thinking about Answers: The Application of Cognitive Processes to Survey Methodology.* San Francisco: Jossey–Bass.

Sudman, S., and G. Kalton. 1986. New developments in the sampling of special populations. *Annual Review of Sociology* 12:401–29.

Sudman, S., M. G. Sirken, and C. D. Cowan. 1988. Sampling rare and elusive populations. *Science* 240:991–96.

Survey Research Center. 1976. *Interviewer's Manual*, rev. ed. Ann Arbor, MI: Institute for Social Research.

Sutton, J. R. 1991. The political economy of madness: The expansion of the asylum in progressive America. *American Sociological Review* 56:665–78.

Talaska, C. A., S. T. Fiske, and S. Chaiken. 2008. Legitimating discrimination: Emotions, not beliefs, best predict discrimination in a meta-analysis. *Social Justice Research* 21:263–96.

Taylor, C. J. 1998. Factors affecting behavior toward people with disabilities. *Journal of Social Psychology* 138:766–71.

Taylor, D. G., P. B. Sheatsley, and A. Greeley. 1978. Attitudes toward racial integration. *Scientific American* 238:42–49.

Taylor, S. J., R. Bogdan, and M. L. DeVault. 2016. *Introduction to Qualitative Research Methods: A Guidebook and Resource*, 4th ed. Hoboken, NJ: Wiley.

Thibodeau, R. 1989. From racism to tokenism: The changing face of blacks in *New Yorker* cartoons. *Public Opinion Quarterly* 53:482–94.

Thomas, W. I., and F. Znaniecki. 1918. *The Polish Peasant in Europe and America.* Boston: Gorham Press.

Tilcsik, A. 2011. Pride and prejudice: Employment discrimination against openly gay men in the United States. *American Journal of Sociology* 115:586–626.

Tilly, C. 1981. *As Sociology Meets History.* New York: Academic Press.

Tinati, R., S. Halford, L. Carr, and C. Pope. 2014. Big data: methodological challenges and approaches for sociological analysis. *Sociology* 48:663–81.

Tourangeau, R., and N. M. Bradburn. 2010. The psychology of survey response. In *Handbook of Survey Research*, 2nd ed. (eds. P. V. Marsden and J. D. Wright), pp. 315–46. Bingley, UK: Emerald Group.

Tourangeau, R., F. G. Conrad, and M. P. Couper. 2013. *The Science of Web Surveys.* New York: Oxford University Press.

Tourangeau, R., L. J. Rips, and K. Rasinski. 2000. *The Psychology of Survey Response.* Cambridge: Cambridge University Press.

Tourangeau, R., and T. W. Smith. 1996. Asking sensitive questions: The impact of data collection mode, question format, and question context. *Public Opinion Quarterly* 60: 275–304.

Traugott, M. W., and J. P. Katosh. 1979. Response validity in surveys of voting behavior. *Public Opinion Quarterly* 43:359–77.

Tremayne, M. 2014. Anatomy of protest in the digital era: A network analysis of Twitter and Occupy Wall Street. *Social Movement Studies* 13:110–26.

Trice, A. D. 1987. Informed consent VIII: Biasing of sensitive self-report data by both consent and information. *Journal of Social Behavior and Personality* 2:369–74.

Tukey, J. W. 1977. *Exploratory Data Analysis.* Reading, MA: Addison–Wesley.

Twenge, J. M., R. F. Baumeister, C. N. DeWall, N. J. Ciarocco, and J. M. Bartels. 2007. Social exclusion decreases prosocial behavior. *Journal of Personality and Social Psychology* 92:56–66.

U.S. Bureau of Labor Statistics. 2013. Women in the labor force: A databook. BLS Reports, Report 1040, February. http://www.bls.gov/cps/wlf-databook-2012.pdf (accessed May 4, 2016).

U.S. Bureau of Labor Statistics. 2016a. Labor Force Statistics from the Current Population Survey. Technical Documentation: Concepts and Methodology. http://www.bls.gov/cps/eetech_methods.pdf (accessed July 18, 2016).

U.S. Bureau of Labor Statistics. 2016b. Occupational outlook handbook: Most new jobs. http://www.bls.gov/ooh/most-new-jobs.htm (accessed May 4, 2016).

U.S. Census Bureau. 1986. Voting and registration in the election of November 1982. *Current Population Reports*, Series P-20, No. 383. Washington, D.C.: U.S. Government Printing Office.

U.S. Census Bureau. 2008. *Statistical Abstract of the United States: 2008*, 127th ed. Washington, D.C.: Author.

U.S. Census Bureau. 2009. *History: 2000 Census of Population and Housing*, Vol. 1. Washington, D.C.: U.S. Government Printing Office.

U.S. Census Bureau. 2012. Census bureau release estimates of undercount and overcount in the 2010 Census. https://www.census.gov/newsroom/releases/archives/2010_census/cb12-95.html (accessed March 13, 2016).

U.S. Department of Health and Human Services. 2016. National Institutes of Health, Certificates of Confidentiality Kiosk. https://humansubjects.nih.gov/coc/index (accessed July 18, 2016).

Valentine, B. 1978. *Hustling and Other Hard Work: Life Styles in the Ghetto*. New York: Free Press.

Van der Zouwen, J., and J. H. Smit. 2004. Evaluating survey questions by analyzing patterns of behavior codes and question-answer sequences: A diagnostic approach. In *Methods for Testing and Evaluating Survey Questionnaires* (eds. S. Presser et al.), pp. 109–130. Hoboken, NJ: Wiley.

Van Poppel, F., and L. H. Day. 1996. A test of Durkheim's theory of suicide—without committing the "ecological fallacy." *American Sociological Review* 61:500–507.

Vasquez, J. M. 2011. *Mexican Americans Across Generations: Immigrant Families, Racial Realities*. New York: New York University Press.

Vaughan, T. R. 1967. Governmental intervention in social research: Political and ethical dimensions in the Wichita jury recordings. In *Ethics, Politics, and Social Research* (ed. G. Sjoberg), pp. 50–77. Cambridge, MA: Schenkman.

Wacquant, L. 2004. *Body and Soul: Notebooks on an Apprentice Boxer*. New York: Oxford University Press.

Wagenaar, A. C. 1983. *Alcohol, Young Drivers, and Traffic Accidents: Effects of Minimum Age Laws*. Lexington, MA: D. C. Heath.

Wagenaar, A., and T. Toomey. 2002. Effects of minimum drinking age laws: Review and analyses of the literature from 1960 to 2000. *Journal of Studies on Alcohol*, Supplement No. 14, 63:206–225.

Waite, L. J., and R. M. Stolzenberg. 1976. Intended childbearing and labor force participation of young women: Insights from nonrecursive models. *American Sociological Review* 41:235–52.

Wallace, W. L. 1971. *The Logic of Science in Sociology*. Chicago: Aldine–Atherton.

Wallis, W. A., and H. V. Roberts. 1956. *Statistics: A New Approach*. New York: Free Press.

Warden, G. B. 1976. Inequality and instability in eighteenth-century Boston: A reappraisal. *Journal of Interdisciplinary History* 6:585–620.

Warr, Mark. 1995. The polls poll trends: Public opinion on crime and punishment. *Public Opinion Quarterly* 59:296–310.

Warren, C. A. B., and P. K. Rasmussen. 1977. Sex and gender in field research. *Urban Life* 6:349–69.

Warren, J. R., and A. Halpern-Manners. 2012. Panel conditioning in longitudinal social science surveys. *Sociological Methods and Research* 41:491–534.

Wasserman, S., and K. Faust. 1994. *Social Network Analysis*. Cambridge: Cambridge University Press.

Watters, J. K., and P. Biernacki. 1989. Targeted sampling: Options for the study of hidden populations. *Social Problems* 36:416–30.

Wax, R. H. 1971. *Doing Fieldwork: Warnings and Advice*. Chicago: University of Chicago Press.

Webb, E. J., D. T. Campbell, R. D. Schwartz, and L. Sechrest. 2000. *Unobtrusive Measures*, rev. ed. Thousand Oaks, CA: Sage.

Weber, M. 1949. *The Methodology of the Social Sciences* (trans. E. A. Shils and H. A. Finch). New York: Free Press.

Weber, R. P. 1984. Computer-aided content analysis: A short primer. *Qualitive Sociology* 7:126–47.

Weber, R. P. 1990. *Basic Content Analysis*, 2nd ed. Beverly Hills, CA: Sage.

Weber, S. J., and T. D. Cook. 1972. Subject effects in laboratory research: An examination of subject roles, demand characteristics, and valid inference. *Psychological Bulletin* 77:273–95.

Wechsler, H., A. Davenport, G. Dowdall, B. Moeykens, and S. Castillo. 1994. Health and behavioral consequences of binge drinking in college: A national survey of students at 140 campuses. *Journal of the American Medical Association* 272:1672–77.

Wechsler, H., and T. F. Nelson. 2008. What we have learned from the Harvard School of Public Health College Alcohol Study: Focusing attention on college student alcohol consumption and the environmental conditions that promote it. *Journal of Studies on Alcohol and Drugs* 69:481–90.

Weick, K. E. 1968. Systematic observational methods. In *The Handbook of Social Psychology*, 2nd ed., vol. II (eds. G. Lindzey and E. Aronson), pp. 357–451. Reading, MA: Addison–Wesley.

Weinberg, E. 1983. Data collection: Planning and management. In *Handbook of Survey Research* (eds. P. H. Rossi, J. D. Wright, and A. B. Anderson), pp. 329–58. New York: Academic Press.

Weinberg, M., and C. J. Williams. 1972. Fieldwork among deviants: Social relations with subjects and others. In *Research on Deviance* (ed. J. D. Douglas), pp. 165–86. New York: Random House.

Weiss, C. H. 1987. Evaluating social programs: What have we learned? *Society* 25(November/December):40–45.

Weiss, R. S. 1966. Alternative approaches in the study of complex situations. *Human Organization* 25:198–206.

West, K. K, and D. J. Fein. 1990. Census undercount: An historical and contemporary sociological issue. *Sociological Inquiry* 60:127–41.

West, S. G., S. P. Gunn, and P. Chernicky. 1975. Ubiquitous Watergate: An attributional analysis. *Journal of Personality and Social Psychology* 32:55–65.

White, H. D. 2009. Scientific communication and literature retrieval. In *The Handbook of Research Synthesis and Meta-Analysis*, 2nd ed. (eds. H. Cooper, L. V. Hedges, and J. C. Valentine), pp. 51–71. New York: Russell Sage Foundation.

Whyte, W. F. 1993. *Street Corner Society: The Social Structure of an Italian Slum*. 4th ed., rev. and enl. Chicago: University of Chicago Press.

Willard, J. C., and C. A. Schoenborn. 1995. Relationship between cigarette smoking and other unhealthy behaviors among our nation's youth: United States, 1992. Advance Data from Vital and Health Statistics, No. 263. Hyattsville, MD: National Center for Health Statistics.

Williams, J. D. 2012. The 2010 Decennial Census: Background and Issues. Washington: Congressional Research Service. https://www.fas.org/sgp/crs/misc/R40551.pdf (accessed March 31, 2016).

Willis, G. B., and J. T. Lessler. 1999. Question Appraisal System QAS-99. Research Triangle Institute. https://www.researchgate.net/publication/259812768_Question_Appraisal_System_QAS_99_Manual (accessed June 10, 2016).

Wimmer, A., and K. Lewis. 2010. Beyond and below racial homophily: ERG models of a friendship network documented on Facebook. *American Journal of Sociology* 116:583–642.

Winfree, L. T., Jr., F. A. Esbensen, and D. W. Osgood. 1996. Evaluating a school-based gang-prevention program: A theoretical perspective. *Evaluation Review* 20:181–203.

Winfree, L. T., Jr., D. Peterson Lynskey, and J. P. Maupin. 1999. Developing local police and federal law enforcement partnerships: G.R.E.A.T. as a case study of policy implementation. *Criminal Justice Review* 24:145–68.

Woodward, J. 2016. Causation in science. In *The Oxford Handbook of Philosophy of Science* (ed. P. Humphreys), pp. 163–84. New York: Oxford University Press.

Wray, M., C. Colen, and B. Pescosolido. 2011. The sociology of suicide. *Annual Review of Sociology* 37:505–528.

Yodanis, C. 2005. Divorce culture and marital gender equality: A cross-national study. *Gender and Society* 19:644–59.

Zeisel, H. 1968. *Say It with Figures*. New York: Harper & Row.

Zelditch, M., Jr. 1962. Some methodological problems of field studies. *American Journal of Sociology* 67:566–76.

Zeller, R. A., and E. G. Carmines. 1980. *Measurement in the Social Sciences: The Link between Theory and Data*. New York: Cambridge University Press.

Zimbardo, P. G. 1973. On the ethics of intervention in human psychological research: With special reference to the Stanford prison study. *Cognition* 2:243–56.

Zimbardo, P. G., C. Haney, W. C. Banks, and D. Jaffe. 1973. The mind is a formidable jailer: A pirandell-ian prison. *New York Times Magazine* 122(April 8):38–60.

Zinkhan, G. M., and L. A. Hayes. 1989. Changing patterns of other-directness: A content analysis of women's magazines. *Journal of Social Psychology* 129:825–31.

Zipp, J. F., and J. Toth. 2002. She said, he said, they said: The impact of spousal presence in survey research. *Public Opinion Quarterly* 66:177–208.

Zito, G. V. 1975. *Methodology and Meanings: Varieties of Sociological Inquiry.* New York: Praeger.

Zoble, E. J., and R. S. Lehman. 1969. Interaction of subject–experimenter expectancy effects in a tone length discrimination task. *Behavioral Science* 14:357–63.

Name Index

Subject Index

Page numbers followed by *f, t,* and *b* refer to figures, tables, and boxes, respectively.

in field research, 356–58
in-depth, 357
intensive, 357
schedule, 273
semistructured, 259
standardized, 283*f,* 288, 289–91*b,* 291–92
telephone, 272*f,* 275–77
thinkaloud, 337
unstructured and semistructured, 356–58
unstructured v. structured, 259–60
See also Cognitive interviewing
Introduction, section of research report, 567
Inverse (negative) relationship, 93
Inverted-funnel sequence, of questions, 326,
    327–28*b*
Investigator error, comparison of approaches, 442*t*
IPUMS project, 401, 422n2
IRB (Institutional review board), 69–70
ISSP (International Social Survey Program), 262, 418
Item nonresponse, 183

J

Jigsaw method, 478, 486n4
Job discrimination and sexual orientation study, 122
Just World Scale, 144*b*

K

Keyboard layout study, 405
Key informants, 365
Knowledge, scientific, 44
    as description, 21–22
    as explanation and prediction, 22–24
    nature of, 41
    as social construction, 42–43
    tentative, 26–27
    as understanding, 24–26
Knowledge Network, 280–81

L

Laboratory experiment, 442*t*
Labor market discrimination, field experiment,
    242–43*b*
Language
    in survey instrumentation, 320–35
    use for questions, 320–27
Laws, scientific, 23
Leading crowd hypothesis, 91, 549
Leading question, 324
Least squares line, 519
Lerner Self-Esteem Scale, 142
Levels of measurement, 126–30
Library of Congress, 397
Library searches, 559–64
Likert scaling, 312, 432–33*b*
Linear relationship, 93, 94*f,* 519
Listwise deletion, 509–10
Literature review, section of research report, 568
Literature searching, 558–64
Logical reasoning, 32–34
Longitudinal designs, 264–67

M

Magazine advertising studies, 84, 392–94, 411
Mail survey. *See* Paper-and-pencil questionnaires
Main effect, 240
Manipulation, 122
    check, 205–6
    experimental, 192–93
Manuscript census, 388, 389–90*b*
Marginal frequencies, 512
Marriage and cohabitation, influenced by abuse,
    440–41
Mass media, as available data source, 392–94
Matching, 194–95, 472–73
Mathematical statements, 107
Maturation, threat to internal validity, 227
Mean, 506
Measurement, 111, 116–48
    attitude, 123–24, 143, 248
    in available data research, problems, 398–99
    composite, 426–31, 427*f*
    conceptualization, 117–18
    control of reactivity, comparison of approaches, 442*t*
    defined, 127
    of dependent variable in experiments, 206–7
    ease of, comparison of approaches, 442*t*
    error, 271
    forms of, in social research, 122–26
    interval, 129–30, 131*t*
    levels of, 126–30
    nominal, 127–28, 131*t*
    nonreactive, 417
    observation, 124–25
    operationalization, 118–20
    ordinal, 128–29, 131*t*
    process of, 117–20
    random, error, 134
    ratio, 130, 131*t*
    reactive effects, 133, 210
    reliability and validity, 131–34, 145
    reliability assessment, 135–38
    in research design, 111, 116–48
    self-reports, 123–24
    sources of error, 132–34, 134*f*
    systematic, error, 132–33
    validity assessment, 138–43, 145
    validity in evaluation research, 478–80
Measures of association, 514, 516–17
Media aids, in survey instrument design, 315
Media influence, 393
Median, 506
Membership role, 368–70
Memory problems, in survey responses, 330–32
Memos, 376
Mental hospital behavioral disturbances study, 350
Meta-analysis, 444–49
    data collection, 447
    data evaluation, 447–48
    interpretation and analysis, 448–49
    problem formulation, 446
    public presentation, 449
"A Methodology for Twenty-first Century
    Sociology," 441